THE YALE EDITIONS OF

The Private Papers of James Boswell

(Research Edition)

Boswell's Correspondence, Volume 2
General Editor: Frederick W. Hilles

THE CORRESPONDENCE
AND OTHER PAPERS OF JAMES BOSWELL
RELATING TO THE MAKING OF THE
LIFE OF JOHNSON

THE CORRESPONDENCE AND OTHER PAPERS

OF

James Boswell

RELATING TO THE MAKING OF THE *LIFE OF JOHNSON*

EDITED WITH AN INTRODUCTION AND NOTES BY

MARSHALL WAINGROW

PROFESSOR OF ENGLISH
CLAREMONT GRADUATE SCHOOL

McGRAW-HILL BOOK COMPANY
NEW YORK   TORONTO

Library of Congress Catalog Card
Number 68–12066

67735

PRINTED IN GREAT BRITAIN

EDITORIAL COMMITTEE

GENERAL EDITORIAL NOTE

THE research edition of the Private Papers of James Boswell will consist of at least three co-ordinated series: Boswell's journal in all its varieties, his correspondence, and the *Life of Johnson* in an arrangement which will show the method and progress of its composition. The undertaking is a co-operative one involving many scholars, and publication will proceed in the order in which the volumes are completed for the press. It is expected that the whole edition will consist of not fewer than thirty volumes.

In the parallel "reading" or "trade" edition, which began publication in 1950 and has now reached its tenth volume, those portions of the papers have been selected which appeared likely to interest the general reading public, and the object of the annotation has been to illuminate the documents themselves as compositions. The annotation in that series may be said to be turned in towards the text.

The annotation of the research edition, on the contrary, is turned out from the text, and is intended to relate the documents to the various areas of scholarship which they are capable of illuminating: history in many of its varieties (literary, linguistic, legal, medical, political, social, local), biography, bibliography, and genealogy. The comprehensiveness and coherence of the papers that Boswell chose to preserve make them almost uniquely useful for such exploitation.

The journal and its related notes and memoranda will be presented in one chronological sequence, but the correspondence will appear in three different kinds of volumes: *subject* volumes, which will select letters relatable to a topic or theme, of which the present volume is a good illustration; *single-correspondence* volumes (for example, Boswell's correspondence with John Johnston of Grange); and *miscellaneous-correspondence* volumes, which will collect the remaining letters in chronological sequence. Since, with all its gaps, the journal provides a more continuous and detailed record of Boswell's life than the correspondence does, it has been taken as the primary document for the annotation of his daily activities and the identification of the persons he met or mentioned. In particular, the volumes of the journal will contain, in alphabetized Biographical Supplements, condensed biographical accounts of all the contemporaries of Boswell whom he mentions in those volumes in more than an allusive way. The correspondence volumes will deal in a more summary fashion with matters that are to receive systematic "depth" annotation in the journal volumes, but will themselves provide "depth" annotation on their own special topics and on persons and events not mentioned in the journal.

FREDERICK W. HILLES
HERMAN W. LIEBERT
FRANK E. TAYLOR

FREDERICK A. POTTLE
Chairman

ACKNOWLEDGEMENTS

JOHNSON wrote to a straitened acquaintance: "Neither the great nor little debts disgrace you. I am sure you have my Esteem for the Courage with which you contracted them, and the Spirit with which you endure them." If this be Johnsonian sophistry, there is humanity in it, and I would hope that some virtue may be allowed to my own debts, both great and little.

My principal creditors are F. W. Hilles, F. A. Pottle, J. L. Clifford, L. F. Powell, H. W. Liebert, Marion S. Pottle, J. D. Fleeman, B. F. Houston, and Harriet Chidester, who have read this book in one or more of its phases and have greatly reduced its level of imperfection.

In addition, I owe various debts of gratitude to many individuals, who collectively have animated for me the meaning of Boswell's phrase, "the general courtesy of literature". They are: W. S. Anderson, Delight Ansley, the late C. H. Bennett, Frank Brady, Gwen W. Brewer, the late R. W. Chapman, B. H. Davis, A. F. Falconer, C. N. Fifer, E. S. Fussell, D. J. Greene, the late Donald Hyde, Mary Hyde, E. R. Kanjo, G. L. Lam, E. L. McAdam, Jr., Martha D. Mench, R. F. Metzdorf, John Oates, J. M. Osborn, R. B. Palmer, J. W. Reed, Robert Smith, W. H. Smith, A. B. Strauss, R. S. Walker, the late Robert Warnock, C. McC. Weis, W. K. Wimsatt, Jr., John Zeigel, and, not the least, the staffs of the Yale and Honnold libraries.

M. W.

CONTENTS

ALPHABETICAL TABLE OF CORRESPONDENTS

Papers transmitted to Boswell directly by hand, and Johnsoniana taken down by him from dictation or memory, are not distinguished from letters in this table.

TABLE OF CORRESPONDENTS

TABLE OF CORRESPONDENTS

XV

TABLE OF CORRESPONDENTS

TABLE OF CORRESPONDENTS

TABLE OF CORRESPONDENTS

TABLE OF CORRESPONDENTS

INTRODUCTION

I. The Documents

THE documentary history of the *Life of Johnson* begins with Boswell's private journal and ends, virtually, with the manuscript he sent to the printer. The first of these massive documents, or the bulk of it, has been produced in a limited edition, is currently being reissued in a popular edition, and will eventually make its third and definitive appearance in an edition for scholars. The second document, substantially a later recovery, is in the process of being edited, and will, like the journal, be published in versions for both the common reader and the poring man.

But for a complete history of the *Life of Johnson* it is necessary to look beyond the journal and behind the manuscript: specifically, at that part of the making of the *Life* which cast Boswell in the roles of researcher, compiler, and editor. The present volume (researched, compiled, and edited to that end) consists of more than four hundred letters and other papers, most of which are in the Yale Collection and most of which are here printed for the first time. The title given to this volume reflects the central but not the entire interest of its contents; for the *Life* is here viewed not only in its "making" but also from the vantage points of its anticipations, its publication, its reception, its revision, and even its posthumous editions.

Geoffrey Scott's study of the making of the *Life* out of the journal and its sources (the sixth volume of the *Private Papers*) is a contribution of the first importance to our projected history. His theme is Boswell as editor of his own papers. Now, with the recovery of the great mass of Boswell's correspondence, a new vista has been opened onto the biographical landscape. The theme of the present volume is Boswell as editor of the contributions of others. The two principal documentary sources—journal and correspondence—may be regarded as posing a common problem to the biographer: that of adapting more or less raw materials to a finished and complete narrative. Yet, it should be evident that for Boswell's purposes the journal was less raw than the materials supplied by his correspondents, and therefore that his editing of what we may call his secondary sources is at least potentially more revealing than his editing of his own record.

Scott's findings are fairly represented by a remark of R. W. Chapman's in a review of the first six volumes of the *Private Papers* (TLS, 6 Feb. 1930):

> . . . when all is said—when the work of revision has been traced through its stages—the conclusion that issues is the altogether welcome conclusion, that there is no surprising revelation. When Boswell's workshop has at last been ransacked, the results previously reached by scholarship are confirmed. We now know for certain . . . that the finished *Life* is substantially the same thing as the contemporary records. The revision, careful and artful though it was, appears as an operation of polishing, not as a structural synthesis.

One might ask, however, whether the structural synthesis that seems lacking in the revision of the journal was not in fact there from the start; whether the Johnsonian record was not shaped in the initial composition by a single perception and a coherent, if not always conscious, conception of the subject's character. What Boswell recorded of Johnson was, after all, what he "thought worthy of preservation" (*Life* i. 461), and it is difficult to imagine how what was considered worth preserving would not be consistent with a certain image or idea of the man.

In any case, Boswell's workshop had not at the time of Scott's study "at last been ransacked". From our present pinnacle we see that Scott enjoyed a paucity of riches. The materials available to him, though not numerous, were happily consanguineous: notably a section of the journal with a corresponding fragment of the *Life* manuscript. Today, the results of continued ransacking have placed students of the *Life of Johnson* in the embarrassing position of having more evidence than a scholar might decently hope for. It is now our fate to be thorough rather than brilliant, and the task that awaits us is to trace the making of the *Life* through all (not some) of its fully (not partially) documented stages. The present volume is a step in the direction of enlarging the definition of what Chapman called "the contemporary records"; the edition of the manuscript *Life* will complete it. But from the present volume alone it is plain that we must revise the judgement that the finished *Life* is substantially the same as its sources. For as we broaden the base of our investigation into Boswell's biographical method, we find in his treatment of other people's versions of Johnson evidences of that structural synthesis which is so difficult to detect in the revision of the journal but which surely is implied in the universal judgement that the *Life of Johnson* is a work of art.

II. *Boswell's Research*

The critical history of the *Life of Johnson* has suffered from a preoccupation with its main attraction, the great conversations. It has often been observed that the shape of the book follows closely the contours of Boswell's own limited acquaintance with his subject, with the result that the *Life*, chronologically speaking, is seriously out of joint. Croker was the first to point out that the dominant matter of the biography, Boswell's record of his meetings and conversations with Johnson, derives from a mere spot of time relative to the lifespan of its subject. However, the estimate of the actual extent of this first-hand element in the *Life* is usually exaggerated. Chapman, for example, succumbed to the common impression, stating that the record of the journal constitutes "by far the greater part of the *Life*". In fact, it constitutes less than half.[1]

Boswell himself took no precautions to forestall a too selective appreciation of his work. At the beginning of the *Life* (i. 31) he declares: "What I consider as the peculiar value of the following work, is, the quantity that it contains of Johnson's conversation." Mrs. Piozzi had anticipated him with a "rationale" for such an emphasis: "To recollect, however, and to repeat the sayings of Dr. Johnson, is almost all that can be done by the writers of his Life: as his life, at least since my acquaintance with him, consisted in little else than talking, when he was not employed in some serious piece of work" (quoted, *Life* iv. 343). But Boswell did not of course submit to so restrictive a conception of his task. Although, like Mrs. Piozzi, he satisfied the Johnsonian requirement for undertaking biography by having "eat and drunk and lived in social intercourse" with his subject (*Life* ii. 166), he knew that no one can write the life of a man from personal experience alone. (Johnson's closest approximation to his own ideal, his *Life of Savage*, is ironically his most conjectural biography.) From a time early in their acquaintance

[1] "BOSWELL. 'How your statement lessens the idea.' JOHNSON. 'That, Sir, is the good of counting. It brings every thing to a certainty, which before floated in the mind indefinitely' " (*Life* iv. 204).

(see the Chronology of the Making of the *Life*, *post* p. li) Boswell is discovered gathering materials quite independently of his journalizing, though not systematically. With the death of Johnson —and the end of the "living" record of the journal—Boswell seems to have sensed that he was far from ready to write the *Life*, as his publisher Dilly proposed. "I answered him that I had a large collection of Materials for his life, but would write it deliberately. I was now uneasy to think that there would be considerable expectations from me of Memoirs of my illustrious Freind; but that habits of indolence and dejection of spirit would probably hinder me from laudable exertion" (Journ. 18 Dec. 1784). The preparation of the Hebrides journal for publication served at once to pacify the public appetite and to provide Boswell with a warm-up for the far greater exertion of writing the *Life*.

The chief materials that lay at hand as he faced the *magnum opus* were: (1) the record in the journal and in loose notes of his meetings and conversations with Johnson (a record marred by numerous lacunae); (2) a quantity of miscellaneous Johnsonian materials written up in more or less finished form which were to be assimilated in the main narrative (called by Boswell "Papers Apart"); (3) Johnson's letters to him (he eventually recovered his letters to Johnson[1]); and (4) lists of Johnson's published writings and assorted anecdotes and data preserved both in notebooks and on loose leaves. But though this was indeed a large collection of materials, it was far from complete: the great stretch of life before Boswell entered it, and the many small gaps in the record thereafter, needed to be filled, or filled more fully.

In January 1785 Boswell launched a systematic appeal to the acquaintances of Johnson's early years for anecdotes, sayings, and letters. At the beginning of his inquiries he was careful to discourage in his prospective informants an attitude of discrimination —on the theory that nothing concerning Johnson, however minute or trivial, could fail to interest. Later, as the work progressed, the circle of correspondents widened and the inquiries tended to become more specific. On the whole Boswell's solicitations met with success. A few persons were reluctant to have their names associated with their contributions, or to have their correspondence with Johnson published. A few failed to supply answers, or satisfactory

---

[1] Apparently not long after Johnson's death. See *post* To Brocklesby, 18 Dec. 1784 (end), and From Brocklesby, 27 Dec. 1784 and n. 23.

answers, to Boswell's queries. But the majority were both able and willing, and Boswell's exertions were amply repaid. With the appearance of the work in print, the initiative in Boswell's correspondence upon this subject was taken over by his readers, who furnished him with numerous corrections and additions.

For much of Boswell's research there is of course no record. The *Life* was composed in London, where countless investigations must have been made in person—only a few of which are mentioned in the journal. It is thus the correspondence that affords the main evidence for Boswell's pursuit of the Johnson that had escaped him in his lifetime. Only the sleuthing reader would have guessed how dependent the writing of the *Life* was upon the writing of letters.

Boswell remarks of Johnson's projected edition of Shakespeare (*Life* i. 319): "he shewed that he perfectly well knew what a variety of research such an undertaking required, but his indolence prevented him from pursuing it with that diligence which alone can collect those scattered facts that genius, however acute, penetrating, and luminous, cannot discover by its own force." The *Life of Johnson* is itself an eminent case of the successful mediation between the labour of diligence and the management of genius. The present volume confirms impressively the claim made by Boswell in the Advertisement to the first edition that his work represented a great effort at research. Even more importantly, because it is less obvious, it confirms, what he never asserted, that there was as much art as matter in it. As Scott observed, Boswell's conscious effort was aimed at authenticity far more than at art. The virtues of which he was pleased to boast as a biographer are the orthodox ones of perseverance, thoroughness, accuracy, and fairness. He may not have recognized—at least he did not articulate—the double standard in literary biography that perplexes the criticism (without inhibiting the practice) of that *genre*; namely, the competition of so-called scientific and aesthetic requirements. Nevertheless, our scrutiny of Boswell at his editorial labours exposes the problem to a strong light, and it is to an assessment of his techniques in coping with the rival claims that this introduction now proceeds.

III. Boswell's Editing

Readers of the Johnsonian persuasion may be expected to look at Boswell's source materials for new light on the subject of the biography. Such a hope would seem to betray a certain lack of confidence in the author: that is, a willingness to believe that he was not always capable of recognizing or discovering the truth, or, worse, that he was capable of suppressing or distorting it. Although it would be rash to claim for Boswell a perfect record on either of these heads,[1] it is important to note how very little in the way of biographical data that are both demonstrably authentic *and* significant can be gleaned from the unused materials. One substantial omission was a part of Johnson's juvenile poetry,[2] but as Boswell projected a complete edition of the poems it is unnecessary to seek a further explanation. Beyond this recovery, we must content ourselves with small rewards: odds and ends about the life, writings, and opinions of Johnson which, for one reason or another, were excluded from the *Life*. In these fragments are the makings of a new collection of Johnsoniana, but it would be idle to catalogue here every item of possible Johnsonian interest; the notes to this volume will serve as a guide to whatever is, or appears to be, new, and students of Johnson biography may help themselves. To make the most of our materials on the present occasion we must subordinate our interest in Johnson's life to our interest in the *Life of Johnson*. Both inquiries, in so far as they are determined by the present documents, rest on the same base: what Boswell left out. But as we cannot separate his omissions from his motives, nor his motives from his general design, our study attracts us inevitably to the Boswellian pole of the work, which is to say, to the *Life of Johnson* as a work of art.

We may begin our survey of how Boswell used his contributions by considering the way in which he used his contributors, for in his practice of acknowledging his authorities we find an epitome of the larger, more complicated editorial problem and its solution. And we also find at least a tentative answer to the question which the

---

[1] Two important suppressions, the evidence for which lies outside the present collection, concern Johnson's alleged incontinence during his early years in London and his decision, taken not long after his wife's death, to remarry. See F. A. Pottle, "The Dark Hints of Sir John Hawkins and Boswell", and Donald and Mary Hyde, "Dr. Johnson's Second Wife", both in *New Light on Dr. Johnson*, ed. F. W. Hilles, 1959. Professor Pottle's article, apart from its ingenious defence of Boswell on both counts, is valuable for its arresting monitions on the subject of biographical speculation.

[2] The texts of all of these *juvenilia* (see *post* From Hector, 1 Feb. 1785) were originally to have been reproduced in this volume, but instead have been transferred to the new edition of Johnson's *Poems* (volume IV of the Yale Edition of the Works of Samuel Johnson, 1964).

exposure of an author's sources inevitably raises: the question of Boswell's candour.

The great majority of the contributions which Boswell received are in the form of personal reminiscence, a circumstance which made verification a superhuman task. Except where there was palpable reason to doubt, or clear opportunity to certify, Boswell did what anyone else must have done: he trusted his contributors. At the same time he insisted that names should accompany contributions; if he could not be absolutely sure of his sources, he would at least make them known. The *Life* is strewn with acknowledgements; the question is how well they define Boswell's indebtedness.

Our papers show that Boswell sometimes fails to make an acknowledgement of his authorities, either directly or indirectly, and that where he does acknowledge them, he frequently fails to indicate precisely the extent of his obligation. But given the mass of particulars which had to be digested into his narrative, such sins of omission will appear venial. Indeed, to have documented every item of second-hand information in a fabric so vast and intricately woven might have laid Boswell open to the worse charge of pedantry. How he met the problem may be seen from a few illustrations.

Late in the *Life* (iv. 311) are found "some particulars . . . collected at various times". The first item is a list of books recommended by Johnson to Astle (*post* From Astle, 23 Jan. 1787), who is duly acknowledged for the communication. There follows a long series of anecdotes without acknowledgement, the first three of which were also transmitted by Astle (*post* Dec. 1786). Similarly, an anecdote contributed by George Strahan appears without his name among illustrations of Johnson's "characteristical manner" during his last days, while a few pages later Strahan is acknowledged for his "agreeable assurance, that, after being in much agitation, Johnson became quite composed, and continued so till his death" (*Life* iv. 411, 416; *post* From George Strahan, 4 Mar. 1791). These illustrations point to a method; Boswell placed his acknowledgements where they counted, identifying his informants whenever it appeared necessary or desirable to lend authority to his information, and letting slide whatever spoke for itself.[1]

---

[1] Compare his practice of grouping anecdotes or sayings "without specifying each scene where it passed. . . . Where the place or the persons do not contribute to the zest of the conversation, it is unnecessary to encumber my page with mentioning them" (*Life* iii. 52; cf. iv. 176).

Moreover, a number of Boswell's omissions of the names of his authorities were dictated by the informants themselves, and if Boswell yielded, it was against his own wishes and better judgement (see, for example, *post* To Malone, 25 Feb. 1791 and n. 3). There is, finally, little evidence that Boswell ever suppressed a source for the purpose of passing the information off as his own.[1] Indeed, it did not serve his purpose to advance himself as sole authority for the life or character of his subject; the more competent witnesses he could bring forward, the more weight his biography would have.

In our examination of Boswell's use of the source materials themselves it will be convenient to distinguish between his revisions and omissions, and to proceed generally from technical to thematic considerations.

Boswell subjected his materials to every conceivable mode of revision: summary, paraphrase, expansion, conflation, interpolation, and so forth. The best explanation for these diverse practices, taken as a whole, is the obvious one: the necessity of accommodating what were essentially raw materials to a finished narrative. Two of Boswell's correspondents anticipated the problem, one in terms of content, the other in terms of style. Maxwell invited Boswell to "just make what Use you think proper" of his collection of Johnsoniana, and in his reply Boswell frankly admitted that he would use his "discretion in separating what is *adventitious*" (*post* 12 May and 4 July 1787). The other correspondent, Mickle, wrote: "If you make any use of it, I beg and adjure you not to print the above hasty Memorandum, but to reduce the heads of it into your own language" (*post* 28 Oct. 1786).

Our first specimen of revision recounts the first performance of *Irene*, as recollected by Dr. Adams. Boswell took it down from conversation in the form of rough notes and soon after filled it out (*post* June 1784). The expansion then served for the revised version in the *Life*.

Rough notes

present first night of Irene Catcalls Then murder etc. Mrs. Pritch obliged to go off alive.

[1] For a possible exception, see *post* From Mylne, 31 Dec. 1789.

Expansion

Dr. Adams told me he was present the first night when *Irene* was acted. There were Catcalls whistling before the Curtain drew up which was alarming. The Prologue soothed the Audience. The Play went off tolerably, till it came to the Conclusion when Mrs. Pritchard was to be strangled upon the Stage, and was to speak two lines with the bowstring round her neck. They cried out Murder Murder. She several times attempted to speak. But in vain. At last she was obliged to go off the Stage alive. Dr. Adams beleives it was altered afterwards.

Life (i. 196–97)

Dr. Adams was present the first night of the representation of *Irene*, and gave me the following account: 'Before the curtain drew up, there were catcalls whistling, which alarmed Johnson's friends. The Prologue, which was written by himself in a manly strain, soothed the audience, and the play went off tolerably, till it came to the conclusion, when Mrs. Pritchard, the heroine of the piece, was to be strangled upon the stage, and was to speak two lines with the bow-string round her neck. The audience cried out *"Murder! Murder!"* She several times attempted to speak; but in vain. At last she was obliged to go off the stage alive.'

The refinement of language was Boswell's confirmed practice, whether he was working with his own texts or those of others; but it was not his custom to call attention to this freedom. On the contrary, it is when he gives a *verbatim* reproduction of his text that he lets the reader know it (as we shall presently see). In a footnote to the present passage Boswell observes: "The expression used by Dr. Adams was 'soothed.' I should rather think the audience was *awed.* . . ." That he should feel obliged to certify that the quotation in this instance was direct testifies to his general practice.

The interpolations discovered in the process of revision are on the whole transparent: "which alarmed Johnson's friends" supplies an unstated reference; "the heroine of the piece" completes an identification; "which was written by himself in a manly strain" provides a cause for the effect. Taken together, the revisions may be understood as filling out an elliptical record and polishing an abbreviated or colloquial style.

While the vehicle of direct quotation in such usages may dismay our modern scholarly instincts, it is apparent that the practice caused neither Boswell nor his contributors any anxiety. There is not a murmur of complaint in the correspondence over being "mis-quoted"; nor is it likely that Boswell would have exposed himself to his own informants by taking liberties which he had reason to believe they would regard as licences.

The letter from Mickle mentioned above will serve to illustrate the extent to which Boswell might go in revising a text not his own. The parts of the letter he prints are given in two forms, summary-paraphrase and direct quotation. It is an extract from the latter that we need for our illustration.

Mickle

I had a few days before been reading the Doctor's Introduction to a *Collection of voyages* (I believe it is intitled) in which he strongly expresses his sentiments as above. I thought myself happy in this opportunity of having the topic discussed, and a dispute of more than an hour ensued. . . . I set about the discussion of that topic with spirit, and took the freedom to cite the Dr. (see Introd. to the *Lusiad* p. 1, 6, 7 and 8) who says in his work above mentioned, "It had been happy for both the old and the new worlds if the East and West Indies had never been discovered." This, you will find, I controvert. . . . Authors, it is said, are bad judges of their own works. Be it so, I am not however ashamed to own to a friend that that disser[ta]tion is my favourite above all I ever attempted in prose. About a month after the *Lusiad* was published I waited on the Dr. at his house. . . . he said with one of his good natured smiles "So I see you have remembered our dispute about Prince Henry (This was more than a year after) and have cited me too." He then handsomely complimented my disser[ta]tion, said I had made the best of my argument, *"but"* added he, *"I am not yet convinced."*

Life (iv. 250–51)

'This sentiment, (says Mr. Mickle,) which is to be found in his

"Introduction to the World displayed," I, in my Dissertation prefixed to the Lusiad, have controverted; and though authours are said to be bad judges of their own works, I am not ashamed to own to a friend, that that dissertation is my favourite above all that I ever attempted in prose. Next year, when the Lusiad was published, I waited on Dr. Johnson, who addressed me with one of his good-humoured smiles:—"Well, you have remembered our dispute about Prince Henry, and have cited me too. You have done your part very well indeed: you have made the best of your argument; but I am not convinced yet."'

Although Mickle himself authorized a free rendering of his letter (as noted above), one is struck by the alteration of words and phrases, the conflation and rearrangement of sentences and parts of sentences, the silent corrections,[1] and the invention of a piece of dialogue—all within quotation marks. Yet the impression of textual anarchy gives way before the recognition that in Boswell's revision there has been no loss or distortion of the essential content of Mickle's letter.

The more closely we look at Boswell's revisions the plainer it appears that he deliberately combined the roles of editor and literary critic. When a text qualified in form and style, he printed it verbatim; when it did not, he simply re-wrote it. Thus, of Thomas Warton's memorial of Johnson's visit to Oxford in 1754 he observes: "though not written with all the care and attention which that learned and elegant writer bestowed on those compositions which he intended for the public eye, [it] is so happily expressed in an easy style, that I should injure it by any alteration" (*Life* i. 271). Again: "Dr. Burney has kindly favoured me with the following memorandum, which I take the liberty to insert in his own genuine easy style" (*Life* i. 328). Boswell's liberties bespeak two concerns: the protection of his informants from indecent exposure and the protection of his readers from a medley of clashing styles.

---

[1] An example of an easily explicable omission in an otherwise faithfully transcribed text may be seen in the printing of Beattie's letter to Boswell, 3 May 1792. Beattie wrote: "As I suppose Your great work will soon be reprinted, I beg leave to trouble You with a remark or two on a passage of it, in which I am a little misrepresented. Be not alarmed; the misrepresentation is not imputable to You; it is in one of Dr. Johnson's letters." In the printing Boswell omitted the last clause—for the simple reason that Beattie's recollection of the context was wrong. The statement could of course have been retained, and corrected; but Boswell took the easier, less pedantic, and more considerate way.

Except for the letters of Johnson, which Boswell regarded as finished products to be faithfully if not perfectly preserved,[1] documents subsidiary to the main narrative were grist for his mill. The *Life* is less a compilation—one of Boswell's favourite and most misleading descriptions of the work—than it is a composition, in the full literary sense of that word.

Our last illustration of Boswell's revisions focuses on content rather than style. The text is Hector's reminiscence of Johnson at school (*post* 1 Feb. 1785), and reads in part:

> The Idler and I were very early school-fellows at Lichd, and for many Years in the same Class. As his uncommon abilities far exceeded us, we endeavour'd by every boyish mode of Flattery to gain his assistance, and three of us by turns us'd to call upon him in a Morning, on one of whose backs He rode triumphantly to School.

Here is the account in the *Life* (i. 47–48):

> His favourites used to receive very liberal assistance from him; and such was the submission and deference with which he was treated, such the desire to obtain his regard, that three of the boys, of whom Mr. Hector was sometimes one, used to come in the morning as his humble attendants, and carry him to school. One in the middle stooped, while he sat upon his back, and one on each side supported him; and thus he was borne triumphant. Such a proof of the early predominance of intellectual vigour is very remarkable, and does honour to human nature.

A comparison of Boswell's version with the original appears at first glance to expose a distortion: flattery is elevated to deference, self-seeking to reverence. But attention to the context of this passage in the *Life* shows that Boswell is here carefully adapting his material to a theme, and to a thesis. The theme is Johnson's intellectual superiority and the tribute voluntarily paid it by his fellows; the thesis—which governs the whole account of Johnson's early years—is that "the boy is the man in miniature":

> That superiority over his fellows, which he maintained with so much dignity in his march through life, was not assumed from vanity and ostentation, but was the natural and constant effect of

---

[1] See Chapman's discussion (*Letters SJ* iii. 306–09) of Boswell's treatment of Johnson's letters in the *Life*.

those extraordinary powers of mind, of which he could not but be conscious by comparison . . . From his earliest years, his superiority was perceived and acknowledged. He was from the beginning *Ἄναξ ἀνδρῶν*, a king of men. . . . In short, he is a memorable instance of what has been often observed, that the boy is the man in miniature: and that the distinguishing characteristicks of each individual are the same, through the whole course of life (*Life* i. 47).

We may note furthermore that Boswell's reinterpretation of Hector's Johnson was not without the authority of Hector himself, who "told me that he had the same extraordinary superiority over boys of the same age with himself that he has now over men" (*Note Book*, p. 4).

An omission from another part of Hector's account shows the same tendency towards reinterpretation on Boswell's part:

I never knew him corrected at School, unless it was for talking, and diverting the other boys from their business, by which perhaps he thought of gaining an ascendancy.

Boswell omitted in the printing the conjectured motive, perhaps (and we should not overlook *Hector's* "perhaps") because it does not easily fit into the picture of Johnson already in the ascendant, which is essentially Hector's own view. From this, and from illustrations to come, it is evident that Boswell, in editing his authorities, was engaged in more than polishing: he was aiming at a unified and coherent portrait.

On the subject of improving his *Ramblers* Johnson observed (*Life* iv. 309) that "there are three ways of making them better;— putting out,—adding,—or correcting." The "putting out" of Boswell's source materials is that activity in the making of the *Life* most likely to tease us into speculation. While revisions and omissions may share a common motive and produce a similar effect (as in the illustrations just given), the revision at least affords two immediate fixed quantities for analysis; the omission on the other hand, except in the rare case where the motive is self-evident (see, for example, *ante* p. xxxi, note), leaves us guessing. Boswell warned in the *Tour to the Hebrides* that "It is in vain to try to find a meaning in every one of [Johnson's] particularities" (*Life* v. 306); in our speculations over Boswell's own particularities as an editor the same warning is apposite. If, theoretically, every move is explicable, practically speaking, a great many of them elude us. Nevertheless, our inquiry into Boswell's motives in omitting certain materials is necessary—because natural curiosity abhors a vacuum—and desirable—because natural suspicion is so precipitate in filling it. In the notes I have offered explanations for omissions wherever the reasons appeared within easy reach; but these instances are few in relation to the sum total of unused materials. Instead of loading the commentary with speculations, I have chosen to discuss, and illustrate, the general problem here by way of introduction. The particular cases, as they turn up in the correspondence, may be more judiciously decided if we approach them with a full sense of the complexity of Boswell's task.

In his occasional remarks upon the subject of biography Boswell puts the claim of authenticity before all others. In the Advertisement to the first edition he declares "that the nature of the work . . . as it consists of innumerable detached particulars, all which, even the most minute, I have spared no pains to ascertain with a scrupulous authenticity, has occasioned a degree of trouble far beyond that of any other species of composition". While the present collection does much to uphold that claim, it at the same time shows it to be misleading in the emphasis it bears. Boswell verified far from all of his "innumerable detached particulars", for the simple reason that far from all of them were verifiable. As I have observed above, for a high proportion of his materials definitive authority was either beyond his reach or non-existent altogether. Reports of Johnson's conversation are a major case in point. Boswell remarked to Johnson in 1775 "that there were very few of his friends so accurate as that I could venture to put down in writing what they told me as his sayings" (*Life* ii. 133). What was true for Johnson's sayings was true for countless other assertions made about him; and where verification was impossible, Boswell had to fall back upon his own experience and knowledge of his subject.[1]

[1] The accuracy of Boswell's own record of Johnson's conversation has been generally accepted but not always construed in the same way. This is not the place to reconsider this question, but the topic presently under discussion encourages me to suggest that both Boswell's short-hand method and his occasional expressions of doubt over particular words and phrases indicate a concern not for overall or complete accuracy but for local verbal precision. In short, the "authentic" Johnsonian matter—and manner—were to be conveyed by key words and phrases, and it was probably their inattention to these vehicles that made Boswell distrustful of other reporters. Cf. F. A. Pottle, *James Boswell: The Earlier Years, 1740–1769*, 1966, p. 91.

The scrupulous authenticity advertised by Boswell is thus only a half-truth. The other half is disclosed in another statement of intention: "I am desirous that my work should be, as much as is consistent with the strictest truth, an antidote to the false and injurious notions of his character, which have been given by others" (*Life* iii. 391). Coming as it did after a succession of diverse biographical attempts, Boswell's *Life* took on a corrective as well as an expository function. In accounting for Boswell's omissions we may therefore expect to find this motive prominent.

Yet these two halves do not make a whole. Materials rejected on the grounds of factual error, doubtful attribution, misinterpretation, and so forth are balanced by another class of unused materials: those which appear to owe their exclusion to factors internal to the composition of the work. Certain formal exigencies obviously affected the editorial process. One of them—the limits of space—must be recognized as a general consideration, even though it cannot explain a particular omission. We know that the work in progress swelled beyond Boswell's expectations, and we may suppose that he exercised some restraint over his impulse to be exhaustive. In this effort he was helped by materials in his collection which duplicated each other or which would have served only to multiply examples; and in such cases we need normally look no further for our explanations.

A factor more difficult to estimate is the significance or worth of a given item of biography. The *Life of Johnson* was written in accordance with the avowed (Johnsonian) desideratum of minute particularity—which makes it peculiarly vulnerable to the charge of triviality. Boswell frequently anticipates the quizzical response: "And sure I am, that, however inconsiderable many of the particulars recorded at this time may appear to some, they will be esteemed by the best part of my readers as genuine traits of his character, contributing together to give a full, fair, and distinct view of it" (*Life* ii. 111). Elsewhere, in the space of two paragraphs, two apologies appear: "I cannot allow any fragment whatever that floats in my memory concerning the great subject of this work to be lost. Though a small particular may appear trifling to some, it will be relished by others; while every little spark adds something to the general blaze. . . . This may be laughed at as too trifling to record; but it is a small characteristick trait in the Flemish picture which I give of my friend, and in which, therefore,

I mark the most minute particulars" (iii. 190, 191). While Boswell in these passages is defending the inclusion of the significant trifle as it is found recorded in his own memoirs, the doctrine ought equally to hold for the memoirs of his correspondents. Yet a difference manifests itself at once: as I have observed, what Boswell adopted from his journal had already virtually passed the test of what the future biographer regarded as significant, whereas what he received from his contributors was still subject to this (admittedly obscure) process of discrimination. In studying the exclusion of materials from the second-hand sources, therefore, we must make allowance for the factor of value even though Boswell's general method creates an illusion of all-inclusiveness.

Finally, and most important in our enumeration of Boswell's editorial motives, we must recognize the factors of focus and emphasis. In so far as the finished *Life* may be supposed to reflect a steadiness of conception, we must assume that the editorial hand which worked upon the source materials was engaged in controlling their effects. The time is past when the praise of Boswell can be seriously construed as the praise of folly—or as sheer good luck. But the blame of Boswell will probably persist, on the grounds that however deliberate his art his focus and emphasis were such that he did not really give us Johnson (in his own ingenuous phrase) "as he really was". The rub for many readers of the present collection will be Boswell's treatment of those materials which deal with Johnson's weaknesses, real and alleged. His indolence, his oddities and asperity of manner, his excesses in eating and drinking, his profanity and bawdy, his sexual lapses, his intellectual narrowness and prejudice, his use of drugs, his insanity—all of these subjects appear among the unused sources, and seem to compose themselves into a pattern of suppression. Yet it is an equally demonstrable fact that all of these subjects are admitted to the published work in one form or another. Whatever construction Boswell may have put upon Johnson's weaknesses, it cannot be said that he concealed either the fact or the issue.

In the specimens that follow no attempt is made to display every possible motive of Boswell's in action; but a few typical cases may prepare the reader for the kinds of omission he will encounter in this volume. The analysis which accompanies them is intended to provide a context for interpretation rather than sure answers to every question. The passages chosen all deal with the "sensitive" subjects—not because omissions of this tenor predominate over others in number (they do not), but because they are the most deceptively self-evident.

In his study of the revision of the journal Scott observed Boswell occasionally suppressing indelicate elements in Johnson's talk and as a consequence giving us "slightly too clerical a picture". But, as Professor Pottle noted (BP x. 173–74), the main evidence for this conclusion is an obscenity which Boswell recorded as hearsay—together, it should be remarked, with the reflection, "The curiosity was that he should pronounce such a saying." The unwilling suspension of disbelief implied here is relevant to two of our passages:

(1) Dr. grew angry flew into a passion—and said, "Damn Maty —little dirty-faced dog. I'll throw him into the Thames (From Adams, June 1784).

In the *Life* (i. 284) "Damn" is omitted and "dirty-faced" altered to "black".

(2) Johnson's translation of the *Messiah* was first printed for his Father, without his knowledge or consent. Johnson told Taylor he was very angry at this and in his violent manner said if it had not been his Father he would have cut his throat (From Taylor, May 1785).

In the *Life* (i. 61) the second half of the last sentence is omitted.

Delicacy for its own sake is an uncertain test in explaining Boswell's revisions, as Scott pointed out. What seems more pertinent in these examples is a contradiction of Boswell's own experience. The only record of Johnson using profanity in Boswell's presence is printed in the *Tour to the Hebrides* (*Life* v. 306): "On Monday we had a dispute at the Captain's, whether sandhills could be fixed down by art. Dr. Johnson said, 'How *the devil* can you do it?' but instantly corrected himself, 'How can you do it?'—I never before heard him use a phrase of that nature." If the lapse is venial, it is all the more significant: Boswell's shock must mean that he had never heard anything worse from Johnson's lips—of that nature or any other.

On the other hand Boswell was not unused to the *attribution* of profanity, bawdy, and low language in general to Johnson. Speaking of a collection of *Johnsoniana, or Bon Mots of Dr.*

Johnson published in 1776, he asks (*Life* ii. 432–33): "Pray Sir, could you have no redress if you were to prosecute a publisher for bringing out, under your name, what you never said, and ascribing to you dull stupid nonsense, or making you swear profanely, as many ignorant relators of your *bon mots* do?" Neither Adams nor Taylor can be fairly put down as an ignorant relater, though in the one case we may note Johnson's caution "against giving implicit faith to Taylor's narratives" (From Taylor, 6 May 1785, n. 1). In any event Boswell was set against propagating a myth, even though the myth might originate in a fact—Johnson's notorious violence of manner and impassioned speech.

Fortifying his own personal experience were Johnson's frequent expressions of disapproval of swearing and bawdy. Among those recorded in the *Life* is a delightful account of Johnson's attack on "a gentleman-farmer" for using the word "damned" in which the offence is conveyed by his own ironic repetition of the word (iii. 189). The nearest thing to an admission by Johnson of the fault in himself occurs in a conversation in 1783 (*Life* iv. 215–16): "JOHNSON. . . . . 'I myself was for some years totally regardless of religion. It had dropped out of my mind. It was at an early part of my life. Sickness brought it back, and I hope I have never lost it since.' BOSWELL. 'My dear Sir, what a man you must have been without religion! Why you must have gone on drinking, and swearing, and—' JOHNSON. (with a smile) 'I drank enough and swore enough, to be sure.' " The *badinage* on Boswell's part seems to be met with a strategic concession rather than a genuine admission on Johnson's. In any case, the point of the conversation for us is what it says about Boswell's view of Johnson as the man he was, not the man he might have been.

From the problem of accurate reporting we proceed to the more central one—both for Boswell as a biographer and for ourselves as his critics—the problem of interpretation. Conflicting estimates of Johnson's character and behaviour would have posed no problem to a mere compiler, but to a true biographer who held firmly to a view of his subject and yet recognized the value of external authority it was a formidable one. At an early stage in the writing of the *Life* Boswell apparently decided to keep personalities out of the argument (see, for example, From Taylor, 6 May 1785, n. 3), unless of course the personalities were Hawkins or Mrs. Piozzi. Instead, he seems to adopt the estimate which (again) accorded with his own knowledge and experience or, where that failed, with his conception of the broad and enduring lines of Johnson's character. This is not to say that he never entertained contradictions; but he obviously did not feel bound to publish every version of Johnson known to him, or to present his choices polemically at every turn. Boswell's omissions—and revisions—are thus the unspoken commentary on his biographical conception.

Omitted from Boswell's account of the Birmingham period is the statement that Johnson "used to be absent and talk to himself and abuse Hector who would then keep aloof upon which Johnson would come and coax him" (*post* From Hector, 28 Mar. 1785). Elsewhere in the *Life* there are narrations of Johnson's absent-mindedness, his habit of talking to himself, his abuse of his friends, and his eager attempts at reconciliation. An example of the last involves Boswell himself (*Life* ii. 106–09), who moralizes: "This little incidental quarrel and reconciliation . . . must be esteemed as one of the many proofs which his friends had, that though he might be charged with *bad humour* at times, he was always a *good-natured* man; and I have heard Sir Joshua Reynolds, a nice and delicate observer of manners, particularly remark, that when upon any occasion Johnson had been rough to any person in company, he took the first opportunity of reconciliation, by drinking to him, or addressing his discourse to him; but if he found his dignified indirect overtures sullenly neglected, he was quite indifferent, and considered himself as having done all that he ought to do, and the other as now in the wrong." Hector's account is not inconsistent with the characterization of Johnson as both bad-humoured and good-natured, but the picture of Johnson *coaxing* his victim clashes with Sir Joshua's (nicer and more delicate?) observation of his "dignified indirect overtures", not to mention Boswell's own general conception of Johnson as a man too great to stoop.[1]

If there is any one aspect of Johnson which Boswell may be said to have pre-empted under his own critical authority, it is the quality of his mind. On this subject we find the biographer firmest in his conviction, even to the extent of overruling the subject

[1] Except—to Boswell's great dismay —before Mrs. Piozzi: see Journ. 7 Mar. 1788. Against the testimony of Reynolds must be put that of his sister, who tells of Johnson coaxing Thomas Barnard (then Dean of Derry, later Bishop of Killaloe) after an offence, "with such a beseeching look for pardon, and with such fond gestures—literally smoothing down his arms and his knees—tokens of penitence" (*Johns. Misc.* ii. 263).

himself. Another part of Hector's account (*post* 28 Mar. 1785) illustrates Boswell's stand on the vexed question of Johnson's alleged insanity:

> When at Birmingham the time now mentioned [1732–34] Hector was affraid of Dr. Johnson's head, and he thought there was the same apprehension after he went to London. Johnson had been conscious of it all along but had been affraid to ask Hector for fear of an answer in the affirmative. When last at Birmingham [1784] he asked Hector if he had observed in him a tendency to be disorde[re]d in his mind. Hector said he had.

The diagnosis—and the whole passage—were rejected out of hand; for Boswell was steadfast in denying all assertions, including Johnson's own, that he was ever afflicted with insanity or even suffered a tendency towards it. Boswell's view was that Johnson confounded melancholy and madness (*Life* i. 35, 65–66, iii. 175). "That his own diseased imagination should have so far deceived him, is strange; but it is stranger still that some of his friends should have given credit to his groundless opinion, when they had such undoubted proofs that it was totally fallacious" (i. 66).

A related omission occurs in the printing of Dr. Brocklesby's account of Johnson's last days (*post* 27 Dec. 1784). Johnson, having learned from his physician that he could not recover, determined to give up taking opiates so that he might render up his soul to God "unclouded". Boswell prints Brocklesby's narrative thus far, but then omits what follows:

> "for" said he "Opiates though they ever lulled my bodily pains yet they usually filld my imagination with horrors and visions that disturbed for several hours my clear judgem[en]t and I should be loth to dy in that state with any overcast to cloud it."

Hawkins, whose account of Johnson's end is rather more lugubrious than Boswell's, reports that Johnson took opium in large quantities, observes that "the fabric of his mind was tottering", and, presumably on Brocklesby's authority, tells of Johnson's fear of dying insane (pp. 540, 541, 585). Boswell had recorded under 23 March 1783 (*Life* iv. 171) the fact that Johnson had "taken opium the night before. He however protested against it, as a remedy that should be given with the utmost reluctance, and only in extreme necessity." It is clear from Johnson's letters that he took opium as sparingly as his health would permit and that he regarded its effects with "terrour". Boswell's suppression of Johnson's past experience of "horrors and visions", though it seems unwarranted in fact, is consistent with his effort to dissociate apparent from real madness. And rather than dwell on Johnson's anxiety in his account of "the death" (as he called it), he emphasizes the characteristic resolution that was summoned to combat it—and the successful result. For eyewitnesses (including Brocklesby) reported that Johnson died composed of mind (*Life* iv. 416, 419).

In addition to a straight report of Johnson's last days Brocklesby offered Boswell a diagnosis of Johnson's intellectual schizophrenia, according to the deistic creed:

> His Religion was the true Δεισιδαιμονία of Plutarch, which narrowed the wonderful powers of his judgement and made his extraordinary talents of mind continually at war with each other, so that in his later days his Philosophy seemed to draw his mind one way and his Religion byassed him to the contrary; and may have occasioned that continual perplexity, and doubts and fears, in which the greater portion of his life was passed.

Boswell omitted the passage[1] but without rejecting all of Brocklesby's views. More than once the narrowing effect of Johnson's orthodox principles is conceded in the *Life*. Commenting upon their argument over predestination and free will in 1769 Boswell observes (*Life* ii. 104): "His supposed orthodoxy here cramped the vigorous powers of his understanding. He was confined by a chain which early imagination and long habit made him think massy and strong, but which, had he ventured to try, he could at once have snapt asunder." And conspicuously, at the very end of the *Life* (iv. 426), in summing up "the capital and distinguishing features of this extraordinary man", he writes: "He was a sincere and zealous Christian, of high Church-of-England and monarchical principles, which he would not tamely suffer to be questioned; and had, perhaps, at an early period, narrowed his mind somewhat too much, both as to religion and politicks." This last observation occurs only a few pages following the contributions of Brocklesby which Boswell did use (iv. 416–17), and it is natural to suppose

---

[1] At the point in the MS. *Life* where Boswell is introducing Brocklesby's testimony on Johnson's religious faith (p. 1032), the following deletion (originally an addition) occurs: "after mentioning the perplexity and doubts in which the Doctor supposes the greater portion of his life was passed".

that Boswell wished to save the mention of this important article for his peroration.

But the implication in Brocklesby's analysis of a radical conflict between Johnson's philosophy and his religion—a not uncommon view both then and now—Boswell refused to accept. Speaking of Johnson's habit of making pious acknowledgements in his prayers (*Life* i. 305), he employs a dubious logic: "If there be any thoughtless enough to suppose such exercises the weakness of a great understanding, let them look up to Johnson and be convinced that what he so earnestly practised must have a rational foundation." More persuasive is his analysis of Johnson's "doubts and fears" respecting death (*Life* ii. 298): "He had, indeed, an awful dread of death, or rather, 'of something after death;' and what rational man, who seriously thinks of quitting all that he has ever known, and going into a new and unknown state of being, can be without that dread? But his fear was from reflection; his courage natural. His fear, in that one instance, was the result of philosophical *and* religious consideration." The italics are mine; the insight Boswell's. In the pre-eminently rational man, all perplexities make sense.

We may conclude our survey of Boswell's editing by looking at two omitted anecdotes which, if inspected for authenticity, relevance, and interest alone, would seem easily to pass muster. The first is from Taylor, the second from Hector (*post* 6 May 1785, 28 Mar. 1785):

(1) When Dr. Johnson was last at Ashbourne he said to Dr. Taylor, "I am resolved to confine myself to a milk diet I see it does you so much good." That very day there was a glorious haunch of vennison at Taylor's table. Dr. Johnson eat and eat again. Alsop who did not like him, wickedly prest him to eat more—which he did. He grew so ill that it was feared he would have died of downright eating, and had not a Surgeon been got to administer to him without delay a glister he must have died. After this, he took to a milk diet, and improved so much in his health that he became quite a new man and beat them all in walking home from church.

(2) Dr. Johnson some years later told me there was no man alive who had seen him drunk. Mr. Hector said—"then he had forgot me." For once when he lived at Birmingham there

came a Relation of his of the name of Ford from Stourbridge
to whom he had been under obligations. He was it seems
a hard drinker and he engaged Johnson and Hector to
spend the evening with him at the Swan Inn. Johnson said
to Hector, "This fellow will make us both drunk. Let us take
him by turns, and get rid of him." It was settled that Hector
should go first. He and Ford had drank three bottles of Port
before Johnson came. When Johnson arrived, Hector found
he had been drinking at Mr. Porter's instead of saving
himself. Hector went to bed at the Swan leaving Johnson to
drink on with Ford. Next morning he perceived that Johnson
who had been his bedfellow had been Very drunk and he
dammed him. Johnson tried to deny the charge. Literally
speaking Hector had not *seen* him drunk, though he was *sure*
of the fact. I said He must have been a monstrous Silenus.

While it is true that incidents such as these are just the sort that
lend themselves to embroidery, there is no evident reason why
Boswell should have suspected the essential veracity of either
account. In the *Life* (i. 468) he gives his own vivid description of
Johnson's coarseness at table, and concludes: "To those whose
sensations were delicate, this could not but be disgusting; and it
was doubtless not very suitable to the character of a philosopher,
who should be distinguished by self-command. But it must be
owned, that Johnson, though he could be rigidly *abstemious*, was not
a *temperate* man either in eating or drinking." Had Boswell wanted
further illustrations of his point, either or both of the present
anecdotes would have served admirably. But he seems to have
realized that he ran the risk of making certain points not wisely but
too well. Such grotesquerie as these materials depicted threatened
to lose the man in the monster. Boswell's artistic dilemma was not
unlike Johnson's personal one: he could refrain, but he could not
use moderately.[1]

It remains to ask whether Boswell's editorial techniques can be
elucidated in terms of a governing principle of biography. We have

[1] A more particular reason for not
printing Hector's anecdote might possibly
be inferred from Boswell's use of it:
"though he loved to exhilarate himself
with wine, he [Hector] never knew him
intoxicated but once" (*Life* i. 94). It is
clear from the source that Hector meant
to answer Johnson's boast, not to support
it by recalling only a single instance to the
contrary. In making his own point, Boswell
blunted Hector's, though Hector
could not but have subscribed to Boswell's
as well.

already noticed Boswell's reticence on the subject of his art, but fortunately he was hurt into criticism by his rival, Mrs. Piozzi. It is in his animadversions upon the *Anecdotes*, if anywhere, that something approaching a statement of principle is to be found. The burden of the critique (articulated with the help of that "nice" critic, Malone) is that the *Anecdotes*, being fragmentary, condensed, and unconnected, give a misleading notion of Johnson's character (*Life* i. 410, iv. 340–47):

> His occasional reproofs of folly, impudence, or impiety, and even the sudden sallies of his constitutional irritability of temper, which have been preserved for the poignancy of their wit, have produced that opinion [of the harshness of his general demeanour] among those who have not considered that such instances, though collected by Mrs. Piozzi into a small volume, and read over in a few hours, were, in fact, scattered through a long series of years; years, in which his time was chiefly spent in instructing and delighting mankind by his writings and conversation, in acts of piety to GOD, and good-will to men.

> . . . wherever an instance of harshness and severity is told, I beg leave to doubt its perfect authenticity; for though there may have been *some* foundation for it, yet . . . it may be so exhibited in the narration as to be very unlike the real fact.

> The evident tendency of the following anecdote is to represent Dr. Johnson as extremely deficient in affection, tenderness, or even common civility.

Perfect authenticity is to be found not in the discrete historical fact, but in its representation—in the control of implications and "evident tendencies". To say this is to recall the commonplace that history, or biography, is ultimately an art, and our discussion seems inevitably to have led us to a point where the problem of Boswell's editorial tactics and the question of his artistry have merged.

IV. Boswell's Johnson

Geoffrey Scott, in concluding his study of the making of the *Life*, preferred the conclusion in which not everything is concluded. His argument is all but irresistible:

> To speak of the final achievement to which all this labour was

directed, would perhaps be a logical, but certainly an impertinent, conclusion. It is a quality of the *Life of Johnson* that its appeal is not less intimate than universal; the praise or comment of a critic, even when we agree with his statement, falls like a hand officiously and needlessly intruded on a private possession. This silencing consideration, if it applies in regard to every reader of the *Life*, has still greater force in the presence of the Johnsonian scholars for whose convenience these documents have been assembled, and who may, with better right, fulfill what is not here attempted.

Like Scott, we have pushed to our own logical conclusion (indeed, the cases are virtually identical), and if we cannot, despite his example, resist speaking of the final achievement, we can only hope that the impertinence will be forgiven by common readers and scholars alike.

This introduction began with the suggestion that the greatness of Boswell's biography owes as much to its wholeness as its fullness, as much to the synthesis of its multitudinous facts as the facts themselves. Any analysis of Boswell's editorial practices must be tested finally against a conception of the finished work; the limited contexts in which we view the particulars of Boswell's method must be enlarged to include the spectacle of the whole.

Admittedly, the spectacle of the whole of the *Life of Johnson* is bewildering. The disjointed and unbalanced narrative deprives the reader of one form of regularity upon which the eye might rest. Moreover, though Boswell's scheme is chronological, it is in no real sense progressive. Instead of the growth of a mind (the absence of which modern critics have repeatedly deplored), Boswell deliberately shows us its unaltered passage through the world. In this light neither completeness nor order matters so much as singleness of impression. Yet Boswell's tireless marking of "the most minute particulars" in his "Flemish picture" conveys an extraordinary variety—or at least the illusion of it. The range of the conversations is probably the principal tributary to this effect; but the conversations themselves illustrate, what Boswell's own narrative so often makes explicit, a certain level of uniformity in Johnson's life.

No trait of Johnson's receives more emphasis in the biography than his intellectual powers and the use to which he put them:

But his superiority over other learned men consisted chiefly in what may be called the art of thinking, the art of using his mind; a certain continual power of seizing the useful substance of all that he knew, and exhibiting it in a clear and forcible manner; so that knowledge, which we often see to be no better than lumber in men of dull understanding, was, in him, true, evident, and actual wisdom (iv. 427–28).

Johnson's pre-eminence of mind is insisted upon throughout. He had "a knowledge of Latin, in which, I believe, he was exceeded by no man of his time" (i. 45). He was the intellectual superior of his fellow-students and indeed of his teachers. In the development of English prose "he appeared to lead the national taste" (i. 222). "In biography there can be no question that he excelled, beyond all who have attempted that species of composition" (i. 256). In the writing of dedications "no man excelled Dr. Johnson" (ii. 1). Johnson enters upon a company and "we were all as quiet as a school upon the entrance of the head-master" (iii. 332).

Goldsmith complained to Boswell "for talking of Johnson as entitled to the honour of unquestionable superiority. 'Sir, (said he,) you are for making a monarchy of what should be a republic'" (ii. 257). The metaphor is in fact Boswell's own favourite way of expressing Johnson's supremacy.[1] We have already noted (*ante* pp. xxxii–iii) the passage in which Johnson the schoolboy, "a king of men", was "borne triumphant". He was "a majestick teacher of moral and religious wisdom" (i. 201). "His majestick expression would have carried down to the latest posterity the glorious achievements of his country" (i. 355). Upon Johnson's writings Boswell reflects: "Tastes may differ as to the violin, the flute, the hautboy, in short, all the lesser instruments: but who can be insensible to the powerful impressions of the majestick organ?" (ii. 335). But the best illustration of this view of Johnson is a dramatic one: the famous interview with the King. For the ironic effect of the episode is to establish the majesty of Johnson, not of George III. It is to Johnson's authority that all questions are put; his also the privilege of stooping to compliment. He "talked to his Majesty with profound respect, but still in his firm manly manner,

[1] Compare Courtenay's *Moral and Literary Character of Dr. Johnson*: "By nature's gifts ordain'd mankind to rule" and "his philosophick throne" (*Life* i. 222–23).

xlvi

with a sonorous voice, and never in that subdued tone which is commonly used at the levee and in the drawing-room. After the King withdrew, Johnson shewed himself highly pleased with his Majesty's conversation and gracious behaviour" (ii. 40).[1]

Goldsmith's complaint is essentially that of all those who, without Goldsmith's personal grievance, charge Boswell with undue veneration of Johnson. Reverence is undoubtedly Boswell's last word on the subject—and indeed the last word of the *Life*. But the attitude of reverence calls for examination before calling for apology (as Carlyle saw). The royal metaphor points to the particular meaning of Boswell's awe: what he worshipped was not the mind for its own sake, but its power to *govern*. That there was a deep private need underlying Boswell's devotion is clear enough:

I complained of a wretched changefulness, so that I could not preserve, for any long continuance, the same views of any thing. It was most comfortable to me to experience, in Dr. Johnson's company, a relief from this uneasiness. His steady vigorous mind held firm before me those objects which my own feeble and tremulous imagination frequently presented, in such a wavering state, that my reason could not judge well of them (iii. 193).

In paying this tribute Boswell lightly passes over Johnson's admission in the preceding paragraph that he was *not* always "the same". The infirmity of Johnson's mind (revealed so strikingly in the diaries) was a fact that his biographer recognized; but the greater fact for him was Johnson's constancy in spite of it.

"To have the management of the mind is a great art", says Johnson (*Life* ii. 440). The mind in this maxim is both object and subject, and the Johnsonian triumph, according to Boswell, is the triumph not only of mind over matter (poverty, neglect, disease) but of mind over mind itself (the dangerous prevalence of imagination).

---

[1] Boswell acknowledges no fewer than five different sources for this narrative, any or all of which may have contributed the suggestion of a reversal of stations. A comparison between Boswell's version and its principal source, the "Caldwell Minute", shows Boswell setting the stage for his drama by sweeping some of the *dramatis personae* off it: namely, other persons present in the library, to whom the King "talked for some time" before turning to Johnson (F. Taylor, *Johnsoniana from the Bagshawe Muniments in the John Rylands Library: Sir James Caldwell, Dr. Hawkesworth, Dr. Johnson, and Boswell's Use of the "Caldwell Minute"*: reprinted from *Bull. Rylands Lib.*, 1952, xxxv. 211–47).

We cannot but admire his spirit when we know, that amidst a complication of bodily and mental distress, he was still animated with the desire of intellectual improvement (ii. 263).

Notwithstanding his afflicted state of body and mind this year, the following correspondence affords a proof . . . of . . . his extraordinary command of clear and forcible expression (iv. 149).

In 1783, he was more severely afflicted than ever . . . but still the same ardour for literature, the same constant piety, the same kindness for his friends, and the same vivacity, both in conversation and writing, distinguished him (iv. 163).

Johnson's weaknesses, as our survey of Boswell's sources disclosed, are methodically viewed under the aspect of his strengths: his indolence together with his energy, his excesses of appetite together with his abstemiousness, even his sexual irregularities together with the force of his conscience (*Life* iv. 395–98). But it was Johnson's "morbid melancholy" that fascinated Boswell most and provided him with his major theme. If the mind is the most powerful weapon for coping with the world, it is also the most vulnerable target for the assailants of life. Johnson's greatest strength and his greatest weakness were near allied: the mind that preys on everything will at times prey upon itself. As we have seen, Boswell emphatically refused the allegation of insanity in Johnson and instead presented him as ever rising above his affliction. One early episode dramatizes the achievement in a striking way: Johnson's diagnosing his own melancholy for his own physician, Dr. Swinfen, in 1729. Boswell comments:

The powers of his great mind might be troubled, and their full exercise suspended at times; but the mind itself was ever entire. As a proof of this, it is only necessary to consider, that, when he was at the very worst, he composed that state of his own case, which shewed an uncommon vigour, not only of fancy and taste, but of judgement (i. 65).

The worst is not, when we can say the worst; and a Johnson can push the paradox further by saying it best.

Saying it best describes Johnson's talk as well as his writings, and his oral prowess may be seen as both a symptom of the radical cause of his melancholy and its palliative. We know that society was for Johnson an escape from the horrors of solitude, but (despite the self-deprecating self-portrait of Mr. Sober in *Idler* 31) talk meant more than distraction: it was action itself. Johnson's conversation "will best display his character", says Boswell (*Life* i. 31); and indeed, as anxiously preserved, or rather re-created, by Boswell, it is the most dramatic expression in the biography of the theme we have been tracing.

The image of Johnson as dogmatist probably owes more to the records of his talk than to his writings, for it is in conversation that he is most opinionated, peremptory, and violent. Yet it is a peculiarity of Johnson's mode of talking that it was deliberately defensive; Boswell tells us that he rarely initiated conversation, which, we may imagine, was for him a microcosm of the world: a flux of sentiments and beliefs, unsettling to a greater or lesser degree, and therefore requiring to be answered. For Johnson was dedicated, nay addicted, to settling notions. "Oglethorpe, Sir, never *completes* what he has to say." "Sir, there is nothing *conclusive* in [Lord Elibank's] talk." "Goldsmith had no settled notions upon any subject; so he always talked at random" (*Life* iii. 56–57, 352). To settle the most minute question was to affirm the authority of the mind, which meant in effect to put the world temporarily back in order. It is only before the great question of the greater order of the "other" world, the question of "futurity", that the mind of Johnson shrank. "He talked to me upon this awful and delicate question in a gentle tone, and as if afraid to be decisive" (*Life* iii. 200; cf. iii. 154, iv. 177). This is the Johnson of private life, of the diaries and prayers—"unsettled and perplexed", as Boswell describes him (*Life* iii. 98). But the Johnson of the *Life* is combative and, though not all-conquering, at least impressively holding his own:

> His mind resembled the vast amphitheatre, the Colisaeum at Rome. In the centre stood his judgment, which, like a mighty gladiator, combated those apprehensions that, like the wild beasts of the *Arena*, were all around in cells, ready to be let out upon him. After a conflict, he drove them back into their dens; but not killing them, they were still assailing him (ii. 106).

Boswell's simile is meant to represent Johnson's fear of death specifically, but it serves as well as an image of the whole tragic striving of his life. For Johnson is surely an eminent case of man girding his constancy before his inevitable change, and presuming to make definitive pronouncements in a finite world. Boswell, who knew how perilous this balance was, could still regard Johnson as *semper idem*, the apotheosis of sanity.

What it took to create such a portrait is pithily suggested in a passage joining in characteristic fashion a Johnsonian saying and a Boswellian reflection:

> Johnson said, "A madman loves to be with people whom he fears; not as a dog fears the lash; but of whom a person stands in awe." I was struck with the justice of this observation. To be with those of whom a person, whose mind is wavering and dejected, stands in awe, represses and composes an uneasy tumult of spirits, and consoles himself with the contemplation of something steady, and at least comparatively great (iii. 176).

Let us do for Boswell what he did for Johnson, and allow his own melancholy to be free of the implication of madness. Yet, in missing the irony of his analogy, did he not hit the mark of his achievement? If Johnson alive was that something steady, and steadying, of which Boswell stood in awesome contemplation, the writing of the *Life* was more than memorial therapy, the patient ministering to himself; the hypochondriac turned artist steadied his own doctor and consoled *us* with the contemplation of something at least comparatively great.

Our judgement of Boswell the editor must ultimately rest, we have argued, upon our judgement of Boswell the biographer— upon, that is, an appreciation of the finished work of art. If the fullness of that work has been more generally remarked than its wholeness, a study of Boswell's sources should subtract something from the one quality and add it to the other. And if the result does nothing to alter the long and widely held view that Boswell's Johnson is an "idealized" portrait, it may help alleviate our suspicion that what is idealized is therefore of necessity untrue. That the *Life* might have contained more truths and fewer errors is of course obvious; and it has been the work of scholarly commentary to bring it progressively to that desired condition. But it is equally obvious that, no matter how many new facts are brought to light, Samuel Johnson will always be somebody's hypothesis. And none has pleased so many, or is likely to please so long, as Boswell's.

CHRONOLOGY OF THE MAKING
OF THE *LIFE*

THIS calendar supplements the record of biographical activity
found in the correspondence and other papers collected in this
volume. I have thought it useful however to repeat here those
statements in Boswell's letters printed below which help date the
progress (real or imagined) of the *Life*. Quotations for which no
reference is given are from the journal.

1768 ?2 May. "As he had objected to a part of one of his letters
being published [in the *Account of Corsica*], I thought it
right to take this opportunity of asking him explicitly
whether it would be improper to publish his letters after
his death. His answer was, 'Nay, Sir, when I am dead, you
may do as you will'" (*Life* ii. 60).

1772 31 Mar. "I have a constant plan to write the *Life* of Mr.
Johnson. I have not told him of it yet; nor do I know if
I should tell him. I said that if it was [not] troublesome
and presuming too much I would beg of him to tell me all
the little circumstances of his life, what schools he attended,
when he came to Oxford, when he came to London etc. etc.
He did not dissapprove of my curiosity as to these
particulars; but said 'They'll come out by degrees'"
(Journ.; later edited as MS. *Life*: *Life* ii. 166).

5 May. "Percy a little and got note of Johns."

7 May. "Percy, note of Johns works."

1773 11 Apr. "I asked him if he could tell when he was born,
when he came to London and such things. Said he, 'You
shall have them (or I'll give you them) all for twopence. I
hope you shall know a great deal more of me, before you
write my *Life*.'" Some particulars follow. Cf. *Life* ii. 217.

1775 1 Apr. "Said I: 'There are few from whom I can put down in
writing your sayings.' JOHNSON. 'Why should you put
down my sayings?' BOSWELL. 'When they are good.'
JOHNSON. 'Nay, you may as well put down the sayings of
any one else that are good.'"

1775 6 Nov. "Dr. Johnson has said nothing to me of my Remarks during my Journey with him which I wish to write. . . . If I do not publish them now, they will be good materials for My *Life of Dr. Johnson*" (To Temple: MS. Pierpont Morgan Lib.).

1776 20 Mar. "I had desired much to see Adams, and once thought of going to Shrewsbury to visit him, supposing that he could tell me a great deal of Dr. Johnson's University life. I got a little from him, which is marked in the little Book of Notes for Dr. Johnson's Life." See *"Note Book"* under Cue Titles and Abbreviations.

22 Mar. "Mr. Hector told me several anecdotes of Dr. Johnson, which I have marked in a Book of Notes concerning the Dr. I wished to be longer with him to get more; for Dr. Johnson said I might pretty well depend on what he related."

24 Mar. "I returned to Peter Garrick's to Coffee and tea while Dr. Johnson went to visit Miss Aston. . . . Peter got into a livelier humour than usual, and told many little anecdotes of his brother's going on the stage, and of Dr. Johnson."

25 Mar. "Mrs. Porter told me a good deal about Dr. Johnson."

15 Apr. "I got [Langton] to talk of Johnson and he told me some particulars which are to be found in the little book which I keep solely for Dr. Johnson's Life. I hope I shall have many of them filled."

9 May. "Percy's at Northumb[erland] House. . . . copied note about Dr. J."

30 Aug. "It would be very kind if you would take the trouble to transmit to me sometimes a few of his admirable sayings which you collect. May I beg of you to mark them down as soon as you can. You know what he says in his *Journey* of 'dilatory notation.' You and I shall make up a Great Treasure between us" (To Mrs. Thrale: MS. Nat. Lib. Scot. 3278, f. 53).

1777 14 Feb. "I wish much that I could make a complete collection of every thing that has been published by you, or concerning you. But I suppose that cannot now be done. I shall get together what I can" (To Johnson).

22 Sept. "my Journal of every portion of time which I have

1777   had the happiness . . . to be with him contains valuable materials for his *Life*."

23 Sept. "He had, at this time, frankly communicated to me many particulars, which are inserted in this work in their proper places" (*Life* iii. 196).

1779 16 Mar. "I then found Mr. Strahan at home, and was pleased with . . . his wish to communicate to me all that he knew concerning Dr. Johnson."

Spring. "During my stay in London this spring, I find I was unaccountably negligent in preserving Johnson's sayings, more so than at any time when I was happy enough to have an opportunity of hearing his wisdom and wit" (*Life* iii. 376).

18–19 Oct. Conversations with the Lichfield friends of Johnson, on the way to Chester (*Life* iii. 411–12).

1780 12 Oct. "I told Erskine I was to write Dr. Johnson's *Life* in Scenes. He approved."

1781 27 Mar. "Stevens told several anecdotes of Dr. Johnson. But I will have them in writing from him, that they may be correctly recorded."

1782 9 July. "Anecdotes of our literary or gay freinds, but particularly of our illustrious Imlac, would delight me" (To Mrs. Thrale: printed *Letters JB* 209; MS. Hyde, a draft).

1784 18 Dec. "In the evening I read two Accounts of Dr. Johnson's death in the *Public Advertiser* and *London Chronicle*. And I had a letter from Mr. Dilly mentioning it, and in the true spirit of *the trade* wanting to know if I could have an Octavo volume of 400 pages of his conversations ready by Febry. I had had a letter from him lately [before Johnson's death] suggesting that I might be the editor of all his works and write his *Life*. I answered him [7 Dec.] that I had a large collection of Materials for his *Life*, but would write it deliberately. I was now uneasy to think that there would be considerable expectations from me of Memoirs of my illustrious Freind; but that habits of indolence and dejection of spirit would probably hinder me from laudable exertion. I wish I could write now, as when I wrote my *Account of Corsica*. But I hoped I should do better than I at first apprehended."

1784 20 Dec. "Mr. Dilly that I should announce my intention to publish the *Life of Dr. Johnson*" (Reg. Let.).

23 Dec. "Mr. Dilly that I intend to publish in the Spring my tour with Dr. Johnson, a good Prelude to my large Work his *Life*. Will he go halves in an edition?" (Reg. Let.).

25 Dec. "Mr. Dilly that the People at large will pay more respect to a life of Dr. Johnson by me than by any of his Executors therefore wishing I may prepare for publication as soon as I can" (Reg. Let.).

1785 11 Jan. "Mr. C. Dilly that I shall first publish my *Journal of a Tour to the Hebrides*. etc." (Reg. Let.).

21 Jan. "I wrote to Mr. Hector at Birmingham Dr. Adams at Oxford and Miss Seward for materials for Dr. Johnson's *Life* and got good packets from all of them."

20 Mar. "It [the *Tour*] will be a Prelude to my large Work, *The Life of Samuel Johnson L.L.D.* for which I have been making collections for upwards of twenty years and which I really hope will be a Valuable treasure of Literary Anecdotes, and of the genuine emanations of his energy of mind. It will be some time before it is ready for publication" (To Bishop Barnard).

1 June. "Breakfasted with Strahan. . . . Gave me a *little* about Dr. Johnson, and promised to look out *some* of his letters and notes."

29 June. "Dined Dr. Brocklesby at 3 . . . Dull a little—till he brought me sixteen letters from Dr. Johnson."

12 July. "Dined worthy Langton . . . Got Letter to Lord Chesterfield."

1 Oct. The first authorized advertisement appeared at the end of the *Tour*.

22 Dec. "Met Dr. Johnson's Frank in the street, and he promised to search for every scrap of his Master's handwriting, and give all to me. It vexed me to be told that he had burnt some letters from Dr. Johnson to Mrs. Johnson."

25 Dec. "I told [Mason] . . . he should appear in the *Life*. . . . I said I would shew him what Dr. Johnson said against him before printing it. He seemed not to desire this; but I shall do it." See *Life* ii. 335, iii. 31–32.

1786 12 Jan. "Lord Monboddo came in to the [Advocates'] Library. I bowed to him, but he did not speak to me. I understood afterwards that he was violent against me. I did not care. I considered that it would make him *fair game* in Dr. Johnson's *Life*."

20 Feb. "Dined Sir Joshua's . . . After dinner wrote some anecdotes of Dr. Johnson dictated by Sir Joshua."

26 Feb. "[THURLOW.] '. . . You are going to publish something more about Dr. Johnson?' B[OSWELL.] 'Yes My Lord. I am going to give *tota vita Senis*.'"

1 Mar. "Then waited on Sir Francis Lumm who had obligingly procured me from Sir John Caldwell a Minute of the conversation between the King and Dr. Johnson which was in the late Sir James Caldwell's repositories. . . . He gave me Lord Carmarthen's Letter to him containing his Majesty's permission that the Minute should be delivered to me to make what use of it I should think proper in my *Life of Dr. Johnson*."

5 June. "At home all forenoon sorting materials for Dr. Johnson's *Life*. Dined at Mr. Taylor's Old Burlington Street with Seward, the Rev. Dr. Maxwell of Ireland who had lived 25 years in London, and been much with Dr. Johnson . . . Mr. Taylor had through Seward asked me to meet Dr. Maxwell. . . . Maxwell had a good deal of Johnson."

8 June. "did a little in sorting Johnsonian Materials."

9 June. "Malone's a little, and got advice as to my *Life of Johnson*—to make a Skeleton with references to the materials, in order of time."

12 June. "I sat at home all day, sorting materials for Johnson's *Life*, and took neither dinner nor tea. This was wrong."

14 June. "Sorted Johnsonian Materials, a little. Went with Sastres, and was introduced to Mrs. [Charlotte Lewis], widow of an irish Dean, who with her sister Miss Cottrel who lives with her but who was not at home were old acquaintances of Dr. Johnson, and made him and Sir Joshua Reynolds acquainted. She could give me no materials for his *Life*."

15 June. "Staid at home all forenoon sorting Johnsonian

1786   materials. But there was something in the weather which relaxed me so that I was quite inactive. However I kept at it. I dined (for the first time) with the Right Hon. William Gerrard Hamilton. . . . The occasion of my being at length invited to his house was my being engaged in writing Dr. Johnson's *Life*. He promised to give me two letters of the Doctor's to him, and some Anecdotes."

22 June. "Resolved to sit all day sorting Johnsonian Materials. [Breaks resolve.] Returned home and sorted till I was stupified."

27 June. "Malone and I walked in the Temple Garden. He then went home with me, and . . . heard me read some Johnsoniana."

28 June. "nothing yet done to Johnson's *Life*."

29 June. "Resolved to fast and try to write. Could do little."

3 July. "My next consideration is Dr. Johnson's *Life*, which it is necessary I should get ready for the press soon, that the publick attention may not be diverted to some other object; and as I have collected a great variety of materials, it will probably be a Work of considerable value. Mr. Malone thinks I can write it no where but in London" (To Margaret Boswell).

9–11 July. "These three days I confined myself to the house and took only tea and dry toast to breakfast and boiled milk and dry toast at night, and this discipline made me quiet, and I did the first part of Dr. Johnson's *Life* and made arrangements for more of it. My resolution now was to put it in such a way that I could carry it on at Auchinleck, and as soon as I had it so, I was to set out, and wrote so to my Wife. . . . I was to return in November to polish and complete the *Life*."

13 July. "Could not rest at home; but did not lose the day for, I went to Malone's and with his assistance traced Dr. Johnson's publications chronologically through the *Gentleman's Magazine*, and wrote their titles under each year. I dined at General Paoli's, and returned to Malone's, and thus pursued my task which entertained me."

14 July. "I staid in till between three and four doing something to Dr. Johnson's *Life*."

18 July. "I did something to Dr. Johnson's *Life*."

1786 20 July. "I was at home, arranging the order of Dr. Johnson's *Life*, part of the morning; I believe indeed the whole."

21 July. "Either yesterday or this day went to Nichols, the Editor of the *Gentleman's Magazine*, who pointed out to me some particulars concerning Dr. Johnson."

25 July. "Did a little to Johnson's *Life*."

29 July. "At home in the forenoon, doing something to Dr. Johnson's *Life*."

Sept.–Oct. "I read almost nothing, and went on very slowly with Dr. Johnson's *Life*."

1 Nov. "wrote some of Johnson's *Life*."

4 Nov. "Wrote some of Johnson's *Life*."

7 Nov. "[Malone] encourages me to go on with Johnson's *Life*. One morning We revised a part of it, which he thought well of, and dispelled my vapourish diffidence; and he surprised me another day with a page of it on two different types, that we might settle how it was to be printed."

11 Nov. "Langton . . . gave me Johnsoniana."

14 Nov. "Did a little of Johnson's *Life*."

1787 6 Jan. "My great Volume will not be finished for some time. I have waited till I should first see Hawkins's compilation. But my friends urge me to dispatch, that the ardour of curiosity may not be allowed to cool" (To Bishop Barnard).

1 Mar. "Breakfasted with Langton and got from him his letters from Johnson. Dined home. Some of the *Life*."

2 Mar. "Home all day—the *Life*."

3 Mar. "Home till the evening. The *Life*."

5 Mar. "Somewhat low, home all day. The *Life*."

6 Mar. "A little of the *Life*."

7 Mar. "Wrote a little of the *Life*."

14 Mar. "Some of *Life*."

17 Mar. "Did a good deal at *Life*."

20 Mar. "Malone who had dined at Sir Joshua's the day before advised me to push him to get Johnson's Diaries from Sir J. Hawkins, that I might see them. I breakfasted with him today and he promised to write for them."

21 Mar. "Did some of *Life*."

1787 22 Mar. "Did a little of the *Life*, having been occupied a good while in searching for Johnson's letters to Dr. Warton which I feared were lost." See *post* From J. Warton, 29 Jan. 1787 and n. 2.

23 Mar. "Did a very little of the *Life*."

26 Mar. "no *Life* done today."

27 Mar. "Some *Life*."

28 Mar. "Some *Life*."

29 Mar. "Laboured at *Life* all day, yet did no more than seven pages."

30 Mar. "Wished to labour at *Life* as I did yesterday. . . . I called on Courtenay, who insisted that we should take a long walk, and that Malone and I should dine with him. I was very sorry to have an idle day, yet I could not resist this cordial invitation, in case Malone should agree. He did, and said he would let me off from my task of Johnson's *Life* for today."

31 Mar. "A little *Life*."

17 Apr. "Did some *Life*."

19 Apr. "Did some *Life*."

23 Apr. "Some *Life*."

24 Apr. "Some *Life*."

1 May. "Breakfasted with Mr. Malone, as usual on the first of a month, and read the Reviews and Magazines on Dr. Johnson's *Life* by Hawkins."

5 May. "This whole week had done no *Life*."

8 May. Expects to have the *Life* in the press in July or Aug., and to publish at the end of this year or the beginning of next (To Forbes).

10 May. "I had for eleven days done nothing to Johnson's *Life*. Wrote some of it today."

11 May. "The King accosted me with a pleasing look: 'How does writing go on?' B[OSWELL.] 'Pretty well Sir.' K[ING.] 'When will you be done?' B[OSWELL.] 'It will be some time yet. I have a good deal to do to correct Sir John Hawkins.' K[ING.] 'I believe he has made many mistakes.' B[OSWELL.] 'A great many Sir, and very injurious to my good friend.'"

May. "The Publick are respectfully informed, that Mr. Boswell's LIFE OF DR. JOHNSON is in great Forwardness.

1787 The Reason of its having been delayed is, that some other Publications on that Subject were promised, from which he expected to obtain much Information, in Addition to the large Store of Materials which he had already accumulated. These Works have now made their Appearance; and, though disappointed in that Expectation, he does not regret the Deliberation with which he has proceeded, as very few circumstances relative to the History of Dr. Johnson's private Life, Writings, or Conversation, have been told with that authentick Precision which alone can render Biography valuable. To correct these erroneous Accounts will be one of his principal Objects; and on reviewing his Materials, he is happy to find that he has Documents in his Possession, which will enable him to do Justice to the Character of his illustrious Friend. He trusts that in the mean Time the Publick will not permit unfavourable Impressions to be made on their minds, whether by the light Effusions of Carelessness and Pique, or the ponderous Labours of solemn Inaccuracy and dark uncharitable Conjecture. London, May, 1787" (Boswell's advertisement in the papers: see *Lit. Car.*, p. 163).

1 June. "Breakfasted at Malone's as usual on the first of the month, and looked at Reviews of Hawkins's *Life of Johnson.*"

2 June. "Dined at home, and did some *Life.*"

9 June. "Did some *Life.*"

c. 10 June. "My Book will not be ready for the press before August" (To Maxwell).

12 June. "Dined at Literary Club. . . . I took care not to introduce Johnson. But Sir Joshua did, and I observed that a great part of our conversation was about him. I indeed took a part, though I would not lead."

13 June. "Some *Life.*"

15 June. "Some *Life.*"

4 July. "It will be in January or February next at soonest that my volume will be ready for publick inspection" (To Maxwell).

20 July. "Then to Nichols. Just going to Hawkins. Went and waited in Storey's gate Coffeehouse till Treasure brought.

1787 [See *post* From Barber, 9 July 1787, n. 1.] Went to Malone's. Not at home. Sir Joshua's; gone from thence— home with the papers."

21 July. "Malone's with some of Johns. Papers."

2 Aug. "You will now be wondering why my *Life of Dr. Johnson* has not yet appeared. The truth is that besides the various avocations which have insensibly hindered it, I have solid reasons for delay, both from the motive of having Sir John Hawkins to precede me that I might profit by his gross faults, and from that of giving time for the accession of materials of which I have received a great addition since I last wrote to you. I am resolved that my work shall be published in the course of the next session of Parliament" (To Blair).

14 Sept. "No packet, or box from Bowles. —What an insufferable procrastinator! almost as great a one as another person of my acquaintance" (From Malone).

10 Oct. "At *Life*."

11 Oct. "At *Life*." —The progress of his book is retarded by a stay of seven weeks in Ayrshire. He will work away until Michaelmas term (To Forbes).

15 Oct. "Some *Life*."

16 Oct. "*Life* all day."

17 Oct. "Breakfasted with Malone and read to him some of the *Life* which I had lately done. He animated me by commending it. Home and continued. General Paoli called. . . . and asked me to dinner, with some foreigners of rank. But I kept to *Life*."

18 Oct. "*Life* all day."

19 Oct. "*Life*."

20 Oct. "Some *Life*, but still hyp'd."

22 Oct. "Some *Life*."

23 Oct. "Some *Life*."

24 Oct. "Some *Life*."

25 Oct. "Some *Life*."

26 Oct. "Met Sharpe [Richard ('Conversation') Sharp] who cheered me as to my *Life*. Was wonderfully relieved. Evening some *Life*."

27 Oct. "*Life*. Was easier."

28 Oct. "Went to Malone's and read him an year's Journal of

1787 Johnson's conversation for *Life*, which I feared was of little value. He cheered me by praising it."

29 Oct. "*Life.*"

30 Oct. "A good deal of *Life.*"

31 Oct. "*Life.*"

1 Nov. "*Life.*"

2 Nov. "Not well—but did some *Life.*"

3 Nov. "I grew so much hyp'd that I could not write any *Life.*"

5 Nov. "A little *Life.*"

10 Nov. "Some *Life.*"

13 Nov. "*Life.*"

14 Nov. "*Life.*"

15 Nov. "Some *Life.*"

16 Nov. "Called on Malone in the morning, and was advised by him to attend [Westminster Hall] laxly this term, and get on diligently with my *Life*. Did some today."

17 Nov. "Some *Life.*"

19 Nov. "I do not mark particularly my *lax* attendance in West. Hall. I did *Life.*"

20 Nov. "Did *Life.*"

23 Nov. "A great deal of *Life.*"

26 Nov. "Some *Life.*"

27 Nov. "Some *Life.*"

29 Nov. "Some *Life.*"

30 Nov. "Did a great deal of *Life*, having laboured all day."

1 Dec. "Some *Life.*"

3 Dec. "Had dreamt some weeks ago of seeing Dr. Johnson cursorily, but without having any conversation."

4 Dec. "Some *Life.*"

5 Dec. "Some *Life.*"

7 Dec. "Some *Life.*"

11 Dec. "Some *Life*. . . . I did some *Life.*"

13 Dec. "Some *Life.*"

14 Dec. "Some *Life.*"

15 Dec. "Some *Life.*"

17 Dec. "Some *Life.*"

1788 9 Feb. "I am ashamed that I have yet seven years to write of his *Life*. I do it chronologically, giving year by year his publications if there were any, his letters, his conversations,

1788 and every thing else that I can collect. It appears to me that mine is the best plan of Biography that can be conceived; for my Readers will as near as may be accompany Johnson in his progress, and as it were see each scene as it happened. I am of opinion that my delay will be for the advantage of the Work" (To Percy).

16 Feb. "Had for I think twelve days not written one line of Johnson's *Life*."

20 Feb. "My dear Wife . . . expostulated with me on the miserable consequences of keeping my family longer in London . . . that indeed I led a life of dissipation and intemperance, so that I did not go on even with my *Life of Dr. Johnson* from which I expected both fame and profit."

25 Feb. "I have been wretchedly dissipated, so that I have not written a line for a forthnight. But today I resume my pen and shall labour vigorously" (To Temple: MS. Pierpont Morgan Lib.). "after a shameful interval of neglect, I resumed Johnson's *Life*. . . . I laboured with alacrity at the *Life*."

1 Mar. "Home and did some *Life*. This week had done 52 pages."

3 Mar. "*Life*." —"It will not be published before September or October" (To Barber).

4 Mar. "Ditto" [i.e. "*Life*"].

5 Mar. "A little *Life*."

10 Mar. "I staid at home all day and worked at Johnson's *Life*, except sitting a short time with Lady Strange." —"I have yet six years of it to write, so that I cannot reckon on having it published earlier than September, or perhaps later" (To Beattie).

11 Mar. "At home all day—*Life*."

12 Mar. "I did some *Life*."

17 Mar. "In the afternoon I did some *Life*."

18 Mar. "I did *Life* with more satisfaction than for some days. In the morning had a short visit of Mr. Dilly, who was very desireous that I should put it fairly into the press."

19 Mar. "In all day. *Life*."

20 Mar. "In all day. *Life*."

28 Mar. "At home and laboured at *Life*."

31 Mar. "Some *Life*."

1788 3 Apr. "Some *Life.*"

4 Apr. "Ditto."

7 Apr. "Did *Life.*"

8 Apr. "Mr. Hoole breakfasted with me, and gave me some letters from Dr. Johnson to him, and some notes of his last days. Did some *Life.*"

9 Apr. "Some *Life.*"

11 Apr. "My *Life* of that illustrious Man has been retarded by several avocations, as well as by depression of mind. But I hope to have it ready for the press next month" (To Anna Seward).

12 Apr. "Was in a great flow of spirits; so that though I had resolved to work at *Life* all day, could not settle . . . called on Seward and drank some coffee with him. Mr. Lysons came, and from him I filled up a great many of the blanks in Dr. Johnson's *Letters to Mrs. Piozzi.*"

15 Apr. "Some *Life.*"

16 Apr. "Some *Life.*"

17 Apr. "Some *Life.*"

19 Apr. "Having received from Francis Barber a letter authorising me to demand from Sir John Hawkins all books or papers that belonged to Dr. Johnson which remained in his possession, of which I had acquainted Sir John, and begged to know when I might wait on him to receive them, I had received from the Knight a very civil answer. . . . I accordingly was with him a few minutes after [eleven]. . . . Sir John and I settled the business . . . in perfect good humour."

26 Apr. "I had not written one line of *Life* this week. Sad idleness."

28 Apr. "Resumed the labour of *Life*. Did so much."

29 Apr. "At home all day—not out of my slippers. Laboured at *Life.*"

30 Apr. "Laboured at *Life* forenoon."

1 May. "[Malone] lectured me upon my intemperance, and on my delaying Johnson's *Life*, on which I was to rest my fame."

2 May. "At home all day. *Life.*"

5 May. "I thought that by carrying with me [to Auchinleck] my Journals of the years 1783 and 1784, and what I had still to copy out and expand of 1783 [1781?], I might

1788   finish Johnson's *Life* in the Country—go the Northern
        Circuit, or part of it—and after holding the Michaelmas
        Sessions at Carlisle, return to London, and revise and
        correct and get all the Work printed."

    12 May. "Then Malone's to meet Courtenay and drink some
        farewell hock. Seward came. Was a little alarmed that my
        Quarto might not sell."

    18 Sept. "Pray then accept of this apology for my silence for
        too long a time, nay for my having done nothing to Dr.
        Johnson's *Life*—Literally nothing—not a single line of the
        remaining part of the first draught which I hoped and
        trusted should be completely finished here [at Auchin-
        leck]. . . . I see that *the Whole* will be of London manufac-
        ture" (To Malone).

    17 Nov. "During all this time I have laboured at the *Life*,
        and what I wonder at, have done very well. I am now half
        done with 1783, so that there remains no more but a year
        and a half of the first draught to do. But then the Con-
        versation with the King is to be formed into a complete
        Scene out of the various minutes—my Correspondence
        with him is to be excerpted—and the whole series of the
        Composition is to be revised and polished. I intend to make
        a Skeleton of the Whole, or a Table of Contents in the
        chronological order, and have it examined by some of the
        most Johnsonian freinds and by steady Reed—that any
        omissions may be supplied. . . . I forgot to mention
        another operation that remains to be performed which is
        selecting and arranging in proper places the Memorabilia
        furnished by Langton[,] Maxwell, Steevens[,] Seward. . . .
        I shall work assiduously to get my Magnum Opus
        concluded" (To Malone).

    5 Dec. "papa is continuing to write his life of the great Dr.
        Johnson and hopes to have it done by Christmas" (James
        Boswell Jr. to his mother).

    12 Dec. He has reached June 1784 in the composition of the
        Life and hopes to publish next May (To Forbes).

1789 10 Jan. "I am now very near the conclusion of my rough
        draught of Johnson's *Life*. On Saturday I finished the
        Introduction and Dedication to Sir Joshua both of which
        had appeared very difficult to be accomplished. I am

1789   confident they are well done. Whenever I have completed the rough draught, by which I mean the Work without nice correction, Malone and I are to prepare one half perfectly, and then it goes to press, where I hope to have it early in february so as to be out by the end of May" (To Temple: MS. Pierpont Morgan Lib.).

28 Jan. "I had . . . Mr. Seward who has been very obliging in getting me materials for Johnson's *Life*. . . . O! if this Book of mine were done. Job says, 'O that mine ennemy *had written* a Book!' I shall rejoice when I can speak in the *past* tense. I *do* hope to be at *Finis* in ten days" (To Margaret Boswell).

9 Feb. "All last week I did none of my Great Work. This vexes me, for it will be a week longer delayed, and I cannot *absolutely* see when I shall be done with it" (To Margaret Boswell).

5 Mar. "I have the pleasure to tell you, that a part of my Magnum Opus is now ready for the press, and that I shall probably begin to print next week" (To Temple: MS. Pierpont Morgan Lib.).

14 Mar. "I am very soon to put my *Life of Dr. Johnson* to the press" (To Mary Cobb).

6 Nov. "Revising *Life*."

17 Nov. "Dined quiet with Malone and revised so much of Johnson."

23 Nov. "at Malone's evening revising Magnum Opus."

27 Nov. "I dined at Lord Lonsdale's . . . As Malone had promised me the whole evening for Johnsonian revision, I wished to send an excuse . . . but Penn told me it was not to be risked, as I had said the day before I would come."

30 Nov. "the revision of my *Life of Johnson* by so acute and knowing a critick as Mr. Malone is of most essential consequence especially as he is *Johnsonianissimus*, and as he is to hasten to Ireland as soon as his *Shakspeare* is fairly published, I must avail myself of him now. His hospitality —and my other invitations—and particularly my attendance at Lord Lonsdale's have lost us many evenings; but I reckon that a third of the Work is *settled*, so that I shall get to press very soon. You cannot imagine what labour, what perplexity what vexation I have endured in arranging

1789   a prodigious multiplicity of materials, in supplying omissions, in searching for papers buried in different masses—and all this besides the exertion of composing and polishing. Many a time have I thought of giving it up" (To Temple: MS. Pierpont Morgan Lib.).

30 Nov. "Dined quietly with Malone and had a long revise of *Life*."

2 Dec. "Awaked in very bad spirits, and doubting if I *could* get *Life* finished . . . With Malone in the evening—revised and grew better."

5 Dec. "Evening Malone's and revised more *Life*."

8 Dec. "Went to Malone's and revised."

9 Dec. "Evening at Malone's and revised."

11 Dec. "Dined quietly at home in order to be at Malone's to revise, having refused invitations from Lord Lonsdale, Penn and General Paoli. Had a long revise, and got into spirits with respect to my Work and resolved to put it to press immediately after Christmas."

13 Dec. "At night was with Malone and had a very little revise, for he had a Dulcinea with him."

14 Dec. "At home till 5 when I dined with Malone tête à tête and had a good revise."

16 Dec. "At home all the rest of the day filling up blanks in my *Life of Johnson*." See *Life* i. 34 and n. 1, 90 and n. 4.

18 Dec. "Sat a while with Malone, and got a quotation from Bacon for my Johnsonian Introduction. Visited Miss Cave grandniece of old Edward Cave, and saw his original letters from Johnson."

21 Dec. "At home after visiting Captain Grose, as also Nichols the Printer, and Lockyer Davis for little Johnsonian particulars. Made insertions in the *Life* in the evening."

22 Dec. "I did something to *Life*. . . . In the evening at Malone's revising."

23 Dec. "In the evening at Malone's. Courtenay was with him at dinner. After Courtenay went we revised." —"My *Life of Dr. Johnson* is at last very near being put to the press" (To Lady Rothes).

26 Dec. "Evening at Malone's revising."

27 Dec. "Dined with Malone tete à tete and revised *Life*."

31 Dec. "At Malone's and revised some *Life*."

1790 1 Jan. "Called at Lockyer Davis's and copied a passage from
Plutarch for Johnson's *Life* [*Life* i. 31–32]. Then delivered
the Introduction of it to Baldwin that I might say my Book
was *at* if not *in* the press on Newyear's day. The honest
friendly Printer was a little gruff about my mode of carrying on the Work, but I made allowance for him. . . . A
little before ten I went to Malones and revised a few pages
of *Life*."

2 Jan. "The Rev. Dr. Coombe an American who had been
Chaplain to Lord Carlisle when Lord Lieutenant of Ireland
waited on me with Dr. Johnson's letter on his Lordship's
Tragedy. . . . Then at Malones, where I found Courtenay,
and after he left us, revised *Life*."

6 Jan. "Passed a part of the morning at Malones, and had the
pleasure of consulting with him and Mr. Selfe the corrector
of Baldwin's press, as to a specimen of my *Magnum Opus*."

7 Jan. "Dined with Malone tete â tete and revised *Life*."

9 Jan. "I had been at Baldwin's before dinner, in consequence
of a letter from him, which shewed me that, by using a
pica instead of an *english* letter in printing my Book, I
might comprise it within such a number of sheets as a
Guinea volume should contain, which I could not do in
english letter unless upon a *medium* instead of a *demy*
paper, so as to have a larger page. I consulted with Dilly,
and carried specimens of both kinds of paper to Baldwin's,
where it was settled that I should on Monday have a
specimen in each way."

11 Jan. "Was at Baldwins and Dillys consulting as to my
Life of Johnson. From the computation of my Manuscript
or *Copy* as it is called, there were 416,000 words, which we
averaged would make too many pages in Quarto even upon
pica, and therefore it was thought by Baldwin that I should
make two Quarto volumes on *English* and sell them at 30
shillings. . . . made calculations as to my book; then went
to Malone's and revised *Life*."

13 Jan. "I had talked of printing my *Life of Johnson* in
Folio, rather than in two volumes. Malone said I might as
well throw it into the Thames, for a folio would not now be
read. His scheme was to print 1,000 on pica in Quarto, in
one volume however thick, and at the same time by

1790 *over-running* the types as it is called to print 1,000 in octavo, which would be kept in *petto* and be in readiness for sale, whenever the Quarto was sold. This scheme pleased me much, and both Dilly and Baldwin approved of it; so I had resolved on it and got a specimen of each; but having talked with Mr. John Nichols the Printer, he satisfied me it was a bad plan. . . . He advised me rather to print 1,500 in quarto, and assured me that I would run no risk of not disposing of that number. This advice was given me *after* this day; but I put the whole history of my publication together. I was much obliged to this worthy, liberal-minded man."

15 Jan. "in the evening revised at Malone's."

18 Jan. "Dined at Malone's . . . and had a long revise of my *Life of Johnson*."

27 Jan. "worked *Life*."

28 Jan. "Up late at *Life*."

31 Jan. "Sent to Malone's in hopes of *Life*. But Courtenay and Kemb[le] and Jep[hson] there."

2 Feb. "Printing House to quicken [the printing]."

3 Feb. "Laboured *Life*."

4 Feb. "Dined at Malone's quiet . . . and revised *Life*."

8 Feb. "I am within a short walk of Mr. Malone, who revises my *Life of Johnson* with me. We have not yet gone over quite a half of it; but it is at last fairly in the press" (To Temple: MS. Pierpont Morgan Lib.).

13 Feb. "Dined quietly at home, and added to *Life*."

14 Feb. "Then Malone's and revised."

12 Mar. "I shall by [next summer] be well advanced in my *Magnum Opus*, of which a hundred pages are now printed" (To Percy: MS. Arthur A. Houghton, Jr.).

27 Mar. "One of my sheets waits for your answer [i. 129–36]. I go on steadily, but cannot be out before October" (To Joseph Warton).

3 Apr. "Malone's to revise."

6 Apr. "revised Malone."

9 Apr. "I have printed twenty sheets of my Magnum Opus" (To Langton).

12 Apr. "revised at Malones."

18 Apr. "dined at Mr. Malones and revised a little."

1790 20 Apr. "Plym[s]ell [Boswell's compositor] breakfasted."

21 Apr. "worked hard at *Life* all the rest of the day."

4 May. "Revised."

18 May. "I repaired to Malone's and revised a small portion of my *Life of Johnson*, but was interrupted by his brother etc."

27 May. "Was at the printing house some time. . . . In the evening I had a long revise of part of Johnson's *Life*, at Malone's."

29 May. "My friend Temple told me fairly that he had never seen any body so idle as I was. I could scarcely take the necessary trouble of preparing my Book for the press."

31 May. "I went to my Printer's and Mr. Dilly's."

7 June. "I staid at home, arranging Dr. Johnson's *Life*."

8 June. "I was as far as Mr. Sewel's in Cornhill to get some little information for Johnson's *Life*. Hundreds of such pieces of trouble have I been obliged to take, in the course of the printing. . . . went to Malone's and revised some of my Work."

10 June. "I dined with Sir William Scott, by appointment, to *sit* upon my Record of the conversation between Johnson and him. . . . We revised my Johnsonian leaves."

11 June. "invitation from Malone . . . We revised a little."

13 June. "I dined tete â tete with Malone and revised 46 pages of my *Life of Johnson*."

14 June. "I breakfasted with honest Baldwin my Printer, and concerted that in case I should be called away for some weeks [to Carlisle], my compositor Plymsell an intelligent and accurate man, should have other employment that he might leave, and resume my Book on my return."

16 June. "Malone upon a message from me came, and we settled that my *Life of Johnson* should go on at press a certain way during my absence."

17 June. "It vexed me that I was dragged away from the printing of my *Life of Johnson*, and that perhaps Malone might be gone to Ireland, before I could get back to London."

30 June. "How shocking is it to think that I . . . was forced to interrupt my *Life of Dr. Johnson* the most important, perhaps *now* the only concern of any consequence that I ever shall have in this world—and what galls me and irritates

1790   me with impatience is the thought that I lose those hours which you could now have given me for revising my M.S. and that perhaps you may be gone before I get back to town" (To Malone).

2 July. Three hundred pages of the book are printed; more than three hundred and fifty pages of the manuscript are not as yet gone over by Malone (To Forbes).

8 July. "Your compositor has gone on very smartly; and has not been delayed by me, though I am so busy. I have never seen more than two proofs. . . . I have had 5 Sheets[:] Rr, Ss, Tt, Uu[,] Xx. The last nearly exhausts Maxwell. It will, I believe, be worked off tomorrow" (From Malone).

19 July. "Had found that by my kind and active friend Malone's aid my Book had gone on in my absence five sheets. I was quite pleased to see another *proof* and to be put in train again."

21 July. "Either today or yesterday had a long revise of Johnson's *Life* with Malone."

24 July. "Went to Baldwin's Printing office, where I was happy to find myself again, though I found neither my friend Baldwin the Master, Selfe the Corrector, nor Plymsell the Compositor. . . . I had a small but disagreable loss tonight, my pocket having been picked of a proof-sheet of my *Life of Johnson*, with the M.S. belonging to it. But this could not be remedied, and luckily all was secured in print but two lines, which I could supply."

25 July. "Dined tete á tete with Malone and had a revise of my Book."

6 Aug. "I think I revised some of Johnson's *Life* at Malone's one of the evenings of this week, I am not sure which."

24 Aug. "Dined at Malone's with only Courtenay, and in the evening read my Journal at Ashbourne with Dr. Johnson in 1777 and heard their remarks."

25 Aug. "Was always doing a little towards the correction and improvement of my Manuscript or *Copy* as it is called of Johnson's *Life*."

27 Aug. "It will be a much larger work than was calculated. I was very desireous to confine it within one quarto volume, though it should be a very thick one; but I now

1790   find that it must be two, and these more than 550 pages each. I have printed as yet only 456; but am next week to put on two compositors, so as to advance in a double ratio" (To Langton).

     30 Aug. "Settled that two Compositors should be put upon my *Magnum Opus* so as that it might be dispatched faster by almost a half."

     2 Sept. "I was busy preparing a quantity of *Copy* for my two compositors."

     4 Sept. "In the evening at Malone's revising Johnson's *Life*."

     8 Sept. "I had now found that my *Magnum Opus* must be in two volumes."

     10 Sept. "My life at present, though for some time my health and spirits have been wonderfully good, is surely as idly spent, as can almost be imagined. I merely attend to the progress of my *Life of Johnson*, and that by no means with great assiduity such as that which Malone employs on Shakspeare."

     27 Sept. "Malone's evening, revised."

     29 Sept. "Mr. Boswell will bring more copy tomorrow 30 Septr" (Boswell's note on the revise for ii. 25 of the first edition: R. W. Chapman, "Boswell's Revises," *Johnson & Boswell Revised*, 1928, p. 27).

     1 Oct. "Printing-house."

     2 Oct. "Printing house."

     5 Oct. "my *Magnum Opus* (of the second Volume of which 56 pages are now printed) requires my presence much" (To Alexander Boswell).

     1 Nov. "I am just come to that part of my Work in which the Letter from Johnson to your Lordship is introduced [ii. 138–39 of the first edition]" (To Hawkesbury).

     4 Dec. "The Magnum Opus advances. I have revised p. 216" (To Malone).

     16 Dec. "My work has met with a delay for a little while— not a whole day however—by an unaccountable neglect in having paper enough in readiness. I have now before me p. 256. My utmost wish is to come forth on Shrove tuesday (8 March)" (To Malone).

1791   18 Jan. "I cannot be out on *Shrove Tuesday* as I flattered

1791   myself. P. 376 of Vol. II is ordered for press and I expect another proof tonight. But I have yet near 200 pages of Copy besides letters[,] and *the death* which is not yet written. My second volume will I see be 40 or 50 pages more than my first" (To Malone).

29 Jan. "Last week they gave me six sheets. I have now before me in *proof* p. 456. Yet I have above 100 pages of my copy remaining, besides his *Death* which is yet to be written, and many insertions were there room. As also seven and thirty letters exclusive of twenty to Dr. Brocklesby most of which will furnish only extracts. I am advised to extract several of those to others and leave out some; for my first volume makes only 516 pages and to have 600 in the second will seem awkward, besides increasing the expence considerably. . . . I have now desired to have but one compositor. Indeed I go sluggishly and comfortlessly about my work. As I pass your door I cast many a longing look" (To Malone).

2 Feb. "After breakfast called on Kemble to get a note of Johnson's conversation with Mrs. Siddons. . . . I went to the Printinghouse a cold raw day; had no pleasure from my Book."

3 Feb. "Kemble came to me in the morning, and made out a note of Dr. Johnson's conversation with Mrs. Siddons, for my Book. He encouraged me to hope that there would be a great sale, of which I now was despairing. Sat at home and laboured at *Life* all the evening."

4 Feb. "Sat again at home all the evening, getting a good deal of Johnson's *Life*, (now advanced to its last year) ready for the press."

5 Feb. "I went early to Sir William Scott and settled with him how I should mention Lord Thurlow's application to the King to enable Johnson to go abroad, and its failure [ii. 520–21, 534–35 of the first edition] . . . I found Dilly at breakfast in his kitchen and shared with him. He did not raise my hopes high of the sale of my Book. . . . Went to Johnson's in St. Paul's Churchyard, and saw two publications to quote from in Johnson's *Life*. Wright the printer happened to come in, and named me, and afterwards Johnson asked me when my Book was to be ready. I told

1791 him in about a month; but that there would be too much of it. 'O no,' said he; 'it will be very entertaining.' I was twice at the printing house."

8 Feb. "Was at Printing House."

9 Feb. "Intended to have worked hard at my *Life*, but called on Courtenay, and he prevailed with me to saunter about with him."

10 Feb. "I have now before me p. 488 in print, the 923 page of the Copy only is exhausted; and there remain 80, besides the Death, as to which I shall be concise though solemn—also many letters.

"Pray how shall I wind up. Shall I give the Character in my *Tour*, somewhat enlarged?" (To Malone).

14 Feb. "My worthy printer Baldwin endeavoured to cheer me with hopes that my *Life of Johnson* might be profitable, though Steevens had thrown cold water on my hopes. . . . the Corrector of his press Mr. Tomlins . . . shewed me a good part of an Index to my *Life of Johnson*, which he had offered to make, and offering to do it very reasonably had been desired by me to go on with it. I intended to *prefix* it as an *Alphabetical Table of Contents* to make my first volume more equal with my second, which had swelled much beyond my computation."

20 Feb. "I met my friend Dilly, and took a walk with him into Lincolns Inn fields, being in great despondency as to *Life of Johnson*. He told me that Stockdale told him it had been depreciated and on being pressed, owned that Steevens had talked against it. It vexed me to think that this malicious man had I feared access to it at the Printing-House. Good Dilly advised me to accept of the £1000 which I was now informed by a letter from Malone had been talked of for it by *Robinson*. I apprehended Malone had been too sanguine in imagining it had been *offered*. I was unwilling to separate myself as an Authour from Dilly with whom my name had been so long connected."

22 Feb. "Courtenay came about ten . . . and obligingly assisted me in *lightening* my animadversions on Mrs. Piozzi in my *Life of Johnson* [ii. 528–34 of the first edition]—for my own credit."

24 Feb. "I became suddenly so well, that I wished to go

1791   into company and be gay. But restrained myself and laboured at *Life.*"

25 Feb. "I meant to publish on Shrove Tuesday. But if I can get out within the month of March, I shall be satisfied. I have now I think *four* or *five* sheets to print which will make my second volume about 575 pages. But I shall have more cancels" (To Malone).

26 Feb. "Sharpe gave me hopes of a great sale for my *Life of Johnson.* He said there were so many people in both the Universities etc. etc. who expected to see themselves, or those whom they knew in it—that they would be eager to have it."

3 Mar. "Dined at W. G. Hamilton's who had fantastically insisted that some passages in my *Life of Johnson* relative to him should be cancelled, and Courtenay and I were with him some time before dinner to talk of this. Courtenay had been plagued with tedious consultations about it, from the anxiety of Hamilton's vanity. I did not like it; but yielded to a certain degree."

4 Mar. "I walked to Islington where by kind invitation, I dined with the Rev. Mr. Strahan, and talked of Dr. Johnson's last illness."

8 Mar. "I hoped to have published today. But it will be about a month yet before I launch. I have now before me in print 560 pages of Vol. 2 and I fear I shall have 20 more" (To Malone).

14 Mar. "I am now *writing* the *last sheet* of my Book. But the whole, including Dedication and Table of contents will not I imagine be all *printed* sooner than this day forthnight. I mean to publish on the 15 of next month" (To Alexander Boswell).

17 Mar. "Mr. Boswell's Life of Johnson is positively finished, and the day of publication will be announced in the course of the present week" (*London Chronicle*).

18 Mar. "My *Life of Johnson* being nearly finished I once thought of asking Robinson fairly as to the offer which he, through Mr. Malone, made for the Copyright, which Mr. Malone understood to be £1000; but apprehending that I might give occasion to its being slighted, I resolved to take the fair chance of the Publick."

1791 19 Mar. "Next month will be published, In two volumes large quarto, Price two guineas in Boards, (Dedicated to Sir Joshua Reynolds,) The Life of Samuel Johnson, LL.D. . . . including his celebrated Letter to the Earl of Chesterfield. . . . By James Boswell, Esq. . . . The extraordinary zeal which has been shown by distinguished persons in all parts of the kingdom, in supplying additional information, authentic manuscripts, and singular Anecdotes of Dr. Johnson, has occasioned such an enlargement of this work, that it has been unavoidably delayed much longer than was intended" (*London Chronicle*).

31 Mar. Advertisement repeated in *London Chronicle*.

6 Apr. "My *Life of Johnson* is at last drawing to a close. I am correcting the last sheet, and have only to write an Advertisement [dated 20 Apr.], to make out a note of Errata and to correct a second sheet of contents, one being done. [He entered the Errata on the last page of the second sheet of Contents.] I really hope to publish it on the 25 current. My old and most intimate friend may be sure that a copy will be sent to him. I am at present in such bad spirits, that I have every fear concerning it—that I may get no profit, nay may lose—that the Publick may be dissappointed and think that I have done it poorly—that I may make many enemies, and even have quarrels.—Yet perhaps the very reverse of all this may happen" (To Temple: MS. Pierpont Morgan Lib.).

6 Apr. "my *Life of Dr. Johnson* is at last on the eve of publication" (To Hector).

30 Apr. "My *Magnum Opus* the *Life of Dr. Johnson* in two Volumes Quarto is to be published on Monday 16 May. . . . I really think it will be the most entertaining Collection that has appeared in this age" (To George Dempster).

30 Apr. *London Chronicle* announces 16 May as day of publication.

13 May. Reports to Forbes that forty-one London booksellers have purchased upwards of four hundred sets of the *Life*.

16 May. The book is published.

22 Aug. "My *Magnum Opus* sells wonderfully. 1200 are now gone and we hope the whole 1700 [cf. 6 Mar. 1793] may

1791   be gone before Christmas" (To Temple: MS. Pierpont Morgan Lib.).

1792 5 Apr. "My Octavo edition is now in the press" (To Churton).

      24 Oct. "Two volumes and a part of a third of an Octavo Edition of Mr. Boswell's *Life of Dr. Johnson* are already printed" (To Agutter).

      11 Nov. "I visited Malone, and revised some additional Johnsoniana."

      24 Nov. "This was the day fixed by Mr. Dilly for settling Accounts with me and Mr. Baldwin as to the Quarto Edition of my *Life of Johnson* etc. . . . he produced to me the clear produce of the sale exclusive of presents, amounting to £1555.18.2. This was very flattering to me as an Authour. We proceeded to Baldwin's, where I cleared off a Bond for £400 . . . and a note of hand for £100 lent to me by himself. There was great satisfaction in thus paying principal and interest to two worthy friends who had assisted me with their credit. I then returned to Mr. Dilly's, and after allowing for various sums which I owed him, there was a ballance due to me of £608."

      29 Nov. "This day I gave a dinner, a kind of feast, two courses and a desert upon the success of my first edition of Dr. Johnson's *Life*—present Mr. Malone, Mr. Deputy Nichols, his son in law the Rev. Mr. Pridden, Mr. Reed, Mr. Dilly, Mr. Baldwin, and his son Charles printer with him, Squire Dilly, my brother T. D., my daughters Veronica and Euphemia and son James. I got into a pretty good state of jovialty, though still dreary at bottom. We drank 'Church and King'—'Health and long life to the *Life of Dr. Johnson*'—'the pious memory of Dr. Johnson' etc. etc."

      21 Dec. "I often called on Malone, and found him fully occupied in historical and biographical researches, on which he was intent, while I had absolutely no pursuit whatever. The delusive hope of *perhaps* getting into some practice at the bar, was *now* dead, or at least torpid. The printing of my second edition of Dr. Johnson's *Life* was the only thing I had to do. That was little, and was now nearly ended."

1793 26 Feb. "I return early in April . . . to publish the second edition of my *Life of Dr. Johnson*, for which I have lately received some more additions of great value" (To Temple: MS. Pierpont Morgan Lib.).

6 Mar. "I will send you my second Edition in three volumes, octavo which will come forth early in April, with corrections and several sheets of additions. . . . I am to publish them separately in Quarto to accommodate the purchasers of the first Edition of which 1689 sets have been sold (the rest of the impression of 1750 having gone to the ent[r]y in Stationershall[,] presents etc.) and many more would have gone off could they have been had" (To Erskine).

20 Mar. Date of Baldwin's colophon at the end of the third volume of the second edition.

3 and 10 Apr. The dates of the plates.

1 July. The date assigned in the third edition to the Advertisement of the second edition.

11 July. "On Wednesday, July 17, will be published, in three large Vols. 8vo. Price 1 £.4s. in boards, The Life of Samuel Johnson, LL.D. By James Boswell, Esq. The Second Edition, corrected, and considerably enlarged by additional Letters and interesting Anecdotes. . . . While no pains have been spared to improve this very popular work, the CORRECTIONS and ADDITIONS are printed separately in quarto, for the accommodation of the purchasers of the First Edition" (*London Chronicle*).

24 July. "Above 400 of the new Johnsonian volumes are already sold. Wonderful man!" (To Langton: MS. Hyde).

6 Aug. "The printing of the *Additions* to my first edition of my *Life of Dr. Johnson* was my only *business* at present."

9 Aug. "called at Baldwin's to see a sheet of my *Additions*."

3 Oct. "Dined at Baldwin's who kindly gave an entertainment on occasion of the second edition of my *Life of Dr. Johnson*. . . . It was an excellent City dinner at which I did my part as well as I could; but my gloom was heavy."

24 Oct. The second edition is selling as well as could be expected (To Forbes).

19 Dec. "The Epitaph on Dr. Adams pleases me much and should my *Life of Dr. Johnson* come to a third edition, it

1793   will be a suitable and agreable addition" (To Stedman).

      27 Dec. "called at Dilly's, and had a pretty good account of the sale of My second edition of Johnson's *Life.*"

1794 11 Jan. "walked to Dilly's, and heard that the sale of my Book was going on as might be expected."

      29 Jan. "Sat a while at Dilly's, and found that the sale of my *Life of Dr. Johnson* had stagnated for some time, which discouraged me."

      17 Mar. "My second edition of Dr. Johnson's *Life* has sold not so rapidly as the first, but as well as I had reason to expect. Eight hundred and odds are gone, and I doubt not but the whole impression will *move* (as the Booksellers say) before this time twelvemonth" (To Alexander Boswell).

1795 19 May. Death of Boswell.

1799 8 Apr. Date of Malone's Advertisement to the third edition.

      18 May. "This day is published, in four volumes 8vo, price 1£.8s. in boards, the 3d. Edit. (revised and augmented), of the Life of Sam. Johnson, LL.D. . . . By James Boswell Esq." (*Morning Chronicle*).

EDITORIAL PROCEDURES

THE TEXTS

A. The Choice of Documents and Their Arrangement

Where I have had a choice between an original and a draft or copy, I have invariably reproduced the original. However, where the original was known to me only in a printed version, I have exercised my judgement as to the superiority of texts. Variants are recorded only when of consequence or interest.

Those letters and other papers which Boswell edited for inclusion in the MS. *Life* (the "Papers Apart") are reproduced here in their original form. (In the edition of the MS. *Life* which Herman W. Liebert and I are preparing, these and other Papers Apart will be reproduced in their edited form, as corresponding in compositional stage to the writing of the manuscript proper.) The nature and extent of Boswell's editing are indicated in the notes.

In order to represent my subject as completely as possible I have included a number of letters which will appear elsewhere in the Yale Edition. In these instances I have printed only those parts that are concerned with the *Life*, though in a few cases those parts made a whole. The purchaser of the entire Edition will perhaps forgive duplication later for the sake of completeness now.

On the assumption that the primary usefulness of the present volume will be to students of the *Life* rather than to investigators of particular persons and their relationships with Boswell, I have adopted a chronological arrangement for the whole collection. This arrangement has made for some disruption of the question-and-answer sequence in individual correspondences—a defect I have tried to remedy by means of cross-references and the provision of an Alphabetical Table of Correspondents at the beginning.

Manuscripts which I have been unable to date, even conjecturally, are collected at the end of the chronological sequence. These in turn are followed by the correspondence of Malone concerning the posthumous editions of the *Life*.

B. The Transcription

The documents in this volume are printed, in conformity with the projected research edition as a whole, in a conservative manner, with certain concessions being made to typographical expediency and others to modern custom where no nuance of meaning may be said to be involved. This is not to say that everything that is preserved is meaningful; but no reader who has considered the question of how to transcribe a text will be unsympathetic to a measure of inconsistency and compromise. Editorial intervention or suppression has been restricted generally to formulary and mechanical elements of the texts. The following editorial practices are, unless otherwise indicated, unaccompanied by sign or note:

Addresses. Elements which appear in the MS. on separate lines are run together, punctuation being supplied according to modern practice. Places and dates appearing on the address side are reproduced along with the address.

Datelines. Places and dates are connected by commas, and are joined at the head of the letter regardless of their position in the MS. Periods following datelines are omitted.

Salutations. Abbreviations occurring in salutations are expanded. Colons are supplied following salutations in the absence of punctuation or in place of any mark of punctuation other than the comma.

Complimentary closes. Elements which appear in the MS. on separate lines are run together and are set off, as in modern convention, by commas. Complimentary closes which are separately paragraphed in the MS. are printed telescoped at the end of the preceding sentence. Abbreviations occurring in complimentary closes are expanded.

Signatures. Periods following signatures are omitted.

Terminal punctuation. Periods are supplied at the end of completed sentences; capital letters at the beginning of new sentences. Dashes, colons, and semi-colons which serve simply as terminal punctuation are replaced by periods. Dashes following periods are omitted unless they appear to serve as a device for signalling transitions (i.e. as a substitute for paragraphing).

Other punctuation. Punctuation in lists, tables, numerical series, etc. is regulated. Punctuation or re-punctuation necessary to relieve ambiguities or to ease awkward transitions is attended by a sign or a note.

Interlineations and marginalia. Interlineations and marginalia are inserted in line with the text.

Deletions. Insignificant deletions are ignored.

Lacunae. Words and letters obliterated by a defect in the MS. are supplied within angular brackets. Words and letters inadvertently omitted by the writer are supplied within square brackets.

Abbreviations, contractions, and symbols. The following abbreviations, contractions, and symbols, and their variant forms, are expanded: abt (about), acct (account), agst (against), Bp (Bishop), compts (compliments), cd (could), Dr (Dear), Fayr (Father), Ld (Lord), Lop (Lordship), recd (received), shd (should), Sr (Sir), wd (would), wt (with), & (and), &c (etc.), y (th). Periods are supplied for all abbreviations and contractions except those for ordinals. Colons following abbreviations are replaced by periods. Obscure or unfamiliar abbreviations and contractions are expanded within square brackets.

Superior letters. Superior letters are lowered.

Titles. Titles of books, literary compositions, periodicals, and newspapers are printed in italics, except where they occur in lists, columns, etc. A capital letter is supplied where lacking for the first word of the title.

Dialogue. Dialogue is printed between double quotation marks. Where a mixture of direct and indirect discourse obstructs normal practice, quotation marks are omitted.

Quotations. Double quotation marks replace single. Overlooked terminal quotation marks are supplied. Lengthy quotations are set off from the rest of the text by means of spacing and indentation.

Brackets. Square brackets in the MS. are replaced by parentheses (the former being reserved for editorial use). Overlooked terminal parentheses are supplied.

Devices of emphasis. Double underscoring and writing in bold strokes are reproduced by small capital letters.

Flourishes. Flourishes, in which category may be included casual, unemphatic underscoring, are ignored.

In a few instances, a text has, for reasons evident or explained, been reproduced *literatim*.

Although the reader may from the foregoing infer the elements of the text that have been preserved, it may be well to specify them.

Spelling is retained, except for patent inadvertencies, which are corrected in the text and recorded in the notes. The accidental use of one word for another is treated in the same way.

Capital letters are retained.

Abbreviations, contractions, and symbols not treated as above are allowed to stand.

Paragraph organization (or disorganization) is preserved. Exception: where a letter is reproduced in extracts, the paragraph immediately following an omission is run in without distinction.

Deletions of any consequence are recorded in the notes.

THE ANNOTATION

Head-notes. Where more than one text is cited, the first mentioned is the one reproduced. Former printings are mentioned only where the original remains untraced. Only date-postmarks are noted. Miscellaneous notations on the address side of a letter, such as "Single Sheet", are ignored. Where an address is not given, it may be assumed that the letter was sent "under cover". Boswell's Register of Letters is cited only where useful: namely, for dates on which letters were received; the date on which a letter was sent when there is disagreement with the date given in the letter itself; and, most important, where it is the only record of a missing letter. Similarly, the abstracts which accompany the entries in the Register are quoted only when they provide new or useful information.

Foot-notes. As in the choice of documents, so in their annotation: the primary aim has been to elucidate the process of the making of the *Life of Johnson*. Allusions to that part of the life of Boswell which is separable from this process have been annotated lightly. The Johnsonian matter is annotated primarily with respect to Boswell's use of it. I have not attempted, in the manner of Hill, to collect all references that might confirm or confute (though I am glad that he did). When Boswell makes use of a given passage, I indicate the fact, and, usually, the manner. When he fails to use material which on the face of it seems serviceable, I indicate that fact also; and where such an omission is balanced in the *Life* by an alternative version, I ask the reader to compare them. In general, however, I have refrained from attempting, in the absence of compelling evidence, to explain all of Boswell's moves, and have reserved the Introduction for a discussion of the editorial side of his biographical method.

Biographical notes follow the axiom that the better known the less needs be said by way of identification—with the proviso that membership in either Johnson's circle or Boswell's constitutes some claim to fame. The notes on the correspondents seek mainly to establish their relationship with the biographer and with the biographer's subject. Commonly the correspondence will itself contribute this kind of information, in which case the first biographical note will be deliberately reticent. Normally a person is identified at his first appearance, but I have sometimes postponed a note until a conspicuous entrance. Persons named in passages which are translated into the *Life* are not normally identified. Such omissions are in keeping with my decision to adopt the superbly annotated Hill-Powell edition of the *Life* for regular reference.

To the common reader who does not possess the Hill-Powell edition I offer two excuses and a palliative. Had I not permitted myself the liberty of taking my departure from this commentary, my own would have been overblown with repetition. Further, as my references are almost always to minute contexts, convenience is better served by volume-and-page, than by date, citations—especially for a work so uneven in its chronological spread. However, by way of compromise I have quoted from the *Life* rather more abundantly than would be appropriate were I annotating for the scholarly reader alone.

Authorities other than the *Dictionary of National Biography* are always announced (as is DNB itself for discrete facts). Manuscripts cited without a source are in the Yale Collection.

A list of cue titles and abbreviations employed in this volume follows.

CUE TITLES AND ABBREVIATIONS

This list omits the more familiar abbreviations of standard works of reference and periodicals, such as DNB, OED, and N & Q.

Note: All manuscripts referred to in the foot-notes without mention of a repository are in the Yale Collection. Catalogue numbers are supplied in some instances in order to facilitate identification.

Adam Cat.: R. B. Adam, *The R. B. Adam Library Relating to Dr. Samuel Johnson and His Era*, 4 vols., 1929–30.

Alum. Cant.: J. and J. A. Venn, *Alumni Cantabrigienses*, 4 vols., 1922–47.

Alum. Oxon.: Joseph Foster, *Alumni Oxonienses*, 4 vols., 1887–88, 1891–92.

Anecdotes: Hester Lynch Piozzi, *Anecdotes of the Late Samuel Johnson, LL.D.*, 1786. References are to the reprint in *Johns. Misc.* i. 141–351.

Army List: *A List of the Officers of the Army*, etc., 1756–.

Boswelliana: *Boswelliana. The Commonplace Book of James Boswell*, ed. Rev. Charles Rogers, 1874.

BP: *Private Papers of James Boswell from Malahide Castle in the Collection of Lt.-Col. R. H. Isham*, ed. Geoffrey Scott and F. A. Pottle, 18 vols., 1928–34. References are to the editorial commentary; see "Journ." in this list.

Chapman-Hazen: R. W. Chapman and A. T. Hazen, *Johnsonian Bibliography, A Supplement to Courtney*, 1938.

Clifford, *Johnson*: J. L. Clifford, *Young Sam Johnson*, 1955.

Clifford, *Piozzi*: J. L. Clifford, *Hester Lynch Piozzi (Mrs. Thrale)*, 2nd ed., 1952.

Comp. Bar.: G. E. C[ockayne], *Complete Baronetage*, 5 vols., 1900–06.

Comp. Peer.: G. E. C[ockayne], *Complete Peerage*, rev. Hon. Vicary Gibbs, H. A. Doubleday, and others, 13 vols., 1910–59.

Cooke: [William Cooke, or Cook,] *The Life of Samuel Johnson, LL.D.*, 1785. References are to the second edition, published the same year as the first.

Courtney: W. P. Courtney and D. N. Smith, *A Bibliography of Samuel Johnson*, 1915; reissued with facsimiles, 1925.

Croker: J. W. Croker's editions of Boswell's *Life of Johnson*, 1831, 1835, 1848.

Diaries: *Samuel Johnson: Diaries, Prayers, and Annals*, ed. E. L. McAdam, Jr. with Donald and Mary Hyde, 1958.

Gent. Mag.: *The Gentleman's Magazine*, 1731–.

Hawkins: Sir John Hawkins, *The Life of Samuel Johnson, LL.D.*, 1787. References are to the second edition, published the same year as the first.

Hazen: A. T. Hazen, *Samuel Johnson's Prefaces & Dedications*, 1937.

Hyde: The Hyde Collection, Somerville, New Jersey.

Johns. Glean.: A. L. Reade, *Johnsonian Gleanings*, 11 vols., 1909–52.

Johns. Misc.: *Johnsonian Miscellanies*, ed. G. B. Hill, 2 vols., 1897.

Johnsoniana: *Johnsoniana; or, Supplement to Boswell*, 1836.

Journ.: Boswell's journal. Transcribed conservatively from the MS.

Judd: G. P. Judd, *Members of Parliament, 1734–1832*, 1955. Entries are cited by number. (Additional information on individual members may be found in Sir Lewis Namier and John Brooke, *The House of Commons, 1754–1790,* 3 vols., 1964.)

Letters JB: *Letters of James Boswell,* ed. C. B. Tinker, 2 vols., 1924. The letters are cited by number.

Letters SJ: *The Letters of Samuel Johnson, with Mrs. Thrale's Genuine Letters to Him,* ed. R. W. Chapman, 3 vols., 1952. The letters are cited by number.

Life: *Boswell's Life of Johnson, Together with Boswell's Journal of a Tour to the Hebrides and Johnson's Diary of a Journey into North Wales,* ed. G. B. Hill, rev. L. F. Powell, 6 vols., 1934–50; vols. v and vi, 2nd ed., 1964. The text of the *Life* is that of the third edition (variorum). My (frequent) references to the first and second editions are spelled out. Malone's editions are indicated by number and year; those of later editors by name and year.

Lit. Anec.: John Nichols, *Literary Anecdotes of the Eighteenth Century,* 9 vols., 1812–15.

Lit. Car.: F. A. Pottle, *The Literary Career of James Boswell, Esq.,* 1929; reprinted 1966.

Lit. Illust.: John Nichols, *Illustrations of the Literary History of the Eighteenth Century,* 8 vols., 1817–58.

Lives: *Lives of the English Poets by Samuel Johnson, LL.D.,* ed. G. B. Hill, 3 vols., 1905.

MS. alt.: An alternative reading in the manuscript.

MS. *Life*: The manuscript of Boswell's *Life of Johnson.*

MS. orig.: The original reading in the manuscript.

Murphy: Arthur Murphy, *An Essay on the Life and Genius of Samuel Johnson, LL.D.,* 1792. References are to the reprint in *Johns. Misc.* i. 353–488.

Musgrave: *Obituary prior to 1800 (as far as Relates to England, Scotland, and Ireland),* comp. Sir William Musgrave, ed. Sir George J. Armytage, 6 vols., 1899–1901.

Note Book: *Boswell's Note Book, 1776–1777, Recording Particulars of Johnson's Early Life,* etc. [ed. R. W. Chapman], 1925.

Papers Apart: The papers subsidiary to the main narrative of the MS. *Life,* kept separately by Boswell.

Plomer: H. R. Plomer and others, *Dictionary of Printers and Booksellers, 1668–1725; 1726–1775,* 2 vols., 1922, 1932.

Poems, ed. Smith and McAdam: *The Poems of Samuel Johnson,* ed. D. N. Smith and E. L. McAdam, Jr., 1941.

Poems, ed. McAdam and Milne: *Samuel Johnson: Poems,* ed. E. L. McAdam, Jr. with George Milne, 1964.

Reades: A. L. Reade, *The Reades of Blackwood Hill . . . with a Full Account of Dr. Johnson's Ancestry,* 1906.

Reg. Let.: Boswell's register of letters sent and received.

Sale Catalogue: *A Catalogue of the Valuable Library of . . . Samuel Johnson,* etc., 1785.

Scots Mag.: *The Scots Magazine,* 1739–.

Scots Peer.: Sir James Balfour Paul, *The Scots Peerage,* 9 vols., 1904–14.

Shaw: [Rev. William Shaw], *Memoirs of the Life and Writings of the Late Dr. Samuel Johnson,* 1785.

Thraliana: *Thraliana: The Diary of Mrs. Hester Lynch Thrale (Later Mrs. Piozzi), 1776–1809,* ed. Katharine C. Balderston, 2 vols., 2nd ed., 1951.

Tour: Boswell's *Journal of a Tour to the Hebrides.* References are to the Hill-Powell edition (see "*Life*" in this list) unless otherwise indicated.

Works: *The Works of Samuel Johnson,* ed. Sir John Hawkins, 11 vols., 1787.

THE CORRESPONDENCE AND OTHER PAPERS
OF JAMES BOSWELL
RELATING TO THE MAKING OF THE
LIFE OF JOHNSON

1772–1779

From Thomas Percy,[1]
Tuesday and Thursday 5 and 7 May 1772[2]

MS. Yale (M 148). In JB's hand. JB's annotations are printed in italic.

The Publications Fugitive Pieces etc. of Mr. Samuel Johnson

Dictionary of the English Language 2 Vols. Folio
The same abridged in 2 vols. 12mo[3]
The Rambler 4 vols. 12mo[4]
The Idler 2 vols. 12mo
Some Papers and most of the Mottos in the Adventurer. *Those marked with a T. are his. He gave them to Dr. Bathurst and therefore would never own them. He even used to say he did not* write *them. But Mrs. Williams told me that he* dictated *them while Bathurst* wrote.[5]
The Prince of Abyssinia a Tale 2 vols. 12mo[6]
Irene a Tragedy 8vo. *Prologue his own. Epil. Sir W. Younge.*[7]
London a Poem in imitation of Juv. 3 Sat. 4to[8]

[1] Thomas Percy, D.D. (1729–1811), author of *Reliques of Ancient English Poetry*, 1765; member of The Club, 1768; Dean of Carlisle, 1778; and Bishop of Dromore, 1782. At this time he was domestic chaplain and secretary to the Duke of Northumberland. On 26 Mar. JB had called on him at Northumberland House. "It was agreable to find Percy in a large room looking into the Strand, and at the same time his room as much a Library, as crowded and even confused with books and papers, as any room in a College. . . . I observed how humbling it was to literary ambition that this man who had so much merit and was so high in fame, should now hardly be known" (Journ.). See *Letters SJ*, *Life*, and Journ. *passim*. Percy contributed notes—and strictures on JB—to Robert Anderson's third edition of his *Life of Johnson* (1815), written for this purpose in an interleaved copy of the second edition (Anderson's Advertisement, pp. vi–vii). The original notes are in the Bodleian Library (MS. Percy d. 11, ff. 6–18).

[2] The dates respectively of the following two entries in JB's journal: "Percy a little and got note of Johns" and "Percy,

note of Johns works." The first "note" may refer to another MS., but my guess is that JB acquired Percy's catalogue of SJ's works in two instalments. A short MS. catalogue of SJ's works in Percy's hand is in the Bodleian Library (MS. Percy 87).

[3] Rather, octavo (1756, 1760, 1766, 1776, etc.).

[4] This describes the fourth edition (1756), as well as most subsequent ones.

[5] Cf. *Life* i. 252–54; and *post* From J. Warton, 30 Mar. 1790. Percy noted (Anderson's *Life of Johnson*, 3rd ed., 1815, p. 190 n.): "Hawkesworth, who was not so well acquainted with the Latin and Greek classics as Johnson, usually sent him each paper, to prefix a motto before it was printed."

[6] Rather, pott octavo.

[7] See *Life* i. 197 and n. 4; and *post* From Anon., n.d., p. 591 and n. 1.

[8] The first appearance of the poem in a quarto edition was in 1750, when it was issued as a companion to *The Vanity of Human Wishes*. The first four editions (1–3, 1738; 4, 1739) were in folio. A "second" edition of 1738 in octavo was, despite the imprint, printed in Edinburgh.

The Vanity of Human Wishes in imit. of Juv. 10 Sat. 4to
Pope's Messiah translated into Latin verse (Gent. Mag. 1752)[9]
Some verses in Mrs. Williams's Poems[10]
The Lives of Mr. Richard Savage, Sir Francis Drake and Admiral
Blake 8vo[11]
Prologue on opening the Theatre in Drury lane 1747
Prologue for Mrs. Foster's benefit fol.[12] *I read this to Lord Hailes
in Mr. Johnson's hearing; and he acquiesced in it by smiling and
saying nothing.*[13]
Miscellaneous observations on the Tragedy of Macbeth, 1745 12mo
Political Debates in the Gentleman's Magazine for the years
1741-2-3. *N.B. Dr. Percy makes them 2-3-4 and 5 but Mr. J.
says as above.*[14]
Several annual Prefaces to that Magazine *viz. for the years*[15]
Introduction to the Literary Magazine[16]
Remarks on some letters of Sir Isaac Newton in that Magazine[17]
Remarks (in ditto) on Soam Jennings's Origin of Evil[18]
In every one of that Magazine to No. 15 is something of Mr.
Johnson's, chiefly in the Account of Books.[19]

[9] This was the second appearance of the poem; it was first printed in John Husbands' *Miscellany of Poems*, Oxford, 1731. See *Poems*, ed. McAdam and Milne, p. 29; and *post* From Taylor, 6 May 1785, n. 40.

[10] *Miscellanies in Prose and Verse*, 1766.

[11] The lives of Drake and Blake, which had originally appeared in *Gent. Mag.* in 1740, were added to the third edition of the *Life of Savage* to form this volume (1767). The collection was re-issued in 1769, 1775, and 1777 (all called the "fourth" edition).

[12] That is, the New Prologue to *Comus*, 1750.

[13] Not mentioned in the *Life*.

[14] "He told me himself, that he was the sole composer of them for those three years only [1741-43]. He was not, however, precisely exact in his statement, which he mentioned from hasty recollection; for it is sufficiently evident, that his composition of them began November 19, 1740, and ended February 23, 1742-43" (*Life* i. 150). See Hill's comments, *ibid.* 509-10; B. B. Hoover, *Samuel Johnson's*

Parliamentary Reporting, 1953, pp. 207 ff.; and D. J. Greene, "Some Notes on Johnson and the *Gentleman's Magazine*", PMLA (1959) lxxiv. 75-84, and *The Politics of Samuel Johnson*, 1960, ch. 5.

[15] In italicizing "*viz. for the years*" I am guessing that JB added the phrase as a memorandum to himself. In the *Life* (i. 16-18) he attributes to SJ on internal evidence the Prefaces to the volumes for 1738 and 1740-44. The "Address to the Reader" which he cites under 1739 appeared in the May number.

[16] That is, the Preliminary Address "To the Public".

[17] *Four Letters from Sir Isaac Newton to Dr. Bentley, Containing Some Arguments in Proof of a Deity*, 1756.

[18] See *post* From Adams, 17 Feb. 1785, n. 20.

[19] "He continued to write in it, with intermissions, till the fifteenth number" (*Life* i. 307). SJ's "original essays" and reviews are then enumerated. See D. J. Greene, "Johnson's Contributions to the Literary Magazine", RES (1956) vii. 367-92.

A Quarto Pamphlet on the Lord Chamberlain's licensing the Play House[20]

Life of John Philip Baratier in 1744 8vo[21]

Life of Sir Thomas Brown prefixed to his Christian Morals 12mo[22]

Life of Boerhave in the Gent. Magaz[in]e

Life of Dr. Sydenham prefixed to Dr. Swan's version[23]

Life of Roger Ascham prefixed to his English Works 4to

Life of Edward[24] Cave in the Gent. Magazine

Vision of Theodore the Hermit published in the Preceptor. *N.B. Dr. Percy writes upon it that he heard Mr. Johnson declare it was the best thing he ever wrote.*[25]

Preface to the Preceptor

Preface to Rolt's Dictionary of Trade and Commerce

Preface to the Translation of Sully's Memoirs [*deleted*]. *Mrs. Williams told me he wrote Mrs. Lenox's Dedications to translations of Sully and Maintenon.*[26]

Proposals for publishing his Eng. Dict. 4to[27]

Proposals for publishing his Shakespeare

Proposals for publishing Osborne's Harleian Miscellany. *The latin accounts of the Books in Osborne's catalogue of the Harleian Library.*[28]

1760 Introduction to the London Chronicle

Introduction to the proceedings of the Committee appointed to

---

[20] That is, *A Complete Vindication of the Licensers of the Stage*, etc., 1739.

[21] A revision of articles in *Gent. Mag.*, 1740–42.

[22] Rather, small octavo.

[23] In the *Life* (i. 153) JB lists this work under SJ's writings for *Gent. Mag.* in 1742, stating that it was "afterwards prefixed" to Swan's edition (i.e. translation) of Sydenham's works. Actually, as Dr. Powell notes, the *Gent. Mag.* printing followed the book, which came out earlier the same year.

[24] MS. orig. "Henry": i.e. David Henry (1710–92), Cave's brother-in-law.

[25] *Life* i. 192.

[26] As the following letter to Percy makes clear, the deletion was on SJ's authority, not Mrs. Williams's. JB records a review by SJ in *The Literary Magazine* of Mrs. Lennox's translation of Sully (*Life* i. 309), but makes no mention of the Dedication. Why he did not take Mrs. Williams's word for it is not evident. Croker (1831, i. 287) attributed the Dedication to SJ, but gave no authority. See Hazen, pp. 110–13. The Dedication to Maintenon similarly goes unnoticed in the *Life*. Miriam Small (*Charlotte Ramsay Lennox: An Eighteenth Century Lady of Letters*, 1935, pp. 21–22, 215) notes that all but the last sentence and signature of the Dedication appears on a leaf which is a cancel, which fact she explains alternatively as owing to a new version by SJ and a change of dedicatee by Mrs. Lennox. Prof. Hazen, who in his book (p. 90 n. 2) doubted SJ's authorship, now suggests to me that SJ may well have revised the second paragraph only.

[27] That is, the *Plan*, 1747.

[28] *Life* i. 153–54.

manage the contributions begun at London Decr. 18, 1758 for cloathing the french Prisoners London 1760[29]

Dedication to Ascham's Eng. Works 4to[30]

Dedication to Kennedy's Chronology 1762 4to also the concluding paragraph p. 728[31]

Dedication to Hoole's Tasso 1763

Account of Collins in Pag. 110, 111, 112 of the XIIth No. of the Poetical Calendar in 1763 (The former part by Jo. Warton)[32]

Thoughts on the Coronation of Geo. 3 1761 folio (The facts by Gwynne an Architect) *Mr. J. only corrected it.*[33]

New Edition of Shakespeare's Plays 8 vols. 8vo 1765

Remarks on the Chaplain Lindsey's Account of the Conquest of Goree in Gent. Mag. *Mr. J. says he never heard of Lindsey nor that Gorree was conquered, so that to the best of his knowledge this cannot be.*[34]

The above list was communicated to me by Dr. Percy who told me he took it down from Mr. Levet while Mr. Johnson sat by, and corrected any mistake.[35]

[29] For new light on this publication, see J. L. Clifford, "Johnson's Obscure Middle Years," *Johnson, Boswell and Their Circle: Essays Presented to Lawrence Fitzroy Powell*, 1965, pp. 102–03.

[30] *Life* i. 22, 464. *The English Works of Roger Ascham*, by James Bennet, appeared in 1761. SJ contributed the life of Ascham and most of the notes. He had also written the Advertisement to Bennet's Proposals of which Strahan printed two editions, first in Dec. 1757 and second in Aug. 1760. See *Life* i. 550–51 and Hazen, pp. 19 ff.

[31] *Life* i. 366.

[32] See *post* To J. Warton, 3 Aug. 1787, n. 3.

[33] *Life* i. 361.

[34] "*Some Account of a Work lately published, entitled,* A Voyage to the Coast of Africa in 1758. *Containing a Narrative of the expedition against* Goree, *under the Hon.* Augustus Keppel. *By the Rev.* John Lindsay, *Chaplain of the* Fougueux" (*Gent. Mag.*, 1759, xxix. 447–51). JB does not mention the review in the *Life*.

[35] "I once got from one of his friends a list, which there was pretty good reason to suppose was accurate, for it was written down in his presence by this friend, who enumerated each article aloud, and had some of them mentioned to him by Mr. Levett, in concert with whom it was made out; and Johnson, who heard all this, did not contradict it. But when I shewed a copy of this list to him, and mentioned the evidence for its exactness, he laughed, and said, 'I was willing to let them go on as they pleased, and never interfered.' Upon which I read it to him, article by article, and got him positively to own or refuse; and then, having obtained certainty so far, I got some other articles confirmed by him directly, and afterwards, from time to time, made additions under his sanction" (*Life* iii. 321–22). See JB's letter to Percy, following, n. 3. According to Mrs. Piozzi (*Thraliana*, p. 173), SJ "purposely suffered" Percy "to be misled, and he has accordingly gleaned up many Things that are not true".

To Thomas Percy,
c. 8–11 May 1772[1]

MS. Hyde.

ADDRESS: To Dr. Percy.

[London, c. 8–11 May 1772]

DEAR SIR: I return you the list of Mr. Johnson's writings with many thanks. I must tell you however that he allowed Levet to dictate to you several errours, as for instance the Conquest of Goree, and the Preface to Sully. He corrected these errours *himself* to me.[2] Mr. Garrick is very desireous to have a copy of the list; but I must ask your permission before I give it; or I would rather wish you should give it yourself. If you do not forbid me, I will give it.[3]

I hope to hear from you at Edinburgh and am Dear Sir, Your obliged humble servant

JAMES BOSWELL

From Thomas Percy,
Thursday 9 May 1776

MS. Yale (M 156:3). In JB's hand.

This[1] is imitated by one Johnson who put in for a Publick School in

[1] Writing to Garrick, 10 Sept. 1772, JB speaks of this letter to Percy as being sent "before I left London". He left London for Scotland immediately after 11 May (BP ix. 101).

[2] On 8 May JB was "With Mr. Johns ... Angry asking as to works" (condensed Journ.).

[3] JB sent a copy of the list with a page and a half of additions in the letter mentioned above, n. 1. In M 148 following the additions appears the memorandum: "Thus far I sent to Mr. Garrick with the following Note

The above Catalogue was mostly copied from one which the Reverend Dr. Percy communicated to me. He told me that it was drawn up by him and Mr. Levet in the hearing of Mr. Johnson who sometimes corrected it; and therefore Dr. Percy concluded that it must be authentick. Mr. Johnson however told me that he allowed Percy and Levet to do the best they could; and put them right only sometimes as the inclination took him; but by no means so often as they were wrong. I prevailed with Mr. Johnson to give me some additional corrections; and from these and what I had from Mr. Langton and Mrs. Williams, I take the above Catalogue to be a very good one. There are however several more things written by Mr. Johnson, particularly in the Gentleman's Magazine which we have not yet discovered. September 1772."

Cf. *Life* iii. 320–21. The MS. continues for several pages enumerating further writings of SJ.

[1] In the MS. *Life* (p. 89) JB re-copied this note by Pope with the direction to the printer: "Print this Note exactly

9

Shropshire; but was Dissappointed. He has an Infirmity of the convulsive kind, that attacks him sometimes, so as to make Him a sad
Spectacle. Mr. P. from the Merit of This Work which was all the
knowledge he had of Him endeavour'd to serve Him without his
own application; & wrote to my L^d. gore, but he did not succeed.
M^r. Johnson publish'd afterw^{ds}. another Poem in Latin with Notes
the whole very Humerous call'd the Norfolk Prophecy.

P.

This Billet was written by Mr. Pope when Mr. Johnson pub-
lished his Imitation of Juvenal entitled London. The merit of that
Poem struck Pope and he inquired of Richardson the Painter if he
knew the Author who told him "it was one Johnson." Upon which
Pope said—"I never heard of him before, but he will be *deterré.*"
Afterwards Pope picked up further particulars about him which
he wrote down on this Billet.[2] Mr. Richardson gave it to Sir
Joshua Reynolds, who gave it to me.[3]

PERCY

Jany. 20 1773

I copied this Note with Dr. Percy's remark from the Originals,
at Northumberland House London, 9 May 1776.

JAMES BOSWELL

To the Rev. Dr. William Adams,[1] Tuesday 28 April 1778

MS. Yale (L 6). JB's copy, headed: "To The Rev. Dr. Adams Master of
Pembroke College Oxford." Sent 29 Apr. (Reg. Let.).[2]

with capitals contractions and false
spelling as written." See *Life* i. 142–43.
The false spelling "Dissapointed"—
doubtless JB's—was corrected. The original of Pope's note is untraced. A contemporary copy, varying from JB's in a
number of accidentals, is in the Hyde
Collection (facsimile in *Adam Cat.*, vol. ii).

[2] *Life* i. 128–29, with acknowledgement to Percy.

[3] *Life* i. 142.

---

[1] William Adams, D.D. (1706–89),
author of *An Essay in Answer to Mr.
Hume's Essay on Miracles* (1752) and
other works, was Master of Pembroke
College, Oxford from 1775 until his death.

When JB in a conversation with SJ on 11
Apr. 1773 suggested that a visit to Adams
might prove rewarding to the future biographer, "Sir," said he, "'tis not worth
while. You know more of me than he does."
Yet, a few months later SJ told Mrs.
Thrale: "the history of my Oxford
exploits lies all between [Dr. Taylor] and
Adams" (*Anecdotes: Johns. Misc.* i. 166;
quoted, *Life* i. 26 n. 1). In his correspondence with JB, Adams is in fact less
informative about SJ's college days than
he is about some later episodes in his
career, and the reason is clear: Adams
became tutor at Pembroke just about
the time SJ left college (see *post* From

London, 28 April 1778

REVEREND SIR: I know not if you will recollect my having been at your house about two years ago with Dr. Johnson. I was received by you with a very polite civility; and I regretted that the Dr.'s hurry to get forward to Lichfield and Ashbourne prevented me from having more of the pleasure of your conversation.[3]

I have thoughts of coming down to Oxford, for a day or two, early in May, if I were sure of finding you there and at leisure.

Will you not think it too much presumption in me when I thus take the liberty to beg that you may let me know.

Be so good as make my compliments acceptable to your Lady and Miss Adams;[4] and beleive me to be with great respect, Reverend Sir, your most obedient humble servant

My Address is at General Paoli's Southaudley Street.[5]

From the Rev. Dr. William Adams, Friday 1 May 1778

MS. Yale (C 11). Received 5 May (Reg. Let.).

ADDRESS: To James Boswell Esqr., at Genl. Paoli's, South Audley Street.

POSTMARK: 2 MA.

Oxford, 1 May 1778

DEAR SIR: You wrong me much in thinking that I can forget Mr.

Adams, 17 Feb. 1785, n. 11–11).—JB visited Adams at Oxford twice in SJ's company: in Mar. 1776 (at which time he was storing Johnsoniana in his *Note Book*) and in June 1784 (Journ. 20 Mar. 1776 and *Life* ii. 441 ff.; *post* From Adams, June 1784 and *Life* iv. 285 ff.). In 1786 he went to Oxford with Malone, and in the following year he called on Adams and his daughter during their stay in London. JB describes Adams as "a most polite, pleasing, communicative man" (*Life* ii. 441), "a little fair man, very civil and communicative" (Journ. 20 Mar. 1776). —In addition to the correspondence there is in the Yale Collection a letter from Adams to SJ about Shenstone for the *Lives of the Poets* (C 12). JB made no use of it.

[2] The Register abstract concludes: "(Intended as a trial if he'd ask me to lodge at his house.)."

[3] They left Oxford on 21 Mar. and arrived the next morning at Birmingham, where JB wished to stay over to talk more with Hector (*post* To Hector, 21 Jan. 1785, n. 1), but SJ "was impatient to reach his native city". They accordingly went on to Lichfield that night, and remained there until the 26th, when their Ashbourne host, Dr. Taylor, sent a coach for them (Journ. Mar. 1776; *Life* ii. 451 ff.).

[4] Adams married Sarah Hunt, of Boreatton, Shropshire, in 1742. Their only surviving child, Sarah, was born in 1746. JB was to cultivate her as well as her father, and for the same purpose: see *post* To S. Adams, 5 May 1786.

[5] JB was the frequent guest of General Paoli in London. In 1778 he made his headquarters at Paoli's house from 18 Mar. to 18 May (Journ.).

11

Boswell the Friend of Dr. Johnson and Genl. Paoli. I shall be happy in seeing you here when ever and as oft as you please.[1] I did myself the honour of waiting on Signr. Paoli when at Shrewsbury,[2] hearing that he had no one to attend him in a Place where he was a Stranger but the Host of the Inn: but had the ill fortune to miss seeing him and being suddenly called into the Country[3] had it not in my power to repeat my Visit. But I afterwards found that he was in better hands—those of Mr. Pulteney,[4] which made me less regret tho' I much regretted losing the pleasure of seeing him. When you see Dr. Johnson I beg my Compliments to him. I am Sir, with great Regard, Your obedient Servant

W. ADAMS

To William Strahan,[1]
Tuesday 17 November 1778

Missing. Sent to London from Edinburgh. Reg. Let.: "William Strahan Esq. that as he will be glad to contribute to the Great Life,[2] I beg he may mark down for me all the particulars which he remembers of Dr. Johnson of every kind."

[1] There is no record of a visit to Oxford at this time. The journal lapses between 30 Apr. and 12 May. If the excursion was made at all, it must have been made between the 5th, when Adams's letter was received, and the 7th, when JB was in London.

[2] Adams's birthplace. He had been curate of St. Chad's from 1732, when he left Pembroke as tutor, until 1775, when he returned as Master (*Johns. Glean.* v. 181). I am not able to account for Paoli's presence at Shrewsbury.

[3] Perhaps to Counde, near Shrewsbury, where Adams was rector.

[4] William Johnstone-Pulteney (1729–1805), M.P. for Cromartyshire, 1768–74, and for Shrewsbury, 1775–1805; fifth Bt. (*Comp. Bar.* iv. 395). "He published in 1778 and 1779 a pamphlet on the Affairs of America and on the Present State of Public Affairs; and in 1783 an Examina-

tion of Mr. Fox's India Bill, which was bought up and distributed in great numbers by the friends of Mr. Pitt" ([——Marshall], *Catalogue of Five Hundred Celebrated Authors of Great Britain, Now Living*, 1788).

[1] William Strahan (1715–85), King's Printer; M.P. for Malmesbury, 1774–80, and for Wootton Bassett, 1780–84. He was SJ's friend, banker, printer, and publisher. See J. A. Cochrane, *Dr. Johnson's Printer: The Life of William Strahan* (1964); *Life* and *Letters SJ passim*. In 1767 Strahan published *The Letters of Lady Jane Douglas*, edited by JB and others (*Lit. Car.* p. 48).

[2] There is no correspondence, or record of one, on this subject. Strahan's offer may have been made in person in the spring of this year, when JB was in London.

From *William Strahan,*
Monday 4 January 1779

MS. Yale (C 2583). Received 8 Jan. (Reg. Let.). At the top of the letter appear two notes in JB's hand, written at different times: (1) "Refers to 1778." and (2) "p. 767X." The first was evidently a guide for filing materials for the *Life*; the second indicates the place in the MS. *Life* where a passage from this letter, marked off by Xs (see n. 3–3), was to be "taken in".

ADDRESS: James Boswell Esqr., Advocate, Edinburgh.

FRANK: ffree W. Strahan.

POSTMARK: 4 IA.

London, Jany. 4, 1779

DEAR SIR: I received yours of the 17th November, and instantly sent the Letter inclosed to Sir John Pringle,[1] our most valuable and worthy Friend.

Dr. Johnson's *Poets* go on but slowly; however I hope we shall be able to publish a good many Volumes soon.[2] [3]The Notes I shewed you that past between him and me were dated in March last.[4] The Matter lay dormant till July 27th when he wrote me as follows.

Sir: It would be very foolish for us to continue Strangers any longer. You can never by Persistency make wrong, right. If I resented too acrimoniously, I resented only to yourself. Nobody ever saw or heard what I wrote. You saw that my

[1] Sir John Pringle, Bt. (1707–82), physician to George III, " 'mine own friend and my Father's friend,' between whom and Dr. Johnson I in vain wished to establish an acquaintance, as I respected and lived in intimacy with both of them, observed to me once, very ingeniously, 'It is not in friendship as in mathematics, where two things, each equal to a third, are equal between themselves. You agree with Johnson as a middle quality, and you agree with me as a middle quality; but Johnson and I should not agree' " (*Life* iii. 65). Pringle was the middle quality in the formula joining him with JB and Lord Auchinleck. JB's letter to

him is untraced, but is noted in Reg. Let. under 17 Nov. 1778: "Sir John Pringle of 31 Octr. from Auchinleck, and Addition of this date (Copy) of my Father etc. Begging he may communicate what he recollects of the Reverend Dr. [David] Cooper [M.D., minister of Auchinleck, 1732–51]." See Journ. 31 Oct., 6 and 17 Nov. 1778.

[2] The first four volumes of SJ's *Prefaces, Biographical and Critical, to the Works of the English Poets* were published in Mar. 1779.

[3–3] Quoted, *Life* iii. 364.

[4] Not recovered.

Anger was over, for in a Day or two, I came to your House. I have given you longer time, and I hope you have made so good Use of it, as to be no longer on evil Terms with, Sir, Your etc.

Sam Johnson

On this I called upon him; and he has since dined with me;[3] but I have not had time to see him lately.

I shall be attentive to note any Particulars that may contribute to your Life of that Great Man;[5] and am, with sincere Esteem, Dear Sir, Your most obedient Servant

WILL. STRAHAN

To Francis Barber,[1]
Friday 22 January 1779

Missing. Sent to London from Edinburgh. Reg. Let.: "Mr. Francis Barber, Dr. Johnson's black servant, reminding him to preserve for me the M.S. and Proof sheets of his Master's *Prefaces Biographical and Critical to the English Poets* (Copy)."[2]

---

[5] JB called on Strahan in London on 16 Mar. of this year "and was pleased with his wealthy plumpness and good animal spirits and his wish to communicate to me all that he knew concerning Dr. Johnson" (Journ.).

---

[1] For the biography of Francis Barber (c. 1742–1801), SJ's Negro servant, see *Johns. Glean.* ii. and viii. 73 ff. His autobiography, of sorts, may be read in the present correspondence with JB, to whom he communicated as many details of his own life as of his master's. Much of this was at JB's request, but even the digressively personal note of Barber's later letters was not entirely gratuitous, for JB openly declared his interest in Barber's welfare after he and his white wife had been abused by Hawkins in his *Life of Johnson* (see *post* To Barber, 29 June 1787, n. 2). Hawkins's daughter Laetitia Matilda contended that Barber "sold

intelligence to Boswell" (*Johns. Glean.* ii. 26). It is true that JB did on one occasion lend Barber £20 which seems to have been forgotten by both, and also that the correspondence comes to a halt in 1790 when JB refuses Barber's second request for a loan and subjoins a mild reproach; but the element of calculation —on both sides—is outweighed by good feelings—on both sides—and JB's treatment of Barber in the *Life* is marked by the same respect shown him in his letters.

[2] On the same day JB wrote to SJ "on several topicks, and mentioned that as he had been so good as to permit me to have the proof sheets of his 'Lives of the Poets,' I had written to his servant, Francis, to take care of them for me" (*Life* iii. 371). The year before, 18 June, he had written to SJ, "I am eager to see more of your Prefaces to the Poets; I solace myself with the few proof-sheets which I have" (*ibid.* 360). See also *Johnsoniana*, p. 264.

From Francis Barber, Friday 19 February 1779

MS. Arthur B. Spingarn, New York.

Sent from London or Streatham (*Letters SJ* 600.1–602). Received 23 Feb. (Reg. Let.).

ADDRESS: James Boswell Esqr., Advocate, Edinburgh.

FRANK: ffree W. Strahan.

POSTMARK: 19 FE.

Friday Feb. 19th 1779

SIR: I am extremely sorry, and also beg pardon for having put you to the necessity of writing, my engagement had not slip'd my memory but found it impracticable to collect the proof sheets regularly as they are work'd off; notwithstand the few which fell in my way I have carefully laid by in order to transmit them to you: however my Master has since order'd me to enform you that you shall shortly have the Books instead of the above sheets[1] and am with due obedience, Your Humble Servant

FRAS. BARBER

[1] SJ wrote to JB a few weeks later: "I shall spare Francis the trouble, by ordering a set of both the Lives and Poets to dear Mrs. Boswell, in acknowledgement of her marmalade" (*Life* iii. 372). Nevertheless, JB did obtain proof sheets of many of the *Lives* (both 1779 and 1781), a number of which are now in the Victoria and Albert Museum and in the Hyde Collection. He also received from SJ "the greatest part of the original" manuscript, now, with the exception of the lives of Rowe and Pope, lost (see *Life* iv. 36, 71, 72, 480). See also J. D. Fleeman, "Some Proofs of Johnson's *Prefaces to the Poets*," *The Library* (1962), xvii. 213–30.

1784

To Francis Barber,
Friday 30 January 1784

MS. Yale (L 27). A copy by John Lawrie, JB's clerk, written on side 3 of a copy of a letter to Drs. Heberden and Brocklesby; headed: "To M[r.] Francis Barber at Dr. S. Johnsons."

Edin., 30 Janry. 1784

MR. FRANCIS: I am in very anxious concern about my much respected friend your Master.[1] And as the accounts which I receive of the state of his health are not by any means so particular as I could wish, I will be obliged to you if you will once a week at least let me know with minute exactness how he is, who are with him and in what manner his time is employed. I long earnestly to be with him. But as that cannot be till the middle or perhaps the end of march[2] I shall in the mean time depend upon full intelligence from you and I trust you will say nothing of this to Dr. Johnson, as it might alarm him. I am, Sir, Your sincere friend

To the Rev. Dr. William Adams,
Monday 7 June 1784

MS. Yale (L 7). JB's copy, headed: "To The Rev. Dr. Adams Master of Pembroke College Oxford."

London, 7 June 1784

REVEREND SIR: I was perfectly sincere when I told you I was sorry to leave your society. But I had a very sufficient reason when my

[1] "In the end of this year [1783] he was seized with a spasmodick asthma of such violence, that he was confined to the house in great pain . . . and there came upon him at the same time that oppressive and fatal disease, a dropsy" (*Life* iv. 255). On 6 Feb. 1784 JB wrote to Sir Joshua Reynolds: "My anxiety about Dr. Johnson is truly great. . . . I intend to be in London next month Chiefly to attend upon him with respectfull affection. But in the mean time, it will be a great favour done me if you who know him so well, will be kind enough to let me know particularly how he is."

[2] On 21 Mar. news reached JB that "Dr. Johnson was wonderfully releived". The next day he set out for London, but learning at Newcastle that Parliament had been dissolved, he returned home to contest the seat for Ayrshire, in which he was unsuccessful. He thereupon set out again for London, and arrived on 5 May (BP xvi. 42 and n., 52).

19

object was to hear the wonderful performance of the *Messiah* in Westminster Abbey.[1]

Mr. Osborn formerly the British minister at the Court of Dresden[2] having engaged General Paoli General Boyd,[3] etc. etc. etc. to dine with him tomorrow *to meet me*, I could not with propriety or indeed in gratitude refuse to accept of an invitation so polite.[4] I trust you will satisfy your *Pupil*[5] that I have done right, though I shall be two days more absent from *College* than I might have been. On Wednesday evening I shall (GOD willing) have the pleasure to be again under your hospitable roof.[6] I beg to have my best compliments presented to Mrs. and Miss Adams and Dr. Johnson. I am, Reverend Sir, your obliged humble servant

[1] "He had now a great desire to go to Oxford, as his first jaunt after his illness; we talked of it for some days, and I had promised to accompany him. He was impatient and fretful to-night [Tuesday 1 June], because I did not at once agree to go with him on Thursday. When I considered how ill he had been, and what allowance should be made for the influence of sickness upon his temper, I resolved to indulge him, though with some inconvenience to myself, as I wished to attend the musical meeting in honour of Handel, in Westminster-Abbey, on the following Saturday. . . . we were received [3 June] with the most polite hospitality at the house of his old friend Dr. Adams, Master of Pembroke College, who had given us a kind invitation. Before we were set down, I communicated to Johnson my having engaged to return to London directly, for the reason I have mentioned, but that I would hasten back to him again" (*Life* iv. 283, 285). The fifth of June was the final day of the performance commemorating the centennial of Handel's birth and the twenty-fifth anniversary of his death. The event is described in Dr. Burney's *Account of the Musical Performances in Westminster-Abbey and the Pantheon . . . in Commemoration of* *Handel* (1785), for which SJ wrote the Dedication to the King. See *Life* iv. 544–46.

[2] John Osborn (b. 1743), envoy extraordinary in Saxony, 1771–75; D.C.L. Oxford, 1777. He was the son of Sir Danvers Osborn, Bt., and the younger brother of Sir George Osborn, Bt., general in the army (D. B. Horn, *British Diplomatic Representatives 1689–1789*, 1932, p. 65; *Alum. Oxon.*; *Comp. Bar.* iii. 243–44). See also Journ. *passim*.

[3] Sir Robert Boyd (1710–94), lieutenant-general and second in command at the defence of Gibraltar from 1779 to 1783; appointed governor of the colony in 1790.

[4] There is no notice of this dinner among JB's meagre records for this period.

[5] See *post* From Adams, 17 Feb. 1785 and n. 7.

[6] "I fulfilled my intention by going to London, and returned to Oxford on Wednesday the 9th of June, when I was happy to find myself again in the same agreeable circle at Pembroke College, with the comfortable prospect of making some stay. Johnson welcomed my return with more than ordinary glee" (*Life* iv. 286).

Johnsoniana Related by the Rev. Dr. William Adams, Oxford, June 1784[1]

MS. Yale (C 13). In JB's hand.

[I]

15 June 1784

Dr. Adams told me Warburton spoke well of the *Dictionary* and desired the Dr. would tell Johnson he honoured him for the spirit with which he refused to dedicate to Lord Chest[erfiel]d and for his letter to him. Dr. Adams told Johnson he was sorry he had written such a letter. "Sir" said Johnson "He is the proudest man that ever existed." "No Sir" said Dr. Adams "I know a prouder man that exists now. And that is yourself." "But" said Johnson "my pride was defensive."[2]

R. Dodsley told Dr. Adams that Lord Chesterfield shewed him Johnson's letter—said this man has great powers—pointed out the severest passages, and observed how well they were expressed.[3] His Lordship said he was unjustly blamed—If Johnson had been ever refused access it must have been from something in his appearance.[4] But his Lordship would have turned off the best servant he

---

[1] Of these three groups of notes only one was dated by JB (15 June 1784, the last day of his visit at Oxford), but it can be shown that all three belong in all probability to the same period. The group which I have designated II contains an anecdote told by Charles Howard, a Lichfield lawyer (printed, *Life* iii. 222–23), and the Register of Letters discloses visits to Lichfield both in Apr. and July of 1784. (Oxford and Lichfield were on the same itinerary in 1776, but on that occasion JB was recording Johnsoniana in the *Note Book*.) As for the third group, both it and the first take up the subject of SJ's *Dictionary* and the quarrel with Chesterfield. Finally, the very fact that these notes have survived affords evidence for their date. It was JB's practice to discard his notes once they were transcribed into the journal, and of his four visits with Adams, only one of them belongs to a period when he failed to keep up his journal—that of June 1784.

[2] The story of SJ's famous quarrel with Chesterfield is told at length, *Life* i. 256 ff. JB's account is based in part on details furnished by Adams, both in these notes and in his letter *post* 17 Feb. 1785. The latter version was preferred. On SJ's "defensive pride", cf. Hawkins, p. 165: "There were not wanting those among his friends who would sometimes hint to him, that the conditions of free conversation imply an equality among those engaged in it, which are violated whenever superiority is assumed: their reproofs he took kindly, and would in excuse for what they called the pride of learning, say, that it was of the defensive kind."

[3] *Life* i. 265, completing the anecdote at the end of group III below ("Dr. Adams mentioned to Dodsley").

[4] Not used.

ever had if he had known he had denied him to Johnson[5]—As to not inquiring after him for years, he had inquired but could not find out where he was.[6] Besides he said it was Johnson's business to inquire after him.[7] He said also he did not know that Johnson's Tragedy *Irene* was brought on the stage.[8]

Dr. Adams told me he was present the first night when *Irene* was acted. There were Catcalls whistling before the Curtain drew up which was alarming. The Prologue soothed the Audience. The Play went off tolerably, till it came to the Conclusion when Mrs. Pritchard was to be strangled upon the Stage, and was to speak two lines with the bowstring round her neck. They cried out Murder Murder. She several times attempted to speak. But in vain. At last she was obliged to go off the Stage alive.[9] Dr. Adams beleives it was altered afterwards.[10]

[II]

Dr. Adams found him at his *Dictionary*. This is a great work Sir. How can you get all the Etymologies. Why there is a Shelf with Junius and Skinner and others and there is a Welch Gentleman who has published a collection of Welsh proverbs would help him with the Welsh. But Sir how can you do this in three years? Yes Sir I can do it in three years. But french Accademy of 40 took 40

[5] *Life* i. 265, conflated with the assertion in the later version (*post* 17 Feb. 1785) that SJ "would have been always more than welcome."

[6] JB uses Adams's later version.

[7] Not used.

[8] This issue is not raised in the *Life*, but it is hard to believe that Chesterfield was ignorant of the performance of *Irene*, which had a respectable run, 6–20 Feb. 1749 (*Life* i. 198 n. 1). Bonamy Dobrée remarks, without reference to the controversy, that "he must have heard of the production of *Irene*" (*Letters of Lord Chesterfield*, 1932, i. 183).

[9] Revised and presented as a direct quotation from Adams, *Life* i. 196–97. See Introduction, pp. xxviii–xxix. The original sketch among JB's rough notes (J 93) reads: "present first night of Irene Catcalls. Then murder murder etc. Mrs. Pritch obliged to go off alive." Hannah

Vaughan Pritchard (1711–68), though one of the toasts of Drury Lane, made no hit with SJ, who disparaged her intellect and character as well as her ability as an actress (*Life* ii. 348–49, iv. 243, v. 126; Journ. 8 Apr. 1775). Burney noted (*Life*, 3rd ed., 1799, i. 167 n.): "there was not the least opposition during the representation, except the first night in the last act, where Irene was to be strangled on the stage, which *John* could not bear, though a dramatick poet may stab or slay by hundreds. The bow-string was not a Christian nor an ancient Greek or Roman death. But this offence was removed after the first night, and Irene went off the stage to be strangled." See *Poems*, ed. Smith and McAdam, pp. 238 ff.

[10] "This passage was afterwards struck out, and she was carried off to be put to death behind the scenes, as the play now has it" (*Life* i. 197).

years. Why Sir thus it is. This is the proportion. Let me see 40
times 40 is 1600—as 3 to 1600 is the proportion of an englishman
to a Frenchman.[11]

Dr. Adams remembers his Father bringing him to College and
was present the first evening when he was introduced to Jorden[12]
his tutor. The mighty Cub! His Father told he was a good scholar
and a poet and wrote latin verses. He appeared strange to them.
Behaved modestly and sat silent till upon something he struck in
and quoted Macrobius. Now they wondered a Schoolboy should
know Macrobius. It was about the last day of October.[13] It was
near the 5 of Novr. which was then kept as a great day at Pembroke.
Exercises were given in. Johnson failed. I[14] am sorry for it—a
Poem by him on the Gunpowder plot would have been sublime. He
gave in an excuse titled *Somnium* a common thought that the muse
came to him and said it did not become him to write on such high
subjects as politicks but should confine himself to humbler themes.
But it was in Virgilian Verse.[15] Then Jordin set him as a task to
translate the *Messiah* which was done in two months after he came
to College.[16] He loved and respected Jordin not for his literature
but said he whenever he gets a young man for his pupil he was his
son.[17]

[III]

Dr. Adams in the year   visited Dr. Johnson at his house
in Gough Square. He found the parlour floor covered with parcels
of foreign Journals and english reviews and he told Dr. Adams he
meant to undertake a Review. "How Sir" said Dr. Adams "can

[11] *Life* i. 186. Cf. Garrick's "On
Johnson's Dictionary. 1755":
    And Johnson, well arm'd, like a
      hero of yore,
    Has beat forty French, and will
      beat forty more.
Cf. also *Anecdotes*: *Johns. Misc.* i. 183.
[12] William Jorden (c. 1686–1739),
Adams's first cousin, attended Pembroke
College, where, like Adams, he was "of
founder's kin". He became tutor and
chaplain to the College in 1720 (*Johns.
Glean.* v. 123–29).
[13] Freely expanded, *Life* i. 59. In the
MS. *Life* (p. 19) the clause "They
wondered that a schoolboy should know
Macrobius;" is marked as having been

left out by the printer (homoeoteleuton);
but it was not restored. In SJ's library
there was a quarto volume of "Macrobii
opera" (*Sale Catalogue*, No. 191). For a
conjecture on the quotation from Macrobius, see C. G. Osgood, MLN (1954)
lxix. 246. JB himself struck in with
Macrobius on one occasion (*Life* iii. 25),
but SJ does not appear to have been
impressed.
[14] JB.
[15] Freely expanded, *Life* i. 60. Cf.
post From Adams, 17 Feb. 1785.
[16] JB uses Adams's later, and fuller,
account (*post* 17 Feb. 1785).
[17] *Life* i. 61.

you think of doing it alone. All branches of knowledge must be considered in it. Do you know mathematicks? Do you know natural history?" Dr. Johnson answered "I must do as well as I can. My chief purpose is to give my countrymen a view of what is doing in literature upon the continent, and I shall have in a good measure the choice of my subjects." Dr. Adams suggested it would be better for him to do the reverse and having a high esteem for Dr. Maty he then mentioned that he had just laid aside his *Bibliotheque Britannique* and Dr. Johnson might do well to take his assistance. Dr. grew angry[18]—and said "Damn Maty—little dirty-faced dog I'll throw him into the Thames."

Dr. Johnson never executed this scheme of a Review.[19]

In the year 1766 he was dreadfully afflicted with low spirits. Dr. Adams called at his house. Mrs. Williams said nobody had been admitted to him for some days but Mr. Langton. But he would see Dr. Adams. He found Mr. Langton with him. He looked miserable[;] his lips moved, tho he was not speaking[;] he could not sit long at a time—was quite restless, sometimes walked up and down the room, sometimes into the next room, and returned immediately. He said to Dr. Adams "I would suffer a limb to be amputated to recover my spirits."[20]

Dr. Adams mentioned to Dodsley that he was sorry Dr. Johnson had written his letter to Lord Chesterfield. Dodsley said he was very sorry too; for that he had a property in the *Dictionary* to which Lord Chesterfield's patronage might be of consequence. He then told Dr. Adams that Lord Chesterfield had shewn him the letter. "I should have imagined" said Dr. Adams "Lord Chesterfield

---

[18] MS. alt. "flew into a passion"

[19] *Life* i. 284, incorporating details from Adams's later, and less dramatic, version (*post* 17 Feb. 1785). In the MS. *Life* (opp. p. 103) the anecdote concludes: "Johnson declared his disapprobation of this in strong [*altered to* contemptuous] terms, and the scheme was dropt"; in the first proofs all but the last two words were deleted and the bolder ending, with some revision, was written in. See Introduction, p. xxxvii. Matthew Maty (1718–76), Ph.D. and M.D., Leyden, was Librarian of the British Museum from 1772. The *Journal Britannique* was published bi-monthly at The Hague, 1750–55. SJ's dislike for Maty arose from his

criticism in the *Journal* of SJ's relations with Chesterfield (Maty was an executor of Chesterfield and was writing his memoirs at the time of his own death) and of the *Dictionary* as well (DNB; *Life* i. 284 n. 3; Journ. 18 Mar. 1776). If Maty literally "had just laid aside his *Bibliotheque Britannique*", Adams's visit to SJ must have taken place at the end of 1755 or the beginning of 1756.

[20] Condensed and extensively revised, *Life* i. 483. JB dates the incident in 1764 rather than 1766, perhaps because of Adams's later allusion to SJ's melancholy "about 20 years before his death" (*post* 12 July 1786).

would have concealed that letter." "Poh!" said Dodsley "do you think a letter from Johnson could hurt Lord Chesterfield? not at all Sir. It lay upon his table where any body might see it. He read it to me, and pointed out the most striking passages of it.[21] But

When Dr. Adams first spoke to Dr. Johnson of his letter to Lord Chesterfield there was somebody present. Dr. Johnson took him into the next room and repeated it from beginning to end.[22]

From Dr. Richard Brocklesby,[1]
Monday 13 December 1784

MS. Yale (C 581). Received 17 Dec. (Reg. Let.).

ADDRESS: To James Boswell Esqr., Advocate, Edinborough, N.B.

POSTMARKS: 13 DE, DE 17.

London, Monday 13th Decr. 1784

DEAR SIR: Your letter 7th Decr.[2] was not sent to my house till late on Saturday night 11th curr[en]t and the approaching Crisis of our great and excellent friend Dr. Johnson determined me not to answer it till by this nights Post, by which time by the rules of

[21] *Life* i. 264–65. See *ante* n. 3. Robert Dodsley (1703–64), bookseller, dramatist, and poet, was one of the seven booksellers to contract for the publication of the *Dictionary*. He appears to have been instrumental in the undertaking from the start (see *post* From J. Dodsley, 29 June 1786) and was responsible for the addressing of the *Plan* to Chesterfield (*Life* i. 182–83; *Letters SJ* 67).

[22] Not used. But cf. *Life* i. 260 and iv. 128.

[1] Richard Brocklesby, M.D. (1722–97), onetime physician to the Army, pioneer in military medicine and sanitation. With SJ he was co-founder of the Essex Head Club (*Life* iv. 254). See W. S. Curran, "Dr. Brocklesby of London (1722–1797): An 18th-Century Physician and Reformer," *Journal of the History of Medicine and Allied Sciences* (1962), xvii. 509–21. An undated rough note in the Yale Collection headed "Johnsoniana/Dr. Brocklesby" (M 155) reads: "Such was his expression of regard for Dr. Brocklesby that one day

when Mr. Langton was present and some conversation had gone on very pleasantly to which Doctor Brocklesby as usual had in a good degree contributed, upon his rising to go Johnson earnestly said 'Nay don't leave us. I think I may apply to your going from me what has been told of a Gentleman who in his eagerness to chide his servant for not coming to him when called said "you seem to me to go ten times down stairs for once that you come up." ' " JB met Brocklesby in SJ's room on 30 Mar. 1783. He "roused us by that flow of spirits just supplied by an active bustling through life. He took to me agreably" (Journ.). Brocklesby appears to have furnished Cooke and Hawkins as well as JB with information about SJ's last days: see *post* From Brocklesby, 27 Dec. 1784 and notes.

[2] In which JB asks anxiously after SJ's health, and also solicits compliments paid SJ by various writers for a book he is planning (not the *Life*); see *Lit. Car.*, p. 306, No. 23. The letter is in the Hyde Collection.

Art I anticipated what hath since happened. About three weeks ago he returned from Litchfield swoln, dejected and giving himself up for a dead Man,[3] he grew daily worse and worse though at intervals he talked of preparing an edition of his works in 12 Volumes in the same type and letter press as his *Lives of the poets* are already printed in large duodecimo. He commissioned me to receive from Cadel[4] and his Coadjutor-brethren the booksellers any or what proposals they should offer but though some whilst Johnson continued in the Country had talked generously, when the proposal came in earnest cooled and grew so selfish, that they represented the value of his literary property as next to nothing, for that he could not legally transfer it to any of the trade, but had reservd it solely for his own supervision. This nettled him and he took a legal opinion about the assignment of his right to 5 or 6 friends to whom he spoke and asked to be concerned in the edition of his whole Works. He asked me among others and I from my heart offerd to take a share to the amount of 4 or 500 £ to build him up the noblest and handsomest monument in a handsome and intire edition of his own works, for we thought they were better and more lasting materials than any monument of brass or Stone in Westm[inste]r Abbey. But whether he has completed his Catalogue and fulfilled his design with Mr. Nichols the printer and the rest I am at present not informed.[5] For he has been for a week past doing little else than burning his manuscripts, though Mr. Stevens took away (as I hear) the Catalogue of his works[6] forty four Articles of which

---

[3] See *Letters SJ* 1037 and following.

[4] Thomas Cadell (1742–1802), one of the many booksellers who published the *Lives*. He espoused the tradition of liberal patronage of authors, including such famous ones as Blackstone, Gibbon —and SJ. According to John Nichols, SJ "was earnestly invited, by his warm friend the late Mr. Alderman Cadell, to publish a volume of *Devotional Exercises*; but this (though he listened to the proposal with much complacency, and a large sum of money was offered for it by Mr. Cadell), he declined, from motives of the sincerest modesty" (*Lit. Anec.* ii. 552).

[5] " 'When talking of a regular edition of his own works, he said, "that he had power, [from the booksellers,] to print such an edition, if his health admitted it; but had no power to assign over any edition, unless he could add notes, and so alter them as to make them new works; which his state of health forbade him to think of. I may possibly live, (said he,) or rather breath, three days, or perhaps three weeks; but find myself daily and gradually weaker" ' " (*Life* iv. 409, quoting Nichols). Cf. *Lit. Anec.* ii. 552.

[6] "An Account of the Writings of Dr. Samuel Johnson" appeared anonymously in *The European Magazine* between Dec. 1784 and Apr. 1785 (vi. 411–13, vii. 9–12, 81–84, 190–92, 249–50). This was probably by Steevens, though he may have been helped by Isaac Reed, the editor of the magazine. Steevens contributed, also anonymously, anecdotes under the title of "Johnsoniana" to the Jan. number (vii. 51–55). See *post* From Steevens, 23 Apr. 1786, n. 1.

I supplyd him with but I kept no Copy of them, but he excepted against two tracts among them, which he said were none of his; He has consignd to Mr. Langton 95 select Epigrams most of them translated into latin verse from the greek Anthologia since his sleepless nights prevented his tranquil hours in bed.[7] But what more he had done as to the conservation of a neat or elegant edition of his works I cannot at present say with precision. His letter to Chesterfield he has consignd to oblivion unless any imperfect Copy appears in print in which case Mr. Langton is impowerd to give the world the original,[8] which is now in Mr. Langston's custody. He asked me on thursday last as a moral man whom he hoped incapable of telling a ly and also competent in my profession whether he could recover. I replied if he could be confident in his own firmness of Mind to hear the whole truth I would not conceal it. He said he insisted on it and then with unfeigned concern I answerd that to the best of my judgement he could not outlive many days on which he repeated a passage from Shakespear and asked where it was. I said in *Macbeth* but added "therein the Patient must minister to himself."[9] He then said he was resolvd against trying any new Doctors whom his friends pressed on him and though Dr. Warren came the following day he beggd pardon but professd he would try no more medicine of any kind[10] and from that time till this even[in]g about 7 oClock he scarse took any

[7] "During his sleepless nights he amused himself by translating into Latin verse, from the Greek, many of the epigrams in the *Anthologia*. These translations, with some other poems by him in Latin, he gave to his friend Mr. Langton, who, having added a few notes, sold them to the booksellers for a small sum, to be given to some of Johnson's relations, which was accordingly done; and they are printed in the collection of his works [*Works* xi. 407–26]" (*Life* iv. 384). Cf. Hawkins, pp. 579–80, 584, 605 n. For a description of Langton's editing, see *Poems*, ed. Smith and McAdam, pp. xviii–xix. Croker obtained the MSS. from Langton's grandson (3rd ed., 1848, p. xviii); but only a few are now extant.

[8] That is, the copy which SJ dictated to Baretti, "with its title and corrections, in his own hand-writing. This he gave to Mr. Langton; adding, that if it were to come into print, he wished it to be from that copy. By Mr. Langton's kindness, I am enabled to enrich my work with a perfect transcript of what the world has so eagerly desired to see" (*Life* i. 260–61). The copy is in the British Museum (Add. MS. 5713): see *post* Malone to Forbes, 3 Mar. 1804. For the copies in the Yale Collection, see *post* From Adams, 17 Feb. 1785, n. 27.

[9] See Brocklesby's expanded version, *post* 27 Dec. 1784.

[10] See the anecdote by Richard Greene, quoted by Hill (from Croker), *Life* iv. 399 n. 5. Richard Warren (1731–97), a member of The Club, received his M.D. at Cambridge in 1762 and in the same year succeeded his father-in-law, Dr. Richard Mead, as physician to George III. He attended members of JB's family and JB himself in his last illness (Journ. *passim; Letters JB* 329).

thing but a little milk and after sleeping 7 or 8 hours he awoke and gave up the Ghost.

Pity that your letter[11] had not the wished for effect, for it was little for the Sovereign to do. No more than as much again as I six months ago long before it was known any application in a certain quarter was to be made did earnestly press him to receive from a man not very rich in worldly goods yet sufficiently rich to afford a great virtuous Man oppressed with infirmities and apprehensions[;] yet he magnanimously rejected my offer of 100 £ per Ann. for life saying he would take such bounty only from the K——.[12] Pray excuse the errors of haste sorrow and much affection for our late good and great friend and allow me a place among yours to subscribe in haste Dear Sir, Your most Obedient Humble Servant

RICHARD BROCKLESBY

From the Rev. Herbert Croft,[1] Thursday 16 December 1784

MS. Yale (C 864). Received Mar. 1785[2] (Reg. Let.).

ADDRESS: To J. Boswell Esqre., at General Paoli's, London.

POSTMARK: 17 DE.

[11] To Lord Thurlow, 24 June 1784, petitioning the King for an addition to SJ's pension, as "his valuable life cannot be preserved long, without the benignant influence of a southern climate". The letter was printed in *The London Chronicle* for 4–6 Jan. 1785, together with an explanatory introduction, over the initials "A.B." For the details of the "pious negociation" (as JB called it), see *Life* iv. 326–28, 336–39, 348–50, 542–43.

[12] See *post* To Brocklesby, 18 Dec. 1784 and n. 2. According to William Windham (*Diary*, ed. Mrs. Henry Baring, 1866, p. 34), SJ, in response to Brocklesby's offer, "pressed his hands and said, 'God bless you through Jesus Christ, but I will take no money but from my sovereign.' This, if I mistake not, was told the King through West" (quoted by Hill, *Life* iv. 338 n. 2). According to Hawkins (p. 574), Brocklesby, while he offered to help, did not approve of SJ's travelling at this time. SJ admitted, in his own letter

to Thurlow, Sept. 1784 (*Life* iv. 349–50), that "My journey to the continent, though I once thought it necessary, was never much encouraged by my physicians."

[1] The Rev. Herbert Croft (1751–1816), barrister, bibliophile, biographer, and (1797) baronet. SJ adopted his *Life of Young* for his *Lives of the Poets* (see *Life* iv. 58, 482). JB's first, and apparently only, meeting with Croft took place on 12 June of this year at Oxford (*Life* iv. 298), where Croft had been pursuing his studies from about 1782. Three days later Croft opened a correspondence, but JB, on the copy of his reply, 28 June, wrote: "N.B. I wished to avoid entering into a regular correspondence with Mr. Croft, as I perceived he was too much inclined to that mode of employing time, which I now cannot well spare."

[2] In Edinburgh.

28

ENDORSEMENT: Rev. Mr. H. Croft that he may speak to the Publick of Johnson and asking materials from me. My Answer Within. [3]

Holywell, Oxford, 16 Decr. 1784

DEAR SIR: Since our great friend's death, I have written to one of his executors, [4] and it is not impossible, on other accounts, that, sooner or later, I may have to speak to the public respecting Johnson. [5]

Your profession, perhaps, employs you too much (and may it employ you much more!) to let you think of saying any thing about our friend. Should this be the case, will you lay any commands on me? If I do any thing of this kind, the communication of any papers or remarks would be an additional favour to that already conferred by your acquaintance (may I say, your friendship?) on, Dear sir, Your obliged and sincere friend,

HERBERT CROFT

To Dr. Richard Brocklesby, Saturday 18 December 1784

MS. Yale (L 272). JB's copy, headed: "To Dr. Brocklesby."

Edinburgh, 18 Decr. 1784

MY DEAR SIR: I am under very great obligations to you for your attention to me upon the melancholy occasion of Dr. Johnson's death, which notwithstanding his advanced age and long and severe illness, hath at last come upon me unexpectedly, and would have given me a sudden shock had I first read it in the Newspapers, which I probably should have done had not you written to me the very evening on which it happened. [1] The full preparation with

---

[3] That is, a copy of the answer enclosed: see *post* 8 Mar. 1785.

[4] The "o" of "one" is formed over an "S"; apparently Croft began to write "Sir" but decided to suppress the reference to—doubtless—Hawkins.

[5] Croft had long projected an English dictionary, and in Mar. 1788 a long, unfinished letter from him to Pitt, pointing out defects in SJ's *Dictionary*, was printed, but not published. Proposals for a new edition of SJ's *Dictionary* in four volumes folio were issued by Croft in 1792, but as they met with a poor subscription, the scheme was dropped (DNB; *Lit. Illust.* v. 213–15).

[1] JB noted in his journal for 17 Dec.: "This must be ever remembered as a melancholy day; for it brought me the dismal news of my great and good Freind, Dr. Samuel Johnson. His Physician Dr. Brocklesby favoured me with a very full letter dated on Monday the 13 the night of his death. I was stunned, and in a kind of amaze. . . . I did not shed tears. I was not tenderly affected. My feeling was just one large expanse of Stupor. I knew that I should afterwards have sorer sensations." The next day he read the accounts in *The Public Advertiser* and *London Chronicle*.

which you have taken the trouble to communicate it I shall ever remember with the warmest gratitude; and as you and I My Dear Sir are now connected by mutual sorrow for the loss of our truly great and good Freind, let us henceforth maintain a cordial intimacy, which I assure you shall be highly valued on my part. You may beleive me perfectly sincere when I inform you that it is a considerable time since you had my warm esteem and affection; For, the day before I left London last summer, Dr. Johnson [in] a glow of feeling communicated to Sir Joshua Reynolds and me the noble offer you had made to him.[2]

I beg you may do me the favour to let me know from your authentick information as many particulars as you can learn concerning him. What was the passage which he repeated from *Macbeth*, when like the Prophet of old you announced to him that in a short time he must die? I should suppose it to be either "Tomorrow tomorrow and tomorrow" Or "Upon this bank and shoal of time." Was he mercifully releived from that fear of death which used so much to distress him? Did the other World seem to brighten upon him as he approached it?

I shall be vexed if he has burnt all his Manuscripts, more especially if he has destroyed two volumes of Memoirs of his life a considerable part of which I have read.[3] He knew that I was for many years assiduous in collecting materials for his life;[4] and I have a large stock which I shall in due time arrange and publish. I have also several pieces in Manuscript which he dictated to me.

As he and I kept up a correspondence by letters for a period of more than twenty years, and I wrote to him as to a Confessor, I

---

[2] "As an instance of extraordinary liberality of friendship, he told us [30 June 1784], that Dr. Brocklesby had upon this occasion, offered him a hundred a year for his life. A grateful tear started into his eye, as he spoke this in a faultering tone" (*Life* iv. 338).

[3] "Two very valuable articles, I am sure, we have lost, which were two quarto volumes, containing a full, fair, and most particular account of his own life, from his earliest recollection. I owned to him, that having accidentally seen them, I had read a great deal in them . . . I said that I had, for once in my life, felt half an inclination to commit theft. It had come

into my mind to carry off those two volumes, and never see him more. Upon my inquiring how this would have affected him, 'Sir, (said he,) I believe I should have gone mad' " (*Life* iv. 405–06). On 5 Dec. of this year Hawkins, by his own account (pp. 586–87), attempted to take the notebooks into protective custody, and provoked SJ to the same dire prophecy. It is to this incident that JB attributes SJ's haste in burning "those precious records" (*Life* iv. 406 n. 1). For a description of the extant autobiographical manuscripts, see *Diaries*, Introduction.

[4] See *Life* i. 25–26.

trust you will mention to those in whose hands his affairs are left, that I depend upon their honour that my letters will be given back to me if they exist. I am My Dear Dr. Brocklesby, Your most faithful friend and humble servant

P.S. This letter was too late for Saturdays post, and yesterday there was none. I not only revered but loved Dr. Johnson so that his loss is particularly afflicting to me. I feel it more now than at first.

To Francis Barber, Thursday 23 December 1784

Missing. Sent to London from Edinburgh. Reg Let.: "Mr. Francis Barber Ditto [i.e. "for particulars concerning Dr. Johnson"] (Copy)."

From Dr. Richard Brocklesby, Monday 27 December 1784

MS. Yale (C 582). Received Jan. 1785 (Reg. Let.).

ADDRESS: To James Boswell Esqr., Advocate in Edinbrough, N.B. 28th Decembr. 1784.

POSTMARKS: 27 DE, DE 31.

[London]

DEAR SIR: I am favoured with your letter of 18th current wherein you manifest the signs of unfeigned concern at the loss of our late valuable, learned and excele[n]t friend Dr. Johnson who hath scarsely left in all Britain his equal behind him. He had the most logical apprehensive, and book informed vigorous Mind, that I have ever known, but withal, his views of Nature and of the Universe and of all the various objects to contemplate which Philosophy invites an unfetterd, speculative mind, were narrow, partial and much confined. [1]His Religion was the true Δεισιδαιμονία of Plutarch,[2] which narrowed the wonderful powers of his judgement and made his extraordinary talents of Mind continually at War with each other, so that in his later days his Philosophy seemed to draw his mind one way and his Religion byassed him to the contrary, and this may have occasioned that continual perplexity, and doubts, and fears, in which the greater portion of his life was

---

[1-1] See Introduction, p. xli.   [2] Περὶ δεισιδαιμονίας ("On Superstition"), in the *Moralia*.

passed,[1] [3]but all such dubious agitations for some time before his death were composed, and all his fears were calmed and absorbed by the prevalence of his faith and his trust in the merits and propitiation of Jesus Christ.[3] During the last three weeks of his life he was earnest with all his friends, in impressing on them, the necessity of religion, and its outward duties;[4] to his Surgeon[5] he injoined going to Church on Sundays; to Sir J. Reynolds he prohibited touching on a Sunday his Pencil or Pallett.[6] He talked often to myself about the necessity of Faith in the Sacrifice of Jesus, as necessary, beyond all good works whatever, for the Salvation of Mankind.[7] He made me on 28th Novr. write down some curious dicta on the Subject and Importance of Faith,[8] which when I had done, he read over again and said it was well and made me sign it and urged me to keep it as long as I live in my own custody and said, if I was led through his means to Salvation it would be ample recompense to me, as well as from him, for all my kindness and attention to him in his Sickness as well as in his health.[9] But with all this [10]he pressed me to study Dr. Clark and to read his Sermons. I[11] asked him why he pressed Dr. Clark an Arian? "Because" said he, "he is fullest on the propitiatory Sacrifice,[10] and that above all things is necessary to believe as Xians." Yet his Superstition at last was not one continual Gloom[;] but the emanations of his learning Wit and Memory often dispelled all darkness by the Sallies of his fanciful Imagination, as in the passage formerly alluded to from *McBeath*. The circumstance was this[:] [12]he was

[3-3] Revised and quoted directly, *Life* iv. 416.

[4] "Indeed he shewed the greatest anxiety for the religious improvement of his friends, to whom he discoursed of its infinite consequence" (*Life* iv. 414.) Cf. Cooke, pp. 103–04.

[5] William Cumberland Cruikshank (1745–1800), anatomist and surgeon; M.A. Glasgow, 1767; associate of Dr. William Hunter in London from 1771. See *Life* and *Letters SJ passim*. SJ gave the same advice from his death-bed to Sir John Scott, later Earl of Eldon (*Life* iv. 414 n. 1).

[6] "He requested three things of Sir Joshua Reynolds—To forgive him thirty pounds which he had borrowed of him;—to read the Bible;—and never to use his pencil on a Sunday. Sir Joshua readily acquiesced" (*Life* iv. 413–14). Cf. *Works* xi. 200 ("Apophthegms, Sentiments, Opinions, &c.").

[7] Quoted directly, *Life* iv. 416. Cf. Cooke, p. 104.

[8] *Post* ?17–18 Apr. 1785.

[9] Revised, *Life* iv. 414. Cf. Cooke, p. 104. In 1775 SJ had referred anonymously to Brocklesby as "a person, originally a Quaker, but now, I am afraid, a Deist" (*Life* ii. 359). "Deist" tones down the phrase in JB's journal, 14 Apr. 1775, "loose in his notions".

[10-10] Quoted directly, *Life* iv. 416.

[11] MS. "Sermons, I"

[12-12] Revised, *Life* iv. 400–01. Cf. Cooke, pp. 73–74 and Hawkins, p. 577.

low and desponding when a few (10 or 8) days before his death I askd in my mornings visit, how he had been the preceding night, to which he replied, "I have been as a dying Man all night." Then he emphatically broke out "Canst thou not minister to minds diseasd pluck from the memory its rooted Sorrow etc." to the end of that Speech. At which he said "What says my Dr." I replied "Therein Sir the Patient must minister to himself," at which he squeezd my hand and exclaimd in rapture, "Aptly enough answerd."[12] Another day after that, seeing him languid and almost spent, he renewd his serious talk and asked me, if I was not in the use and habit of prayer, to which I answerd, I always prayd from my heart, in the sentiment of Juvenal, "Orandum est ut sit mens sana in corpore sano, fortem posce animum mortis terrore carentem, qui spatium Vitæ extremum inter munera ponat Naturæ etc." to the end of Satyr 10th but in running it glibly over I pronouncd supremum for extremum, at which his critical ear was so offended, that he broke in with a long parenthesis on the unmetrical effect of such a lapse and at that instant was replete as full as ever with the Grammarians Spirit.[13] 3 days before his death [14]he asked me as an honest professional Man in whom he confided most, whether he could recover. "Give a direct answer." To which I said "You must first tell me whether you can bear the whole truth which way soever it may lead?" He said he could. I then declared in my opinion he could not without a miracle recover. "Then" says he "Ill take no more Physick, not even my opiates any more for I have earnestly prayed to render up my Soul to God just as it may be unclouded[14] and simple, for" said he "Opiates though they ever lulled my bodily pains yet they usually filld my imagination with horrors and visions that disturbed for several hours my clear judgem[en]t and I should be loth to dy in that state with any overcast to cloud it."[15]

[13] Revised, *Life* iv. 401. Brocklesby should have been on guard. In a letter to Mrs. Thrale, 20 June 1783, SJ wrote: ". . . when I waked I found Dr Broaclesby sitting by me, and fell to talking to him in such a manner as made me glad, and, I hope, made me thankful. The Dr fell to repeating Juvenal's tenth satire, but I let him see that the province was mine" (*Letters SJ* 851).

[14-14] Revised, *Life* iv. 415.

[15] Not used. See Introduction, p. xl. Hawkins noted (pp. 584, 585) that on 4 Dec. SJ "Complained of great weakness, and of phantoms that haunted his imagination," and the next day, after receiving the sacrament, "he said, that he dreaded to meet God in a state of idiocy, or with opium in his head; and, that having now communicated with the effects of a dose upon him, he doubted if his exertions were the genuine operations of his mind."

The last time all the Drs. consulted together when we enterd his room he[16] began thus from Swift,[17] "The Doctors tender of their Fame, wisely on me lay all the blame, We own indeed his case was nice, but He would never take advice, Had he been ruld, for what appears He might have livd these twenty Years, for when we opend him we found[18] his vital parts were sound."

"Now" says he, "Brocklesby will lay my death to disobedience and my taking lately 4 times as much Squills as he advisd[19] and Dr. Heberden will say, I disturbed Natures operation in the outlet she made spontaneously in one leg, when I maugre all advice punctured my self the other leg which never ouzed any, but stopped by not ouzing the curr[en]t of tother."[20] So he playfully interposd gaiety with the gravity of his conduct and in 100 instances exhibited how various a System the purest and best of us are compounded of. I shall have much pleasure in orally relating to you divers particulars more when we next meet in London.[21] The good Man had his wishes answerd for at last he dyed possessd of his mind, in as full vigour as ever and reconciled to the final close. As[22] soon as he was convinced of the Necessity that pressed him he sealed up all your letters in a bag and wrote on the outside to be deliverd to you.[23] He burnt all[24] written memoirs of himself and his life, but left in Mr. Langston's custody near 100 Epigrams translated into elegant latin verse in the time of his last sickness and some latin odes to be publishd by that Gentleman,[25] but you and every lover of letters

[16] MS. "room. He"
[17] "Verses on the Death of Dr. Swift," *ad libitum*.
[18] MS. "that all" deleted. Brocklesby appears to have voluntarily sacrificed correctness of meter to accuracy of diagnosis. The anecdote was not used. For a diagnosis of the condition of SJ's "vital parts" at his death, see P. P. Chase, M.D., "The Ailments and Physicians of Dr. Johnson," *Yale Journal of Biology and Medicine* (1951), xxiii. 375.
[19] Cf. *Letters SJ* 1033.1, 1037, and *passim*.
[20] Not used. Two other versions are recorded by Hawkins and William Windham (reprinted, *Johns. Misc.* ii. 7, 386). For SJ's autosurgery, see *Life* iv. 399 and n. 6. William Heberden (1710–1801) was "one of the most eminent English physicians of the eighteenth century"

(DNB). SJ is said to have described him as *"ultimus Romanorum*, the last of the learned physicians", but also, in connection with this incident, as *"timidorum timidissimus"* (*Life* iv. 399 nn. 4 and 6). See *Letters SJ passim*.
[21] See *post* From Brocklesby, ?17–18 Apr. 1785, n. 1.
[22] MS. "close, as"
[23] ". . . which was accordingly done" (*Life* ii. 2). Only six of JB's letters to SJ (including a fragment and two drafts) have been recovered. See *Letters SJ* iii. 277 ff.
[24] Not all: see *Diaries*, Introduction; and Donald and Mary Hyde, "Johnson and Journals", *The New Colophon* (1950) iii. 165 ff.
[25] See *ante* From Brocklesby, 13 Dec. 1784 and n. 7.

will lament the loss of many beautiful things besides committed to the fire. His life is now writing by six Authors Sir J. Hawkins among the rest[26] near London but you know more facts than all the rest. He was so agitated till the day I pronouncd he could not live, that he forgot to mention in his Will made in that time of perplexity the names of Boswell Strahan Murphy etc. whom he lovd sincerely but forgot their mention.[27] But I know he lov'd and respected you sincerely, though he often bewaild his Animal infirmity, that Sickness had made him a peevish selfish ungrateful snarling Dog was his word, but in that S. Johnson[28] was no more for his life was generous bountiful kind and good even to the wicked, his philanthropy so much excelled his Religion. I fear I have tired your Patience but I with pleasure describe the picture of the Man belovd by you and by Dear Sir, Your faithful and Obedient Humble Servant

RICHARD BROCKLESBY

[26] Mrs. Piozzi noted on 25 Jan. 1785: "Six People have already undertaken to write his Life I hear [from Samuel Lysons], of which Sr. John Hawkins, Mr. Boswell, Tom Davies and Dr. Kippis are four. Piozzi says he would have me add to the Number" (*Thraliana*, p. 625). Rumours apart, the following "lives" actually appeared between SJ's death and JB's *Life*: (1) *A Biographical Sketch of Dr. Samuel Johnson*, 1785, by Thomas Tyers. The first version was published in *Gent. Mag.*, Dec. 1784 and Feb. 1785 (liv. 899–911, 982, lv. 85–87); see G. D. Meyer's Introduction to the edition by the Augustan Reprint Society (No. 34, 1952). (2) *The Life of Samuel Johnson, LL.D.*, 1785, attributed to William Cooke (Cook), published by George Kearsley (Kearsly). It was "just published" according to *St. James's Chronicle*, 28–30 Dec. 1784. (3) *Memoirs of the Life and Writings of the Late Dr. Samuel Johnson*, 1785, by the Rev. William

Shaw (anonymously). (4) JB's *Tour to the Hebrides*, 1785. (5) Mrs. Piozzi's *Anecdotes*, 1786. (6) *An Essay on the Life, Character, and Writings of Dr. Samuel Johnson*, 1786, by Joseph Towers. (7) Hawkins's *Life of Johnson*, 1787. See Walter Raleigh, *Six Essays on Johnson*, 1910, pp. 40–43.

[27] "This may be accounted for by considering, that as he was very near his dissolution at the time, he probably mentioned such as happened to occur to him; and that he may have recollected, that he had formerly shewn others such proofs of his regard, that it was not necessary to crowd his Will with their names" (*Life* iv. 404 n.). When JB first read the will, in an English newspaper on 28 Dec., he felt "a little uneasy". "But I considered that I had several Books in a present from him and many more valuable tokens" (Journ.).

[28] MS. "Johnnson"

1785

From the Rev. William Johnson Temple,[1]
Thursday 6 January 1785

MS. Yale (C 2829).

ADDRESS: To James Boswell Esqr., Edinburgh.

POSTMARK: 10 IA.

Gluvias Vicarage, January 6th, 1785

MY DEAR BOSWELL, The death of Dr. Johnson, will, I fear, increase the depression of spirits you complain of. You will be deprived of his society and conversation, and of *something*, which you derived from your known intimacy with him. Yet as to himself, he had reached a good old age, and his fame and his faculties were as vigorous as at any former period of his Life. This event, may in some degree cool your ardour for your London Settlement, as perhaps the Doctor was somehow connected with it.

I have read his *Will* in the News Papers and am disappointed and angry at not seeing your name in it. Your partial and even enthusiastick attachment to him well deserved some fond memorial. I fully expected he would have left his Papers to your care, and desired as the last act of a long friendship that you would be his editor and historian. Think of making his Will on the very night on which he died, and leaving so large a sum to a Negroe.[2] An annuity of £20 or £30 would have been a more suitable Legacy for him to give or the other to receive. Is the old blind Lady dead that he does not mention her?[3] Even Mrs. Thrale, to whom he owed so many civilities so much Devotion and so many delicate suppers is not honoured with a picture or a book. Indeed, I cannot help accusing him of insensibility and ingratitude.

The News Writers threaten us with many Lives of him. Your long and intire intimacy with him well qualify you to satisfy completely the public curiosity and I hope you will give us a correct and elegant edition of all his writings. Such an undertaking will bring you both profit and fame. If you will insert it, I will supply you with his character.[4] . . .

---

[1] The Rev. William Johnson Temple (1739–96), JB's most intimate friend. See Journ. *passim* and James Gray, "Boswell's Brother Confessor: William Johnson Temple," *Tennessee Studies in Literature* (1959), iv. 61–71.

[2] See *post* From Hector, 19 June 1787,

n. 2. SJ's will was made on the 8th and 9th of Dec. (*Life* iv. 402 n. 2); he died on the 13th.

[3] Anna Williams had died 6 Sept. 1783.

[4] Temple's offer does not appear to have been taken up.

From the Rev. Dr. Thomas Campbell,[1]
Friday 7 January 1785

MS. Yale (C 755). Received 21 Jan. (Reg. Let.).

ADDRESS: James Boswell Esqr., At Mr. Dillys, Bookseller, Poultry, London.

POSTMARKS: JA 7, 12 IA.

No. 34 Kildare Street, Dublin, Jany. 7th 1785

DEAR SIR: Having heard, not many months ago, from Mr. Dilly (who, by the bye, from his epistolary style seems to be an egregious *cockney*) that you purposed to settle soon in London, I therefore write *at you* there. And having long persuaded myself that you would sometime or other publish Memoirs of the life of Dr. Johnson —being also confirmed in this opinion by seeing your intention notifyed (not however as from yourself) in the English prints,[2] I could not help recalling to my memory an Anecdote of that illustrious name in literature, which (as I conceive) does honour to his heart—and of course I could wish it to be communicated through your channel rather than any other. Sitting with him one morning alone, he asked me if I had known Dr. Madden (I need scarcely tell you that Dr. Madden was author of the Premium scheme in Ireland).[3] On my answering in the affirmative, and also that I had for some years lived in his neighbourhood etc. etc. he begged of me

---

[1] Thomas Campbell, D.D. (1733–95), preacher, diarist, author. "On Wednesday, April 5, [1775] I dined with [SJ] at Messieurs Dilly's, with ... Dr. Thomas Campbell, an Irish Clergyman, whom I took the liberty of inviting to Mr. Dilly's table, having seen him at Mr. Thrale's, and been told that he had come to England chiefly with a view to see Dr. Johnson, for whom he entertained the highest veneration. He has since published 'A Philosophical Survey of the South of Ireland,' a very entertaining book, which has, however, one fault;—that it assumes the fictitious character of an Englishman" (*Life* ii. 338–39). See J. L. Clifford's account of Campbell in his edition of *Dr. Campbell's Diary of a Visit to England in 1775* (1947).

[2] For example, *St. James's Chronicle*, 14–16 Dec. 1784: "Biographers are very busy in preparing Materials for the Life of Dr. Samuel Johnson. Many, we are told, are the Candidates, but the principal which are mentioned are Sir John Hawkins, and James Boswell, Esq. his itinerant Companion through the Highlands of Scotland."

[3] Samuel Madden, D.D. (1686–1765), "a name which Ireland ought to remember" (*Lives* ii. 131). The "Premium Scheme", providing for prizes in recognition of academic excellence, was set forth in *A Proposal for the General Encouragement of Learning in Dublin-College* (Dublin, 1731). See Malone's explanatory note, *Life*, 4th ed., 1804, i. 286 n. *.

that, when I returned to Ireland, I would endeavour to procure for him a Poem of Dr. Madden's called *Boulters Monument*. "The reason," adds he, "why I wish for it is this—When Dr. Madden came to London A.D. —— he submitted that work to my castigation and I remember that I blotted a great many lines, and might have blotted many more, without making the Poem the worse; However, the Doctor (Madden) was very thankful and very generous, for he gave me Ten guineas—*which was to me, at that time, a great Sum*." [4]

Whether you may think with me concerning the value of this anecdote I dont know—but if you do, I can furnish you with another of a political turn, which strongly marks his partiality to England; and evinces that with him Justice had one Standard for England, but a very different one for Ireland. But as this would not tend so much to the credit of his memory, I shall not press it upon you, especially as my note which I took of the conversation (when last in London June 1781) [5] is among my papers in the country, whence I came to this town very lately, in almost a total oblivion of all such matters.

I can never forget the civilities I received from you when first in London [6] and therefore shall be forever your most grateful servant

THO. CAMPBELL

*N.B. Boulter was Primate of Ireland and died 1742. [7]

[4] Quoted directly, with minor revision, *Life* i. 318. Cf. Hawkins, p. 391 and Percy, *Johns. Misc.* ii. 211–12. Madden did not acknowledge SJ's help: see *Life* i. 545. On 1 July JB wrote to Bishop Barnard: "There was a Dr. Madan of Ireland with whom Dr. Johnson was very intimate. Perhaps some Letters and other materials for the *Life* may be recovered from his heirs." In answering JB's letter Barnard did not reply to this inquiry.

[5] The conversation, which took place on 11 June, is recorded at length in Campbell's *Diary* (ed. Clifford, pp. 94–96). Still another account is given in his *Strictures on the History of Ireland* (1789, p. 336; extracts reprinted in *Johns. Misc.* ii. 56 n. 2).

[6] JB and Campbell first met at the Thrales's on 1 Apr. 1775. On 5 Apr. JB told Mrs. Thrale "that I had asked Dr. Campbell, the irish Clergyman, to dine today at Dilly's, as he was so desireous to see Mr. Johnson, was so goodhumoured a man, and so thankful for any civilities. That he was quite like a *pet* sheep . . . went with the cows, walked about the house, and every body, even the children, gave him clover or a handful of corn or a piece of bread out of their pockets. Every body gave something to Campbell—'Poor Campbell.' She thought my idea a very good one" (Journ.).

[7] Hugh Boulter, D.D. (1672–1742), Archbishop of Armagh.

EE*

To the Rev. Dr. William Adams,
Friday 21 January 1785

MS. Hyde. MS. Yale (L 8): a copy by John Johnston of Grange,[1] headed by JB: "To The Reverend Dr. Adams Master of Pembroke College Oxford."

ENDORSEMENT: Mr. Boswell 15 Jan.[2] 1785 [*in another hand:*] to Dr. Adams Master of Pembroke Coll. Oxford.

Edinburgh, 21 January 1785

REVEREND SIR: I most sincerely condole with you on the death of our valuable Freind Dr. Johnson.

As I am engaged in writing his Life, it will be very obliging if you will favour me with communications concerning him, in addition to those with which you have allready favoured me. The more minute your narrative is the better. And if you will send me any letters from him of which you are possessed, your kindness shall be thankfully acknowledged. Please put your packets[3] under cover to Sir Charles Preston Baronet M.P.[4] London, who will forward them to me.

I offer my best compliments to Mrs. and Miss Adams, and I ever am with most sincere regard, Dear Sir, Your much obliged humble servant

JAMES BOSWELL

To Edmund Hector,[1]
Friday 21 January 1785

MS. Yale (L 636). A copy by Johnston of Grange, endorsed by him: "Copy of two Letters To The Reverend Mr. [*altered to* Dr. *by JB*]

---

[1] John Johnston of Grange (d. 1786), for whom the London journal of 1762–63 was written, was one of JB's closest friends. Like JB he suffered from fits of depression, and his acting as amanuensis, particularly at this time, may well have been therapeutic. See Journ. 13 Jan.

[2] Adams appears to have confused his dates; see also *post* To Adams, 22 Dec. 1785, n. 2, and From Adams, 12 July 1786, n. 1.

[3] Copy, "letters"

[4] Sir Charles Preston, Bt. (c. 1735–1800), of Valleyfield, in Fife; a major in the 26th Foot; M.P. for the Dysart Burghs, 1784–90 (*Comp. Bar.* ii. 426; Judd 3759). He and JB were first cousins once removed. See Journ. *passim*.

[1] Edmund Hector was born in Lichfield in 1708, attended the grammar school with SJ, and c. 1729 removed to

Adams and Mr. [Careless *deleted*; *see n. 1*] Hector both dated 21st January 1785"; headed by JB: "To Mr. Hector Surgeon in Birmingham."

Edinr., 21st January 1785

SIR: I most Sincerely Condole with you on the death of our valuable Friend Dr. Johnson. As I am engaged in writing his Life it will be very obliging if you will favour me with Communications Concerning him from his earliest years in addition to those with which you have already favoured me. The more minute your Narrative is the better, and if you will Send me any Letters from him of which you are possessed, as also his *Juvenilia* which you have preserved,[2] your Kindness Shall be thankfully acknowledged, please put your packets (etc. as in the above Letter).[3] I offerr my best Compliments to Mrs. Careless and I am Dear Sir your most obedient humble Servant

(Signed) JAMES BOSWELL

Birmingham, where he lived and practised as a surgeon until his death in 1794. (See Joseph Hill and R. K. Dent, *Memorials of the Old Square*, Birmingham, 1897, pp. 25 ff., 135, and *Reades*, pp. 151 ff. for detailed accounts of Hector and his family.) The close association between SJ and Hector, begun during their early school days and interrupted by SJ's subsequent academic excursions, was renewed in 1732, when SJ went to live in Birmingham for about a year and a half. In later life, between the years 1772 and 1784, SJ visited Hector on at least six occasions, and received at least one visit in return. Of their correspondence, which ranges between 1755 and 1784, only SJ's letters have been recovered.

Two other Hectors deserve at least passing notice by reason of their Johnsonian connections: Hector's uncle, George Hector, "a man-midwife of great reputation", who assisted at SJ's difficult birth (see *Diaries*, p. 3), and Hector's sister Ann (Mrs. Carless or Careless), of whom SJ confessed to JB: "She was the first woman with whom I was in love. It dropt out of my head imperceptibly; but she and I shall always have a kindness for each other" (*Life* ii. 460).

JB first met Hector on 22 Mar. 1776, at the time of his jaunt with SJ to Oxford, Birmingham, Lichfield, and Ashbourne (*Life* ii. 456 ff.; Journ.). He had been advised by Mr. Thrale that Hector "could tell a great deal about" SJ, and SJ himself had assured him that he "might pretty well depend on what he related" (Journ. 8 Apr. 1775, 22 Mar. 1776). What Hector related was duly recorded in the *Note Book*. The next, and apparently last, meeting between them took place, again in Birmingham, on 28 Mar. 1785, and yielded an abundance of "Particulars" (see *post*). Their correspondence, however, continued until the year of Hector's death (and the year before JB's). —Mrs. Piozzi, in the spring of the present year, attempted from Italy (using Samuel Lysons as intermediary) to collect materials for her *Anecdotes* from Hector, and other of SJ's early acquaintances, but she failed. See Clifford, *Piozzi*, pp. 243–44.

[2] "Mr. Hector told me he had many of Dr. Johnson's Juvenilia, little things written when he was very young and had copied them fairly for preservation" (*Note Book*, p. 4).

[3] To Adams. The parentheses are JB's.

To *Anna Seward*,[1]
Friday 21 January 1785

MS. Yale (L 1147). A copy by Johnston of Grange, endorsed by him: "Copy Letter To Miss Seward 21st January 1785"; headed by JB: "To Miss Seward at Lichfield."

Edinburgh, 21st January 1785

DEAR MADAM: How I have been detained from London this Winter with a variety of other topicks I reserve till I have the pleasure of again waiting on you at Lichfield, which I hope to do in March next.[2]

At present I presume to Solicit your liberal and freindly Assistance in procuring additional materials for the *Life of Dr. Samuel Johnson* to whose name it would be Superfluous to Join any epithet when I write to Miss Seward.

Dr. Johnson knew that I was his Biographer, and gave me a thousand particulars which will be interwoven into my narrative. But I am desirous to have every thing that can be had. You perfectly understand me, and I Shall depend upon receiving from you many valuable Communications. Be so good as write down all that you have been told of him with your Authoritys, and all that you Yourself recollect of his Sayings. I Shall be Sorry if his death is not lamented by that Charming Muse of whose excellence even He acknowledged himself to be Sensible as I Shall record.[3]

Be pleased to Seal and deliver the enclosed to Mrs. Porter,[4] I would write to Mrs. Aston,[5] did I not fear it would be unavailing. From many people in Lichfield you may Collect at least Small

---

[1] JB first met the Lichfield poetess on 24 Mar. 1776, on the same jaunt that introduced him to Dr. Adams and Hector. See Journ. and *Life* ii. 467. The story of their mutual attraction and subsequent falling-out, with the figure of SJ forming the apex of the triangle, is dramatically unfolded in their correspondence, selections from which are given here. I owe a number of my notes to the late Percy Laithwaite and R. F. Metzdorf.

[2] See *post* From Seward, 25 Mar. 1785, head-note.

[3] *Life* iv. 331.

[4] "The Letter to Mrs. Porter was I think verbatim the same with that to Dr. Adams" (JB's note). See next letter.

[5] Elizabeth Aston (1708–85), third daughter of Sir Thomas Aston, died unmarried on 25 Nov. of this year at her house, Stowe Hill, Lichfield, and was buried in the Cathedral. She was a lifelong friend and correspondent of SJ (*Johns. Glean.* v. 249–51; *Letters SJ passim*). JB had called on her during his visit to Lichfield in Oct. 1779 (*Life* iii. 412).

Anectdotes. All his Letters that can be found will be valuable.

I beg to have my best respects presented to Mr. Seward[6] and I ever am, Dear Madam, your very faithfull and obliged humble Servant—

(Signed) JAMES BOSWELL

Please put your packets under cover to Sir Charles Preston Baronet M.P. London, who will forward them to me.

To Lucy Porter,[1]
Friday 21 January 1785

MS. William Andrews Clark Library, University of California at Los Angeles. Enclosed in the preceding.

ADDRESS: To Mrs. Porter at Lichfield.

Edinburgh, 21 Janry. 1785

DEAR MADAM: I most sincerely condole with you on the death of our valuable Freind Dr. Johnson.

As I am engaged in writing his Life it will be very obliging if you will favour me with communications concerning him in addition to those with which you have allready favoured me.[2] The more minute your narrative is the better. And if you will send me any letters from him of which you are possessed your kindness shall be thankfully acknowledged. Please put your packets under cover to Sir Charles Preston Bart. M.P. London who will forward them to me. I am, Dear Madam, Your most obedient humble servant

JAMES BOSWELL

---

[6] The Rev. Thomas Seward (1708–90), Canon of Lichfield, Anna Seward's father. See *Life* ii. 467, iii. 412.

---

[1] Lucy Porter (1715–86), SJ's step-daughter. See *Reades*, pp. 241–43; *Letters SJ passim*. JB was introduced to her by SJ at Lichfield on 23 Mar. 1776 and visited her again in Oct. 1779 (*Life* ii. 462, iii. 412).

[2] The information obtained by JB in 1776 was recorded in his *Note Book* (pp. 3, 10, 11). There is no journal for the time of his second visit, in Oct. 1779, to indicate how much, if any, new material he acquired; but all of the acknowledged communications from Miss Porter in the *Life* are accounted for by the record of the earlier visit.

From Henry Baldwin,[1]
Tuesday 25 January 1785

MS. Yale (C 61). Received 29 Jan. (Reg. Let.).

ADDRESS: James Boswell, Esqr., Edinburgh.

POSTMARK: 25 IA.

London, 25th Jany., 1785

DEAR SIR, That no Time might be lost I have given Inst⌈an⌉t Room to your Letter in this Evening's *St. Jas. Chronicle*;[2] but I have just found an Opportunity of speaking to the Gentleman in Question, who has empowered me to divulge to you his Name, but in confidence that it shall go no farther. To be short then, the whole (almost) have been the Communications of Mr. Steevens of Hampstead, (Dr. Johnson's Colleague).[3] He seems to be a great Friend to your Undertaking, and expresses a Readiness to serve you in it, and would even revise the Press was the *Life* printed in Town. He says you will of course print the Book you are now about in Scotland;[4] but thinks you would find your Account in printing *The Life* in Town; in which case he could render you some Assistance.

[1] Henry Baldwin (c. 1734–1813), printer of the *Tour* and the *Life*, "now Master of the Worshipful Company of Stationers, whom I have long known as a worthy man and an obliging friend" (Advertisement to the Second Edition, *Life* i. 10). "As a Printer, he was of the Old School; bred under Mr. Justice Ackers of Clerkenwell, the original Printer of 'The London Magazine'; and he commenced business for himself under the most promising auspices . . . Connected with a phalanx of the first-rate Wits, Bonnel Thornton, Garrick, Colman, Steevens, etc. etc. he set up, with the success it so well deserved, a literary News-paper, 'The St. James's Chronicle' . . . and had the satisfaction of conducting it to a height of eminence unknown to any preceding Journal, nor exceeded by any of its successors—with whom sheer Wit and Literature are no longer the prominent features" (*Lit. Anec.* viii. 478–79; the account, by Nichols, continues with a eulogy on Baldwin's character). JB noted

in his journal, 1 Jan. 1790, that "The honest, friendly Printer was a little gruff about my mode of carrying on the Work, but I made allowance for him." See also Journ. *passim*.

[2] 22–25 Jan. JB provides his own summary in his journal, c. Feb.: "There was a great deal of writing about my *Life of Dr. Johnson* in The St. James's *Chronicle*. I was highly praised, and thought it proper to write in that Paper declaring that since Dr. Johnson's death I had not sent a single paragraph concerning him, nor should send one that was not signed with my name. I begged that the Writer of such praise as animated my mind to its best exertions would have the generosity to avow himself publickly, or at least would let me know privately to whom I was obliged."

[3] See *post* From Steevens, 23 Apr. 1786, n. 1.

[4] The *Tour*, published 1 Oct., in London (*Lit. Car.* pp. 121–22). Baldwin was himself the printer.

And now, Sir, give me Leave to take this Opportunity of hinting to you that this Gentleman (together with Mr. Colman and some others of Respectability) is a General in our News-Paper Army, and it is my Wish to form an invincible Phalanx, by adding a few Recruits. You shewed once an Inclination to such Undertakings, by embarking in the *London Magazine*,[5] which has proved unprofitable; but the *St. Jas. Chronicle* is at present in the highest State of Respectability and Profit; and as you lately informed me of your Intention to settle in London, it might probably prove an agreeable Connection to you. —Favour me with a Line on this Subject, Sir, and let me know if it would be agreeable to you that I should sound our Partners on the Business.[6] You know all that is expected of Gentlemen Partners in such Undertakings. I am, Sir, most respectfully and cordially, Your very humble Servant

H. BALDWIN

From Anna Seward,
end of January–beginning of February 1785

Missing. Sent to Edinburgh via London from Lichfield. Received 11 Feb. (Reg. Let.): "Miss Seward with Anecdotes of Dr. Johnson." See *post* To Seward, 15 Feb. 1785 and n. 2.

From Edmund Hector,
Tuesday 1 February 1785

MS. Yale (C 1523). Hector's draft of this letter, owned by F. W. Hilles, contains many variants, but only one (which I have noted) is of any significance.

ADDRESS: James Boswell Esqr.

[Birmingham,] Feb. 1, 85

SIR: Our much lamented Friend Dr. Johnson spent two or three days with me here in his return to Lond.[1] I did not then think him so near his latter end.

---

[5] Both as contributor and partner. See Journ. Notes, 3 Oct. 1769, 14 Oct. 1769; Journ. 1 Jan. 1777; and Charles Dilly to JB, 15 Dec. 1778 (C 1043).

[6] JB replied on 11 Mar. "acknowledging my obligations to him and Mr. Steevens, that I am to be soon in London, and shall confer with them" (Reg. Let.). On 2 May JB put his copy of the *Tour* to

Baldwin's press (Journ). I have found no further mention of the *St. James's Chronicle* matter.

[1] During the second week of Nov. 1784. SJ wrote to Hector from London on the 17th, the day after arriving home (*Letters SJ* 1035–37).

[2]He was very sollicitous with me to recollect some of our most early transactions and transmit them to him; for I perceiv'd nothing gave him greater pleasure, than calling to mind, those days of our Innocence. I comply'd with his request and He only receiv'd them a few days before his death.[2] I had expressd an earnest desire to know how He did, and his particular friend[3] was so obliging, as to inform me, He died without a Groan or a Sigh.[4]

I have transcribd, for your inspection, exactly the Minutes i wrote to him,[5] except what relates to his being under the care of a Mr. Wentworth, and the occasion of his Latinizing Popes *Messiah*.

His Juvenilia proper for the Publick are all inclos'd[6] as you desire. I shall inclose the dates of them very near the time they were wrote.

I most sincerely wish you success and Honour in your attempt of writing the life of so great, so worthy a Man and subscribe myself Your oblig'd humble Servant

EDM. HECTOR

The Daffodaill was wrote between his 15th and 16th Year. As it was not characteristick of the Flower He never much lik'd it.[7] *Integer Vitae* was translated at School. The next Year some Young Ladies at Lich. had a mind to act *The Distress'd Mother*, for whom

---

[2]–[2] Quoted, *Life* iv. 375.

[3] Probably Mrs. Desmoulins, one of SJ's famous tribe of dependants. She was the daughter of Samuel Swinfen (Swynfen), SJ's godfather, who was a physician in Lichfield and Birmingham, and she herself was at one time a resident of Birmingham, where she may have become acquainted with Hector. Along with Francis Barber, she was in attendance when SJ died and was therefore peculiarly qualified to give a circumstantial account. Both JB and William Shaw, SJ's early biographer, found her communicative (*Reades*, p. 230; *Life passim*; Shaw, Preface). In the Yale Collection is a MS. entitled "Extraordinary Johnsoniana—Tacenda", dated "Easter day 1783" (J 88). It is a record of a conversation between JB, Mauritius Lowe, the painter, and Mrs. Desmoulins, carried on while SJ was napping. The topics, relentlessly pursued by JB and Lowe,

were SJ's sexual relations with his wife, his passionate nature in general, and his overtures to Mrs. Desmoulins in particular. With respect to the last, it appears that SJ's conscience always prevailed over his appetite. In the exploitation of this material, JB's discretion prevailed over his knowledge. See Introduction, p. xlviii.

[4] Cf. Shaw, pp. 183–84 and *Johnsoniana*, p. 276. JB writes: " . . . he expired, about seven o'clock in the evening, with so little apparent pain that his attendants hardly perceived when his dissolution took place" (*Life* iv. 417).

[5] Quoted, *Life* iv. 375.

[6] For the texts of the poems, see *Poems*, ed. McAdam and Milne.

[7] Hector, some six years later, sent JB another copy of the same poem, together with a similar comment (*post* 31 Oct. 1791).

he wrote the *Epilogue* and gave it me to convey privately to them. The *Ode on Freindship* was much about the same time.

To a Lady, on her Birth-day, was made, as I was present, almost impromptu. As was the *Epigram*, the first line being propos'd by Dr. James,[8] the company call'd upon him to finish it.

The Young Authour I shou'd have mentiond before the two last.[9]

I have many of his Letters, but shall only inclose his last,[10] which breaths the most ardent piety and sincere religion.

[Enclosure]
The Copy sent to Dr. Johnson[11]

The Idler and I were very early School-fellows at Lichd., and for many Years in the same Class.[12] As[13] his uncommon abilities far exceeded us, we endeavour'd by every boyish mode of Flattery to gain his assistance, and three of us by turns us'd to call upon him in a Morning, on one of whose backs He rode triumphantly to School.[14] He never associated with us in any of our diversions that were in season, unless in Winter, when the Ice was firm to be drawn by a Boy barefoot.[15] His ambition to excell was great, tho his application to books, as far as it appear'd, was very trifling.[16]

[8] Robert James, M.D. (1705–76), of fever-powder fame (and notoriety), was brought up near Lichfield and attended the grammar school. Although he left for Oxford in 1722, when SJ was but thirteen years old, SJ told Mrs. Thrale that "Doctor James can give a better Account of my early Days than most Folks, except Mr. Hector of Birmingham & little Doctor Adams" (*Thraliana*, p. 173). SJ, whose opinion of James's professional competence wavered, nevertheless defended his nostrum in print; he also helped with the Proposals, wrote the Dedication, and contributed articles to his *Medicinal Dictionary* (1743). See *Johns. Glean.* iii. 124; F. A. Pottle, "James's Powders", N & Q (1925) cxlix. 11; and Hazen, pp. 68–73.

[9] Draft, "and *The Young Author* was wrote in his 20th year"

[10] 17 Nov. 1784 (*Life* iv. 378; *Letters SJ* 1037). JB eventually acquired two others (*Life* iv. 146 ff.; *Letters SJ* 771, 772). The three were found at Fetter-

cairn and are now in the Hyde Collection. Altogether sixteen letters from SJ to Hector have been recovered (*Letters SJ passim*).

[11] That is, a copy of the original, which, as JB points out, *Life* iv. 375, fell into the hands of Hawkins, who incorporated it into his *Life of Johnson* (pp. 7–8). The differences between the two versions are, with one exception to be noted, insignificant.

[12] "Hector is likewise an old Friend the only companion of my childhood that passed through the school with me. We have always loved one another" (*Diaries*, p. 310; quoted, *Life* iv. 135).

[13] MS. "Class, as"

[14] *Life* i. 47, combined with details from the *Note Book* (p. 4). See Introduction, p. xxxii.

[15] *Life* i. 48, combined with a detail from Hector's later version of the anecdote (*post* 28 Mar. 1785).

[16] *Life* i. 48. JB paraphrases the first clause and for the rest of the sentence

I cou'd not oblige him more, than by sauntring away every vacation that occur'd, in the fields during which time he was more engag'd in talking to himself, than his Companion.[17] Verses, or Themes he wou'd dictate to his favourites, but never wou'd be at the trouble of writing them; His aversion to business was so great, that he wou'd procrastinate his exercise to the last hour, and I have known him after a long Vacation, in which we were rigidly task'd, return an hour earlier in the Morn. to School, and begin one Theme, or Copy of Verses, in which he purposely left a fault, to gain time to finish another.[18] I never knew him corrected at School, unless it was for talking, and diverting other boys from their business, by which perhaps he thought of gaining an ascendancy,[19] He was uncommonly inquisitive, and his memory so tenacious, that what little he read or heard, he never forgot. I rem[em]ber rehearsing to him eighteen Verses, which after a little pause, he repeated verbatim, except one Epithet which improv'd the line.[20]

After a long absence from Lich.[21] when he return'd, I was fearfull there was something wrong in his constitution, which might impair his Intellects or shorten[22] his Life.[23]

Dr.[24] Johnson in his 15th year was remov'd by the recommendation of his realation the Revd. Mr. Ford[25] to a School at Stower-

substitutes: "which roused him to counteract his indolence." That SJ in his youth was more studious than he appeared is clear from his own testimony: see *Life* i. 445 and n. 3, 446.

[17] *Life* i. 48. The awkward phrasing is improved, and the whole presented as an indirect quotation.

[18] Not used. Cf. *Life* i. 47: "for though indolence and procrastination were inherent in his constitution, whenever he made an exertion he did more than any one else."

[19] *Life* i. 47. The conjectured motive was originally included in the MS. *Life* (opp. p. 12), but was deleted. See Introduction, p. xxxiii.

[20] *Life* i. 48. For JB's preference for Hector's account of SJ's school-days over that of another schoolmate, see *post* From Taylor, 6 May 1785 and n. 3.

[21] SJ's year at Oxford, Oct. 1728–Dec. 1729, is apparently meant.

[22] MS. "shortnen"

[23] JB, who was at pains to distinguish between madness and melancholy (see e.g. *Life* i. 65), rejects this and also a later remark of Hector's on SJ's mental state (*post* 28 Mar. 1785). The present passage is quoted by Hill, from the original "Minutes" as printed by Hawkins, in connection with JB's account of SJ's attack of "morbid melancholy", *Life* i. 63 and n. 1. In the original "Minutes" the sentence continues: "but, thanks to Almighty God my fears have proved false." This observation, being no longer apposite, was naturally omitted in the copy made for JB.

[24] This last section is differentiated from the preceding transcript of the "Minutes" sent to SJ by means of vertical strokes in the left-hand margin of the MS. See the third paragraph of the letter proper.

[25] The Rev. Cornelius ("Parson") Ford (1694–1731) was SJ's first cousin on his mother's side. In 1724 he married

bridge under the care of a Mr. Wentworth, a Gentleman Eminent for classical learning, where he continu'd about one Year, a difference arising between his Master and him about the purity of a phrase in his exercise.[26]

When he was at Oxford, Dr. Pantin the master of the College[27] seeing him frequently idling about had twice imposd him,[28] without effect, the Dr. call'd him up and once more assur'd him if he did not comply with his request, he shou'd take no farther notice of him, the Dr. promis'd, and performd. He told me, that afternoon at the first heat he finishd more than one half and in the Morn. concluded the translation of Popes *Messiah*.[29]

Judith Crowley, daughter of a wealthy Quaker ironmaster of Stourbridge, Worcestershire, and in the autumn of the next year SJ visited them at their home in Pedmore, overstaying his vacation by several months. Under Ford's tutelage SJ, in Reade's view, absorbed the ideals of cultivating general knowledge and conversational ability. The well-attested virtues of this convivial, witty, and learned cleric appear to have been offset by some equally well-attested moral lapses, and he is perhaps best remembered in two notorious roles: supposedly the punch-dispensing parson in Hogarth's *Midnight Modern Conversation*, and the protagonist in a widely circulated ghost-story. See *Reades*, pp. 158 ff.; *Johns. Glean.* iii. 144 ff., ix. 1 ff., x. 198–99; Journ. 23 Mar. 1775; *Life* iii. 348–49; Hawkins, p. 2; and *Anecdotes*: *Johns. Misc.* i. 154–55.

[26] JB's (brief) account of this chapter in SJ's history, *Life* i. 49–50, is based upon Percy's narrative, *post* 6 Mar. 1787, and upon SJ's own account, recorded in the journal, 24 Apr. 1772: "Then at —— in Worcestershire with Wentworth. Very good Master, but did not agree. Was idle, mischievous, and stole. 'I was too good a scholar. He could get no honour by me. Saw I would ascribe all to my own labour or former Master.' " From Hector JB may have taken the estimate of a year's residence; SJ himself has dated the stay well enough in his "Annales" (*Diaries*,

p. 24): "1725 Mensibus Autumnal. S.J. ad se vocavit C.F. a quo, anno proxime insequenti, Pentecostes feriis Lichfieldiam rediit." The Rev. John Wentworth (c. 1677–1741) was Headmaster of the Stourbridge school from 1704 to 1732, when he was discharged for absenteeism, etc. (*Johns. Glean.* iii. 155–56; see also [H.] J. Haden, "Dr. Johnson's Headmaster at Stourbridge", *The Birmingham Post*, 16 Sept. 1952).

[27] Matthew Panting, D.D. (c. 1683–1739) became Master of Pembroke College in 1715. SJ called him "a fine Jacobite fellow", an appellation well earned if only by his sermon preached on the day of George I's accession, in which the event is scarcely acknowledged (Douglas Macleane, *History of Pembroke College, Oxford*, 1897, p. 321; *Note Book*, pp. 7–8; *Life* i. 72 and n. 3, 73).

[28] That is, punished him by an imposition (OED).

[29] JB had heard the anecdote from Hector in 1776 and had recorded it in his *Note Book* (p. 9): "Mr Hector told me that the Master of Pembroke used to see him idling away his time in the quadrangle & that he set him a task to turn Pope's Messiah into Latin. Upon which Mr Johnson produced his admirable version of that Poem. It was first published in a Miscellany at Oxford by one Husbands." In a marginal note to the first sentence, added later, appears the correction: "wrong. He was asked very

51

From Thomas Barnard, Bishop of Killaloe,[1]
Thursday 10 February 1785

MS. Yale (C 83). Received Mar. (Reg. Let.).

ADDRESS: James Boswell Esqr., Honble. General Paoli's, South Audley Street, London.

POSTMARK: 18 FE.

Henrietta Street, Dublin, Feby. 10th 1785

... I am Vex'd and ashamed to read the Paltry accounts of the Life and Conversation of that excellent Man with which the Papers have been Stuffed since his Decease. It is Reserved for you to Vindicate his Fame: You have Collected Materials to do it; you have formerly Declar'd it to be your Intention: The Publick, Expects it from you: and I (as one of them) call upon you to perform your Promise, and give to the World the Memorables of the Modern Socrates for his Honour as well as your own. ...

To Mrs. Mary Cobb,[1]
Tuesday 15 February 1785

MS. Yale (L 373). A copy by Johnston of Grange, endorsed by him:

civilly by Jorden to do it." This upon the authority of Dr. Adams, whose version of the story (*post* 17 Feb. 1785) provides the basis for JB's account in the *Life*. On 14–17 Feb. 1777 JB wrote to SJ from Edinburgh: "I bought at an auction here the other day Husbands's *Miscellany* printed at Oxford in 1731, as your old friend Mr. Hector informed me, if I recollect right, that your first appearance in print was in that Collection—Your *Messia*. I like to have this Book, and I wish much that I could make a complete collection of every thing that has been published by you, or concerning you. But I suppose that cannot now be done. I shall get together what I can." See *post* From Taylor, 6 May 1785 and n. 40.

[1] Thomas Barnard, D.D. (1728–1806), Dean of Derry, 1769, Bishop of Killaloe, 1780, Bishop of Limerick, 1794; member of The Club. JB prints SJ's complimentary charade upon his name, *Life* iv. 195, and in the same passage speaks of him as one "who has been pleased for many years to treat me with so much intimacy and social ease, that I may presume to call him not only my Right Reverend, but my very dear Friend." See Journ. *passim*.

[1] Mary ("Moll") Cobb (1718–93) was the widow of Thomas Cobb (d. 1772), a Lichfield mercer; the younger daughter of Richard Hammond (d. 1738), a Lichfield apothecary; and aunt to Mary Adey

"Copy Letter To Mrs. Cobb's 15th February 1785"; headed by JB: "To Mrs. Cobb Lichfield."

Edinr., 15th February 1785

DEAR MADAM: As I am engaged in writing the life of our great and good friend Dr. Johnson, I presume to Solicit the Communications which you can give me Concerning him. I am already indebted to you for his verses on Friendship[2] and his Letter to Dr. Taylor when under a Stroke of the palsy.[3] You will oblige me much, and will help me to oblige the World, if you will take the trouble to write down and Send to me every anectdote Concerning him, from his earliest years, and every one of his Sayings that you recollect. The utmost Minuteness will be desireable. Garrick, in one of his Prologues or Epilogues Speaking of Shakespeare has this Expression.

Nor lose one drop of that immortal Man.[4]

We may adopt it when Collecting all we can of the wonderfull genius of Lichfield.

I shall make no apology for this application, because I trust it will not be disapproved of by a Lady of whose respect for Dr. Johnson, I have long been well Convinced.

Please put your packets under cover etc. I am etc.

(see next letter). SJ and JB visited Mrs. Cobb (and Miss Adey) at her house, called The Friary, on 24 Mar. 1776, JB remarking that "She was a sensible wellbred Woman." Anna Seward's description of her, and SJ's own (according to Miss Seward), are less complimentary. On 19 Oct. 1779 JB revisited The Friary, this time by himself (*Johns. Glean.* i. 12–13, viii. 168; *Life* ii. 466, 522, iii. 412; *Journ.* 24 Mar. 1776). JB's correspondence with Mrs. Cobb begins with an exchange of letters, 11 and 13 June 1784, in which JB, suspecting strained relations between SJ and Lucy Porter, solicits from Mrs. Cobb an invitation to SJ to stay at her house during his projected visit to Lichfield in July; and in which Mrs. Cobb, in deference to Miss Porter, declines to assume the latter's traditional role of hostess to SJ. On 26 July SJ wrote to JB from Ashbourne: "On the 14th I came to Lichfield, and found every body glad to see me" (*Life* iv. 378). JB himself stopped at Lichfield on the 4th and 5th, on his return to Scotland (Reg. Let.).

[2] Missing. See *Poems*, ed. McAdam and Milne, p. 70.

[3] *Life* iv. 228. A copy, in an unidentified hand, appears in the MS. *Life* (Paper Apart for p. 913). JB may have acquired both this letter and the missing "verses on Friendship" during his brief visit to Lichfield the summer before.

[4] "To lose no drop of that immortal Man" (Prologue to *Florizel and Perdita*).

To Mary Adey,[1]
Tuesday 15 February 1785

MS. Yale (L 9). A copy by Johnston of Grange, endorsed by him: "Copy Letter To Miss Adey 15th February 1785"; headed by JB: "To Miss Adye Lichfield."

Edinr., 14th [*sic*] February 1785

DEAR MADAM: Though I have by this post Solicited Mrs. Cobb's communications of Anectdotes[2] and Sayings of our great and good friend Dr. Johnson, I beg your kind assistance also in Collecting materials for his life. Every thing that you can Send me Concerning him will be valuable; and therefore pray think nothing too Small, you have been so much with him, have had so lively a perception of his Wisdom and Wit, and can reflect it so well, that I am Sure you may enrich my work if you will be so good as take the trouble to write down all that you remember.

Please put your packets under Cover etc.

To Anna Seward,
Tuesday 15 February 1785

MS. Maine Historical Society, J.S.H. Fogg Collection. MS. Yale (L 1148): a copy by Johnston of Grange, endorsed by him: "Copy Letter To Miss Seward 15th February 1785."

ADDRESS: To Miss Seward at Lichfield.

Edinburgh, 15th Febry. 1785

DEAR MADAM: Your goodness to me has equalled my expectations. I received first your short letter[1] which obligingly appeased my impatience; and then came your valuable treasure[2] for which I am exceedingly indebted to you. Yet I still presume to solicit more of that delightful liberality to which I glow with gratitude. I wish to

---

[1] Mary Adey (1742–1830), daughter of Joseph Adey (1704–63), Town Clerk of Lichfield, and Felicia Hammond (d. 1778), sister of Mrs. Cobb. She was living with her aunt previous to the death of her mother (Journ. 24–25 Mar. 1776), and in 1793 inherited the bulk of her property. The following year she married John Sneyd (1734–1809), High Sheriff of Staffordshire (*Reades*, p. 212 n. 4, 229; *Life* ii. 522).

[2] MS. "Ancetdotes"

---

[1] Missing.
[2] After his falling-out with Miss Seward, JB was to write of this contribution: "This lady, as she herself has stated, did indeed *cover several sheets of paper* with the *few* anecdotes, concerning Dr. Johnson, which she did me the honour to communicate to me. They were, however, not only poetically luxuriant, but, I could

have (without the name) Dr. Johnson's well-poised attack upon a Lady—"When thy Mother told thee that A—— was" etc.[3] Also his reproof to a *Miss* who asked him to recommend a Book to her;[4] and, if you can recollect it, his tremendous Commination at Mr. Dilly's when we talked of the "odious wench" who turned Quaker.[5] If from your relation to Mr. Hunter[6] by whom He was first led upon classical ground, you have any little anecdotes of his boyish years, any traits of the infant Hercules, let us preserve them.

easily perceive, were tinctured with a strong prejudice against the person to whom they related. . . . I was therefore obliged to reduce, into a very narrow compass indeed, what Miss Seward's fluent pen had expanded over many sheets" (*Gent. Mag.*, 1793, ii. 1009). And again: ". . . I committed to the flames those sheets of '*Johnsonian Narratives,*' with which I was favoured by her . . . I however first extracted from those sheets all that I could possibly consider to be authentic" (*ibid.* 1794, i. 32).

[3] See *post* From Seward, 25 Mar. 1785.

[4] Ignored, or overlooked, by Miss Seward in her reply.

[5] The incident, which Miss Seward merely touches upon in her letter to JB, 22 May 1784, is recounted at length, *Life* iii. 298–99. The printed version represents only a slight expansion, apparently owing something to Miss Seward, of JB's journal for 15 Apr. 1778. Since JB already possessed an adequate record of the conversation, a record in which he later professed the greatest confidence (*Life* iii. 299 n. 2), the present request, like much else in the correspondence, shows JB cultivating the informant as much as the information. —On 27 Mar., two days after her reply to the present letter, Miss Seward wrote to Mrs. Knowles, SJ's principal antagonist in the conversation, that JB "desires I will send him the minutes I made at the time of that, as he justly calls it, tremendous conversation [*sic*] at Dilly's, between you and him, on the subject of Miss Harry's commencing quaker. Boswell had so often spoke to me, with regret, over the ferocious, reasonless, and unchristian

violence of his idol that night, it looks impartial beyond my hopes, that he requests me to arrange it. I had omitted to send it in the first collection, from my hopelessness that Mr. Boswell would insert it in his life of the Colossus" (*Letters of Anna Seward*, 1811, i. 48). A foot-note adds : "Mr. Boswell has strangely mutilated, abridged, and changed the minutes sent him of this conversation. The reader will find them faithfully given in a letter further on, addressed to Mrs. Mompesson, and dated December 31, 1785 [p. 97]." The fact is that Miss Seward mutilated her correspondence for publication: see *post* 25 Mar. 1785, n. 1. JB received from Mrs. Knowles her own version of the conversation, which he mentions in the second edition only to reject as totally discrepant from his own record (*Life* iii. 299 n. 2). It was printed in *Gent. Mag.* (1791) lxi. 500–02, and reprinted as a pamphlet in 1799 and again in 1805. See also *Gent. Mag.* (1796), lxvi. 924 and 1074.

[6] John Hunter (c. 1674–1741), Headmaster of the Free Grammar School at Lichfield from 1704 until his death. He was Miss Seward's grandfather by his first marriage, to Ann Norton, and Harry Porter's brother-in-law by his second, to Lucy Porter the elder. SJ considered Hunter a cruel but competent master (*Reades*, pp. 243 ff.; *Johns. Glean.* iii. 110 ff.; *Life* i. 44 ff., ii. 146; *Johns. Misc.* i. 159). According to one anecdotist, "He had a remarkably stern look, and Dr. Johnson said, he could tremble at the sight of Miss Seward, she was so like her grandfather" (*ibid.* ii. 414).

I shall certainly not mention in my *Life of Dr. Johnson* the circumstance in his daughter in law's behaviour which displeased me.[7] Your defence of her satisfies me; and if it did not, your request would be a law. But I wish much to have Dr. Johnson's letters to her. Be they ever so short, or upon a subject so barren, their *manner* must be capital.

I thank you for your hint to apply to Mrs. Cobb and Miss Adey. I have written to both of them, and I shall hope for favourable answers. . . .

From the Rev. Dr. William Adams, Thursday 17 February 1785

MS. Yale (C 14). Received 26 Feb. (Reg. Let.).

Oxford, Feb. 17. 1785

DEAR SIR, Your Letter found me in Gloucester where I am obliged to reside two months in the year.[1] On my Return hither I searched our College Books and am going to give you all the little Materials that I am able to furnish you with concerning our late excellent Friend.

Dr. Johnson's Father was a Bookseller in Lichfield who failed in business either before or soon after his Son came to Oxford.[2] He had been educated under an eminent Schoolmaster Mr. Hunter from whose School came out about the same time Dr. Green late Bishop of Lincoln[3] Dr. Newton Bishop of Bristol[4] and the cele-

[7] Apparently her grudging hospitality to SJ (*ante* To Cobb, 15 Feb. 1785, n. 1). Years before, 6 Oct. 1772, SJ had written to Dr. Taylor: "Miss Porter will be satisfied with a very little of my company" (*Letters SJ* 278). In the *Life* (ii. 462) JB wrote: "She reverenced him, and he had a parental tenderness for her."

[1] A prebend of Gloucester was then and until quite recently attached to the office of Master of Pembroke College.

[2] Cf. *Life* i. 78; Hawkins, p. 17; *Johns. Glean.* iii. 179–80.

[3] John Green, D.D. (?1706–79), successively Professor of Divinity, Master of Corpus Christi College, and Vice-Chancellor, Cambridge. In 1761 he was raised to the bishopric of Lincoln. Adams

erred in implying both that Green was a pupil at the school and that, as such, he was a contemporary of SJ's. His position was that of usher and he held it at a time (c. 1729–30) when SJ had been long out of school. But it is not impossible that they became acquainted during this period, for SJ had returned home from Oxford in Dec. 1729 (*Life* i. 45; *Johns. Glean.* vi. 49–50).

[4] Thomas Newton, D.D. (1704–82), Bishop of Bristol and Dean of St. Paul's; Milton scholar and author of theological treatises, the best known of which is a *Dissertation on the Prophecies* (1754–58). He was a native of Lichfield and attended the grammar school; but if he was a fellow-pupil of SJ's it could not have been for long, as he left the year SJ entered

brated Mr. Garrick.[5] He was enterd Commoner of Pembroke College Oxford on the 31st of October 1728[6] under the Tuition of Mr. Jorden. His Tutour leaving College some time after I had the honour for a time to call him my Pupil.[7] He was immediately distinguished in College by one of his first Exercises a Copy of Latin Verses which were so much in the Virgilian Style[8] that his Tutour was induced by it to give him for a Christmas Exercise Mr. Pope's *Messiah* to translate: which he performd so well that it was soon after printed; and meeting with general applause his Character became established.[9] He was caressed and loved by all about him and contracted on his part a Love for the College which he retained to the last. This was I am persuaded the happiest part of his Life.[10] But it was not of very long continuance. [11]His

—1717. Newton's criticism of the *Lives of the Poets* as malevolent in spirit provoked SJ to a counterblast against his own writings and character (*Johns. Glean.* iii. 123; *Life* iv. 285–86, 532). See also *Johns. Glean.* vi. 50–51 and *Life* i. 227 and n. 3.

[5] Garrick, according to his biographers, did not enter the school until SJ had left it (*Johns. Glean.* iii. 132).

[6] *Life* i. 58. Cf. *Johns. Glean.* v. 5.

[7] Cf. *Note Book*, p. 8 and *Life* i. 79. As JB explains, Adams *"would have been his tutor"* had SJ remained at Oxford after Jorden's departure; but believing that SJ had continued in the College until 1731, JB dates Jorden's departure in that year. Actually, Jorden left in Dec. 1729, to be inducted as Rector of Standon, in Staffordshire (*Johns. Glean.* v. 56). And since SJ left in the very same week (see *post* n. 11–11), the distinction claimed by Adams is most tenuous.

[8] Cf. *ante* From Adams, June 1784 and n. 15.

[9] *Life* i. 61. Cf. *ante* From Adams, June 1784, and From Hector, 1 Feb. 1785 and n. 29. JB rejected not only Hector's version of the poem's origin but two other divergent accounts: according to Hawkins (p. 13) the exercise was imposed by Jorden as a penalty for "absenting himself from early prayers," while according to Steevens (*Johns. Misc.* ii. 312–13) it was written "rather

to shew the tutors what I could do, than what I was willing should be done." For the publication of the poem, see *post* From Taylor, 6 May 1785 and n. 40.

[10] "Dr. Adams told me that Johnson, while he was at Pembroke College, 'was caressed and loved by all about him, was a gay and frolicksome fellow, and passed there the happiest part of his life.' . . . I do not find that he formed any close intimacies with his fellow-collegians. But Dr. Adams told me, that he contracted a love and regard for Pembroke College, which he retained to the last" (*Life* i. 73, 74). The interpolation "was a gay and frolicksome fellow" is derived from one of JB's notes of the Oxford conversations of June 1784 (J 93): "When I told Dr. Johnson that Dr. Adams told me that he was a gay and frolicksome fellow when first at Oxford the Dr. said 'I was rude and violent it was bitterness which they mistook for frolick.' " Ironically, JB, who was at pains to correct the suspicion of insanity in SJ (see *post* From Hector, 28 Mar. 1785 and n. 37), misread his own writing and reproduced SJ's confession in the *Life* as: "Ah, Sir, I was mad and violent."

[11–11] *Life* i. 77–78. In JB's revision of the passage, MS. *Life*, p. 35, "December" is changed to "autumn", clearly in an attempt to adjust Adams's chronology to the date of Michael Johnson's death, which JB knew occurred some time in

Remittances from the Country fell short, His Debts in College tho' not great were increasing: and he found it necessary to retire in hopes of raising the Supplies he wanted. The Res angusta domi[12] robbed his Father of the power of helping him; a Friend who, it was said, had promised to assist him, deceived him:[13] and for these tyrannical reasons he was obliged to leave the College in December 1731 having been a member little more than three years.[11]

A few years after this I was applied to by a common Friend to know whether a Master of Arts degree could be granted him as a Favour from the University, to qualify him for a School masters Place which was then offerd him. But this, tho' his character in the literary world began to rise was thought too much to be asked.[14]

His manner of Life when he repaird to London—among the Booksellers etc. you are probably better acquainted with than I.[15] [16]It was I think early in this period that I was employed by

Dec. (*Life* i. 79–80). But Adams was wrong as to the year, not the month. As Reade has conclusively shown in his exhaustive study of the problem of SJ's residence at Oxford (*Johns. Glean.* v. chs. 3 and 4 and App. H), SJ left Oxford in Dec. 1729 and did not return. We know now that it was Adams and not (as was supposed) Hawkins (pp. 14–15) who led JB astray. Adams's authority appears to have been "our College Books" (opening paragraph). The only sure evidence of residence is to be found in the College "buttery books", which record the regular weekly charges for board and in addition certain other levies and fines. Charges against SJ of the first class cease in Dec. 1729, while charges against him of the second class continue until 8 Oct. 1731. However, "all the charges against Johnson after 12 December 1729 are exactly matched by identical charges entered against numbers of other commoners who were obviously out of residence, and, therefore, instead of providing an argument against his having left College for good in December 1729, they actually prove that he never returned after that date" (*Johns. Glean.* v. 53). If, then, Adams did consult, and misinterpret, the data in the buttery books, why did he report that SJ left the College in December rather than in October, the

month of the last entry bearing his name? I can only suggest an inadvertent conflation of (1) the *month* in which the regular board charges cease, and (2) the *year* in which the name is dropped from the books altogether.

[12] JB applies the phrase (Juvenal, *Satires* iii. 164) to himself in the journal, 3 Dec. 1787.

[13] See *post* From Taylor, 6 May 1785 and n. 29.

[14] *Life* i. 132–33. The school was at Appleby, in Leicestershire. See *post* To and From Hector, 15 July 1786 and n. 19. Adams elaborates upon the episode *post* 12 July 1786.

[15] How SJ "employed himself upon his first coming to London is not particularly known" (*Life* i. 102). See however *Johns. Glean.* vi. 55 ff. and Clifford, *Johnson*, pp. 175 ff. The phrase "among the booksellers" is, if we exclude Cave, more precisely descriptive of a somewhat later phase of SJ's career.

[16-16] *Life* i. 134. For SJ's regrets see *ibid.* iii. 309–10. Against this might be set the rather dimmer view of the chances of success in the legal profession given SJ by "a very sensible lawyer", *ibid.* iii. 179. SJ's attorney-biographer Hawkins remarks (p. 15): "If nature could be said to have pointed out a profession for him, that of the bar seems to have been it."

58

him to consult Dr. Smalbroke of the Commons[17] whether a Person might be admitted to practise as an Advocate there without a Doctors degree in Civil Law. "I am" said he "a total stranger to these Studies but whatever is a Profession and maintains Numbers must be within the reach of common Abilities and some degree of Industry." This was in my opinion a happy Thought. He would no doubt have shone in this Profession. But here again the Degree was an insurmountable Bar.[16]

It was I think before he began his *Dictionary* that he had formd a design of writing a literary Journal.[18] I found his Parlour Floor in Gough Square coverd with Bundles of foreign Bibliotheques, the *Journals des Savans*, and the like in English; out of which he was to form his Plan.[19] Dr. Maty had just then finished his *Bibliotheque Britannique*, a well designd and well executed work, to convey to the literati of other Countries an idea of the most valuable British Publications. I recommended him to Johnson as One that might be an able and useful Assistant to him in this Design, being well skilled in those parts of Science where he was most deficient. But he declined having any Partner in the work: intending as he said to give his judgement, with a short Account chiefly of foreign Writers: among which he could select such as he could well understand, and best deservd notice. This Design came to nothing. Only he has left us a Specimen of his Talents for this sort of writing in his admirable Review of Mr. S. Jennings *Origin of Evil*, and of some other Publications occasionally inserted in a weekly Paper called, if I remember right, *The Literary Magazine*.[20]

[17] Richard Smalbroke (c. 1716–1805), Chancellor of the Diocese of Lichfield. He did not receive his degree until 1745, and therefore could not have been practising as an advocate of Doctors' Commons "early in this period," or as JB dates the episode, in 1738 (DNB s.v. Richard Smalbroke, 1672–1749; *Johns. Glean.* vi. 116).

[18] SJ does not appear to have turned his attention to the project until the *Dictionary* was near completion: see *Life* i. 283. The account that follows repeats that of the Oxford conversations of June 1784 (*ante*). JB places this project under 25 Mar. 1755, the date of a letter from SJ to Thomas Warton in which he says: "I intend in the winter to open a *Bibliothèque*, and remember, that you are to subscribe a sheet a year" (*Life* i. 283–84). He had originally placed it under 1746 (MS. *Life*, p. opp. p. 103); but among his notes for revising the MS. *Life* appears, deleted, the following: "See if the Bibliotheque be not 1755. See Warton [i.e. SJ's letter to Warton] and trans[fer] whence it now is."

[19] See *Life* i. 285, 543. SJ states the function of the literary journal in his introduction to the first number of *The London Chronicle*. For his conversation with the King on the subject of literary journals, see *Life* ii. 39–40 and Journ. 10 Apr. 1776.

[20] Croker believed that *The Literary Magazine* was itself the result of SJ's plan to undertake a *Bibliothèque*. The magazine

At this time a favourite Object which he had in contemplation was the Life of Alfred: in which, from the warmth with which he spoke about it, he would I believe, had he been Master of his own Will, have engaged himself rather than on any other Subject.[21]

The History of his *Dictionary* and of the Quarrel which it occasiond betwixt him and Lord Chesterfield you are I dare say well acquainted with:[22] and therefore the Story which I am going to tell you may probably be of little or no Use.

When the *Dictionary* was finished and near Publication there appeared two Papers in a periodical Work called *The World*, congratulating the Publick upon The near Prospect of seeing a Work so interesting to the honour of the Nation, and executed by so able an hand etc.[23] These were known to be written by Lord Chesterfield and were understood by Dr. Johnson's Friends as an intimation that he would be glad to have the Books dedicated to himself,[24] and to be thought the Patron of the Author and the Work. But this Compliment was ill receivd by Johnson; who had thought himself shamefully neglected by his Lordship: who after urging him in the most flattering manner to undertake this Work, had taken no farther notice of him; from whom he had not once heard for several years; and to whom he had been denied admittance when at his Door.[25] In stead therefore of dedicating the *Dictionary* He ad-

---

was published monthly, not weekly, and SJ was engaged to superintend its beginnings in 1756, as well as to contribute essays and reviews. Soame Jenyns's *Free Enquiry into the Nature and Origin of Evil* was published anonymously in 1757, and in three successive numbers of the magazine for that year SJ attacked "Jenyns's version of the official optimism of the eighteenth century" (Basil Willey). The fourth edition of the work (1761) included a long preface answering the review, and after SJ's death, according to JB, Jenyns printed an abusive epitaph "very unworthy of that gentleman, who had quietly submitted to the critical lash, while Johnson lived". The epitaph was answered in kind, though prematurely, by (presumably) JB himself. See *Life* i. 307, 315–16 and nn.; Courtney, pp. 75 ff.; Hazen, pp. 125 ff.; Willey, *Eighteenth Century Background*, 1949, p. 48; and D. J. Greene, "Johnson's Contributions

to the *Literary Magazine*", RES (1956) vii. 367–92.

[21] Quoted directly, *Life* i. 177.

[22] Adams appears to forget that he had already delivered himself upon this subject in June 1784 (*ante*).

[23] Adams's abstract is descriptive of only the first of these papers, 28 Nov. 1754. The second, 5 Dec., consists of a satirical analysis of the linguistic foibles of the *beau monde* and an ironic recommendation to SJ to compile a supplementary volume designed only for the genteel reader.

[24] Cf. *Life* i. 257. According to Shaw (p. 119 n.), "*Moore* [Edward Moore], author of the World, and the creature of this nobleman, was employed by him to sound Johnson on the subject of a Dedication."

[25] Cf. the letter to Chesterfield, *Life* i. 261.

dressd a severe Letter to him, thanking him in a sarcastick manner for this late recommendation of his work and expostulating with him on the little Regard which had been paid to him. [26]While this was the Talk of the Town I happend to visit Dr. Warburton: who finding that I was acquainted with Johnson desired me earnestly to carry his Compliments and to tell him that he honourd him for his manly behaviour in rejecting these condescensions of Lord Chesterfield, and for resenting the treatment he had receivd from him with a proper spirit. Johnson was visibly pleasd with this Compliment for he had always an high opinion of Warburton;[26] and immediately entertaind me with the long Letter that he had written to Lord Chesterfield. It was indeed an Entertainment being written in a lofty style that became the Spirit of it, and full of keen well pointed Satyr.[27] [28]I was however sorry for the Breech betwixt our Friend and this noble Peer who certainly wishd to shew himself his Friend and Patron: and was far from being convinced that he had intentionally been guilty of the Charges brought against him. My Doubts were grounded as I told Johnson on his known condescension and affability, and his easiness of Access especially to Men of Letters etc. "That is not Lord Chesterfield" says Johnson. "Lord Ch. is the proudest Man this day existing." "No," said I, "there is one Person at least as proud: I think by your own account you are the prouder Man of the two." "But mine," replied he

[26-26] Quoted directly, *Life* i. 263. (Through an error in the printing of Hill's edition, uncorrected in Dr. Powell's revision, the sentence that follows in the printed text is included as part of the quotation.) Of Warburton "a very grateful remembrance was ever entertained by Johnson, who said, 'He praised me at a time when praise was of value to me.'" The occasion was the publication of SJ's *Miscellaneous Observations on the Tragedy of Macbeth* (1745), which Warburton judged to be the work of "a man of parts and genius" (*Life* i. 175–76). For SJ's high though not undiscriminating regard for Warburton, see *ibid.* ii. 36–37, iv. 46 ff., 288, v. 80–81.

[27] Cf. *Life* i. 264. In one of JB's undated MSS. containing Johnsoniana appears the note: "Dr. Douglas [John Douglas, Bishop of Salisbury] told me that he was confident from memory that

Johnson's letter to Lord Chesterfield was more pointed than in the copy which he dictated many years after it was written." The original has not been recovered. In the Yale Collection is the version that JB wrote from SJ's dictation in 1781 (C 1596) and also a transcript in the hand of one of JB's children (probably Alexander) of the version SJ dictated to Baretti and later presented to Langton (see *ante* From Brocklesby, 13 Dec. 1784 and n. 8). The transcript, to which is attached a paper containing JB's introductory remarks, was plainly used as printer's copy. See *Letters SJ* i. xxxi–xxxv. Other copies of the famous letter are in the Hyde Collection and the Huntington Library (HM 17356).

[28-28] *Life* i. 265–66, combining details from Adams's earlier account (*ante* June 1784).

instantly, "was defensive Pride." This was One of those happy Turns for which he was so remarkably ready.[28] [29]I learnd afterwards from Dodsley to whom Lord Ch. had shewn this Letter and pointed out some of the finer Strokes in it, that his Lordship denied every one of the Facts charged against him: asserting that he had, when Secretary of State,[30] never been knowingly denied to the meanest Reptile that came to his Door—that Dr. Johnson would have been always more than welcome—that he had sent frequently to invite him but that he had changed his Lodgings or could not be found etc.[29]

I give you this long Detail to shew how willing I am tho' it is little in my power to enrich your work with any valuable Materials. Our Friend was created Master of Arts in Feb. 1755 by Diploma; an honour very sparingly conferred in this University:[31] and afterwards made Doctor of Law, by Diploma May 30. 1775.[32] [33]His last Visit was, I believe, to my House; which he left after a stay of four or five days on the 22d (17) of November. We had much serious Talk together, for which I ought to be the better as long as I live. You will remember some discourse which we had in the Summer upon the Subject of Prayer and the difficulty of this sort of Composition.[34] He reminded me of this and of my having wished him to try his hand and to give us a Specimen of the Style and manner that he approved. He added that he was now in a right frame of mind and as he could not possibly employ his time better he would in earnest set about it. But I find upon inquiry that no Papers of this sort were left behind him, except a few short ejaculatory Forms suitable to his present situation.[33] [35]He sent us

[29-29] Cf. *Life* i. 265.

[30] 1746–48. SJ's *Plan* was published in 1747.

[31] JB gives "the whole progress of this well-earned academical honour", including the correspondence relating to it, *Life* i. 278–83. For an account of the difficulty in obtaining the M.A. degree at Oxford, see A. D. Godley, *Oxford in the Eighteenth Century*, 2nd ed., 1908, pp. 183–84.

[32] The diploma is dated 30 Mar. 1775; SJ received it on 1 Apr. (*Life* ii. 332; Journ. 1 Apr. 1775).

[33-33] Quoted directly, *Life* iv. 376, omitting Adams's uncertain dating of the visit. The exact length of SJ's stay at Oxford—12–16 Nov.—is indicated in his

letter to Hector from London, 17 Nov., which JB prints two pages later. Adams had written to Dr. Scott on 8 Feb. 1785: "The Doctor's last visit was, I believe, to this College. We had much serious Talk together during the few days that he staid with me; for which I ought to be the better as long as I live" (*Adam Cat.* iii. 2; *Johns. Misc.* ii. 461–62). For the papers left behind, their publication, and Adams's reaction, see *post* From Adams, 12 July 1786 and n. 15.

[34] *Life* iv. 293–94. See also *Diaries*, pp. 412–14.

[35-35] *Life* i. 74–75, omitting the details of the house's value and the charge upon it; adding "and he bequeathed it to some poor relations" (cf. Hawkins, p. 588);

a little before his Death a valuable Mark of his Affection for the College in a Present of all his Works, to be deposited in our Library.[36] And was about leaving as a Legacy to the College a House which he had in Lichfield; but which being of no great value and having a Charge upon it the Friends that were about him very properly dissuaded him from.[35]

I have thus put down in a rough manner every thing that at pres[en]t occurs to me. If I can be of any farther use upon this or any other occasion I hope you will freely and without reserve command Your affectionate and obedient Servant

W. ADAMS

My Wife and Daughter present their best Respects.

From Mary Adey,
Saturday 26 February 1785

MS. Yale (C 19). Received Mar. (Reg. Let.).

Lichfield, Febry. th[e] 26: 1785

DEAR SIR: I need not tell you that every word and sentiment of our much lamented Friend the Great and Good Doctor Johnson ought to have been remember'd. I have frequently enjoy'd the Pleasure of his Company, and listen'd with delight to his instructive Conversation, but alas! I have not treasur'd it in my Memory as I *ought* to have done, perhaps from too Volatile a disposition of my own, or from knowing that when I wish'd to think of him in Absence I cou'd fly to his *Ramblers* and his other Works where he still lives. My Aunt was so much affected by his Death that I am convinced it is neither a good understanding, nor a well order'd Mind that can excuse the Possesors of them from feeling *painful* Sensibilities of Friendship. One of her greatest consolations is that you undertake to write his Life, as We have every reason to believe that *You* will do Justice to his Merits, his Great, his Inspired Mind.

We often talk of you as the Friend of *our* Friend, and beg of you to Accept that share of our Regard which we find with regret return upon our hands. You request that we wou'd send you some

putting in effect a different construction upon the matter. For the conveyance of the house and the disposition of the proceeds, see *Johns. Glean.* iv. 20 ff. For the works presented to Pembroke, see *Letters SJ* 1038 and *Life* i. 527.

[36] Cf. Adams to Scott (*Adam Cat.* iii. 2; *Johns. Misc.* ii. 460).

Anecdotes. I know of few but what the News Papers have related, but as you desire me to think nothing too small and encourage me in the wish to oblige you I will Send you all I *can*, but Pray don't expose my Letters, and excuse every inaccuracy of my Pen. I inclose you a Letter which I am sure you know how to value. I will repeat to you an Anecdote which Mrs. Cobb mention'd to me the other Day. When the famous Doctor Sachaverel was at Lichfield Johnson was not quite 3 Years old. My Grandfather Hammond observ'd him at the Cathedral perch'd upon his Fathers Shoulder listning and gazing at the much celebrated Preacher. Mr. Hammond ask'd Mr. Johnson how he cou'd possibly think of bringing Such an Infant to Church and in the Midst of so Great a Croud. He answer'd because it was impossible to keep him at home for young as he was he believ'd he had caught the Public Spirit and zeal for Sachaverel and woud have staid forever in the Church Satisfied with beholding him.[1]

Certainly there was something very Peculiar in this for so young an Infant. Miss Seward I hear has sent you his Epitaph on his Duck,[2] it is needless in me to repeat it. Mrs. Gastrel[3] tells me he

[1] Quoted directly, with a trifling omission, *Life* i. 38–39.

[2] Apparently among the communications which JB destroyed: see *ante* To Seward, 15 Feb. 1785, n. 2. For Miss Seward's confirmation of the anecdote, see *post* 25 Mar. 1785. JB had first heard the story from Lucy Porter on 25 Mar. 1776, on the authority of SJ's mother. SJ asserted that his father composed half of the epitaph, but JB nevertheless wrote in his *Note Book* (pp. 3–4): "I trust to his mother's relation of what happened in his childhood rather than to his own recollection; and Miss Porter assured him in my presence upon his mother's authority that he had made this epitaph himself." The next year, however, JB added in the margin (p. 4): "But he assures me 21 Septr. 1777 that he remembers his Father's making it. So I am convinced." In the *Life* (i. 40 n. 3) JB quotes Miss Seward's "ingenious and fanciful reflections" on the verses (see *post* 25 Mar. 1785 and n. 12–12) only to discredit them as being "deduced from a supposed fact, which is, indeed, a fiction". Nevertheless, the text of the verses which he prints, as it differs from Miss Porter's (*Note Book*, p. 3), Mrs. Piozzi's (*Anecdotes: Johns. Misc.* i. 153, where, by the way, the point is blunted by her failure to mention the number of ducks), and Hawkins's (p. 6), may well have been Miss Seward's version. Mrs. Piozzi had the epitaph ("just arrived from Lichfield") in a letter from Lysons, 25 Feb. See Clifford, *Piozzi*, p. 243 and n. 2.

[3] Jane (Aston) Gastrell (1710–91), sister of Elizabeth Aston. She married the Rev. Francis Gastrell, Vicar of Frodsham, Cheshire, in 1752, and was widowed in 1772. As the last surviving member of the family she left a considerable fortune at her death (*Johns. Glean.* v. 252–54). In the Hyde Collection is a presentation copy of *The Rambler* inscribed by SJ: "To Mrs. Gastrel in memory of a long friendship and in acknowledgment of many favours these volumes are presented by Her most obedient and most humble servant The Authour" (*Life* ii. 540). JB dined with Mrs. Gastrell and Miss Aston at Lichfield

was one Day expressing to her his great dislike to any indecency of Conversation. He told her, if he kept a Whore and the Hussey was to talk impudently to him he wou'd kick her out of Doors.[4]

One of the last pleasant things I heard him Say was of your Friend Mr. Greene,[5] but you must not Publish it as it is a reflection upon poor Greenes Eloquence, tho a Just compliment on that good humour and Airy lightness of Mind which he certainly Possesses. I was with them both at Mrs. Porters. Doctor Johnson was *particularly* civil to Mr. Greene. When Greene had made his Exit Madam Porter gave Johnson a look of dis-approbation but utter'd not a Word. Johnson understood her meaning and addressd her as follows. I remember it most perfectly. "Greene cannot talk my Dear. Greene cannot even tell what he does—but if Greene *cou'd* talk, you wou'd follow him my Love as you wou'd do a Pipe or a Fiddle."[6] Oh! how it diverted me, and what Pleasure did I receive from observing some return of that charming vivacity, which I so often found suppress'd by Sickness and Pain and overwhelmn'd by gloomy reflections. Indeed I cannot express what I felt for his Sufferings. He is now a Partaker of Endless Bliss.

The Pow'r whose Just rewards are Sure
Thought Earth for his deserts too Poor
And Snatch'd him to the Skies.[7]

Mrs. Porter was very attentive and obliging to him when he was *last* at Lichfield.[8] I am surprized he did not leave her some little rememberance,[9] and We are not Pleas'd that you was not rememberd in his Will. I am sure he loved you—I never heard him speak of you but with Praise and Love.[10]

Mrs. Porter is very Ill, a Friend of mine who has some Wit says that Lucy is impatient to follow her Father in Law.[11]

on 25 Mar. 1776 and found them "substantial old women". "Mrs. Gastrell appeared to me as a good, chatty, hospitable Lady" (Journ.). He called on her again in the autumn of 1779 while making a round of visits in Lichfield (*Life* iii. 412).

[4] Not used.

[5] Richard Greene, another of JB's Lichfield correspondents. See *post* To Greene, 29 June 1787.

[6] Not used.

[7] Not identified. Apparently an ode.

[8] See *ante* To Cobb, 15 Feb. 1785, n. 1.

[9] See *Life* iv. 405 n. A MS. note in a group of JB's "Johnsonian Additions" (M 157) reads: "Mrs. Lucy Porter was much offended. I argued with her. It afterwards appeared that though rich she had not put him into her Will."

[10] Cf. *ante* From Brocklesby, 27 Dec. 1784 and n. 27.

[11] That is, step-father. She died 13 Jan. 1786 at the age of 70 (*Johns. Glean.* vii. 111).

Some Years Ago Doctor Johnson was Speaking to me of a young Lady who had an attachment contrary to the approbation of her Parents. I pleaded for her, and I dare Say utterd many Silly things on the Passion of Love. He told me a Courtship of Passion was a very *pretty* thing, but if I married, he hoped it woud be a Match of approbation.[12]

I have Scribbled till I am tired. I cannot recollect at present any thing more worth Sending. If my Packet proves Acceptable it will make me very happy. My Aunts best respects attend you. Believe me Dear Sir with respect and regard Your Sincere Friend and Humble Servant

MARY ADEY

Poor Mrs. Aston is confined to her Bed. Mrs. Gastrel is a most attentive Nurse.

My Friends Mr. and Mrs. Patton have been the whole of this Winter at St. Andrews. I hope they will soon Pass thro Edingburgh in their Way to the South. She is a very Sensible amiable Woman. Her Children are with Mr. and Mrs. Docksey. She has a Sweet little Girl whom we doat upon. She is entirely a Garrick.[13] Such a comic droll little thing I never beheld, and very pretty.

Mr. Inge who banish'd Mrs. Cobb and myself from our Dear Friary is dead.[14] He was the Idol of Lichfield, and I believe a good Man. I pity the affliction of his Family.

---

[12] Not used. Cf. SJ's advice to Baretti, *Life* i. 381–82.

[13] On his visit to Lichfield in Mar. 1776 JB "walked with Miss Adey and Miss Docksy, the only Child of the sister of the Garricks, in Mr. Docksy's garden" (Journ. 24 Mar.). On 13 Nov. 1779 SJ wrote to JB at Edinburgh, enclosing "a petition from Lucy Porter" to JB, "Requesting me to inquire concerning the family of a gentleman who was then paying his addresses to Miss Doxy" (*Life* iii. 417 and n. 2). The principals in this romance, which issued in marriage on 13 Jan. 1780 at St. Chad's, Lichfield, were Merrial Docksey, daughter of Thomas and Eliza (Garrick) Docksey, and James Susanna(h) Patton (1753–1812), of Clatto, Fife, and the Priory, Lichfield (*Life* iii. 536; Percy Fitzgerald, *Life of David Garrick*, 1899, i. xvii). In her will, dated 25 Apr. 1805, Miss Adey (then Mrs. Sneyd) bequeathed: "To James Susanna Patton, of Lichfield, esq., £50, and the picture of Susanna to his wife, and £100 to his dau. Merrial Patton, and £400 to his dau. Anna Maria Patton" (*Johns. Glean.* iv. 138).

[14] "A little West of Bridgestreet is a pleasant town mansion called the Friary; Which was formerly a monastery, conventual church, or religious house, (of Grey-Friars, Franciscans, or Friars Minor,) founded about the year 1229, by Alexander Stavensby, then bishop of Coventry and Lichfield. . . . The friary is an extraparochial place, and has been the seat of many gentlemen since it has been converted into a mansion-house. . . . The rooms are spacious and pleasant, having been recently improved and modernised for the residence of that highly-respected

Johnson said every Man was a Fool who attempted to Modernize an old House. I can never cease to lament the destroying those beautiful Relics of Antiquity.[15] You must know I am not without Superstition, and I sometimes think that some old Friar with his *Brushy Beard* came and tickel'd Poor Mr. Inge out of his Sleep at Midnight, for his Rest was disturb'd, and he has never enjoy'd health Since he Modernized The Friary. We lived at it 23 Years in Peace and tranquility.

And never Physician lifted the Latch.[16]

Thank God we still enjoy a good share of health and Spirits. I hope I am thankful for So great a blessing.

It will give us Pleasure to hear that Mrs. Boswell and your Family are well.

[Enclosure]
An original Letter from Doctor Johnson To Joseph Simpson Esqr.[17]

and much-lamented magistrate, the late William Inge, esq. who was many years chairman of the Quarter-sessions at Stafford, till his death in 1785. That great luminary of the law, lord Mansfield, declared that Mr. Inge's abilities, impartiality, and integrity, would have been an ornament to any bench" (Stebbing Shaw, *History and Antiquities of Staffordshire*, 1798, i. 320–22). See also Thomas Harwood, *History and Antiquities of the Church and City of Lichfield*, 1806, pp. 480 ff., and *Life* ii. 539. Inge was baptized 8 Mar. 1736/37 and was buried at Thorpe 19 Feb. 1785. He had been justice of the peace and Sheriff of the County, as well as Chairman of the Sessions. He was survived by his wife, Ann (Hall) Inge, a son, and two daughters (Shaw, *Staffordshire* i. 409). The lessee of The Friary before Inge was Thomas Cobb, Mrs. Cobb's husband. In 1801 the lease passed to James Susanna(h) Patton (Harwood, *Lichfield*, p. 486).

[15] Miss Adey wrote to Mrs. Piozzi on 29 Oct. 1787 (see n. 17): "We remember with *Pleasure* the agreeable Hours we have *formerly* Past with you at our dear Friary from whence we were *banished*.—

I verily believe we felt as much as our first Parents when they were expel'd Paradise, not from *Shame*, but *Sorrow*, and we still lament that our *old* Mansion is divested of all its relic's of Antiquity, *all* its Gothic grandure, and has *now* not one Sentiment more about it than a *Modern* fine Lady."

[16] Not identified.

[17] Used by JB as printer's copy for *Life* i. 346–47 (MS. *Life*, Paper Apart for p. 190). The letter is there assigned to 1759, though in a notebook on SJ's publications JB had entered under 1755: "Letter to J. Simpson Esq. (I suppose this year)." See Hill's speculations, *Life* i. 346 n. 1, and Chapman's, *Letters SJ* 134 n. At least three other copies of this letter are known: (1) another by Miss Adey, sent, with another and rather more informative commentary, on 29 Oct. 1787 to Mrs. Piozzi, who had requested it the previous summer for her edition of SJ's letters: see J. L. Clifford, "Further Letters of the Johnson Circle", *Bull. Rylands Lib.* (1936) xx. 280–82, and Clifford, *Piozzi*, p. 310 and n. 4; extract, *Johns. Glean.* viii. 68; (2) by the Rev. Daniel Astle, sent to JB in Dec. 1786 (*post*); and (3) by "Mrs. Clerke",

Dear Sr.

Your[18] Fathers Inexorability not only grieves but amazes me, he is your Father, he was always accounted a Wise Man nor do I remember any thing to the disadvantage of his good nature, but in his refusal to assist you, there is neither good nature, Fatherhood nor Wisdom. It is the practice of good Nature to over look Faults which have already by the consequences[19] punish'd the[20] Delinquent. It is natural for a Father to think more favorably than others of[21] Children, and it is always wise to give Assistance while a little help will prevent the Necessity of greater; If you married imprudently, you miscarried[22] at your own hazard at an Age when you had a right of choice, It wou'd be hard if the[23] Man might not chuse

sent to "Miss Simpson", dated "Tuesday Night Septr. 21st [?1802: watermark 1799]", presented by Chapman to Col. Isham in 1947 (*C 793). Variants are recorded in the notes following. See also *Letters SJ* i. 430.

Joseph Simpson (1721–before 12 July 1773), the eldest son of Stephen Simpson and Jane Adey of Lichfield, was "a schoolfellow of Dr. Johnson's, a barrister at law, of good parts, but who fell into a dissipated course of life, incompatible with that success in his profession which he once had" (*Life* iii. 28). His first marriage, to Elizabeth Gravenor, the daughter of a silk merchant of Coventry, though opposed by his parents, appears to have been both socially and financially advantageous; the imprudent marriage which SJ speaks of in his letter was presumably his second. Mrs. Piozzi relates that he "paid a clergyman to marry him to a fellow-lodger in the wretched house they all inhabited, and got so drunk over the guinea bowl of punch the evening of his wedding-day, that having many years lost the use of one leg, he now contrived to fall from the top of the stairs to the bottom, and break his arm, in which condition his companions left him to call Mr. Johnson, who relating the series of his tragicomical distresses, obtained from the Literary Club a seasonable relief" (*Anecdotes: Johns. Misc.* i. 228–29). See *Johns. Glean.* iv. 155 ff., viii. 67 ff. JB was first made

acquainted with "the history of Joe Simpson" on 10 Apr. 1776 at the Thrales's, where Arthur Murphy was holding forth. "Murphy said his life would be very instructive. . . . The Dr. seemed willing to write Joe's life, and wished to have materials collected" (Journ.).

[18] Mrs. Piozzi's text begins: "Communicate your letters regularly." The oddity of this sentence is illuminated by (1) Astle's copy, which reads: "Mr. Simpson communicates your Letters regularly" and (2) Miss Adey's request to Mrs. Piozzi "not to Publish the name of *Simpson*" (*Bull. Rylands Lib.* xx. 280). Whether the untidy truncation was Mrs. Piozzi's doing, or the work of Lysons or the printer following her instructions, is not apparent (her copy has not been recovered). Miss Adey's precaution in omitting the sentence altogether from the copy sent to JB ironically failed of its purpose: JB gives the full name of the addressee, Mrs. Piozzi only the initials (see *post* n. 41). "Mr. Simpson" was probably Joseph's brother Charles (1732–96), who succeeded his uncle, Joseph Adey, as Coroner and Town Clerk of Lichfield in 1764 (*Johns. Glean.* iv. 167).

[19] Piozzi and Astle, "consequence"

[20] Astle, "their"

[21] *Life* and Astle, "of his"

[22] Piozzi and Astle, "married"

[23] Clerke, "a"

his own Wife who has a right to plead before the Judges of his Country.[24]

If your imprudence has ended in difficulties and inconveniences,[25] you are yourself to support them,[26] and with the help of a little better health you wou'd Support them & conquer them. Surely that want which Accident & Sickness produces[27] is to be supported[28] in every Region of Humanity, tho' there were neither Friends nor Fathers in the World, You have certainly from your Father the highest claim of Charity tho' none[29] of right, and therefore I wou'd counsel you to omit no decent nor Manly degree of Importunity. Your debts in the whole are not large, and of the whole but a small part is troublesome.[30] Small debts are like small shot, they are ratling on[31] every Side, & can scarcely be Escaped without a Wound. Great debts are like Cannon of loud Noise but little danger. You must therefore be enabled to discharge petty debts[32] that you may have leisure with Security to Struggle with the rest.[33] Neither the great nor little debts disgrace you. I am sure you have my Esteem for the Courage with which you contracted them, and the Spirit with which you endure them. I wish my Esteem cou'd be of more use. I have been invited, or have invited Myself to Several parts of the Kingdom, and will not incommode my Dear Lucy by coming to Lichfield while her present Lodging is of any use to her.[34] I hope in a few Days to be at leisure & to make

[24] In Astle's copy this sentence is followed by the quotation: "Cui se clientum Capita fortunae/fides tutanda credunt" ("One ought to assume that a man is responsible if clients entrust their lives and fortunes to him"). I have not been able to locate it.

[25] Astle, "inconvenience"

[26] Astle, "and to conquer them" (homoeoteleuton).

[27] Piozzi, "produce"

[28] Astle, "succoured". See Letters SJ i. 430.

[29] Clerke, "to none"

[30] See Life i. 346 n. 1; Johns. Glean. iv. 158 n.

[31] Clerke, "in"

[32] Piozzi and Astle, "demands"

[33] "He [Simpson] said to Murphy that Dr. Johnson told him 'A man is not so much in danger from great creditors. They have a liberality of mind. It is small creditors that distress a man. Few are killed in a battel by cannon. It is small shot that does the execution. Therefore try to get all your debts concentrated in a few hands.' So poor Joe's plan was to borrow more money of his great creditors to pay his small ones, as if they would lend it to him for that purpose" (Journ. 10 Apr. 1776).

[34] "Poor Doctor Johnson was always in fears of Incommoding his Dear Lucy. —I have heard him often say no Person ever kept him in so much order as Lucy. —I am sure he was ever attentive and kind to her, and she has frequently behaved most ungraciously to him, but she was a strange woman as her last will testify'd, but this is entre nouns [sic]" (Miss Adey to Mrs. Piozzi, Bull. Rylands Lib. xx. 281–82).

Visits. Wither I shall fly is Matter[35] of no Importance, A Man unconnected is at home every where, unless he may be said to be at home no where.

I am sorry Dear Sr.[36] that where you have Parents, a Man of your Merits[37] shou'd not have an[38] home. I wish I cou'd give it you.

I am my Dear Sr.[39]

Affectionately Yours

Saml. Johnson[40]

I can not resist sending you this charming Letter, tho' I have some Scruples of conscience in doing it as I make you Acquainted with the failings of my near Relations. Mr. Joseph Simpson was my first Cousin. He was a Man of distinguished abilities, a very eloquent Pleader, and Great in the Profession of the Law. His good humour and Pleasantry were delightful, but his imprudent conduct render'd his Life miserable. He died neglected by almost all his Friends except our Dear Johnson whose Merit of Genius fell short of that of his friendly and compassionate Heart. He loved my Cousin, and thought with many others that his Parents Shew'd too little lenity to the distresses of their Child, even tho' they were of his own Acquiring. Let these particulars remain a Secret, as his Brother is an Inhabitant of this Place and might with reason be hurt at any reflection cast upon his Parents,[41] but alas! they were too Cruel, and I am sorry to Say my Aunt Simpson was more implacable than my Uncle, which was very Strange, as She had generosity

---

[35] Astle, "a matter"

[36] Astle, "dear Simpson". Cf. nn. 39 and 41.

[37] Astle, "merit"

[38] Piozzi, "a"

[39] Piozzi, "I am, Dear Sir,"; Astle, "I am/Dear Simpson". For the rarity of the latter in SJ's epistolary style, see R. W. Chapman, "The Formal Parts of Johnson's Letters", *Essays on the Eighteenth Century Presented to David Nichol Smith*, 1945, pp. 147 ff.

[40] MS. "Johson"; corrected by JB. Astle and Clerke, "Sam Johnson"; Piozzi, no signature (as usual).

[41] "... be so kind not to Publish the name of *Simpson*, for as they are our very near Relations, and it casts a reflexion upon my *Uncle* for his unkindness to his son, we would not wish the *present* Family who resides *here*, and with whom we live upon friendly terms, to know you had *this* Letter from *us*. —My Aunt gave it to Mr. Boswell with the same Injunction" (Miss Adey to Mrs. Piozzi, *Bull. Rylands Lib.* xx. 280–81; *Johns. Glean.* viii. 68). If Miss Adey's memory did not fail her, we may interpret both parts of this last sentence broadly. The injunction to JB was not so explicit, and whether JB was justified or not in publishing the name of Simpson, he at least kept Miss Adey's own particulars a secret.

and Charity to *others*, and was Esteem'd a very Sensible Polite Woman.

Adieu! I shall inclose this in my first Packet. Yours

MARY ADEY

From the Rev. Dr. Hugh Blair,[1] Monday 7 March 1785

MS. Yale (C 161).

ADDRESS: Mr. James Boswell, Advocate, James's Court.

DEAR SIR: The Subject of Dr. Johnson, in which you engaged me, suggested the inclosed Letter; which I do not mean for publication in any Shape; and do not allow you to make that use of it. But as you had Started the Objection in Conversation,[2] I have written this letter simply for your Satisfaction, and for the Satisfaction of any other of the Dr.s friends, to whom any thing of this nature may have occurred. Yours

H.B.

7 March 1785, Edinb.

DEAR SIR: I was Surprized when you told me that I had been attacked by some Anonymous Critic for having omitted in my printed Lectures[3] certain Strictures on the Style of *The Rambler* which Some Years ago I had given in my class.[4] This appeared to me a strange Attack. I was certainly Master of my own Lectures, to publish, or to omit publishing, what parts of them I pleased. Several Observations might appear to me proper to be deliverd in a meeting of College Students, which were not suited to the publick

---

[1] Hugh Blair, D.D. (1718–1800), critic; one of the ministers of the High Church, Edinburgh from 1758. "He [SJ] said today [19 Sept. 1777] at Dr. Butter's that Dr. Blair at Edinburgh was a very great man, which I thought too high an epithet for him, and which I imagine was heedlessly uttered; for I have heard Dr. Johnson talk of him in a strain by no means consistent with greatness. But he had been talking now of his Sermons which were not published, when he talked in a different strain of Blair. He said Strahan had no opinion of the sermons till

he got an opinion from *Him* much in their praise. But he said they would not be reprinted after seven years, at least not after Blair's death" (Journ.). See *Life* iii. 97–98, 486, iv. 98, and Journ. *passim*.

[2] "On sunday [6 Mar.] I heard Dr. Blair in the forenoon—sat a good part of the afternoon at Grange's with him" (Journ.).

[3] *Lectures on the Rhetoric and Belles Lettres*, 1783.

[4] Blair was Regius Professor of Rhetoric and Belles Lettres at the University of Edinburgh, 1762–83.

Eye; and Accordingly various passages were omitted[5] in Several parts of the Course, some were changed and Corrected; nay one or two whole Lectures were left out in the publication which I had read in the College. Who had any title to find fault with me for making my book as useful or Unexceptionable as I could?

The plain fact with regard to Dr. Johnson was, that as the Style of his *Rambler* always appeared to me turgid, unnecessarily crowded with words of Latin derivation, and too full of Antithesis, I took the Liberty, for some Years,' of reprehending these faults in his Style, and opposing it by Exemplification to the more chaste and Simple Style of Mr. Addison. In giving College Lectures to young men in this part of the Kingdom, where you know we are accustomed in Conversation to a provincial dialect, and are obliged to form our Style by Studying the best English Authors, this Attention occurred to me as useful; and accordingly I exercised a liberty of the same kind in criticising some of Mr. Addisons in-acuracies. But when in Process of time, Copies of my Lectures began to be circulated abroad in manuscript, I became sensible of an impropriety in my circulating a Censure upon a Living Author, (which in every other instance of living Authors I had carefully avoided) and an Author too with whom by that time I was in habits of Acquaintance, and mutual Esteem. I saw that this might be considerd as petulant; and therefore for some Years before my giving over to read Lectures in the University, I entirely omitted these Strictures upon Dr. Johnson, and deleted from the Manu-script which I read to the Students the passages which contained them. Afterwards, when his *Lives of the Poets* were published, it was Universally acknowledged that his Style was much improved, and cleared from its former defects.[6] I cordially joined my Suffrage to the publick Voice that the *Lives of the Poets* was one of the best books of Criticism in the English Language. In this Strain accordingly I Speak of it in my printed Lectures;[7] and there, when I was address-ing my Self, not to a meeting of Scotch Students, but to the publick at large, to have revived the Strictures upon the Style of *The*

---

[5] Three passages of animadversion on SJ's style have been recovered from copies of students' notes: see R. M. Schmitz, *Hugh Blair*, 1948, pp. 107–08, and John Butt in the *Johnsonian News Letter* (Mar. 1960) xx. 9–10.

[6] Cf. Cooke (p. 60): "His style [in the *Lives*] too, which in *The Rambler* more particularly, was thought *turgid*, was admitted to be much improved."

[7] Lecture XXIV, on the prose style of Swift, makes a passing bow to SJ, "a very able critic".

Rambler, which for Several Years I had disused, would justly have been held to be envious and illiberal.[8]

This plain Account will Satisfy you that any attack upon me for not returning in a publication to Observations which I had given up in the Lectures when read, proceeded from no Source but impotent Malevolence. 'Tis very well if an Author can answer for all that he publishes. Nothing can be more absurd than to accuse him for not publishing all that on any occasion he has written. I am with much respect and Esteem, Dear Sir, Your most Obedient and most humble Servant

HUGH BLAIR

To the Rev. Herbert Croft, Tuesday 8 March 1785

MS. Yale (L 397). A copy by Johnston of Grange, endorsed: "Copy Letter To [*in JB's hand:* The Rev. Mr. Herbert Croft] 8th March 1785." Sent according to Reg. Let. on the 11th.

Edinr., 8th March 1785

DEAR SIR: Your Letter directed for me at London was transmitted to me here, where from particular Circumstances with which I Shall not trouble you at present, I have remained this winter instead of prosecuting the Ambitious Scheme of which we talked at Oxford,[1] but of which I have not yet given up *thoughts*. I[2] Shall be in London next month, and Shall certainly avail myself of your obliging introduction to Mr. Osgood.[3]

Concerning our illustrious departed friend Dr. Johnson, you will please be informed that for upwards of twenty Years, I with his knowledge Collected materials for writing his life, which will be a large work, and require a Considerable time to make it ready for publication. I have therefore occasion for all my papers. But I

---

[8] Following, but not quoting, Blair's letter, JB gives a summary defence of his position, *Life* iii. 172 n. 2.

[1] Doubtless JB's scheme of coming to the English bar.

[2] MS. "*thoughts*, I"

[3] William Osgoode (1754–1824), said to be a natural son of George II, was the author of *Remarks on the Laws of Descent* (1779), criticizing Blackstone. He became Chief Justice of Upper Canada in 1791 and of Lower Canada in 1794; in 1801 he returned to England. Croft had written to Osgoode in Lincoln's Inn, 15 June 1784, introducing JB, who called "but did not find him" (JB to Croft, 28 June 1784).

Shall be very glad if you also favour the World with your Account of that great and good man. I am Dear Sir, Your obliged and most obedient humble Servant

(Signed) JAMES BOSWELL

To the Rev. Dr. William Adams, Friday 11 March 1785

Missing. Sent to Oxford from Edinburgh. Reg. Let.: "Rev. Dr. Adams returning my best thanks for his communications concerning Dr. Johnson. Wishing much to see all the Dr.'s letters to him that are not confidential. Hoping to be with him soon."[1]

To Edmund Hector, Friday 11 March 1785

Missing. Sent to Birmingham from Edinburgh. Reg. Let.: "Mr. Hector to the same effect."

To Thomas Barnard, Bishop of Killaloe, Sunday 20 March 1785

MS. Yale (L 41). A copy by the Rev. Alexander Millar, JB's chaplain, endorsed by him: "Copy Letter To The Bishop of Kilaloe 20th March 1785."

Auchinleck, 20th March 1785

... Your Lordship encourages me much when you call upon me as one who is able in your opinion to do justice to the memory of that great and good Man. I own it is my Ambition. I have long had it in View; and our illustrious departed Friend was well informed of my design. I am soon to publish my *Journal of a Tour to the Hebrides* in company with him which he read and liked, and which will exhibit a specimen of that Wonderful conversation in which Wisdom and Wit were equally conspicuous. It will be a Prelude to my large Work, *The Life of Samuel Johnson L.L.D.* for which I have been making collections for upwards of twenty years and which I really hope will be a Valuable treasure of Literary Anecdotes, and of the

---

[1] JB left for London on the 21st, stopping at Lichfield and Birmingham, but not at Oxford (Journ.).

74

genuine emanations of his energy of mind. It will be some time before it is ready for publication; and as I am anxious to make it as perfect as I possibly can, I will be much obliged to your Lords[h]ip if you will send me any particulars concerning him which you may recollect; and pray let me have his character drawn by your Lordships pen. I shall not fail to do justice to your Lordship in the course of my Work. You won Dr. Johnsons heart and his serious esteem; and it is truely pleasing to me to think that I was a benevolent negotiator between you and helped to remove a little misunderstanding.[1] . . .

To Thomas Percy, Bishop of Dromore, Sunday 20 March 1785

Missing. Printed, *Lit. Illust.* vii. 303–04.

Auchinleck, 20 March, 1785

. . . It is a great consolation to me now, that I was so assiduous in collecting the wisdom and wit of that wonderful man. It is long since I resolved to write his life—I may say his life and conversation. He was well informed of my intention, and communicated to me a thousand particulars from his earliest years upwards to that dignified intellectual state in which we have beheld him with awe and admiration.

I am first to publish the *Journal of a Tour to the Hebrides*, in company with him, which will exhibit a specimen of that wonderful

---

[1] ". . . the Dean told me at the dinner of the Royal Academicians 22 April 1776 that he had a very great respect for Johnson. I love him said he; but he does not love me. & he complained of his rough harsh manners saying that when he smiled he shewed the teeth at the corner of his mouth like a dog who is going to bite. He said Johnson is right ninety nine times in a hundred. I think with him but—you do not feel with him said I 'No, said the Dean. 'In short he is not a Gentleman' [cf. Journ. 23 Apr. 1776]. The Dean told me he thought of answering Gibbons & would be glad to talk with Johnson of it. When I came to Bath, Johnson said the Dean was mistaken. He loved him very well, though he dissap-proved of his being out of place, by living so much among wits & being member of a midnight Club—(that was ours) He was pleased with his design of answering Gibbons & said he would be glad to talk with him. I said the Dean appeared to me to be in earnest. Dr Johnson said he thought so too. I was happy in thinking that I could contribute to the reconciliation of two Christians" (*Note Book*, p. 18). The trouble seems to have started with the "pretty smart altercation between Dr. Barnard and him, upon a question, whether a man could improve himself after the age of forty-five" (*Life* iv. 115 n. 4). See *ibid.* 431–33; *Note Book*, p. 18; and Dixon Wecter, *Edmund Burke and His Kinsmen* (1939), pp. 68–69.

conversation in which wisdom and wit were equally conspicuous. My talent for recording conversation is handsomely acknowledged by your Lordship upon the blank leaf of Selden's *Table Talk*, with which you was so good as present me.[1] The *Life* will be a large work enriched with letters and other original pieces of Dr. Johnson's composition; and, as I wish to have the most ample collection I can make, it will be some time before it is ready for publication.

I am indebted to your Lordship for a copy of "Pope's Note" concerning him,[2] and for a list of some of his works[3] which was indeed written down in his presence uncontradicted; but he corrected it for me when I pressed him. If your Lordship will favour me with any thing else of or concerning him I shall be much obliged to you. You must certainly recollect a number of anecdotes. Be pleased to write them down, as you so well can do, and send them to me. . . .

From Anna Seward, Friday 25 March 1785

Missing. Printed, *Letters of Anna Seward*, 1811,[1] i. 38–45. JB stopped at Lichfield on 26–27 Mar. on his way to London (Journ.), and sent a note (L 1149) to Miss Seward upon arriving. In her reply (C 2471) she remarks: "I was just sending away a paquet for you, but am much better pleas'd to deliver it to you in person."

Lichfield, March 25, 1785

I regret that it is not in my power to collect more anecdotes of Dr. Johnson's infancy. My mother passed her days of girlhood with an uncle at Warwick,[2] consequently was absent from home in the school-boy days of the great man; neither did I ever hear her

---

[1] The volume appeared in the catalogue of Hodgson Co., 14 Jan. 1932, Lot 373.

[2] *Ante* 9 May 1776.

[3] *Ante* 5 and 7 May 1772.

---

[1] See J. L. Clifford, "The Authenticity of Anna Seward's Published Correspondence", MP (1941) xxxix. 113–22; reprinted, *Studies in the Literature of the Augustan Age . . . in Honor of Arthur Ellicott Case*, ed. R. C. Boys (1952), pp. 50 ff. ("the 1811 edition cannot be implicitly trusted for facts or contemporary opinions and not even for a strict chronology of the period").

[2] Miss Seward's mother, Elizabeth (Hunter) Seward (1712–80), was the daughter of the Rev. John Hunter, SJ's schoolmaster at Lichfield (*Johns. Glean.* vii. 176). Her uncle, the Rev. Thomas Norton (?1676–1743), was Vicar of Budbrooke, Warwick (*Johns. Glean.* i. 19, vii. 150).

mention any of the promissory sparkles which doubtless burst
forth, though no records of them are within my knowledge. I
cannot meet with any contemporary of those his *very* youthful days.
They are all, I fear, like my poor mother, gone to their eternal
home, and thus are our fountains of juvenile intelligence dried up.
Mrs. Lucy Porter, who, were she in health, could communicate
more than she would take the trouble of doing, is following apace
her illustrious father-in-law.[3] She is now too ill to be accessible to
any of her friends, except Mr. Pearson; and were it otherwise, I do
not believe that a kneeling world would obtain from her the
letters you wish for.[4]

On inquiring after Dr. Johnson, she has often read one of his
recent epistles. As she read, I secretly wondered to perceive that
they contained no traces of genius. They might have been *any*
person's composition. When this is the case, it is injudicious to
publish such inconclusive testimonies. Several letters of his have
appeared in the *Gentleman's Magazine*,[5] that could interest no one
by their intrinsic vigour. They will be eagerly read because they
are Johnson's; but I have often thought, that we never rise from
any composition by the pen of the illustrious, with exactly the
same degree of respect for the talents of the author with which we
sat down to peruse it; our mass of admiration is either increased or
diminished. If it is but by a single *grain*, that grain is something.

His letter to the Chancellor is a very stiff, indifferent performance, tinctured with a sort of covert resentment to the King, that
looks ungrateful for past obligations. I wonder how he could bear
the thoughts of such a request being made to his Majesty, since he
had a capital of three thousand pounds, out of which he might have
drawn to support the expence of continental travelling.[6]

You request the conversation that passed between Johnson and

---

[3] Cf. *ante* From Adey, 26 Feb. 1785
and n. 11.

[4] JB obtained twelve letters written
by SJ to Lucy Porter from Pearson (*post*
2 Apr. 1785), and one from an unknown
source (*Life* iv. 203). Altogether, forty-
nine have been recovered: see *Letters SJ*
iii. 315. (The text of 635.1, now in the
Hyde Collection, is printed in Mary Hyde,
"Not in Chapman," *Johnson, Boswell and
Their Circle*, pp. 311–12.)

[5] (1784) liv. 892–94; (1785) lv. 3 ff.

[6] SJ's letter to Lord Thurlow, 9 Sept.
1784, gratefully declining his offer to
sponsor his migration, was printed in
Gent. Mag. (liv. 892–93), and reprinted
by JB, *Life* iv. 349–50. For JB's part in
the same cause, see *ante* From Brocklesby,
13 Dec. 1784 and n. 11. Miss Seward's
figure of £3000 doubtless reflects the
inflationary spiral of local gossip: the
value of SJ's estate was nearer to £2000
(see *Life* iv. 402 n. 2).

myself in company, on the subject of Mrs. Elizabeth Aston of Stowe Hill,[7] then living, with whom he always past so much time when he was in Lichfield, and for whom he professed so great a friendship.

"I have often heard my mother say, Doctor, that Mrs. Elizabeth Aston was, in her youth, a very beautiful woman; and that with all the censoriousness and spiteful spleen of a very bad temper, she had great powers of pleasing; that she was lively, insinuating, and intelligent.

"I knew her not till the vivacity of her youth had long been extinguished, and I confess I looked in vain for the traces of former ability. I wish to have *your* opinion, Sir, of what she was, *you* who knew her so well in her *best* days."

"My dear, when thy mother told thee Aston was handsome, thy mother told thee truth: She was very handsome. When thy mother told thee that Aston loved to abuse her neighbours, she told thee truth; but when thy mother told thee that Aston had any marked ability in that same abusive business, that wit gave it zest, or imagination colour, thy mother did not tell thee truth. No, no, Madam, Aston's understanding was not of any strength, either native or acquired."

"But, Sir, I have heard you say, that her sister's husband, Mr. Walmsley,[8] was a man of bright parts, and extensive knowledge; that he was also a man of strong passions, and, though benevolent in a thousand instances, yet irascible in as many. It is well known, that Mr. Walmsley was considerably governed by this lady; as witness Mr. Hinton's[9] constant visits, and presence at his table, in despite of its master's

[7] "This conversation, though requested by Mr Boswell, the author believes is not inserted in that Gentleman's Life of Johnson; at least, not in the first edition. Mrs. Aston's sister, Mrs. Gastrill, being alive when it was published, was, doubtless, the reason why this anecdote was suppressed" (*Seward Letters* i. 40 n.). Mrs. Gastrell died 30 Oct. 1791 (*Johns. Glean.* v. 252). Cf. *post* From Jones, 29 Aug. 1791, n. 6.

[8] Gilbert Walmesley (?1680–1751), Registrar of the Ecclesiastical Court, Lichfield, was SJ's "first friend" and patron. He married Magdalen Aston (1709–86), fourth daughter of Sir Thomas Aston, in 1736 (*Johns. Glean.* iii. 174, v. 251). For SJ's portrait of Walmesley, "drawn in the glowing colours of gratitude", see *Life* i. 81. See also Clifford, *Johnson*, p. 169.

[9] The Rev. Thomas Hinton (?1710–57), Curate of St. Chad's, Lichfield, Canon of Windsor. He is said to have built Stowe House (1737), later acquired by Mrs. Gastrell (*Johns. Glean.* v. 251, ix. 218–19).

avowed aversion. Could it be, that, without some marked intellectual powers, she could obtain absolute dominion over such a man?"

"Madam, I have said, and truly, that Walmsley had bright and extensive powers of mind; that they had been cultivated by familiarity with the best authors, and by connections with the learned and polite. It is a fact, that Aston obtained nearly absolute dominion over his will; it is no less a fact, that his disposition was irritable and violent. But Walmsley was a man; and there is no man who can resist the repeated attacks of a furious woman. Walmsley had no alternative but to submit, or turn her out of doors."

I have procured, from Mr. Levett, of this city, the inclosed copy of an original letter of Dr. Johnson's.[10] Though its style may not bear the stamp of its author's genius, yet it is illumed with a soft ray of filial piety, which cannot fail to cast its portion of additional lustre, however small, on the amiable side of the Johnsonian medal.

The genuine lovers of the poetic science look with anxious eyes to Mr. Boswell, desiring that every merit of the stupendous mortal may be shewn in its fairest light; but expecting also, that impartial justice, so worthy of a generous mind, which the popular cry cannot influence to flatter the object of discrimination, nor yet the yearnings of remembered amity induce, to invest that object with unreal perfection, injurious, from the severity of his censures, to the rights of others.

There can be no doubt of the authenticity of that little anecdote of Johnson's infancy; the verses he made at three years old, on having killed, by treading upon it, his eleventh duck.[11] Mrs. Lucy Porter is a woman of the strictest veracity; and a more conscientious creature could not live than old Mrs. Johnson, who, I have heard Mrs. Porter say, has often mentioned the circumstance to her. [12]It is curious to remark, in these little verses, the poetic seed

---

[10] Theophilus Levett (1693–1746), Town Clerk of Lichfield. He was the mortgagee of the Johnson house in Lichfield (*Johns. Glean.* iv. 8–11, 182, 190). JB prints the letter, *Life* i. 160–61, "the original of which lies now before me". The copy actually sent to the printer (MS. *Life*, Paper Apart for p. 96) was an erratic one by (probably) JB's daughter Veronica,

which JB corrected from the original. See *Letters SJ* 19.

[11] See *ante* From Adey, 26 Feb. 1785 and n. 2.

[12–12] A comparison of this passage with JB's quotation of Miss Seward's "ingenious and fanciful reflections", *Life* i. 40 n. 3, shows to what extent her printed letters diverge from the originals.

which afterwards bore plenteous fruits, of so rich a lustre and flavour. Every thing Johnson wrote was poetry; for the poetic essence consists not in rhyme and measure, which are only its trappings, but in that strength, and glow of the fancy, to which all the works of art and nature stand in prompt administration; in that rich harmony of period,

> More tunable than needs the metric powers
> To add more sweetness.[13]

We observe, also, in those infant verses, the seeds of that superstition which grew with his growth, and operated so strongly through his future life.[12]

I have often heard my mother say she perfectly remembered his wife. He has recorded of her that beauty which existed only in his imagination. She had a very red face, and very indifferent features; and her manners in advanced life, for her children were all grown up when Johnson first saw her, had an unbecoming excess of girlish levity, and disgusting affectation.[14] The rustic prettiness, and artless manners of her daughter, the present Mrs. Lucy Porter, had won Johnson's youthful heart, when she was upon a visit at my grandfather's in Johnson's school-days.[15] Disgusted by his unsightly form, she had a personal aversion to him, nor could the beautiful verses he addressed to her,[16] teach her to endure him. The nymph, at length, returned to her parents at Birmingham, and was soon forgotten. Business taking Johnson to Birmingham, on the death of his own father, and calling upon his coy mistress there, he found her father dying.[17] He passed all his leisure hours at Mr. Porter's, attending his sick-bed, and, in a few months after his

---

[13] "More tuneable than needed lute or harp/To add more sweetness" (*Paradise Lost* v. 151).

[14] Not used. But cf. Garrick's equally unflattering description, *Life* i. 99, which JB discounts as "probably ... considerably aggravated". See also Clifford, *Johnson*, pp. 310–12.

[15] Reade calls this account Miss Seward's "absurd romance" (*Johns. Glean.* v. 103).

[16] "See the Verses on receiving a

myrtle from a Lady, inserted in Mr. Boswell's Life of Johnson" (*Seward Letters* i. 44 n.). See rather *post* From Hector, 9 Aug. 1791 and n. 2.

[17] "Her statements have so often been traversed that they can have practically no biographical value. Perhaps it is scarcely fair to apply strict chronological tests to stories of this kind, but it is legitimate to point out that nearly three years elapsed between the deaths of Michael Johnson and Harry Porter" (*Johns. Glean.* v. 103).

death, [18]asked Mrs. Johnson's consent to marry the old widow. After expressing her surprise at a request so extraordinary— "no, Sam, my willing consent you will never have to so preposterous a union. You are not twenty-five, and she is turned fifty. If she had any prudence, this request had never been made to me. Where are your means of subsistence? Porter has died poor, in consequence of his wife's expensive habits.[18] You have great talents, but, as yet, have turned them into no profitable channel." —"Mother, I have not deceived Mrs. Porter: I have told her the worst of me; that I am of mean extraction;[19] that I have no money; and that I have had an uncle hanged. She replied, that she valued no one more or less for his descent; that she had no more money than myself; and that, though she had not a relation hanged, she had fifty who deserved hanging."

And thus became accomplished this very curious amour. Adieu, Sir, go on and prosper in your arduous task of presenting to the world the portrait of Johnson's mind and manners. If faithful, brilliant will be its light, but deep its shades.[20]

[18-18] Cf. *Life* i. 95–96 and n. 2.

[19] In the MS. *Life* (p. 1) JB originally wrote of Michael Johnson that he was "of low extraction", but in revision altered the phrase to "of obscure extraction" (*Life* i. 34).

[20] In a letter to Mrs. Knowles, dated 27 Mar. 1785 (*Seward Letters* i. 47–48), Miss Seward wrote: "Mr Boswell has applied to me for Johnsonian records for his life of the despot. If he inserts them unmutilated, as I have arranged them, they will contribute to display Johnson's real character to the public; that strange compound of great talents, weak and absurd prejudices, strong, but unfruitful devotion; intolerant fierceness; compassionate munificence, and corroding envy. [Cf. *post* From Astle, Dec. 1786 and n. 46.] I was fearful that Mr. Boswell's personal attachment would have scrupled to throw in those dark shades which truth commands should be employed in drawing the Johnsonian portrait; but these fears are considerably dissipated by the style of Mr Boswell's acknowledgments for the materials I had sent him, and for the perfect impartiality with which I had spoken of Johnson's virtues and faults." By 10 Apr. she had become fearful again, writing to William Hayley (*ibid.* i. 62): "Mr. Boswell lately passed a few days in Lichfield. I did not find him quite so candid and ingenuous on the subject of Johnson, as I had hoped from the style of his letters. He affected to distinguish, in the despot's favour, between envy and literary jealousy." The warning should be repeated that in reading Anna Seward's published correspondence one must always allow for the possibility of a redaction.

From the Rev. Dr. William Adams, Monday 28 March 1785

MS. Yale (C 15).

ADDRESS (by Sir Charles Preston): James Boswell Esqr., James's Court, Edinburgh.[1]

FRANK: London twenty ninth March 1785. Free Chas. Preston.

POSTMARK: 29 MR.

Oxford, Mar. 28. 1785

DEAR SIR: I have no Letters of Dr. Johnson that will be of any use to you. Most of those that I have received here have been Recommendations of a Foreigner or two or some other Friend to whom he wished the Civilities of shewing the Place etc. might be paid.[2] He sent me last Summer a Packet of Letters from Mr. Cooper the Prior of the English Benedictines in Paris[3] desiring me to answer the two last of these Letters. These related to the Collation of two Mss. in the Kings Library of Xenophon's *Memorabilia Socratis* which Dr. Edwards a common Friend of ours (now dead) was printing here.[4] This brings to my mind what may perhaps be worth your mentioning—the Respect which had been paid to our Friend by this learned Society and which you may remember he spoke of in my house with seeming great pleasure. "I dined" said he "in their Refectory, studied in their Library, and had a Cell allotted me in their College which is my own at this day."[5] One of this Society, a Mr. Wilkes now settled in Staffordshire, a very

---

[1] JB arrived in London from Birmingham the day after the letter was forwarded (Journ.).

[2] Only one such letter has been recovered: see *post* n. 6.

[3] William Cowley (not Cooper) became a monk of St. Laurence's, Dieulwart in 1749, taking the name Dom Gregory; became Prior in 1765; and Prior of the monastery of St. Edmund the King at Paris in 1773 (*Chronological Notes on the English Congregation of the Order of St. Benedict*, 1881, Appendix, pp. 14, 17, 20). See SJ's French Journal, *Life* ii. 390, 397, 398, 399.

[4] See SJ to Adams, 11 July 1784 (*Letters SJ* 974). On 30 Mar. 1784 SJ

had written to Adams: "In my letter to you of the miscarriage of which I can no[t] account, was inclosed a letter from the Prior of the Benedictines, informing me, that the collation of the manuscripts in the King's library at Paris for the use of Dr. Edwards is finished, and that of the manuscripts two had never been collated before, and to desire directions how to transmit the papers" (*ibid.* 946.1). Edward Edwards, D.D. (c. 1726–83), was Vice-Principal of Jesus College, Oxford. His edition of Xenophon's *Memorabilia* was published posthumously in 1785 (*Life* iii. 367 n. 2, 529).

[5] Cf. *Life* ii. 402.

learned and agreeable Man I was obliged to him for recommending to me here.[6]

I believe I told you[7] that the Doctor a little before his Death made our College a Present of all his Works. Dr. Scott has since informd me that "a few days before his Death he expressd his cordial Regard for the College and his Wish to have his Name rememberd there. His specific intention was to have left his House in Lichfield to the College on condition of their paying the Rent to his Servant during his Life and afterwards applying it as an Exhibition or for any other College purpose." "This" says the Doctor "he told me only the week before his Death. But his Will was at last made under the apprehension of an immediate Dissolution and without the benefit of sufficient assistance. And when I came," says he, "the next day I found it rather too late to recall his attention to business of that nature."[8]

I am now going to trouble you with a delicate, but I hope not disagreeable Commission. This is an inquiry about a Gentleman of the name of *Grieves* who is said to be of a respectable Family in Scotland—to have studied at Edinburgh—to have since practised as a Physician with great Success and Character at Petersburgh[9]—and to be well known to the Provost and Dr. Robertson of Edinburgh.[10]

---

[6] See SJ to Adams, 29 May 1776 (*Letters SJ* 484). SJ later wrote to Mrs. Thrale: "Father Wilkes, when he was amongst us, took Oxford in his way. I recommended him to Dr. Adams, on whom he impressed a high opinion of his Learning" (*ibid.* 551). Joseph Wilks, of Coughton, Warwickshire, became a monk of St. Edmund's in 1746, taking the name Dom Cuthbert (*Chronological Notes*, Appendix, p. 23). He served as chaplain to Basil Fitzherbert, of Swinnerton in Staffordshire, was later at Bath, and about 1788 left England to pass his remaining years on the Continent (*Johnsoniana*, p. 31, n. 3). See also *Life* ii. 399; *Letters SJ* 483, 483.1.

[7] *Ante* 17 Feb. 1785.

[8] The will is dated 8 Dec. 1784, five days before SJ's death, and the codicil, which provided for the disposition of the house, is dated the 9th (*Life* iv. 402 n. 2), or the day when Scott "found it rather too late to recall his attention to business

of that nature." Hawkins, by his own account (pp. 576–77, 580, 588), furnished, along with Strahan, whatever assistance there was.

[9] John Grieve (1742–1806), a native of Peeblesshire, received his M.D. at Glasgow in 1777, was licensed by the Royal College of Physicians in London in 1786, and became a fellow of the Royal Society of Edinburgh in 1794. Both he and his brother James (d. 1773) served as physicians with the Russian army. The *Royal Kalendar* lists a London address for him from 1787 to 1799, and Russia from 1801. He died at St. Petersburg (Burke's *Landed Gentry*, 1937, p. 979; William Munk, *Roll of the Royal College of Physicians*, 1878, ii. 360; *Scots Mag.*, 1806, lxviii. 318). He is probably the Dr. Grieve in whose company JB dined on 28 Apr. 1788 in London (Journ.).

[10] The Provost of Edinburgh at this time was Sir James Hunter-Blair, Bt. (1741–87), who attended college with JB

A valuable Friend of mine supposing me to be more acquainted than I am with Dr. Robertson has requested me in very modest but pressing terms to make the best inquiry I can about this Gentleman. My Acquaintance with the Doctor will scarcely warrant this liberty. My Friend has given me no reasons for this inquiry: but that he has good and laudable ones I cannot doubt. Nor has he specified any Particulars to be inquired into. I therefore suppose he wishes to know what may be learnd of his Character in general and of his History at home and abroad. If therefore you can learn anything of this from the Provost or Dr. Robertson, I shall be much obliged to you for as early and as particular and full intelligence as you can conveniently give me. If you find it proper to mention me to the latter you will assure him of my real and great Respect for him. My Friend is so studious of Privacy in this Affair that he seems almost afraid of trusting me with this Commission and assures me that I may depend upon his Caution with respect to any Answers that may be receivd.[11]

Dr. Scott informs me that Dr. Johnson was very industrious in destroying Papers before he died and had committed his Life written by himself to the Flames.[12] Many of the first Copies of his Writings he had preservd the Executors intended to deposite in our Library. But it is well if these are not lost in the Fire at Sir Jn. Hawkins's.[13] Your affectionate and obedient Servant

W. ADAMS

and later became his banker (Journ. 10 Dec. 1774). William Robertson, D.D. (1721–93), the historian, was Principal of the University of Edinburgh; see *Life* and especially *Tour passim*.

[11] Towards the end of Apr. 1785 JB wrote to "Principal Robertson to inform me about Dr. Grieve of Russia" (Reg. Let.). Neither the letter nor the reply has been recovered. His next move was to write to Sir Alexander Dick (Reg. Let., 2 May), Dick replying on 1 June with a favourable account of Grieve (MS. Yale C 997).

[12] See *ante* From Brocklesby, 27 Dec. 1784 and n. 24.

[13] On 23 Feb., at Queen's Square, Westminster (*London Chronicle*, 22–24 Feb. 1785). *The St. James's Chronicle*, 24–26 Feb., reported the rumour that several of SJ's MSS. were lost. Hawkins wrote to Cadell, his publisher, on 26 Feb., assuring him that he had preserved SJ's papers and what was already written of the *Life*; but he does not positively deny a loss. See B. H. Davis, *Johnson Before Boswell* (1960), pp. 11–12.

Johnsoniana Related by Edmund Hector, Birmingham, Monday 28 March[1] 1785

MS. Yale (C 1524). In JB's hand.

Particulars of Dr. Johnson's Life communicated to me by Mr. Hector at Birmingham 1785[2]

Sir John Floyer Physician at Lichfield recommended to Dr. Johnson's Parents to have their son carried to London and touched by Queen Anne which was done. He was very well when he came to school, and had only the scars.[3]

When at school he never engaged in any of the boyish sports. But in frost he used to go upon Stowpool and make a boy pull off his stockings and shoes and put a garter round him and draw him on the ice.[4]

[1] Dated from the journal.

[2] A later expansion of the original heading: "Dr. Johnson."

[3] Sir John Floyer, Kt. (1649–1734), was renowned for his studies of the pulse, his advocacy of cold baths, and his research on asthma, with which he was himself afflicted (though he "panted on to ninety": *Life* iv. 267). A number of his works were printed for Michael Johnson at Lichfield. SJ, a fellow-asthmatic, read Floyer on the subject with a critical eye (*Johns. Glean.* iii. 10, 19, 115; *Life* i. 91 and n. 1, iv. 353, 543–44). JB's account of SJ's scrofula and of the royal therapy, *Life* i. 42–43, is based on other sources; but as an afterthought (MS. *Life*, opp. p. 8) he included, with an acknowledgement to Hector, the information concerning Floyer's role in the affair. For expert reconstructions of this event in SJ's childhood, see *Johns. Glean.* iii. 61 ff. and Clifford, *Johnson*, pp. 10–13.

[4] Cf. Hector's earlier version (*ante* 1 Feb. 1785), and see Introduction, p. xxxii. JB revised the anecdote to read: "He never joined with the other boys in their ordinary diversions: his only amusement was in winter, when he took a pleasure in being drawn upon the ice by a boy bare-footed, who pulled him along by a garter around him . . ." (*Life* i. 48). Guy

Boas ("Dr. Johnson on Schools and Schoolmasters", *English*, 1937, i. 540) asks bemusedly: "How did the boy who pulled him enjoy walking barefooted upon the ice, and for how long did he have to keep it up? Was it until his feet were turned to ice-blocks, and his toes to stalactites?" If the alleged action is incredible, JB's insensibility in reporting it is scarcely less so. Prof. Pottle has suggested to me that Hector meant only to say that SJ was on skates and the other boy wasn't, and that JB in a fit of literalness took the phrase "by a Boy barefoot" (as he set it down in the first MS. version) to mean by a boy without shoes and stockings (detail of the picture in the second MS. version). This is an ingenious and tempting explanation (cf. "barefootclogs" meaning "clogs without irons", *English Dialect Dictionary*), but it leaves some difficulties. If the removal of the boy's shoes and stockings was a spontaneous imaginative act on JB's part, prompted by the "barefoot" condition mentioned by Hector, was the use to which JB put one of the now useless garters an act of premeditated invention? Hector, it is true, may have described the business of the garter along with the condition of the boy, without, in *his* view, implying denudation at all. But if the

When he returned from Oxford he remained some time at Lichfield.[5] Then went to Bosworth as under Master of the school. This situation was very irksom to him. He remained there about a year and a half.[6]

Mr. Hector had been settled at Birmingham about three years. Johnson came there to visit him.[7] Mr. Hector had appartments at the house of Mr. Warren Bookseller in the highstreet opposite to where the Swan Inn now is. Mr. Warren was the first established Bookseller in Birmingham.[8] Before he opened a shop there, Dr. Johnson's Father used to come every market day and open a shop

bizarre picture was of JB's making, why then, in the revision of the anecdote for the *Life*, did he omit the detail of the removal of the shoes and stockings? (He kept the garter.) It can't be inferred from this omission that he eventually saw the light, for he still describes the boy as "barefooted"; and if it be conjectured that he came to understand this to mean (in this context) "without skates", one would have to ask why he would not take care to prevent the very misconstruction he himself fell victim to. Some alternative sense can be made of the anecdote, and of JB's revision of it, if we regard the omission of the removal of the shoes and stockings as a suppression, and note that it is accompanied by an alteration of "make a boy" etc. into "took a pleasure" etc. If the revision was in fact an attempt to touch up the picture, it was crude in its method and obviously unsuccessful in its effect. Show the boy barefooted, and you show SJ playing the bully in this "sport" ("He never joined with the other boys in their ordinary diversions", the anecdote begins). But show SJ playing the bully, and the barefoot boy, however much at a disadvantage in playing *his* part, is at least plausible. Taking "barefoot" literally, then, as JB did, we may imagine SJ not on skates but in his shoes, and the action that of *sliding*—which (not to justify this variation of it) would make the pulling operation one more of necessity than of convenience.

[5] From the end of Dec. 1729 to the beginning of Mar. 1732. For JB's attempt to set the chronological record straight, see *post* To and From Hector, 15 July 1786.

[6] JB's account of the Bosworth episode, *Life* i. 84–85, is based mainly on the fuller information later supplied by Hector (*post* 15 July 1786). SJ's "Annales" fixes the term at Bosworth from 9 Mar. to July 1732. JB, who saw the "Annales", but also saw "one of his little fragments of a diary", misinterpreted the signs. See *Diaries*, pp. 28–29 and n.

[7] Hill and Dent (*Memorials of the Old Square*, p. 25) date Hector's arrival in Birmingham c. 1731 and SJ's visit in 1732, but they give no authorities. Reade (*Johns. Glean.* v. 96) argues for the end of 1732 as the time of SJ's arrival. See *post* n. 10. The Birmingham chapter in SJ's history is briefly set down in the *Note Book* (p. 10), and is elaborated in the *Life* (i. 85 ff.), chiefly from the materials which follow.

[8] MS. orig. "Lichfield". Thomas Warren was a printer as well as a bookseller (but not the first established in Birmingham). He was in business in Birmingham at least from 1727, and died in 1767 "greatly advanced in years". In 1743 he suffered bankruptcy as a result of his association with Lewis Paul's cotton-spinning venture (*Johns. Glean.* v. 93–94; *Life* i. 528). See also *Letters SJ* 13, 14, 69, 179; and *post* n. 25. SJ and JB lodged at the Swan Inn during their visit to Birmingham in 1776 (Journ. 22 Mar. 1776).

for books and stationary ware.[9] Mr. Hector invited him to live with him which he did—not knowing then whether he might stay a forthnight or a month or what time.[10] He was Mr. Hector's guest at the boarding table of Mr. Warren who was also very civil to him on account of the great use Dr. Johnson was to him with his advice in his trade.[11] Warren in his Newspaper began a Periodical paper. Johnson furnished some numbers.[12] About six months after he took lodgings for himself in the lower part of the town.[13] Johnson mentioned that he had read at Pembroke College Lobosts History of Abyssinia and thought an Abridgement and Translation of it might do well.[14] How to get the book was the question. Hector borrowed it of the Library of Pembroke.[15] Johnson was very indolent.[16]

[9] Cf. *Note Book*, p. 4 and *Life* i. 36.

[10] He seems to have stayed about a year and a half, returning to Lichfield early in 1734, but revisiting Birmingham towards the end of that year (*Johns. Glean.* v. 100, 104).

[11] ". . . by his knowledge of literature" (*Life* i. 85).

[12] *Life* i. 85. "After very diligent inquiry, I have not been able to recover those early specimens of that particular mode of writing by which Johnson afterwards so greatly distinguished himself." Nor have succeeding biographers. For a description of *The Birmingham Journal*, see Clifford, *Johnson*, pp. 143–44.

[13] *Life* i. 85–86. In his "Annales" SJ wrote: "1733 Junii 1mo apud F. Jervis Birminghamiae habitare incepi" (*Diaries*, p. 31). Cf. Hawkins, p. 21.

[14] *Life* i. 86. JB adds that SJ was "urged" to the undertaking by Hector and Warren. The story of SJ's first literary project (of any scope) had been related by Hector in 1776, and is recorded in very brief form in the *Note Book* (p. 10). See H. W. Liebert, "Dr. Johnson's First Book", *Yale University Library Gazette* (1950) xxv. 23 ff. JB's criticism of the book as undistinguished except for the Preface and Dedication seems reminiscent of Hawkins (p. 22).

"On Sunday, March 31, [1776] I called on him, and shewed him as a curiosity which I had discovered, his 'Translation of Lobo's Account of Abyssinia,' which Sir John Pringle had lent

me, it being then little known as one of his works. He said, 'Take no notice of it,' or 'don't talk of it.' He seemed to think it beneath him, though done at six-and-twenty. I said to him, 'Your style, Sir, is much improved since you translated this.' He answered with a sort of triumphant smile, 'Sir, I hope it is' " (*Life* iii. 7).

Father Jerome Lobo (1593–1678) was a Portuguese Jesuit missionary to India and Abyssinia. His own account of his travels was apparently never published, but the MS. was translated into French in 1728 by Abbé Joachim le Grand and entitled *Voyage* (or *Relation*) *historique d'Abissinie*. It was this edition which SJ abridged and translated into English. See J. J. Gold, "Johnson's Translation of Lobo", PMLA (1965) lxxx. 51–61.

[15] *Life* i. 86, where the borrower is SJ rather than Hector, who, Dr. Powell informs me, was not entitled to borrow a book from Pembroke. There is, in any case, no record of the book in the College library (*Life* i. 528). The omission of the word "library" in JB's account enabled Reade to suggest (*Johns. Glean.* v. 108) that the book may have been borrowed from a private source at the College. In the *Note Book* version SJ is said to have read the book at Warren's.

[16] "From that kind of melancholy indisposition which I had when we lived together at Birmingham, I have never been free" (SJ to Hector, 7 Oct. 1756: *Letters SJ* 103).

Osborn the Printer employed by Warren could not get other work till it was finished and Johnson furnished him with copy only progressively. Hector went to Johnson and told him how the poor Printer and his family suffered. He lay in bed—got the book before him and dictated while Hector wrote.[17] Hector wrote it over almost the whole of it and carried it to the Press, and Johnson saw little of the proofsheets. Hector corrected most of them.[18] He had five guineas for this Work.[19] Johnson was then very idle lounged about with Hector and had a few acquaintances Mr. Porter and Mr. Taylor who afterwards acquired an immense fortune.[20] He would sometimes steal an hour and read but had a vanity in concealing that he ever studied. It was all to be from his own mind.[21] When at Stourbridge he was much enamoured of a fair young Quaker Olivia LLoyd on whom he wrote a copy of verses.[22] The story which

---

[17] *Life* i. 86–87. Lysons wrote to Mrs. Piozzi at Florence, 14 July 1785: "I saw Boswell lately at Banks's for the first time and cannot say, that I saw any thing very engaging in his manner—He said that Mr. Hector told him that when Johnson was translating Le Bo's Abyssinia which was the first work he engaged in, he lay in bed and was too lazy to write, but dictated to Hector who was then his Amanuensis—" (J. L. Clifford, "Further Letters of the Johnson Circle", *Bull. Rylands Lib.* 1936, xx. 276–77). The story was duly incorporated in the *Anecdotes* (*Johns. Misc.* i. 178).

[18] *Life* i. 87, omitting the detail of Hector's rewriting.

[19] *Life* i. 87. As an afterthought (MS. *Life*, p. 43) JB interpolated the phrase "only the sum of". See however *Johns. Glean.* v. 97 for a more realistic estimate.

[20] *Life* i. 86. The first part of the sentence is replaced by the remark that he "had no settled plan of life". The phrase "had a few acquaintances" was improved by stages in the MS. *Life* (p. 40): from "had a few good acquaintances" to "made some valuable acquaintances". Harry Porter (d. 1734), the husband of SJ's future wife, was a mercer or woollen draper, established in a house in the High Street which Warren was to occupy

after his death (*Johns. Glean.* v. 99, 102, 106). John Taylor (1711–75), "the Shakespeare or Newton of Birmingham", lived on the same street, in a house now occupied by Lloyds bank. He was High Sheriff of Warwickshire in 1756, and with Sampson Lloyd the Third founded in 1765 the first regular banking-house in Birmingham. He was best known, however, as the inventor and manufacturer of the gilt button and enamelled snuff-box, and as the possessor of a fortune of £200,000 (Hill and Dent, *Memorials of the Old Square*, pp. 101–02; *Johns. Glean.* v. 97–98; *Life* i. 86 n. 3). See also *Letters SJ* 179 and Journ. 22 Mar. 1776.

[21] Not used. Cf. JB's account of SJ's reading, *Life* i. 70–71.

[22] "which I have not been able to recover" (*Life* i. 92). Olivia Lloyd (1707–75) was the youngest child of Sampson Lloyd the First of Birmingham by his second wife, Mary Crowley of Stourbridge. SJ may have met her through his cousin "Parson" Ford and his wife, Judith Crowley, Olivia's aunt. She was also related (remotely) to the Carlesses, and hence to Hector himself. In 1735 she married Thomas Kirton of Brimton, Berkshire (*Reades*, p. 151; *Johns. Glean.* iii. 159–60; *Life* i. 529).

Peter Garrick[23] was told by Victor[24] that Johnson was one of the three gallants of the dissolute Wife of Mr. Paul (Gimcrack)[25] was not true. Dr. James[,][26] Victor and Johnson were said by Victor to be the Triumvirate and Victor said the Lady told him Johnson was the most seducing man she had ever known.[27] Johnson never was at Birmingham till James left it.[28] James was fond of her— then grew tired—and to get rid of her he *palmed* her on Dr. Larkin[29] by giving her a guinea to fee him that he might be catched. Larkin

[23] Peter Garrick (1710–95), "the elder brother of David, strongly resembling him in countenance and voice, but of more sedate and placid manners" (*Life* ii. 311). "He was David with a sourdine: the same instrument, but not so loud or sharp" (Journ. 23 Mar. 1776). According to David, he was SJ's "prime favourite" (*Letters of David Garrick*, ed. D. M. Little and G. M. Kahrl, 1963, iii. 1084). Peter was a wine merchant in Lichfield, where he played host to SJ and the Thrales in July 1774 and to SJ and JB in Mar. 1776 (*Life* ii. 462, 466, v. 429; Journ. 23–24 Mar. 1776).

[24] Benjamin Victor (d. 1778), Poet Laureate of Ireland, theatre manager, and historian of the stage. JB met "old Victor" in 1762 and wrote of him: "He is an honest, indolent, conversable man, and has a great many anecdotes" (Journ. 30 Nov. 1762).

[25] Lewis Paul (d. 1759), the inventor, was the son of a French refugee druggist in London and the ward of the third Earl of Shaftesbury. In 1738 he took out a patent for a roller-spinning machine (which appears actually to have been the invention of John Wyatt) and set up a mill at Birmingham, with the assistance of Wyatt, Warren the printer, Cave, Dr. James, and Mrs. Desmoulins. Although the enterprise failed (it was successfully developed by Arkwright ten years later), Paul persisted in his researches on cotton-carding and cotton-spinning machines. SJ acted as intermediary for Paul and his financial backers. See *John Wyatt, Master Carpenter & Inventor*, 1885; R. K. Dent, "The Sorrows of an Inventor", *Central Literary Maga-*

zine (Birmingham), 1917, xxiii. 482–86; *Letters SJ passim*; and Clifford, *Johnson*, pp. 241–42. Paul was married in Feb. 1728 to Sarah Bull Meade, a widow, who died in Sept. of the next year. The term "Gym crack" was used by Wyatt, in letters to his brother, as early as 1733 for the "fly shuttle".

[26] See *ante* From Hector, 1 Feb. 1785 and n. 8. For James's sexual indulgences, see Journ. 1 Apr. 1775 and *Dr. Campbell's Diary*, ed. Clifford, pp. 68–69.

[27] JB had heard a very similar tale ten years earlier from Peter Garrick. "He said a Lady, a very fine woman, said to him that Mr. Johnson was a very seducing man among the women when he chose it; and he added that it was suspected he had seduced her. This was not very probable" (Journ. 24 Mar. 1775). JB makes use of the first part of Garrick's anecdote in order to enforce his claim that SJ was not unattractive to women, *Life* iv. 57 n. 3. Cf. *ibid.* 73.

[28] It is not known just when James left Birmingham (he was married there in 1737), but I have seen no evidence to preclude the possibility of either James's or SJ's having known Mrs. Paul. She was Mrs. Paul from Feb. 1728 and died in Sept. 1729; SJ was at leisure in Lichfield from the fall of 1726 to the fall of 1728, and had many relatives in and around Birmingham whom he could have visited. See *Johns. Glean.* iii. 124 n., 164, 177 ff.

[29] Perhaps George Larkin (b. c. 1702), of Bristol. He was a bachelor of medicine at this time, and did not become an M.D. until 1737 (*Alum. Oxon.*).

said to Hector[30] "Now here is a guinea which I beleive James has given her to give to me." Yet with his eyes open he was taken in. Mr. Hector said Johnson never was given to Women.[31] Yet he then did not appear to have much Religion.[32] He drank freely particularly Bishop[33] with a roasted Orange in it. He used to be absent and talk to himself and take peevish fits and abuse Hector who would then keep aloof upon which Johnson would come and coax him.[34] Sir Harry Gough told Hector he was obliged to put him out of one of his houses in Gough Square for the Neighbours complained they could not get rest for a man who walked all night and talked to himself.[35] When at Birmingham the time now mentioned[36] Hector was affraid of Dr. Johnson's head, and he thought

[30] Hector's appearance among the dramatis personae helps fix the time of his residence in Birmingham: see *ante* n. 7. Larkin, who was not one of the original "Triumvirate", probably became involved in 1729. SJ spent this year at Oxford.

[31] Meaning that he was chaste—not indifferent. At least so JB interpreted it: "His juvenile attachments to the fair sex were, however, very transient; and it is certain, that he formed no criminal connection whatsoever. Mr. Hector, who lived with him in his younger days in the utmost intimacy and social freedom, has assured me, that even at that ardent season his conduct was strictly virtuous in that respect" (*Life* i. 93–94). Cf. *ibid*. iv. 395–96, where JB belatedly mentions, "(with all possible respect and delicacy, however,) that his conduct, after he came to London, and had associated with Savage and others, was not so strictly virtuous, in one respect, as when he was a younger man". See F. A. Pottle, "The Dark Hints of Sir John Hawkins and Boswell", *New Light on Dr. Johnson*, ed. F. W. Hilles, 1959, pp. 153–162.

[32] SJ dated his religious reawakening from a sickness suffered (he thought) when he was twenty-two (Journ. 30 Apr. 1783); altered to "at an early part of my life" (*Life* iv. 215). For JB's attempt to date SJ's first serious attack of "morbid melancholy", see *post* To and From Hector, 15 July 1786.

[33] "that liquor called *Bishop*, which Johnson had always liked" (*Life* i. 251). Hill noted (n. 1) the definition given in SJ's *Dictionary*: "A cant word for a mixture of wine, oranges, and sugar."

[34] Not used. See Introduction, p. xxxix.

[35] Not used. SJ lived at No. 17 Gough Square from 1747 until 23 Mar. 1759, when he moved to Staple Inn (Clifford, *Johnson*, p. 293; *Life* iii. 535). According to Hawkins (p. 365) he was compelled to leave his house in Gough Square for lack of funds; but Hector's story gains some support from an entry in SJ's *Prayers and Meditations*, dated 25 Mar. 1759: "callest me to a . . . reformation of my thoughts words and practices. . . . let the change which I am now making in outward things, produce in [me] . . . a change of manners" (*Diaries*, p. 68). In one of his notebooks on SJ's writings, JB alludes to this passage with the query: "what was the *change* he was going to make?"

Sir Henry Gough, Bt. (d. 1798) added in 1788 the name of his maternal uncle, Sir Henry Calthorpe, whose estates he had inherited, and in 1796 he became Baron Calthorpe of Calthorpe (Norfolk) (*Comp. Peer*. ii. 490). Hector's acquaintance with Gough may be accounted for by the fact that Gough was brought up in Edgbaston, which forms the west district of Birmingham.

[36] 1732–34.

there was the same apprehension after he went to London. Johnson had been conscious of it all along but had been affraid to ask Hector for fear of an answer in the affirmative. When last at Birmingham he asked Hector if he had observed in him a tendency to be disorde[re]d in his mind. Hector said he had.[37] Hector did not think he would have died so soon. As Water had been carried from his scrotum by punctures he suggested it might be taken by the same means from his legs and that he might grow better.[38] Johnson gave a spring of joy, and said "You have given me another twig." Parson Ford a Relation of his by the mother's side recommended to him to be sent to Stourbridge School.[39] Dr. Johnson some years ago told me there was no man alive who had seen him drunk. Mr. Hector said—"Then he had forgot me." For once when he lived at Birmingham there came a Relation of his of the name of Ford from Stourbridge[40] to whom he had been under obligations. He was it seems a hard drinker and he engaged Johnson and Hector to spend the evening with him at the Swan Inn. Johnson said to Hector "This fellow will make[41] us both drunk. Let us take him by turns, and get rid of him." It was settled that Hector should go first. He and Ford had drank three bottles of Port before Johnson came. When Johnson arrived, Hector found he had been drinking at Mr. Porter's instead of saving himself. Hector went to bed at the Swan leaving Johnson to drink on with Ford. Next morning he perceived that Johnson who had been his bedfellow had been Very drunk and he damned him. Johnson tried to deny the charge. *Literally* speaking Hector had not *seen* him drunk, though he was *sure* of the fact.[42] I said He must have been a monstrous Silenus.

[37] Not used; cf. *ante* From Hector, 1 Feb. 1785 and n. 23. JB carefully explains that SJ himself had confounded madness with melancholy, and shows impatience with those who "have given credit to his groundless opinion" (*Life* i. 66, iii. 98–99, 175). See Introduction, p. xl.

[38] See *Life* iv. 399 and n. 6, 418 n. 1.

[39] See *ante* From Hector, 1 Feb. 1785 and n. 26.

[40] "Parson" Ford, to whom SJ was surely "under obligations" and of whom it was said "that no liquor could fluster him" (*Johns. Glean.* ix. 1), would qualify eminently, had he not died in 1731, or a year before SJ was living in Birmingham. It is clear in any case from the context that another Ford is meant: perhaps SJ's maternal uncle, Cornelius Ford (1674–?buried 1734 at Old Swinford, near Stourbridge), famous as a broad-jumper (*Reades*, pp. 156–57; *Anecdotes: Johns. Misc.* i. 149), or Gregory Ford (1706–48), of Stourbridge, SJ's first cousin (*Reades*, Tabular Pedigree xxix).

[41] MS. orig. "fill"

[42] Not used. See Introduction, pp. xlii–xliii. Reynolds was another who is said never to have seen SJ intoxicated but once (*Life* i. 379 n. 2). See also Journ. 24 Apr. 1779.

From the Rev. John Batteridge Pearson,[1] Saturday 2 April 1785

MS. Hyde.

ADDRESS: James Boswell Esqe.

Lichfield, April 2nd 1785[2]

DEAR SIR, I hope you will re[c]eive safe, enclosed in three Covers, twelve Letters from Dr. Johnson to Mrs. Porter. Mrs. P. has examined her Papers, but did not find any others that are material. She gives you liberty to publish as many of them as you think proper.[3]

She joins with me in best Respects and Wishes to you. I am, Dear Sir, with much esteem, your most obedient

J. B. PEARSON

Mrs. Porter begs you will return the Letters as soon as you have done with them.[4]

To the Rev. John Batteridge Pearson, Thursday 7 April 1785

MS. Mrs. Sherburne Prescott of Greenwich, Connecticut.

ADDRESS (by Sir Charles Preston): Revd. Mr. Pearson, Litchfield.

FRANK: London seventh April 1785. free Chas. Preston.

London, 7 April 1785

REVEREND AND DEAR SIR: I am favoured with the Packets containing Dr. Johnson's letters to Mrs. Porter twelve in number of which

---

[1] The Rev. John Batteridge Pearson (1749–1808), Perpetual Curate of St. Michael's, Lichfield, 1774–82, and later Prebendary of Pipe Parva in Lichfield Cathedral. He was Lucy Porter's principal heir and executor. See *Johns. Glean.* i. 14 ff. JB met him at Lichfield 25 Mar. 1776 and described him as "a modest, well behaved young man much esteemed by Mrs. Porter" (Journ.).

[2] MS. "1784"

[3] See *ante* From Seward, 25 Mar. 1785 and n. 4. JB published ten, stating (*Life*

ii. 387 n. 3) that none of SJ's letters to Lucy Porter written before 1775 had been preserved; but a number of these early letters were printed by Malone and by Croker (who acquired them from Pearson's widow through the agency of Dr. Harwood). See *Life* i. 512–16; Croker, 1831, i. xviii.

[4] Miss Porter died in 1786, and the letters were never returned. They were recovered at Fettercairn and are now in the Hyde Collection.

I shall be very careful, and shall return them, as soon as I have published my Memoirs of that great Man in which I intend to introduce them; for, they all do credit at least to his heart. As it may be some time before my Work is ready for the press, I shall (if Mrs. Porter be impatient to have the letters again) return them sooner.

I beg you may present my best compliments to her with thanks for this favour. You will please accept of the same yourself for the trouble you have been pleased to take. I will be still more obliged to you, if you will write down and send me, all the Anecdotes and sayings of Dr. Johnson which you can perfectly recollect, let them be ever so minute. Will you also do me the kindness to put Mr. Henry White[1] in mind of his promise to let me have all that he recollects. I wish to preserve all we can. I am with sincere regard, Dear Sir, Your most humble servant,

JAMES BOSWELL

From Dr. Richard Brocklesby, ?17–18 April 1785[1]

MSS. Yale (C 583, C 580). The first is in JB's hand and is endorsed (by ?Malone): "Dr. Brocklesby"; the second is in Brocklesby's hand.

[I]

Dr. Brocklesby

Sir if you were driven by a storm of rain to take shelter under an oak tree in company with Burke, he would describe the shower of rain though a very common thing—he would describe it in so

---

[1] The Rev. Henry White (1761–1836), grandson of John Hunter by his second wife, Lucy Porter (1690–1768). He succeeded his father, the Rev. Thomas White (c. 1711–84), as Sacrist of Lichfield Cathedral in 1784, and was Perpetual Curate of St. Chad's, Lichfield, from 1814 until his death (*Life* iv. 547).

[1] In his letter of 27 Dec. 1784 (*ante*) Brocklesby had informed JB that he possessed SJ's "curious dicta on the Subject and Importance of Faith" (the second of the present MSS.) and had promised "divers particulars more when we next meet in London". I have conjecturally assigned the MSS. to 17 and 18 Apr., the first of several recorded meetings between JB and Brocklesby this spring. On 29 June Brocklesby turned over sixteen of SJ's letters (Journ.); on 29 Jan. 1791 JB reports to Malone that he has twenty (*post*). Extracts from sixteen are printed in *Life* iv. 353 ff.; all twenty were found at Fettercairn and are now in the Hyde Collection. For the complete texts, see *Letters SJ passim*.

animated and lively a picture that to hear him go on you would be contented for the pleasure he gave you to be wet to the skin.[2]

Dr. Johnson often expressed the feelings and uncertainties of his mind to Dr. Brocklesby. But about a forthnight before his death he one morning in rapture of exultation said "My Freind I am fully persuaded that to be a good Christian is the sheet anchor of our hope. There is nothing that will stand the test in the hours of trial but a firm confidence in the truth of the christian religion. And if you are unacquainted with Dr. Clarks writings let me conjure you to read them with a diligent and earnest desire to be convinced." Upon which he repeated the greatest part of the following passage from the 9th volume 5 Sermon of Dr. Clarke on perfection

And is it then possible etc.[3]

and recommended to the Dr. to buy Clarke's sermons and study what he had said upon the expiatory sacrifice of Jesus Christ.[4]

He then went on nearly to the following purpose and made Dr. Brocklesby[5] write it down and read it over to him,[6]

[II]

In a conversation with the pious Mr. Johnson 28th Novr. he repeated his concern about the speculative Opinions I entertained about Xianity; the good Man apprehended, I had too loosely considerd the Doctrines of our Religion, and with love of my Soul he pressed me to turn the subject most seriously over and over in my mind: "For" added he, "besides the extraordinary good laws, and moral precepts in the Gospel, it is highly necessary to believe that Our Saviour Jesus Christ was sent by God himself into this world, by his death to approve himself an expiatory Sacrifice for lost and undone Mankind and as all Nations of the World have entertained

---

[2] SJ's compliment to Burke was known to JB in at least three other versions: the one recorded in the journal for 15 Aug. 1773, the one which replaced it in the printing of the *Tour* (*Life* v. 34), and the one (actually two in succession) in the *Life* under 15 May 1784 (iv. 275). See also BP vi. 172–73; *Tour*, ed. F. A. Pottle and C. H. Bennett, rev. ed. 1961, p. 19, n. 15 and additional note, p. 409; and *Johns. Misc.* i. 290 and 421.

[3] "And is it then possible that mortal man, should in any Sense attain unto *Perfection?*" etc. (*Sermons* ix, 1731, 95 ff.).

[4] See *ante* From Brocklesby, 27 Dec. 1784 and n. 10–10.

[5] MS. "Brocklesby"

[6] JB originally intended to print Brocklesby's account, and edited the MS. (for style and emphasis). Instead, he summarizes, *Life* iv. 414. Cf. SJ's "advices" to Sastres, *post* 22 Feb. 1786.

faith in bloody Sacrifices to the offended Majesty of Heaven so as good Christians we ought to and must believe that the death of our Saviour on our account was the Seal or final Sacrifice to be made for our Redemption": and then in a fervent Strain of extemporary unpremeditated devotion he prayed that these doctrines might lay a deep hold on my heart, and that they might do away whatever difficulties had lain in my way to which He wished me seriously to say Amen.[7] He added many friendly wishes, and expressions of his Sense of my kindness in his Sickness and on other occasions, and wished the conviction of these doctrines through his means might overtake and rest with me which he said would be ample and abundant recompense for all or more, than I had ever done for him, and this he again prayed devoutly for, in the name and through the Grace of our Lord and Saviour Jesus Christ.

N.B. He insisted on my instantly committing as nearly as I could collect my sense of this conversation to black and white, with which I complied as above, and shewed the same by his own desire to himself and he approved the same.

RICHARD BROCKLESBY

From Thomas Percy, Bishop of Dromore, Saturday 23 April 1785

MS. Yale (C 2232).

ADDRESS: To James Boswell Esqr., of Auchenlech, at Edenburgh.[1]

POSTMARKS: AP 23, AP 28.

Dublin, April 23. 1785

. . .—I am truly glad that you continue the Intention of giving your Johnsoniana to the World. —I will try to rub up my Memory and will transmit to you every thing worth notice, that I can recollect of this extraordinary Man. —I unfortunately neglected to commit to Paper his *Dicta* as they occur'd to me, so that I fear I shall [not]

---

[7] According to Hannah More (*Memoirs* i. 393), SJ "caught hold of his hand with great earnestness, and cried, 'Doctor! you do not say *Amen*.' The Doctor looked foolish, but after a pause, cried '*Amen*'" (quoted by Hill, *Life* iv. 414 n. 3).

[1] Despite JB's instructions at the end of his letter of 20 Mar. to write to him at Gen. Paoli's in London. On 1 July JB wrote to Percy from London that the letter came to his house at Edinburgh but had got lost, "so I have not received it".

preserve many of these worth your notice. —But I recollect a few facts that I have heard of his early years which are peculiar and characteristic; and as I do not see them retailed in any of the periodical Publications, they may possibly be new to *you also*: These I shall commit to Paper and whatever else I think will answer your purpose and do all I can to *scrattle*[2] for you. —I have a few Letters of his, but they were meer short Billets and not of consequence to merit Publication.[3] . . .

To Anna Seward, Saturday 30 April 1785

MS. Yale (L 1150). JB's copy, headed: "To Miss Seward."

London, 30 April 1785

MY DEAR MADAM: I am quite ashamed that I have not e'er now returned one of your jewels which you kindly lent me—the enclosed letter from Mr. Hayley, out of which I have taken what I wanted for my Great Biographical Monument.[1] I tell every body it will be an Egyptian Pyramid in which there will be a compleat mummy of Johnson that Literary Monarch.

Be so kind as put your cousin Mr. Henry White as also Mr. Pearson in mind of their obliging promise to write down and send me *All* that they recollect of the Mighty Sage. . . .

[2] Keep on scratching (OED).

[3] Thirteen letters, ranging between 1760 and 1776 (one undated), have been recovered (*Letters SJ passim*). Percy's estimate of them is accurate.

[1] JB's transcript, headed "Dr. Johnson/ Mr. Hayley to Miss Seward/March 18— 1785", reads: "I am highly pleased with your character of the Old Lion. Pray tell your Freind Boswell with my compliments that I hope he will insert it entire in the biographical Work which the World expects from him with all the eagerness of literary affection./It delights me to hear that my impromptu on the Colossal Critick entertained you so much. In return for your tenderness to this Liliputian Poem I give you full permission to send it to your freind Boswell if you think it will please him in any degree. He may tack it if he pleases to your character of the fallen Colossus. I shall be proud to attend you in any post either as your Gentleman Usher or your page." The extract was not used. JB's subsequent quarrel with Miss Seward necessarily meant a quarrel with her fellow poet and alter ego. In *Gent. Mag.* for Nov. 1793 (lxiii. 1011) he wrote: "What are we to think of the scraps of letters between her and Mr. Hayley, impotently attempting to undermine the noble pedestal on which the public opinion has placed Dr. Johnson?" Miss Seward's "character of the Old Lion" appeared in *The General Evening Post* for 27 Dec. 1784—"without my name; because my friend, his daughter-in-law, Mrs. Lucy Porter, would resent the fidelity of the portrait. She thinks he was almost next to the Deity in perfection" (To Sophia Weston,

From the Rev. Richard George Robinson,[1] ?April 1785

MS. Yale (C 2396).

ADDRESS: James Boswell Esqr., General Paoli's, Seymour Street, Portman square.

ENDORSEMENT: Rev. R. G. Robinson.

[London]

DEAR SIR: I did myself the honor of inquiring for you at the general's a few days ago, to communicate to you an anecdote of your late friend, which I have picked up since I had the pleasure of seeing you;[2] and which was told me by Mr. Howard of Lichfield,[3] whose father[4] was the doctor's schoolfellow, and from whom he had the relation. Whenever the doctor was in a state of delinquency, from whatever cause, he used to enter the school with his back to his master, and to sneak along to his seat in that direction. Being a favorite with Mr. Hunter, either from being a boy of genius, or because their political principles were congenial, he seldom took any other notice of him, than by a smile, though a remarkably severe disciplinarian.[5] As you wish, Sir, to know every, the most minute circumstance relative to him, I will take this opportunity of giving you his opinion, in his own words, of Mrs. Macaulay's statue being placed in St. Stephen's church. About the time of its removal I dined with him at Mr. Seward's, and wishing to know his opinion, desired Mr. Seward to ask it. Being absorbed in deep contemplation, he did not at first understand the question; but upon its being repeated, exclaimed with great energy, "Oh! aye, aye, poor foolish Wilson! aye, aye. Sir, the man was a fool for doing it,

23 Mar. 1785: *Seward Letters* i. 35–36). For earlier versions of her characterization of SJ, see *post* From Astle, Dec. 1786, n. 46.

[1] The Rev. Richard George Robinson (?1737–1825), B.C.L., Chancellor's Vicar of Lichfield Cathedral (*Johns. Glean.* ix. 99–100). In 1794 he wrote to *Gent. Mag.* (lxiv. 875–76) protesting SJ's characterization of Thomas Seward as a valetudinarian (*Life* iii. 152). The letter was plainly intended as ammunition in support of

Anna Seward's paper war with JB (see *post* From Hector, 9 Jan. 1794 and n. 6).

[2] Apparently 26–27 Mar., when JB was in Lichfield. The journal does not mention Robinson, but: "27 Received the holy sacrament in Lichfield Cathedral."

[3] See *ante* From Adams, June 1784, n. 1.

[4] Charles Howard (1707–71), Proctor in the Ecclesiastical Court of Lichfield (*Johns. Glean.* iv. 112 ff.). See *Life* i. 80.

[5] Not used. Cf. *ante* To Seward, 15 Feb. 1785, n. 6.

and she was as great a one for permitting it."[6] The conversation concerning Dr. Dodd, which I wrote down for Miss Seward passed the same afternoon.[7]

If you deem these little anecdotes worth being communicated, it will give great pleasure to, Sir, your most obedient humble Servant

RICH. GEO. ROBINSON

I have had the pleasure of meeting Mr. Hamilton[8] several times.

Johnsoniana Related by the Rev. Dr. John Taylor,[1] London, Friday 6 May 1785

MS. Yale (C 2641). In JB's hand.

[6] Not used. The statue of Catharine Macaulay (1731–91), in the character of History, was placed within the altar-rails of St. Stephen Walbrook on 8 Sept. 1777 by her friend and patron, Dr. Thomas Wilson (1703–84), the Rector. According to DNB (s.v. Macaulay), he had it removed after her second marriage —on 17 Dec. 1778 to William Graham, a twenty-one-year-old surgeon's mate (see Journ. 9 Sept. 1790). According to DNB (s.v. Wilson), the vestry ordered him to remove it, the date not being specified. In any case, a discrepancy remains between the date of the removal of the statue, or indeed even of its installation, and the supposed date of SJ's observation (see next note).

[7] Between 7 and 29 Aug. 1777 (Letters SJ). A record of this conversation was communicated to Croker by the Rev. Hastings Robinson, Rector of Great Warley, Essex, son of JB's correspondent. According to this version, Anna Seward was herself present (Johns. Misc. ii. 417). The next month, at Ashbourne, SJ gave JB an account of Dr. Dodd (Life iii. 139 ff.).

[8] Probably Alexander Hamilton, of Grange, who accompanied JB to London 21 Mar. (Journ.).

[1] John Taylor, D.D. (1711–88), SJ's schoolmate at Lichfield and life-long friend. He held a number of preferments in the Church, the last (from 1784) being the rectorship of St. Margaret's, Westminster. SJ visited him almost annually at his estate in Ashbourne, and was joined by JB in 1776 and 1777 (Life ii. 473 ff., iii. 135 ff.; Journ. 26–27 Mar. 1776, 14–24 Sept. 1777; see also Note Book, passim). "He is an excellent Justice of Peace, and has a considerable political interest which he gives to the Devonshire Family. He is like the Father or Sovereign of Ashburn. He last winter gave away £200 among it's inhabitants who were in want of assistance. He keeps a good deal of land in his own hand, breeds horses and remarkable large cattel and game fowls. He has no wit, but, as Dr. Johnson observed, a very strong understanding" (Journ. 26 Mar. 1776). See the abusive character of Taylor by JB's correspondent, the Rev. Daniel Astle, post Dec. 1786. On 6 May 1785 JB "Dined with Dr. Taylor of West[minste]r tete a tete, and he dictated a greal deal about Dr. Johnson which I wrote down" (Journ.). The present MS. is doubtless the result, and though it is substantial enough, it is strange that Taylor did not make, or JB solicit, a larger contribution to the Life. Perhaps the fact that "Dr. Johnson had cautioned" him in 1777 "against giving implicit faith to Taylor's narratives" (Journ. 18 Sept.) accounts for the absence in this case of JB's characteristic importunity in dealing with SJ's old friends. But it cannot account for the paucity of letters from SJ to

Communications concerning Dr. Johnson
from the Rev. Dr. Taylor[2]

When at School he was not remarkable for he was very idle.[3] It was a practice for one boy to get the lesson to construe it and teach the rest. Johnson till towards the latter end of his being at School could not do it. His exertion was roused by his pride being hurt. Lowe[4] once refused to assist him. This made him resolve to be independent. [5]In the same form with him were Lowe

Taylor (only three) which JB printed in the *Life*. Taylor was one of SJ's principal correspondents throughout his lifetime (see *Letters SJ passim* and Mary Hyde, "Not in Chapman," *Johnson, Boswell and Their Circle*, pp. 310, 312, 317), and faithfully preserved his letters, three of which he published in 1787 along with his own (and perhaps partly SJ's: see Chapman in RES, 1926, ii. 338–39) *Letter to Samuel Johnson, LL.D. on the Subject of a Future State*. It is easier to believe, in the absence of records, that JB was refused SJ's letters than that he did not solicit them, and if so, the reasons are at hand. First, many of the letters deal quite candidly with Taylor's personal affairs, and second, Taylor appears to have contemplated publishing them himself. That these reasons are not contradictory is clear from the number of erasures of intimate passages in the original MSS.: see *Letters SJ*, App. D. On 22 Mar. Mrs. Piozzi wrote to Lysons from Florence: "Do you know who Dr. Taylor gives his Anecdotes to? Mr. Johnson bid me once ask *him* for Memoirs if I was the survivor [cf. *Anecdotes: Johns. Misc.* i. 166 and *Thraliana*, pp. 173, 625–26], & so I would, but I am afraid of a Refusal, as I guess Sir Jno. Hawkins is already in possession of all that Dr. Taylor has to bestow" (Clifford, *Piozzi*, p. 243). Whether or not Hawkins was already in possession of all he certainly was eventually in possession of some: namely, those anecdotes which the present MS. shows to have been independently transmitted to Hawkins and JB. As neither biographer acknowledged his source, it might easily have been supposed that JB

copied from Hawkins. Mrs. Piozzi managed to tap Taylor finally (see *Thraliana*, p. 690)—too late for her *Anecdotes* (1786) but in time for supplementing her *Letters To and From the Late Samuel Johnson, LL.D.* (1788): see the anecdotes at ii. 381–82, 384–85; and *post* n. 21.

[2] The title is a later addition.

[3] In the MS. *Life* (opp. p. 12—the second so numbered) occurs the following cancelled passage: "The Reverend Dr. Taylor Prebendary of Westminster who was also his schoolfellow differs from Mr. Hector in his account [*alternatively* has given me a different account from that of Mr. Hector in his recollection] alledging that he made no distinguished figure being very idle. But Johnson's extraordinary powers might well shew themselves conspicuously though his application was remiss, and Mr. Hector's recollection appeared to me clearer and more distinct. But besides thus ballancing the testimony of one schoolfellow against the other, and perceiving the greater weight in the scale of Mr. Hector, I have perfect conviction on that side from Johnson's own authority which all who knew him allowed to be true in the full sense of the word to a degree far beyond the common authenticity of Relation." See *ante* From Hector, 1 Feb. 1785.

[4] The Rev. Theophilus Lowe (c. 1708–69), Rector of Merton and Stiffkey, Canon of Windsor (*Johns. Glean.* iii. 125–26).

[5-5] *Life* i. 45. William Connolly of Ireland became lord of the manor of Congreve, at Stretton, in 1751 (L. Margaret Midgley, *A History of the County of Stafford*, 1958, iv. 165).

afterwards Canon of Windsor and Tutor to Lord Townshend[6] and Charles[7] who never thought highly of Johnson, till he burst upon the World as an Authour. Congreve[8] who was Chaplain to Arch Bishop Boulter[9] and got good preferment in Ireland. He was a younger son of the Ancient family of Congreve in Staffordshire.[10] His brother sold the Estate to Mr. Connoly.[5]

When Dr. Johnson was last at Ashbourne[11] he said to Dr. Taylor, "I am resolved to confine myself to a milk diet I see it does you so much good."[12] That very day there was a glorious haunch of vennison at Taylor's table. Dr. Johnson eat and eat again. Alsop[13] who did not like him, wickedly prest him to eat more— which he did. He grew so ill that it was feared he would have died of downright eating, and had not a Surgeon been got to administer to him without delay a Glister he must have died. After this, he took to a milk diet, and he improved so much in his health that he became quite a new man and beat them all in walking home from church.[14]

The last time Dr. Taylor saw him was on the saturday before his death.[15] He was then very ill and looked ghastly. There were in the room Mrs. Hoole[16] and the Reverend Mr. Evans Rector of St. Olaves Southwark.[17] He said to Dr. Taylor, "Dr. you now see

[6] George Townshend, fourth Viscount and first Marquess Townshend (1724–1807), Lord Lieutenant of Ireland.

[7] Charles Townshend (1725–67), Chancellor of the Exchequer.

[8] The Rev. Charles Congreve (1708–77), Archdeacon of Armagh and Vicar-General of Ireland. See *Life* ii. 460, 537–38.

[9] See *ante* From T. Campbell, 7 Jan. 1785 and n. 7.

[10] Charles and Richard (1714–82) were born at Stretton, the sons of John Congreve, of Congreve, first cousin to William, the dramatist (*Johns. Glean.* iii. 126–27). See SJ's *Life of Congreve: Lives* ii. 212; *Letters SJ* 3.2, 75.2, and *passim*.

[11] 20 July–18 Sept. 1784 (*Life* iii. 455).

[12] Cf. *Letters SJ* 747, 749.

[13] John Alsop (c. 1726–1804) was one of the governors of the Ashbourne Grammar School and a justice of the peace for Derbyshire (*Life* iii. 504–05). In Dec. 1779 JB made a list of people he used to see at Taylor's. It includes:

"Mr. & Mrs. Alsop—The name is pronounced here *Awsop*. *He* is a roun-headed Squire, & I was told this of him . . . that when he is asked—Jack—What time do you go to bed? He answers—I don't know. About the time one gets drunk I think" (Journ.).

[14] Not used; see Introduction, p. xlii. For SJ's intemperance in eating, see *Life* i. 468, iv. 72 and 330–31.

[15] 11 Dec. 1784. Taylor's statement is confirmed by John Hoole's record of SJ's last days (*Johns. Misc.* ii. 158). Taylor's account, however, is conspicuously missing from JB's own narrative, based on several sources, of the final illness, *Life* iv. 399 ff.

[16] Susannah (Smith) Hoole. She, her husband (see *post* From Hoole, 17 June 1790), and her son, the Rev. Samuel Hoole, all attended SJ during his last days (*Johns. Misc.* ii. 146 ff.).

[17] The Rev. James Evans (d. c. 1786), Rector of St. Saviour's and St. Olave's, Southwark, "an intimate acquaintance"

me[18] My Physicians have now left me and I am in the hands of
GOD only." Dr. Taylor said "You cannot be in better hands; and I
hope GOD will be merciful to you." Dr. Johnson then uttered aloud
an extempore prayer of some length which he concluded with
imploring GOD to accept his imperfect repentance and grant him a
most humble place in his Kingdom of Heaven, to which the Company all said Amen.[19] Dr. Taylor then began to apologise for being
so long without making him a visit; but he hoped Dr. Butter[20]
had told him how ill he had been and that it was not possible for
him to go out of his house. Dr. Johnson (who thought Dr. Taylor
more a Malade imaginaire than really ill and when he took a fancy
of whatever sort into his head, there was no beating it out) answered "Sir I will tell you a story; though it ill becomes me in my
present situation to tell stories. A Lady whom a Cancer had with
the most excruciating torture brought to the verge of the grave
into which to end her torment She was eager to escape, sent
several messages to another Lady her old freind whom she was
impatient to see whose conversation allways gave her the greatest
pleasure and of whose judgement she had the highest opinion.
At last when she came she was full of excuses; lamented much that
it had not been in her power to come sooner for She herself had
been afflicted with a most painful disorder. She had had a Whitlow."
Considering Dr. Johnson's fancy as to Dr. Taylor's illness this was
an Excellent Allegory An Admirable *de te fabula narratur*.[21] —Dr.
Johnson then said "My Dear Doctor dont go yet; for I have very
much to say to you." —The Company most improperly did not take
the hint. Dr. Taylor staid till another person whom he forgets
came into the room—and then he went away—and he never saw his
old freind Dr. Johnson any more.[22]

[23]Dr. Taylor tells me that Hunter was an excellent Master. His
Ushers were eminent men. Holbrook was one of the most ingenious

of SJ and Mrs. Thrale (*Anecdotes: Johns.
Misc.* i. 252–53; *Letters SJ*, Index). See
also *Life* iii. 537.

[18] A short space is left blank in the MS.
[19] Cf. *Diaries*, pp. 417–18.
[20] William Butter, M.D. (1726–1805),
one of Taylor's physicians, also attended
SJ in his last illness. He was educated at
Edinburgh, migrated to Derby, and from
1781 practised in London. His wife was
related to JB (*Life* iii. 467–68, 163).
See also *ibid*. ii. 474–75, iv. 110, 492.

[21] Horace, *Satires* I. i. 69. The anecdote
was printed by Mrs. Piozzi in her *Letters
To and From Johnson* (ii. 382).
[22] Taylor's signature appears at this
point in the MS. ". . . he, at my request,
signed his name, to give it authenticity"
(*Life* iv. 375–76).
[23-23] *Life* i. 44–45, combined with the
passage in the opening paragraph on
SJ's classmates.

men best scholars and best preachers of his time. He married Mrs. Hunter's sister Aunt to Mrs. Seward Mother of the celebrated Poetess.[24] He was Usher the greatest part of the time that Johnson was at School. Then came Hague[25] of whom as much may be said with the addition that he was an elegant Poet. Green afterwards Bishop of Lincoln[26] succeeded Hague and his character in the learned World is well known.[23]

Dr. Taylor had a little quarrel with Dr. Johnson when they were both at School. Taylor at breakfast in the kitchen repeated the following Epigram in presence of Mrs. Hunter[27] and some of the boys

> Here lies honest Sam as quiet's a Lamb
> Who in his life ne'er did much evil
> His bones are here laid but his soul I'm afraid
> Is gone to the high road to the Devil.

One of the boys told Johnson and he was very angry. Dr. Taylor bid me say *he did not know who wrote this Epigram* and I promised to him *upon my honour* I should not say *he* did.[28]

Johnson never would have thought of going to Oxford nor would his Father have thought of sending him, the expence being so great had it not been that Andrew Corbet Esquire his schoolfellow a Shropshire Gentleman (who afterwards had the great fortune of his relation Corbet Kynaston Esquire of the same county left to him) spontaneously undertaken [*sic*] to defray his charges in order to have him as his companion in his studies. Johnson accordingly went to Oxford, and took possession of the rooms in Pembroke College which Corbet had hired—(the rooms over the gate which I have visited with veneration). But Corbet who had been at Oxford a year or two before, never returned to it, and it is known that he never advanced one shilling for Johnson.[29] [30]About a year

[24] This sentence is omitted. The Rev. Edward Holbrook (1695–1772), Vicar of St. Mary's, Lichfield from 1744, married in 1723 Israel Norton (b. 1685), sister of Hunter's first wife, Ann Norton (*Johns. Glean.* ii. 114, iii. 113).

[25] Not further identified. Musgrave lists William Hague (d. 1789) and —— Hague (d. 1794)—both schoolmasters.

[26] See *ante* From Adams, 17 Feb. 1785 and n. 3.

[27] The first Mrs. Hunter, who died c. 1722. Hunter did not remarry until

1726, when SJ was out of school (*Johns. Glean.* i. 19, 33).

[28] The anecdote was not used.

[29] *Life* i. 58. Cf. *ante* From Adams, 17 Feb. 1785. Andrew Corbet (1709–41), whose name is omitted from JB's account, matriculated 3 May 1727 from Pembroke College, but took no degree. "The Buttery Books show that his normal battels ceased after 1 Nov. 1728, the very week when Johnson's began . . . and that, though his name is still among the gentlemen commoners down to Oct.

after Johnson had gone to Oxford[31] Dr. Taylor was taken by his Father Thomas Taylor Esq. of Ashbourne with intention to enter him of Pembroke that he might be with Johnson as had been agreed between the two freinds in letters on account of their great intimacy which had been kept up by a constant correspondence by letters. The moment that young Taylor lighted at the Crown Inn he hastened to his freind who took him directly into his room and upon Dr. Taylor's announcing to him that he had obtained his Father's consent to be admitted of the same College with him, Johnson with that conscientiousness which attended him through life immediately objected and said "I cannot in conscience suffer you to enter here. For the Tutor under whom you must be[32] is such a Blockhead that you will not be five minutes at his lectures till you find out what a fool he is and upbraid me with your looks for recommending you to him." The plan therefore was changed. Johnson made inquiry all through the University and from what he collected found that Mr. Bateman[33] of Christ Church was the most celebrated tutor, and Taylor was accordingly entered of Christ Church.[34] Bateman's lectures upon the Classicks Logick and Ethicks and preparatory to the Mathematicks in Algebra were so excellent that Johnson came every day and had them at second hand from Taylor. At last Johnson was so poor that he had not shoes to his feet, but his toes were seen naked. Some of the Christchurchmen smoaked this while he stood upon the pavement of Peckwater[35] and Johnson saw this. He therefore would never again come to Christ church. His pride or rather dignity of mind[36] was such that it was in vain to offer him money and some person (supposed to be Vyse of Lichfield afterwards Canon of that Cathedral a most respectable man and father of Dr. Vyse Prebendary of Canterbury and of the amiable and worthy Colonel Vyse)[37] having set a pair of shoes at his door he

1731 . . . he was never in residence again" (*Johns. Glean.* v. 121–22). He succeeded to several estates in Shropshire under the will of his relation, Corbet Kynaston, of Hordley (1690–1740), M.P. for Shrewsbury, 1714–23, and for Shropshire, 1734–40 (*ibid.* v. 122–23; Judd 2636).

30–30 *Life* i. 76–77.

31 It was nearer to four months (*Johns. Glean.* v. 13).

32 William Jorden (*ante* From Adams, June 1784 and nn. 12, 17).

33 The Rev. Edmund Bateman (1704–

51), later a prebendary of Lichfield and Chancellor of Lichfield Cathedral (*Johns. Glean.* v. 13–14).

34 Matriculating 10 Mar. 1729, aged 17 (*Johns. Glean.* v. 13).

35 Peckwater Quad, Christ Church.

36 Probably JB's distinction.

37 (1) William Vyse (1709–70), Treasurer of Lichfield Cathedral, 1734; later Archdeacon of Salop and Rector of St. Philip's, Birmingham. He matriculated from Pembroke College on 11 Feb. 1727. (2) His elder son, William Vyse, D.C.L.

threw them away with indignation.[30] [38]Taylor then in the hand-somest manner without seeming to know his reason for not coming to Christ Church said to Johnson that he'd come to him at his own college, and repeat Bateman's lectures which he did as long as John-son staid. The last lecture which he meant to carry him was the solu-tion of a Problem in Algebra. Taylor however had lost it. He went to two or three of his fellow students who had lost it likewise. He then went to the chambers of Mr. Whitehorn,[39] a Gentleman Commoner, a west Indian, and there Mr. Bateman happened to be who seeing Taylor come in immediately asked him what he came there for. Taylor who had the book in his hand told him he had forgot the Solution of the Problem in that day's lecture and wished to recover it. Upon which Mr. Bateman with a most obliging complacency immediately went over it again. Taylor then run to Johnson, but could not report it so precisely as to make him understand it. A few days after this Johnson being miserably poor set out for Lichfield very early in a morning having hid his toes in a pair of large boots. Taylor went with him as far as Banbury and returned at night.[38]

Johnson's translation of the *Messiah* was first printed for his Father, without his knowledge or consent. Johnson told Taylor he was very angry at this and in his violent manner said if it had not been his Father he would have cut his throat;[40] for he wished to have some freind first to introduce it to Pope. He was told that

(1742–1816), Rector of Lambeth, 1777, and Chancellor of Lichfield, 1798; see *post* From Hector, 8 Apr. 1791. (3) His younger son, Richard Vyse (1746–1825), a colonel in 1781, a general in 1812 (*Johns. Glean.* v. 21–22; *Letters SJ*, Index; DNB s.v. Richard William Howard Vyse).

[38-38] Not used.

[39] William Whitehorne, of St. Ann's, Jamaica. He matriculated 10 Oct. 1727, aged 16 (*Alum. Oxon.*).

[40] Toned down, *Life* i. 61; see Intro-duction, p. xxxvii. What follows concern-ing Pope was not used. JB states simply: "It is said, that Mr. Pope expressed him-self concerning it in terms of strong appro-bation." Cf. Hawkins, p. 13. In the MS. *Life* (p. 22) JB noted in the margin: "Investigate the time of its being printed in Husbands' Miscellany and Taylor's Account of his Father's having it done

etc." A fuller memorandum occurs, deleted, among some notes for revising the MS. *Life*: "⟨P.⟩ 22 Adjust as to his translation of Messiah Taylors story of his Father publishing it and then its coming out in a Miscellany at Oxford by J. Husbands A.M. with this modest motto from Scaliger's Poeticks Ex alieno ingenio Poeta, ex suo tantum versifi-cator." JB was not able to adjust the two publications, and nothing more is known "of his Father publishing it". Hawkins (p. 13) identified the "some-body" who showed the poem to Pope as "a son of Dr. Arbuthnot, then a gentle-man-commoner of Christchurch": i.e. Charles Arbuthnot, who matriculated 5 June 1724, aged 19, took his B.A. in 1728, his M.A. "in holy orders" in 1731, and died the same year, 1 Dec., in Dublin (*Alum. Oxon.*).

when somebody did shew it to Pope, Pope said it was very finely done, but that he had seen it before, and said nothing more either of it or its Authour which disgusted Johnson very much and made him express himself strongly as above. When Johnson's *London a Poem* came out it is said Mr. Lyttelton carried it to Pope and insisted it was his, and would not be persuaded but that it was his till the real Authour was discovered.[41] Johnson sent this admirable performance to Dr. Taylor in manuscript that he might read it over, which he did, but made nor suggested no Alterations.

His Scheme of translating Father Paul's *History of the Council of Trent* was rendered abortive by its being taken up by another Samuel Johnson Librarian of St. Martins and Curate of that parish, and as the Clergy particularly Pearce afterwards Bishop of Rochester patronised him, Our Johnson dropt his scheme and the other Johnson did not go on with his. Several squibs in Advertisements etc. passed between the two.[42] He then took up his design of compiling the English Dictionary. He sent his Plan to Dr. Taylor in the country* and desired his opinion of it. Dr. Taylor was coming to London and did come immediately and the very day after his arrival who should come to make him a visit but Whitehead the late Poet Laureat. The Plan was lying upon the table and Taylor shewed it to Whitehead who was much pleased with so much of it as he had time to read and as Dr. Taylor was obliged to go out, begged

* Dr. Taylor has that copy of the Plan still. It was returned to Dr. Johnson and he gave it again to Taylor within a few years of his death. It is written in a bad hand but more legible than Johnson's own.[43]

[41] Not used. Cf. Hawkins, p. 60.

[42] *Life* i. 135. SJ's rival was the Rev. *John* Johnson. Taylor had misinformed Hawkins also (pp. 64–65). For the circumstances of this abortive competition, see Edward Ruhe, "The Two Samuel Johnsons," N & Q (1954) cxcix. 432–35, and Clifford, *Johnson*, pp. 200–01, 345 n. 12; and for a description of the Proposals (preserved in the Manchester Univ. Lib.), J. A. V. Chapple, "Samuel Johnson's Proposals for Printing the History of the Council of Trent," *Bull. Rylands Lib.* (1963), xlv. 340–69.

[43] Cf. Hawkins, p. 176. JB's foot-note was a later addition, and corrects the statement in the text that the copy was

not recovered. There were actually two versions, a holograph (the "Scheme") and a fair copy of the Plan by an amanuensis, now both in the Hyde Collection. The holograph bears numerous annotations by (presumably) Taylor and a few by a second reader; the copy bears revisions in SJ's hand and annotations by Chesterfield and (presumably) Villiers. Both MSS. were in the library of JB Jr. (*Bibliotheca Boswelliana*, etc., 1825, p. 99); but if they were originally in JB's library, he does not appear to have made use of them. See J. H. Sledd and G. J. Kolb, *Dr. Johnson's Dictionary*, 1955, chs. 2 and 3 for a description of the two MSS. and an estimate of their significance.

leave to carry it home with him promising faithfully to return it that night. He failed in his promise, and though Dr. Taylor hunted him for a week he never could find him or recover it; and in the mean time Johnson hunted Taylor and found him; and upon Taylors very fairly telling him how the fact stood "then" said Johnson "I can tell you the rest. For" said he "Whitehead has carried it to Mr. Villers (now Earl of Clarendon,) and Mr. Villers has taken it to my Lord Chesterfield in whose hands it now is." Dr. Taylor said he thought all this might be an advantage to his design. "No Sir" said Johnson. "It would have come out with more bloom if it had not been seen before by any body."[44]

Dr. Taylor has his *Irene* in the very state it was in when he brought it first to London. The Copy Dr. Taylor has is written in a Woman's hand.[45] Johnson afterwards at the desire of Garrick made several alterations. There was a violent quarrel between them before he would agree to make any alterations at all. Garrick made interest with Dr. Taylor to interfere. It was with difficulty he could prevail on Johnson to comply. "Sir" said he "the fellow wants me to make Mahomet run mad, that he may have an opportunity of tossing his hands and kicking his heels." He however was prevailed on by Dr. Taylor to make the Alterations[46] which appear upon comparing Dr. Taylor's copy with the Play as now printed.

When Garrick had played for some little time at Goodman's fields Johnson and Taylor went to see him and afterwards passed the evening at a tavern with him and old Giffard. Johnson who had all his life a contempt for stage playing, after censuring some mistakes of emphasis in Garrick's acting that night said to both him and Giffard that the Players had got a kind of rant with which they run forward without any regard either to accent or emphasis. They were both offended at this reflection and endeavoured to contradict it. Upon which Johnson said—"Well now I'll give you something

[44] *Life* i. 184–85. Cf. Hawkins, p. 176.
[45] In Aug. 1742 SJ wrote to Taylor at Market Bosworth, where Taylor was rector: "Keep Irene close, You may send it back at your leisure" (*Letters SJ* 17). JB makes no mention of this MS. in the *Life*; instead, he gives extracts from a copy of "the original unformed sketch of this tragedy, in his own hand-writing" which SJ gave to Langton, who in turn presented it to the King (*Life* i. 108 ff.). The original and Langton's own copy are now in the British Museum (*ibid.* 108 n. 1). A recently recovered holograph notebook containing notes and draft speeches for part of Act V of the play is in the Hyde Collection. See *Poems*, ed. McAdam and Milne, pp. 109–10, 218–39.
[46] *Life* i. 196.

to speak with which you are little acquainted and then we shall see how just my Observation is. That shall be the Criterion. Now" said he "let me hear you repeat the Ninth Commandment. Thou shalt not bear false witness against thy neighbour."—Both tried at it and both mistook the emphasis which should be upon *not* and *false witness*. After having them put right, he triumphed very much.[47]

Johnsoniana Related by William Strahan, London, Wednesday 1 June 1785[1]

MS. Yale (C 2584). In JB's hand.

Mr. Strahan of Dr. Johnson

The Contractors for the Dict[iona]ry were Millar Dodsley Longman Knapton and Hitch.[2] Ja. Dodsley[3] brother of R. Dodsley and Longman nephew[4] of Mr. Longman or Mr. Cadel may perhaps furnish particulars.

Mr. Strahan knew him when he lived in Fetter lane and was writing for the *Gentlemans Magazine*.[5]

[47] *Life* i. 168–69. "I suspect Dr. Taylor was inaccurate in this statement. The emphasis should be equally upon *shalt* and *not*, as both concur to form the negative injunction; and *false witness*, like the other acts prohibited in the Decalogue, should not be marked by any peculiar emphasis, but only be distinctly enunciated" (JB's note). Dr. Kearney noted (*Life*, 4th ed., 1804, i. 144 n. 3): "A moderate emphasis should be placed on *false*." Hawkins (p. 426 n.) gives the anecdote with different ingredients, notably the Seventh Commandment instead of the Ninth. See also *Life* i. 326 n. 1 for a similar injunction by SJ to Mrs. Bellamy.

[1] On this day JB "Breakfasted with Strahan . . . Gave me a *little* about Dr. Johnson, and promised to look out some of his letters and notes" (Journ.). Strahan died on 9 July of this year. JB printed only one letter from SJ to Strahan (*ante* From Strahan, 4 Jan. 1779 and

n. 3–3), a sentence from another (*Life* iii. 97), two letters to Mrs. Strahan (*ibid.* iv. 100, 140), and a letter to Humphry Heely "as a voucher" to Strahan (*ibid.* iv. 371). Thirty-three letters to Strahan and three to his wife have been recovered (see *Letters SJ* iii. 317–18). JB also printed from Strahan's own copy his letter recommending SJ for a seat in Parliament (MS. *Life*, Paper Apart for p. 365: *Life* ii. 137).

[2] Cf. *Life* i. 183. The original contract, dated 18 June 1746, came into Hawkins's possession (p. 345 n. †). For the parts played by these various booksellers, see Sledd and Kolb, *Dr. Johnson's Dictionary, passim*.

[3] A contributor to the *Life*: see *post* From Dodsley, 29 June 1786.

[4] Thomas Longman II (1731–97), junior partner of T. & T. Longman (Plomer).

[5] SJ's residence changed several times during 1738–45, the period when he was writing for *Gent. Mag.* See *Life* iii. 405 and n. 6, 534–35.

Dr. Johnson brought his *Rasselas* to Mr. Strahan[6] which Mr. Strahan says it is well known he wrote to defray the expences of his mothers funeral and to pay some little debts she had left. It was purchased by Messieurs Strahan Johnston and Dodsley for £100.[7]

He printed his Pamphlets on his own Account. Mr. Cadel can shew me the particulars.[8]

He used at one period of his life to be very much at Mr. Strahan's House. But on his acquaintance with Mrs. Thrale he in a great measure deserted all his old friends.[9]

One day talking with Mr. Strahan of money-getting men he said He did not know how a man could be more innocently employed than in getting money. A deep reflection the justness of which appears the more the more one thinks of it.[10]

From William Bowles,[1]
Thursday 2 June 1785

MS. Yale (C 555).

ADDRESS: James Boswell Esqr. [*completed by George Dempster:*] at Genl. Paoli's, Upper Seymour Street, London.

POSTMARK: 3 IU.

Heale, near Salisbury, June 2d 85

MY DEAR SIR, I hope you will not infer from my omitting to write that I have forgotten the task you were pleased to impose on me, or that I am become unmindful of the sincere pleasure I received from your conversation this Spring in London.[2] So far otherwise, I have been setting down several new things of our friend which I

---

[6] MS. "and told him he had written it to" deleted.

[7] *Life* i. 341.

[8] Cadell published SJ's political pamphlets.

[9] *Life* iii. 225.

[10] Introduced into the conversations at Strahan's, 27 Mar. 1775, *Life* ii. 323. It does not appear in JB's journal for that day but is among the rough notes for the journal (J 64), 18 Apr. 1779.

[1] William Bowles (1755–1826), of Heale House, Wiltshire, was the son of the Rev. William Bowles (1716–88), Canon of Salisbury, and the third cousin

of William Lisle Bowles (1762–1850), the poet. In 1779 he married Dinah Frankland, daughter of Admiral Sir Thomas Frankland, Bt., a descendant of Cromwell. In 1782 Bowles became Sheriff of Wiltshire (*Life* iv. 235 n. 5, 523; Sir Richard Colt Hoare, *History of Modern Wiltshire*, "Hundred of Chalk", 1833, pp. 36–37). See *Letters SJ passim*.

[2] Bowles is nowhere named in the journal; but the conversation may have taken place at the Essex Head Club, either on 27 Apr. or 11 May (Journ.). Bowles was elected, having been proposed by SJ, the year before (*Letters SJ* 935.1).

beleive you will think worth noting, and I hope earnestly for the pleasure of seeing you here. You shall sleep in the bed that your friend slept in and sit upon the bench in the garden that was erected for him.[3] I shall be glad to know when you think you can favor me with a visit. I have been thinking that you will not find it so expedient to mention the names of those persons who supply you with materials: the world must so far have faith in you as to beleive that you have examined the authenticity of what is sent you. I apprehend most persons would object to the mention of their names on such an occasion.

Mrs. Bowles begs to present her Compliments. I rest Dear Sir, with great truth, Your most humble Servant

W. Bowles

From Joseph Cooper Walker,[1] Sunday 5 June 1785

MS. Yale (C 3050).

ADDRESS: James Boswell Esqr., Auchinleck, Ayrshire, Scotland.

Treasury Chambers, Dublin, 5th June 1785

SIR, I am rejoiced to find that the elegant Author of *An Account of Corsica* meditates a Life of the late Dr. Johnson. You have chosen, Sir, a fine Subject for Biography, and will, I am sure, do it justice.

If you mean to publish the Doctor's epistolary Correspondence, I shall have great pleasure in searching for his private Letters amongst the Literati of this City, and in communicating to You Copies of so many of them as I may find. An original Letter from him to my venerable friend, Charles O Conor, now lies before me, of which you may command a Copy. This Letter is alluded to in the Preface to the Second Edition of Mr. O Conor's *Dissertations on the*

---

[3] SJ visited Bowles at Heale from 28 Aug. to 18 Sept. 1783 (*Letters SJ* 878–882). For a description and history of the house and estate, see *Life* iv. 522–23.

[1] Joseph Cooper Walker (1761–1810), Irish antiquary. "While almost a boy, he got an employment in his Majesty's Treasury of Ireland, where he has arrived to the rank of Third Clerk . . . Though fond of the favourite amusements of the age, he pays the strictest attention to the duties of his office; whilst in office, he is the man of business; after the hours of business, his time is devoted to pleasure or books" (*Lit. Anec.* ix. 654–55). See also *Lit. Illust.* vii. 681.

History of Ireland, p. 3. I have Mr. O C.'s permission to publish this Letter.[2]

Historical Memoirs of our Bards and Music,[3] engross, at present, my thoughts and *private* Pen. As the history of the Irish Music involves that of the Scots, I shall most thankfully receive any communications with which you may be so good as to favour me, respecting the latter. Was the *Crwdd*[4] ever in use amongst the Scots? I know a representation of it was found amongst the outside Ornaments of the Abbey of Melross.

While I write, Volunteer Corps are pouring into this City from different parts of the Kingdom. Tomorrow a general Review is to be held in Phoenix Park.[5] I am, Sir, Your most obedient, humble Servant,

JOSEPH COOPER WALKER

To *William Bowles,*
Tuesday 14 June 1785

MS. Yale (L 264). JB's draft.

London, 14 June 1785

DEAR SIR: I am very much obliged to you for your kind invitation, and should be happy to accept of it.[1] But I fear I cannot have that pleasure this year. I am detained in London to superintend the printing of my *Tour to the Hebrides* which I am anxious should be very accurately done; and by the time it is finished I believe it will be necessary for me to go to Scotland.[2] I hope to [be] under your roof at some future time.[3]

[2] See *post* From Walker, 13 Nov. 1785 and n. 1. For SJ's relations with O'Conor, see Alexander Napier's edition of the *Life* (1884) ii. 566–69.

[3] *Historical Memoirs of the Irish Bards Interspersed with Anecdotes of and Occasional Observations on the Music of Ireland. Also an Historical . . . Account of the Musical Instruments of the Ancient Irish,* etc., 1786.

[4] Or crwth (crowd): "an ancient Celtic instrument of the viol class" (OED, "Crowd," sb[1]).

[5] "On the 8th of June there was a review in the Phoenix Park, Dublin, before General Ld. Charlemont, of the City and County corps of Volunteers,

strengthened by the junction of several country corps, in number about 1200. They made a fine appearance, and went through their exercise with great exactness" (*Gent. Mag.* lv. 479).

[1] MS. orig. "and should I am sure be happy at a place of which Dr. Johnson thought highly".

[2] JB informed the King on 21 Sept. that the work would be finished the next day. Its publication was announced for 1 Oct., by which time JB was on his way to Scotland (Journ.; *Lit. Car.* p. 122).

[3] MS. orig. "If however I can find time to wait on you at Heale, I shall take the liberty to let you know."

In the Great Literary Monument which I am ambitious to erect to the memory of our illustrious departed Friend, I wish that those who are able to bear an honourable part, should each have a pillar inscribed with his own name. To speak without a metaphor The World is to have Dr. Adams's Communications Mr. Malone's Communications Dr. Brocklesby's Communications etc. etc. etc. etc. They and several more are thus to unite their labours of love with mine; and I hope Mr. Bowles will give me leave to authenticate his kind communications in the same manner.

In the mean time in the Course of my Hebridian Tour where[4] mention is to be made of Dr. Samuel Clarke,[5] may I not promise "ample information concerning that great man with which I am to be favoured by my worthy Mr. Bowles of Heale Wiltshire."

Bis dat qui cito dat.[6]—Though you are to have a separate place for yourself,[7] yet as in the progress of my work the Letters and other materials with which you are to furnish me may be of good service in correcting and illustrating my narrative, It will be very kind if you will send me what you have without delay, under cover of George Dempster Esq. M.P.[8] London. I offer my best compliments to Mrs. Bowles, and am with much regard Dear Sir, Your most obedient humble servant

To Joseph Cooper Walker, Friday 1 July 1785

MS. Hyde. MS. Yale (L 1265): JB's copy, written on side 3 of Walker's letter of 5 June (*ante*), headed: "Answer."

ADDRESS: To Joseph Cooper Walker Esq., Treasury Chambers, Dublin.

POSTMARKS: 1 JY, J—Y 6.

London, 1 July 1785

SIR: I am very much obliged to you for your polite attention in offering to collect for me among the Literati of Dublin such private letters of Dr. Johnson as have been preserved. All that you can send me will be very acceptable; for, it is my design in writing the

---

[4] MS. "where" deleted. The final form of this sentence is recorded in Bowles's quotation, *post* 30 Aug. 1785.

[5] *Life* v. 287–88.

[6] "He gives twice who gives soon": proverbial; attributed to Publilius Syrus (*Oxford Dictionary of Quotations*, 2nd ed.,

1953, p. 526). JB uses the saying in his letter to SJ, 19 Jan. 1775 (*Life* ii. 290).

[7] MS. "⟨?⟩ longum" [?at length] deleted.

[8] George Dempster (1732–1818), who represented the Perth burghs, 1761–68, 1769–90 (Judd 1287). See Journ. *passim*.

Life of that Great and Good Man, to put as it were into a Mausoleum all of his precious remains[1] that I can gather. Be pleased Sir to
transmit your packets for me to the care of Mr. Dilly Bookseller
London.

I should ill deserve the liberal aid you are to afford me, did I not
endeavour to procure for you in return what communications I can
get for your Historical Memoirs of the Bards and Musick of Ireland.
I myself am very ill informed upon that subject. But when I get
back to Scotland which will be some time in Autumn next, my
exertions shall not be wanting.[2] I am Sir, Your most obedient
humble servant

JAMES BOSWELL

From the Rev. Dr. William Adams, Monday 18 July 1785

MS. Yale (C 16).

ADDRESS: James Boswell Esqr., at Genl. Paoli's, Portman Square.

POSTMARK: 19 IY.

Oxford, July 18. 1785

DEAR SIR, I am obliged to advertise you of another Journey which
will again deprive me of the hopes of seeing you soon in Oxford.[1]
My Daughter and I[2] are just setting out (at Five in the morning)
for Shropshire where we shall probably stay till the beginning of
October. Our Residence there is at Counde[3] near Shrewsbury:
where I shall be glad to see you or to receive your Commands by
Letter. Your affectionate humble Servant

W. ADAMS

[1] MS. "which have not vanished"
deleted.

[2] At the foot of the page of JB's copy
appears the note (L 1266): "20 Decr.
1785. Sent him references to several
publications on the subject, communicated
to me by Sir William Forbes." See
Letters JB 233.

[1] See *ante* To Adams, 11 Mar. 1785
and n. 1. That there is a loss at this point
in the correspondence is clear not only

from the tenor of this opening sentence
but also from the fact that Adams knew
JB's new address in London. JB must
have written some time after hearing from
Sir Alexander Dick about Dr. Grieve
(see *ante* From Adams, 28 Mar. 1785
and n. 11), and he must also, in that or in
another letter, have expressed his wish
to visit Adams at Oxford in July.

[2] Mrs. Adams had died in Apr.
(*Johns. Glean.* v. 181).

[3] Where Adams was rector.

From Joseph Cooper Walker, Monday 18 July 1785

MS. Yale (C 3051).

ADDRESS: James Boswell Esqr., Mr. Dilly's, Bookseller, London.

POSTMARKS: JY 23, 28 IY.

Treasury Chambers, [Dublin,] 18th July 1785

SIR: My present situation is a delicate One. When it was generally known that Sir J. Hawkins had undertaken to publish an Edition of Dr. Johnson's Works, my friend Mr. O Conor (Author of *Diss. on the Hist. of Ireland*) sent me a Letter he had received from the Doctor, a Copy of which he directed me to offer to Sir John, in case he intended to publish the Doctor's Epist[olar]y Correspondence. I immediately wrote to Sir John agreeably to my friend's directions. The learned Knight politely refused the Offer, declaring at the same time, that he had determined *not* to publish any of the Doctor's private Letters. Happening about this time to hear that you meditated a Life of Doctor Johnson, I took the liberty to offer you my services in collecting such of his Letters as I could discover in this Kingdom.[1] While I waited your Answer Mr. Cadell[2] wrote to inform me that Sir John had been prevailed upon to promise a Selection of Dr. J.'s Letters, and requested I would communicate any that were in my possession. This Letter lay unheeded in my Closet till I began to conclude from your Silence (almost two Months having elapsed from the time I wrote to you)[3] that the tender I had made you of my services was not acceptable. Possessed with this Idea, I sent a Copy of the Letter with which Mr. O Conor had intrusted me, to Mr. Cadell[4] the day preceding the one on which I was honor'd with your polite favor. I then repented of my rash conclusion, and was puzzled how to act. At length I resolved to send you also a Copy of that Letter, and have now the pleasure to do so.[5] This may be an imprudent step; but I am sure you will

[1] *Ante* 5 June 1785.

[2] With Andrew Strahan, publisher-in-chief of the *Life* and *Works* (1787).

[3] The postmarks show that only one month elapsed between the exchange of letters (*ante* 1 July).

[4] It was not printed by Hawkins, who seems to have stuck by his original determination. Few of SJ's letters, "pri-

vate" or otherwise, are included in his *Life*.

[5] Not the letter mentioned in Walker's first communication to JB (*ante* 5 June 1785; see end of the present letter), but a later one. JB used Walker's transcript (sides 1 and 2 of the present letter) as printer's copy, quoting in a note his accompanying sketch of O'Conor (Paper

not avail yourself of it, unless you can do so with some degree of propriety.

As I should be happy to see Dr. Johnson's remains elegantly and splendidly deposited, I shall strain every Nerve in collecting such of them as are scattered thro' this Kingdom, for the Mausoleum you mean to raise. Unfortunately all my literary friends have retired to the Country—But I will importune them with Letters. Be assured I shall be zealous—(I wish I cou'd add, and successful).

Your intention of serving me in Scotland has my warmest thanks. Any Communications with which you may be pleased to honor me will be gratefully acknowledged by, Sir, Your most obedient humble servant

J. C. WALKER

P.S. I hope to sit down to the fair Copy of my little Work next month.—When will you publish?

N.B. Mr. O Connor has mislaid Dr. J.'s first Letter to him—if he finds it, I'll send you a Copy.[6]

From Joseph Cooper Walker, Tuesday 26 July 1785

MS. Yale (C 3052).

ADDRESS: James Boswell Esq., Mr. Dilly's, Bookseller, London.

POSTMARKS: JY 29, 3 AU.

Treasury Chambers, Dublin, 26th July 1785

SIR, I have not been idle since I did myself the honor to write to you on the 18th inst.

Having heard an eminent Divine of this City[1] numbered with the Friends of Dr. Johnson, I had application made to him for Copies of such private Letters of the Doctor as he might have preserved—But in vain. He had lived in friendship with the Doctor, but had not corresponded with him.

I then wrote to my learned friend, Col[one]l Vallancey[2] with

---

Apart for p. 618: *Life* iii. 111–12 and n. 4). The printer omitted from SJ's letter the word "times" in the parenthesis "for such times there were". Thomas Campbell, who printed an extract of the letter in his *Strictures on the . . . History of England* (1790, p. 1), has it "if such times there were". See *Life* iii. 489 and *Letters SJ* 517 n. 4.

[6] See *post* 13 Nov. 1785.

[1] Thomas Leland, D.D. See *post* From John Leland, 29 July 1786.

[2] Charles Vallancey (1721–1812), the antiquary. JB was in his and SJ's company on 9, 15, and 17 May of the preceding year (*Life* iv. 272, 273, 278).

better hopes of success. This was the Colonel's Answer.—"I have no Letters of Dr. Johnston—only some literary Observations on the dialect of the Barony of Forth, which I mean to publish with the Vocabulary of it.[3] The Doctor promised me a long Letter for publication in my next Number (of *Collectanea de Rebus Hibernicis*)[4] on the necessity of printing all our ancient Mss at the public expence. This promise was made a little before his death. If you will mention this to Mr. Boswell, I will thank you—perhaps the rough draft of such a Letter may be found amongst the Doctor's Papers—"[5] Permit me Sir, *as an Irishman*, to request you will search, and also prevail on Sir John Hawkins to search, for this Letter. If you find it, I trust you will give it a place. It might serve to awaken the Curiosity of the Public to the neglected Antiquities of this Country.

Be assured, Sir, I shall continue *my* Search with the zeal of a friend. I am, Sir, Your most obedient humble servant

J. C. WALKER

P.S. When your *Life of Johnson* is ready for publication let me recommend it to you, to make a bargain with the Dublin Booksellers, else the work will appear here almost as soon as in London, without your enjoying any advantage from it.

From *William Bowles,*
Wednesday 17 August 1785

MS. Yale (C 556).

ADDRESS: James Boswell Esqr. [*completed by George Dempster:*] No. 1 Portman Square, London.

POSTMARK: 19 AU.

Weymouth, Aug. 17. 1785

DEAR SIR, I have been favored with your letter,[1] and truly regret the circumstances whatever they are, that hinder me from enjoying the pleasure of your company in Wiltshire, but I will still cherish the hope of seeing you at a future period not I trust, very remote.

---

[3] Not published.

[4] 6 vols., 1770–1804. Walker contributed "Anecdotes of Chess in Ireland" to vol. v (1790).

[5] Not found.

[1] *Ante* 14 June 1785.

I shall be a little fearful of being the known and professed writer of a part of your book and the more so as what I can communicate will be trifling: but yet I shall be willing to comply with your wishes as much as possible. I have not yet recollected all I can; bus'ness and avocations of one kind or other have intervened to take up my time. As I am sure I shall have nothing that will be of service as to the *main body* of the History, I am the less in haste. In the mean time I am desirous of interesting you in behalf of a little publication that I hope and beleive will be prepared in this neighbourhood. "Memoirs of the late Dutchess of Queensberry."[2]

If you could communicate any thing respecting her, or prevail with any one of your acquaintance to communicate any particulars I should be much obliged to you. Much is already known and many people are marked out as contributors. I see that Mr. George Strahan has published our good friends devotional writings[3] and I shall be glad to see them as I hope they will differ in most respects from similar performances of other people. I have been here a few days and am returning to Heale almost immediately. I remain Dear Sir with great regard and respect, Your most humble Servant

W. Bowles

From Joseph Cooper Walker, Saturday 20 August 1785

MS. Yale (C 3053).

ADDRESS: James Boswell Esqr., at Mr. Dilly's, Bookseller, London.

Dublin, Treasury Chambers, 20 Aug. 1785

SIR, Since I did myself the honor to write to you last Month, I have not been so fortunate as either to procure or discover another Letter of Dr. Johnson. But I do not despair. With Winter my Friends will return.

---

[2] Catherine Hyde, Duchess of Queensberry (1701–77), Prior's "Female Phaeton" and the patroness of Gay. The undertaking appears to have been abortive. In her cousin Mrs. Delany's journal for 9 Dec. 1783 is found the entry: "After tea I read, and *begun* ye answer to ye Dss of Marlborough's *account*, memoirs supposed to be written by ye late Dss of Queensberry" (*Autobiography and Correspondence of Mary Granville, Mrs. Delany*, ed. Lady Llanover, 2nd ser., 1862, iii. 169).

[3] The *Prayers and Meditations*. For Strahan's contributions to the *Life*, see *post* 4 Mar. 1791.

Having had occasion to write to the Bishop of Dromore lately,[1] I took that opportunity of urging him to afford you his Aid. I believe he lived in friendship and corresponded with Dr. Johnson. The Bishop is preparing a Life of Dr. Goldsmith for the Press, which, with his Poetical Works, is to be published by Subscription. I enclose the Proposals.[2]

I also enclose a kind of *Prospectus* of an Academy lately instituted in Dublin.[3]

I am rejoiced to find that your *Journey to the Hebridies* is gone to Press. I promise myself much pleasure from the perusal of it.

To my last Letter I added an hasty, and, I fear, an inaccurate Postscript. This was my meaning. The Booksellers here will publish your *Life of Johnson* almost as soon as Mr. Dilly; and, unless you make a bargain with one of them, they will enjoy *all* the profits arising from the sale of it.[4]

I dined yesterday in Company with Mr. Woodfall,[5] and was delighted with his Conversation. His head teems with Anecdotes.

This, I suppose, will find you returned from Scotland. If you made any musical Discoveries during your Excursion, be so good as to communicate them to, Sir, Your most obedient humble servant

J. C. WALKER

---

[1] Walker's letters to Percy (beginning in 1787) are printed in *Lit. Illust.* vii. 702 ff.

[2] Missing. The Proposals are dated "Dublin, June 1, 1785": see Katharine C. Balderston, *History & Sources of Percy's Memoir of Goldsmith*, 1926, p. 24.

[3] The Royal Irish Academy: see *post* From Walker, 13 Nov. 1785. The Prospectus is missing.

[4] Walker repeated his warning a second time in his letter of 31 Dec.: "Soon as your *Life of Dr. Johnson* shall appear in London, it is the intention of the Dublin Booksellers to set about printing it in octavo." JB replied, 31 May 1786: "It is very discouraging to Authours here, that your irish Booksellers lye in wait to publish a cheap edition of every Book as soon as they can get it over. You tell me I am to be served so when my *Life of Dr. Johnson* comes out. There is no help for it. But *durum est.*" (As these letters concern the *Life* only in the most incidental way, they will appear in another volume in the present series.) Walker was to show a similar solicitude over the publication of Horace Walpole's *The Mysterious Mother* (*Letters of Horace Walpole*, ed. Mrs. Paget Toynbee, 1903–05, xiv. 374, xv. 125; unpublished letters of Walpole and Walker, 26 Feb. and 23 Mar. 1791, W. S. Lewis Collection; *Lit. Illust.* vii. 734).

[5] William Woodfall (1746–1803), journalist and drama critic. He was famous for his full reporting of the debates in Parliament from memory. "In 1784 he was invited to Dublin, to report the debates upon the Commercial Propositions" (*Lit. Anec.* i. 303–04).

From William Bowles,
Tuesday 30 August 1785

MS. Yale (C 557).

ADDRESS: James Boswell Esqr. [*completed by George Dempster:*] No. 1 Portman Square, London.

POSTMARK: 1 SE.

Heale, Aug. 30 1785

DEAR SIR, In my letter to you from Weymouth,[1] I recollect that I omitted answering what you said respecting Dr. Clarke. The passage in your letter[2] it is proper for me to transcribe as amidst your concerns it is most probable you have nearly forgotten it.

> In the mean time, as in the course of my Hebridian Tour mention is to be made of Dr. Clarke may I not promise interesting information concerning that great man to be communicated by William Bowles Esqr.

Now Sir, in answer to the above I am to tell you that I have nothing to communicate on the subject of Dr. Clarke and you must in a great degree have misunderstood what passed between us[3] on the matter. But something there is which you may communicate to the publick and which in my judgement they will be much obliged to you for.

When Dr. Johnson was at this House he paid a visit to a very worthy friend[4] of mine who married a neice[4] of Dr. Clarke's and who became afterwards Executor to the only son of the Doctor.[5] He was shewn by this gentleman all Dr. C.'s unpublished papers (of which as far as he red Dr. Johnson thought highly) and the copies of some of the printed works especially the Homer. Dr. Johnson recommended a careful inspection of all the unedited papers and said that the London booksellers would pay high for them. He also requested the family to recollect any anecdotes they could of Dr. Clarke before they were irrecoverable.[6]

[1] *Ante* 17 Aug. 1785.
[2] *Ante* 14 June 1785.
[3] In conversation: see *ante* From Bowles, 2 June 1785 and n. 2.
[4] Not identified.
[5] Samuel Clarke, B.A. 1721, M.A. 1724, Jesus College, Cambridge; admitted to the Inner Temple, 1716; F.R.S.,

1735 (*Alum. Cant.*); died, 1778 (Musgrave).
[6] Anecdotes of Dr. Clarke by the Rev. J. Jones of Welwyn were contributed to the *Gent. Mag.* for Mar. 1783 (liii. 227)—anticipating SJ's recommendation by about six months.

The Papers will certainly be inspected with all possible attention and will probably be published: this with Dr. Johnson's opinion it will be good to communicate[7] and the family will give you many thanks.

With regard to the Life of our great friend I was thinking a few days ago that Francis must know a great deal. The Dr. wrote often to him when he was absent, ⟨and⟩ those letters are probably curious, if happily the fellow had sense to preserve them.[8]

I shall hope to hear from you soon. If you frequent the Club (as I hope you do) pray remember me kindly to my friends who belong to it.[9] I feel a great regard for all Dr. Johnson's friends.

Mrs. B. begs to present her best Compliments. I rest Dear Sir, most truly, Your affectionate humble Servant

W. BOWLES

From Sir Joshua Reynolds,[1] October 1785

MSS.[2] Yale (M 145, C 2368). The first MS. is printed, Life i. 144–45.

[I]

Such they appear'd to me, but since the former Edition Sir Joshua Reynolds has observed to me that those motions or tricks of Dr. Johnson are improperly called convulsions, that he could sit

---

[7] Not mentioned in the Life.
[8] See post From Barber, 7 Jan. 1786.
[9] Bowles was one of the "constant members" of the Essex Head Club at the time of SJ's death (Lit. Anec. ii. 553).

---

[1] Sir Joshua Reynolds is one of those members of the Johnson Circle whose very intimacy with JB makes it difficult to estimate the extent of their contributions to the Life. His name appears in the Life (from the Dedication onward) with the frequency one would expect, and frequently in ways that suggest the part of an informant; but except for the present texts (and SJ's letters to him) the MS. originals of his contributions have not been recovered. The most extended contribution of Johnsoniana from Reynolds was added in the second edition

(Life iv. 182 ff.), but the MS., like most of those belonging to the second edition, is missing. The journal tells us that JB took down some anecdotes from Reynolds's dictation on 20 Feb. 1786; whether they were used or not remains a question. In any case, the reader may be confident that there is more of Sir Joshua in the Life than meets the eye. For an account of SJ's letters to him printed by JB, see Letters SJ iii. 315–16.

[2] The two MSS. were originally one folio, written on all four sides. The leaves were cut so that the first half might be sent to the printer (Paper Apart "R" for p. 89). A version of this MS. is printed in Portraits by Sir Joshua Reynolds, ed. F. W. Hilles, 1952, pp. 68–69, together with an account of its genesis. JB did not print the second MS. but drew upon it for

motionless, when he was told to do so as well as any other man, his opinion was that it proceeded from a habit he had indulged himself in, of accompanying his thoughts with certain untoward actions and that those actions allways appeared to him, as if he reprobated some part of his past conduct. That whenever his mind was not engaged in conversation such thoughts were sure to rush in to his mind, and for this reason, any company any employment whatever, he preferred to his being alone. The great business of his life he said was to escape from himself; this disposition he considerd as the disease of his mind which nothing cured but company.

Sir Joshua in the course of conversation gave some instances of

his narrative of SJ's being "discovered" by Pope, *Life* i. 128–29 and 142–43. The first MS., which was edited by JB, is here given in its original form. The following account of the circumstances of its composition and incorporation into the *Life* is derived from Prof. Hilles's: While Malone was preparing the second edition of the *Tour* for the press, he wrote to JB in Scotland, 5 Oct. 1785: "Don't forget Sir Joshua R.'s observation about Johnson's extraordinary motions not being *involuntary*; and therefore not exactly described [in the *Tour*: *Life* v. 18]." JB replied, 13 Oct.: "I still remain of opinion that Dr. Johnson's extraordinary motions were *involuntary*. Had not that been the case, he surely would have restrained them in the publick streets. I therefore cannot omit or alter that part of his character. If you think it proper there may be a note to convulsive contractions as follows. *Sir Joshua Reynolds is of opinion that Dr. Johnson's extraordinary gesticulations [alternatively gestures] were not involuntary. But I still think they were; for had not that been the case etc. as above."* On 19 Oct. Malone wrote again: "I drew up what I conceived to be Sir J. R.'s idea about them by way of note and sent it to him. He approved, but sent me a much larger and very valuable discussion of the subject [the present MS.], which I shall enclose with the letter. It could not have been got in without a good deal of trouble; besides I thought it too valuable to be thrown away [i.e. in a foot-note], and better to

be reserved for the *Life*. His solution of the shoutings and gestures being connected with ideas from which he shrank, is surely very ingenious. It meets with your observations about his not restraining these motions in the street, for such ideas were as likely to intrude into such a mind there as any where else; —in reverie. However I have added what you sent as you will see by the enclosed. It will do very well for the present." See *Life* v. 18 n. 4. Finally, on 27 Oct. JB replied: "The *contractions* are well stated for the present. Sir Joshua's note at *large* will be admirable in the *Life*; But it must be in Sir Joshua's own name." Reynolds had written the account as if by JB, with references to himself in the third person; in editing the MS. JB translated it into the first person, making the necessary adjustments along the way. At the end of the MS. appears a note in Malone's hand: "Mem. what Mr. Langton says about Dr. Johnson's *owning* that his gestures or habits or whatever they may be called were very similar to those of the *kissing* Dr. Barton of Christchurch, Oxford." This observation was not included in the *Life*. In the fifth edition (1807, i. 122 n. 6) Malone remarked: "Sir Joshua Reynolds's notion on this subject is confirmed by what Johnson himself said to a young lady, the niece of his friend Christopher Smart. See a note by Mr. Boswell on some particulars communicated by Reynolds, in vol. iv under March 30, 1783 [*Life* iv. 183 n. 2]." —For Frances Reynolds's

Dr. Johnsons absensce which as they are characteristic of the man may be worth relating. When He and the Doctor took a journey together in the West they visited the late Mr. Banks of Dorsetshire. The Conversation turning upon Pictures which the Doctor could not see, he retired to a corner of the room stretching out his right leg as far as he could reach before him, then bringing up his left leg, and stretching his right still further on. The old Gentleman observing him went up to him and in a very courteous manner told the Doctor, that tho it was not a new house, he assured him the flooring was perfectly safe. The Doctor started from his reverie like a person waked out of his sleep, but spoke not a word.

[II]

It appears that Mr. Pope had entertained the same opinion with myself[3] of Dr. Johnsons convulsions. Sir J. Reynolds had a note in his possesion[4] written by Pope where-in he says that he had recommended the Author of *London a Poem* to Lord Gore to be preceptor to his Son, merely on account of the excellence of that Poem, but without success, for that he had been informed he was troubled with convulsions that made him at times a hideous spectacle.[5]

Sir Joshua told Dr. Johnson of this note which he had in his possesion but allways avoided shewing it to him on account of the last words, tho he often enquired after it. Sir Joshua observed to him that he seemed to be much flatterd with Mr. Popes attention to him. "Who," says he, "would not be flatter'd with the sollicitous enquiry of such a man as Pope?"[6] Mr. Richardson told Sir Joshua that Pope had earnestly desired him to enquire who was the

account of SJ's "extraordinary gestures or anticks with his hands and feet" (including her version of the anecdote that concludes the first MS.), see *Johns. Misc.* ii. 273–75. See also L. C. McHenry, Jr., "Samuel Johnson's Tics and Gesticulations," *Journal of the History of Medicine and Allied Sciences* (1967), xxii. 152–68.

[3] That is, JB.

[4] "to whom it was given by the son of Mr. Richardson the painter, the person to whom it was addressed" (*Life* i. 142). See *ante* From Percy, 9 May 1776.

[5] Pope's note does not mention the

preceptorship, but rather "a Publick School in Shropshire"—actually Appleby School, in Leicestershire (see *post* To and From Hector, 15 July 1786 and n. 19). Nor does Pope explicitly say that SJ's infirmity was the reason he failed to secure the appointment. There is certainly no hint of this infirmity in Gower's letter to "a friend of Dean Swift", applying in SJ's behalf for an M.A. from Dublin to make the appointment possible (*Life* i. 133–34).

[6] Quoted, with revision, *Life* i. 143.

Author and that when he informed him that his name was Johnson an obscure man Pope answerd "he will soon be deterrè"[7]—the event has fully justified the prediction.

From Thomas Barnard, Bishop of Killaloe, Saturday 15 October 1785

MS. Yale (C 87).

ADDRESS: To James Boswell Esqr., Aughinleck, Kilmarnock, North Britain. By way of Portpatrick.

POSTMARK: OC 21.

Killaloe, Octr. 15th 1785

. . . I have been beating my Brains to no purpose to find anecdotes or aphorisms to enrich your Life of Johnson, and can think of none but such as I am sure you are in Possession. Except an Expression of his in Praise of the Irish Nation, deliverd to myself in a Conversation above ten years ago, soon after[1] the Publication of his Tour to Scotland. When Speaking of his Taking another Tour to Ireland as a thing not impossible; I said that I did not Know whether we ought to wish for his Company; as from the Severity of his observations on the Scots, we had reason to dread a Similar, or perhaps a still less Favourable representation of our Manners and Character. "Sir" Sais he "you have no reason to be afraid of me. The Irish are not in a Conspiracy to cheat the World by false Representations of the merits of their Countrymen: No Sir; the Irish are a Fair People. I never heard them Speak well of one another."[2] These were as nearly his words as I can recollect. But how pleasing it may be to either Nation to publish them, I leave to your Judgement.

The Round Robin we sent to him from Sir J. Reynolds's to persuade him to alter Goldsmiths Epitaph; might be an anecdote so far worthy of notice, as it serves to shew how much he was fear'd by his most Intimate Freinds; who, tho' they agreed in their

---

[7] *Life* i. 128–29.

[1] MS. "ago soon, after"

[2] *Life* ii. 307, slightly revised. Cooke (pp. 129–30) records an anecdote calculated to confirm Barnard's worst fears. SJ tells a company, in which JB is present, of giving a shilling to a peasant at Skye, who asked whether he meant it all for him. When a laugh is raised against JB, SJ turns to an Irishman, saying that had it happened in *his* country, "the probability is, that he would not know *what a shilling was*".

gaieté de Coeur to pen a Remonstrance against his Composition, yet no one of the Company had the Courage to present it, or even to appear as a Ring leader in the Transaction. Sir William Forbes took the Copy of the original Round Robin when he was in Dublin at my house;[3] and will give you all the particulars of the Business, (being then one of the Subscribing parties) if you think it worthy of inserting.

From Thomas Warton,[1]
Saturday 5 November 1785

MS. Yale (C 3071).

ADDRESS: To James Boswell Esq., at Mr. Dilly's Bookseller, in the Poultry, London.

POSTMARK: 7 NO.

Trin. Coll. Oxon., Nov. 5, 1785

DEAR SIR, As I am informed that you mean to print a Collection of Dr. Johnson's Letters by way of Appendix to his *Life*, I take the liberty to acquaint you, that I have about twenty of Dr. Johnson's

---

[3] "I know not the time when I have spent so many happy hours so happily as in the worthy Bishop's Company.— Among other things he showed me the original *Round Robin*, Quorum pars (I cannot say *magna*) fui [*Aeneid* ii. 5]: and I have brought with me a Copy of it, which shall be at your Service, as a literary Curiosity, connected with the life of Dr. Johnson, If you chuse to make any use of it" (Forbes to JB, 16 Sept. 1785, C 1275). See *post* From Forbes, 19 Oct. 1787.

[1] JB was introduced to Thomas Warton by SJ at Oxford on 20 Mar. 1776. "Then we went to Mr. Thomas Warton of Trinity, whom I had long wished to see. We found him in a very elegant appartment ornamented with good prints, and with wax or spermacetti candles before him. All this surprised me, because I had heard that Tom kept low drunken company, and I expected to see a confused dusty room and a little, fat, laughing fellow. In place of which I found a good,

sizeable man, with most decent clothes and darkish periwig, one who might figure as a Canon. He did not say much; but as Dr. Johnson had some time ago given him a memorandum from me to inquire about an ancient Ballad for Lord Hailes, he very obligingly told me that he should send me it, and asked to have my address. There was no vivacity broke forth—no poetick flash. . . . Dr. Johnson said to me afterwards that Warton did not like to be with us. He was not at his ease. He liked only company in which he could reign. 'I am sure,' said I, 'I should have willingly let him reign.' 'Ay, but he would not have reigned before us,' said he, 'for all men who have that love of low company are also timid' " (Journ.; see also *Life* ii. 446 ff.). For SJ's strictures on Warton's poetry, see *ibid.* iii. 158–59. From the journal it appears that JB and Warton did not meet again until ten years later, 29 Apr. 1786, when JB visited Oxford with Malone. Thereafter, they frequently dined in each other's company.

Letters written to me in the years 1755, 1756.[2] If you wish to print them, I will transcribe and send them to you. They are short, but I think they should not be witheld from the Public; and they illustrate a part of his Life when he conversed but little with the world.[3] I am, Dear Sir, Your most obedient humble servant

THOS. WARTON

From Joseph Cooper Walker, Sunday 13 November 1785

MS. Yale (C 3054).

ADDRESS: James Boswell Esq., Mr. Dilly's, Bookseller, London.

POSTMARK: NO 15.

Dublin, Treasury Chambers, Nov. 13th 1785

SIR, My venerable and amiable friend, Mr. O Conor, sent me, a few days ago, Dr. Johnsons first Letter to him; desiring me, at the same time, to forward a copy of it to Sir Jn. Hawkins. I complied with his desire. And I have now the honor to send you a copy of it.[1]

Your *Journal of a Tour to the Hebrides* was published here yesterday, in the same size of the London Edition.[2] It is exquisitely entertaining. I have hardly ate, drank or slept since I got it. It was with pain I laid it down to take up my Pen.—I am promised a translation of the Ode to Mrs. Thrale,[3] of which (if I get it and like it) I will send you a copy for your next Edition.

You say, that after the prospect from Constantinople and the Bay

---

[2] Twenty-one letters from SJ to Warton have been recovered (*Letters SJ passim*), of which JB acquired and printed eighteen (see *post* To T. Warton, 13 Apr. 1786 and n. 1).

[3] *Life* i. 270.

---

[1] See *ante* From Walker, 5 June and 18 July 1785. Like the copy of the second letter (sent first), this was used by JB as printer's copy (Paper Apart for MS. *Life*, p. 179: *Life* i. 321). Following the transcription (sides 1 and 2 of the present letter) is a note by Walker, which JB did not use: "Mr. O Conor in the Letter which covered the above, says, 'I had almost forgot to inform you, that

at this time (tho' in an infirm state) I am following Dr. Johnsons Directions in drawing up a Memoir on the ancient State of this Island.' " Chapman prints this letter from another copy by Walker, now in the Hyde Collection (*Letters SJ* 107). Except for one slip of the pen, there are no substantive variants between it and the text printed by JB.

[2] "The book is practically a line for line reprint of the first edition, which it resembles very closely in appearance. Unlike many of the Irish piracies, it is printed on a fine quality of paper, and in every respect is worthy of comparison with the genuine edition" (*Lit. Car.* p. 116).

[3] *Life* v. 158.

of Naples, the view from the Castle-Hill of Edinburgh, is the finest prospect in Europe.[4] But you have not seen the Bay of Dublin.[5] It is generally allowed *not* to be inferior to the Bay of Naples. I wish, *avec tout mon Cœur*, you would visit it. I wish too you would give the world "a Tour in Ireland." No Man is more equal to the Task. Ireland is almost *Virgin-Ground*. Come then amongst us. You will find us more civilized, and not less hospitable than the Corsicans. But you must not expect a *Paoli*!

I am sure you will be glad to hear that His Majesty has been pleased to incorporate the Irish Academy.[6]

But I must attend Dr. Johnson to the Isle of Skie. Adieu. I am, Sir, with great respect, Your much obliged and most obedient humble servant

JOSEPH C. WALKER

P.S. Hearing that Dr. Johnson and the late Dr. Leland corresponded, I endeavoured, but in vain, to get copies of Dr. J.'s Letters *for you*.[7]—I request you will command my poor services in this City.

From the Rev. Dr. William Adams, Thursday 17 November 1785

Missing, except for two small fragments, Yale (C 17). Sent to London(?) from Oxford. Printed, *Life* i. 8 and iv. 416 n. 2. Text transcribed from MS. *Life*, Advertisement, p. 6 and opp. p. 1033.[1]

[4] *Life* v. 54.

[5] He must have seen it—on his visit to Dublin in May 1769.

[6] See *ante* From Walker, 20 Aug. 1785. The Royal Irish Academy was incorporated by George III by Royal Charter, 28 Jan. 1786 (*Proceedings of the Royal Irish Academy*, Dublin, 1862, vii, "Charter, Statutes, etc."). In the first volume of its *Transactions* (1787) appeared the excellent essay on SJ's prose style by the Rev. Robert Burrowes (see *Life* iv. 385–86).

[7] See *ante* From Walker, 26 July 1785, and *post* JB's correspondence with John Leland, 11 and 29 July 1786.

[1] I have joined these two fragments on the evidence of their form and content; the place and date are given by JB with

the first extract only. Following the second extract, the letter proceeded with a criticism of Strahan for publishing the *Prayers*, to which JB appended a footnote: "Dr. Adams is here i⟨n⟩ an errour. The *Prayers* ⟨and⟩ *Meditations* Mr. Strahan ⟨told⟩ me were directed to hi⟨m in his⟩ own handwriting and h⟨e⟩ promised to Johnson ⟨?that he would publish them.⟩" Apparently JB intended to use the letter as printer's copy (see *post* From Adams, 12 July 1786, n. 15) and dissected it accordingly. A prior intention, however, can be discovered from a deleted passage at the end of the Advertisement, which originally concluded: "Such a sanction to my faculty of giving a just representation of Dr. Johnson is of great value; and I deposited the letter in the British Museum."

DEAR SIR: I hazard this Letter, not knowing where it will find you,[2] to thank you for your very agreable *Tour* which I found here on my return from the Country, and in which you have depicted our Friend so perfectly to my Fancy in every attitude, every scene and situation, that I have thought myself in the company, and of the party almost throughout. It has given very general satisfaction; and those who have found most fault with a passage here and there have agreed that they could not help going through and being entertained through[3] the whole. I wish indeed some few gross expressions had been softened, and a few of our Hero's foibles had been a little more shaded; but it is useful to see the weaknesses incident to great minds; and you have given us Dr. Johnson's Authority that in history all ought to be told.[4]

*   *   *

The Doctor's prejudices were the strongest, and certainly in another sense the weakest that ever possessed a sensible man. You know his extreme zeal for orthodoxy. But did you ever hear what he told me[5] himself that he had made it a rule not to admit Dr. Clarke's name in his *Dictionary*. This however wore off. At some distance of time he advised with me what Books he should read in defence of the Christian Religion. I recommended Clarke's *Evidences of Natural and Revealed Religion* as the best of the kind, and I find in what is called his *Prayers and Meditations* that he was frequently employed in the latter part of his time in reading Clarke's Sermons.[6]

[2] JB arrived in London on the day this letter was written. As was his custom, he stopped first at Dilly's, where he remained until the 21st, and then went to Gen. Paoli's (Journ.). If Adams directed the letter to Paoli's in Portman Square, as he did his last (*ante* 18 July 1785), there should have been little delay in its delivery.

[3] *Life*, "with"

[4] "'M'Leod asked, if it was not wrong in Orrery to expose the defects of a man with whom he lived in intimacy. —*Johnson*. 'Why no, sir, after the man is dead; for then it is done historically' " (*Life* v. 238).

[5] MS. "told me told me"

[6] See *Diaries, passim*. In SJ's library were two volumes of "Clarke's sermons, &c." (*Sale Catalogue*, Items 242 and 251). SJ himself recommended reading Clarke "to every man whose faith is yet unsettled" (*Life* i. 398; see also *ibid*. iii. 248, iv. 524, and *ante* From Brocklesby, 27 Dec. 1784 and ?17–18 Apr. 1785). Clarke's *Evidences* consists of the two Boyle Lectures delivered by him in 1704 and 1705. The volume was published under the title, *A Discourse Concerning the Being and Attributes of God, the Obligations of Natural Religion, and the Truth and Certainty of the Christian Revelation*, etc. JB owned a copy.

To Thomas Warton,
Friday 18 November 1785

MS. Yale (L 1273). JB's copy, headed (later): "To The Rev. Mr. Tho. Warton."

London, 18 Novr. 1785

REVEREND SIR: I arrived here yesterday, and this day found at Mr. Dilly's your letter which was lying for me.

I am very much obliged to you for your kind offer of Dr. Johnson's letters to you, which I thankfully accept, and shall be glad to have them as soon as you can conveniently let me have them, as my plan is to carry on his Life chronologically, with letters interweaved. I am with great regard, Dear Sir, Your much obliged humble servant

From Thomas Warton,
Saturday 19 November 1785

MS. Yale (C 3072). A message from Dilly to JB written on the address side is heavily scored through.

ADDRESS: To James Boswell Esq., at Mr. Dilly's Bookseller, in the Poultry, London.

POSTMARK: 22 NO.

Trin. Coll. Oxon., Nov. 19th, 1785

DEAR SIR: You shall receive Dr. Johnson's Letters to me, before the sixteenth day of next Month. I hope I do not mention too late a day; and am with true regard, Dear Sir, Your most obedient humble servant

THOS. WARTON

To the Rev. Dr. William Adams, Thursday 22 December 1785

MS. Hyde.

ADDRESS: To The Reverend Dr. Adams, Master of Pembroke College, Oxford.[1]

POSTMARK: 23 DE.

ENDORSEMENT: Mr. Boswell Dec. 12.[2] 1785.

London, 22 Decr. 1785

REVEREND SIR: Your obliging approbation of my Tour with our great friend has given me a very high satisfaction; for, besides the value of praise *a laudato viro*,[3] you are peculiarly *competent* (as we say in the law) to judge of what I have done to preserve Dr. Johnson really "as he was."

You have favoured me with several interesting Anecdotes for his Life. May I beg that in addition to that goodness, you may be pleased to let me have what letters he wrote to you, however short, that my Collection may be enriched with them. You mentioned to me[4] that they are chiefly recommendations of visitors to your University. But they will be of value. So pray send them to me, to the care of Mr. Dilly Bookseller London.

I am going down to Scotland to pass the Christmas Holidays with my Wife and Children, and I hope to be here again early in february,[5] that I may go on with my large Work, for which I solicit more communications from you.

I shall at all times be happy in an opportunity of enjoying your conversation. I beg to have my best compliments presented to Miss Adams, and I remain with most sincere respect, My Dear Sir, Your much obliged and faithful humble servant

JAMES BOSWELL

[1] "Oxford" is deleted and "Gloucester" added in another hand. See *ante* From Adams, 17 Feb. 1785 and n. 1.

[2] Again, Adams seems to have confused his dates; see *ante* To Adams, 21 Jan. 1785 and *post* From Adams, 12 July 1786.

[3] Naevius, *Hector Proficiscens*; quoted by Cicero, *Tusculan Disputations* iv. 31. Quoted by JB again, *Life* iv. 423.

[4] *Ante* 28 Mar. 1785.

[5] JB left London this day, after stopping overnight at Dilly's, and arrived in Edinburgh on the 28th. He spent Christmas in York as the guest of the poet William Mason, and enjoyed some very spirited conversation. On 1 Feb. he was back in London (Journ.). A codicil to his will, dated 22 Dec. 1785, puts the materials for the *Life* in Malone's charge.

From Thomas Warton,
Thursday 22 December 1785

MS. Yale (C 3073). Received 2 Jan. (Reg. Let.).

ADDRESS: To James Boswell Esq., at Mr. Dilly's Bookseller, in the Poultry, London.

POSTMARK: 23 DE.

Trin. Coll. Oxon., Dec. 22, 1785

DEAR SIR: I shall be in town within a fortnight, when I will bring the Letters with me. But if wanted sooner, I will send them almost immediately.—In the mean time, I am to beg pardon for not sending them before the 16th instant, according to promise. But the hurry of an Election (in which I have succeeded)[1] deranged everything. I hope you will admitt this excuse; and am Dear Sir, Your most obedient Servant

T. WARTON

P.S. Excuse my awkward direction of this—I know not your address exactly.

---

[1] MS., apparently, "suceeded". Warton was elected Camden Professor of History on 1 Dec. 1785, succeeding Dr. Scott (H. Stuart Jones, "The Foundation and History of the Camden Chair", *Oxoniensia*, 1943–44, viii–ix. 187). I owe this reference, which corrects DNB, to Dr. Powell.

1786

From Francis Barber,
Saturday 7 January 1786

MS. Hyde.

ADDRESS: Mr. Boswell.[1]

ENDORSEMENT: Mr. Barber No. 47 St. John Street Smithfield.

[London,] Saturday January 7th 1786

SIR: These are all the Letters I now have in my possession in my late Master's hand,[2] I had more, but in removing from Bolt Court[3] the rest were by some means or other lost. I return you many thanks for your *Tour* which I had by your order from Mr. Dilley. I am Sir, your humble Servant

FRAS. BARBER

From Francesco Sastres,[1]
London, Wednesday 22 February 1786[2]

MS. Yale (C 2430). Note by JB at end: "Mr. Sastres has eleven letters from Dr. Johnson of which I am to have copies."[3]

[1] On 22 Dec. 1785, the day JB left London for Edinburgh, he "Met Dr. Johnson's Frank in the street, and he promised to search for every scrap of his Master's handwriting, and give all to me. It vexed me to be told that he had burnt some letters from Dr. Johnson to Mrs. Johnson" (Journ.). In the expectation of returning to London in the near future JB probably instructed Barber to deposit whatever he found with Dilly.

[2] *Life* ii. 62, 115, 116; *Letters SJ* 207, 238, 241. The MSS. are now in the Hyde Collection. See Mary Hyde, "Not in Chapman," *Johnson, Boswell and Their Circle*, p. 319.

[3] SJ lived at No. 8 Bolt Court from Mar. 1776 until his death (*Life* iii. 536).

[1] Francesco Sastres (fl. 1776–1822), Italian teacher and translator, Consul-General to the Kingdom of the Two Sicilies from 1796. See *Life* iv. 443 and Elizabeth H. Thorne, "Francesco Sastres," *English Miscellany* (1964) xv. 175–93. The journal records several meetings

between JB and Sastres, beginning 10 Apr. 1779 at SJ's house. On 14 June of the present year Sastres led JB on an unsuccessful mission to obtain Johnsonian materials from Mrs. Charlotte (Cotterell) Lewis and her sister Frances (Journ.; see also *Life* i. 244–45 and *Thraliana*, p. 579 n. 4).

[2] The MS. consists of two main parts, written at different times. The first, Sastres's record of SJ's "advices", is headed with the date of the interview and was probably written the same night, as SJ urged, or soon thereafter. The second part, Sastres's reflections on the character of SJ, is evidently a later addition composed for JB. The two last anecdotes appear to have been written still later. The date I have assigned to the MS. as a whole is the probable date of presentation to JB. It was on this day that the two met at the Essex Head Club, after which "Sastres walked home with me" (Journ.). Four days later JB told Lord Thurlow of the compliment paid him by SJ, according to Sastres (Journ.).

[3] See *post* From Sastres, c. Feb. 1788.

Sunday the 28 Novr. 1784. At 10 o'clock at night.
Dr. Samuel Johnson's Advices to Francesco Sastres.

Mr. Sastres. We are now by ourselves (Mr. Hoole[4] only in the room[4a] besides the Dr. and me) and nobody hears us. No one has shown more affection to me than you have in the course of our friendship. You have constantly called upon me and been very kind and very good to me—let me now be good to you also.

In your Situation in life you must Struggle for your livelyhood in the world. You have however a profession and you discharge the duties of it, as I beleive, with fedelity innocence and purity: and give, as far as I can find, great Satisfaction. Do always so and never lose the character of an honest man. As long as you live do all the good you can and never do any harm. Think how short is life and how long eternity! Never suffer yourself to be tempted by pleasures that are against virtue. These are the ways of the Devil and lead to hell. You are a Roman chatholick; you was born so. If you practise the duties of your religion you may, as I think, be saved; and we shall, I hope, meet in heaven:—for I beleave thousands of your persuasion are saved. But if the true light of heaven should come upon you and make you think more rightly, then become one of us. But dont do it unless you are quite convinced of the superiority of our religion over yours. Dont do it through hypocritical principles. You may read the controversy between the two religions and come at the truth of the matter.[5] Let no worldly prospect or the hope of the favour of the great ever induce you to do it. Consider how little and insignificant are the advantages and views of this life compared with those of a life to come. What can the world do now for me in my present situation? I am upon the brink of eternity! I recollect my past offences, I repent of having committed them and only hope to be saved through the merits and the mediation of our Saviour Jesus Christ. You are, my dear Sastres, the third person to whom I Speak in this free way.[6] Remember what I have now told you in this solemn manner and when you get home write it down with the

---

[4] See *ante* From Taylor, 6 May 1785 and n. 16; and Hoole's version of SJ's exhortation to Sastres, *Johns. Misc.* ii. 151–52.

[4a] MS. "roon"

[5] In his will SJ bequeathed "to Mr. Sastres, the Italian master, the sum of five pounds, to be laid out in books of piety for his own use" (*Life* iv. 403 n.).

[6] The others being Hoole and Dr. Brocklesby: see *Johns. Misc.* ii. 152 n. 2; *Life* iv. 414; *ante* From Brocklesby, 27 Dec. 1784 and ?17–18 Apr. 1785.

date of the year. God bless you* and protect you through Jesus Christ—Amen. [7]

This truly great man breathed his last Monday the 13th Decr. 1784, about half an hour after seven in the evening whilest I was alone in the dining room waiting to see Franc in order to ask him how his master was.

*The concluding words after *God b[l]ess you* are of the preceding night (Saturday the 27) when I was taking my leave of my great and worthy friend at about eleven o'clock. I have hadded them to the conclusion of the above truly excellent advices, because I am proud of so solemn a blessing from so great, so virtous and so excellent a man; whose equal many centuries will perhaps not see. For, considering his exalted mind, his astonishing and very exstensive Knowledge, his rigid love of truth, his constant practise of every moral and religious virtue, and (what is very extraordinary for so great a philosopher and celebrated author) his examplary piety and unspotted character as a christian, who can name his equal[8] and match[9] him with any of the first characters (in the same sphere of life) either in antient or modern history? He was a bulwark of religion, a colosse of litterature and a very zelous champion for virtue. What he professed in theory and in speculation he was the first to put rigidly in practice; and his own bright example constantly accompanied his precepts. It may justly be said upon the whole that he was one of those rare characters that are now and then send by heaven into the world in order to show how far men may advance during their lives in Wisdom and Knowledge, in moral and religious excellence. It may be reckoned as one among the many praises that are due to him that he had friends among the great without having at any time flattered any of them. He was very sollicitous in doing good even when he was far from being well, and he always did it without ostentation and with great simplicity. Those who have only felt the severity of his criticism will naturally speak of him as they feel; but those who have had the good fortune of knowing him intimately well will for ever lament and sensibly feel his loss. And whenever they comtemplate the high excellency of his mind and the great goodness of his heart will be induced to think with me that Nature in forming great and good men, destined to

[7] Not used.
[8] MS. "(excepting Socrates)" deleted.
[9] MS. "macth" (perhaps not inadvertently).

enlighten the world and to serve as examples to the rest of mankind, will with difficulty form again such a man as Dr. Samuel Johnson.

As to his faults (for who is obsolutely free from them?), when fairly and impartially weighed with every thing that was good excellent and great in him, [they] may be considered as a feather in one scale against a pound weight in the other: or, perhaps more justly, as small rivers compared to the main ocean. They will only prove (altho' it is the duty of every one and highly worthy of praise to endevour to be as perfect as possible in every thing) that there is no obsolute perfection in this life. If strictly speaking there was such a thing in the world as obsolute perfection in man, it would be a melancholy consideration indeed; and the atheists (if such beings really exist) and the enemies of religion might then[10] overthrow one of the strongest arguments in favour of a future state "drawn from the perpetual progress of the soul to its perfection, without a possibility of ever arriving at it."*[11]

He had the highest opinion of Lord Thorlow. I heard him once say in a company at his own house—"I'll prepare myself for the company of no man in England except My Lord Thorlow's—as to him I should like to know a day before I am to meet him."[12]

The las year before he died when he was forming the Essex Head Club he invented a new word to express at once a good member of such a society. He having said that Mr. Boswel should be one of the number I observed that there could be no better member—upon which Dr. Johnson replied "to be sure, Sir, Boswel is a very *clubable man* he will bring and he will carry away."[13]

* Adison.

To *William Bowles,*
Monday 27 February 1786

MS. Yale (L 265). JB's copy, headed: "To Wm. Bowles Esq."

London, 27 febry. 1786

DEAR SIR: Since I last had the pleasure of corresponding with you, I have been twice in Scotland, and am at last called to the english bar;[1] so that I hope to have more frequent opportunities of meeting you.

---

[10] MS. "them"
[11] Not used. The quotation is from *Spectator* No. 111.

[12] *Life* iv. 327. See *ante* n. 2.
[13] *Life* iv. 254 n. 2.
[1] See Journ. 9 Feb. and following.

Our Johnsonian Club in Essex Street goes on exceedingly well, and I doubt not of its continuing for many many years to be an instructive and entertaining Society.[2]

I will now, Sir, be much obliged to you, if you will send me Dr. Johnson's letters to you, and the Anecdotes of him, according to your kind promise. They will be interweaved in his Life chronologically, and I hope you will give me leave to authenticate the Anecdotes with your name.

The packets may be sent under cover of John Courtenay Esq.[3] M.P. London. I am Dear Sir, your most obedient humble servant

To Thomas Warton, Monday 27 February 1786

Missing. Sent to Oxford from London. Reg. Let.: "Rev. Mr. Tho. Warton begging he may now send me his letters from Dr. Johnson."

From Thomas Warton, Monday 27 February 1786

MS. Yale (C 3074). Received 3 Mar. (Reg. Let.).

ADDRESS: To James Boswell Esqr., London.

Oxon., Feb. 27th, 1786

DEAR SIR: You will receive the Papers on Monday or Tuesday next, by the hands of Mr. Hamilton (late Printer)[1] of Princes Street Bedford Row.

[2] "I believe there are few societies where there is better conversation or more decorum. Several of us resolved to continue it after our great founder was removed by death. Other members were added; and now, above eight years since that loss, we go on happily" (*Life* iv. 254 n. 2).

[3] John Courtenay (1738–1816), Irish-born poet, essayist, and politician, was an intimate friend of both SJ and JB, and a member of The Club. He was M.P. for Tamworth, 1780–96, and for Appleby, 1796–1807, 1812–12 (Judd 1095). His speeches in Parliament were notable for candour and a strong satiric strain

(see e.g. *Gent. Mag.*, 1785, lv. 869–70); nevertheless, it was he who, says JB (Journ. 22 Feb. 1791), "obligingly assisted me in *lightening* my animadversions on Mrs. Piozzi in my *Life of Johnson*—for my own credit". Courtenay's *Poetical Review of the Literary and Moral Character of the Late Samuel Johnson, LL.D.* was published this spring.

[1] Archibald Hamilton (c. 1719–93), founder of *The Critical Review*, partner in the management of the University Press at Oxford (*Life* iii. 475; Plomer). See Journ. 19 Apr. 1783; *Gent. Mag.* (1793) lxiii. 285.

HH*

I am exceedingly obliged to you for the Present of your most entertaining *Tour*.[2] I was very unfortunate in not finding you in town.[3] I am with great Regard, Dear Sir, your most faithful and obedient Servant

T. WARTON

From William Bowles, Wednesday 22 March 1786

MS. Yale (C 558). Received 30 Mar. (Reg. Let.).

ADDRESS: James Boswell Esqr.

Heale near Sarum, Mar. 22. 1786

DEAR SIR, I am to ask pardon for my delay in acknowledging your fav[o]r of Feb. 27. I have had bus'ness at our Assizes which has hindered me and I have been also very disagreably taken up with illness in my family. I have got ready what you ask for respecting our old friend; but in a few days I expect an old friend of his[1] on a visit and shall wish to shew him what I have written. It will be probably of advantage to the Papers. You must do as you please respecting my name, but I would wish not to have my name mentioned: it may be said "communicated by a member of the club in Essex street." I should be better content with this.

It would be a great pleasure to me to have the honor of waiting on you here at any time. In the mean time (with Mrs. Bowles's best Compliments) I am Dear Sir, Your most obedient and humble Servant

W. BOWLES

To Edmond Malone,[1] Wednesday 22 March 1786

MS. Yale (L 932). JB's copy. Misdated 20 Mar. in Reg. Let.

[2] Ordered by Malone to be sent "on account of his budget of letters" (Malone to JB, 3 Jan. 1786).

[3] See *ante* From T. Warton, 22 Dec. 1785. JB did not return to London from Edinburgh until 1 Feb. (Journ.).

[1] W. J. Mickle? See *post* From Bowles, 1 Mar. 1787.

[1] JB's friend, critic, executor, and editor; editor of Shakespeare; member of The Club. See *Life* and Journ. *passim* and J. M. Osborn, "Edmond Malone and Dr. Johnson," *Johnson, Boswell and Their Circle*, pp. 1 ff. Malone's MS. strictures on Hawkins's *Life of Johnson*, nowhere mentioned in his correspondence or in JB's journal, are preserved in the William Salt Library, Stafford. They are printed in Davis, *Johnson before Boswell*, pp. 188–94.

TO MALONE, 22 MARCH 1786

. . . Courtenay once proposed that an Action should be brought against the Publisher of Peter Pindar's Attack which we have now repelled.[3] But what would you think of prosecuting him for the Post[s]cript in which he falsely asserts that a conversation passed between *him* and Dr. Johnson in which the Doctor spoke of me in the most contemptous manner, and *particularly* enlarged on my being incapable to write his Life.[4] Absurdly malignant as this really is, it *may* be believed by many people, and therefore *may* injure the success of my GREAT WORK. I own I am not much affraid of this. But if I thought that a verdict would be obtained merely to proclaim the faleshood of the fellow and punish him in the most *tender* part of his *purse*, I certainly should prosecute. And you will consider if this would not give an opportunity to announce the Work in the most splendid manner. Erskine[5] would expatiate upon it as not only to be the Life and Conversation of the first Genius etc. etc. etc. but the History of Literature and Literary Men during a considerable period.[6] A letter or two of Dr. Johnson's to me

[2] Where JB was attending the Assizes, on the northern Circuit. See BP xvi. 179–80.

[3] *A Poetical and Congratulatory Epistle to James Boswell, Esq. on his Journal of a Tour to the Hebrides, with the Celebrated Doctor Johnson,* by "Peter Pindar" (John Wolcot) was published in Feb. "Read in the hackney coach as I drove along a scurrilous attack in verse upon me under the name of Peter Pindar" (Journ. 24 Feb.). Pindar charged JB with cowardly submission to Lord Macdonald's "severe remonstrance" over "scandalous passages" in the *Tour*. JB replied in the newspapers in Mar. and in *Gent. Mag.* for Apr. (lvi. 285). In his *Bozzy and Piozzi*, published 24 Apr., Pindar renewed the charge. See Prof. Pottle's full account of the controversy between JB and Lord Macdonald, BP xvi. 221–59.

[4] "Whenever Bozzy expires, he will create no *vacuum* in the region of literature—he seems strongly affected by the *cacoethes scribendi* ["itch for writing": Juvenal, *Satires* vii. 52] . . . The account

[*Corsica*] is a farrago of disgusting egotism and pompous inanity. . . . were I sure that James Boswell would write *my* life, I do not know whether I would not anticipate the measure, by taking *his*. . . . He dares not—he would make a scarecrow of me. I give him liberty to fire his blunderbuss in *his own* face, but not murder *me*. Sir, I heed not *his* αυτος εφα [*ipse dixit*]—Boswell write my life! why the fellow possesses not abilities for writing the life of an *ephemeron*."

[5] Thomas Erskine (1750–1823), barrister; Lord Chancellor and first Baron Erskine of Restormel, 1806. See Journ. *passim.* Erskine was a distant cousin of JB's and very helpful to him when he was called to the English bar. JB is suggesting that he be engaged to plead the proposed libel action against the publisher. —I owe this note to Prof. Pottle.

[6] ". . . the whole exhibiting a view of literature and literary men in Great-Britain, for near half a century, during which he flourished" (title-page).

might be *proved* and read;[7] as might Dr. Blair's to me,[8] and if necessary a good deal of parole evidence might be produced to shew how gross the calumny is. Perhaps even Lord Carmarthen's letter containing the polite approbation of a Great Personage[9] might be introduced. Do consult with Mr. Courtenay as to this; for, it appears to me a very good use might be made of such an Action. . . .

From Edmond Malone, Monday 27 March 1786

MS. Yale (C 1907).

London, March 27, 1786

. . . I have read Mrs. Piozzi's book twice through[1]; there is a great deal of good stuff in it; but many of your stories, not half so well told. The story of Graham, whom she ignorantly calls *Eaton* Graham, is murdered;[2]—as are some others, but many are told well. I suppose you have got it by this time and found yourself in p. 261.[3]

[7] None of SJ's known letters to JB—which means essentially those printed (frequently extracted) in the *Life*—mentions the biography. But JB is probably thinking rather of the doubt cast by Pindar on SJ's esteem for him; and any of a dozen letters would have served in refutation.

[8] Of 3 Mar. 1785, quoted in the *Tour* (*Life* v. 398).

[9] On 1 Mar. JB had "waited on Sir Francis Lumm who had obligingly procured me from Sir John Caldwell a Minute of the conversation between the King and Dr. Johnson which was in the late Sir James Caldwell's repositories. . . . He gave me Lord Carmarthen's Letter to him containing his Majesty's permission that the Minute should be delivered to me to make what use of it I should think proper in my *Life of Dr. Johnson*" (Journ.). JB quotes the letter, *Life* ii. 34 n. 1. See also *ante* Introduction, p. xlvii, note.

[1] *Anecdotes of the Late Samuel Johnson, LL.D.* was published 25 Mar.

[2] "They [SJ and Goldsmith] had spent an evening with Eaton Graham too,

I remember hearing it was at some tavern; his heart was open, and he began inviting away; told what he could do to make his college agreeable, and begged the visit might not be delayed. Goldsmith thanked him, and proposed setting out with Mr. Johnson for Buckinghamshire in a fortnight; 'Nay hold, Dr. *Minor* (says the other), I did not invite you' " (*Johns. Misc.* i. 270). Malone, in his copy of the *Anecdotes* (lent Dr. Powell—my informant—by Mr. Urquhart of Balliol College), underlined "Eaton" and noted in the margin: "Mr. Graham, author of 'Telemachus a Masque,' and one of the tutors at Eton . . . See this story much better told in Boswell *Tour to the Hebrides*, 2nd edit. p. 100 [*Life* v. 97]."

[3] "I fancy Mr. B—— has not forgotten, that though his friend one evening in a gay humour talked in praise of wine as one of the blessings permitted by heaven, when used with moderation, to lighten the load of life, and give men strength to endure it; yet, when in consequence of such talk *he* thought fit to make a Bacchanalian discourse in its favour, Mr. Johnson contradicted him

I think the conclusion is *pointed*, on purpose to gratify Mrs. Mountague.[4] I long to see your *report* of the same story. She seems clearly to mean that it should be understood that Dr. J. called you a *liar*; whereas it is manifest that his argument is *general*, and not ad hominem—otherwise than thus: "if you wish to avail yourself of that position (*in vino veritas*), to make it of any use to you you must confess yourself not a man of truth, when you are sober. I do not say this is the case, but such is the dilemma you are driven to, to give your argument any weight." —Such I think was his meaning. She does not, I think, write about Johnson *cordato animo*;[5]—and there is an evident weakness, and flimzy statement, when she comes at the end to account for her going to Bath. She contradicts all the former part of her book, and would have the reader think that the eighteen years intercourse with J. was a *bondage*, which she endured *to please Mr. Thrale*, but when he was dead it became insupportable;—and so she was forced to fly to Bath:[6]—when in truth she was flying not *from* Dr. J. but *to* a new husband; who does not appear upon the canvass.

She hints at a quarrel between Dr. J. and Master Pepys, but does not tell the particulars. I think you have them.[7] I can't guess which of the members of the Club it was that was so completely *down'd* in p. 202.[8] . . .

---

somewhat roughly as I remember; and when to assure himself of conquest he added these words, You must allow me, Sir, at least that it produces truth; *in vino veritas*, you know, Sir—'That (replied Mr. Johnson) would be useless to a man who knew he was not a liar when he was sober'" (*Johns. Misc.* i. 320–21). Malone noted (later) in his copy: "This story was told to Mrs. Thrale by Mr. Boswell himself and she (as usual) has not recorded half the circumstances attending it. See Boswell's *Life of Johnson* i. 377 4to ii. 45 8° 1793 [*Life* ii. 187–88]."

[4] See next letter.

[5] With a judicious spirit. I am unable to locate this quotation, if it *is* a quotation.

[6] *Johns. Misc.* i. 339–41. Malone noted (later) in his copy: "The whole of the account given in this [p. 291] and the two following pages is false. See Boswell's

Life of Johnson, ii. 528 et seq. iii. 605 8vo edit. 1793 [*Life* iv. 340]."

[7] *Johns. Misc.* i. 244–45. JB does not appear to have had the particulars: see *Life* iv. 82 and n. 1. For Pepys's own account of the quarrel, which was over SJ's *Life of Lyttelton*, see *Johns. Misc.* ii. 416–17; for Fanny Burney's account, *Life* iv. 65 n. 1. See also *ibid.* 487–88.

[8] "One gentleman however, who dined at a nobleman's house in his company and that of Mr. Thrale, to whom I was obliged for the anecdote, was willing to enter the lists in defence of King William's character, and having opposed and contradicted Johnson two or three times petulantly enough; the master of the house began to feel uneasy, and expected disagreeable consequences: to avoid which he said, loud enough for the Doctor to hear, Our friend here has no meaning now in all this, except just to

To Edmond Malone,
Friday 31 March 1786

MS. Yale (L 934). JB's copy.

Lanc⟨aster,⟩ 31 March 1786

. . . And now for La Signora Piozzi. I received her by the coach only last night *Thursday*, and her journey down cost me within 6d of her original price.[1] I however did not grudge the cost, and *devoured* her as you say. I had before the Book arrived, two *whets* in the *Herald*.[2] She is a little artful impudent malignant Devil. She relates that Johnson in reference to her *littleness* said Insects have gay colours.[3] I will add Insects are often *venomous* have often *stings*. It is *clear* that she *means* to bite me as much as she can, that she may curry favour with Mrs. Montague.[4] P. 44 is *undoubtedly* levelled at me; for, it *describes* what the Jade has often seen me do—but with Dr. Johnson's *approbation*; for he at all times was flattered by my preserving what fell from his mind when shaken by conversation, so there was nothing *like* treachery.[5] I must have the patience of

relate at club to-morrow how he teized Johnson at dinner to-day—this is all to do himself *honour*. No, upon my word, replied the other, I see no *honour* in it, whatever you may do. 'Well, Sir! (returned Mr. Johnson sternly) if you do not *see* the *honour*, I am sure I *feel* the *disgrace*' " (*Johns. Misc.* i. 285). Malone's inference that the combatant was a member of *The* Club is clearly unwarranted, as he must have come to realize when he later identified him, in a note to his copy of the *Anecdotes*, as "Mr. Poltinger" —whom I have been unable to identify further.

———

[1] Four shillings (Clifford, *Piozzi*, p. 263, n. 3).

[2] There were actually four "whets"— or instalments—of "Leaves, collected from the Piozzian Wreath, lately woven to adorn the Shrine of the departed Dr. Johnson" (*Morning Herald*, 27–30 Mar.).

[3] *Johns. Misc.* i. 331; quoted, *Life* i. 495.

[4] The reference is to Mrs. Piozzi's embarrassment over SJ's statement in the *Tour* (*Life* v. 245) that she was unable to read through Mrs. Montagu's

Essay on Shakespear. In a Postscript to the *Anecdotes* she made an equivocal denial (actually composed by Sir Lucas Pepys and Cadell, but using her own words from her letter to Pepys). JB, assisted by Malone and Courtenay (Journ. 15 Apr. 1786), replied in the newspapers on 18 and 20 Apr., and again in a foot-note to the third edition of the *Tour* (*Life* v. 245 n. 2). For a full account of this episode, see J. L. Clifford, "The Printing of Mrs. Piozzi's *Anecdotes of Dr. Johnson*", *Bull. Rylands Lib.* (1936) xx. 157–59. Towards the end of the present letter JB discusses the provocative passage at some length, but as it has no direct bearing on the *Life* I have omitted it.

[5] "This I thought a thing so very particular, that I begged his leave to write it down directly, before any thing could intervene that might make me forget the force of the expressions: a trick, which I have however seen played on common occasions, of sitting steadily down at the other end of the room to write at the moment what should be said in company, either *by* Dr. Johnson or *to* him, I never practised myself, nor approved of in

Job to bear the Book of *Esther*. But I shall trim her *recitativo* and all her *airs*.[6]

The *retort* upon *in vino veritas* which she affects to *remember* as if she had been *present* was told to her by myself,[7] and she has either forgotten or misrepresented the true state of it. The argument in favour of drinking was maintained by me one evening at the Crown & Anchor where Dr. Johnson supt with Lord Binning and his tutor, Langton, myself, and ⟨?one or two⟩ more. But I have it all in writing. It was I think in ⟨?1772. ?My⟩ Journal will ascertain it all exactly. I am pretty certain his answer to *in vino veritas* was "Sir a fellow is not much to be regarded who cannot speak truth till you fill him drunk." I am *sure* he did not *point* his fire personally to *me*, till after I had teased him long, to bring out all I could. When I at last said, "But Sir would not you drink to forget care, to forget every thing disagreable?" *Johns.* "Yes,—if I sat next *you*."[8] *Madam* as *Sam* said "has no care about truth." . . . *Eaton* Graham is I fancy only an errour of the press; for, he was an under Master or Usher at Eton School.

She seems to have had no *affection* for our great friend, but merely the attachment of vanity.

She describes him as barbarous and dirty. The story of spitting her relations is I suppose exagerated;[9] or she must have provoked him confoundedly by *affectation* of grief. The Book however has a great deal of valuable memorabilia, which prove themselves genuine. But there is seldom the true *zest*. She puts cherries in the brandy. . . .

another. There is something so ill-bred, and so inclining to treachery in this conduct, that were it commonly adopted, all confidence would soon be exiled from society, and a conversation assembly-room would become tremendous as a court of justice" (*Johns. Misc.* i. 175).

[6] In allusion now to Handel's oratorio, *Esther*.

[7] Repeated, *Life* ii. 188 n. 3. Cf. *ibid.* 193 n. 1.

[8] JB's recollection was substantially correct. But in translating the journal (15 Apr. 1772) into the *Life*, he separated the conversation into two parts (ii. 188–89 and 193), inserting in the first the phrase "in general" to clarify (taking his cue from Malone) the intent of SJ's remark,

and changing "I" to "A gentleman" in the second to avoid undermining his case against Mrs. Piozzi's representation (ii. 188 n.3). Hill astutely saw through the device (ii. 193 n. 1). Mrs. Piozzi saw through the anonym (*loc. cit.*).

[9] "When I one day lamented the loss of a first cousin killed in America—'Prithee, my dear (said he), have done with canting: how would the world be worse for it, I may ask, if all your relations were at once spitted like larks, and roasted for Presto's supper?' " (*Johns. Misc. i.* 189). JB quotes the anecdote, and sets against it Baretti's version for the purpose of exposing its "exaggeration and distortion" (*Life* iv. 347).

To Thomas Warton,
Thursday 13 April 1786

Missing. Sent to Oxford from London. Reg. Let.: "Rev. Mr. Tho. Warton thanking him for his valuable communications concerning Dr. Johnson[1]—putting a few queries—begging to know if I can be of any service to him to make some return.[2] May perhaps be a week at Oxford this vacation."

From Thomas Warton,
Saturday 15 April 1786

MS. Yale (C 3075). Received 16 Apr. (Reg. Let.).

ADDRESS: To James Boswell Esq., at Mr. Dilly's Bookseller, in the Poultry, London.

POSTMARK: 15 AP.

Oxon., April 15th, 1786

DEAR SIR: Miss Jones[1] lived at Oxford, and was often of our parties. She was a very ingenious poetess, and published a volume of poems; and on the whole was a most sensible, agreeable, and amiable woman. She was sister of the Rev. Oliver Jones,[2] Chantor of Christ Church Cathedral at Oxford, and Johnson used to call her the *Chantress*. I have heard him often address her in this passage from *Il Penseroso*,

> Thee, Chantress, oft the woods among
> I woo, etc.

She died, unmarried, about fifteen years ago.

Of Miss Roberts,[3] if you please, we will say nothing more.

---

[1] A notebook containing Warton's transcripts of eighteen letters from SJ to him and one to Sir Robert Chambers. It was used as printer's copy for the *Life* (*passim*). The originals are at Trinity College, Oxford (see *Letters SJ passim*).

[2] MS. "returned"

printed, *ibid*. n. 4. For a list of Miss Jones's writings, see *ibid*. 545–46.

[2] Misread by JB "River" Jones, and so printed; corrected, *Life* vi (1964), 489 (Errata). Oliver Jones (c. 1706–75) received his B.A., 1726, and M.A., 1729, at Oxford (*Alum. Oxon*.). In his obituary, *Gent. Mag.* xlv. 255, he is designated "Senior Chaplain of Christ Church, Oxford".

---

[1] Mary Jones (fl. 1740–71), mentioned in SJ's letter to Warton, 21 June 1757 (*Life* i. 322). The whole of this paragraph but the last phrase was transcribed by JB into Warton's notebook as a gloss, and

[3] Miss Roberts (fl. 1758–63) was Bennet Langton's first cousin. She is mentioned in SJ's letter to Warton, 14 Apr. 1758 (*Life* i. 336). See also *ibid*. 430. Warton's reticence is unexplained.

My *Spenserian design* was hindered by taking pupils in this College.[4]

I suppose Johnson means, that my *kind intention* of being the *first* to give him the good news of the Degree being granted, was *frustrated*, because Dr. King brought it before my intelligence arrived.[5]

I must forever most heartily regret, that I neglected to committ to paper many of his conversations, now totally forgotten; for in his earlier visits at Oxford, he lived with me almost intirely.[6] And in town, I have passed much time with him. I am, Dear Sir, your most faithful humble Servant

T. WARTON

P.S. Excuse my Address, as I do not exactly know when you are in town.

To the Rev. Dr. William Adams, Monday 17 April 1786

Missing. Sent to Oxford from London. Reg. Let.: "Rev. Dr. Adams Oxford hoping to see him at Oxford next week—begging to know if he will be there."

From the Rev. Dr. William Adams, c. Tuesday 18 April 1786

Missing. Sent to London from Oxford. Received 19 Apr. (Reg. Let.): "Rev. Dr. Adams Oxford, that he will be glad to welcome me there. Wishing to know a day before I come."

To the Rev. Dr. Hugh Blair, Friday 21 April 1786

MS. Yale (L 60). JB's copy.

London, 21 April 1786

. . . A third edition of my *Tour to the Hebrides* is in the press; and I am preparing for my Great Work the *Life of Dr. Johnson*, which

---

[4] SJ to Warton, 28 Nov. 1754 (*Life* i. 276). JB combines Warton's gloss in the notebook with that of the present letter, *ibid.* n. 3.

[5] SJ to Warton, Feb. 1755 (*Life* i. 280 and n. 1). The degree was the M.A. conferred by Oxford.

[6] Cf. *Life* i. 270 n. 5. Warton later (perhaps 29 Apr.: see Journ.) supplied JB with a long "memorial" of SJ's visit with him in 1754 (Paper Apart for MS. *Life*, p. 155: *Life* i. 271–74).

will be, I trust, a very valuable acquisition to the Philo[lo]gical World. I am still receiving additional materials. Mr. Thomas Warton lately sent me a series of Dr. Johnson's letters to him, with notes explaining and illustrating them. His Majesty has been pleased to signify by a letter from Lord Carmarthen to Sir Francis Lumm who favoured me with communications which were in the possession of the late Sir James Caldwell, that I have permission to publish the minute of the Conversation between the King and Dr. Johnson.[1] I will venture to promise that my Life of my revered Friend will be the richest piece of Biography that has ever appeared. The Bullion will be immense, whatever defects there may be in the workmanship.

You have no doubt read Mrs. Piozzis *Anecdotes*, and probably have seen my Retort courteous to her Postscript.[2] Her Book is very entertaining, and she has preserved a good deal of genuine Johnsoniana; but she has proved herself to be a wicked, false, ungrateful little vixen. . . .

To the Rev. Dr. William Adams, Saturday 22 April 1786

Missing. Sent to Oxford from London. Reg. Let.: "Rev. Dr. Adams Oxford that I shall be there on thursday the 27. Mr. Malone is to come with me, and we are to stay till monday or tuesday."

From George Steevens,[1] Sunday 23 April 1786

ADDRESS: James Boswell Esqr., Great Queen Street, Lincolns Inn Fields.

ENDORSEMENT: From Mr. Steevens.

MS. Yale (C 2543). This letter, clearly written in response to a request for information, anecdotes, and letters, points to a missing letter from JB. The journal records no meeting with Steevens about this time, but does tell us that JB was "writing letters" on the 20th.

---

[1] See *ante* To Malone, 22 Mar. 1786 and n. 9.

[2] See *ante* To Malone, 31 Mar. 1786 and n. 3.

---

[1] George Steevens (1736–1800), editor of Shakespeare, had lived on intimate terms with SJ, revising his edition of Shakespeare in 1773 and supplying him with anecdotes and quotations for the *Lives of the Poets*. A compulsive and anonymous contributor to the newspapers and magazines, he was certainly or very probably the author of the following: (1) a review of Tyers's *Biographical Sketch of Dr. Samuel Johnson* in *The St. James's Chronicle* for 8–11 Jan. 1785; (2) a collection of Johnsoniana in

[Hampstead Heath,] Sunday Evening April 23

DEAR SIR: In the eleventh book and second chapter of *Tom Jones* (3d edit. 12° Vol. 8. p. 179) you will find the following passage.— "The other, who, like a Ghost, only wanted to be spoke to, readily answered, etc."

As for Tom Tyers, or Tom Tit, I am always happy to assist at what our late friend would have styled the *deplumation* of a thievish bird, who wishes to parade in borrowed feathers, nay receives compliments on their beauty, without once acknowledging whence he had them. [2]

I enclose a few anecdotes set down in the first words that offered. You may either burn these papers, or take such hints from them as you judge to be worth notice. I wish you may find a niche for the earliest of the two letters, [3] as [4] it tends to prove that Dr. Johnson was not wholly disgusted by the encrease of the club, to which he himself contributed at the very time when Mrs. P. represents him

---

The European Magazine for Jan. 1785 (vii. 51–55; reprinted, *Johns. Misc.* ii. 312 ff.), which was incorporated with alterations in the eleventh volume of SJ's *Works* (1787, pp. 212–16); (3) the Johnsonian bibliography which appeared in the same magazine serially from Dec. 1784 to Apr. 1785 (see *ante* From Brocklesby, 13 Dec. 1784 and n. 6); and (4) the strictures on Hawkins's *Life* (by "Philo Johnson") in the same magazine for Apr. and May 1787 (xi. 223–27, 310–13). See Davis, *Johnson Before Boswell*, pp. 21–22.

On 27 Mar. (under 28 Mar.) 1781 at The Club "Stevens told several anecdotes of Dr. Johnson. But I will have them in writing from him, that they may be correctly recorded" (Journ.). Two years later JB took down some anecdotes following an interview with Steevens (Journ. 30 Apr. 1783); if the MS. is among the Boswell Papers, it is not identified. The correspondence appears to begin with the present letter, or exchange, and to end, abruptly, in 1791, when Steevens, after discouraging JB over the prospective sale of the *Life*, proceeded to take an active part in fulfilling the prediction by depreciating the

work (see *post* To Malone, 25 Feb. 1791 and n. 1). For Steevens's malignity, see also *Life* iii. 281–82, iv. 274; BP xiii. 243; and Journ. 28 Mar. 1781.

[2] In the *Tour* SJ is quoted as saying: "Tom Tyers described me the best. He once said to me, 'Sir, you are like a ghost: you never speak till you are spoken to' " (*Life* v. 73). In a foot-note to the passage in the third edition, which appeared late this year, JB gives the source of Tyers's epigram, following Steevens, but without acknowledgement. The figurative use of "deplumation" would not have been original with SJ, had he said it: see OED and his own *Dictionary*. Steevens's witticism, in any case, may have been inspired (as Dr. Powell suggests to me) by SJ's brilliant "depeditation" of Foote, which Steevens would have read in the *Tour* (*Life* v. 130). SJ's characterization of Tyers as Tom Restless in *Idler* No. 48 tends to support Steevens's charge. For JB's account of Tyers and his writings, see *Life* iii. 308–09.

[3] Apparently those of 21 Feb. and 5 Mar. 1774 (*Life* ii. 273–74). The originals are now in the Hyde Collection.

[4] MS. "at"

as having lost all confidence in it, on account of the introduction of "new faces."[5]

I think I shall find other Letters etc. for you, and am always, Your very faithful and obedient

G. STEEVENS

[Enclosure]

I am convinced that Johnson and Garrick had no reciprocal affection. In private they frequently owned their disgust at each other's conduct and manners.[6] The Rambler was envied by the Hero of the Stage, who at once foresaw the extent and durability of his tutor's reputation, and the narrowness and brief existence of his own. The Player's wealth and patrons, were an equal source of discontent to the Moralist, who silently wished for the same advantages, because he knew he could have rendered them more beneficial to mankind. —After Johnson had dined with Garrick at Hampton, the latter would complain that he took insufficient notice of the improvements about his house and gardens;[7] and when Garrick had called on Johnson in Fleetstreet, the former rarely failed to observe how little comfort was to be met with in the society of a man absorbed in thought, and inattentive to his visitants. Johnson heartily despised the profession of Garrick;[8] allowed in conversation that the character of Prospero[9] was designed

---

[5] In the letter SJ informs Steevens: "We are thinking to augment our club, and I am desirous of nominating you." Mrs. Piozzi's recollection of SJ's changing attitude towards The Club is somewhat vague, but she suggests the date of 1775 or 1776 as the turning-point (*Anecdotes: Johns. Misc.* i. 229). However, the fact that SJ contributed to the enlargement of The Club does not necessarily mean that he approved the course it was taking. See Journ. 16 Mar. 1776 and especially *Life* iii. 106.

[6] Cf. Percy (Anderson's *Life of Johnson*, 3rd ed., 1815, p. 50 n.): "There was no great cordiality between Garrick and Johnson; and as the latter kept him much in awe when present, Garrick, when his back was turned, repaid the restraint with ridicule of him and his dulcinea. . . ." At the Shakespeare Jubilee at Stratford-on-Avon in 1769 JB "particularly lamented that [SJ] had not that warmth of friendship for his brilliant pupil, which we may suppose would have had a benignant effect on both" (*Life* ii. 69).

[7] Although SJ frequently ridiculed Garrick's estate, he confessed to him once that "it is the leaving of such places that makes a deathbed terrible" (Margaret Barton, *Garrick*, 1948, p. 160; no authority is cited, but cf. *Johns. Misc.* ii. 394).

[8] *Life* i. 167 and *passim*.

[9] *Rambler* No. 200. See *Life* i. 216 and n. 2.

for him; in the Preface to Shakspeare took care to hint that his ancient copies of that Poet's dramas were inaccessible to their Editor; and was offended with Mr. S—— for telling a different story on a similiar occasion.[10] —Garrick observed that he was the only contemporary Author of eminence who had furnished no public testimony to his powers on the stage. "This," said Johnson, "is a Lie; for neither Akinside, Mason, or Gray, have once recorded his name."[11] —"Now I have quitted the theatre," cries Garrick, "I will sit down and read Shakspeare." " 'Tis time you should," exclaimed Johnson, "for I much doubt if you ever examined one of his plays with diligence from the first scene to the last."[12] —Johnson declared he would never renew his acquaintance with the theatre, because Garrick's indiscriminate banishment of Gentlemen from behind the scenes, had taken away a privilege which he demanded as the writer of *Irene*, and would accept on no other terms.[13] —"Such, Sir," said Johnson, "are the benefits of wealth, that no one ventures to stile Garrick an illiterate man; and yet what does he know? He is not a linguist, he is not a reasoner.[14]

[10] JB quotes the passage in the Preface containing the hint and proceeds to clear Garrick of the charge, *Life* ii. 192. See also Journ. 15 Apr. 1772. In the Advertisement to his and SJ's edition of Shakespeare Steevens writes: "I should be remiss, I am sure, were I to forget my acknowledgments to [Garrick], to whose benevolence I owe the use of several of the scarcest quartos, which I could not otherwise have obtained." See *Life* ii. 192 n. 2, and Hawkins, p. 444. For Steevens's treachery to Garrick, see *Life* iii. 281 n. 3.

[11] Another version of the anecdote appeared among the Johnsoniana Steevens contributed to *The European Magazine* (*Johns. Misc.* ii. 326–27). Garrick is named in Mason's *An Heroic Postscript to the Public* (1774), but as a writer, not as an actor.

[12] Quoted, with the omission of the phrase "with diligence", in a foot-note to the third edition of the *Tour* (*Life* v. 244 n. 2). Steevens is there acknowledged not by name but as "one of the ablest commentators on Shakspeare, who knew much of Dr. Johnson". See *Life* v (1964), 542.

[13] As co-manager of Drury Lane Garrick attempted in 1747 to abolish the practice of admitting gentlemen behind the scenes, but with little success (A. S. Turberville, *Johnson's England*, 1933, ii. 183–84). The published version of Steevens's anecdote clarifies the nature of SJ's grievance: "Sir, while I had, in common with other dramatic authors, the liberty of the scenes, without considering my admission behind them as a favour, I was frequently at the theatre" (*Johns. Misc.* ii. 318).

[14] See however *Life* ii. 377 n. 2, and Thomas Davies, *Memoirs of Garrick*, 1808, ii. 394–95, 397–98. The difficulty of ascertaining SJ's true feeling for Garrick is aggravated by his disposition to take the opposite side whenever Garrick was either praised or censured (*Life* iii. 312)—a mannerism delightfully illustrated by Reynolds in his *Johnson and Garrick* (printed for private circulation, 1816; reprinted, *Johns. Misc.* ii. 232 ff.; see Journ. 9 Sept. 1790). See also Hawkins, pp. 425 ff.; Murphy: *Johns. Misc.* i. 456–57.

A pleasant companion he is;[15] but the mere power of exciting laughter is an unsubstantial talent; and who rises up contented from a table on which whipt syllabub was the principal dish?"[16] —Nor would Garrick's appetite for commendation have been highly gratified by such as Johnson bestowed on him after his death. That this event "eclipsed the gaiety of nations, and impoverished the publick stock of harmless pleasure," sounds to my ear like the chill though elegant praise of one who lamented the actor, but not the man,[17] and proclaimed what was equally true of Shuter[18] and of Garrick. In short, the declarations of the Philosopher and the Player in each others favour, whether in company, or in print, were but specious coverings for a rooted enmity which betrayed itself to those who were the occasional confidants of them both.[19]

It is unfortunate, however, for Johnson that his peculiarities and frailties can be more distinctly traced than his good and amiable exertions. Could the many bounties he studiously concealed, the many acts of humanity he performed in private, be displayed with equal circumstantiality, his defects would be so far lost in the blaze of his virtues, that the latter only would be regarded.[20]

---

[15] SJ called Garrick "the cheerfullest man of his age" (*Life* iii. 387).

[16] "JOHNSON. 'Garrick's conversation is gay and grotesque. It is a dish of all sorts, but all good things. There is no solid meat in it' " (*Life* ii. 464).

[17] SJ's famous epitaph on Garrick, printed in his *Life of Edmund Smith* (*Lives* ii. 21), was the subject of a spirited critical encounter between SJ and JB at a dinner-party on 24 Apr. 1779. Steevens was present (*Life* iii. 386 ff.; Journ.).

[18] Edward ("Comical Ned") Shuter (?1728–76) acted under Garrick at Drury Lane until 1753, when he transferred his services to Covent Garden. He played the original roles of Hardcastle in *She Stoops to Conquer* (1773) and Sir Anthony Absolute in *The Rivals* (1775).

[19] Steevens was not noted for a magnanimous view of human nature, and perhaps he makes his point too severely. Cf. Journ. 15 Apr. 1772.

[20] Steevens had remarked to JB at The Club on 7 Apr. 1775 "that it was a pity Mr. Johnson was so rough, as it prevented many people from knowing his excellence (or some such expression)" (Journ.). This last paragraph of Steevens's first enclosure was copied by JB at the end of the text of the second enclosure, where it is introduced by the statement: "Mr. Steevens adds this testimony." The whole of the second enclosure, thus augmented, served as printer's copy for *Life* iv. 324–25. In copying, JB altered "peculiarities" to "particularities", but not to shade the meaning: the two words are practically interchangeable in the *Life* (e.g. i. 396, ii. 330, iii. 154, iv. 183). The printed text shows some minor revisions, which may have been made by JB in proof, or indeed even by the printer.

[Enclosure]

One evening, previous to the trial of Baretti,[21] a consultation of his friends was held at the house of Mr. Cox the solicitor[22] in Southhampton Buildings, Chancery Lane. Among others present were Mr. Burke and Dr. Johnson, who differed in sentiments concerning the tendency of some part of the defence the Prisoner was to make. When the meeting was over, Mr. Steevens observed that the question between him and his friend had been agitated with rather too much warmth. "It may be so, Sir," replied the Doctor; "for Burke and I should have been of one opinion, if we had no audience."

Dr. Johnson once assumed a character in which perhaps even Mr. Boswell never saw him. His curiosity having been excited by the praises bestowed on the celebrated Torre's fireworks at Marybone gardens,[23] he desired Mr. Steevens to accompany him thither. The evening had proved showery; and soon after the few people present were assembled, publick notice was given that the conductors to the wheels, suns, stars, etc. were so thoroughly water-soaked, that it was impossible any part of the exhibition should be made. "This is a mere excuse," says the Doctor, "to save their crackers for a more profitable company. Let us but hold up our sticks, and threaten to break those coloured Lamps that surround the Orchestra, and we shall soon have our wishes gratified. The core of the fireworks cannot be injured. Let the different pieces be touched in their respective centers, and they will do their offices as well as ever." Some young men who overheard him,

[21] Which took place on 20 Oct. 1769, with SJ, Burke, Reynolds, Garrick, and Goldsmith testifying in Baretti's behalf. See H. W. Liebert, *A Constellation of Genius; Being a Full Account Of the Trial of Joseph Baretti*, etc. (printed for private circulation, New Haven, 1958). JB, whose dislike of Baretti was reciprocated, thought him guilty of murder, even after his acquittal (*Life* ii. 96 ff.; Journ. 5 Apr. 1776). However, in a draft of a letter dated "Autumn 1769" and headed "To Joseph Baretti/a weak absurd letter", JB admits to having been prejudiced and apologizes for his conduct.

[22] Tentatively identified by Dr. Powell (*Life* Index) as Samuel Cox (d. 1776). Cf. *Johns. Misc.* i. 105 and n. 1.
[23] "Signor" Torré, a London print-seller, conducted his pyrotechnics at Marylebone Gardens from 1772 to 1774. A riot took place during one of the displays in 1774, but SJ's name has not been connected with it (*Life* iv. 539). According to Tyers, SJ composed a Latin poem on Torré's fireworks, but there is no trace of it (*Johns. Misc.* ii. 377).

immediately began the violence he had recommended, and an attempt was speedily made to fire some of the wheels which appeared to have received the smallest damage; but to little purpose were they lighted, for most of them completely failed. The Author of *The Rambler*, however, may be considered on this occasion as the ringleader of a successful riot, though not as a skilful pyrotechnist.

It has been supposed that Dr. Johnson, so far as fashion was concerned, was careless of his appearance in public. But this is not altogether true, as the following slight instance may show. Goldsmith's last Comedy was to [be] represented during some Court-mourning;[24] and Mr. S. appointed to call on Dr. Johnson and carry him to the tavern where he was to dine with other of the Poet's friends. The Doctor was ready dressed, but in coloured cloaths; yet being told that he would find every one else in black, received the intelligence with a profusion of thanks, hastened to change his attire, all the while repeating his gratitude for the information that had saved him from an appearance so improper in the front row of a front box. "I would not," added he, "for ten pounds, have seemed so retrograde to any general observance."[25]

He would sometimes found his dislikes on very slender circumstances. Happening one day to mention Mr. Flexman, a dissenting minister, with some compliment to his exact memory in chronological matters, the Dr. replied, "let me hear no more of him, Sir. That is the fellow who made the index to my *Ramblers*, and set down the name of Milton, thus—"Milton. *Mr.* John."[26]

From the Rev. Dr. William Adams, c. Monday 24 April 1786

Missing. Sent to London from Oxford. Received 25 Apr. (Reg. Let.): "Rev. Dr. Adams Oxford, a kind invitation."[1]

---

[24] *She Stoops to Conquer* was first performed on 15 Mar. 1773, about three weeks after the death of the King of Sardinia (*Life* iv. 325 n. 1).

[25] See *Life* iv. 540.

[26] See *Life* iv. 325 n. 3, 540.

[1] JB and Malone set out on the 27th as planned. On the 28th: "Dined Adams's and supt." 29th: "Break[fasted] Inn. [The] Laureat [Thomas Warton] dined with us. Supt Adams." 30th: "Felt dreary. With Malone to St. Mary's. Dr. Weatherell's, etc. Dined Adams, tea Walls Visit Adye sup Adams." 1 May: "To London" (Journ.).

From Thomas Warton,
Wednesday 3 May 1786

MS. Yale (C 3076). Received 6 May (Reg. Let.).

ADDRESS: To James Boswell Esq., at Mr. Dilly's Bookseller, in the Poultry, London.

POSTMARK: 4 MA.

Oxon., May 3d 1786

DEAR SIR: I have just recovered Dr. Johnson's Letter of Thanks for his Doctor's Diploma from Oxford, 1775.[1] I have sent it, as I thought you might wish to see it as soon as possible. Very faithfully Your most obedient

T. WARTON

From the Rev. Dr. Hugh Blair,
Thursday 4 May 1786

MS. Yale (C 162). Received 9 May (Reg. Let.).

ADDRESS: James Boswell of Auchinleck Esqr., London.

4th May 1786, Edinb.

. . . As much as I wish you to attend steadily to what belongs to the business of your Profession, I confess a strong wish to have your great biographical Work given as speedily as you can to the World: and this not only from my own desire of entertainment from it, but upon account of its Success. You must not allow the Memory of the Doctor to languish away upon the Publick; lest their appetite for him, by delay, should fall off. For consider that tho' Dr. Jn. was, really and truly, *a great man*; yet there was much broad mixture in his character, and if the disagreable parts of it, should come to strike the public too strongly, according to the Common Vicissitudes of luck, they might take a disgust, and tire of hearing more about him. I have another reason too for wishing that work published, that then you might have done with Dr. Johnson altogether, and apply close to your Profession. . . . Mrs. Piozzi's

---

[1] *Life* ii. 333. The letter, copied by Dr. Fothergill, with Warton's endorsement, served as printer's copy (Paper Apart for MS. *Life*, p. 452). See *post* From Wetherell, 30 Mar. 1787.

Performance is diverting. She has indeed placed many of the Drs. imperfections in a strong light; and the impression of his Character upon the whole which her book leaves on the reader, is not at all pleasing. Indeed of all the Drs. imperfections, the one which hurts me the most, and which she has put in a strong light, is his extreme arrogance. He certainly put forward higher claims than I think any human Being is entitled to among his Equals. No Respect was sufficient to please him. Had he possessed the abilities of an Archangel I could not have lived with him so much as you did. Mrs. Piozzi's own Character does not appear to advantage in her work: and yet I am not surprized that she wanted at length to get free of him. A Strong, Comprehensive and Vigorous Mind he had, as ever was bestowed on man; but I should think it better to read him, and admire him at a distance like a stupendous object, than to have been too near him. It was a sort of threatening Colossus. This however is a good figure to be displayed to Publick View; and I dare say when properly erected by you and placed on its Pedestal, it will Command our Veneration.

Your *retort Courteous* as you justly Call it to Mrs. Piozzi I have read and admired. Nothing of that kind was ever more happily thrown off. Her apparent denial of the charge, is, as you point out, a mere equivocation: and by her having before read your Mss. you have clenched her fully. At the same time all your expressions are Civil and properly Courteous. I could not but recollect one of the Johnstoniana which you told me[:] "Sir, since Thrale's bridle was off her neck, she has never done one thing that was right."[1] . . .

To the Rev. Dr. William Adams, Friday 5 May 1786

Missing. Sent to Oxford from London. Reg. Let.: "Rev. Dr. Adams Oxford begging to have Dr. Johnson's Letters to him, as also his College exercises; desireous to hear how he is."

[1] "On Sunday, May 16, [1784] I found him alone; he talked of Mrs. Thrale with much concern, saying, 'Sir, she has done every thing wrong, since Thrale's bridle was off her neck'" (*Life* iv. 277).

To Sarah Adams,[1]
Friday 5 May 1786

MS. Yale (L 5). JB's copy, headed: "To Miss Adams Oxford."

London, 5 May 1786

DEAR MADAM: Dr. Adams was so good as to say that he would look for any letters he had from Dr. Johnson, and let me have them to illustrate the Life of our great friend. I will be very much obliged to you if you will do me the favour to assist me in this matter. No letter of Johnson's however short should be lost. If I could also obtain such of his college exercises as still remain in Dr. Adams's possession I should value them as proofs of that extraordinary vigour of mind which shewed itself at all times in a greater or less degree. You who had his *heart* must do all you can to preserve him.

If it is not an improper request, Mr. Malone and I would beg to have a copy of the Rules of the O'Neale Society.[2] We are both very sensible of your polite attention to us, and join in best compliments. I am, Dear Madam, Your most obedient humble servant

From Sarah Adams,
Tuesday 9 May 1786

MS. Yale (C 9). Received 11 May (Reg. Let.).

ADDRESS: James Boswell Esqr., London.

ENDORSEMENT: Miss Adams about Dr. Johnson. 1786.

Oxford, May 9th—86

DEAR SIR: I send you inclosed a Copy of the Rules to be observed at Shanes Castle,[1] as you desired; and I much wish I could also

---

[1] Dr. Adams's daughter (1746–1804), "who was, as [John Gwynn the architect] told me, a very fine scholar" (Journ. 20 Mar. 1776). JB records her part in the Oxford conversations of 10 June 1784, *Life* iv. 291–92, where he speaks of her "good qualities, merit, and accomplishments". She married Benjamin Hyett, of Gloucester, in 1788 (*Johns. Glean.* v. 181).

[2] The O'Neill Society was formed under the aegis of John O'Neill, first Viscount O'Neill (1740–98) in behalf of "the independency and rights of Ireland":

see Historical Manuscripts Commission, Thirteenth Report, Appendix, Part VIII, *The Manuscripts and Correspondence of James, First Earl of Charlemont*, 1894, ii. 31–32. (I owe this reference to J. M. Osborn.) Neither Miss Adams's connexion with the society nor JB's interest in it is explained. The request for the rules may have been Malone's more than JB's.

---

[1] Missing. Perhaps turned over to Malone.

comply with your wishes in procuring any Letters or Papers relating to our ever honor'd friend Dr. Johnson. But my Father assures me he has not anything of the kind here, and if he has preserved any of his Letters he apprehends they must be left in the Country, but he is by no means certain that he has any; and indeed he has been too indifferent of late to be able to exert himself in search of them if they were here, which he hopes will also be admitted as an Apology for his not answering at present the favor of your Letter. If anything should hereafter be found worth communicating to you, I am sure he will be very glad to do it, and I shall not fail to remind him.

I hope I may say my Father is better than when you saw him, tho' not yet perfectly recovered. He joins with me in best compliments to yourself and Mr. Malone, and in regretting that he was not more able to enjoy the pleasure of such agreeable Society whilst you stayed in Oxford.

Mrs. and Miss Hunt[2] and Mrs. Kennicott[3] desire to add their Compliments. I am, Sir, your much obliged humble Servant

S. Adams

To William Bowles, Wednesday 31 May 1786

MS. Yale (L 266). JB's copy, written on side 2 of Bowles's letter of 22 Mar. (*ante*).

London, 31 May 1786

Dear Sir: I beg you may not take it amiss that I renew my solicitation for the performance of your very obliging promise to send me Dr. Johnson's Letters to you, and your Collectanea concerning him. Your last favour which is dated 22 March gave me hopes that in a few days they would be ready. I have now occasion for them, and shall take it very kind if you will be so good as to transmit them without delay, either in packets under cover of John Courtenay

---

[2] Probably Mary (Wells) Hunt (d. 1801), second wife and widow of Rowland Hunt (1707–85), Rector of Stoke Doyle, the late Mrs. Adams's brother, and their only daughter, Mary (1764–1834), preceptress, under the Countess of Elgin, to Princess Charlotte (*Johns. Glean.* v. 194).

[3] Mrs. Ann Kennicott (d. 1830), widow of Benjamin Kennicott (1718–83), the Biblical scholar. She was in SJ's company at Oxford in 1782, when her husband was still living, and again in June 1784, when JB was also present (*Life* iv. 151 n. 2, 285, 288).

Esq. M.P. or in a parcel to be left at my Bookseller's Mr. Dilly in the Poultry.

I look forward with an affectionate wish to the time when I shall make one in your pious society as described to me by our departed Friend. I offer my best respects to Mrs. Bowles and am, Dear Sir, Your most obedient humble servant

From William Thomas Hervey,[1] Monday 5 June 1786

MS. Yale (C 1537).

ADDRESS: James Boswell Esqr., at De Paolis, Upper Seymour Street, Portman Square.

No. 15, George Street, Portland Chapel, June 5th 1786

SIR: Particular business, and indispensable engagement, prevented me for some days looking over my dear Mothers papers; I was very sorry when I did so, to find it fruitless. The letter[2] Sir, I had the honor to mention to you,[3] wou'd have encreased the honor of the wise and enlightened Author. I am sure, Sir, your

---

[1] Son of the Hon. Thomas Hervey (1699–1775) and Ann Coghlan (d. 13 Jan. 1786), daughter of Francis Coghlan, a counsellor-at-law in Ireland (*Gent. Mag.* 1786, lvi. 84). The DNB (s.v. Thomas Hervey) confuses him with his illegitimate half-brother, George Bartman, who was killed at Ticonderoga in 1758. Tom Hervey had another natural son, by Elizabeth Lady Hanmer before he married her. He too was a military man, rose to the rank of colonel, and died c. 1783. William, who was disinherited by his father, is said to have died without issue in 1791, thus bringing to an end the legitimate line of Tom Hervey's descendants. See *Journals of the Hon. William Hervey . . . From 1755 to 1814*, ed. [the Rev.] S. H. A. H[ervey], Bury St. Edmunds, 1906 (Suffolk Green Books, No. XIV), pp. xlii–xlvii. I am indebted to the Hon. David Erskine for calling my attention to this source.

In *Boswelliana* (p. 324) appears the following anecdote credited to Langton:

"A certain young clergyman used to come about Dr. Johnson. The Doctor said it vexed him to be in his company, his ignorance was so hopeless. 'Sir,' said Mr. Langton, 'his coming about you shows he wishes to help his ignorance.' 'Sir,' said the Doctor, 'his ignorance is so great, I am afraid to show him the bottom of it.' " A cancellation in the MS. of *Boswelliana* (Hyde Collection) identifies him as "Tom Harvey's son", and there can be little doubt that he and JB's correspondent are one and the same. (The journal for 30 Apr. 1783 notes that "Tom Harvey's son" came to SJ's as JB was leaving, but he is not further identified.)

[2] Doubtless the "letter of expostulation, which I have not been able to find", which SJ wrote to Tom Hervey over the threatened separation from his wife (*Life* ii. 32). For Hervey's open letter in reply, see *ibid.* 480.

[3] When, or where, is nowhere indicated in JB's papers.

157

Portrait will truly resemble the Original, and we his Friends may thank Heaven for having given him a very happy Nature, which render'd him very useful to Society; and not like the bright Lord Bolingbroke,[4] a mischievous Being. Tho He is represented by his Enemies under the denomination[5] of a Samoiede, yet we his Friends know him every thing great, magnanimous and good. I long Sir to see your work, I know his Character is forcibly impressed on your mind, and that you are perfectly Capable of elucidating all his Virtues. My Heart will enjoy the praises you will bestow on one, who whilst he held the Cornucopia of literature, in the other hand held the balance of humanity. Sir, with respect, I have the honor to be your most Obedient Servant,

WILLIAM THOMAS HERVEY

Johnsoniana Related by James Dodsley,[1] Thursday 29 June 1786

MS. Yale (C 1091). In JB's hand, except for Dodsley's signature.

[2]Novr. 25 1748.

I received of Mr. Dodsley fifteen guineas for which I assign to him the right of copy of an imitation of the tenth Satire of Juvenal written by me, reserving to myself the right of printing one Edition.

SAM. JOHNSON

London, 29 June 1786[3]

A true copy from the original in Dr. Johnson's handwriting.

JAS. DODSLEY[2]

Septr. 8 1749. There is in Mr. Robert Dodsley's handwriting, and signed by Dr. Johnson a receipt for one hundred pounds for all his right and property in his Traged[y] entitled *Irene* reserving to himself the right of printing one impression.[4]

[4] Henry St. John, first Viscount Bolingbroke (1678–1751). See *Life* i. 268.

[5] MS. "demonination": an unconscious portmanteau?

[1] James Dodsley (1724–97), bookseller; younger member of the firm of R. & J. Dodsley. JB dined with him at Dilly's on 26 Mar. 1787 (Journ.).

[2-2] Printed, *Life* i. 193 n. 1. The original receipt is in the Hyde Collection.

[3] The journal entry for this day makes no mention of Dodsley.

[4] *Life* i. 198. The original receipt is in the Pierpont Morgan Library.

Mr. James Dodsley recollects that one day when Dr. Johnson was sitting upon a bench in his brother Mr. Robert Dodsley's shop, Mr. Robert Dodsley suggested to him that a Dictionary of the english language would be a work which would be well received by the Publick; or words to that effect. Johnson seemed to catch at the idea; but after a pause, said in his manner "I believe I shan't undertake it."[5]

To John Leland,[1]
Tuesday 11 July 1786

Missing. Sent to Dublin from London. Reg. Let.: "John Leland Esq. Ditto [i.e. "for materials for Dr. Johnson's Life"]." Dated from Leland's reply, *post* 29 July 1786.

From the Rev. Dr. William Adams,
Wednesday 12 July 1786

MS. Yale (C 18). Received 24 July[1] (Reg. Let.).

ADDRESS: James Boswell Esqr.

ENDORSEMENT: Rev. Dr. Adams.

Oxford, 12 July 1786

DEAR SIR, I am a sad Fellow and take Shame to myself for having been so long in your Debt. You left me[2] half dead; and I am still very imperfectly recoverd. After long continuing the Use of the Bark[3] and declining both Company and Business, I got strength enough to undertake a Journey which I had despaired of making, and from which I am very lately returnd: I have looked repeatedly for Letters of Dr. Johnson but find none that will be of the least use to you.[4] The Subject of our last Correspondence was an Edition of

[5] *Life* i. 182.

[1] John Leland, Irish barrister; son of Thomas Leland (*ante* From Walker, 26 July and 13 Nov. 1785). He is named among the company at Reynolds's, 25 Apr. 1778 (*Life* iii. 318); the corresponding journal reveals little more of him—only that he "read Lady Lucan's Verses on Ireland".

[1] Adams may have mis-dated the letter; cf. *ante* To Adams, 21 Jan. and 22 Dec. 1785, endorsements.

[2] See *ante* From Adams, c. 24 Apr. 1786, n. 1.

[3] One of SJ's favourite remedies: see *Letters SJ* 79, 118, 140, 309, 967. He had commented on its efficacy in Adams's company at Oxford, 10 June 1784 (*Life* iv. 293).

[4] JB's persistent attempts to obtain SJ's letters to Adams appear to have failed. Four of the letters, and possibly a fifth, have come down to us through other channels (*Letters SJ* 484, 570 [see Addenda, ii. 529], 946.1, 963.1, 974).

Xenophon's *Memorabilia Socratis*, undertaken by a Friend of his and mine, who died before it was finished.[5] Some Mss were collating for this work in Paris and Dr. Johnson engaged the Prior of the English Benedictines there to get these Collations finished. Several Letters past betwixt him, and the Prior, and a very excellent Scholar one of the Collators. These Letters with the Collations the Doctor sent to me when he was ill in Derbyshire;[6] desiring me to return an Answer for him to the Prior; and to send with it an Account of a MS which he the Prior inquired after in the Bodley Library.[7] These Collations are printed in the Book: and the Letters which I thought I had brought with them from the Country I have looked for in vain. I may probably find them there but believe that neither they nor any thing of the Doctors in my keeping will be of much use to you. If I can answer any inquiries which you may wish to make I shall be happy in doing it. I believe I informd you that one of the first Expedients which our Friend thought of after his leaving College for raising money was to publish Politian's poetical works: for which he sollicited Subscriptions but meeting with no great encouragement he dropped the Design.[8] After this he applied for a Masters Degree to qualify him for a School which not being to be procured in this University Lord Gower exerted his interest to get from Dublin; and a very handsome Letter of his Lordship to the then Lord Lieutenant on this subject was lately published in the London Papers.[9] He then at some distance of time conceivd a

[5] See *ante* From Adams, 28 Mar. 1785 and n. 4.

[6] They were apparently sent from London, shortly before SJ set out for Staffordshire and Derbyshire (*Letters SJ* 974).

[7] See *Letters SJ* 974 and n. 2.

[8] This sentence appears in the MS. *Life* (opp. p. 36) in a close paraphrase under the year 1731; but JB subsequently acquired the printed proposals for the work, deleted the original account, and rewrote it under Aug. 1734, when, according to JB, the proposals were published (MS. *Life*, opp. p. 45: *Life* i. 90 and n. 2). They are not among the recovered Boswell Papers. Hawkins wrote (p. 445 n.): "Among the books in his library, at the time of his disease [*sic*], I found a very old and curious edition of the works of Politian, which appeared to be-

long to Pembroke college, Oxford. It was probably taken out of the library when he was preparing to publish a part of that author, viz. in 1734, and had been used as his own for upwards of fifty years." Later in the *Life* (iv. 371 n. 2) JB takes Hawkins to task for this "most unfavourable insinuation". Hawkins does not say whether he returned the book to Pembroke College; in any event, it is not now there.

[9] See *ante* From Adams, 17 Feb. 1785 and n. 14. In the MS. *Life* (p. 82) JB directed the printer to "Kearseley's *Life* p. 12": i.e. the *Life of Johnson* published in 1785 by George Kearsley and attributed to William Cooke (the page reference is to the second edition, brought out the same year). The letter had appeared in print as early as 1782 (*The Beauties of Johnson*, 5th ed., Pt. II,

160

Thought of becoming an Advocate in Doctor's Commons and employed me to inquire of Dr. Smalbroke whether this might be without his taking a Doctors Degree. But this, which he seemd to feel as a great disappointment, could not be dispensed with.[10] The History of his Melancholy about 20 years before his death, which was indeed dreadful to see,[11] I am not enough acquainted with: but I always conjectured it to be owing to the sudden transition from water drinking, which was his Habit invariably for 15 years or more, to drinking Wine, in which by his own Account he indulged himself very liberally.[12] He has given my Daughter an Account of his Writings distinguishing those composed during his Water Regimen from those when he was a Wine drinker. The first Talk the Doctor and I had together upon the Subject of Prayer you were I think a witness to.[13] In the last Visit which he paid me just before his Death he renewd the Subject and would for some time talk of nothing else.[14] The Prayers which Mr. Strahan has so unadvisedly published were designd, and in the Envelope were directed to me, as Dr. Scott told me: and were I am confident intended to shew me that he had not forgot his promise of writing to me upon that Subject tho' not well enough to attempt it. How Mr. Strahan came to think himself authorised and even directed to publish them (which must be impossible) I think I can form some not wholly improbable conjecture.[15] I hope Sir Jn. Hawkins will not publish these among

pp. ix–x; this work also attributed to Cooke) and was frequently reprinted, always with variants. JB originally included Adams's identification of the addressee but later deleted it in favour of the designation (following Cooke) "a friend of Dean Swift". He also corrected the date to 1 Aug. 1739 (Cooke's first edition has it 1737, the second 1738, apparently following European Magazine, 1785, vi. 413), at which time the Lord Lieutenant of Ireland was William Cavendish, Duke of Devonshire. The writer of the letter, John Leveson-Gower (1694–1754), first Earl Gower and Lord Privy Seal, is the former Jacobite whose name SJ intended to use in his Dictionary as a synonym for "renegade", "but the printer had more wit than I, and struck it out" (Life i. 296; cf. Note Book, p. 1).

[10] See ante From Adams, 17 Feb. 1785 and nn. 16–16, 17.

[11] See ante From Adams, June 1784 and n. 20.

[12] Cf. Life iii. 305, i. 103 n. 3.

[13] MS. "too". See ante From Adams, 17 Feb. 1785 and n. 34.

[14] See ante From Adams, 17 Feb. 1785 and n. 33–33.

[15] Adams's suspicions probably arose from the fact that Strahan attended SJ's deathbed: see post From G. Strahan, 4 Mar. 1791. In the preface to his edition of the Prayers and Meditations Strahan (who censored the MS.) states that SJ composed his devotions "without any view to their publication. But being last summer on a visit at Oxford to the Reverend Dr. Adams, and that Gentleman urging him repeatedly to engage in some work of this kind, he then first conceived a design to revise these pious

his works.[16] We propose setting out for Counde in Shropshire on Monday sevennight where, et partout toujours, I shall be glad to receive your Commands. My Daughter presents her Compliments with those of Your obedient Servant

W. ADAMS

Mrs. Piozzi is mistaken in saying that Johnson never attended his Tutours Lectures. He attended these and ⟨?the⟩ Lectures in the College Hall very regularly.[17] His Translation of Popes *Messiah* which soon appeard in print was an Exercise set him within a few weeks after he enterd, by his Tutour of whom, tho' he professd no Esteem for his literary Abilities, he also spoke with Regard and even Affection.[18]

To Thomas Percy, Bishop of Dromore, Wednesday 12 July 1786

Missing. Printed, *Lit. Illust.* vii. 304–05.

effusions, and bequeath them, with enlargements, to the use and benefit of others" (*Johns. Misc.* i. 4, corrected from the original edition). A review of the volume in *Gent. Mag.* for Sept. 1785 (lv. 724) begins: "This publication appears to have been at the instance of Dr. Adams, master of Pembroke College, Oxford." Adams replied in the Oct. number (lv. 755), disclaiming any responsibility for the publication and indeed expressing his disapproval of it. The reception of the work was generally hostile or embarrassed: see M. J. Quinlan, JEGP (1953) lii. 125–139. The critical remarks in the present letter (supplementary to those in the missing portion of Adams's letter of 17 Nov. 1785: see *ante* n. 1 to that letter) were originally included in the MS. *Life* (Paper Apart for p. 1009) to follow Adams's account of SJ's last visit with him. At the end of the quotation appears the memorandum "(Here respectfully differ, and commend the Prayers.)." But JB decided to suppress Adams's criticism, and deleted the quotation and the introductory remarks which preceded it. The revised account, defending the

publication, is essentially the same as that printed, *Life* iv. 376–77. Cf. Hawkins, pp. 447, 451. Croker renewed the attack on Strahan, and Percy Fitzgerald in prosecuting Croker came to Strahan's defence (*Croker's Boswell and Boswell*, 1880, pp. 124–27). For a description of the MSS. that make up the *Prayers and Meditations*, and of Strahan's editing, see *Diaries*, pp. xvi–xviii. J. D. Fleeman informs me that the MSS. were presented to Pembroke College by Strahan's daughter in 1826, two years after her father's death.

[16] Six "Prayers and Devotional Exercises" were included (*Works* xi. 191 ff.), three of which—those dated 1 Aug., 18 Sept., and 5 Dec. 1784—had appeared in Strahan's edition.

[17] *Life* i. 60 n. 3. See *Anecdotes: Johns. Misc.* i. 164, and cf. Hawkins, pp. 9 and 11–12.

[18] See *ante* From Adams, June 1784 and nn. 16, 17. Adams's remarks are aimed at refuting Mrs. Piozzi's insinuation that SJ had no respect for Jorden—who, it will be remembered, was Adams's cousin.

London, July 12th, 1786

. . . I beg leave to renew my solicitation, and to remind your Lordship of your obliging promise to let me have any materials in your possession that can illustrate the *Life of Dr. Johnson*, which I am now preparing for the press. I beg that your Lordship may be kind enough to favour me with them as soon as you can, as I now have occasion for all that I can get. Be pleased to direct for me at Mr. Dilly's, bookseller, London. Though the magnitude and lustre of his character make Dr. Johnson an object of the public attention longer than almost any person whom we have known, yet there is some danger that if the publication of his life be delayed too long, curiosity may be fainter.[1] I am, therefore, anxious to bring forth my quarto. Pray, then, send me your kind communications without delay. . . .

To Anna Seward, Saturday 15 July 1786

Missing. Sent to Lichfield from London. For the date, see next letter. Reg. Let.: "Miss Seward Ditto [i.e. "for materials for Dr. Johnson's Life"]." Miss Seward's reply is not extant.

To and From Francis Barber,[1] Saturday 15 July 1786

MS. Yale (L 28).

ADDRESS: To Mr. Francis Barber at Lichfield.

London, 15 July 1786

GOOD MR. FRANCIS: I beg you may oblige me with Answers to the following Questions for the Life of your late excellent Master,

---

[1] Cf. *ante* From Blair, 4 May 1786.

[1] The letter, which was folded but not sealed, was enclosed, I think, in the preceding letter to Anna Seward. The answers to JB's questions are supplied in his own hand; the letter therefore must have been returned and the inquiry conducted in person—perhaps at the London address which JB had noted on the back of Barber's last letter to him (*ante* 7 Jan. 1786, head-note). Barber had delivered to JB Miss Seward's letter of 12 Oct. 1785 (to be included in another volume in this series), in which she indicated that Barber was then in the process of establishing residence in Lichfield, but this appears not to have been realized until Aug. 1786 (*Johns. Glean.* ii. 65).

which you will be pleased to write under each question.[2] I am Sir your sincere friend

JAMES BOSWELL

1. Where was you born? When did you come to England? How was you introduced to Dr. Johnson? At what age did you become his servant? Was you then free?[3]

Born in Jamaica. Came to England with Colonel Bathurst father of Dr. Bathurst[4] in 1750. Was seven or eight year old.[5] His Master and he went and lived with Dr. Bathurst. He was then sent to the Rev. Mr. Jackson's school at Barton in Yorkshire. Was there between two and three years.[6] Col. Bathurst made him free in his Will. Then he came up from School was with Dr. Bathurst a short time and then went to Dr. Johnson in Gough square as his servant.[7] But the Dr. first put him to board at Mrs. Coxeter's[8] that he might

[2] "It is very rare to find any person who is able to give a distinct account of the life even of one whom he has known intimately, without questions being put to them. My friend, Dr. Kippis, has told me, that on this account it is a practice with him to draw out a biographical catechism" (*Life* iv. 376).

[3] In his account of SJ's state of mind after his wife's death (*Life* i. 239) JB cites Barber as a trustworthy witness and in a foot-note presents a biographical sketch of him derived from the following record.

[4] Richard Bathurst (d. c. 1754–56), of Lincolnshire, appears to have spent most of his life in Jamaica, where he was a planter and an officer in the militia. His return to England in his later years was the result of financial difficulties (*Johns. Glean.* ii. 2 ff.). His son, Dr. Richard Bathurst (d. 1762), "though a Physician of no inconsiderable merit, had not the good fortune to get much practice in London. He was, therefore, willing to accept of employment abroad, and, to the regret of all who knew him, fell a sacrifice to the destructive climate, in the expedition against the Havannah" (*Life* i. 242 n. 1). Long after the event SJ remembered him in his prayers (*Diaries*, pp. 79, 92, 150, 156). Bathurst was a member of the Ivy Lane Club, a reputed associate of SJ's in *The Adventurer*, and the

projector of an apparently abortive geographical dictionary (*Letters SJ* 47; Hill's ed. of the *Life*, 1887, vi. xxii ff.).

[5] Not used. Cooke (p. 100) states that Barber "was but ten years old when he took him under his care". Cf. *Johns. Glean.* ii. 6.

[6] The Rev. William Jackson (c. 1701– 84) was Perpetual Curate of Barton, Yorkshire, from 1737 until his death (*Johns. Glean.* ii. 9–10). Barber's term at the school must have been nearer two years than three, for by the spring of 1752 he was living with SJ (*Life* i. 239). JB carefully substitutes "for some time" for Barber's estimate. According to Cooke (pp. 100–01) it was SJ who sent Barber to school in Yorkshire, intending to train him to be a missionary, "in order to instruct his countrymen in the principles of the Christian religion. His parts, however, after repeated and extraordinary trials, not admitting this cultivation, he took him into his service, where he experienced in the Doctor, rather the friend than the master."

[7] Col. Bathurst's will is dated 24 Apr. 1754, some two years after Barber went to live with SJ (*Johns. Glean.* ii. 3 n., 5).

[8] "Mrs." Coxeter may have been the orphan daughter of Thomas Coxeter (1689–1747), the antiquary, whose children SJ is known to have befriended (*Life* iii. 158 n. 1).

go to Blackfriars school. He went one day only for he caught the small pox. After being in the Dr.'s service he went to Mr. Desmoulins writing school.[9]

2. How long was you at sea? In what year did he send[10] you to school in the country? How long did you continue there? Under whose care was you? What were you taught?[11]

He lived with Dr. Johnson from 1752 to about 1757—when upon some difference he left him[12] and served a Mr. Farren Apothecary in Cheapside for about two years during which he called some times on his Master and was well received and was to return to him. But having an inclination to go to sea, he went accordingly and continued till the end of 1760 three days before Geo. II died, having been discharged thro' Dr. Johnson's application, without any wish of his own.[13] Found the Dr. in the Temple and returned to his service.[14]

3. Where did your Master and Mistress live when you first came to Dr. Johnson? If in London in what part? Had they not a

[9] Mr. Desmoulins, the husband of SJ's dependant (*ante* From Hector, 1 Feb. 1785, n. 3), was "a Hugenot refugee and a writing master, most probably engaged at the Birmingham Free Grammar School" (Hill and Dent, *Memorials of the Old Square*, pp. 38–39).

[10] MS. "sent"

[11] The three letters from SJ to Barber enclosed in Barber's letter to JB *ante* 7 Jan. 1786 show that Barber was away at school in 1768 and 1770. It will be noticed that all four of JB's questions concerning this episode in Barber's career are unanswered, and that the information given appears to be the result of a different line of questioning. Given the fact of an oral inquiry, one cannot be sure that the questions about Barber's schooling were actually put to him; no doubt JB was led by some of Barber's answers to improvise some new questions. In any case, the investigation into Barber's schooling was pursued two years later in a letter to Bishop Percy (*post* 9 Feb. 1788), on the false assumption that the school was at Easton Mauduit, Northamptonshire, where Percy had been rector.

[12] "... my Boy is run away" (SJ to Lewis Paul, ?1756: *Letters SJ* 100).

[13] This episode is given fuller treatment, *Life* i. 348 ff. Barber joined the Navy 7 July 1758 and was discharged 8 Aug. 1760. The allusion to George II's death, omitted in the second edition (see *post* From Reed, c. Nov. 1792 and n. 18), creates a chronological confusion: the King died 25 Oct. 1760, more than two months after Barber's discharge. However, as Reade suggests, the Oct. date may indicate the time that Barber actually left his ship (*Life* i. 350 n. 1; *Johns. Glean.* ii. 13–14, viii. 73). SJ's first application to obtain Barber's discharge was made to Smollett (because of his Jamaican as well as Navy connexions?); Smollett wrote to John Wilkes; Wilkes applied to Sir George Hay of the Admiralty. The order for the discharge was apparently made out, but was not executed because of SJ's absence from London at the time. SJ's second application was made (directly to Hay?) in a letter dated 9 Nov. 1759 (*Johns. Glean.* ii. 13–14; *Letters SJ* 132.3).

[14] SJ resided at No. 1 Inner Temple Lane from Aug. 1760 until July 1765 (*Life* iii. 535).

lodging at Hampstead? Did they both live there? or did she live there alone?[15]

Mrs. Johnson was dead a forthnight or three weeks before he came to the Dr.[16] The Dr. was in great affliction. Mrs. Williams was then living in his house which was in Gough Square.[17]

4. What kind of tempered woman was she? Did they appear to live happily together? What company chiefly frequented the house during her lifetime?[18]

5. What particulars can you give of her last illness and death and of your master's behaviour on that occasion? Was not you sent the night she died, to bring Dr. Taylor to your master?[19] Do you remember what passed?

6. When did Mrs. Williams come to live in your Master's House?

She used to come to the house often in Mrs. Johnson's lifetime, and came to live in it immediately after Mrs. Johnson's death.[20]

7. What were the names of your Master's Barber Taylor and Shoemaker, and where do they live?

Barber Mr. Collet[21] lives in plumbtree court shoelane; his taylor for many years was Mr. Harrison upon Ludgate hill—But he having died he employed Mr. Cooke in King Street Bloomsbury who made one suit for himself and one for Francis. His shoemaker

---

[15] Mrs. Johnson lived for long periods at Hampstead, apparently for reasons of health, from 1748 or earlier until her death in 1752. SJ lived at Gough Square from 1747 or earlier, but according to JB he "resorted occasionally" to Hampstead (*Life* i. 192, 238, iv. 377 n. 1; Clifford, *Johnson*, p. 293).

[16] Life i. 239. This fact accounts of course for the incomplete answer to No. 3 and the complete absence of answers to Nos. 4 and 5.

[17] JB transposes the two foregoing sentences to the beginning of the long passage with which the letter ends, *Life* i. 241. See *post* n. 23.

[18] Mrs. Johnson has been variously portrayed in contemporary accounts, and the success of the marriage much disputed. See Hawkins, pp. 313 ff.; Shaw, pp. 110–11; *Anecdotes: Johns. Misc.* i. 247 ff.; Murphy: *Johns. Misc.* i. 376; *Life passim*; and *Johns. Glean.* vi. 122. According to

Hawkins, SJ invited few of his friends to the house while Mrs. Johnson was living: among them Garrick and Hawkesworth.

[19] This question must have been prompted by Mrs. Piozzi's account (from Taylor) of how "when he lost his wife, the negro Francis ran away, though in the middle of the night, to Westminster, to fetch Dr. Taylor to his master, who was all but wild with excess of sorrow, and scarce knew him when he arrived" (*Johns. Misc.* i. 257–58). Taylor's relation of the same incident recorded in the journal, 18 Sept. 1777, does not mention Barber. It is the latter account which JB used, *Life* i. 238. Mrs. Piozzi may have confused this summons to Taylor with a later one, when SJ suffered his paralytic stroke (*Life* iv. 228–30).

[20] *Life* i. 232.

[21] See *Diaries*, pp. 284, 326, 355; *Letters SJ* 815.2; Journ. 16 Mar. 1779.

was Owen in Bonds stables fetter lane—dead but the business carried on by his daughter.[22]

8. What other particulars can you tell concerning your Master?[23]

When he came to him the Dr. was busy with the *Dictionary*. The younger Macbean[24] brother of the Duke of Argyll's Librarian[25] and Mr. Peyton a linguist who taught foreigners, (both whom and his Wife Dr. Johnson afterwards buried)[26] then wrote to him.[27] The elder Macbean and Mr. Maitland[28] Mr. Stewart[29] and Mr. Shiels[30] who had all written to him before used to come about him.

[22] None of this information was admitted to the *Life*; but JB was probably inquiring into further *sources* of information: thus, "where do they live?"

[23] The following narrative is extensively revised and presented as Barber's "authentick and artless account of the situation in which he found him recently after his wife's death," *Life* i. 241–42.

[24] William Macbean wrote to James Dodsley on 13 May 1785, sounding him out on a supplementary volume to SJ's *Dictionary* and referring to himself as the last survivor of the "laborious brethren the Dr.'s amanuenses" (*Adam Cat.* iii. 160). Nothing else is known of him.

[25] Alexander Macbean (d. 1784), "a very learned Highlander", was employed on the *Dictionary* c. 1748–54 and as librarian to Archibald Campbell, third Duke of Argyll, c. 1758–61 ("but was left without a shilling": *Life* i. 187). In 1773 he published *A Dictionary of Ancient Geography*, for which SJ wrote the Preface. He also compiled the Index (1780) to the *Works of the English Poets*. In 1781, through SJ's efforts, he was admitted to the Charterhouse, where he died (DNB; Hazen, pp. 132 ff.; *Letters SJ passim*). See also *Diaries, passim*; Journ. 7 Apr. 1776, 15 Apr. 1781: *Life* iii. 25–26, iv. 94.

[26] "Poor Peyton expired this morning. He probably during many years for which he sat starving by the bed of a Wife not only useless, but almost motionless, condemned by poverty to personal attendance, and by the necessity of such attendance chained down to poverty, he probably thought often how lightly he should tread the path of life without his burthen. Of this thought the admission was unavoidable, and the indulgence might be forgiven to frailty and distress. His Wife died at last, and before she was buried he was seized by a fever, and is now going to the grave" (SJ to Mrs. Thrale, 1 Apr. 1776: *Letters SJ* 467). JB believed that Peyton "taught French, and published some elementary tracts" (*Life* i. 187). For his identification as V. J. Peyton, author of linguistic works in French and English, see *Life* Index (2nd ed., 1964) and Dr. Powell's revision of *Life* i. 536.

[27] That is, to his dictation, or for him; altered to "for him" in the *Life*. For this idiom, cf. the *Life of Savage*: *Lives* ii. 412.

[28] Not identified.

[29] Francis Stewart, "son of Mr. George Stewart, bookseller at Edinburgh", appears to have died before the *Dictionary* was finished. An early receipt for work on the *Dictionary* as an amanuensis, signed by him and dated 1746, is in the Hyde Collection. SJ remembered him long afterwards as "an ingenious and worthy man" (*Life* i. 187, iii. 421; *Letters SJ* 39). See also *Life* i. 536, and for SJ's negotiations with JB in behalf of Stewart's sister, *ibid*. iii. 418, 421, iv. 262, 265.

[30] Robert Shiels (d. 1753) was the author of *The Power of Beauty*, a poem in praise of SJ's *Irene*, and *Musidorus*, an elegy on James Thomson. His slight fame rests, however, on his controversial role in the compilation of *The Lives of the Poets of Great Britain and Ireland to the Time of Dean Swift* (1753), which bore the name of "Mr. Cibber" on the title-

Though the Dr. had then little to himself Francis frequently carried money from him to Shiels when in distress. The friends who came about him then were chiefly Dr. Bathurst—and Mr. Diamond an Apothecary in Cork street Burlington gardens. There was a talk of the Dr.'s going to Iceland with him, which he supposes would have happened had Mr. Diamond lived.[31] Mr. Cave—Dr. Hawkesworth[32]—Mr. Ryland Merchant Court Towerhill[33]—Mrs. Masters the Poetess[34] (who lived with Mr. Cave)—Mrs. Carter[35] and Mrs. Mcaulay[36] some times also Mrs. Gardiner Wife of a tallow chandler on Snowhill, not in the learned way, but a worthy good woman.[37] Mr. (now Sir Joshua) Reynolds[38] Mess. Millar R.

page (*Life* iii. 29–30, 30 n.). The collection included SJ's *Life of Savage* (or most of it) anonymously. SJ wrote of Shiels that he was "a man of very acute understanding, though with little scholastick education, who, not long after the publication of his work, died in London of a consumption. His life was virtuous, and his end was pious" (*Lives* ii. 312–13). See also Journ. 10–11 Apr. 1776.

[31] These two sentences are combined with the last sentence but one. Mr. (or Dr.) Diamond is not further identified.

[32] John Hawkesworth, LL.D. (1715–73), at this time engaged in the conduct of *The Adventurer*, to which SJ was one of the chief contributors. See *Life* i. 233–34, 252 ff., 540; and *post* From J. Warton, 30 Mar. 1790.

[33] John Ryland (?1717–98), Hawkesworth's brother-in-law, was a West India merchant of Muscovy Court, Tower Hill, London, and a contributor to *Gent. Mag.*, of which he occasionally served as director. He was a member of both the Ivy Lane and Essex Head Clubs, and was a constant visitor during SJ's last illness. See *Letters SJ, passim* and Mary Hyde, "Not in Chapman," *Johnson, Boswell and Their Circle*, p. 318.

[34] Mrs. Mary Masters (d. 1771) was the author of *Poems on Several Occasions* (1733) and *Familiar Letters and Poems on Several Occasions* (1755), both of which contain contributions by her friends. Her later volume, to which SJ was a subscriber, was published by Richard Cave, Edward

Cave's nephew, and David Henry, who was married to Cave's sister. Cave himself had died the year before the work appeared. See DNB and *Life* iv. 246, 525–26.

[35] Elizabeth Carter (1717–1806) was introduced to SJ through Cave, a friend of her father and the publisher of her first volume of poems. She contributed to *Gent. Mag.* under the name of "Eliza", and was the author of two papers in *The Rambler*, Nos. 44 and 100. For SJ's relations with her, see Edward Ruhe, "Birch, Johnson, and Elizabeth Carter: an Episode of 1738–39", PMLA (1958) lxxiii. 491–500.

[36] Croker pointed out that at this time she was Miss Sawbridge: see *Life* i. 242 n. 4.

[37] In one of his notebooks containing materials for the *Life*, JB instructed himself to "End 1783 with attention to Mrs. Gardener introduced to him by Mrs. Masters." See *Life* iv. 245–46. She was another constant visitor during SJ's last illness, and was left a book in his will (*Johns. Misc.* ii. 147, 155–56, 158–59; *Life* iv. 403 n.). See also *Diaries, passim*, and F. M. Smith, *Some Friends of Doctor Johnson* [1934], pp. 149 ff.

[38] While the date which unites this catalogue of acquaintances is clearly approximate, JB nevertheless places the first meeting between SJ and Reynolds under the year 1752 (*Life* i. 244–45)—or about three to four years too early. See F. W. Hilles, *Literary Career of Sir Joshua Reynolds*, 1936, p. 12 n. 2.

Dodsley Bouquet[39] and Paine[40] of paternoster row Booksellers
Mr. Strahan—Earl of Orrery[41]—Lord Southwell[42]—Mr. Garrick.
He and Mrs. Williams generally dined every sunday with Dr.
Diamond. Used to be disturbed by people calling frequently for
money which he could not pay.[43]

To and From Edmund Hector, Saturday 15 July 1786

MS. Yale (L 637). Returned by Hector with his reply of the next day.

London, 15 July 1786

DEAR SIR: I beg you may be so good as to favour me with Answers
to the following questions for the life of our late excellent friend
Dr. Johnson, and write the answers underneath each question.
Please to enclose to me under cover of John Courtenay Esq., M.P.
London. I am with sincere regard, Dear Sir, your obliged humble
servant

JAMES BOSWELL

1. In one of the letters to you with which you favoured me,[1] Dr.
Johnson says that he had not enjoyed a day's health since his
twentieth year. *That* may refer to the first vacation he spent at home
after being entered in Pembroke College. Was it *then* that he was
first seised with a strong fit of "morbid melancholy"? or was it
later? I *know* it was *about* that period.[2] He never got entirely rid of
it. What particulars can you tell of it? and where was you then?

[39] Joseph Bouquet (see Plomer), in partnership with John Payne, published *The Rambler*.

[40] John Payne (d. 1787), a member of the Ivy Lane Club, was the publisher of *The Rambler* (with Bouquet), *The Adventurer*, and the first numbers of *The Universal Chronicle* (for a time called *Payne's Universal Chronicle*), in which *The Idler* first appeared. From 1744 he was employed in the Bank of England, becoming chief accountant in 1780. SJ wrote the Preface to his *New Tables of Interest*, 1758 (Hazen, pp. 142, 205).

[41] John Boyle (1707–62), fifth Earl of Orrery, 1731, and fifth Earl of Cork, 1753; author of *Remarks on the Life and Writings of Swift* (1751). See *Life* i. 185, v. 238.

[42] Thomas Southwell (1698–1766),

second Baron Southwell of Castle Mattress, Limerick. SJ described him as "the highest-bred man without insolence that I ever was in company with; the most *qualitied* I ever saw" (*Life* iv. 173–74).

[43] JB omits this final sentence in his quotation. SJ was arrested for debt in Mar. 1756: see *Letters SJ* 90 and 94 (and n., i. 426). An earlier arrest—some time before the death of SJ's rescuer, Henry Hervey, in 1748—is reported, and confirmed by SJ, *Life* iii. 195.

[1] *Life* iv. 147–48. See *ante* From Hector, 1 Feb. 1785 and n. 10.

[2] "*Johnson* I once walked a good deal. I left it off at two and twenty when I grew melancholy" (MS. *Life*, p. 883: cancelled). A corroborating statement is

1st Q.

If that Letter does not carry its own date, I cannot ascertain it. The time He complains of his morbid melancholy must be dated from his first fixing in London and his acquaintance with Mr. Thrale.[3]

2. Upon his return to Lichfield from Oxford finally, from want of money,[4] how long did he continue there idle? When did he come to Birmingham? and how long was he there?[5]

Soon after He left Oxford, He was invited to Bosworth in Leicestershire[6] to be under master in a Grammar School, where He continu'd about one Year, from whence He wrote me word, his business was to teach Lillies Grammar to a few Boys, and it was hard to say whose difficulty was greatest He to explain Nonsense, or they to understand it.[7]

3. Did he make applications for employment in any way?[8] How

found in Steevens's published anecdotes of SJ (*Johns. Misc.* ii. 322): "Every change, however, in his habits, had invariable reference to that insanity which, from his two-and-twentieth year, he had taught himself to apprehend." But JB decided for 1729 (*Life* i. 63). See also *Johns. Glean.* v. 25. The term "morbid melancholy" was SJ's own (*Diaries*, p. 257; cf. Hawkins, pp. 287, 454).

[3] This answer must have exasperated JB. SJ's acquaintance with the Thrales began in 1765 (*Life* i. 522), or some twenty-five years after his settling in London. Furthermore, JB was obviously inquiring into a much earlier manifestation of SJ's melancholy. But perhaps Hector did not recognize the term "morbid melancholy" as descriptive of SJ's affliction as *he* knew it. In any case, his association of SJ's melancholy with the Thrales may be explained by a passage in Mrs. Piozzi's *Anecdotes* (*Johns. Misc.* i. 233–34): "in the year 1766 his health, which he had always complained of, grew . . . exceedingly bad . . . Mr. Thrale's attentions and my own now became so acceptable to him, that he often lamented to us the horrible condition of his mind, which he said was nearly distracted."

[4] See *ante* From Adams, 17 Feb. 1785.

[5] It will be noted that here and elsewhere Hector fails to supply complete answers to JB's questions. For the answers to this group of questions, see *ante* From Hector, 28 Mar. 1785, nn. 5, 7, and 10.

[6] MS. "Leiscershire"

[7] *Life* i. 84, where the last part of this answer and the first part of the next are conflated, and the whole freely revised. Hector's estimate of the term of employment is rejected (see *ante* From Hector, 28 Mar. 1785, and n. 6), and the name of the textbook is omitted—perhaps because JB was unable to decipher Hector's scrawl. From SJ's own account of his early schooling at Lichfield Grammar School it is evident that he learned his Latin from a late version of Lily's text, which had the rules in Latin jingles. He was merely teaching what he himself had been taught (Clifford, *Johnson*, p. 47).

[8] SJ made at least five applications for academic employment—all unsuccessful, one of which Hector mentions in his reply to the last question in the letter. The other four were made: in 1731, for the ushership in the grammar school at Stourbridge, which he had attended in 1726 (*ante* From Hector, 1 Feb. 1785

did he come to be engaged in Bosworth School.[9] How long did he continue there? Was he ever engaged in any other school?[10] What became of him when he quitted Bosworth?[11] Why did he quit it?

Martial, writes He, shall sum up the var[i]eties of such a life—Vitam continet una dies.[12] He told me the occasion of his leaving Bosworth arose from a difference between Sir Wolleston Dixie the Patron of the School and him.[13]

I believe[14]

and n. 26); in 1732, for the ushership in the grammar school at Ashbourne; in 1735, for the mastership of the Solihull school, in Warwickshire; and in 1736, for the assistant mastership of the grammar school at Brewood, in Staffordshire. JB seems to have known of only the last (*Johns. Glean.* v. 64–65, 88–89, vi. 29–30, 46 ff.; *Life* i. 531, iv. 407 n. 4).

[9] Reade uncovered social relations between the family of Sir Wolstan Dixie, the patron of the school, and three families with which SJ had associations (*Johns. Glean.* v. 86).

[10] Two of JB's predecessors laid false trails on this ground: (1) Shaw (pp. 23–24), following the first edition of Davies's *Memoirs of Garrick* (1780), stated that in the beginning of 1735 SJ "undertook the instruction of young gentlemen in the Belles Letters at Litchfield", and proceeded, wrongly, to distinguish this venture from the school at Edial (*post* n. 18). The year was changed to 1736 in succeeding editions of Davies's *Memoirs*. (2) Hawkins (p. 163) assigned the entry in SJ's Diary for "Friday, August 27th" —"attended the school in the morning" —to 1734; but this too probably refers to the school at Edial, and therefore belongs to 1736 (when the 27th did fall on Friday). See Clifford, *Johnson*, p. 163 and n. 31; *Diaries*, pp. 35, 36 n.

[11] Unenlightened by Hector, JB passes over the interval between SJ's departure from Market Bosworth and his visit to Birmingham with the remark that he was "now again totally unoccupied" (*Life* i. 85). See *Johns. Glean.* v. 90.

[12] ". . . Mr. Hector recollects his

writing 'that the poet had described the dull sameness of his existence in these words, "*Vitam continet una dies*" (one day contains the whole of my life); that it was unvaried as the note of the cuckow . . .'" (*Life* i. 84). The translation of the line and the interpolated comment "that it was unvaried as the note of the cuckow" appear in the MS. *Life* (p. 38) as additions. The interpolation may have been a recollection of what Taylor related about this episode: it is written with the same quill that was used in expanding the first draft to include the details of SJ's misery at the school, clearly derived from Taylor's account (see next note). In proof JB changed "Martial" to "the poet". The quotation has eluded me (and others) also. See, however, Chapman's analysis of the line, *Letters SJ* 1.1 n. 1. Chapman guessed that the translation was Hector's, as it was not characteristic of JB to translate SJ's Latin. But perhaps the translation was in earnest of an identification.

[13] *Life* i. 84–85. Following Taylor (see *Note Book*, p. 10), JB emphasizes the "complicated misery" of SJ's situation. Sir Wolstan Dixie (c. 1701–67), fourth Baronet of Bosworth Park, was descended from Sir Wolstan Dixie, Kt. (1525–94), Lord Mayor of London and founder of the grammar school at Market Bosworth (John Nichols, *History of the County of Leicester*, 1811, iv. 503, 506–07). Reade presents abundant evidence to show that SJ's low opinion of Dixie was fully justified (*Johns. Glean.* v. 82 ff.). See also Clifford, *Johnson*, pp. 136–39.

[14] The sentence breaks off.

4. Was he not Tutor to a Mr. Whitby? When and how long was that? What was the name of Mr. Whitby's Estate? In what County was it?

I know nothing of his being Tutor to Mr. Whitby nor do I believe he ever was, that Gentleman liv'd at great Haywood Staffordshire.[15]

5. Were these engagements previous to his living with you at Birmingham? or was he with you at various times?

These engagements were previous to his living here with me.

In the Year thirty three I find him at Birmingham engag'd in the following Work. A translation of Jerom Lobo's *Voyage to Abyssynia* publish'd the following Year as appears by that Book now before me.[16]

6. In general I wish to have from you with as exact chronology as may be, the particulars of his life after his return from Oxford in the end of 1731[17] to the time of his settling in London in 1737.

If Dr. Johnson fix'd in London in 37, He must have marry'd the Widow in 35 for soon after He took an House at Ediall a place about two miles from Lichfield in order to instruct Youth in Classical learning, where having only three Pupils viz. Garrick and two Mr. Offleys, He broke up and immediately remov'd to London.[18] I remember He stood Candidate for

---

[15] This series of questions was aimed at completing the record of the *Note Book* (p. 10): "He then was Tutor to the son of Mr. Whitby of   in   shire. His pupil did not live to inherit the estate. I am not sure whether this was before he went to live at Birmingham. I think it must, as he married there." (SJ was married at Derby; JB has it right on the next page.) If JB's informant was Lucy Porter (*ibid.* pp. 10–11), it was now too late to turn to her for a verification of the record, for she died in Jan. of this year (*Johns. Glean.* vii. 111). In any case, JB unluckily deferred to Hector's opinion and omitted the matter from the *Life.* SJ served as tutor to John Whitby (1716–51), son of Thomas Whitby (c. 1672–1747), of Great Haywood, Staffordshire, some time between 10 May and 9 July (the day of his marriage) 1735

(*Johns. Glean.* v. 108 ff., 257–58; *Life* i. 84 n. 2).

[16] This statement appears to have been JB's authority for dating SJ's visit to Birmingham, *Life* i. 85; but see *ante* From Hector, 28 Mar. 1785, nn. 7, 10. The book was published in 1735, not 1734, as Hector, with the aid of his spectacles, soon came to perceive.

[17] For the date of SJ's return from Oxford, see *ante* From Adams, 17 Feb. 1785, n. 11–11.

[18] Cf. *Life* i. 96 ff., which is based on other sources, including the *Note Book* (p. 11: Lucy Porter). The Edial venture was probably not undertaken until after 30 Aug. 1735, when SJ's application for the mastership of the Solihull school was rejected. According to the account in the *Note Book* there were two Garricks and one Offley: "He had as Pupils Mr Offaly

Appleby School then vacant in Leicestershire which He lost by a single Vote, I think this was sometime after He left the Country.[19]

From Edmund Hector, Sunday 16 July 1786

MS. Yale (C 1525). A cover for the preceding. Received 19 July (Reg. Let.).

ADDRESS: James Boswell Esqr.

Birm[ingha]m, July 16/86

DEAR SIR: Inclos'd you will find I have answer'd all your Queries (to the best of my remembrance) in the manner you pointed out to me in your Letter, and with that expedition which your present undertaking may stand in need of.

I thank you for the Copy of your *Journall*[1] you was so kind to

David & George Garricks." Lawrence Offley was the younger son of Crewe Offley, of Wichnor Park, near Lichfield. He matriculated at Cambridge in 1737, and died in 1749 at the age of thirty. His brother John, who was about a year older, lived to 1784 (*Johns. Glean.* vi. 43 ff., v. 240).

[19] Cf. *Life* i. 132–33, where JB went astray by failing to heed Hector and the corroborating account in Hawkins (pp. 61–62). Instead, he took the tack of not naming the school in his text, but correcting in a foot-note (first edition, i. 67) Pope's placing of it in Shropshire (*ante* From Percy, 9 May 1776). JB's conjecture, based on a phrase in Earl Gower's letter, that the school must have been in Staffordshire might have been supported by Percy's identification of the school as that of Trysull ("Tresull") in that county (*post* 6 Mar. 1787). But while it is odd that JB makes no reference to this authority, it was just as well. In the second edition (i. 107–08) the original foot-note was revised and expanded to include another attempt at an identification, this one by "Mr. Spearing, attorney-at-law", who argues the case for a school in New-

port, Shropshire. Again, it is odd that JB would present this speculation without taking note of the fact that SJ had unsuccessfully applied to (doubtless) this same school "as a scholar and assistant" some fifteen years before (*Life* i. 50: on Percy's authority, *post* 6 Mar. 1787). But, again, the less said the better, as it turned out. For, the correct identification, already within JB's reach if not in his grasp, was to be confirmed by a letter to *Gent. Mag.* for May 1793 from one of the masters of the Appleby School. JB was able to include this last word on the matter among his "Corrections" prefixed to the first volume of the second edition; for the third edition, the foot-note was further adjusted for unity (as in *Life* i. 132 n. 1). A detailed account of the Appleby episode is given in *Johns. Glean.* vi. 96 ff. According to Reade, no vote was cast. The rival candidate, being "of founder's kin" and therefore entitled to the preference, was appointed by the Bishop of Lincoln, to whom the governors, lacking a quorum, delegated their power.

_____

[1] The *Journal of a Tour to the Hebrides*.

present me with, I wish you as good nay better success with your present undertaking and am with the most ardent wishes for your Health Fame and happiness Your oblig'd humble Servant to command

E. HECTOR

From Edmund Hector, Monday 17 July 1786

MS. Yale (C 1526).

ADDRESS: James Boswell Esqr.

[Birmingham,] July 17/86

DEAR SIR: I find a mistake in my last to you for want of my Spectacles. Jerom Lobo was not publisd untill 35. I thought it necessary to set you right in that date and hope you will excuse this oversight and the trouble I give you, and am, Dear Sir, Your obligd humble Servant

E. HECTOR

From John Leland, Saturday 29 July 1786

MS. Yale (C 1724). Received 4 Aug. (Reg. Let.).

ADDRESS: James Boswell Esqr., [British Coffee House, London *deleted*] Great Queen Street, Lincolns Inn Fields.

POSTMARKS: ⟨JY⟩ 29, 2 AU.

ENDORSEMENT: Counsellor Leland about Dr. Johnson.

No. 10 Aungier Street, Dublin, July 29th 1786

SIR, I had the honour of receiving your Letter of the 11th Inst. the day before yesterday; I immediately applyed to some of the Gentlemen of the College for a Copy of Doctor Johnson's Diploma,[1] but have been informed that it is not usual with them to keep any copies of the Diplomas they grant, and that there is in their Registry, only a short memorandum of the Degree having

---

[1] The diploma of Trinity College, Dublin, conferring upon him the degree of Doctor of Laws. See *Life* i. 488–89.

been granted to him: however in this matter, I dare say Doctor Kearney[2] will be able to give you more particular information, than any I have been able to obtain. I have Doctor Johnson's letter to Doctor Leland on receiving the Diploma, which I will send you with great pleasure, but at present it is in the hands of a particular friend of my Father's, who has undertaken the publication of some things that he has left behind him, and who has an intention of writing an account of his life, to be prefixed to some of his Posthumous Works.[3] As the Gentleman is at present at a great distance from Dublin, it will not be in my power to send it to you for some little time, but as soon as I can get it from him, I shall feel great pleasure in being able to communicate any thing to you, that can in the least degree tend to forward so laudable a work as that in which you are engaged.[4] The other Letter you mention I am afraid it will be impossible to recover,[5] I never heard of it, and have not been able to find it amongst any of my fathers papers; but if ever I should be able to discover it, I'll certainly do every thing in my power to obtain it for you. I am Sir, your most obedient humble Servant

JOHN LELAND

[2] Michael Kearney, D.D. (1733–1814), Archdeacon of Raphoe, formerly a fellow and professor at Trinity. He was one of the signers of the diploma (*Life* i. 489). JB had dined with Kearney at Malone's on 10 June of this year (Journ.), which fact he probably mentioned in his letter to Leland. It is reasonably certain from the context that Leland does not here refer to Michael's brother, John Kearney, D.D., also, and at this date, a fellow and professor at Trinity: this despite the fact that Malone was later to ask Lord Charlemont to seek *John* Kearney's help in recovering the letter mentioned at n. 5 (see *post* To Malone, 29 Jan. 1791, n. 8).

[3] Dr. Leland's only posthumous publication appears to have been his *Sermons on Various Subjects* (Dublin, 1788), but it contains no account of his life nor any sign of his editor's identity.

[4] "Johnson acknowledged the favour in a letter to Dr. Leland, one of their number; but I have not been able to obtain a copy of it" (*Life* i. 489). (In the

first proofs JB altered this to read: "though his son has been so good as to make a search it has not yet been found", but decided to let it stand.) Malone applied to Lord Charlemont on 7 Nov. 1787 for his help in locating both this letter and the one mentioned in the next sentence (Historical Manuscripts Commission, Thirteenth Report, Appendix, Part VIII, *The Manuscripts and Correspondence of James, First Earl of Charlemont*, 1894, ii. 62). It was not, however, until many years later that the letter to Dr. Leland was recovered, and transmitted by his son to Malone, who printed it in the fifth edition of the *Life* (1807, i. 467). A copy is at Trinity College. See *Life* i. 518; *Letters SJ* 178.

[5] Doubtless the letter from SJ to "the College cook": see *post* To Malone, 29 Jan. 1791 and n. 8. The only other known letter from SJ to Dr. Leland is an unrecovered letter of introduction alluded to in SJ to Mrs. Thrale, 12 May 1775 (*Letters SJ* 390).

From Edmond Malone, Monday 4 September 1786

MS. Yale (C 1909).

ADDRESS (by Courtenay): James Boswell Esqr., Auchinleck, Cumnock, Dumfries.

FRANK: London Septembr. fourth 1786. Free J. Courtenay.

POSTMARK: 4 SP.

ENDORSEMENT: Mr. Malone about Dr. Johnson's Life.

London, Sep. 4, 1786

. . . I hope the *Life* goes on well. Did you attend to a laboured attack in the *Pub. A.* against S.J. signed *Erica*.[1] It has all a *foundation*, but is monstrously exaggerated; the surest, and most wounding kind of abuse. I have no doubt it is Macpherson's. When he speaks toward the end of Ossian, he lets the Cat out.—Yet you were tender about this fellow—surely with[ou]t any reason. Pray keep that paper. I think towards the end of the *Life*, where the smaller traits of character are to be investigated, it would be very right to answer this and Mrs. Piozzi,[2] and all other artful *misrepresentations* that are well done; and to mark distinctly how far true and where the falsehood commences. . . .

---

[1] *Public Advertiser* for 26 Aug. 1786, "Observations on the Character of Dr. Johnson". I have not seen the letter, but Prof. Clifford has and kindly reports: "It is a well-written long tirade against what the biographers had shown Johnson's true character to be. The next Saturday, Sept. 2, there was another letter, signed 'M.M.', which highly praised Erica's letter. M.M. writes: 'In short, Sir, had Mr. Boswell and Mrs. Piozzi left the rising generation to judge of Johnson from his writings, his memory would have been revered; but his two warmest friends have d——d his fame in this world past all redemption; for it has brought forth Erica's real character of that motley-minded man, and proves that poor Sam Johnson was not only "Blinking Sam" in person, but likewise "blinking Sam" in mind. . . .' " For "Blinking Sam" in anecdote (Mrs. Piozzi's), see *Johns. Misc.* i. 313 (quoted by Hill, *Life* iii. 273 n. 1). For an account of the Reynolds portrait to which the anecdote probably refers, see *Life* iv. 449–50.

[2] Mrs. Piozzi is answered, *Life* iv. 340–47. As JB's editors have supposed, the anonymous critic quoted in pp. 341–43 was Malone himself (cancelled passage in MS. *Life*, p. 986). "Erica" is not noticed. JB kept a file of newspaper clippings dealing with SJ, but this letter is not among them.

From *William Julius Mickle*,[1]
Saturday 28 October 1786

MS. Yale (C 2014).

ADDRESS: James Boswell Esqr., No. 56, Great Queen Street, Lincoln's Inn fields, London.

POSTMARK: 31 OC.

ENDORSEMENT: Mr. Mickle of Dr. Johnson.

Wheatley, Octr. 28. 1786

. . . My[2] anecdotes of Dr. Johnson are not many, and you was present at most of them.[3] One when you was not present, tho' it concerns myself is perhaps worth repeating, as it does the good Doctor in my opinion much honour and shews his temper in a milder light than is generally conceived of him. It requires some narrative. We were dining at Mr. Hoole's, Henry Fielding happened to be mentioned. The Doctor inveighed against his moral character.[4] I said he had done good. The Dr. said he never could find it out. I mentioned his instituting the marine society. The Dr. "The worst thing ever he did." —The Dr.[5] now enlarged for more than a quarter of an hour in execrating the sea life; he once slept on board a man of war in the river and thought he was in Hell. He said it was corrupting the morals of boys to send them on board a man of war. M. "The destitute pickpocket wicked boys of the streets of London?" Johnson. "Yes, even them Sir. A man of war will make them ten times worse."[6] Here I urged no farther, and the Doctor proceeded. "It had been happy for the world, Sir,

---

[1] William Julius Mickle (1735–88), Scottish poet and translator of the *Lusiad* (1776). See *Life* ii. 495 and Journ. *passim.*

[2] Mickle's letter, from this point to the end of the paragraph beginning "Previous to publishing", was marked by JB with asterisks—apparently for direct quotation in the *Life*. But see n. 5.

[3] The journal records two occasions on which SJ, JB, and Mickle were together: the first, 4 May 1772, when JB introduced Mickle to SJ; the second, 11 Apr. 1776, when the three met at Hoole's. The *Life* records a third,

14 or 15 June (JB forgot which) 1784, at Wheatley, "a very pretty country place a few miles from Oxford" (iv. 308, 536).

[4] Cf. *Life* ii. 49.

[5] From this point to near the end of the letter (as here printed), Mickle's observations are freely rendered (at his own invitation: see end of paragraph), *Life* iv. 250–52, in the form of summary, paraphrase, and direct quotation (revised). See Introduction, pp. xxviii, xxx–xxxi.

[6] SJ's remarks on the man-of-war are omitted. See *Life* v. 514–15 for Cornelia Knight's account of SJ's stay aboard her father's ship in 1770.

if your Hero Gama, Prince Henry of Portugal, and Columbus had never been born, or that their schemes had never gone farther than their own imaginations." I was at this time beginning the Introduction to the *Lusiad*, and had that very point in contemplation, but strongly inclined to the other side of the question. I had also a few days before been reading the Doctor's Introduction to a *Collection of voyages* (I believe it is intitled)[7] in which he strongly expresses his sentiments as above. I thought myself happy in this opportunity of having the topic discussed, and a dispute of more than an hour ensued, in all which the Dr. conducted himself with the utmost politeness, not one uncivil or overbearing word escaped him, though we ended, as disputes usually do, each tenacious of his own opinion. Rather fortified in my own by the prejudices which I thought I could discover in his arguments, (not an unusual result of disputes) I set about the discussion of that topic with spirit, and took the freedom to cite the Dr. (see Introd. to the *Lusiad* p. 1, 6, 7, and 8) who says in his work above mentioned, "It had been happy for both the old and the new worlds if the East and West Indies had never been discovered." This, you will find, I controvert, and deficient as my dissertation on that head may be, the stimulus I received from the Dr. contributed greatly to make it so well as it is. Authors, it is said, are bad judges of their own works. Be it so, I am not however ashamed to own to a friend that that disser[ta]tion is my favourite above all I ever attempted in prose. About a month after the *Lusiad* was publishd I waited on the Dr. at his own house. He had a Levee as usual. After[8] kindly enquiring about the sale, he said with one of his good natured smiles "So I see you have remembered our dispute about Prince Henry (This was more than an year after) and have cited me too." He then handsomely complimented my disser[ta]tion, said I had made the best of my arguments, *"but,"* added he, *"I am not yet convinced."* He expressed himself in the same manner to me about a month after at Mr. Hoole's, and with the same Candour and good-nature. As I said before this anecdote-narrative shews the Dr.'s character in a much more candid and amiable light than is generally conceived of him. If you make any use of it, I beg and adjure you not to print the above hasty Memorandum, but to reduce the heads of it into your own language.

[7] Silently altered by JB to "Introduction to the World displayed". For the variant form of the title, see Hazen, p. 219.

[8] MS. "usual, after"

I was some months upwards of Twelve years acquainted with the Dr., during which time, except when I was abroad, I was frequent[l]y with him every year. I always talked with ease to him, and can truly say that I never received from him one rough word, or according to the homely phrase, *one rap on the knuckles.*[9]

Previous to publishing the *Lusiad*, I sent Mr. Hoole a proof of that part of the Introd. where I make mention of you and other well-wishers[10] to the work, among whom I named Dr. Johnson, but I begged Mr. Hoole to shew it to him for his consent ere I would venture to publish it. Mr. Hoole did so, and the Dr. in place of the simple mention I had made of him, dictated the sentence to Mr. Hoole as it stands in print, who transmitted it to me.

When I was first ⟨introd⟩uced to the Dr. (it was early in Spring 1772,[11] after I had published the first book and other specimens of the *Lusiad*) he told me that about 20 years ago he had a design of translating the *Lusiad* himself (and spoke highly of the merit of the Original) but that a multitude of other avocations prevented him, and that he had recommended it to Dr. Goldsmith; but who for the same reasons did not attempt it.[12]

I hope you have taken a Memorandum of the Dr.'s conversation[12a] the last time that he, yourself and I met at Mr. Hoole's table. The topic led me to observe that it was a maxim of the English Law, "Better some villains excape than that one innocent person should be capitally punished." As I know your liberality of sentiment I take the freedom to remind you that you rather blamed the maxim, and Mr. Nicol the Bookseller[13] quite scanted it, called it the most paltry of all maxims. M. "What would you have an innocent man

---

[9] Cf. JB's answer to the general notion of SJ's manners, *Life* iii. 80–81.

[10] "It is with particular pleasure that the translator renews his acknowledgements to those gentlemen who have patronised his work. . . . To James Boswell, esq. he confesses many obligations. And while thus he recollects with pleasure the names of many gentlemen from whom he has received assistance or encouragement, he is happy to be enabled to add Dr. Johnson to the number of those, whose kindness for the man, and good wishes for the translation, call for his sincerest gratitude.

Nor must a tribute to the memory of Dr. Goldsmith be neglected. He saw a part of this version; but he cannot now receive the thanks of the translator" (Mickle's "Dissertation on the *Lusiad*, and Observations on Epic Poetry," quoted from *The Works of the English Poets, from Chaucer to Cowper*, 1810, xxi. 622–23).

[11] See above n. 3.

[12] The reference to Goldsmith is omitted.

[12a] MS. "consersation"

[13] George Nicol (c. 1741–1829), bookseller to the King. See Plomer; *Life* iv. 365, 466; *Letters SJ* 965.3.

179

hanged?" N. "Ay, rather than ten rogues escape." The Dr. was appealed to, who in a speech of some length, equal in my opinion to the best of his *Ramblers* which may be classed with the subject; discussed the topic, every sentence carried clear conviction; that Government owed the innocent protection he placed in various and irresistible lights, etc. etc.—and I had the pleasure to retort a little severely on Mr. Nicol. I have often been sorry that I did not that evening write down, to the best of my recollection the Dr.'s speech, but I hope you have done it.[14]. . .

From the Rev. Daniel Astle,[1] December 1786

MS. Yale (C 43). A notebook.[2]

ADDRESS: To James Boswell Esquire, London. (From the Revd. Mr. Astle, Ashbourne, Derbyshire.)

[Ashbourne,] December 1786

SIR, I have read your elegant and entertaining *Journal of a Tour to the Hebrides* with a very sensible pleasure; and agreeable to your

---

[14] He didn't.

[1] The Rev. Daniel Astle, according to a contemporary "a most excentrick character", was the younger brother of Thomas Astle, the antiquary and paleographer. He was born about 1743, the son of Daniel Astle, keeper of Byrkley Lodge in Needwood Forest, Staffordshire, and was educated at Barton-under-Needwood. From 1769 or earlier until 1778 he held a commission in the 46th Foot, attaining the rank of captain and serving under Gen. Howe at Bunker Hill. In 1780 he published a topographical study, *A Prospect from Barrow Hill near Rocester, in Staffordshire.* By 1786, when his correspondence with JB opens, he was living at Ashbourne, where, according to the church register, a son was born to him in Aug. 1788 (for his marriage see end of letter proper and n. 44). From 1804 until his death in 1826 he was Rector of Bramshall, near Uttoxeter (*Life* iv. 536–37). In addition to the correspondence there are in the Yale Collection several documents with which Astle's name is associated: (1) copies in his hand of letters from SJ to Cave and to Thomas Astle (see *post* To Astle, 14 Feb. 1787, n. 2); (2) a copy of a letter from SJ to George Nicol in Nicol's hand, endorsed by JB: "This belongs to the Rev. Mr. Astle" (see *Life* iv. 365; *Letters SJ* 994); and (3) anecdotes of SJ in the hand of one —— Baldwin Esqre.", endorsed by Astle: "Revd. Mr Astle"— Astle being the transmitter, not the author (see *post* p. 587).

[2] The notebook is made up of twenty-six leaves, with only the last page left blank. Astle revised the MS. extensively and also included a number of suggestions for revision, aimed not at JB but at a London acquaintance (see *post* From Astle, 23 Jan. 1787). The proposed revisions, which were not executed, are indicated in three ways: (1) by the direction "Correct this"; (2) by the inclusion of alternative expressions; and (3) by underscorings and other devices apparently designed to call attention to

desire expressed in[3] the end of it that those persons who might have had the honour of being numbered among the friends and acquaintances of the late Doctor Samuel Johnson would be so obliging as to furnish you with whatever particulars they might have in their possession relative to that extraordinary personage,[4] I here take the liberty of sending You a few Anecdotes to insert, if you think them deserving of your notice in that Account of the Life of the Doctor with which you propose to favour the public.

The first particular I shall transmit to you, is the copy of a letter from the Doctor to his learned friend the unfortunate Joseph Simpson Esquire Barrister at Law:[5] a person whose necessities I have known the Doctor not only highly to commiserate but frequently relieve.

Next I shall give You two original Fragments that carry with them evident testimony of the rich mine from whence they sprung.[6]

My first introduction to this great genius was at a tavern in London in the year 1765; where I had the honour of dining with him and two other persons of the clerical Order. At this time he appeared more inclined than usual to display that satyrical turn for which he was so famous—a turn which I never thought originated from a splenetic disposition, but purely from an honest indignation at the follies and vices of mankind. One of the company informed the Doctor that I indulged to an unjustifiable degree, a passion for Theatrical Diversions; and that I had the ambition to walk with a Cane. On mentioning the former charge, he declared— That it would afford him more entertainment to sit up to the chin in water for an hour than be obliged to listen to the whining, daggle-tail Cibber, during the tedious representation of a fulsome tragedy without the possibility of receiving from it either pleasure or instruction.[7] As to my delinquency respecting the Cane he

---

questionable usages. These last are both idiosyncratic and uninteresting, and I have not taken note of them. There are several blanks in the MS. which appear also to be the result of Astle's doubts as to spelling and grammatical usage.

[3] MS. alt. "at"

[4] The Advertisement to the second edition of the *Tour* includes a request for SJ's letters to his friends.

[5] A collation of the various texts of this letter is given *ante* From Adey, 26 Feb.

1785; Astle's text is therefore omitted here.

[6] For these fragments of sermons, see the Appendix.

[7] See *Life* v. 38 and n. 1. "Cibber" is Mrs. Susannah Cibber (1714–66), who comes off rather better in SJ's remark in the *Tour* (*Life* v. 126): "Mrs. Cibber, I think, got more reputation than she deserved, as she had a great sameness; though her expression was undoubtedly very fine."

facetiously observed—That I put him in mind of a young fellow of his acquaintance whose daily practice it was to take his stick where he even did not think it worth his while to take his hat, and then positively assured me that in less than three weeks I should not know what to do with my right hand, without a stick. Upon pleading for the custom of carrying it as a weapon of defence,[8] he vociferated "why such an emphasis about a stick? Why such an emphasis about a stick?" and hence took occasion to animadvert on all puerile and foppish habits with a manly spirit.

The same person then intimated to him—That a certain north country gentleman of his acquaintance had expressed considerable uneasiness on account of a feature in the complexion of his family which he feared might prove an insuperable bar to his son's promotion.

The deficiency so dreadfully apprehended was no less than an invincible sheepishness and timidity; and the father was so strongly prepossessed with the idea of his son's labouring under this infirmity that he thought it adviseable to place him at some eminent public school with a view of fortifying his mind with such a competent proportion of that confidence which he esteemed so indispensibly requisite to the advancement of his family.

Our philosopher, hereupon, expressing his surprize at the person's wonderful sagacity in discovering what could not but appear obvious to the most common observer, said, the expedient suggested to remove the apprehended infirmity, was of all others the most preposterous, maintaining that a disposition so effeminate as that alluded to ought to have been cultivated in the shade, and that placing the youth in so conspicuous a station as that at a public school was like forcing an owl upon day.[9]

A few years after this I passed some time in company with the Doctor at my Father's habitation—situate within the deep embowering shades of   Forest.[10]

---

[8] A custom that SJ himself honoured in the observance on at least one occasion: see *ante* From Steevens, 23 Apr. 1786 (second enclosure). See also *Life* ii. 300.

[9] This is the first of three anecdotes related by Astle which were admitted to the *Life*. They appear consecutively under June 1784, in a section made up of "some particulars which I collected at various times" (iv. 311, 312). JB's ability to extract the essence from a verbose anecdote and to present it in dramatic form is well illustrated by his revision of the present passage.

[10] See *ante* n. 1. SJ's visit took place in July 1770 en route to Ashbourne. He remained at the lodge one night (*Letters SJ* 236). Astle's curious taste for anonymous and semi-anonymous designations runs rampant at the end of the letter.

The rural scenery of this recess being *then* remarkably fine, I was disposed to lavish on it more exalted encomiums than our rigid visitor was willing to admit of.

However, a strong partiality for my native place, gave me courage to direct his view one very fine evening to a large grove of stately and well-shaped oaks that presented themselves to advantage on the side of a hill immediately before the windows of the house; just when their verdant tops were beautifully gilded by the last glowing rays of the setting sun. Add to this the harmony of a thousand singing birds warbling among the trees, the appearance of deer and other animals feeding in different directions joined with the plaintive murmurs of a clear stream that watered a sequester'd valley below—But here I experienced no little mortification; for this pleasing assemblage of sylvan imagery had no other effect on the sage than to produce from him this dry, solitary remark,— That there was just timber enough to put one in mind of the want of it.

If the Doctor's temper betrayed a mixture of the acid in its composition, this acidity was compensated by the most laudable motive—a constant desire to apply the medicine of correction to all who stood in need of it; and no person was more competent to judge when and where to make the application.

Many were the sallies of wit and humour that emanated[11] from the Doctor at this visit, but the precious sayings have now slipped my memory[12]—one circumstance, however, I well remember, which is this—A monkey that was chained to a piece of heavy wood in a yard adjoining the house was observed by our curious guest to afford an instance of singular dexterity—by compelling the log to submit to his inclination so far as to gratify him with a portion of that liberty it was intended to deprive him of. And such was the artfulness of this cunning creature that he frequently put it into his power to liberate himself from his confinement by a contrivance which could only have been suggested by a faculty not inferior to reason itself.

The end of the chain which confined him was united by a slender leather thong to an iron staple fixed in the aforesaid piece of wood.

I have frequently made him a prisoner myself by means of

[11] MS. alt. "burst"
[12] MS. alt. "fallen a sacrifice to a treacherous memory"

this thong which often I tied of above a dozen hard knots always proportioning the number of knots to the strength of the creature.[13]

These embarrassments he attacked with astonishing acuteness and resolution, and never failed in the end compleatly to effect his enlargement. On mentioning this fact to the Doctor he treated the possibility of it with derision, and insisted that I must be mistaken in the matter, "For, Sir," (said he) "you might as well tell me that the monkey can extract metal from the ore as to [14]perform an exploit of a nature that required the intervention of reason to effect it."[14]

Being young and inexperienced at the time my Father was honoured with this visit from Doctor Johnson I happened in the course of conversation to advance an opinion in contradiction to my Father, and in support of it rudely offered to lay him a wager. This impropriety, you may be sure, did not pass without a severe reprimand from the Doctor, who to his honour be it spoken,[15] omitted no occasion of inculcating on the minds of young people, the strictest lessons of morality and decorum.

A considerable time after this I passed several weeks in the Doctor's company in the country. Here he told me that he had remarked a particularity in his host[16] that he was not able to

---

[13] MS. alt. "the creature's strength"

[14]–[14] JB himself got into the spirit of things by venturing at this point the simple alternative "disentangle those knots". He did not however, as the revision might suggest, use the anecdote. Cf. SJ's argument with Goldsmith, *Life* ii. 248–49.

[15] MS. alt. "remembered"

[16] The anonymous host so sarcastically portrayed in the following account is readily indentified as Dr. Taylor of Ashbourne. The date of the visit is more problematic, but the summer of 1777 meets most of the requirements. For instance, the report of Taylor's dispute with a neighbour at the time of the visit can be matched with the testimony of both SJ and JB that in Sept. 1777 Taylor was quarrelling with the Rev. William Langley, Headmaster of the Ashbourne grammar school (*Letters SJ* 541.1, 548; Journ. 16 Sept. 1777). The only difficulty

in so dating the visit lies in Astle's statement that he was in SJ's company several weeks. In 1777 SJ was at Ashbourne from 30 Aug. until about 29 Sept., but JB joined him there on the 14th (*Letters SJ* 540, 553; *Life* iii. 135, 208), and we know that Astle and JB had not met (end of letter proper). However, Astle could have been with SJ for two weeks before JB's arrival, and it is perhaps unreasonable to insist upon too literal an accounting in such cases.

An explanation for Astle's venomous characterization of Taylor is to be found in an event of 1776: a lawsuit involving Taylor on the one side and Astle's sister Mary and her second husband, Anthony Rhudde, on the other, over the disposition of the estates of Mrs. Rhudde's first husband, Ralph Wood, a nephew of Taylor's first wife. Astle was a witness for the defendants, and although the decision was in their favour (see Rev.

account for—this was his appearing with a book in his hand, and looking uncommonly studious. On being asked, if this was his practice when not favoured with the Doctor's presence I replied[17] in the negative. Whereupon the Doctor hastily said that he himself was of that Opinion, for to his knowledge he never relished a book in his earlier days,[18] and now he unfortunately begun[19] at the wrong end. "Besides, Sir, there are not Books sufficient in the house to preserve common decency if we consider his profession"—and, moreover, said the Doctor there were two improprieties he had detected in his house—the want of a Bible among his books,[20] and the want of[20a] a Clergyman among his guests: adding that a decent companion was a rara avis at his table. He concluded the conversation by saying that *Rags* would always make their appearance where they had a right to do it.[21]

The person at whose house we were had been bred [22]to the profession of the Law,[22] and was of so litigious a disposition as frequently to involve himself in disputes with his neighbours. One of these taking place during our visit,[23] the Doctor did not hesitate to tell him, that if he continued to indulge such despicable habits he would inevitably incur the contempt of all his friends, and justly[24] be deemed the *very* Bull Dog of his country.[25] And truly it must be observed by the bye that for the last fifty years of his life this

---

Thomas Taylor, *A Life of John Taylor* [1910], pp. 63 ff.), he seems to have nursed his grievance against Taylor—though apparently not to the extent of refusing his hospitality.

[17] MS. alt. "On my being asked . . . he [*sic*] replied"

[18] Perhaps with an oblique allusion to Taylor's delinquency in caring for SJ's books after SJ left Oxford. See *Johns. Glean.* v. 27.

[19] MS. alt. "had begun"

[20] This particular cause for complaint must have been removed by the time of SJ's visit in Nov. 1781: see *Letters SJ* 807 and *Life* iii. 454.

[20a] MS. alt. "and of"

[21] *Life* iv. 312. While JB repeated the apophthegm he himself held a higher opinion of Taylor's guests. See *Life* iii. 138–39. And in the journal, 20 Sept. 1777 (a note added Dec. 1779), he thought it

worth while to record a list of the company at Taylor's house. See Dr. Powell's commentary on this list, *Life* iii. 504–06 and E. A. Sadler, *Dr. Johnson's Ashbourne Friends*, 1939.

[22–22] MS. alt. "an Attorney". —"It had been his intention to follow his father's profession of the law and it is not improbable that for some years after leaving Oxford he did follow that profession. So much indeed is suggested by the ill natured remark of which Taylor was the butt, that a broken attorney made a notable parson" (Thomas Taylor, *Life of John Taylor*, p. 15).

[23] See *ante* n. 16.

[24] MS. alt. "very justly"

[25] Beside the metaphorical meaning is an allusion to Taylor's devoted practice of animal husbandry and in particular to his proud possession of a prize bulldog. See *Life* iii. 189–90.

limb of the Law had been distinguished for little else but Bull baitings Cockfighting Lawsu[its][26] and Intrigues.

Desirous of learning my honoured companion's sentiments respecting some improvements attempted to be made about our host's premises—He observed to me in general that all was of a Piece, for that nothing was *right within* doors, or *without*.[27]

And this he illustrated[28] by the following Quotation

For what has   painted, built, and planted?
Only to show how many *tastes* he wanted.[29]

The very servants themselves, he said instead of doing what they were bid stood gaping on the Guests in idle Clusters round the table, which he thought they were as ill calculated to attend as they were to steer a man of war.[30] As a confirmation of the truth of one part of this Remark, I shall (parvis componere magna)[31] mention an extraordinary contrivance that was intended to give the appearance of a River to a small patch of water at the bottom of a little Grass Plot behind the house.

The terminations of this patch of water are hid from view by two shabby brick buildings erected in defiance of all taste, opposite each other, and so near, as barely to admit the waters being seen between them. These buildings have, however, their respective uses—one being devoted to the laudable purpose of raising Bull Dogs and Game-cocks and the other designed to prevent the sight without excluding the stench of a tan yard.

Behind the garden wall at a small space from the water, is erected an immense pole towering as high almost as the mast of a first rate man of war. And this they had bedizened out in imitation of the rigging of a ship, with a view to excite the idea of a vessel lying at anchor; but it is so very disproportionate to the puddle of

---

[26] The blank in the MS. may indicate a wavering between "Lawsuits" and "Lawsuites", though the latter spelling seems to have gone out by the eighteenth century. See OED.

[27] SJ's opinion of Taylor's estate changed from admiration to scorn as a result of the improvements made over the years. See for example *Letters SJ* 236 and 981. For descriptions of both the house and its surroundings see *Life* ii. 542, iii. 498–99, iv. 548–49, and Thomas Taylor, *Life of John Taylor*, pp. 19 ff.

[28] MS. alt. "corroberated"

[29] "For what has Virro painted," etc. (Pope, *Moral Essays* iv. 13–14).

[30] *Life* iv. 312. Hill conjectured that the unnamed "gentleman" of the *Life* was Sir Joshua Reynolds. Dr. Powell has corrected the identification, *Life* vi (2nd ed., 1964), Table of Anonymous Persons, No. 467, and Errata, p. 493 (where for "David Astle" read "Daniel Astle").

[31] "to compare great things with small": Virgil, *Eclogues* i. 23.

water that appears beneath that the impostor is too gross to pass for a deception. Improvements these sufficient to immortalize the Taste of their elegant projector! Our Connoissieur on this occasion declared that it was not easy to imagine how any man at so advanced a season of life could condescend to amuse himself with so absurd a bauble; or consent to exhibit so flagrant an instance of levity to the neighbourhood, as to put up a stick and then call it a ship, and to dignify the Pit wherein it is fixed with the name of a River. "Pray, Captain," said he, "take a speedy opportunity of advising him to cut it down by the Board.[32] The Owner ought to be ashamed of it, for it is not the Thing it pretends *to be*; it is a Falsehood realized; and a Lie may be *acted* as well as told; but the former is the more malignant of the two.[33] In short," continued he, "it seems to be an established maxim here to take the *short way* to every thing: but deception, indeed, is as natural to some dispositions as noxious weeds are to the soil that spontaneously produces them.[34]

It perhaps may here be incumbent on me to apologize for [35]having enumerated a few[35] trifling Circumstances that principally relate to a Character whose obscure Situation in Life necessarily places him and his atrocious Conduct within the Precincts of a most confined Circle.

However, the Reference they have to your old Friend the Doctor will render them at least admissible in your Eyes, though they cannot altogether exempt me from Censure in my own. (Pray physic and bleed the above into common Sense; and endeavour to introduce the following 7 Lines. From Pope.)[36]

---

[32] This device is not mentioned in any descriptions of the estate that I have seen.

[33] Cf. the anecdote by Mr. Wickins ("a respectable draper in Lichfield"), *Johns. Misc.* ii. 427–28: "Walking one day with him in my garden at Lichfield, we entered a small meandering shrubbery, whose 'vista not lengthened to the sight,' gave promise of a larger extent. I observed, that he might perhaps conceive that he was entering an extensive labyrinth, but that it would prove a deception, though I hoped not an unpardonable one. 'Sir,' said he, 'don't tell me of deception; a lie, Sir, is a lie, whether it be a lie to the eye or a lie to the ear.' "

[34] At this point in the MS. a strip of paper with writing on both sides has been inserted. It is folded horizontally and the top half is pasted to the leaf, concealing a portion of the original writing. On the front of the strip appear the two paragraphs that follow in the text; on the page proper beneath the lower half of the strip is written the beginning of the quotation from Pope; and on the back of the strip the quotation is concluded.

[35-35] MS. alt. "enumerating"

[36] Originally only the first three lines were written, followed by "A hireling etc." and accompanied in the margin by the direction "Insert here 7 lines from

A knave's a knave to me in ev'ry state:
Alike my scorn, if he succeed or fail,
Sporus at court, or Japhet in a jail,
A hireling scribbler, or a hireling peer,
Knight of the post corrupt, or of the shire;
If on a pillory, or near a throne,
He gain his prince's ear, or lose his own.

The Doctor recommended to my perusal a variety of Books of which he gave me a List in his own handwriting. He often desired me to read to him aloud—and when I did he pointed out to me the beauties of any author as they occurred. On producing a Quarto volume of miscellaneous poems that was published some years since in the neighbourhood where we then were, he observed that they were not the spontaneous productions of any particular man's mind, but that they were the produce of some person's Pen
had read other Performances of the same kind of which there are published multitudes every day. (Correct this.) He then repeated in an emphatical manner, the following Lines from Doctor Young's *Love of Fame*.[37]

Ye Bards! why will you sing, tho' uninspir'd?
Ye Bards! why will you starve to be admir'd?
Defunct by Phoebus' laws, beyond redress,
Why will your spectres haunt the frighted press?
Bad metre, that excrescence of the head,
Like hair, will sprout altho' the poet's dead.

(Correct this)[38]

On shewing him a Translation of Dryden's Latin Exercise (which he wrote at School) respecting our Saviour's Miracle of changing water into wine, I observed the Line viz.; "The modest Water saw its God and blush'd,"[39] was not happily expressed: the Word *its* appearing to weaken the Personification. Our Critic after a few Moments Consideration approved the Justness of my Remark.

P—e". But Astle must have decided to complete the quotation himself rather than trouble his London acquaintance, for the last four lines are written in on the back of the inserted strip. The quotation is from the *Epistle to Dr. Arbuthnot*, 361–67.

[37] Satire IV. Cf. *Letters SJ* 252 and *Life* v. 270.

[38] The lines are quoted correctly.

[39] The line, variously attributed, is from an Epigram by Crashaw. See *Life* iii. 304, and *post* From Reed, c. Nov. 1792 and n. 45. "Dryden's" is a later addition in the MS.

Though the Doctor thought proper to commend me for this specimen I gave of critical acuteness, I must confess I have suffered so much from his animadversions in the early part of our acquaintance that I have often been strongly tempted to retaliate the wounds inflicted on me by caricaturing the rigid Censor[40] when Disparity in Age, Difference of Profession, or other Circumstance would not well admit of a politer Species of Retort.

It perhaps may carry the air of vanity to select for my Commendation a Passage from your admired *Journal* that is particularly interesting to myself—so deeply interesting that I cannot pass it over in Silence.

The Passage I mean[41] is—where your Fellow traveller so liberally bestows his Offerings of Gratitude to the Shrine of generous and polite Hospitality erected at S—— Castle.[42]

The accomplished Master of that venerable Mansion took to his second Wife the eldest Daughter of the late Sir William C——, of E—— in N——d, who is the present Countess of E——, and Sister to the Honourable Mrs. M——, Lady to the Commander in Chief in S——d.[43] The respectable Testimony afforded by our learned Traveller to the Merits of these Worthies, has induced me to communicate to You a Circumstance that relates to my Connection with this Family, and which I shall ever esteem the happiest of my Life. What I mean is my entering into the holy Estate of Matrimony with the youngest Daughter of the late Colonel George C——,[44] second Brother to Sir William. This will account

---

[40] For a pen-and-ink sketch of SJ, attributed to Astle, see Francis Redfern, *History of the Town of Uttoxeter* (1865), p. 119.

[41] MS. alt. "allude to"

[42] Slains Castle, Aberdeenshire, which SJ and JB visited on 24–25 Aug. 1773 (*Life* v. 97 ff.). No such passage as that described by Astle is to be found in the *Tour*; perhaps he was thinking of SJ's *Journey to the Western Islands of Scotland* (ed. R. W. Chapman, 1924, p. 18): "Next morning we continued our journey, pleased with our reception at Slains Castle, of which we had now leisure to recount the grandeur and the elegance."

[43] The "master" of Slains Castle was James Boyd (1726–78), son of William Boyd, fourth Earl of Kilmarnock. He assumed the name of Hay upon his succession to the earldom of Erroll in 1758. His second wife was Isabella Carr (1742–1808), elder daughter of Sir William Carr (c. 1705–77), of Etal, Northumberland, who, though he styled himself a baronet, disclaimed the title in a codicil to his will. Carr's younger daughter, Margaret (b. 1747), was married in 1770 to Alexander Mackay (d. 1789), son of George, third Lord Reay. He was appointed Commander-in-Chief of the forces in Scotland in 1780 (*Scots Peer.* iii. 580–81, vii. 175; *Comp. Peer.* v. 100; *Comp. Bar.* ii. 429; Northumberland County History Committee, *History of Northumberland, 1893–1940*, xi. 459).

[44] George Carr (1705–72) married Elizabeth Reid in 1740. The youngest of

for my expatiating so warmly on this part of your *Journal*, and I flatter myself, will acquit me of any Imputation of being too Officious or intrusive by the Freedom of this Epistle; a Freedom that may stand in need of some Apology as being taken by one who has not the Honour, of being personally known to You. I am, Sir, Your obedient, and very humble Servant,[45]

SIR, In addition to my Engagement to You, as specified In my Letter, I shall take the liberty herewith to enclose you, an original sketch of Doctor Johnson's character, writ by a Person of some eminence in the literary world. I am, Sir, your obedient, and Very humble Servant

To James Boswell Esq.

Doctor Johnson's Character in a Letter to a Friend[46]

He is a Being of all others I ever knew, the most heterogeniously constructed—at once the most liberal and the most ungenerous; the most dark and most enlightened; the most compassionate and the most merciless; the most friendly and the least sincere; the best temper'd and the most acrimonious; the most soothing and the most abusive of mankind.

I know him well, he was a native of Lichfield, his Parents extremely poor; my Mother's Father, a Clergyman and an

their three daughters was named Jane (*History of Northumberland* xi. 459–60). Carr was appointed major in the 72nd Foot (Invalids) in 1762; no higher rank, regimental or army, is assigned to him in the *Army List*.

[45] Unsigned. SJ's letter to Simpson (see *ante* From Adey, 26 Feb. 1785, n. 17) and the fragments of sermons (see Appendix) mentioned by Astle at the beginning of his letter appear next in the notebook. These are followed by the remainder of the text as printed here.

[46] The writer was Anna Seward and the recipient Thomas Sedgwick Whalley, D.D. (1746–1828), "the true picture of a sensible, well-informed and educated, polished, old, well-beneficed, nobleman's and gentleman's house-frequenting, literary and chess-playing divine" (DNB). The original letter, dated 22 Nov. 1781 and printed in the Rev. Hill Wickham's

edition of Whalley's *Journals and Correspondence* (1863, i. 346 ff.), is an almost verbatim rendering of extracts from Miss Seward's correspondence with William Hayley, printed in *Gent. Mag.* (1793, lxiii. 197 ff.). The date of the exchange is there given as 1782, but as Miss Seward quotes a passage from one of Hayley's letters in writing to Whalley, it must have been 1781 or earlier. (See Clifford, *Piozzi*, p. xviii n. 2, 306 n. 2, and *ante* From Seward, 25 Mar. 1785, nn. 1 and 12–12, for her re-writing and re-dating of her letters for publication.) In one extract, dated 3 Oct., Miss Seward writes that SJ "has been in Lichfield 10 days". SJ did not visit Lichfield in 1782; in 1781 he was there from 19 Oct. until 9 Nov. (*Life* iii. 454; *Letters SJ* 742–47). Apparently none of the dates assigned to the extracts in *Gent. Mag.* is to be trusted. Another copy of the

eminent Schoolmaster, gave him his Education,[47] and without the most distant Idea of ever receiving a Penny on his Account, took pains with him as with the Sons of the wealthiest Gentlemen.

He comes down for a Month every two Years[48] the Guest of his Daughter in Law, an old Friend of ours.

Doctor Johnson may be called the most Liberal of men because he is open-handed to all who need it: and has been known to divide his last guinea with the distress'd, when all he possessed was earned from Day to day by his Writings.

Ungenerous, because he has no mercy upon reputation of any sort, and sickens with envy over every literary fame, as his Works, (*The Lives of the Poets*) evince.

The most dark, for his Bigotry and Superstition pass Credibility, they are malign and violent.

The most enlightened, since his prodigious genius and immense knowledge can throw lustre even on the gloom of his own malignancy.

Compassionate, because he will weep for the unfortunate, provided their miseries arise either from sickness, or poverty: and he will exert himself to relieve them.

Merciless, for that he exults over the anguish and despair of every person whose party, or religious principles have been different to his own.

Friendly, because he will kindly commiserate and serve with activity those who seek his good offices.

The least sincere, because he delights to sneer and render contemptible those very people whose society he seeks; whom he caresses with tenderness, and whose interests he promotes.

Soothing, for no man's manners are more affectionate, as long as implicit assent is given to his declamations.

Abusive, because from the instant that the slightest opposition is made to his Opinions, he exalts his voice into thunder, and, "don't talk nonsense," and, "Sir," or, "madam it is false," and, "if you think so, you think like a fool," becomes the language he uses, and

character sent to Whalley, by Sophia Weston Pennington, Miss Seward's correspondent, is in the Yale Collection. It is, unlike Astle's copy, virtually identical with the printed version. Hawkins (p. 601 n.) describes an anonymous letter he found among SJ's papers which, if it was not Miss Seward's, sounds like a carbon copy of it. For JB's own antithetical portrait of SJ, see *Life* iv. 426 ff.

[47] See *ante* To Seward, 15 Feb. 1785 and n. 6.

[48] Every two years between 1777 and 1781. See *Life* iii. 454.

with which he interlards his imperious Dogmas: while to the pliability of yielding fear, and unletter'd simplicity, he is ever easy, cheerful, kind, and indulgent.

Grateful, because he *dedicates* his *time* and exerts his good offices even to the *most stupid people* from *whom*, (or whose Families) he has received kindness *in the days of his Youth*.

Ungrateful, because he would as soon expose the failings of his liberal benefactors, as those of the most indifferent persons, magnify them into faults, and lavish on them all the Epithets of Blockhead, Fool, and Rascal.

I heard him pronounce Beattie's charming *Minstrell*, a dull, heavy, uninteresting Fragment whose second Book he could never prevail upon himself to look into.

Mason's *English Garden* he calls a very miserable Piece of labour'd Insignificance.

Mr. Haley stiles him the noble Leviathan of Criticism, who lashes the troubled waters into a sublime, but mischievous Storm of Turbulence and Mud; yet allows that with all his mighty powers, he is a very odd Fish; though he says he reverences him as the Lord of his Element and is welcome to tear his Poems, as the Lion tears the Kid.

From the Publication of *The Lives of the Poets*, I date the Downfall of just poetic Taste in this Kingdom: the splendour of Johnson's literary Fame and *Ignis Fatuis Reasoning* co-operating with the natural Envy of the Ignorant or rather half-learned, will inlist a numerous Army under his Banners; overpowering by their numbers, and by their Eloquence, the generous few, who have juster perceptions of excellence who dare think for Themselves.

To the Rev. Daniel Astle,
Thursday 28 December 1786

MS. Yale (L 19). JB's copy, headed: "To The Rev. Mr. Astle Ashbourne Derbyshire."

London, 28 Decr. 1786

REVEREND SIR: On my return home from the election at Carlisle which occasioned me a month's absence[1] I found your communica-

---

[1] From 25 Nov. to 22 Dec. (Reg. Let.). JB attended the election as counsel to Lord Lonsdale (Journ. 23 Nov.).

tions concerning Dr. Johnson, for which be pleased to accept of my thanks.

As you have been so obliging, I shall make no apology for giving you more trouble.

Pray what is become of the list of Books which Dr. Johnson gave you. If you have preserved it, I should be very glad to have it.

I had some time ago a copy of the letter to Mr. Simpson.

As to the Fragments,—I am sure you will not take it amiss that as I pledge myself to the Publick for a most scrupulous attention to authenticity,[2] I request of you to inform me where the originals are, and if you are possessed of them or can procure them, to favour me with a sight of them.

Letters to me may be sent under cover of John Courtenay Esq. M.P. London. I am Reverend Sir, Your most obedient humble servant

[2] See the Advertisement to the first edition, *Life* i. 6–7.

1787

To Thomas Barnard, Bishop of Killaloe, Saturday 6 January 1787

MS. Yale (L 47). JB's copy, headed: "To The Bishop of Kilaloe."

Great Queen Street, Lincolns Inn Fields, 6 Janry. 1786 [*sic*]
. . . Sir John Hawkins's edition of Dr. Johnson's *Works* with his *Life* will be published in a few weeks. The *Life* is a large Octavo volume, of above 600 pages. It has been printed off several months.[1] I have seen no part of it; but Mr. Langton has read it all, and tells me that he must not anticipate particulars; but that upon the whole it is very en[ter]taining. I understand it is full of digressions, in the Knights manner of writing, which somebody very well characterised by *a rigmarole way*.[2] My great Volume will not be finished for some time. I have waited till I should first see Hawkins's compilation. But my friends urge me to dispatch, that the ardour of curiosity may not be allowed to cool. . . .

From the Rev. Daniel Astle, Tuesday 23 January 1787

MS. Yale (C 44). Received 27 Jan. (Reg. Let.).

Ashbourne, Jany. 23d 1787
SIR, Please to accept my acknowledgements for your very obliging Favour of the 29th[1] of last month, which the distance of time makes necessary for me to apologize to you for not having returned a more expeditious answer. However, in compliance with your request, I have omitted no opportunity of exerting my best endeavours to furnish you with the list of Books, which I intimated to you, in my former letter, Doctor Johnson many years ago gave me: but either through improper treatment, or accidental injury,

[1] In a letter to Bishop Percy, 8 Dec. 1786, Hawkins reports that his *Life of Johnson* is finished and printed, and that it, together with his edition of the *Works*, will appear early in the spring (*Lit. Illust.* viii. 243). They were published on 20 March.

[2] "Rigmarole" is the title of one of the categories of Malone's strictures on

Hawkins's *Life* (Davis, *Johnson before Boswell*, p. 192). JB adopts the term in his answer to Hawkins's account of the Blackfriars Bridge controversy, *Life* i. 351 n. 1 (see *post* From Mylne, 31 Dec. 1789 and n. 2).

[1] JB's copy is dated the 28th.

I am concerned that it has suffered in so extreme a degree, as to be scarcely worth your acceptance.

Whatever I have been able to collect of it shall now be enclosed, as a small earnest of the good offices I would render you, were my ability in any respect proportioned to the inclination I have to oblige you.

Being an inhabitant of Ashbourne, you will, perhaps, suspect that I have more of the Doctor's productions to present you with, since an anonymous correspondent in one of the public papers has lately pointed out a person in this place as the fortunate possessor of many of the Doctor's valuable originals:[2] but my residence here has been of short continuance, and I have not the smallest acquaintance with the person before hinted at; so that nothing is likely to be derived through the channel of my interest even from this very copious source.

The papers which I have already communicated to you, were long ago intrusted to me under a strict injunction of secrecy; so that you may safely rely upon their being authentic. The Originals from whence these were taken, are now in London,[3] where it is not in my power to obtain access to them.

Should I hereafter be possessed of any papers that were the genuine offspring of your late friend's masterly pen, you may depend upon their being transmitted to you by, Sir, your obedient, and very humble Servant,

DANIEL ASTLE

P.S. The pacquet you received sometime ago from me, was sent to an acquaintance in London for correction, before it was delivered to you; the great haste with which it was dispatched from hence, not affording me any opportunity for that purpose: but, I was concerned to find, that my request could not be complied with, on account of other engagements.

---

[2] I have not located the letter from the anonymous correspondent, but guess that the "valuable originals" were SJ's letters to Hill Boothby, and the "fortunate possessor" her brother, Sir Brooke Boothby of Ashbourne Hall. The letters were deposited with Taylor at this time: see *post* From Malone, 14 Sept. 1787, n. 4.

[3] See Appendix, Introductory Note.

[Enclosure][4]

Universal History (ancient) 20 vols.[5]
Rollin's Ancient History[6]
Puffendorfs Introduction to History[7]
Vertot's Hist. of Knights of Malta Fol. 2 vols.[8]
Vertot's Revolution of Portugal[8]
Vertots Revolutions of Sweden[8]
Carte's Hist. of England. 3 vols. fol.[9]
Present State of England[10]
Geographical Grammar[11]
Prideaux's Connection[12]
Nelsons Feasts and Fasts[13]
Duty of Man[14]
Gentleman's Religion[15]

[4] The MS. is now in the Hyde Collection. Despite Astle's apology for its condition and the suggestion of a loss, it appears to be intact, though much mended. It is possible, however, that the original consisted of more than the single leaf that has survived. JB prints the list with minor changes, *Life* iv. 311–12.

[5] *An Universal History from the Earliest Account of Time to the Present*, 23 vols., 1736–65. SJ must have been thinking of the edition of 1746–66 in 64 vols., since a little less than a third of the work is devoted to ancient history. According to Tyers (*Johns. Misc.* ii. 372), SJ was invited to collaborate on the project, but declined. See also *Life* iv. 382–83, 550.

[6] Charles Rollin, *The Ancient History of the Egyptians, Carthaginians*, etc., 10 vols., 1734–36 (translated from the French).

[7] Baron Samuel von Pufendorf, *An Introduction to the History of the Principal Kingdoms and States of Europe*, 1695 (translated from the German). See *Life* ii. 157, 430.

[8] Abbé René Aubert de Vertot d'Auboeuf, *The History of the Knights of Malta*, 2 vols., 1728; *The History of the Revolution in Portugal*, 1700; and *The*

History of the Revolutions in Sweden, 1696 (translated from the French). See *Life* ii. 237.

[9] Thomas Carte, *A General History of England*, 4 vols., 1747–55 (the fourth volume was published posthumously). See *Life* i. 42 n. 3, v. 296.

[10] [Edward Chamberlayne,] *Angliae Notitia, or the Present State of England*, 1669. See TLS, 26 July 1928, leading article.

[11] Probably *A New Geographical, Historical and Commercial Grammar*, etc., 1770, by William Guthrie.

[12] Humphrey Prideaux, *The Old and New Testament Connected*, etc., 2 vols., 1716–18.

[13] Robert Nelson, *A Companion for the Festivals and Fasts of the Church of England*, 1704. See *Life* ii. 458 and n. 3; *Diaries*, p. 91; *Letters SJ* 609 and n., 1121.

[14] [?Richard Allestree,] *The Whole Duty of Man*, 1658. See *Life* i. 67, 527, ii. 239; *Journ.* 30 Apr. 1773, 14 Oct. 1774, 3 Mar. 1777; *Letters SJ* 609 and n., 1121.

[15] [Edward Synge, Archbishop of Tuam,] *A Gentleman's Religion*, 1693. See *Lit. Anec.* i. 378 n.

Clarendon's History[16]
Watts's Improvement of the Mind[17]
Watts's Logick[17]
Nature Displayed[18]
Lowths English Grammar[19]
Blackwal on the Classicks[20]
Sherlock's Sermon's[21]
Burnets Life of Hale[22]
Dupin's History of the Church 4 vols. 12mo[23]
Shuckford's Connection[24]
Law's Serious Call[25]
Waltons Complete Angler[26]
Sandy's Travels[27]
Sprat's Hist. of the royal Society[28]
England's Gazetteer 3 vols. 12mo[29]
Goldsmith's Roman History[30]
Some Commentaries on the Bible[31]

[16] Edward Hyde, Earl of Clarendon, *The History of the Rebellion and Civil Wars in England*, 3 vols., 1702–04. See *Life* ii.79, iii. 257–58; *Journ.* 28 Sept. 1776.

[17] Isaac Watts, *Logick*, etc., 1725; *The Improvement of the Mind*, etc., 1741. See *Lives* iii. 308–09; *Life* i. 312, iii. 126, 358, 370; JB to Alexander Boswell, 7 Feb. 1794.

[18] Abbé Noel Antoine Pluche, *Spectacle de la Nature, or Nature Displayed*, 1733 (translated from the French). See *Life* iv. 537.

[19] [Robert Lowth, Bishop of London,] *A Short Introduction to English Grammar*, 1762. See *Life* ii. 37, v. 57 n. 3, 81, 125, 423; *Journ.* 11 Apr. 1772; *Letters SJ* 686.1.

[20] Rev. Anthony Blackwall, *An Introduction to the Classics*, 1718. See *Life* i. 84; *Johns. Glean.* v. 75 ff.

[21] William Sherlock, Dean of St. Paul's, *Sermons Preached upon Several Occasions*, 2 vols., 1719. See *Life* iii. 248.

[22] Gilbert Burnet, Bishop of Salisbury, *The Life and Death of Sir Matthew Hale*, 1681.

[23] Louis Ellies Dupin, *A Compendious History of the Church*, 4 vols., 1713 (translated from the French).

[24] Samuel Shuckford, Prebendary of Canterbury, *The Sacred and Profane History of the World Connected*, 2 vols., 1728.

[25] William Law, *A Serious Call to a Devout and Holy Life*, 1729. See *Life* i. 69 and n. 2; *Journ.* 8 Dec. 1793; and *post* From G. Strahan, 4 Mar. 1791 and n. 8.

[26] See N & Q (1925) cxlix. 79–80, 170.

[27] George Sandys, *A Relation of a Journey Begun Anno Dom. 1610*, 1615. The work appeared as *Sandys Travailes* in 1652.

[28] Thomas Sprat, Bishop of Rochester, *The History of the Royal-Society of London*, 1667.

[29] [Stephen Whatley,] *England's Gazetter*, etc., 3 vols., 1751.

[30] *The Roman History, from the Foundation of the City of Rome to the Destruction of the Western Empire*, 2 vols., 1769. See *Life* ii. 236–37; *Journ.* 30 Apr. 1773.

[31] See *Life* iii. 58.

From Joseph Warton,[1]
Sunday 29 January 1787

MS. Yale (C 3063).

ADDRESS: James Boswell Esqr.

ENDORSEMENT: Rev. Dr. Joseph Warton.

Winchester College, Jan. 29 1787

DEAR SIR, I Here send you the Two Letters which I mentioned of our old Freind Dr. Johnson, of which you may make what use you please.[2] I long very much to see your work. . . .

From the Rev. Daniel Astle,
Thursday 8 February 1787

MS. Yale (C 45).

ADDRESS: To James Boswell Esqre., [*inserted in Courtenay's hand:* Great Queen Street, Lincoln's Inn Fields] London.

Ashbourne, Feby. 8th 1787

SIR, In compliance with your Request, I sometime ago did myself the Pleasure of enclosing to you (under Cover of Mr. Courtenay) the list of Books I intimated to You was given me by Doctor Johnson. I have not received your Acknowledgement of the Receipt thereof, and therefore wish to know whether it has been delivered. I remain, Sir, Your obedient, and very humble Servant

DANL. ASTLE

P.S. It may not be unacceptable to you to be informed that Mr. Astle of the Treasury is possessed of some Materials that might be serviceable to you, in your present Undertaking, respecting Dr. Johnson.

[1] Joseph Warton, D.D. (1722–1800), poet and critic; Headmaster of Winchester College, 1766–93; member of The Club. See *Life*, Journ., and *Letters SJ* passim.

[2] Printed, *Life* i. 253, ii. 115. In the first, SJ solicits from Warton a regular contribution to *The Adventurer* (see *post* From J. Warton, 30 Mar. 1790); in the second, he invites him to correct a misrepresentation of his opinion of *King Lear* for the SJ-Steevens Shakespeare (it went unchanged). The originals are now in the Hyde Collection.

To the Rev. Daniel Astle,
Wednesday 14 February 1787

MS. Hyde. MS. Yale (L 20): JB's draft, written on the verso of the preceding letter from Astle.

London, 14 Febry. 1787

REVEREND SIR: I should have sooner acknowledged the list of Books by Dr. Johnson, but thought it might be giving you needless trouble. I am much obliged to you for it. I *guess* at the way in which the *Fragments* are known to be authentick; but I shall not express it in my Compilation.[1] I shall apply to Mr. Astle of the Treasury[2] to whom I am a little known, and I beg you may accept of my hearty thanks for your favours. I am, Reverend Sir, Your most obedient humble servant,

JAMES BOSWELL

From William Bowles,
Thursday 1 March 1787

MS. Yale (C 559). Received 3 Mar. (Reg. Let.).

ADDRESS: James Boswell Esqr., Great Queen Street, Lincolns Inn fields, London.

POSTMARK: MARCH 3.

ENDORSEMENT: Mr. Bowles 1 March 1787.

Heale, Mar. 1. 1787

DEAR SIR, I confess myself extremely to blame in not having earlier acknowledged the honor of your letters,[1] and I sincerely ask pardon for my neglect and seeming inattention.

I have waited in hopes of seeing Mr. Mickle[2] at my house; but

---

[1] See Appendix, Introductory Note.

[2] JB acquired copies of three of SJ's letters: (1) to Thomas Astle (*Life* iv. 133) and (2) and (3) to Cave (*Life* i. 155–57). The first two are in the hand of Daniel Astle, the third in JB's. JB had originally noted on (2): "Copy of Dr. Johnson's Letter. The Original is in the Possession of Thos. Astle Esqr. N.B. Compare it and try to fill up the Blanks, by reading his handwriting better." The blanks were filled up, and apparently the copy of (3) was made at the same time.

---

[1] In the extant correspondence only one letter of JB's (*ante* 31 May 1786) is unacknowledged.

[2] Despite the lapse of almost a year between letters, Mickle seems to be the unnamed "old friend" of SJ's whose visit Bowles was expecting 22 Mar. 1786 (*ante*) and who, he hoped, would verify his "Collectanea."

he has been every day coming and continually detained by what I apprehend would detain any man and keep him in uncertainty—a Cause in chancery.[3]

I understand by your several letters that no communications respecting Dr. Johnson will be of use to you excepting those which are authenticated by a name. This being the case I have been led to compare my little collection pretty scrupulously with the published accounts of Mrs. Thrale and others, and I find that the Doctor communicated to her almost all the particulars of his life which he mentioned to me.

I cannot therefore but fear that if my account appears to be a repetition of what has been communicated to the publick already, that I shall be charged with vanity.

I was in hopes about a fortnight ago that I should have been able to communicate to you some of our friends school exercises, having accidentally met with the son of his schoolmaster:[4] I pressed him with the utmost force of entreaty and he seemed willing to give me the exercises which he thought his father had preserved: after a few days he assured me they were not to be found. He told me however that his father had not kept, after leaving his school, any more exercises than those of Dr. Johnson and one other boy.

A Lecturer in Nat. Philosophy (Mr. Warltire)[5] told me that at Litchfield when he red his course, the Dr. once attended, and on his entrance into the room observing a large party of ladies, he said "I am happy to see here so many of my countrywomen; Ladies, it does you honor."[6]

I am perfectly willing to communicate to you all that I know of the *Life and opinions* of our friend if you will excuse my name and mention the particulars as from yourself.

I am a good deal concerned at the delay of my letter, and shall therefore venture to trouble you with what I am not forward to mention a word or[7] two respecting the state of my own family. My father is now 70 and[8] infirm in mind as well as out of health;

---

[3] To recover part of his wife's fortune (DNB).

[4] John Wentworth (b. c. 1708), of Magdalen Hall, Oxford; B.C.L. 1733. He was the nephew rather than the son of SJ's schoolmaster, the Rev. John Wentworth (*ante* From Hector, 1 Feb. 1785 and n. 26). His father was Thomas

Wentworth, Mayor of Salisbury in 1719 (*Johns. Glean.* iii. 156 n.).

[5] Not identified. The spelling is reasonably clear, unlikely as the name may be.

[6] The anecdote was not used.

[7] MS. "a"

[8] MS. "very" deleted.

all his bus'ness devolves on me and for six months past he has been engaged in an affair which has interested every part of his family and is extremely difficult and embarassing. My own time has been almost wholly taken up and my spirits have been so much engrossed by this matter that I have hardly had resolution to attend to any other ⟨one⟩. Use me so much like a friend as not to speak of this: I would not have troubled you with it but to shew you that I have not without reason neglected your kind letters.

I hope you are well and that your removal to London is as pleasant and agreable a circumstance as you could have imagined it. I am Dear Sir, with much regard, Your most obedient humble Servant

WM. BOWLES

From Thomas Percy, Bishop of Dromore, Tuesday 6 March 1787

MS. Yale (C 2233). A draft of this letter, dated 5 Mar. and printed in *Lit. Illust.* vii. 305–08, is in the C. B. Tinker Collection at Yale.

ADDRESS: James Boswell Esqr., at Mr. Dilly's, Bookseller in the Poultry, London.

POSTMARKS: MR 6, MARCH 10.

Dublin, March 6th 1787

DEAR SIR: My delay in answering your obliging Letters, I beg you will ascribe to the true Cause; the not being able to satisfy myself, That any Particulars I could recover concerning our friend Dr. Johnson were worth your Notice,[1] much less would answer the Expectations I had formed to myself, or excited in you, when we regarded the Subject at a Distance. Yet I have often reproached myself for not submitting them to you; and at length have determined to send them such as they are; with the addition of a Greek

---

[1] On 17 Oct. 1786 Percy had written to Malone: "If you see Mr. Boswell, pray tell him I received his very obliging Letter and only delayed acknowledging it in hopes I should have recollected something worth his notice concerning Johnson's Infancy and early Life. But when I came to bring together what little matters I could remember, they were either anticipated by Mrs. Piozzi, or too trivial and indistinct for Transmission" (*Correspondence of Thomas Percy & Edmond Malone*, ed. Arthur Tillotson, 1944, pp. 42–43). Percy nevertheless proceeds to give a brief account of SJ's connexions (real and supposed) with the schools at Stourbridge and Trysull, as in the present letter.

Epitaph made by Dr. Johnson on poor Oliver Goldsmith, which I lately procured from a Gentleman in this Country to whom Johnson gave it himself, (Mr. Archdall[2] who had been educated under Dr. Sumner[3] at Harrow). I send you Mr. Archdall's own Transcript of it,[4] hoping it will prove a Peace-Offering and restore to me the pleasure of your Correspondence.

In Conversations of Dr. Johnson and Mrs. Williams,[5] I have heard them mention the following Circumstances of his Childhood: That he was put to learn to read, or improve his reading, to a School-Dame at Litchfield: Who upon Account of the Defect in his Eyesight, usually followed him home lest he should be run over in the Streets: And he was so near sighted, that he was obliged to stoop down on his hands and knees to take a View of the Kennell before he ventur'd to step over it; but if he observed the Old Woman following him, he would turn back in anger and kick her Shins.[6] This Old Dame lived to hear that he was a great Author, and once when he came to Litchfield brought him a Pound of Gingerbread declaring He was the best Scholar she had ever had.[7]

When he was a boy he was immoderately[8] fond of reading Romances of Chivalry, and he retained this fondness thro' Life, so that spending part of the Summer of 1764,[9] at my Parsonage

[2] Richard Archdall, Irish barrister and M.P. He attended Harrow c. 1766 and took his B.A. at Trinity College, Dublin, in 1772 (*Harrow School Register, 1571–1800*, ed. W. T. J. Gun, 1934, p. 1). He was, with Percy, a member of the Royal Irish Academy (*Transactions of the Royal Irish Academy, 1787* [1787], p. 164).

[3] Robert Carey Sumner, D.D. (1729–71), Master of Harrow. See *Johns. Misc.* i. 161, ii. 4.

[4] The MS. was sent to the printer as part of a Paper Apart for p. 615 of the MS. *Life* (along with the Round Robin on Goldsmith). It appears in the first edition at ii. 93, but was withdrawn in the rearrangement of the third edition, as the text had meanwhile made a second appearance in a letter from SJ to Langton, added belatedly and out of place in the second edition (ii. 613). See *Life* ii. 282. The epitaph was first printed in Malone's anonymous life of Goldsmith prefixed to his edition of his *Poems* (Dublin, 1777).

[5] At Easton Mauduit during the summer of 1764 (*Life* i. 553–54; *Johns. Misc.* ii. 217).

[6] Percy had told JB this anecdote ten years before, at which time JB compared it with "a more accurate edition" from SJ himself (or rather, from his mother's recollection) related at Bath in 1776 (*Note Book*, p. 12). Nevertheless, JB takes as much from Percy as from SJ in *Life* i. 39.

[7] JB's version, *Life* i. 43, again derives from SJ, and combines condensed Journ. 24 Apr. 1772 and Journ. 11 Apr. 1773. Anne Oliver (d. 1731) was the widow of Peter Oliver, a Lichfield shoemaker. She appears to have been a confectioner as well as a schoolmistress (*Reades*, p. 246), but which led to which remains a nice point for conjecture.

[8] MS. orig. "extravagantly"

[9] MS. "1784". See *ante* n. 5. In the MS. *Life* (opp. p. 14) JB left the two last digits blank; in print he omitted the year entirely.

House in the Country, he chose for his regular Reading the Old Spanish Romance of *Felixmarte of Hircania*, in folio, which he read quite through. Yet I have heard him attribute to these Extravagant Fictions that unsettled Turn of mind which prevented his ever fixing in any Profession.[10]

After he had gone thro' Dr. Hunter's School in Litchfield, his Father removed him to that at Stourbridge,[11] where he was received as a kind of assistant, [12]who was to have his own Instruction gratis[12] for teaching the Lesser Boys. I have heard him remark, That at one of these he learnt much in the School, but little from the Master: in the other, much from the Master, but little in the School. Not far from Stourbridge is the endowed Grammar School of Tresull in Staffordshire; Of which, I believe, Pope endeavour'd to procure him to be elected Master thro' the Interest of Lord Gower, as is mentioned in the Billet written by Pope to Richardson the Painter, of which you have a Copy.[13]

Dr. Johnson's Father, before he was received at Stourbridge, applied to have him admitted as a Scholar and Assistant to the Revd. Samuel Lea, M.A. Head Master of Newport School in Shropshire[14] (a very diligent good Teacher, at that time in high Reputation; under whom Mr. Hollis is said in the Memoirs of his Life to have been also educated).*[15] This application to Mr. Lea was not successful; but Johnson had afterwards the supreme Gratification to hear, that this Old Gentleman, who lived to a very advanced age, mentioned it as one of the most memorable events of his Life that he was *very near* having "that great Man for his Scholar."[16]

* As was also your humble Servant many years afterw[ar]ds.

[10] The paragraph is slightly revised and presented as a direct quotation, *Life* i. 49.

[11] JB's account of this episode, *Life* i. 49–50, combines other sources with Percy's narrative. See *ante* From Hector, 1 Feb. 1785 and n. 26.

[12]–[12] Omitted from the *Life*.

[13] *Ante* From Percy, 9 May 1776. See also *ante* To and From Hector, 15 July 1786 and n. 19.

[14] The Rev. Samuel Lea (?1689–1773), M.A. Jesus College, Cambridge, became Headmaster of the Newport Grammar School in May 1725 (*Reades*, pp. 247–48; *Johns Glean.* i. 27–29).

[15] Thomas Hollis (1720–74), "the strenuous Whig, who used to send over Europe presents of democratical books, with their boards stamped with daggers and caps of liberty" (*Life* iv. 97; cf. Journ. 30 Nov. 1764). His *Memoirs* were written by the Rev. Francis Blackburne and published in two volumes in 1780. For Hollis's relations with SJ see *Life* iv. 490–91, and J. L. Clifford, "Johnson's Obscure Middle Years," *Johnson, Boswell and Their Circle*, pp. 101–06.

[16] The paragraph is quoted directly, *Life* i. 50.

S. Johnson was at length admitted of Pembroke College in Oxford, where [17]the pleasure he took in vexing the Tutors and Fellows, has been often mentioned. But I have heard him say, what ought to be recorded to the honour of the present venerable Master of that College, the Reverend William Adams D.D. who was then very young and one of the junior fellows, That the Mild, but judicious Expostulations of this Worthy Man, whose Virtue awed him, and whose Learning he revered, made him really ashamed of himself, "Tho' I fear," said he, "I was too proud to own it."

I have heard from some of his Cotemporaries That he was generally seen *lounging* at the College Gate, with a Circle of young Students round him, whom he was entertaining with his Wit and keeping from their Studies; if not spiriting them up to Rebellion against the College Discipline: which in his maturer years he so much extoll'd.[17]

He ascertain'd the Æra of his coming to London, by recollecting that it happen'd within a Day or two of the Catastrophe of Eustace Budgell[18] the Relation and Friend of Addison, who having loaded his pocket with Stones, called for a Boat and in the midst of the Thames leap'd over and was drown'd.

He remember'd also to have once walk'd thro' the New Exchange ⟨in⟩ the Strand, among the Milleners' Shops mentiond in *The Spectator*,[19] before that building was pulled down and converted into private houses.

When in 1756 or 7[20] I became acquainted with him, he told me [he] had lived 20 years in London but *not very happily*.[21]

The above Particulars are what I chiefly remember to have heard him mention of his Early Life; and you see how little they are worth recording. The subsequent Part you know as well as myself.

Having a treacherous Memory and neglecting at the time to

[17-17] Quoted directly, *Life* i. 74.

[18] 4 May 1737. JB preferred the evidence of Gilbert Walmesley's letter of introduction, dated 2 Mar. 1737, which announces that SJ (and Garrick) "set out this morning for London together" (*Life* i. 102).

[19] No. 454.

[20] Apparently 1756: see *Life* i. 48 n. 2.

[21] In a letter to Baretti, 20 July 1762, SJ speaks of London as "a place, where, if there is not much happiness, there is, at least, such a diversity of good and evil, that slight vexations do not fix upon the heart" (*Life* i. 371). Cf. *ibid*. iii. 178, 378.

commit his *Bon Mots* to writing (which I now regret,)[22] I cannot add much to your Treasures of that sort, of which you have so rich a Store: Yet I will conclude with One, which I heard fall from him, and I hope I have not heard it in vain. —I was in his Company once, when a Person told him of a Friend of his, who had very fine Gardens, but had been obliged to sue to his Neighbour, with whom he was not upon very cordial Terms, for a Small piece of adjoining Ground, which he thought necessary to compleat them. —"See," said the Sage, "how inordinate Desires enslave a Man! One can hardly imagine a more innocent Indulgence than to have a fine Walk in a Garden: Yet observe, even the Desire of this slight Gratification, if carried to excess, how it humiliates and Enthralls the proudest Mind: Here is a Man submits to beg a favour from one he does not love, because he has made a Garden-Walk essential to his happiness."[23] I am, Dear Sir, Your most obedient Servant

THO. DROMORE ...

From Thomas Harwood,[1] Monday 12 March 1787

MS. Yale (C 1502). Received 14 Mar. (Reg. Let.).

ADDRESS: James Boswell Esqr.

ENDORSEMENTS: Tho. Harwood about Dr. Johnson.
March 12. 87 Answer Within.

Lavenham, Suffolk, March 12. 87

SIR: Having drawn up many Observations on the Writings and Genius of Dr. Johnson, with some Remarks on Dr. Towers' Book

---

[22] JB says of Percy that he "was long intimately acquainted with him, and has preserved a few anecdotes concerning him, regretting that he was not a more diligent collector" (*Life* i. 48).

[23] Not used. Another version of this anecdote appears among Percy's strictures on JB's *Life* printed in the third edition of Anderson's *Life of Johnson* (1815); reprinted, *Johns. Misc.* ii. 208 ff. Hill suggested that the subject of the anecdote was Shenstone.

[1] Thomas Harwood (1767–1842) attended Eton and Oxford, and later Cambridge, where he took a B.D. in 1811 and D.D. in 1822. He became Headmaster of the Lichfield grammar school in 1791, and in 1806 published his *History and Antiquities of the Church and City of Lichfield*. His residence at Lavenham, near Sudbury, Suffolk, at this date is confirmed by *Biographia Dramatica*, 1812, i. 313. See n. 3.

on a similar Subject;[2] I am emboldened to trouble you with my Request: being wholly unknown in the literary World, and equally unacquainted with the Arts of Publication,[3] would you permit the Pamp[h]let to appear under the Sanction of your Authority by receiving its Dedication, it will be a lasting Honour conferred on the Authour, and will ever be consider'd in the highest Degree obliging. As I have had frequent Recourse to your Name, you may perhaps wish to peruse it; if you will take the Trouble to communicate to me by Letter the Result of your Inclination, I will proceed accordingly.

I hope you be so good as to excuse the Liberty I have taken, and pardon the Freedom of this Address. I am, Sir, Your much obliged Servant

THOMAS HARWOOD[4]

To the Rev. Dr. William Maxwell,[1] Monday 19 March 1787

MS. Yale (L 959). JB's copy, headed: "To The Reverend Dr. Maxwell Falkland Tynan Ireland."

London, 19 March 1787

REVEREND SIR: You kindly promised to send me several sayings of Dr. Johnson's recorded in a Journal which you kept at the time when you lived much with that great man, as also a few letters which you had from him.

As my Life of our illustrious Friend is in great forwardness, I

---

[2] "... which is very well written, making a proper allowance for the democratical bigotry of its authour; whom I cannot however but admire for his liberality in speaking thus of my illustrious friend: ..." (*Life* iv. 41 n. 1). See *ante* From Brocklesby, 27 Dec. 1784, n. 26. Previously Towers had attacked SJ's political pamphleteering in *A Letter to Dr. Samuel Johnson*, etc.: see *Life* ii. 316.

[3] Harwood published this year a verse tragedy, *The Death of Dion*, and in 1788, at Bury St. Edmunds, another entitled *The Noble Slave*.

[4] At the foot of the page JB has written: "Answer on the other side"—for which, see *post* 20 Mar. 1787.

[1] William Maxwell, D.D. (1732–1818), Reader of the Temple Church, Rector of Mount Temple, co. Westmeath. He was introduced to SJ in 1754 by George Grierson, the government printer at Dublin (*Life* ii. 116). JB met Maxwell in London on 5 June 1786: "At home all forenoon sorting materials for Dr. Johnson's *Life*. Dined at Mr. Taylor's Old Burlington Street with Seward, the Rev. Dr. Maxwell of Ireland who had lived 25 years in London, and been much with Dr. Johnson. . . . Mr. Taylor had through Seward asked me to meet Dr. Maxwell, and had called on me in the forenoon. . . . Maxwell had a good deal of Johnson" (Journ.).

earnestly request that you may be pleased without delay to send these additional illuminations addressed to me Great Queen Street Lincolns Inn Fields.

Do, My Dear Sir, be so good as to comply with my wish, and oblige Your faithful and most obedient humble servant

To Thomas Harwood, Tuesday 20 March 1787

MS. Yale (L 625). JB's copy, written on side 2 of Harwood's letter of 12 Mar.

London, 20 March 1787

SIR: I thank you for your obliging offer; but I beg leave to decline accepting of it, as from the nature of your work, it will with more delicacy and propriety be addressed to some other person, and I wish to have it in my power to say that I did not see it till after it was published.[1] I am Sir, Your most obedient humble servant

To the Rev. Dr. Nathan Wetherell,[1] Tuesday 27 March 1787

Missing. Sent to Oxford from London. Reg. Let.: "Rev. Dr. Wetherell, for Dr. Johnson's Letters to him."

From the Rev. Dr. William Maxwell, Thursday 29 March 1787

MS. Yale (C 1985). Received 4 Apr. (Reg. Let.).

ADDRESS: ——Boswell Esqr., Great Queen Street, Lincoln's Inn Fields, London.

POSTMARK: APRIL 2.

Dublin, March 29th 1787

DEAR SIR: The Favour of your Obliging letter, was transmitted to

[1] It was apparently never published. Harwood's account of SJ in his *History of Lichfield* (pp. 448–53) is almost entirely derivative. Years later, he was to make a more notable contribution—to Croker: see *ante* From Pearson, 2 Apr. 1785, n. 3.

[1] Nathan Wetherell, D.D. (1726–1807), Master of University College, Oxford, 1768; Vice-Chancellor, 1768–72; Dean of Hereford, 1771. JB had visited him at Oxford on 20 Mar. 1776 and 14 or 15 June 1784 with SJ, and on 30 Apr. 1786 with Malone (Journ.; *Life* ii. 440–41, iv. 307–08). See also *post* From Wetherell, 30 Mar. 1787, n. 2.

me yesterday from the Country. Before I left Falkland, I tryed to recover a few of Dr. Johnson's letters, but to no purpose; I apprehend They were lost, with many other Things, which Paul Jones captured in a ship He took, bound from London to Dublin.[1] I lost goods to the Amount of £300 upon that Occasion. Indeed I never had more than two or Three letters in my Life from him, and Those not very Material upon common Occurrences. I often Noted in my Journals his Observations on Life and Manners, some of which I still retain, but many were lost when I suffered That Unfortunate Capture. When I return to the Country, about three weeks hence, I shall have the Hon[ou]r to send you, such of his Observations as I can collect, tho many perhaps are in the Mouths of the Publick and well known to yourself. I Applaud your Zeal for the Hon[ou]r of our Illustrious Friend, and you will deserve the best thanks of the Publick, as you well did upon a former Occasion.

I wish Myself restored to the Society of my English Friends. There I made my happiest Connexions, and there I left my desires. The Scene is much alter'd with me, but I still say, *Vitæ me redde priori.*[2]

I beg my part[icula]r regards to our Fr[ien]ds Mr. and Mrs. Taylor, to whom I was indebted for the Hon[ou]r of your Acquaintance.[3] I entreat you to believe me, Dear Sir, with the most Sincere Esteem, your most Faithfull and Obedient Humble Servant

WM. MAXWELL

From the Rev. Dr. Nathan Wetherell, Friday 30 March 1787

MS. Yale (C 3085). Received 4 Apr. (Reg. Let.).

ADDRESS: James Boswell, Esqr., London.

ENDORSEMENT: Rev. Dr. Wetherell Oxford.

Univ. Coll. Oxford, March 30th 1787

In good truth, my Dear Sir, I have no Letters from Dr. Johnson,

[1] John Paul Jones's raids in Irish waters occurred in 1778–79 (DAB). No correspondence between Maxwell and SJ has been recovered.

[2] "Take me back to my earlier life" (Horace, *Epistles* I. vii. 95).

[3] See *ante* To Maxwell, 19 Mar. 1787,

n. 1. Edward Taylor (d. 1820) was at this time a clerk in the Court of Exchequer; later second deputy King's Remembrancer (*Royal Kalendar*, 1786, p. 176; *Gent. Mag.*, 1820, xc. 93; *Universal British Directory*, 1791, i. 399). See also Journ. 5 June 1786.

with which to enrich your Collection.[1] The enclosed Latin Epistle I have procured from Dr. Fothergill, which was addressed to him as Vice Chan[cello]r from our Friend soon after his having the Degree of LL.D. conferred upon him.[2] Most sincerely wishing you success in the Publication of the Life of our great and good Friend, I am with great regard, Dear Sir, Your faithful Humble Servant

N. WETHERELL

From George Steevens, Thursday 12 April 1787

MS. Yale (C 2544).

ADDRESS: James Boswell Esqr., Great Queen Street, Lincolns Inn Fields.
ENDORSEMENT: From Mr. Steevens.

Hampstead Heath April 12th 1787

DEAR SIR: One of the inclosed letters, and the note, are additional proofs[1] of the attention shown by our late friend to the club. The other letter refers to a sum raised by him toward the relief of a female relation of Dr. Goldsmith.[2] I am, Dear Sir, very faithfully Yours

G. STEEVENS

---

[1] JB had made a copy, at Oxford in 1776, of SJ's letter to Wetherell, dated 12 Mar. of that year, on the subject of the management of the Clarendon Press, of which Wetherell was a trustee, or delegate (*Life* ii. 424–26; MS. *Life*, Paper Apart for p. 496; see *Letters SJ* 463 and n.). For a second letter to Wetherell, see *ibid.* 618.1.

[2] The enclosure is missing. Fothergill had previously made a copy, which Thomas Warton transmitted to JB: see *ante* 3 May 1786 and n. 1. The original is untraced. In 1775 Wetherell had informed JB in London "that he had managed the getting Mr. Johnson's

Diploma from Oxford, as in so numerous a Body some management was required to unite them. I could gather that there were at Oxford some who did not admire and reverence Mr. Johnson as some of us do" (*Journ.* 14 Apr.).

---

[1] To those enclosed *ante* 23 Apr. 1786.

[2] For the letter concerning Goldsmith's relative see *Life* iii. 100 (*Letters SJ* 508). The other letter is not identified, but the note is almost certainly that to Sir Joshua printed by JB, *Life* iv. 84. On the verso, in Steevens's hand, is "Note to the Club, on Mr. Thrale's Death" (C 1603).

From the Rev. Dr. William Maxwell, Friday 4 May 1787

MS. Yale (C 1986).

ADDRESS: James Boswell Esqr., Great Queen Street, Lincoln's Inn Fields, London. By Donaghadee.

POSTMARK: MA 9 87.

Hillsboro', May 4th 1787

MY DEAR SIR: By next Thursday's post I shall have the Hon[ou]r to send you Six Sheets of Anecdotes and remarks of Dr. Johnson. The Letters after the most diligent Search I could not recover, but really They were not very Material, written merely on Common Occasions. The Anecdotes I flatter Myself you will think worth recording. They are most Unquestionably Genuine, and you may Use my Name as you think proper. I hope I am not too late for the Press. I most heartily wish you the most Ample Success in your most laudable Undertaking. Your *Tour to the Hebrides* was A delicious repast. I scribble these lines from An Inn, Apprehensive you might think me too Dilatory. I have the Hon[ou]r to be, Dear Sir, with Sincerest Esteem, Your most Obedient and Faithfull Servant

WM. MAXWELL

To Sir William Forbes,[1] Tuesday 8 May 1787

MS. estate of the late Lord Clinton.[2] MS. Yale (L 544): JB's copy of a part and summary of the rest. JB explains the delay in the publication of the *Life*, hopes to have it in the press in July or Aug. Requests the facsimile of the Round Robin (see *ante* From T. Barnard, 15 Oct. 1785 and n. 3) and (not to be used in the *Life*) the exchange of letters between Forbes and SJ concerning JB's coming to the English bar.

[1] Sir William Forbes, Bt. (1739–1806), banker, biographer of Beattie, and one of JB's executors. See Journ. *passim*.

[2] Nine of JB's letters to Forbes, and two from Malone to Forbes, all be-longing to the estate of the late Lord Clinton were not available for publication in this volume. I give instead summaries of those parts concerned with the *Life*.

From the Rev. Dr. William Maxwell, Saturday 12 May 1787

MS. Yale (C 1987).

ADDRESS: James Boswell Esqr., Great Queen Street, Lincoln's Inn Fields, London.

POSTMARK: MA 19 87.

Donene, Saty. May 12th 1787

DEAR SIR: By this very post I have the Hon[ou]r to send you some Anecdotes of our Invaluable Fr[ien]d. They are contained in 8 or 9 Q° Sheets of letter paper, such as this, written on all Sides.[1] Any little Inaccuracies, you will please to correct, as I had no time for Revision, Being on a Journey, and Seperated from my Papers. Had I thought you could have waited, I had sent this little Narrative, more Ample and Correct, but I Apprehended I should have been too late for the Press. When at Leisure, please to acknowledge by a line, addressed to me at Falkland, Tynan, the Receit of the Papers, of which you will just make what Use you think proper. That All Imaginable Success may attend your meritorious labours, is the fervent and Sincere Desire of, Dear Sir, Your most Faithfull and Obedient Humble Servant

WM. MAXWELL

P.S. Please to rem[embe]r me very Affect[ionatel]y to the Taylors.

From the Rev. Dr. William Vyse,[1] Saturday 9 June 1787

Missing. Printed, *Life* iii. 125.

Lambeth, June 9, 1787

SIR, I have searched in vain for the letter which I spoke of, and which I wished, at your desire, to communicate to you. It was from Dr. Johnson, to return me thanks for my application to Arch-

---

[1] Only the wrapper, postmarked like the letter 19 May 1787, remains. For the printing of the anecdotes, see *post* From Malone, 8 July 1790 and n. 9.

[1] See *ante* From Taylor, 6 May 1785 and n. 37. JB dined in Vyse's company at Bishop Porteus's on 15 May of this year (Journ.).

bishop Cornwallis in favour of poor De Groot.[2] He rejoices at the success it met with, and is lavish in the praise he bestows upon his favourite, Hugo Grotius. I am really sorry that I cannot find this letter, as it is worthy of the writer.[3] That which I send you enclosed[4] is at your service. It is very short, and will not perhaps be thought of any consequence, unless you should judge proper to consider it as a proof of the very humane part which Dr. Johnson took in behalf of a distressed and deserving person. I am, Sir, Your most obedient humble servant,

W. Vyse

To the Rev. Dr. William Maxwell, c. Sunday 10 June[1] 1787

MS. Yale (L 960). JB's copy, headed: "To The Rev. Dr. Maxwell Falkland by Tynan Ireland." [*Later:*] "I fancy June [or July *deleted*] 1787."

[London]

Reverend Sir: Your packets have come safely, and I am very much obliged to you for them. They contain genuine highflavoured *Johnsoniana*. I shall, in consequence of your kind permission, make such use of your communications as will suit the plan of my Work, and shall not fail to record your intimacy with the great subject of it.[2]

[2] Isaac de Groot (c. 1694–1779), descendant of Grotius, was a penurious painter, whose last years SJ sought to make easy. The application to Frederick Cornwallis (1713–83), Archbishop of Canterbury, was in his capacity as Governor of the Charterhouse.

[3] The letter is untraced; it is mentioned again in Vyse's letter to Malone, 23 Apr. 1800 (*Life*, 4th ed., 1804, iii. 135). Vyse furnished Malone with four other letters from SJ to himself: see *Letters SJ* 531, 711, 720, 1039.

[4] SJ's letter to Vyse requesting his assistance in the cause just mentioned. JB printed it preceding the letter from Vyse to himself. Still another contribution was received from Vyse: a letter from Charles Simpson, Town Clerk of Lichfield. to Vyse, 27 Jan. 1790, telling of the

Corporation of Lichfield's unsolicited renewal of the lease on SJ's father's house out of "respect and veneration". It was edited by JB (MS. *Life*, Paper Apart for the verso of p. 1002) and printed, *Life* iv. 372 n. 2.

[1] Maxwell's letter of 16 June 1787 (*post*) was clearly written in answer to the present letter.

[2] As Maxwell's MS. is missing (presumably it was returned), there is no way of knowing to what extent the anecdotes were edited, though in both the present letter and a subsequent one (*post* 4 July 1787) JB indicates his intention of using them freely. He did not, however, as he says here, "interweave" them: they are rather printed as a block (including the materials which were to

My Book will not be ready for the press before August; and as you mention that if you had been amongst your papers, you could have supplied me with more particulars, I intreat that now when at home you may be pleased to transcribe from your Journals *the very words of Johnson taken down at the time* whether of those Apothegms already transmitted to me from your memory, or of any others, as you know how peculiarly excellent his expression was; and pray be so good as also to favour me with any Memoirs you have in writing, or can distinctly recollect, of his manner of life, occupations and the people with whom he chiefly lived, when you first obtained his acquaintance, and thereafter progressively.

As you are polite enough to allow me to make what use I please of the materials which you furnish, I shall just interweave what according to my opinion may be proper.

I beg that whatever you send may come speedily; and, with hopes of having the pleasure to be better acquainted with you, I remain very sincerely, Dear Sir, Your obliged and affectionate humble servant

Pray sit down immediately on receipt of this, and write for me.

From Sarah Adams, Wednesday 13 June 1787

MS. Yale (C 10). Received 14 June (Reg. Let.).

ADDRESS: James Boswell Esqr., Great Queen Street, London.

POSTMARK: JU 14 87.

ENDORSEMENT: Miss Adams of Oxford.

Oxford, June 13th 1787

DEAR SIR: In consequence of your wish to see the little Memorandum I made from Dr. Johnson's information respecting the Regimen he was in at different periods of his Life and Writings[1] I have looked for it since I left London,[2] and am very sorry to say I can no

follow) at the end of the year 1770, and are introduced as "some *Collectanea*, obligingly furnished to me by the Rev. Dr. Maxwell ... for many years the social friend of Johnson, who spoke of him with a very kind regard" (*Life* ii. 116). JB ingenuously explains his choice of the year 1770 as the point of insertion

for these extensive and undated anecdotes as serving to supply the gap left by the absence of any correspondence or meeting between himself and SJ.

[1] See *ante* From Adams, 12 July 1786.
[2] JB visited Miss Adams in London on the 6th of this month (Journ.).

where find it; and conclude I must have either lost it, or left it in the Country; if I find it there, I will take the liberty of sending it to you, tho' you probably will think it scarcely worth recording; nor am I quite satisfied that I act fairly in noting down what dropped from him in the familiarity of easy, friendly Conversation, and merely in answer to the (perhaps impertinent) questions we put to him. But of that I must leave you to judge. Mrs. Kennicott is not in Oxford, or she perhaps could have helped me out.

Have you seen the 13th Number of a Paper called the *Olla Podrida*, upon the Subject of Johnson and his Biographers? It is understood to be written by the Dean of Canterbury.[3] If I had a frank I would inclose it, but it is sold at Faulder's[4] in New Bond St[ree]t and at Hayes's No. 332 Oxford-street and I dare say you will be pleased with it.

I thought myself very unfortunate in missing the pleasure of seeing Mrs. and Miss Boswells when I was in Town[5]—I beg to present my Compliments to them, in which my Father desires to join and to add his to yourself. I am, Sir, Your obliged and very humble Servant

S. ADAMS

P.S. May I beg the favor of you to send a Message to your Neighbour Mr. Opie, and desire, if Dr. Adams's Picture is ready,[6] that he will send it immediately by Ward's Waggon from the Green

---

[3] The *Olla Podrida* was published weekly at Oxford from 17 Mar. 1787 to 12 Jan. 1788. Its editor is thought to have been Thomas Monro, and among the contributors were Richard Graves and George Monck Berkeley (Walter Graham, *English Literary Periodicals*, 1930, pp. 137–38). George Horne (1730–92), Dean of Canterbury, 1781, and Bishop of Norwich, 1790, was host to SJ and JB at Oxford in 1776, at which time he was President of Magdalen College (*Life* ii. 445–46). The paper he contributed to the *Olla Podrida* was reprinted in *Gent. Mag.* (1787, lvii. 559) and in his *Essays* (1808). JB quotes an "eminently happy" passage from it, *Life* iv. 426 n. 3. On 28 June JB sent a copy of No. 13 to Courtenay (Reg. Let.).

[4] Robert Faulder was the publisher of JB's *Ode by Dr. Samuel Johnson to Mrs. Thrale* (1788, dated 1784) and *No Abolition of Slavery* (1791). See *Lit. Car.* pp. 131, 144.

[5] JB, his wife, and his daughters called on Miss Adams on the 2nd of this month (Journ.).

[6] John Opie (1761–1807), the painter, lived for a time in Great Queen Street, a popular residence of literary and theatrical persons (Ada Earland, *John Opie and His Circle*, 1911, p. 52). His portrait of Adams, which is reproduced in Roger Ingpen's ed. of the *Life* (1907, ii. 578), was painted between 1782 and 1789. A copy is at Pembroke College, Oxford (J. Jope Rogers, *Opie and His Works*, 1878, p. 66; Mrs. R. L. Poole, *Catalogue of Oxford Portraits*, 1926, iii. 246). For an account of Opie's portrait (portraits?) of SJ, see *Life* iv. 455 ff.

Man and Still, Oxford-Street.[7] The Waggon comes out of Town before 12 o'clock every Monday, tuesday and friday—I hope it will come by that which sets out *next friday*, as we shall leave Oxford early in next week.

From George Steevens, Wednesday 13 June 1787

MS. Yale (C 2545).

ADDRESS: James Boswell Esqr., Great Queen Street, Lincolns Inn Fields·

[Hampstead Heath,] June 13th 1787

DEAR SIR: I have just now been informed, by a letter out of Sussex, that the Dialogues of Lord Chesterfield and Dr. Johnson,[1] are the Production of Mr. Hayley. Yours very faithfully

G. Steevens

To *Alexander Wedderburn, Baron Loughborough*,[1] Thursday 14 June 1787

MS. Yale (L 891). JB's copy.

G[reat] Q[ueen] St., L[incoln's] I[nn] F[ields,]
Thurs. 14 June

Mr. B. pres[en]ts his compliments to Lord Loughborough. Being anxious to ascertain with perfect authenticity some particulars

---

[7] "Ward's Waggons" operated between London and Oxford. "It is particularly desired that all goods for the above waggons be sent to the inns by ten o'clock, and to the Green Man and Still warehouse, Oxford-road, by twelve o'clock; where the above waggons call going in and coming out of London" (*Universal British Directory*, 1791, iv. 145).

---

[1] *Two Dialogues Containing a Comparative View of the Lives, Characters, and Writings of Philip, the Late Earl of Chesterfield, and Dr. Samuel Johnson*, 1787.

[1] Alexander Wedderburn (1733–1805), first Baron Loughborough, afterwards first Earl of Rosslyn. A protégé of Bute, he was appointed Solicitor-General in 1771 and Attorney-General in 1778. According to JB, it was he who first suggested that SJ be given a pension (*Life* i. 373; see also *ibid*. i. 386–87, iv. 178–79). JB told Malone, 26 Apr. 1788, "I was tortured to see Lord Thurlow, Lord Loughborough, Lord Amherst, and all who had risen to high situation while I was nothing; but I trusted that my being so tortured was a sign that I was made for something great, and that it would come" (Journ.).

concer[nin]g Dr. J.'s pension, he will be much obliged to his Lordship if he will give him leave to have the hon[ou]r of waiting on
him for a quarter of an hour at any time his Lordship shall be pleased
to appoint.[2]

From the Rev. Dr. William Maxwell, Saturday 16 June 1787

MS. Yale (C 1988). Received 25 June (Reg. Let.).

ADDRESS: Jam[e]s Boswell Esqr., Great Queen Street, Lincoln's Inn
Fields, London.

POSTMARKS: JU 18, JU 22 87.

Falkland, June 16th 1787

My DEAR SIR: I had the Hon[ou]r to send you a few days since
some Anecdotes relating to the Private Life of our Incomparable
Fr[ien]d.[1] By this Post I transmit 4 Sides of Q° Paper,[2] containing
the most Memorable Observations I could recollect, *in his own
proper Words.* In the former pacquet I never Varied his expression,
where I could clearly remember it, which was almost always the
Case, as his Language made lasting Impression. I hope the Papers
will arrive safe, and if your Important labours leave you any leisure,
Be so kind to acknowledge the receit, *even by A Line.* You highly
gratifyed us before, and I doubt not will again. Your very Faithfull and Affectionate Friend and Servant

WM. MAXWELL

---

[2] The journal records a chance meeting
with Loughborough on 27 May, but none
thereafter. In any case, the story of the
pension, and of Loughborough's part in it,
as given in the *Life* (i. 373–74), is fully
accounted for in JB's record of his visit at
Court, 16 May 1781 (Journ.).

[1] Missing, but acknowledged by JB,
along with the present communications,
post 4 July 1787.
[2] Only the wrapper, with the same
postmarks as the letter, remains. Cf. *ante*
From Maxwell, 12 May 1787 and n. 1.

From Edmund Hector,
Tuesday 19 June 1787

MS. Yale (C 1527). Received 30 June (Reg. Let.).

ADDRESS: James Boswell Esqr. [*completed by Courtenay:*] Great Queen St., Lincolns Inn fields.

POSTMARK: JU 27 87.

Birm[ingha]m, June 19 (1787)[1]

DEAR SIR: As an Apology for troubling you at this time, I saw a Post[s]cript in your Knight's History of our much respected friend, reflecting severely on his memory, ascribing his general benevolence to ostentatious bounty.[2]

He had only a few relations, and those very remote. The story of Heely, who formerly liv'd in my Neighbourhood is false, he was no more related to the Doctor than to his Biographer.[3] This (and some other gossiping Tales I coud point out), have been thought a proper present for Majesty.[4] I have sent you a transcript of some Verses publis'd in one of our weekly papers,[5] perhaps as coming from Lichfield. May not this infamous story of our illustrious Friend be washd away by a Postscript in yours,[6] as inserted by a post[s]cript of the Knights. I shou'd be very happy, if, when you travel into the North, you cou'd make Birm[ingha]m your road, to chat over some of these fine things, in the mean time I wish you all happiness, and all health to finish the labourious Task you have imposd upon yourself, with the applause of the Publick and with

---

[1] The year is in JB's hand.

[2] Hawkins's Postscript (pp. 599 ff.) attempts to expose SJ's "short-sightedness" and "ill-directed benevolence" in providing so liberally in his will for Francis Barber, to the neglect of the urgent needs of his "relation", Humphry Heely (see next note). It concludes: "The above facts are so connected with the transactions of Dr. Johnson, in the latter days of his life, that they are part of his history; and the mention of them may serve as a caveat against ostentatious bounty, *favour to negroes*, and testamentary dispositions *in extremis*."

[3] Humphry Heely (1714–c. 1796) was the husband of Betty Ford, SJ's first cousin, and though he remarried, SJ continued to regard him as a (poor) relation (*Johns. Glean.* iv. 51; *Life* iv. 370–71, 547).

[4] Hawkins's edition of SJ's *Works*, including the *Life*, was dedicated to George III.

[5] Transcribed at the end of the letter. A search conducted for me in the Birmingham Library has failed to locate the verses.

[6] JB's answer to Hawkins is inserted, without strict regard for chronology, towards the end of the *Life* (iv. 370–71). See also *ibid.* ii. 31 n. 1.

emolument and satisfaction to yourself. I am Dear Sir, Your oblig'd humble Servant

E. HECTOR

> After much toil, strong Pains and feeble Throe's
> A Book! a mighty Book! at last arose!
> Anounc'd with Title fair, and said to be
> The life of Samuel Johnson LLD.

> Where was Piozzi say? Or Boswell where
> To stop the hand of his Biographer?
> And suffer Dullness to pollute his Fame
> With the insidious Tale of Helys name.

To Francis Barber, Friday 29 June 1787

MS. The Johnson Birthplace. Enclosed in the following letter to Greene. MS. Yale (L 29): JB's copy. The original was seen by Hawkins's daughter Laetitia Matilda in July 1827 and epitomized in her "Travelling Diary" (N & Q, 1943, clxxxv. 373–74).

London, 29 June 1787

DEAR SIR: Sir John Hawkins having done gross injustice to the character of the great and good Dr. Johnson,[1] and having written so injuriously of you and Mrs. Barber,[2] as to deserve severe

[1] See *Life* i. 28, iv. 370–71. JB was not alone, among SJ's friends, in being repelled by Hawkins's biography. On 27 Nov. he "Dined at the Literary Club with Sir Joshua Reynolds, Mr. Malone, Mr. Steevens, Dr. Burney, Sir Charles Bunbury, Dr. Fordyce, Mr. Wyndham. . . . Wyndham was indignant against Sir John Hawkins, and expressed a strong desire to attack him. Malone suggested an admirable thought, which was to have a solemn Protest drawn up and signed by Dr. Johnson's friends, to go down to Posterity, declaring that Hawkins's was a false and injurious Account. Sir Joshua alone hesitated. But it was generally approved. I resolved it should not sleep" (Journ.). See also *ibid*. 30 Mar. and 11 May 1787.

[2] "It was hinted to me many years ago, by his master, that he was a loose fellow; and I learned from others, that, after an absence from his service of some years, he married. In his search of a wife, he picked up one of those creatures with whom, in the disposal of themselves, no contrariety of colour is an obstacle. It is said, that soon after his marriage, he became jealous, and, it may be supposed, that he continued so, till, by presenting him with a daughter of her own colour, his wife put an end to all doubts on that score" (Hawkins, p. 589 n.). See *Johns. Glean*. ii. 28, 31, 81. In JB's file of newspaper clippings is one beginning: "Sir John Hawkins—is to be *translated* into *English*: This is the work of Johnson's black footman. The motto, '*Hic Niger*,'

animadversion, and perhaps to be brought before the spiritual court,[3] I cannot doubt of your inclination to afford me all the helps you can to state the truth fairly, in the Work which I am now preparing for the press.

I therefore beg that you will without delay write three Copies of the Letter No. 1 which I enclose, directing one to Sir Joshua Reynolds, one to Dr. Scott and one to Sir John Hawkins putting to each the *date* of which you write, and enclose them to me, together with a Letter to me in the words of No. 2.[4] I have mentioned the business to Sir Joshua and Dr. Scott. When I have received the said letters distinctly written out by you, I shall proceed in an effectual manner.

Please to enclose your packet to me under cover of The Honourable William Ward M.P.[5] London.

You may at the same time let me have a private letter informing me how you are, and mentioning any thing that occurs to yourself. Be assured that I am ever sincerely concerned for your welfare. I send my compliments to Mrs. Barber and am with much regard, Dear Sir, Your steady friend

JAMES BOSWELL

[Enclosure][6]

SIR: As residuary legatee of the late Dr. Samuel Johnson I do now request that his Diary and every other book or paper in his handwriting in the possession of his Executors or any of them may be

applying to Hawkins himself./Besides the watch and cane [see *post* From Barber, 12 Mar. 1788 and n. 2], there are to be free enquiries and a commentary. As, which page may be without a fact, and what fact without a falsehood." The work referred to is the scurrilous satire, *More Last Words of Dr. Johnson* (1787), by "Francis, Barber".

[3] "Boswell's suggestion is that Hawkins might be proceeded against in the Spiritual Court, which had jurisdiction in cases of libel and slander where the allegation concerned offences which rendered one liable to a suit in that court, such as heresy, unchastity, and, more particularly, adultery" (*Johns. Glean.* ii. 66 n.).

[4] The copy of the present letter includes

a transcript of only the first of the two enclosures; the second doubtless authorized JB to take possession of the materials released by SJ's executors (cf. *post* To Barber, 3 Mar. 1788). On 20 Mar. Malone had advised JB to urge Sir Joshua "to get Johnson's Diaries from Sir J. Hawkins" (Journ.).

[5] William Ward (1750–1823), afterwards third Viscount Dudley and Ward of Dudley, was M.P. for Worcester City, 1780–88 (Judd). He was married to Julia Bosville, younger daughter of Godfrey Bosville, of Gunthwaite, JB's "Yorkshire Chief" (*Life* iii. 540–41).

[6] Transcribed from JB's draft accompanying his copy of the present letter to Barber.

delivered to[7]   on my account as I understand them to be an undoubted part of my property. I am, Sir, your
most obedient humble servant

P.S. I have written in the same terms to each of the other
executors.

To Richard Greene,[1]
Friday 29 June 1787

Missing. Printed, Maggs Bros., Summer 1927, No. 492, Lot 710, with a
facsimile of the second page (frontispiece). MS. Yale (L 590): JB's copy,
headed: "To Mr. Green."

London, 29 June 1787[2]

DEAR SIR:[2] I trouble you with the safe delivery of the enclosed to
Mr. Francis Barber, to whom I hope to do justice in my Life of
his illustrious Master.

Will you be so kind as to send me a copy of Dr. Johnson's letter
to you which I have seen in your hands; as[3] also any anecdotes of
him that you can recollect.

It appears from his Meditations or rather Memorandums[4] that
he used to correspond with Mrs. Aston of[5] Stowhill.[6] Will you do
me the favour to inquire if she has preserved his letters, and if she
would[7] enable me to enrich my[8] Book with them.

I depend much on your obliging disposition, you see. If you will
let me know how to send it I will beg your acceptance of my engraved Portrait.

I long to see your Museum again.[9] Please to present my best

---

[7] Presumably to be supplied with the
name of the intermediary. See *post* To
Barber, 3 Mar. 1788.

---

[1] Richard Greene, or Green (1716–93),
Lichfield apothecary and antiquary, "a
bustling, good-humoured little man"
(Journ. 23 Mar. 1776). See *ante* From
Adey, 26 Feb. 1785. Greene claimed a
relationship to SJ (*post* 8 July 1787;
Life ii. 465), but not even Reade could
discover it (*Reades*, p. 145; *Johns. Glean.*
viii. 122 ff.).

[2] The dateline and salutation, omitted
in the print, are here transcribed from the
copy.

[3] Copy, "&"

[4] Correcting Strahan's misleading title,
Prayers and Meditations.

[5] Copy, "at"

[6] See *Diaries*, pp. 314, 318.

[7] Copy, "will"

[8] From this point to the end, my transcription follows the facsimile.

[9] JB visited Greene's Museum in Mar.
1776, with SJ, and again in Oct. 1779
(*Life* ii. 465, iii. 412).

compliments to all my friends at Lichfield, whom I long still more to see—if you will forgive the preference, you being one of them.[10] I am Dear Sir, Your very faithful humble servant[11]

JAMES BOSWELL

Please to write to me under cover of The Hon. William Ward M.P. London.

To the Rev. Dr. William Maxwell, Wednesday 4 July 1787

MS. Yale (L 961). A copy by JB's son, Alexander, headed by JB: "To The Rev. Dr. Maxwell."

London, 4 July 1787[1]

DEAR SIR: I thankfully acknowledge the receipt of your two additional packets concerning Dr. Johnson.[2] I ought to apoligise for having given you so much trouble; but I had *understood* that you had *minutes* of his conversation and I was anxious to have had transcrips of them because however strong the faculty of memory may some times[3] be I am persuaded that no recollection can be so authentick as a Relation committed to writing *at the time*. We are apt to imagine that we have *heard* what has been conveyed to us through some other medium. I am sure you will forgive my frankness when I give you as an instance of this what you communicate in the belief of its being a saying of his as to Scottish education which is indeed a sentence in his *Journey to the Western Islands*.[4] I am much obliged to you Dear Sir for your supplies from the great Fountain head and as I shall use my discretion in separating what is *adven[ti]tious* I hold myself additionally indebted to your liberality in permitting me that liberty. It will be in January or February

---

[10] The facsimile shows the polish of this sentence to be the outcome of some careful insertions: (1) ". . . if you will forgive Your very faithful" etc. (2) ". . . if you will forgive the preference. I am Dear Sir, Your very faithful" etc. (3) ". . . if you will forgive the preference, you being one of them. I am" etc.

[11] The copy stops at this point.

[1] Dateline in JB's hand.

[2] See *ante* 16 June 1787 and n. 1. Alexander originally wrote "Jonson", and then inserted the "h" after the "n".

[3] MS. "timees"

[4] There are a number of observations on Scottish education and learning in SJ's *Journey*, but as JB did not print Maxwell's anecdote—presumably for the reason indicated—we are left in the dark. One of them is repeated, *Life* ii. 363.

next at soonest that my volume[5] will be ready for publick inspection. I am with great regard, Dear Sir, Your most obedient humble servant

From Richard Greene, Sunday 8 July 1787

MS. Yale (C 1397). Received 12 July (Reg. Let.).

ADDRESS: James Boswell Esqr.

ENDORSEMENT: Mr. Green Lichfield 8 July 1787.

Lichfield, 8 July 1787

DEAR SIR: Your obliging Letter came Safe to hand, and in conformity to your desire I Send you a Copy of the late Dr. Johnsons Letter, I believe one of the last he ever wrote;[1] the inscription you will find in the *Gentlemans Magazine* Vol. 55, January 1785 page 9.[2]

I wish it were in my power to furnish you with any Letters or anecdotes[3] relative to my late relation, the Doctor.[4] Mrs. Eliz. Aston has been dead these two years; her papers, and indeed all her property ⟨were⟩ left to her Sister Walmesley, who died in Novemr. ⟨?last⟩ and left her effects to her Sister the Widow Gastrel,[5] to whom I have applied for the Letters from Dr. Johnson to her Sister.[6] She thinks a Correspondence of a private Nature ought not to be published, I therefore have little hopes of Success from that quarter. However I will use my utmost endeavour to have a peep at them.

I delivered F. Barbers Letter, who desires me to present his best respects, and to acquaint you, that he will attend to your directions; he, poor man, has been much hurt by Sir J. Hawkins's

---

[5] The copy is completed in JB's hand.

[1] Dated 2 Dec. 1784, arranging for a gravestone and enclosing the epitaphs for his father, mother, and brother, *Life* iv. 393.

[2] That is, the epitaphs, contributed by John Nichols, to whom they were transmitted by "a friend at Lichfield"; reprinted, *Life* iv. 393 n. 2.

[3] Only one other letter from SJ to Greene is known, but it has not been recovered: see *Letters SJ* 412. As for

anecdotes, three came into Croker's hands: see *Johns. Misc.* ii. 397–99.

[4] See *ante* To Greene, 29 June 1787, n. 1.

[5] For the several legacies, see *Johns. Glean.* v. 249–53.

[6] Twelve letters from SJ to Elizabeth Aston, and three addressed jointly to her and her sister Jane Gastrell have been recovered (*Letters SJ passim*). JB did not see—at least he did not print—any of them.

illiberal treatment: I have great hopes of reaping a fund of entertainment from your intended publication, and shall be happy to
receive your portrait which will come Safe, if left (directed to me)
with Mr. Wilson Druggist at the Red Cross on Snow Hill, to
whom I shall soon Send an Order for Druggs.

My Museum improves daily, owing to the bounty of my
Friends, among which number, I shall always place my dear and
worthy friend Mr. Boswell.

That Success may ever attend your publications, is the Sincere
wish of my dear Sir, Your ever obliged, and faithful humble Servant

RICHD. GREENE

The Doctor never came to Lichfield without paying a visit to my
Museum, and seem'd astonished at my Collection. "Pray Sir how
long have you been collecting the articles in this Room?" "About
forty four years Sir"; "I Should as Soon thought of building a
first rate man of war, as making Such a Collection."[7]

From Francis Barber,
Monday 9 July 1787

MS. Yale (C 65). Received 12 July (Reg. Let.).[1] The original draft, with
corrections and additions in another hand, is printed, *Johns. Glean.* viii.
75.

ADDRESS: To James Boswell Esqr., Barrister at Law.

Lichfield, Monday July 9th 1787

SIR: I had the unspeakable Satisfaction of receiving your Letter
on saturday last by the care of Mr. Green, and agreeable to your
request with a heart full of Joy and gratitude I took Pen in hand to

[7] Greene had already told JB this
anecdote, 23 Mar. 1776, at Lichfield
(Journ.). It is quoted, *Life* ii. 465.

[1] "Mr. Francis Barber two letters
concerning Dr. Johnson—One giving me
his manuscripts": namely, (1) the present
letter—"a private letter informing me
how you are, and mentioning any thing
that occurs to yourself", and (2) Barber's
letter authorizing JB to take possession

of SJ's literary remains, and enclosing
the three letters to his executors (*ante*
To Barber, 29 June 1787). In the journal
for 13 July JB notes the receipt of "Letters
to Sir Joshua, etc., from Frank". One
week later John Nichols, acting for JB
and presumably armed with the letter
directed to Hawkins, succeeded in
obtaining some if not all of SJ's papers
from him. See Chronology of the Making
of the *Life*, 20 July 1787 (*ante*, p. lix), and
post From Hawkins, 17 Apr. 1788.

enform you that I am happy to find there is still remaining[2] a friend who has the memory of my late good Master at heart that will endeavour to vindicate his cause in opposition to the unfriendly proceedings of his Enimies; as I myself am incapable to undertake such a task. The aspersions Sir John has thrown out against my Master as having been his own Murderer are intirely groundless,[3] as also his assertion concerning Mr. Heley's applying to me for releif, he never did,[4] neither was he any ways allied to my Master but by having been married to a[5] relation of his who has been long dead; notwithstanding which my Master never withdrew his friendship but was always very kind to him in every respect. I have not had the mortification to fall in with that impious production of Sir John Hawkins relating to the Life of my Dear Master, but assure yourself Dear Sir it will be to me a subject of the greatest happiness to render abortive the unworthy and false pro[c]eedings of the above mention'd Gentleman and from hence you may justly infer[6] that fuller exposition of that basest of Mortals in as much as he has reflected not only[7] on me and my consort, but on the unsullyed Character of the best of beings my affectionate and unparallel Master: if necessity should require it, if God spare my Life (for I am at present very poorly) I would willingly attest what I have related personally[8] with which I beg leave to subscribe myself, your most obedient humble Servant

FRA:S BARBER

[2] MS. "remaing"

[3] Barber, who had not himself read Hawkins's book (see next sentence), was misinformed. Hawkins wrote (pp. 590–92): "At eleven, the same evening, Mr. Langton came to me, and, in an agony of mind, gave me to understand, that our friend had wounded himself in several parts of the body. I was shocked at the news; but, upon being told that he had not touched any vital part, was easily able to account for an action, which would else have given us the deepest concern. . . . That this act was not done to hasten his end, but to discharge the water that he conceived to be in him, I have not the least doubt." At the same time Hawkins cites Barber as his authority for "all the particulars of this transaction", one of which depicts Barber as entreating his master "not to do a rash action" (p. 591). JB, perhaps yielding to Barber's suggestion, nevertheless accuses Hawkins of equivocating, *Life* iv. 399 n. 6.

[4] Hawkins does not say that Heely applied to Barber for relief; but he does take Barber to task for his alleged refusal to provide for him (p. 599).

[5] MS. "distant" deleted. See *ante* From Hector, 19 June 1787, n. 3.

[6] Barber seems to use the word to mean "count on".

[7] The words "not only" are inserted in JB's hand; he perhaps intended to print the letter.

[8] See *ante* To Barber, 29 June 1787 and n. 3.

To the Rev. John Hussey,[1]
Monday 9 July 1787

MS. Yale (L 648). JB's copy, headed: "To The Rev. Mr. Hussey near Sandwich Kent."

London, 9 July 1787

REVEREND SIR: I beg pardon for presuming to take this liberty but being informed that you were one of Dr. Johnson's friends, I trust you will excuse it, as its intention is to obtain more materials for illustrating his fame in the Life which I am now preparing for the press.

If you will be kind enough to favour me with any anecdotes of him which you know, any of his sayings which you recollect, and any of his letters which may be in your possession, you will much oblige, Reverend Sir, your most obedient humble servant

P.S. Please to write to me under cover of The Honourable William Ward M.P. London.

From William Bowles,
Friday 20 July 1787

MS. Yale (C 560). Received 22 July (Reg. Let.).
ADDRESS: James Boswell Esqr.
ENDORSEMENT: Mr. Bowles 20 July 1787.

Heale House, July 20. 87

MY DEAR SIR, You have doubtless wondered at not hearing, but I received no answer from Mr. Wentworth[1] and beleived from what I did hear, that he would not part with the papers. At length a few days ago I met with him and represented the reasonableness of your request and it happened luckily that fortune favored us and that I fell into the *mollia tempora fandi*,[2] and being near his own lodging

---

[1] The Rev. John Hussey (1751–99), of Hertford College (*Alum. Oxon.*), Chaplain to the English Factory at Aleppo (*Life*, Index). He "had been some time in trade, and was then a clergyman of the Church of England" (*Life* iii. 369).

[1] See *ante* From Bowles, 1 Mar. 1787 and n. 4.

[2] "mollissima fandi/Tempora" (the most opportune moment for speaking): *Aeneid* iv. 293–94. JB uses the phrase, *Life* iv. 309.

I went with him and took them of him immediately. They will be a great addition indeed to your work—Some original compositions, several translations from Horace, Virgil, Homer *etca*: capitally executed, as I understand before he was 16.

I am sending some things of consequence in a small box to town, which will be ready to go from hence in a week or ten days at furthest and will be directed to a particular friend of mine. With these I send if you please the Memoirs and exercises: if you choose them sooner let me hear. I am Dear Sir, Your most humble Servant

W.B.

To John Nichols,[1]
Monday ?23 July 1787

MS. Hyde.

ADDRESS: To Mr. Nichols Printer, Red Lion Court, Fleet Street.

Great Queen Street, Monday morning

DEAR SIR: I send you a frank for Mr. Green.[2] You will please to observe that Sir John Hawkins in Dr. Johnson's *Life* near the beginning (for I have it not by me at present) *admits possession* of his *Adversaria* extending to six folio volumes. I beg you may send a note to him to deliver that part which he has *kept back*.[3] I am with sincere regard, Dear Sir, Your obliged humble servant

JAMES BOSWELL

[1] John Nichols (1745–1826), compiler of the *Literary Anecdotes* and *Illustrations*; printer of the *Lives of the Poets*; editor of *The Gentleman's Magazine*; member of the Essex Head Club. See *Life* and *Letters SJ*, *passim* and A. H. Smith, "John Nichols, Printer and Publisher," *The Library* (1963) xviii. 169–90. For an account of Nichols's contributions to the *Life*—mainly materials which first appeared in *Gent. Mag.*—see Edward Hart, PMLA (1952) lxvii. 391–410.

[2] Not identified, unless the reference is to Nichols himself, who used the pseudonym "Green" in *Gent. Mag.*

[3] See *ante* From Barber, 9 July 1787, n. 1. Hawkins had written (p. 12) that "The heads of science, to the extent of six folio volumes, are copiously branched throughout it; but, as is generally the case with young students, the blank far exceed in number the written leaves." From the account in the *Life* (i. 205 ff.) we learn that JB became satisfied of the scantiness of the collection, but it is not clear how much of it he actually acquired. See *post* From Hawkins, 17 Apr. 1788.

From the Rev. John Hussey, Thursday 26 July 1787

MS. Yale (C 1568). Received 29 July (Reg. Let.).

ADDRESS: To James Boswell Esq., Great Queen Street, Lincolns Inn Fields, London.

ENDORSEMENT: Rev. Mr. J. Hussey.

Newington near Folkstone, Kent, Thursday 26th July 1787

SIR: On my return from Town late last Saturday night I received your letter of the ninth current. I have been so tormented with an incessant headach for some time past, that I am scarce able to recollect any thing, and hardly know what I now write. It is probable I may be in London again within this fortnight; if so I will do myself the honour to call on you, and if I do not go to Town, I will write to you again, if I can meet with, or think of any anecdotes etc. respecting the good Dr. Johnson that may be worth communicating. I have the honour to be, Sir, your most humble Servant

JOHN HUSSEY

To the Rev. Dr. Hugh Blair, Thursday 2 August 1787

MS. Yale (L 61). JB's copy, headed: "To The Rev. Dr. Blair Edinburgh."

London, 2 August 1787

... You will now be wondering why my *Life of Dr. Johnson* has not yet appeared. The truth is that besides the various avocations which have insensibly hindered it, I have solid reasons for delay, both from the motive of having Sir John Hawkins to precede me that I might profit by his gross faults, and from that of giving time for the accession of materials of which I have received a great addition since I last wrote to you. I am resolved that my work shall be published in the course of the next session of Parliament. Believe me the Johnsonian enthusiasm is as warm as ever.

I will be much obliged to you for an extract from your Journal in 1763 as to your introduction to Dr. Johnson and conversation with him; and also for the name of the Poem written by Mr.

Ballantine and you which was impudently assumed by a Dr. Douglas.[1] . . .

To Joseph Warton, Friday 3 August 1787

MS. Yale (L 1270). JB's copy, headed: "To The Revd. Dr. Joseph Warton."

London, 3 August 1787

REVEREND SIR: I am certainly very much to blame for not hav[in]g long ago acknowl[edge]d, the favour of your oblig[in]g letter with two to you from Dr. Johnson.[1] My only excuse is that I waited from time to time for something to communicate by way of making you a return and now I can only heartily thank you.

The Life of our great Friend in which his letters are to be introduced chronologically is not yet so near to its conclusion as you may suppose. Profess[iona]l and social avocat[io]ns have retarded my progress. But the work will cert[ain]ly be published in the course of the next sess[ion] of Par[liamen]t.

I think Sir you men[tione]d to me that you might perhaps find among your pap[er]s something concern[ing] Collins.[2] If you do I beg you may favour me with it. Pray was the orig[inal] *Life of Collins* all written by Johnson or did you furnish a part of it as I have been told?[3]

---

[1] See *post* From Blair, 25 Aug. 1787.

---

[1] *Ante* 29 Jan. 1787. See also Chronology of the Making of the *Life*, 22 Mar. 1787 (*ante*, p. lviii).

[2] SJ's letters to both Wartons in 1754 contain anxious inquiries about Collins (*Letters SJ* 51, 55, 56, 57). Thomas Warton glossed one of these references for JB: "Collins (the poet) was this time at Oxford, on a visit to Mr. Warton; but labouring under the most deplorable languor of body, and dejection of mind" (*Life* i. 276 n. 2). Joseph Warton and Collins were schoolmates at Winchester, and remained friends to the last. In Dec. 1746 they published simultaneously their collections of odes.

[3] Two anonymous accounts of Collins

appeared in *The Poetical Calendar* (ed. the Rev. Francis Fawkes and William Woty, 1763, xii. 107–09 and 110–12). The first has been attributed to another Winchester schoolmate, James Hampton (1721–78), the translator of Polybius (E. G. Ainsworth Jr., *Poor Collins*, 1937, p. 227). SJ printed the second as his own in his *Life of Collins* (*Lives* iii. 337–39), and it is designated by JB as one of his acknowledged works (*Life* i. 22, 382). Warton, who, according to Percy (*ante* 5 and 7 May 1772) was the author of the first account, is acknowledged by SJ at the beginning of the *Life of Collins* as an informant. Unfortunately, we do not have Warton's reply to JB's query. For SJ's revisions of the early version for the *Lives*, see H. W. Liebert in the *Johnsonian News Letter* (Apr. 1951) xi. 2.

You were so good as to say that you would give me some partic[ular]s which you recollected of Dr. J.s convers[ation] with the King. Will you let me have them now? or will it be better to wait till I have drawn up that article—as completely as I can from the materials of which I am allready possessed so that you may see it.[4] . . .

From the Rev. Dr. Hugh Blair, Saturday 25 August 1787

MS. Yale (C 163).

ADDRESS: James Boswell of Auchinleck Esqr., London.

Restalrig, 25 Augt. 1787

. . . I wish you may not be mistaken as to the Johnstonean Enthusiasm still keeping warm with the Publick. However I make no doubt but with your pleasing manner of writing you will make such a book as will attract general attention. The sooner you set it out, certainly now the better. Sir John Hawkin's work is miserably stupid, and upon the whole very degrading to Johnston. The Journal of mine that you speak of[1] I have not here (I am in Summer quarters at Restalrig, having been obliged to quit Merchiston) and am not in case at present to go in search of it. But I am sure there is nothing in it that would be of any consequence to you, or that would at all be proper for publishing. The Juvenile Poem written by Geo. Bannatine (my Brother in law) and me, when we were at College, and afterwards foolishly published under the name of a Dr. or Mr. Douglas (who was a man midwife) in 3 Cantos was entitled *The Resurrection*. But this is an Anecdote too trifling to be put into your Book; and I do not at all wish it to appear.[2] . . .

---

[4] JB had from Langton SJ's own account of the interview, which was retailed to Warton and others at Sir Joshua's. See *Life* ii. 33 ff. and 34 n. 1.

[1] MS. "off"

[2] But it did: *Life* i. 360. In one of his rough notes JB wrote: "Dr. [*James deleted*] William Douglas who assumed Blair and Bannatyne's Resurrection was of conside[r]able service to the opposi-

tion party in the Westminster Election and was made Physician to the Prince of Wales. He dedicated the Poem to the Princess of Wales." William Douglas (b. c. 1711) studied at Leyden, received his M.D. at Rheims in 1738, became man-midwife to Middlesex Hospital in 1749 and physician in 1750, resigning in 1752 (R. W. Innes Smith, *English-Speaking Students of Medicine at the University of Leyden*, 1932, p. 7).

"Memorandums" from the Rev. John Hussey, August 1787[1]

MS. Yale (C 1569).

ENDORSEMENT: Reverend Mr. Hussey.

Memorandums on reading Hawkins's *Life of Johnson*[2]

Page 43. *Mr. Wilcox a Bookseller in the Strand.* Soon after his first arrival in Town, Johnson strolled accidentally into the Shop of Mr. Wilcox, who (enquiring his business) was solicited by the Doctor for some employment in the literary line.[3] Wilcox surveying Johnsons Person observed he was of an athleetic[4] form, and if his constitution were equal to his appearance, he would recommend him to set out in Life as a Porter, for he would not find the carrying of heavy Loads so burdensome a task as becoming an Author or Translator; besides he might then be sure of a hearty Meal and a good draught of Beer at night; which in a literary occupation would be frequently scanty and often uncertain. "The truth of what Wilcox told me" (said Johnson with a sigh about 1777) "I have since bitterly experienced, and however humiliating the advice might be at the time, I never hear his name but I consider him as my Friend."[5]

Page 56. *In it he anticipated the departure of his friend Thales, i.e. Savage.* Johnson told me, that when he imitated the third Satire of Juvenal, he did not intend to characterise any one under the name of Thales, and further said, the Poem was written and published before he was acquainted with Savage.[6]

[1] In his letter to Hussey, 15 Oct. 1787 (*post*), JB acknowledges the receipt of his "Miscellany", which "was left at my house carefully sealed up, when I went to Scotland, supposing that you were to call for it". JB left London for Auchinleck the week of 13 Aug. (Journ.).

[2] Both editions were published by this date; however, for the passages Hussey cites (printed here in italics) the page references are the same.—Many of the following notes reappear in Hussey's annotated copy of JB's *Life* (now in the D. Nichol Smith Collection in the National Library of Australia, Canberra), which Hill drew upon in annotating his *Johnsonian Miscellanies*, and Dr. Powell in his revision of Hill's edition of the *Life*.

[3] MS. "either as a Translator or original Compositor" deleted. For SJ's disapproval of this use of "line", see *post* From Langton, 17 Dec. 1790 and n. 26.

[4] Though in both Greek and Latin the *e* is long, I do not find it so in eighteenth-century English pronunciation.

[5] JB gives a similar though briefer version of this anecdote, attributing it to John Nichols, *Life* i. 102 n. 2 (first introduced in the second edition of the *Life*). Cf. *Lit. Anec.* viii. 416.

[6] JB draws upon this testimony, without acknowledgement to Hussey, in rebuttal to Hawkins, *Life* i. 125 n. 4. Hussey's note in his copy of the *Life*

Page 62. *with a mistaken date of the year viz. 1737.* From the foregoing note, I believe there is no mistake in the date of Lord Gowers letter. [7]

Page 86. *The event is antedated in the Poem of London* etc. corrected by the 2 preceeding articles. [8]

Page 89. *the year 1738 when Johnson conceived a thought of enriching the Magazine with a biographical article* etc. Johnson not only wrote occasionally for, but was the actual editor of the *Gentlemans Magazine* from 1738 to 1745 part of both years inclusive; when he told me this, he could not recollect what month he resigned his employ, but I think he said he took the management of the Magazine upon him at Midsummer. [9]

Page 97. *dismissing Guthrie* etc. I doubt Guthries having any thing to do with the arrangement of the Magazine in the years 1740–1. [10]

Page 177. *he forbore not ever after to speak of him in terms of the greatest contempt.* Not true. Mem. Lord Lyttelton and Lord Chest. [11]

Page 191. *he expressed in a Letter to his Lordship himself his re-*

reads: "Johnson told me that London was written many years before he was acquainted with Savage, and that it was even published before he knew him—of which I informed Mr. Boswell, who did not think proper to believe me—Johnson also said that by Thales he did not mean any particular person" (quoted, *ibid.* 533). As JB wrote essentially what Hussey told him, the complaint seems groundless. Modern scholars have generally accepted the identification of Thales and Savage and have offered various explanations for the chronological discrepancies: see Hill, *ibid.* 125 n. 4; *Johns. Glean.* vi. 77–83; *Poems*, ed. Smith and McAdam, p. 8 n.; Clarence Tracy, *The Artificial Bastard: A Biography of Richard Savage*, 1953, p. 137, n. 12; Clifford, *Johnson*, pp. 207–08; and Davis, *Johnson Before Boswell*, p. 151, n. 25. See also F. V. Bernard, N & Q (1958), cciii. 398–99.

[7] Which mentions SJ as the author of *London*. Hawkins refers to the date as given in Cooke's *Life of Johnson*, though he does not name the source. Cooke was wrong, Hawkins right, and Hussey wrong. See *ante* From Adams, 12 July 1786, n. 9.

[8] "If the departure mentioned in it was the departure of Savage, the event was not *antedated* but *foreseen*" (*Life* i. 125 n. 4).

[9] JB states, *Life* i. 115, that in the spring of 1738 SJ was "enlisted by Mr. Cave as a regular coadjutor in his magazine". Hussey repeated his assertion in his copy of the *Life*, quoted *ibid.* 532.

[10] When, according to Hawkins, SJ replaced William Guthrie (1708–70) as the writer of the Parliamentary Debates. See *ante* From Percy, 5 and 7 May 1772 and n. 14. A long memorial of Guthrie by his brother Hary, dated 8 July 1776, is in the Yale Collection. It was sent at JB's request, but very little if any of it was used for the *Life*.

[11] "him" is Lord Chesterfield. I cannot explain Hussey's memorandum. In his copy of the *Life* Hussey noted: "Dr Johnson once spoke to me very warmly in commendation of Lord Chesterfield and said that he was the politest man he ever knew—but added 'indeed he did not think it worth his while to treat me like a Gentleman' " (quoted, *Life* i. 541).

sentment of the affront etc. This Letter I could never procure a sight of though he kept a copy; but Doctor Johnson assured me that so far from being couched in disrespectful terms; his Lordship had returned his thanks for it and added that it was the Letter of a Scholar and a Gentleman.[12]

Page 313. *more than old enough to be his Mother* etc. I have been told that Johnsons wife was 49 when he married.[13]

Page 491. As Johnson kept none, so no accurate copy can be given of his letter to Macpherson but from the original if it is not destroyed; That which the Doctor dictated at the request of his Majesty differs somewhat from this preserved by Hawkins.[14]

Page 519. Prologue for Mrs. Kelly. line 9th for renew'd hostilities, read, resentful petulance.[15]

From Richard Greene, Sunday 9 September 1787

MS. Yale (C 1398).

ADDRESS: James Boswell Esqr.

ENDORSEMENT: Mr. Greene Lichfield.

Lichfield, 9 Sepr. 1787

DEAR SIR: I take this early Opportunity to acquaint you, that I have just received your very valuable present, which I shall ever esteem, not only for the exact resemblance it bears of you, my generous and worthy Friend, but, from the excellency of the performance;[1] I assure you I shall place it in the most conspicuous part of my room,

[12] Cf. *Life* i. 264–65 and 541 (Hussey's note).

[13] She was forty-seven and SJ was just under twenty-six. JB says: "Mrs. Porter was double the age of Johnson" (*Life* i. 95). Cf. *ibid*. n. 2 and p. 529.

[14] JB prints the letter "as dictated to me by himself, written down in his presence, and authenticated by a note in his own hand-writing, 'This, I think, *is a true copy*' " (*Life* ii. 297). But see *ibid*. n. 2. JB's transcript is missing. The original is in the Hyde Collection. For other versions, see *Letters SJ* 373n. and p. 528. To this account should be added yet another version, given to Reynolds, among the Clinton Papers at the University of Durham.

[15] The Prologue was to a benefit performance on 29 May 1777 of *A Word to the Wise* by Hugh Kelly, who had died in Feb. Hussey's note in his copy of the *Life* reads: "On reading over this Prologue to Dr. Johnson, the morning after it was spoken, the Doctor told me instead of *renew'd hostilities* he wrote *revengeful* [*sic*] *petulance*, and did not seem pleased with the alteration" (*Life* iii. 490). JB followed Hawkins, ignoring Hussey and various printed versions. Smith and McAdam adopt "resentful petulance" (*Poems*, p. 61).

[1] The mezzotint engraving by John Jones, 1786, of the Reynolds portrait.

and near to the Portrait of my illustrious relation, the late Dr. Johnson, which you, Sometime Since presented to me.[2]

When ever I look on these Pictures, I reflect with pleasure on the many obligation[s] you have confer'd on, Dear worthy Sir, Your very affectionate Obedient Servant

RICHD. GREENE

P.S. My Museum flourishes greatly, and I assure you, nothing would give me greater Satisfaction than to be able to take you by the Hand in it: Mr. and Mr[s]. Piozzi honour'd it lately with their presence with Miss Thrale;[3] they, I am inform'd, express'd great Satisfaction at the Sight; but, alas! I was at the Birmingham Music Meeting at the time.'[4]

From the Rev. John Hussey, Sunday 9 September 1787

Missing. See *post* To Hussey, 15 Oct. 1787. Hussey's letter apparently enclosed a letter of SJ's.

From Edmond Malone, Friday 14 September 1787

MS. Yale (C 1911).

London, Sep. 14, 1787

. . . I have received from Dr. Farmer[1] Johnson's letter to Dr. Lawrence, and a few extracts from other letters of his, made by his daughter, chiefly relative to his health.[2] Mr. Windham has also

---

[2] There is no record of this presentation. Greene presented JB with his own portrait (*Life* ii. 466).

[3] See *Thraliana*, pp. 689–90, 689 n. 1. Mrs. Piozzi was at the time seeking additional materials with which to eke out her second volume of SJ's letters, then in the press. She, Mr. Thrale, and SJ had visited the Museum together on 7 July 1774, on their journey into Wales (*Life* v. 428).

[4] The Birmingham Music Festivals originated in 1768 as a concert series to raise funds for the General Hospital, and became a regular triennial event beginning in 1784. The second Triennial Festival opened on 22 Aug. 1787. See R. K. Dent, *The Making of Birmingham*, 1894, p. 264.

[1] Richard Farmer, D.D. (1735–97), Shakespearean scholar and Master of Emmanuel College, Cambridge. See *Life passim*.

[2] JB printed three letters (and possibly a missing fourth) from SJ to Lawrence, extracts of three others addressed to "one of his daughters", and a memorial of SJ by an anonymous lady—all from an undated and unsigned MS. in the hand of (presumably) Elizabeth Lawrence (d. 1790): *Life* i. 82–84, ii. 296, iii. 419, iv. 143–44 and n. 3. Malone's description falls considerably short of the contents of this MS., and it may be that the MS. received from Farmer was not the same.

sent me three letters to himself, which are all that he ever received.[3] They are of no great value, but do him honour. —Mrs. Thrale [deleted] Piozzi, I should say, has, I find, been applying to Mrs. Boothby at Litchfield for letters, but will not I am told succeed.[4] . . . The true cause I perceive, of B[urke]'s coldness, is that he thinks your habit of recording throws a restraint on convivial ease and negligence. I think after once your great work is done, which you seem to refer ad Græcas Calendas,[5] it will be of consequence to declare, that you have no thoughts of that kind more. . . . No packet, or box from Bowles. —What an insufferable procrastinator! almost as great a one as another person of my acquaintance. . . .

To the Rev. Hugh Blair, Sunday 16 September 1787

MS. Yale (L 62). JB's draft.

Auchinleck, 16 Septr. 1787

. . . If upon looking into your London Journal you find any Johnsonian fragments, I shall be obliged to you for them. I recollect your picturesque description of being conducted by Dr. James Fordyce into "the Giant's den."[1] . . .

[3] William Windham (1750–1810), statesman, "whom, though a Whig, [SJ] highly valued"; member of The Club and of the Essex Head Club. See *Life* and *Journ. passim.* The three letters are printed, *Life* iv. 227, 362–63; the originals are in the Hyde Collection. Windham is credited in the *Life* with a number of anecdotes, but no MSS. have survived.

[4] Malone has garbled his information. Mrs. Piozzi, on her visit to Lichfield in Aug., had secured Miss Seward's promise to apply to Sir Brooke Boothby of Ashbourne Hall for copies of SJ's letters to his sister Hill (1708–56). (Miss Seward had made the same promise to JB shortly before this time.) Passing through Ashbourne, Mrs. Piozzi discovered that the letters had been deposited with Dr. Taylor, who was reluctant to part with

them. Sir Brooke was also reluctant to act, without the permission of his son Brooke, who was in Paris. Miss Seward wrote to the son, a member of her literary circle in Lichfield, and the letters were eventually acquired, and printed in Mrs. Piozzi's collection (1788), ii. 391 ff. For a full account of the proceedings, see J. L. Clifford, "Further Letters of the Johnson Circle", *Bull. Rylands Lib.* (1936) xx. 278–80. JB never received the promised copies. He prints one (from Mrs. Piozzi), *Life* iv. 57 n. 3, and deprecates the others.

[5] *ad Kalendas Graecas,* i.e. never (Suetonius, *Divus Augustus,* 87).

[1] *Life* i. 395–96. This account was added to the MS. *Life* subsequent to the first draft, but I have found no MS. source.

From Edmond Malone,
Friday 28 September 1787

MS. Yale (C 1912).

ADDRESS: James Boswell Esqre.

ENDORSEMENT: Mr. Malone.

[London,] Friday Night, Sep. 28. 1787

. . . I have still a moment at Eleven at night, to tell you, your Johnsonian letters are all safe in my drawer, and that you are in high luck, for here is Mr. Humphry the painter just come from India, who has three more letters for you.[1] . . .

To William Bowles,
Thursday 11 October 1787

MS. Yale (L 267). JB's copy, written on side 2 of Bowles's letter of 20 July 1787 (*ante*).

[London,] 11 October 1787

Your letter of 20 July is now before me in which you mention that you had actually received from Mr. Wentworth Dr. Johnson's juvenile exercises, and you add "I am sending etc."

Since that time which is now within nine days of *three months* ago, I have been in Scotland, and on my return[1] could not doubt that your Communications so obligingly promised would certainly be at my house. But they have never yet appeared. I am quite at a

---

[1] Ozias Humphry (1742–1810) had gone to India in 1785 to mend his fortunes, but was obliged to return to England to mend his health (DNB). See also *Life* iv. 528–29; and for some anecdotes of SJ by Humphry, *Johns. Misc.* ii. 400–02. Yale has a copy of JB Jr.'s *Biographical Memoir of the Late Edmond Malone, Esq.* (1814) in which is mounted Malone's letter to Humphry, dated "Saturday Morning", requesting "the letters of Dr. Johnson to you,—for Mr. Boswell". JB dined at Malone's with Humphry and others on 5 Nov. of this year; thereafter they were frequent dinner companions both at home and abroad (Journ.; see also Joseph Farington, *The Farington Diary*, ed. James Greig, 1932, i. 14). The letters from SJ, in behalf of his godson Samuel Paterson, Jr., a young painter seeking instruction, are printed, *Life* iv. 268–69. JB returned the letters on 3 Jan. 1791 (*post*). Humphry "executed a beautiful miniature in enamel" after Reynolds's 1769 portrait of SJ (*Life* iv. 421 n. 2, 449; vi [2nd ed., 1964], 494, Errata); the *Johnsonian News Letter* (July 1957) xvii. 4–5 reported the painting by William Combe of a modern oil after Humphry.

---

[1] 29 Sept. (Journ.).

loss what to conjecture, and you may believe, a good deal uneasy. I intreat then that I may be so no longer.

To Sir William Forbes, Thursday 11 October 1787

MS. estate of the late Lord Clinton. JB again asks for the Round Robin and SJ's letter. Expects to work diligently on the *Life* until the beginning of Michaelmas term. Regards his achievement as mainly that of a collector.

To the Rev. John Hussey, Monday 15 October 1787

MS. in Hussey's interleaved copy of the *Life*, D. Nichol Smith Collection in the National Library of Australia, Canberra.

London, 15 October 1787

DEAR SIR: Your Miscellany[1] for the communication of which I thank you, was left at my house carefully sealed up, when I went to Scotland, supposing that you were to call for it. I have found it on my return, as also your obliging favour of 9th Septr.[2] I return you Dr. Johnson's letter of which I have taken a copy,[3] and your Miscellany shall be left at Mr. Ruston's.[4] I am Dear Sir[5]

From Sir William Forbes, Friday 19 October 1787

MS. Yale (C 1279).

ADDRESS: James Boswell Esqr., No. 56 Great Queenstreet, Lincoln's Innfields, London.

POSTMARKS: OC 19, OC 22 8⟨7⟩.

ENDORSEMENT: Sir. W. Forbes 12 [*sic*] Octr. 1787.

Edinb., 19 Octr. 1787

... [1]I likewise inclose the *Round Robin*. This jeu d'esprit took its

[1] *Ante* Aug. 1787.
[2] Missing.
[3] Printed, *Life* iii. 369.
[4] Not identified. Why the "Miscellany" was not left, or not picked up, is not explained. This is the last letter in the extant correspondence.
[5] Signature cut away.

[1-1] Revised and quoted, *Life* iii. 83–85.

rise one day at dinner at our friend Sir Joshua Reynolds's in Spring 1776, when it was in agitation to erect a monument in Westminster-Abbey to the memory of Dr. Goldsmith. All the Company present, except myself, were friends and acquaintance of Dr. Goldsmith's. The Epitaph written by Dr. Johnson became the Subject of Conversation, and various emendations were Suggested, which it was agreed Should be Submitted to the Dr.'s consideration; but the question was, who should have the Courage to Propose them to him. At last it was hinted that there could be no way so good as that of a *Round Robin* as the Sailors call it, which they make use of when they enter into a Conspiracy, so as not to let it be known who puts his hand first or last to the paper. This proposition was instantly assented to; and the Bishop of Killaloe drew up an Address to Dr. Johnson on the Occasion, replete with wit and humour; but which it was feared the Dr. might think treated the Subject with too much levity. Mr. Burke then proposed the address as it stands in the paper; in writing which I had the honor to officiate as Clerk. Sir Joshua agreed to carry it to Dr. Johnson, who received it with much good humour; and desired Sir Joshua to tell the Gentlemen that he would alter the inscription in any manner they pleased as to the Sense of it; but *he would never consent*, he said, *to disgrace the walls of Westminster-Abbey with an inscription in English*. It was accordingly put up, I believe, on the monument, as originally written by Dr. Johnson. I consider this *Round Robin*, as a species of literary Curiosity, worth preserving; as it marks in a certain degree Dr. Johnson's Character.[1] The inclosed is a faithful transcript which the Bishop of Killaloe who has the original in his possession, was so good as allow me to make, when I was in Dublin two years ago.[2] Should you think it worth while to make a *Fac Simile* of it, to be inserted in your life of Dr. Johnson, for the sake of showing the Subscriptions, I dare say the good Bishop will let you have the use of the original for that purpose.[3] . . .

---

[2] See *ante* From T. Barnard, 15 Oct. 1785 and n. 3. The transcript bears a note in JB's hand: "When he saw Dr. Joseph Warton's name he said 'I did not think Joe a scholar by profession, would have been such a fool.' " This too was revised and printed, *Life* iii. 84 n. 2. JB's informant was doubtless Sir Joshua Reynolds, the only signer of the Round Robin present when Forbes's transcript was received: see *post* To Forbes, 7 Nov. 1787.

[3] See *post* From T. Barnard, 20 Dec. 1790.

To James Beattie,[1]
Tuesday 30 October 1787

MS. University Library, King's College, Aberdeen.

ENDORSEMENT (in an unidentified hand):[2] From James Boswell, London, 30th Octr. 1787, Asking Dr. Beattie to send him any letters he has of Dr. Johnson's that he may publish them in his life which he is writing.

London, 30 October 1787

. . . While I am recording Dr. Johnson's praise of you, it gives me some concern that in your Evidences of our Holy Religion, his name does not appear in your enumeration of eminent laymen who were Christians.[3] I understand from Mr. Dilly that you are in possession of some letters from him, and that you kindly said you would let me have them to insert in his *Life*—which I am preparing for the press. I shall be much obliged to you if you will be so good as to send them to me, without delay, under cover of John Courtenay Esq. M.P. London; and if you can at the same time favour me with any anecdotes or fragments of his conversation,[4] I beg you may do it. . . .

To Dr. John Mudge,[1]
Tuesday 30 October 1787

Missing. Sent to Plymouth from London. Reg. Let.: "Dr. Mudge for Letters of Dr. Johnson's."

[1] James Beattie (1735–1803), poet and philosopher. See *Life passim*. JB introduced him to SJ, at the request of Sir William Forbes, in a letter from Edinburgh, 27 July 1771 (*Life* ii. 141–42).

[2] On a wrapper dated 10 Sept. 1794.

[3] "I read Dr. Beattie's *Evidences of the Christian Religion*, and was much dissatisfied that the Book was so superficial and so dear; and it struck me as a servile compliment to Mrs. Montagu that among the great names of whom he boasts as believers, he did not mention Johnson" (Journ. 5 Nov. 1786). The work was published this year in two volumes at six shillings.

[4] On 12 Aug. 1782 Beattie had told JB "a striking anecdote of Dr. Johnson, to account for his being often unwilling to go to church. He mentioned to Dr.

Johnson his being at times troubled with shocking impious thoughts, of which he could not get rid. 'Sir,' said Dr. Johnson, 'if I was to divide my life into three parts, two of them have been filled with such thoughts'" (Journ.). The anecdote was not used in the *Life*.

[1] John Mudge, M.D. (1721–93), physician of Plymouth. He is described by JB as "the celebrated surgeon . . . not more distinguished for quickness of parts and variety of knowledge, than loved and esteemed for his amiable manners" (*Life* i. 378). His son, Major-Gen. William Mudge (1762–1820), was SJ's godson. For SJ's character of his father, the Rev. Zachariah Mudge (1694–1769), see *Life* iv. 77.

To *William Bowles*, Wednesday 7 November 1787

Missing. Sent to Heale from London. Reg. Let.: "Mr. Bowles to remind him of his Johnsonian Communications."

To *Sir William Forbes*, Wednesday 7 November 1787

MS. estate of the late Lord Clinton. JB reports having received the Round Robin opportunely for the entertainment of his dinner guests, including Sir Joshua.

From *James Beattie*, Thursday 8 November 1787

MS. Yale (C 108). Received 12 Nov. (Reg. Let.).

ADDRESS: To James Boswell Esqr., London.

ENDORSEMENT: Dr. Beattie.

Aberdeen, 8 Novr. 1787

. . . Nor impute it to any want of respect for our ever-memorable Friend, that in my brief account of the Evidences of our Holy Religion, I did not name Dr. Johnson as one of those eminent laymen who had distinguished themselves in the cause of Christianity. Dr. Johnson was alive, when that was written: and You will observe, that all the persons there named (who are but a very small number in comparison of those who might have been named) had been dead for some considerable time; Lord Lyttelton, the last in my little list, having died in 1773.[1] In zeal for Dr. Johnson's honour I cannot yield to any body: in what I write I seldom miss a good opportunity of bringing him in: many a time, in this country, have I bellowed in his vindication, (for among the greater part of Scotchmen You know he is not a favourite character): and while, with peculiar satisfaction, I call to mind the many instances of

---

[1] SJ was dead by the time the work was published. Beattie's list (ch. 2, sect. 3: "The Gospel History is True") names Bacon, Grotius, Newton, Boyle, Hooker, Clarke, Butler, Stillingfleet, Milton, Clarendon, Addison, Arbuthnot, and Lyttleton [*sic*]. Cf. SJ's observation, 28 July 1763, on the evidence for the Christian religion "from the number of great men who have been convinced of its truth [naming Grotius and Newton]" (*Life* i. 454–55).

friendship with which he honoured me, I can never, My Dear Sir, forget what I owe to You for introducing me to his acquaintance.

I have found two of his letters. The one, relating to a private matter, is wholly unfit for the publick eye.[2] Of the other I send You an exact copy.[3] Though short, it is characteristical, and does me much honour:—only [4]I wish he had omitted the suspicion expressed in the last line; though I believe he meant nothing but jocularity; for, though he and I differed sometimes in opinion, he well knew how much I loved and revered him.[4]

I should willingly set down, and send You, some particulars of his conversation, if I thought that by so doing I could tell You any thing which You do not already know. But one circumstance discourages me. Your talent, of remembering his words so exactly, I do not possess at all; though I can retain pretty well the sentiments and opinions I may hear in conversation. And therefore, in recapitulating his thoughts, I must do it in my own words, if I do it at all; and I need not tell You how much this would take away from their elegance and energy. I beg You will inform me, about what time Your *Life of Johnson* will be ready for the press. Some other lives of him I have read, with no great pleasure. From Yours I expect a great deal of instruction and amusement. . . .

From William Bowles,
Friday 9 November 1787

MS. Yale (C 561). Received 10 Nov. (Reg. Let.).

ADDRESS: James Boswell Esqr., Great Queen Street, Lincolns Inn fields, London.

POSTMARK: NO 10 87.

ENDORSEMENT: Wm. Bowles Esq.

Heale, Nov. 9. 87

DEAR SIR, In answer to your letter[1] give me leave to inform you that the reason of my not having sent Dr. Johnson's exercises was my not having received any answer to the letter in which I

---

[2] Probably that of 5 Aug. 1773, on the subject of Beattie's financial difficulties (*Letters SJ* 316.1).

[3] Used as printer's copy for *Life* iii. 434–35.

[4-4] Quoted, slightly revised, *Life* iii. 435 n. 1. The end of SJ's letter reads:

"More news I have not to tell you, and therefore you must be contented with hearing, what I know not whether you much wish to hear, that I am, Sir, Your most humble servant, Sam. Johnson."

[1] *Ante* 11 Oct. 1787.

informed you of my having procured them from Mr. Wentworth.[2]
I do not mean that my letter absolutely required an answer, perhaps it seemed not at all to demand one: but from your silence my
inference certainly was that you were gone the circuit, and that I
had better not send the papers to your house in your absence.
Your silence continuing, I supposed precisely what I find to have
been the case, that you were gone to Scotland; and I assured myself that I should hear from you on your return. I must intreat
your pardon for the delay of the last fortnight because I have both
been from home and had my house full of company who left me not
till yesterday, so that I have had not a moment to write or even to
read a page since I was favored with your letter. I send by the
coach this evening 12 exercises of Dr. Johnson and 2 of a schoolfellow of his: they are numbred, and Mr. Wentworth begs to have
the MSS. returned to him.[3] My own papers accompany them,
which I beg you will look over carefully for I am afraid they are
carelessly compiled. I have a few more things to im⟨part⟩ which
I will communicate as they arise.

Permit me to assure you that I expect great entertainment from
your work: some fastidious people affect to complain that they
are never to hear the last of Dr. Johnson, but surely nothing so
interesting or instructive as what we have heard of him even from
bad writers, has been to be met with since his decease: and it is a
solid proof of the power of his name that it has helped such nonsense as we have seen out of the shops. I am ever Dear Sir, very
truly Your obedient humble Servant

WM. BOWLES

P.S. Amongst the Papers you will find a letter to our friend Mr.
Hoole[4] who I beleive has been as much surprized at not hearing

---

[2] *Ante* 20 July 1787.
[3] In the Yale Collection are transcripts
by JB's servant, James Ross, of eleven of
these exercises, endorsed by JB: "Copy
of Dr. Johnson's Juvenilia being exercises
when at Mr. Wentworth's school. From
the originals communicated to me by his
son through William Bowles Esq. of
Heale, Wiltshire." No transcripts of the
exercises by SJ's schoolfellow appear to
have been made. Two of the exercises,
and a part of a third, were included by JB,
along with a selection from the juvenilia

contributed by Hector (*ante* 1 Feb. 1785),
in a "Paper Marked J" for MS. *Life*,
p. 15, and printed as specimens of SJ's
"poetical genius", *Life* i. 51 ff. For the
texts of the poems, see *Poems*, ed.
McAdam and Milne.
[4] See *post* From Hoole, 17 June 1790.
The letter Bowles speaks of is, as the
remainder of the postscript gradually
makes clear, one from himself—not SJ—
to Hoole. The "Office" is of course the
Post Office.

from me as yourself. Will you obligingly allow your servant to put the said letter into the Office?—Let me have a line to assure me of the arrival of the packett.

From William Bowles, Friday 9 November 1787[1]

MS. Yale (M 145): satellite Paper Apart for MS. *Life*, p. 914. Printed in part, *Life* iv. 235–39.[2] An earlier, smaller, but to some extent parallel, collection of "Memorandums" made by Bowles in 1784 (before SJ's death) is in the Library of Pembroke College, Oxford. Selections from it are printed by Dr. Powell, *Life* iv. 523–24.

Dr. Johnson went to school at Stourbridge in Worcestershire, and took leave of his instructor at about the age of 16. During his stay there he distinguished himself by his compositions of which it is certain from the information of the Master's nephew that many were carefully preserved tho' unfortunately they are now lost. The Dr. and one other of his contemporary school-fellows were peculiarly honored by the regard shewn by their Praeceptor in the selection and preservation of their exercises.[3]

He declared himself that he became religious first at the University by attending the Communion in conformity with the College rules.[4]

When *The Gentleman's magazine* was first published, the parliamentary debates were written by the Doctor who acknowledged that he compiled them frequently without any knowledge and generally without accurate intelligence of what the Speakers actually delivered.[5] Being once interrogated whether he thought such a

---

[1] The date on which the MS. was sent to JB, according to the preceding letter. As the correspondence shows, the materials were compiled over a period of more than two years.

[2] Yielding to Bowles's insistence that he not be named in the *Life*, JB introduces "a few particulars" from the present MS. as coming from "one of [SJ's] friends".

[3] Cf. *Life* i. 49–50. Note that Bowles failed to correct his statement that the exercises, transmitted along with the

present MS., "are now lost". In his "Memorandums" Bowles had written of these exercises: "Some were in English verse. The majority are destroyed." Note also that here the donor of the exercises is properly identified as Wentworth's *nephew* (see *ante* From Bowles, 1 Mar. 1787 and n. 4).

[4] Cf. *Life* i. 68 and n. 1.

[5] Cf. *Life* i. 115–18. For a full account of the Debates in Parliament and of SJ's share in them, see *ibid.*, Appendix A.

conduct was right he answered "No, I think not very right."[6]
"Francis (added he) the translator of Horace at last let it all out,
and[7] in one of his notes told the world that the Speeches generally
supposed to be spoken in Parliament were not made there but in a
garret in the Strand by a man whom he was sorry for the honor of
the nation to see writing for his bread."[8] "I wrote the famous Speech
of Pitt(said he) against Hor. Walpole.[9] Pitt I beleive did say something about his being a young man and Walpole's being an old rogue
but not just what I made him say."[10]—"There were two speeches
of Lord Chesterfield's published in the debates, and the people
said, one was in the style of Cicero and the other in the true spirit
of Demosthenes; they came both from the Garret where I thought
neither of Demosthenes nor Cicero, but only of my dinner."[11]

He said his letter to Lord Chesterfield so much spoken of was
not uncivil and that Lord C. was not known to have thought it so.[12]

---

[6] "Johnson told me, that as soon as he found that the speeches were thought genuine, he determined that he would write no more of them; for 'he would not be accessary to the propagation of falsehood.' And such was the tenderness of his conscience, that a short time before his death he expressed a regret for his having been the authour of fictions, which had passed for realities" (*Life* i. 152).

[7] MS. "& and"

[8] Dr. Powell and I have both searched in vain for such a note either in Francis's Horace or in his Demosthenes. See Arthur Murphy's account of SJ informing an amazed company, including Francis, of his authorship of the Debates: quoted, *Life* i. 504.

[9] Horace Walpole (1678–1757), first Baron Walpole of Wolterton, Sir Robert's brother.

[10] "Mr. Pitt replied:—Sir, the atrocious crime of being a young man, which the honourable gentleman has with such spirit and decency charged upon me, I shall neither attempt to palliate nor deny, but content myself with wishing that I may be one of those whose follies may cease with their youth, and not of that number, who are ignorant in spite of experience.

"Whether youth can be imputed to any man as a reproach, I will not, Sir, assume the province of determining; but surely age may become justly contemptible, if the opportunities which it brings have passed away without improvement, and vice appears to prevail when the passions have subsided. The wretch that, after having seen the consequences of a thousand errors, continues still to blunder, and whose age has only added obstinacy to stupidity, is surely the object of either abhorrence or contempt, and deserves not that his grey head should secure him from insults.

"Much more, Sir, is he to be abhorred, who, as he has advanced in age, has receded from virtue, and becomes more wicked with less temptation; who prostitutes himself for money which he cannot enjoy, and spends the remains of his life in the ruin of his country" (*Works* xii. 306–07: from *Gent. Mag.*, Nov. 1741, xi. 569). Tyers wrote that the speech "was much talked of, and considered as genuine" (*Johns. Misc.* ii. 342).

[11] "Looking at Messrs. Dilly's splendid edition of Lord Chesterfield's miscellaneous works, he laughed, and said, 'Here now are two speeches ascribed to him, both of which were written by me: and the best of it is, they have found out that one is like Demosthenes, and the other like Cicero'" (*Life* iii. 351). See *ibid.* n. 1.

[12] Cf. *ante* From Adams, June 1784.

He had once conceived the design of writing the Life of Oliver Cromwell thinking as he declared that it must be highly curious to trace his extraordinary rise to the supreme power from so obscure a beginning. He at length laid aside his scheme on discovering that all that can be told of him is already in print and that it is impracticable to procure any authentick information in addition to what the world is already possessed of.[13]

He had likewise projected but at what part of his life is not known, a work to shew how small a quantity of *Real fiction* there is in the world and how the same images with very little variation have served all the writers who have ever written.[14]

He often praised Lord Chesterfield's letters to Mr. Stanhope and at the same time enlarged upon the necessity of Politeness and the difficulty of acquiring it. "Every man almost would (says he) be polite, but how few are so! which proves that to be polite is not easy."[15]

He often said that Wine promoted ease and freedom of conversation and instanced in the different behaviour of the company before and after dinner.[16] He had formerly drank a good deal (often two bottles at a sitting) and had often stayed in company till he was unable to walk out of it but he never found liquor affect his powers of thinking it affected only his limbs. Whilst he was speaking of the fashion of drinking he often observed that he had known many able men drink constantly without impairing their minds.[17] Dr. James[18] was an instance of this, who was generally drunk every evening; "yet I remember" says the Doctor laughing,

[13] Quoted, with minor revision, *Life* iv. 235–36.

[14] Quoted, with minor revision, *Life* iv. 236. See *ibid.* 524.

[15] " 'Lord Chesterfield's Letters to his son, I think, might be made a very pretty book. Take out the immorality, and it should be put into the hands of every young gentleman. An elegant manner and easiness of behaviour are acquired gradually and imperceptibly. No man can say, "I'll be genteel" ' " (*Life* iii. 53). See *ibid.* 479.

[16] SJ takes a contrary, or at least much qualified, stand on this subject at the Crown and Anchor, 12 Apr. 1776: "We discussed the question whether drinking improved conversation and benevolence.

Sir Joshua maintained it did. JOHNSON. 'No, Sir: before dinner men meet with great inequality of understanding; and those who are conscious of their inferiority, have the modesty not to talk. When they have drunk wine, every man feels himself happy, and loses that modesty, and grows impudent and vociferous: but he is not improved; he is only not sensible of his defects' " (*Life* iii. 41).

[17] " 'I indeed allow that there have been a very few men of talents who were improved by drinking; but I maintain that I am right as to the effects of drinking in general' " (*Life* iii. 42).

[18] See *ante* From Hector, 1 Feb. 1785, n. 8; 28 Mar. 1785, n. 26.

"James often declared to me most seriously that he had never been drunk since he came to reside in London, and" added he laughing still more, "there are abundance of men who say they are never drunk whom yet every body else thinks they can never catch sober."[19]

The Doctor used to recommend Plutarch's treatise on education and thought it contained every precept of importance on the subject, in which perhaps he said rather too much. He was no advocate for our publick schools and being asked what method of education he thought best he said a mixed one, partly at a school and partly at the father's house.[20]

His thoughts in the latter part of his life were frequently employed on his deceased friends. He often muttered these or such like sentences "Poor man, and then he died."[21]

The death of Mrs. Williams his old friend and companion happened when he was on a visit in Wiltshire. He[22] received the news of it with a laudable mixture of feeling and fortitude. Amongst his Prayers published by Mr. Strahan is a thank[s]giving "for the comforts he had received from the friendship of Anna Williams"[23] and in a letter written a few weeks after her death he says "my companion is gone, so that tho' well I am solitary; at seventy four it is too late to adopt another."[24]

Speaking once of a literary friend "he is a very pompous puzzling fellow" says the Dr. "he lent me a letter once that somebody had written him, no matter what it was about; but he wanted to have the letter back and expressed a mighty value for it, he hoped it was to be met with again, he would not lose it for a thousand pound. I layed my hand upon it soon after and gave it him, I beleive I said I was very glad to have met with it: Oh then he did not know that it signified any thing: So you see when the letter was lost it was worth a thousand pound and when it was found it was not worth a farthing."[25]

[19] Not used. Cf. *ante* From Hector, 28 Mar. 1785 (end).

[20] Not used. SJ advocated the public schools, though not without some reservations. See *Life* ii. 407, iii. 12.

[21] Quoted, *Life* iv. 236.

[22] MS. "Wiltshire he"

[23] *Diaries*, p. 364. Mentioned by JB, *Life* iv. 235.

[24] SJ to Bowles, 7 Oct. 1783, paraphrased (*Letters SJ* 891.1). In Bowles's "Memorandums" a note of doubt is sounded: ". . . but her unfortunate temper (of which I have heard since) had probably rendered her less an object with him than I imagined." Mrs. Williams's "peevishness" is mentioned a number of times in the *Life*.

[25] Quoted, with minor revision, *Life* iv. 236. Dr. Powell suggests that the literary friend was Joseph Warton.

The Style and character of the Doctor's conversation is pretty generally known; it was certainly conducted in conformity with a precept of Lord Bacon, but it is not clear I apprehend that this conformity was either perceived or intended by Dr. Johnson. The precept alluded to is as follows, "In all kinds of speech either pleasant, grave, severe, or ordinary it is convenient to speak leisurely and rather drawingly than hastily: because hasty speech confounds the memory and oftentimes besides the unseemliness drives a man either to a stammering, a non plus or harping on that which should follow; whereas a slow speech confirmeth the memory addeth a conceit of wisdom to the hearers, besides a seemliness of speech and countenance." Dr. Johnson's method of conversation was certainly calculated to excite attention, and to amuse or instruct (as it happened) without wearying or confusing his company; he was always most perfectly clear and perspicuous; and his language was so correct and his sentences so neatly constructed that his conversation might have been all printed without wanting any correction. At the same time it was easy and natural: the accuracy of it had no appearance of labour constraint or stiffness, he seemed more correct than others by the force of habit and the customary exercise of his powerful mind.[26]

At one period of his life he used to frequent the Office of a Justice of Peace, under the idea that much of real life is to be learned at such places. He discontinued his attendance however after no very considerable interval, from finding a great sameness in the complaints, and observing that most of them were frivolous and uninteresting.[27]

Few English writers were more cordially approved and admired by Dr. Johnson than Dr. Samuel Clarke. The great variety of his intelligence was particularly admired by the Dr.[28]

During his visit in Wiltshire in 1783 he had an opportunity of

[26] Quoted, with minor revision, *Life* iv. 236–37. Hill located Bacon's precept in *Short Notes for Civil Conversation* (*Works*, 1859, vii. 109).

[27] JB had SJ's own account of the episode: *Life* iii. 216. The Justice of the Peace was Saunders Welch, the place Westminster, and the interval "a whole winter".

[28] According to William Seward, "in the opinion of Dr. Johnson, Dr. Samuel Clarke was the most complete literary character that England ever produced" (quoted by Hill, *Life* i. 3 n. 2). Bowles's earlier version reads: "Of Dr. Clarke he spoke with great commendation for his Universality and seemed not disposed to censure him for his Heterodoxy. He held, he said, the Eternity of the Son, and that was being far from Heretical." Cf. *Life* iii. 248, iv. 416, and *ante* From Brocklesby, 27 Dec. 1784, ?17–18 Apr. 1785; From Adams, 17 Nov. 1785.

seeing the MS. of the Homer, the corrected Liturgy and several MS letters to and from Dr. Clarke. He strongly urged the immediate examination and revision of all the unedited MS. of Dr. Clarke under the impression that many might be highly deserving of the publick view.—(The hurry of a laborious profession has obliged the respectable person in whose possession these papers are, to postpone but without intending to decline this task.)[29]

It is very singular that Dr. Johnson had no idea of the use of a Barometer and that he even obstinately maintained that no man living that he knew thought it of any use. To the variations of the Thurmometer he was pretty constantly attentive.[30]

The Dr. valued himself a good deal on being able to do every thing for himself. He visited without a servant when he went to stay at the houses of his friends, and found few or no occasions to employ the servants belonging to the family. He knew how to mend his own stockings to darn his linen or to sew on a button on his cloaths. "I am not (he would often say) an helpless man."[31]

He spoke often in praise of French literature, and "the french are excellent in this" he would say "they have a book on[32] every subject." From what he had seen of them he denied them the praise of superior politeness, and mentioned with very visible disgust the custom they have of spitting on the floors of their apartments. "This" says the Doctor, "is as gross a thing as can well be done, and one wonders how any man or set of men can persist in so offensive a practise for a whole day together, one should expect that the first effort toward civilization would remove it[33] even amongst savages."[34]

Of Sermons at the sollicitation of friends he had written several (about 40).[35] The first he ever wrote was on the subject of Pride begun after dinner and sent away by one of the night coaches to the

---

[29] See *ante* From Bowles, 30 Aug. 1785. The last sentence of this paragraph is deleted, perhaps signifying that the project was eventually given up.

[30] Not used.

[31] Deleted in proof, with the remark, "I doubt this, therefore let it go out."

[32] MS. "almost" deleted.

[33] MS. "wherever it had existed" deleted.

[34] Quoted, with minor revision, *Life* iv. 237.

[35] "We shall in vain endeavour to know with exact precision every production of Johnson's pen. He owned to me, that he had written about forty sermons; but as I understood that he had given or sold them to different persons, who were to preach them as their own, he did not consider himself at liberty to acknowledge them" (*Life* iv. 383 n.). See also *ibid.* iii. 507.

preacher for whose use it was intended.[36] This expedition the
doctor said was not difficult to one who had filled his head with the
common topicks of the subject. He spoke sometimes of another
sermon against the Romanists[37] delivered at St. James's Church on
the Anniversary of the Powder Plot. Secker[38] was at that time the
Rector and being zealous for the credit of his pulpit and having
small confidence in the preacher who was (as the Dr. said) no
great controversialist, requested to see the Sermon before it was
preached. Secker's fear was lest more should be said against the
Papists than was known or could be proved: but on perusing the
discourse he returned it with much approbation and said that nothing was advanced that could not be fully maintained.

Dr. Johnson professed that he had not been a very diligent
reader: "I have red few books through, they are generally so
repulsive that I cannot.[39] Xenophon's *Cyropædia* I did read fairly
from beginning to end for the sake of the language."[40] "I told the
King," added the Dr. "that I had red very little in comparison
with many others."[41]

Of Mr. Thrale he appeared to preserve very tender sentiments: "Poor dear Mr. Thrale" were words often in his
mouth.[42]

---

[36] Cf. Sermon VI in *Sermons Left for
Publication by the Rev. John Taylor, LL.D.*
(1788, 1789), and see *post* Appendix,
Introductory Note. SJ remarked to Dr.
Watson and JB at St. Andrews: "I myself have composed about forty sermons.
I have begun a sermon after dinner, and
sent it off by the post that night" (*Life*
v. 57).

[37] Not among the *Sermons*. The anecdote that follows was not used.

[38] Thomas Secker, D.D. (1693–1768),
Archbishop of Canterbury. "He expressed
a great opinion of Abp. Secker but said
he pretended to no great knowledge of
books" (Bowles's "Memorandums", *Life*
iv. 524).

[39] Cf. *Life* ii. 226, iv. 308. But SJ "had
a peculiar facility in seizing at once what
was valuable in any book, without submitting to the labour of perusing it from
beginning to end" (*ibid*. i. 71).

[40] Not used. Bowles's earlier version
reads: "In Greek he told me that the

Cyropædia was the only author wᶜʰ he
ever fairly red thro', & that was for the
sake of the language."

[41] "His Majesty having observed to
him that he supposed he must have read
a great deal; Johnson answered, that he
thought more than he read; that he had
read a great deal in the early part of his
life, but having fallen into ill health, he
had not been able to read much, compared
with others: for instance, he said he had
not read much, compared with Dr.
Warburton" (*Life* ii. 36).

[42] Not used. Bowles's earlier version
continues: "Of Mrs. Thrale he was
silent; she was at Weymouth [in Aug.
1783] whilst the Doctor was with me,
meaning to gratifie him I proposed
the going thither for a few days, but I
found he had no great mind to see Mrs.
Thrale. The event of this year [her marriage to Piozzi, 23 July 1784] foreseen
at that time possibly by him explains the
reason."

Of the American war after its termination he spoke without the heat and prejudice of a partizan. Said it should by all means have been a naval war and to confirm this idea he used to quote a maxim of the King of Prussia's[43] (who to be sure says the Dr. when he talks of War must be allowed to talk of what he knows)[;] his maxim was that when a Prince had a mind to triumph completely over an enemy he should let him come to battle in his own kingdom.[44]

The Doctor never[45] shewed on any other occasion the same degree of pleasure as when he recounted the marks of respect and benignity which he had received from those whom he had made by his own behaviour his enemies. "Mr. Jenyns" said he "(to whom I have not been too civil) after my illness in 1783 told me with great kindness that he was glad to see me abroad again,[46] and Mr. Wilkes (with whom I had a very rough bout) called upon me soon after my recovery and sat with me some time. He asked me to give him my books which he said he should be glad to have but was too poor to buy them, so you may be sure he had them."[47]

Baxter's *Reasons of the Xtian Religion* he thought contained the best collection of the evidences of the divinity of the Xtian System.[48]

The letter signed SUNDAY in *The Rambler* was written the Dr. said by Miss Talbot whilst she resided at Lambeth in the family of Archbishop Secker.[49]

Dr. Dodd was formerly known to Dr. Johnson who drew the petition presented to the King in his favor[,] the speech which he made at his Tryal and his Address to the Convicts in Newgate a few days before his execution. He was in the confidence of those who endeavoured to save the Dr.'s life: immense offers he said were

---

[43] MS. "the Prussia's"

[44] Not used.

[45] MS. "seldom" deleted.

[46] Not used. The example of Jenyns proved an unhappy one: see *ante* From Adams, 17 Feb. 1785, n. 20.

[47] "Mr. Wilkes said to me, loud enough for Dr. Johnson to hear, 'Dr. Johnson should make me a present of his "Lives of the Poets," as I am a poor patriot, who cannot afford to buy them.' Johnson seemed to take no notice of this hint; but in a little while, he called to Mr. Dilly, 'Pray, Sir, be so good as to

send a set of my Lives to Mr. Wilkes, with my compliments.' This was accordingly done; and Mr. Wilkes paid Dr. Johnson a visit, was courteously received, and sat with him a long time" (*Life* iv. 107).

[48] Quoted, *Life* iv. 237.

[49] Catharine Talbot (1721–70) is credited with *Rambler* No. 30, *Life* i. 203. She and her mother lived with Secker (who had been a protégé of her father) from 1725 until his death in 1768 (DNB).

made to the turnkeys the evening before the execution, and every
possible effort was made to restore life afterwards, Dr. Johnson
was not sure but he beleived without effect. Dodd's piety he
conceived to have been at first sincere, but he set up to despise the
world before he knew what the world was. He appeared however
perfectly to concur in opinion with the late Bishop of Bristol
(Newton) who said that Dodd was hanged for the least of his
crimes.[50]

Chymistry was always an interesting pursuit with Dr. Johnson:
whilst he was in Wiltshire he attended some experiments that
were made by a Physician at Salisbury on the new kinds of Air. In
the course of the experiments frequent mention being made of Dr.
Priestley, Dr. Johnson knit his brows and in a stern manner enquired "Why do we hear so much of Dr. Priestley?" This was the
effect of his religious bigotry. He was very properly answered
"Sir because we are indebted to him for these important discoveries." On this Dr. Johnson appeared well content and replyed
"Well, well, I beleive we are, and let every man have the honour
he has merited."[51]

A friend was one day about two years before his death struck
with some instance of Dr. Johnson's great candour: "Well Sir"
says he "I will always say that you are a very candid man." "Will
you" replied the Dr. "I doubt then you will be very singular. But
indeed Sir" continued he "I look upon myself to be a man very
much misunderstood. I am not an uncandid nor am I a severe man. I
have sometimes sallies and say more than I mean in jest, and people
are apt to beleive me serious: however I beleive I am more candid
than I was when I was *younger*: as I know more of mankind I
beleive I expect less of them and am ready now to call a man *a good
man* upon easier terms than I was formerly."[52] Speaking to the
same person at another time, he said "I never judge too much of
men from what they say; some people get a strange way of rattling,
and others say any thing that serves a present turn."

The Doctor's notion of conversation was this[:] that almost all
that was wanting was to keep up the Ball of talk. "Nobody" said he

---

[50] Cf. *Life* iii. 140 ff., 166.

[51] Quoted, *Life* iv. 237–38, with the
omission of the sentence (deleted by JB
in the MS.) "This was the effect of his
religious bigotry."

[52] Quoted, with minor revision, *Life*
iv. 239. (The words "have", "sallies",
and "and" were deleted by JB in the MS.).
None of the remaining particulars was
admitted to the *Life*.

"does ill in conversation (You may be sure I[53] mean on fit subjects) but otherwise I say nobody does ill in company except he that says nothing. Talk what you will, 'tis pretty certain you'l make somebody else speak and whatever you may do[54] he may say something of value." I apprehend this idea governed in great[55] measure his own conversation.[56]

Dr. Johnson was asked whether Dr. Percy meant to write in the controversy about Rowley and Chatterton. "Write Sir about Rowley and Chatterton, no to be sure, why he ought to have his lawn sleeves burned about his ears if he did."[57]

Whilst Dr. Johnson was in Wiltshire he viewed Stonehenge which he declared surpassed his ideas and was more curious than he expected to have found it.[58]

Of the writings of Erasmus he entertained a very high opinion and frequently red[59] them.

Speaking one day of making Indexes; "Sir" said the doctor "there is no secret in the matter[;] only take paper enough and you may go on very dexterously with the Index."[60]

It is very well known that in the latter part of Dr. Johnson's life he became much dejected with gloomy apprehensions respecting his reception in a future world.[61] That he was a firm beleiver in Revelation is past a doubt, and all his fears therefore arose from an idea of his own defective conduct. He was known to say that he only doubted whether he had fulfilled the terms of salvation. That the good Xtian would be recompensed he was clear, and only feared whether he was to be numbred amongst such.[62] His *Prayers and meditations* are an exact portrait of the religious state of his mind and from them we see that his great object was to do every thing upon reflexion and conscience. He wished to employ all his

---

[53] MS. "except vicious talkers" deleted.

[54] MS. "deserve" deleted.

[55] MS. "some" deleted.

[56] SJ states the requirements of good conversation, *Life* iv. 166.

[57] He didn't. For others of the Johnson Circle who did, see *Life* iii. 50 and n. 5, 478.

[58] SJ wrote Mrs. Thrale a detailed archaeological opinion, *Letters SJ* 892.

[59] MS. "parts of" deleted. See *Life passim*.

[60] Cf. SJ's remark in his Preface to the *General Index to the First Twenty Volumes of the Gentleman's Magazine* (1753): "to the Perfection of an Index little more is necessary than can be produced by Diligence and Labour". I owe this reference to Dr. Powell, who announced this work as SJ's in *Essays and Studies by Members of the English Association*, 1942, xxviii. 38–41.

[61] Cf. *Life* iii. 154, iv. 395.

[62] Cf. *Life* iii. 294–95, 299.

time on the best possible subjects and not on those which happened to be most attractive. He wished to govern his mind and conduct altogether upon evangelical principles and therefore saw the necessity of an exact and frequent study of the Bible.[63] Sickness, bus'ness, indolence and those amusements which he had a taste for intervened and prevented him from applying to matters that he had decided to be of more importance. The recollection of this produced regret, and regret produced a number of struggles which tho' often unsuccessful were certainly at all times very beneficial to his mind and conduct. By aiming at more than others often do, he did more than others often do, tho' without attaining exactly to what he intended. It must be admitted however that his seasons of self examination were too rare. The Pythagoreans fixed it to every evening, and whoever will look into one of the last chapters of Law's *Serious call*[64] will find good reasons why this practise should not be adopted less frequently. That Dr. Johnson's melancholy proceeded from his apprehension of future judgement is past a doubt.[65]

I have something more to add concerning this subject.[66]

From Dr. John Mudge, Tuesday 13 November 1787

MS. Yale (C 2061).

ADDRESS: To James Boswell Esqr.

ENDORSEMENT: Dr. Mudge.

Plym[ou]th, Tuesday Nov. 13 1787

DEAR SIR: I perswade myself you will be concern'd that I have so cogent an Apology to make for my not having before fulfill'd my promise; and also for not answering your obliging Letter[1] sooner; in truth, I have been extremely ill, ever since my return into the

[63] The *Diaries* are full of SJ's resolutions to read the Bible.

[64] "Of Evening prayer. Of the nature and necessity of examination. How we are to be particular in the confession of all our sins. How we are to fill our minds with a just horror and dread of all sin" (1729, ch. 23).

[65] JB puts it the other way around: "Johnson's temperament was melancholy, of which such direful apprehensions of futurity are often a common effect" (*Life* iv. 300). But Bowles was surely right.

[66] Nothing more has been recovered.

[1] *Ante* 30 Oct. 1787.

Country, and tho now somewhat better, and I hope, on the recovery, I am, however, so weak as not to be able to attend to
Business. I am much concern'd to find that several Letters of Dr.
Johnsons, which I received from him soon after his return to Town
from his excursions, with Sir Joshua, to this place,[2] are missing; I
have exammined all my papers very carefully, and I fear they were
lost on my removal from my former House, about twelve Months
since. The three enclosed[3] I receiv'd from him, on account of an
alarming complaint he had some time before his Death, for which
he consulted me; but I think the subject of them too delicate to
permit them to be made any use of.[4] I am Dear Sir with great
respect, Your Obliged Humble Servant

JOHN MUDGE

From William Bowles, Wednesday 14 November 1787

MS. Yale (C 562).

ADDRESS: James Boswell Esqr., G. Queen Street, Lincolns Innfields,
London.

POSTMARK: NO 15 87.

Heale, Nov. 14 1787

DEAR SIR, I thought we had agreed in London that many of the
letters of Dr. Johnson to me were not fit for the publick eye.[1] You
will please to remember that several of them were only intended to
give me information concerning a complaint, the situation and
circumstances of which I think you will hardly choose to dilate

---

[2] In the summer of 1762 (*Life* i. 378).
Mudge was a friend of Reynolds (who
painted him as a young man), and was
instrumental in placing James Northcote
in his studio (DNB).

[3] 9 and 23 Sept. and 9 Oct. 1783
(*Letters SJ* 874(1), 884.2, 874(2)). The
originals are now in the Hyde Collection.

[4] JB prints extracts from the first and
last—"such passages as shew either a
felicity of expression, or the undaunted
state of his mind" (*Life* iv. 240). SJ's
complaint was a painful swelling of the
left testicle, which his doctors diagnosed

as malignant and at first proposed to
cut out.

[1] No meeting is recorded in the
journal, but the conversation may have
taken place at the Essex Head Club (see
ante From Bowles, 2 June 1785, n. 2).
JB habitually recorded the names of those
present, but in some instances (e.g. 23
and 30 May 1787) not all. In a missing
letter JB had presumably acknowledged
the receipt of Bowles's communications,
and renewed his request for SJ's letters to
him (see *ante* 27 Feb. and 31 May 1786).

upon in your publication. Mr. Pott[2] possibly may notice it in some paper or other: I think I heard he intended it. When the letters on this subject are separated from the rest, there will remain but a small number, and in these there are so many particulars respecting myself, my wife and children that they certainly could not be published without impropriety nor without giving much uneasiness to myself, my own family, and my connexions. The letters you intend to publish are I make no doubt very different in their general character from those in question. The persons written to were older friends of Dr. Johnson than myself, and I presume too, from their rank in the learned world that the letters all turn on subjects of discussion that are generally interesting and important. The letters to me are in my judgement precisely those which should not be printed, I mean letters of friendship merely, which are valuable only to particular persons, at particular times.

There is not a single passage in any of my letters that can assist towards the knowledge of *Life or opinions*. Unwilling, as I am sure I feel myself to refuse any request made to me by you, I have just perused the letters with the hope of being able to transmit a few worth your acceptance and the notice of the publick: but I see none that I can class under that description. There are a few more particulars that I can perhaps furnish and they shall be sent in a short time with the address you have given me. The particulars I mean are such as I do not possess at present myself but which some friends who saw Dr. Johnson here are sometimes telling me of. One thing I know is a conversation *on Duelling* in which he apologized for the practice and declared it necessary in the present state of Society.[3]

---

[2] Percivall Pott (1714–88), the surgeon. See *Letters SJ passim*. He treated SJ for his sarcocele, and JB for the usual venereal ailment (*Life* iv. 239; Journ. 12 May 1768, 22 July 1785; F. A. Pottle, *James Boswell: The Earlier Years 1740–1769*, 1966, *passim*).

[3] Cf. *Life* ii. 179–80: "Sir, as men become in a high degree refined, various causes of offence arise; which are considered to be of such importance, that life must be staked to atone for them, though in reality they are not so. A body that has received a very fine polish may be easily hurt. Before men arrive at this artificial refinement, if one tells his neighbour he lies, his neighbour tells him he lies; if one gives his neighbour a blow, his neighbour gives him a blow: but in a state of highly polished society, an affront is held to be a serious injury. It must, therefore, be resented, or rather a duel must be fought upon it; as men have agreed to banish from their society one who puts up with an affront without fighting a duel. Now, Sir, it is never unlawful to fight in self-defence. He, then, who fights a duel, does not fight from passion against his antagonist, but out of self-defence; to avert the stigma

If you have any questions that you think I can resolve, or any facts that you can imagine me to be acquainted with on being reminded of them, let me hear as often as you like. I am sure not to be from home for some months, and shall be quite at liberty. I beg to present my best respects to all the Club: I shall always be happy to continue a member whilst the Club exists. Mr. Poore[4] will have the goodness to settle my arrears.

I hope Dear Sir, you will sometimes set your face towards the West of England, and that we shall see you in Wiltshire, where I hope you will find me alive notwithstanding the frequent fears you have had of my death. I am ever Dear Sir, very truly and faithfully yours

Wм. Bowles

To William Bowles, after 14 November 1787

MS. Yale (L 268). A copy by JB's son Alexander, endorsed: "Copy of a Letter To William Bowles Esqr."

[London]

Dear Sir: Your objections to the publication of Dr. Johnsons Letters to you have much weight. But in my humble opinion a distinction and separation may be made so as to avoid what you put so forcibly. There are no doubt in his Letters expressions which mark his fortitude under an alarming complaint and others which afford evidence of his tender and affectionate heart which in his peculiar style are admirably framed. These I am confident might be selected in such a manner that you and your family and friends should feel no uneasiness. If you will place such confidence in me as to send me the Letters I give you my word and honour that they shall be faithfully returned—that I shall not copy them—but that

of the world, and to prevent himself from being driven out of society. I could wish there was not that superfluity of refinement; but while such notions prevail, no doubt a man may lawfully fight a duel." Cf. also *ibid.* ii. 226–27, iv. 211 and n. 4.

4 Along with Bowles, one of the "constant members" of the Essex Head Club at the time of SJ's death (*Lit. Anec.* ii. 553). In the Hyde Collection is a letter from Poore to SJ, 9 May 1780, soliciting

his nomination for membership; it is endorsed by SJ: "Mr. Poore is a very proper man, and a man of great knowledge." JB mentions him in the journal once—among those in attendance at the club on 22 Feb. 1786. He may have been Edward Poore, of Rushall, Wiltshire, "in the commission of the peace, and a deputy lieutenant for that county", who died 10 Apr. 1788, aged 73 (*Gent. Mag.* lviii. 371).

I shall only make excerp[t]⟨s⟩ and that those excerpts[1] shall not be published till they have been submitted to your consideration and been approved by you.[2]

Your goodness[3] already shewn to me encourages me to make this request with which I entreat your compliance, and am Dear Sir your faithfull and most obedient humble Servant

JAMES BOSWELL

[1] MS. orig. "these excerps"; corrected by (I think) JB.

[2] None of SJ's letters to Bowles—not even excerpts—are printed in the *Life*; and no further correspondence between JB and Bowles is extant. Sixteen letters from SJ to Bowles, written between Oct. 1782 and Sept. 1784, have been recovered. The majority of them deal with SJ's illnesses. See *Letters SJ* 871.2 and following, and Mary Hyde, "Not in Chapman," *Johnson, Boswell and Their Circle*, p. 315

[3] MS. "goodness to me"

1788

Johnsoniana Related by William Gerard Hamilton,[1] Wednesday 6 February 1788[2]

MS. Yale (C 1493). In JB's hand, both headed and endorsed: "Right Hon. W. G. Hamilton."

He has made a chasm which not only nothing can fill up but which nothing has a tendency to fill up. Johnson is gone let us go to the next best. Nobody. No man can be said to put you in mind of Dr. Johnson.[3]

---

[1] William Gerard ("Single-speech") Hamilton (1729–96), politician. SJ was long acquainted with him and was employed by him as a consultant on political questions: see *Life* i. 489–90, 519–20, and D. J. Greene, *The Politics of Samuel Johnson*, 1960, pp. 197–99. Prof. Clifford informs me that Thomas Birch, in a letter to Lord Hardwicke, 3 Aug. 1765 (British Museum Add. MS. 35,400, f. 268), while mentioning Burke's writing of Hamilton's speeches in Ireland, refers to "the *single* one made in England, which I hear to have been the performance of Sam. Johnson, with whom, I know, he is very intimate". But the rumour remains to be substantiated. On 15 June 1786 JB "dined (for the first time) with the Right Hon. William Gerrard Hamilton, with Courtenay and Malone . . . I was pleased to think that so able and so elegant a man as Hamilton was my second Cousin. The occasion of my being at length invited to his house was my being engaged in writing Dr. Johnson's *Life*. He promised to give me two letters of the Doctor's to him [*Life* iv. 245, 263–64], and some Anecdotes. The elegance of Hamilton's House, table, and manners, and particularly his beautiful language and pronunciation, pleased me very much. . . . I pleased myself that I might have one of my sons such a Man as Hamilton" (Journ.). JB was not at all pleased when, in 1791, Hamilton objected to the publication of some of these anecdotes (see *post* To Malone, 25 Feb. 1791). This incident may help explain the sardonic tone of some

verses on Hamilton which JB wrote on the blank pages of a letter from Charles Dilly, dated 14 May [1792]. A few lines may be quoted:

> Sure single speech may boast of blood
> For Hamilton's as old's the flood
> His bloods debas'd cries Abercorn
> In Lincoln's Inn the man was born
> His Father Will was in the law
> Thence got his pedigree a flaw
> This I admit but all things weighd
> His cards he surely well has played
> First having been by Johnson taught
> A seat in Parliament he bought
> There by one speech as Holland said
> Irish Vice Treasurer was made
> Then Gerard had the cunning sense
> From Burke to borrow eloquence [*sic*]

[2] The MS. is undated. I assign it to this date on the basis of an entry in the journal for that day: ". . . at Malone's on Ash Wednesday with Hamilton [and others] when we had a great deal of conversation about Johnson, and Hamilton well observed What a proof it was of his merit that this Company had been talking of him so long, as probably other companies were. He said, 'There is no such man; *Nec viget quicquam simile aut secundum*' ["Nothing that resembles him, nothing that comes near to him": Horace, *Odes* I. xii. 18]." The MS. bears signs of having at one time been intended as printer's copy; but as the items which JB used are widely separated in the *Life*, it is clear why he decided against it.

[3] Quoted, with revision, *Life* iv. 420–21. JB identifies his informant only as "an eminent friend".

We are not talking of a man but of a[4] particular being who had a great deal above human nature and many things beneath it.[5]

He said when he waited on Lord Bute he paid him many compliments on his talents and expatiated how unfortunate the situation of literary men often was[,] "a subject, (smiling) which was not new to me and on which I could have talked as much as his Lordship."[6]

Of Sir Joshua Reynolds if he had a month given to him to find fault with him he should at the end of the month be as much at a loss as at the beginning.[7]

Warburton said of him "I admire him, but I cannot bear his style." This being told to Johnson he said "that is exactly my case with[8] him. I admire him, but cannot bear his Style." And he did admire Warburton very much. He said "the table is allways full Sir. He brings things from the north and the south and from every quarter. In his *Divine Legation* you are allways entertained. He carries you round and round without carrying you forward to the point. But you have no wish to be carried on."[9]

[10]He complained that his pension having been given to him as a Literary character he had been applied to by Administration to write political pamphlets [11]and that he had received no reward or additional consideration for having written them, which seemed to imply that this was a command,[11] and he was even so much irritated that he declared to a friend his resolution to resign his pension. His friend shewed him the impropriety of this and he afterwards expressed his gratitude and said he had received good advice.

In conversation[12] he expressed a wish to have his pension secured to him for his life.[10]

Talking how prudent it was for a man who had not been accus-

---

[4] MS. "great" deleted.

[5] Not used.

[6] Not used. It is surprising that JB records no conversation of SJ's on this subject—a recurring one in his writings.

[7] Not used.

[8] MS. alt. "as to"

[9] Quoted, with revision, *Life* iv. 48–49. A cancelled leaf in the first edition named Hamilton as the informant: see *ibid.* 556 and *post* To Malone, 25 Feb. 1791 and n. 3.

[10–10] Quoted, with revision, *Life* ii.

317. JB identifies his informant as "a Right Honourable friend of distinguished talents and very elegant manners, with whom he maintained a long intimacy, and whose generosity towards him will afterwards appear".

[11–11] Deleted in MS. In the *Life* it is replaced, following the last sentence of the quoted passage, by: "but he neither asked nor received from government any reward whatsoever for his political labours".

[12] MS. orig. "In several conversations"

tomed to speak in publick to begin as plainly as possible, he acknowledged that he rose in some speaking society to deliver a speech which he had prepared "but" said he "I found that all my rhetorical flowers forsook me."[13]

To Thomas Percy, Bishop of Dromore, Saturday 9 February 1788

MS. New York Public Library, Berg Collection.

ADDRESS: To The Lord Bishop of Dromore, [Dublin *deleted and*] Dromore [*added in another hand*].

POSTMARK: FE 11 88.

London, Great Queen Street, Lincolns Inn Fields, 9 Febry. 1788

... I am really uneasy to think how long it is since I was favoured with your Lordships communications concerning Dr. Johnson,[1] which though few are valuable, and will contribute to increase my store. I am ashamed that I have yet seven years to write of his Life. I do it chronologically, giving year by year his publications if there were any, his letters, his conversations, and every thing else that I can collect. It appears to me that mine is the best plan of Biography that can be conceived; for my Readers will as near as may be accompany Johnson in his progress, and as it were see each scene as it happened. I am of opinion that my delay will be for the advantage of the Work, though perhaps not for the advantage of the Authour, both because his fame may suffer from too great expectation, and the Sale may be worse from the subject being comparatively old. But I mean to do my duty as well as I can. Mrs. (Thrale) Piozzi's Collection of his letters will be out soon, and will be a rich addition to the Johnsonian Memorabilia. I saw a sheet at the printing House yesterday and observed Letter CCCXXX, so that we may expect much entertainment.[2] It is

[13] Quoted, with revision, *Life* ii. 139, where Hamilton is acknowledged by name. "rhetorical" is a later addition in the MS.

[1] *Ante* 6 Mar. 1787.
[2] On the day before publication, 7 Mar.,

JB received a copy of the edition from Dilly and "read with assiduity till I had finished both Volumes. I was disappointed a good deal, both in finding less able and brilliant writing than I expected, and in having a proof of his fawning on a woman whom he did not esteem—because he had luxurious living in her husband's house,

wonderful what avidity there still is for every thing relative to
Johnson. I dined at Mr. Malone's on Wednesday with Mr. W. G.
Hamilton, Mr. Flood,[3] Mr. Wyndham Mr. Courtenay etc.:
And Mr. Hamilton observed very well, what a proof it was of
Johnson's merit, that we had been talking of him almost all the
afternoon.[4] But Your Lordship needs no refreshment upon that
subject.

I have two or three letters from him to Francis Barber while
that faithful Negro was at school at Easter Mauduit.[5] Can your
Lordship give me any particulars of Johnson's conduct in that
benevolent business? . . .

From William Johnson Temple,
Saturday 9 February 1788

MS. Yale (C 2855).

Gluvias Vicarage, February 9th 1788

. . . Have you the vanity to think your Biography preferable to
Mason's? I'll tell you what I think when I have read his Memoirs of
Whitehead. I suppose his method is very different from yours:
rather an account of his writings and the occasions of them, than
a picture of conversation pieces, and of witty and sententious sayings. Does Sir J. Hawkins misrepresent so much as you allege.
Does he not give one a pretty faithful idea of his great friend? The

and in order that this fawning might not
be counteracted, treating me and other
friends much more lightly than we had
reason to expect. This publication *cooled*
my warmth of enthusiasm for 'my illustrious friend' a good deal. I felt myself
degraded from the consequence of an
ancient Baron to the state of an humble
attendant on an Authour, and what vexed
me, thought that my collecting so much
of his conversation had made the World
shun me as a dangerous companion"
(Journ.).

[3] Henry Flood (1732–91), Irish statesman and orator. He was a subscriber to
SJ's monument and the author of
"sepulchral verses" memorializing SJ's

contribution to the English language
(*Life* iv. 424, 469).

[4] See *ante* From Hamilton, 6 Feb.
1788, n. 2.

[5] See *ante* From Barber, 7 Jan. 1786.
JB appears to have forgotten that all
three letters were addressed at Mrs.
Clapp's in Bishop Stortford, Hertfordshire. The error of "Easter" for "Easton"
probably represents a misreading of SJ's
hand in his letter to Reynolds of Aug.
1764, printed *Life* i. 486. Although the
spelling is clear in Percy's reply (*post*
29 Feb. 1788), JB repeated the error in
composing his narrative which precedes
the letter to Reynolds (MS. *Life*, p. 294).
It was, however, corrected in the printing.

lines perhaps are rather strong, but are they not true? What does Sir Joshua, what does Mr. Burke think?[1] They are more impartial judges. . . .

To *William Johnson Temple,* *Sunday–Monday 24–25 February 1788*

MS. Pierpont Morgan Library.

ADDRESS (by Courtenay): Revrd. Mr. Temple. Penryn.

FRANK: London Febry. Twenty fifth 1788. Free J. Courtenay.

POSTMARK: FE 25 88.

London, Sunday 24 Febry.[1] 1788

. . . Mason's *Life of Gray* is excellent, because it is interspersed with Letters which shew us the *Man.*[2] His *Life of Whitehead* is not a Life at all; for there is neither a letter nor a saying from first to last.[3] I am absolutely certain that *my* mode of Biography which gives not only a *History* of Johnson's *visible* progress through the World, and of his Publications, but a *View* of his mind, in his Letters, and Conversations is the most perfect that can be conceived, and will be *more* of a *Life* than any Work that has ever yet appeared. I have been wretchedly dissipated, so that I have not

---

[1] Sir Joshua "hesitated", if he did not dissent, when Malone proposed a vote of censure at The Club: see *ante* To Barber, 29 June 1787, n. 1. Burke was not present, and I have not seen his opinion recorded; but he would not have been predisposed in Hawkins's favour. JB explains Hawkins's "secession" from The Club: "he one evening attacked Mr. Burke, in so rude a manner, that all the company testified their displeasure; and at their next meeting his reception was such, that he never came again" (*Life* i. 479–80).

[1] "Monday 25 Febry." is inserted at the top of the second page of the letter.

[2] ". . . I have resolved to adopt and enlarge upon the excellent plan of Mr. Mason, in his Memoirs of Gray. Wher-

ever narrative is necessary to explain, connect, and supply, I furnish it to the best of my abilities; but in the chronological series of Johnson's life, which I trace as distinctly as I can, year by year, I produce, wherever it is in my power, his own minutes, letters, or conversation, being convinced that this mode is more lively, and will make my readers better acquainted with him, than even most of those who actually knew him, but could know him only partially . . . Indeed I cannot conceive a more perfect mode of writing any man's life, than not only relating all the most important events of it in their order, but interweaving what he privately wrote, and said, and thought . . ." (*Life* i. 29–30).

[3] ". . . there is literally no *Life,* but a mere dry narrative of facts" (*Life* i. 31).

267

written a line for a forthnight. But today I resume my pen and shall labour vigorously. . . .

From Thomas Percy, Bishop of Dromore, Friday 29 February 1788

MS. Yale (C 2234). Received 6 Mar. (Reg. Let.). Percy's draft, dated 28 Feb., is printed, *Lit. Illust.* vii. 310–12.

ADDRESS: James Boswell Esqr., Great Queen's Street, Lincoln's Inn Fields, London.

POSTMARKS: MR 3, MR 7 88.

Dromore House, Feb. 29. 1788

. . . With regard to our departed Friend Johnson, He spent a good part of the Summer of 1764 at my Vicarage House at Easton Mauduit in Northamptonshire,[1] and was there attended by his black Servant Francis Barber: but he returned with him to London, and never was at School there. He had formerly, I believe been placed by his Master at one of the cheap Schools in Yorkshire: and after 1764 at a School at Bishops Stortford in Hertfordshire;[2] where poor Frank I fear, never got beyond his accidence. But I know nothing of the Particulars.

I found lately a Memorandum of the time of my admission into the Club at the Turks Head in Gerrard Street etc. and I shall[3] here collect some other particulars on that subject;[4] concerning which Mention has been made both by Sir John Hawkins and Madm. Piozzi.[5] But both of them have omitted what I have heard Johnson assign as the Reason why the Club was at first begun with so small a Number as 8 or 9; and for many Years was not allowed to Exceed that of TWELVE Members: He said It was intended the Club should consist of SUCH men, as that if only Two of them chanced to meet, they should be able to entertain each other, without wanting the addition of more Company to pass the Evening agreeably.

---

[1] *Life* i. 486.
[2] See *Life* i. 239 n. 1, and *ante* To Percy, 9 Feb. 1788 and n. 5.
[3] MS. "shall shall"
[4] A parallel but fuller version of Percy's memorandum is included in his life of Goldsmith prefixed to the *Miscellaneous Works* (1801, i. 70–73); cf.

Annals of the Club 1764–1914, 1914, pp. 7–8. Malone corrected some errors in a letter to Percy, 25 Sept. 1807 (*Percy-Malone Correspondence*, pp. 234–36). JB's account, *Life* i. 477–80, is based on other sources.
[5] Hawkins, pp. 423–25; *Anecdotes: Johns. Misc.* i. 229–30.

Whether they answer'd this Expectation must be judged from the following List of their Names as it was compleated soon after the beginning of the year 1768 When (in Consequence of Sir John Hawkins's secession)[6] the remaining Members agreed to extend their Number to Twelve, at which it remained fixed for some years; who then more or fewer constantly supped and spent the evening at the Turk's Head every *Monday* in the Winter and Spring Months. This was afterw[ar]ds changed I think to *Friday* Even[in]g.[7]

The List alphabetically was as follows. 1. Topham Beauclerc Esq. 2. Edmund Burke Esq. 3. Mr. Robert Chambers, then Vinerian Professor of Law in Oxford, now Sir Robt. the Judge in India. 4. Anthony Chamier Esqr. sometime Under Secretary (query) at War.[8] 5. Geo. Colman Esq. 6. —— Dyer Esq. (a great Friend of the Burke's,* and apparently a very amiable agreeable Man).[9] 7. Dr. Oliver Goldsmith. 8. Dr. Samuel Johnson. 9. Bennet Langton Esqr. 10. Dr. Nugent (Father of Mr. Burke's Wife).[10] 11. Revd. Thomas Percy. 12. Mr. Reynolds, now Sir Joshua Reynolds.

I was first admitted into the Club on 15th Feb. 1768, and about the same time Mr. Colman and Mr. Chambers were elected New Members also: the rest I believe were original Members. But Mr. Beauclerc had for sometime left the Club, and afterw[ar]ds returned to it. —For further Particulars I must refer you to Sir Joshua Reynolds, Mr. Langton and Mr. Burke, who are the only original Members now remaining. It was not I think till after the Deaths, 1st of Mr. Dyer 2dly of Mr. Chamier, that the Number of

* If desired I believe I could procure and send you the Eloge which Mr. Edmund Burke published in the Papers on Dyer's Death.[11]

---

[6] See *ante* From Temple, 9 Feb. 1788, n. 1.

[7] In Dec. 1772, according to Percy's later version.

[8] Chamier (1725–80) was appointed deputy secretary at war in 1772 and under-secretary of state in 1775.

[9] Samuel Dyer (1725–72), translator. According to Sir James Prior's *Life of Malone* (1860, p. 424), Percy told Malone "that they all at the Club had such a high opinion of Mr. Dyer's knowledge and

respect for his judgment as to appeal to him constantly, and that his sentence was final" (quoted, *Life* iv. 11 n. 1). Malone, in his *Life of Dryden* (1800, i. 181), defended Dyer's character against Hawkins's attack.

[10] Christopher Nugent, M.D. (d. 1775). See SJ's letter of condolence to his daughter, Jane Burke (d. 1812), *Letters SJ* 437.1.

[11] *Public Advertiser*, 17 Sept. 1772.

Members was extended to more than 12.[12] Nor had it the name of the *Literary Club,* till on the death of Garrick, it was so called in the Account of his Funeral given in the Papers.[13] I am, Dear Sir, Your very faithful Servant

THO. DROMORE

N.B. In the old Club Room at the Turk's Head was a book of entries and Forfeitures of absent Members which would show the variable State of the Club for many Years.

From Francesco Sastres, c. February 1788

MS. Yale (C 2431).

ADDRESS: James Boswell Esqre., No. 59 Great Queen Street, Lincoln's Inn-Fields.

ENDORSEMENT: Sastres.

[London]

DEAR SIR, I have very often taken the liberty of calling on you with our Dear great Friend's letters to me in my pocket, but having been always so unfortunate as never to find you at home nor hearing any thing from you, I began to think that you considered them of little consequence, and was not very desirous to have them. I have been at the same time earnestly Solicitad by Mrs. Piozzi to give the said letters to her, to publish them with the rest of Johnson's to herself. I have been informed, Dear Sir, that your life of Johnson is not yet ready for the press, whereas Mrs. Piozzi's book will be published in a very short time; and considering within my mind that you may make the same use of the said letters from Mrs. Piozzi's publication as from the Manuscript, and trusting on your goodness to excuse me, by considering the many obligations I

---

[12] See Percy's revised computation in his life of Goldsmith (i. 72), Malone's correction of it (*Percy-Malone Correspondence,* pp. 234–35), and Croker's information (quoted, *Life* i. 552).

[13] *London Chronicle,* 2–4 Feb. 1779; *Life* i. 477. On 25 Feb. JB wrote to Langton: "Garrick's death affected me much. . . . I regretted my not being in London to make one in the Funeral procession which did so much honour to his memory. I was pleased to see as one of the Divisions *Gentlemen of the Literary Club.* I beleive it had not a name before except the Alehouse designation as Beauclerc says,—of the Turkshead Club." Cf. Hawkins, p. 424.

have to that lady, I have been induced to deliver them into her hands.[1] I hope, Dear Sir, that this will not be interpreted by you as a disregard from me, the reverse of it being the real truth. I will endevour to recollect as many of Johnson's Sentiments, just as I have heard them from his own mouth, as I can and transmit them to you, which will, I think, serve more your purpose—they will stand in need of no other authenticity than the peculiar Johnsonian energy which will accompany them. Mrs. Piozzi has done me the honor to show me, already printed, many of Johnson's letters, in which I have had the pleasure to read many very fine passages in praise of you. Whenever these uccur Mrs. Piozzi has inserted your name in full length, and on the contrary when some passages have been thought by her otherwise she has even left out the initial.[2] I beg you will freely command me in any thing I can Serve you, and believe me, Dear Sir, Your unfeigned friend and very humble Servant

FRANCESCO SASTRES

To Francis Barber, Monday 3 March 1788

Missing. Facsimile of first page (through signature) and text of remainder, Maggs Bros., Spring 1922, Cat. 421, frontispiece and p. 16, Lot 58.

London, 3 March 1788

DEAR SIR: You have been so obliging, that I trouble you with a farther application, which is to copy, date, and subscribe the enclosed,[1] and transmit it to me under cover of J. B. Garforth Esq.

---

[1] Five letters from SJ to Sastres appear at the end of the second volume of Mrs. Piozzi's *Letters To and From Johnson*, published 8 Mar. of this year (*Thraliana*, p. 711). Sastres also furnished a few observations on SJ's last days (ii. 383). For Mrs. Piozzi's efforts to fill out the second volume, see J. L. Clifford, "Further Letters of the Johnson Circle", *Bull. Rylands Lib.* (1936) xx. 278–82; *Thraliana*, p. 689 n. 1. JB made no use of these letters to Sastres.

[2] The references to JB in SJ's letters to Mrs. Thrale are collected in *Letters SJ*, Index II, Boswell, James, Section 10.

Chapman speaks of "HLP's oscillations between preserving and suppressing J's praises of JB . . . Her malice, it is fair to note, was not strong enough to reach consistency" (*ibid*. Letter 408 n. 6).

---

[1] ". . . a letter for him to copy sign and address to Sir John Hawkins to deliver to Mr. T. D. Boswell the Diplomas from Dublin and Oxford and all other papers or Books in his possession which belonged to Dr. Johnson, and are in his possession, except what were bequeathed to him" (Reg. Let.).

M.P.[2] London. You will be so good as at the same time to author-ise me to receive from my brother[3] what Sir John Hawkins delivers to him. I do not expect any thing but the Diplomas. It is however as well to make the demand general. I do not employ Mr. Nichols's friendly interposition at present, as he is in distress on account of the death of his Wife.[4]

Please to Send your letter to Sir John *unsealed* that my brother may see his authority.

I shall be glad to hear particularly how you go on, and I send my compliments to Mrs. Barber. I am with sincere regard, Dear Sir, Your friend and humble servant

JAMES BOSWELL

I flatter myself that my Book will do justice to the character of your excellent Master. It will not be published before September or October. Be so good as to present my best compliments to all at Lichfield who do me the honour of remembering me. It is very long since I had the honour of hearing from Miss Seward.

From Edmond Malone, Saturday 8 March 1788

MS. Yale (C 1913).

ADDRESS: Mr. Boswell.

ENDORSEMENTS: Mr. Malone on reading Dr. Johnson's Letters to Mrs. Thrale *and* Mr. Malone on reading Mrs. Thrale's Collection of Johnson's Letters.

[London,] March 8

I sat up till four o'clock reading away as hard as I could, and then my candle went out and I could read no more; yet I was not able to finish the first Volume. The letters are, I think, in general very

---

[2] John Baynes Garforth (c. 1722–1808), solicitor in London, steward to Lord Lonsdale, and representative of two of the Lowthers' pocket boroughs in Parliament: Cockermouth, Cumberland, 1780–84 and 1790–1802, and Haslemere, Surrey, 1784–90 (*Johns. Glean.* ii. 68 n.; Judd 297). See also Journ. 23 Nov. 1786.

[3] (Thomas) David Boswell (1748–1826), JB's younger brother and his business agent, was a Spanish merchant and later an inspector in the Navy Pay Office.

[4] Nichols's second wife, Martha, died on 28 Feb. (*Johns. Glean.* viii. 77 n.). For his friendly interposition of the year before, see *ante* From Barber, 9 July 1787, n. 1.

pleasing and exactly what I expected. I think you rate them too low.[1] I would not have one of them omitted.

I see she has got one of your letters; about the Son who married against his father's consent; where he talks of *small-shot debts.* How comes this?[2]

I love him still more than ever. He had a most tender heart; and as much virtue, I believe, as falls to the lot of humanity. I hope heartily *Madam* will be trimm'd well for her suppression, and evident imposition with respect to his answer to her matrimonial notification.[3] All his documents concerning the value of truth, have been thrown away upon her. . . .

To James Beattie, Monday 10 March 1788

MS. University Library, King's College, Aberdeen.

ADDRESS (by Courtenay): Doctr. Beattie, Aberdeen.

FRANK: London March tenth 1788. Free J. Courtenay.

POSTMARK: MR 10 88.

ENDORSEMENT (in an unidentified hand): From James Boswell, London. 10th March 1788. Thanking for a letter of Dr. Johnson's, asking him to write any Sayings of Dr. J.s he may recollect. Expects his *Life of Johnson* to be out in Septr. asking Dr. B. to pray for the recovery of his (Boswell's) wife.

London, 10 March 1788

DEAR SIR: I thank you for Dr. Johnson's Letter to you, which I do not think the worse for the little *quarrel of kindness.*[1] It will come in

---

[1] JB dined the next day at Malone's with Courtenay. "They both thought better of Johnson's letters to Mrs. Thrale than I did, though upon looking at some of them again on saturday, they improved upon me" (Journ.).

[2] See *ante* From Adey, 26 Feb. 1785 and n. 17.

[3] Mrs. Piozzi printed only (1) her conciliatory letter to SJ, dated 30 June 1784, which covered a copy of the circular letter sent to Mr. Thrale's executors, and (2) SJ's letter to her, dated 8 July (Nos. CCCLIII and CCCLIV; *Letters SJ*

969a and 972). She suppressed (3) SJ's "rough" letter of 2 July and (4) her strong answer to it of 4 July (*Letters SJ* 970 and 970.1a). Malone could have read the spurious version (see Hawkins, p. 569) of 2 July in *Gent. Mag.* (Dec. 1784, liv. 893). JB commented, *Life* iv. 339, "If she would publish the whole of the correspondence that passed between Dr. Johnson and her on the subject, we should have a full view of his real sentiments."

---

[1] See *ante* From Beattie, 8 Nov. 1787.

its place in my chronological history of him; for such my Work is to be. I have yet six years of it to write, so that I cannot reckon on having it published earlier than September, or perhaps later. I trust it will give much satisfaction to Johnson's friends who knew him well.

May I beg that you will be so kind as to favour me with any of his sayings which you have retained; for although they may not be preserved in his very words which were allways wonderfully choice, they will be valuable as Opinions or sallies of which the *substance* at least will remain.

Mrs. Thrale's (Piozzis) Collection of his Letters contains a great deal of what is good, though there are many letters, and many passages which should have been left out.[2] They are printed shamefully wide, so as to be sold for twelve shillings,[3] when they might fairly have been contained in a six shillings volume. . . .

You have satisfied me as to the omission of Johnson in your *Christian Evidences.* I ever am, Dear Sir, your faithful and obedient humble servant

JAMES BOSWELL

Please to address under cover of John Courtenay Esq. M.P.

Pray send me all the sayings you have; for though some of them may seem trifling they must be all characteristical, dense and brilliant at least lucid. Do oblige me.

From Francis Barber,
Wednesday 12 March 1788

MS. Yale (C 66).

ADDRESS: James Boswell Esq'r., at Mr. Boswell's,[1] Thanet place near Temple Barr, London.

POSTMARK: MR 14 88.

Lichfield, wed. March 12: 1788

SIR: I should have Answer'd your's before now but not having been very well prevented me. I don't know that Sir John has at present

---

[2] Echoing the criticism of some of the newspapers. See Clifford, *Piozzi*, p. 314.
[3] That is, in two volumes.

[1] T. D. Boswell's, whose address is known from his letter to JB, 2 June 1784.

This address was presumably given in the enclosure to JB's letter of 3 Mar. (*ante*)—but for Hawkins's information, not Barber's. JB had in that letter instructed Barber to write to him in care of Garforth.

any thing in his Custody of mine except a gold headed Cane which was never accounted for;[2] as to the Diploma I have one which I beleive is what you have mention'd, if not, if you can enform me either of that, or any other Paper or Papers which he has in his possession belonging to me as residuary Legatee please to give me a Line or two and shall upon the receipt of which impower you to demand them from Sir John Hawkins. I am greatly oblige to you, and also return you many thanks for the friendly part in which you have took in favour of my poor decease'd Master; which (as long as life last) shall ever be acknowledged as a particular favour done (Dear Sir) to your Sincere humble Servant FRAS. BARBER

P.S. I have not had it[3] in my power to see Miss seward since I receiv'd your Letter but shall take the first opportunity to present your Compliments to her.

From Richard Clark,[1] Wednesday 12 March 1788

MS. Yale (C 790).

ADDRESS: James Boswell Esqr., Great Queen Street, Lincolns Inn Fields.

ENDORSEMENTS: Johnsonian and Alderman Clark.

New Bridge Street, 12 March 1788

DEAR SIR: I have to lament that it is out of my power to assist Mr. Temples Nephew with a presentation to Christs Hospital[2]—

[2] According to Malone, the cane, which "some one had by accident" left in SJ's house, was confiscated by Hawkins, who, unmoved by the legal arguments of his fellow-executors, refused to give it up to Barber, and later alleged that it was consumed in the fire at his house (*Johns. Glean.* ii. 53). However, JB, in recounting his interview with Hawkins on 19 Apr. of this year, writes: "He defended himself, I thought very well, from the charge of the gold-headed cane which Francis's letter mentioned" (Journ.).

[3] MS. "in"

[1] Richard Clark (1739–1831), "a gentleman for whom [SJ] deservedly

entertained a great regard" (*Life* iv. 258) was Alderman of London, 1776–98, Lord Mayor in 1784, and City Chamberlain, 1798–1831.

[2] Temple had written to JB on 18 Feb. for his help in placing the ten-year-old son of his widowed sister in Christ's Hospital. JB replied on the 24th that he had received from his brother David "a list of the governours, so many of whom marked with asterisks have a right (about once in two years) to present a boy not a son of a freeman of London; and amongst these I find Alderman Clark, who was a friend of Dr. Johnson's, to whom I shall apply" (*Letters JB* 248). See also *ibid.* ii. 354, 367.

mine has been long engaged or it should have been much at your Service.

About a week ago I called at your House to inform you that I had pick'd up two or three Notes of our Friend Dr. Johnson[3]—if you will do me the favor to call upon [me] when you have occasion to come this way I shall be happy to communicate them to you. I am, Dear Sir, Your faithful humble Servant

R. Clark

To Francis Barber, Thursday 20 March 1788

MS. The Johnson Birthplace.

London, 20 March 1788

Dear Sir: I thank you for your attention. Be so good as to send me the Diploma which you have by first sure opportunity, directed to me No. 56 Great Queen Street Lincolns Inn Fields.

And as I cannot specify exactly what papers Sir John Hawkins may yet have, you[1] will please to write to me thus

> Sir. I hereby authorise you to demand from Sir John Hawkins all books or papers of any sort which belonged to the late Dr. Samuel Johnson, that may be in his possession, and your receipt to him shall be sufficient on my account as residuary legatee. I am Sir, your most humble servant

Let this be copied over in your own hand, dated and signed and addressed to me. I give you a great deal of trouble; but I am very desireous to collect all I can concerning your excellent Master. I enclose you the funeral sermon which he composed for Mrs. Johnson.[2] You will read it with serious advantage I doubt not.

---

[3] Seven letters from SJ to Clark have been recovered (*Letters SJ passim*). JB prints only one, that of 27 Jan. 1784 notifying him of his turn as president of the Essex Head Club (*Life* iv. 258). On one occasion SJ too had requested Clark's support of a candidate for Christ's Hospital (*Letters SJ* 574.2).

---

[1] MS. "have. You"

[2] *A Sermon, Written by the Late Samuel Johnson, LL.D. for the Funeral of His Wife*, published this month by the Rev. Samuel Hayes. See *Life* i. 241. Taylor appears to have told Mrs. Piozzi (*Letters To and From Johnson* ii. 384–85) that he refused, first, to compose the sermon, second, to preach it, and third, to publish it—all on the grounds of his disrespect for Mrs. Johnson's character. Cf. Murphy: *Johns. Misc.* i 476.

My compliments to Mrs. Barber. I am Dear Sir, your sincere freind

JAMES BOSWELL

Put your letters to me under cover of J. B. Garforth Esq. M.P. London.

From Francis Barber, Wednesday 2 April 1788

MS. Yale (C 67). Received 5 Apr. (Reg. Let.).
ADDRESS: James Boswell Esqr.

Lichfield, wed. April[1] the 2: 1788

SIR: I would have complyed with your request immidiately but having had return of my old complaint,[2] and not having a convenient opportunity of sending the Diploma prevented me from writing till now; a few days ago having mention'd the above affair to mr. Green he recommended me to a Gentleman who will take care to delivere it safe to you, he I beleive leave Lichfield the Latter end of this week. My disorder together with that of three of my Children lately having had the Small pox, has been very expensive to me, so that I am at present rather distressed, and find some difficulty to discharge my Rent for this year; for which reason I shall ever acknowledge as a particular favour if you would advance me Ten pound (which I will repay as I can turn myself about) to release me from my present uneasy situation. I am sir, your sincere humble servant

FRANCIS BARBER

P.S. I return you many thanks for the Sermon you sent me which I will read with attention as soon as I am able.

Sir: I hereby autherrise to demand from Sir John Hawkins all Books or papers of any sort which belonged to my late Master Dr. Samuel Johnson, that may be in his possession, and receipt to him

---

[1] MS. "March"
[2] "He [SJ] says the boy is a sickly lad, of a delicate frame, and particularly sub- ject to a malady in his throat" (Smollett to Wilkes, 16 Mar. 1759; quoted, *Life* i. 349).

277

shall be sufficient on my account as residuary Legatee. I am sir, your most humble Servant

F. BARBER

To Francis Barber, Friday 11 April 1788

MS. The Johnson Birthplace.

London, 11 April 1788

DEAR SIR: I have received both your letters, and shall demand from Sir John Hawkins what papers or Books you have authorised me to receive.

As I am very sensible of your obliging disposition towards me, I am glad that I can accomodate you with the sum which you want, for which I enclose you a Bank Post Bill.

Please to deliver the enclosed to Miss Seward, and to present my best compliments to Mr. Green.

Some of your old Master's friends have thought that your opening a little shop for a few books and stationary wares in Lichfield might be a good thing for you. You may consult, and consider of it. I am, Dear Sir, your sincere friend

JAMES BOSWELL

Write to me under cover of J. B. Garforth Esq. M.P. London.

To Anna Seward, Friday 11 April 1788

MS. The Johnson Birthplace. MS. Yale (L 1152): JB's copy, headed: "To Miss Seward."

London, 11 April[1] 1788

. . . What a variety of publications have there been concerning Johnson. Never was there a Man whose reputation remained so long in such luxuriant freshness, as his does. How very envious of this do the "little stars" of Literature seem to be, though bright

---

[1] Misdated 11 Mar. in the copy: perhaps influenced by Barber's error (*ante* 2 Apr. 1788).

themselves in their due proportion.[2] My Life of that illustrious Man has been retarded by several avocations, as well as by depression of mind.[3] But I hope to have it ready for the press next month. I flatter myself it will exhibit him more completely than any person ancient or modern has yet been preserved, and whatever merit I may be allowed, the World will at least owe to my assiduity the possession of a rich intellectual treasure. . . .

From William Johnson Temple, Monday 14 April 1788

MS. Yale (C 2858).

G[luvias] V[icarage,] 14th April, 1788

MY DEAR BOSWELL, I wish your account of Mrs. Piozzis publication, or rather imposition had come sooner; but I thought the woman had a greater regard for her friends memory than to give us any thing of his that would not increase his celebrity: I suppose the literate Signora could not resist the temptation of making it known how much She was in the Criticks thoughts: I do not like her at all and can hardly suppose she felt either for her husband, her children or the man she affected so much to admire. Do not you observe that his own account and Hawkins account of his paralytic seizure do not quite agree?[1] Though the Letters are trifling and such as any sensible person would write to one whom he regarded and at whose house he wished to be well received, yet they bear all the marks of a good mind, and now and then *The Idler* and *The Rambler* break in upon us. Indeed nobody but a vain woman or needy collector would have thought of obtruding such trifles on the publick. The subject of those from the Hebrides had already been anticipated by your and his *Tour* and there is nothing in the others that one wishes to know—Certainly every thing now has appeared

---

[2] Notably Miss Seward herself? With "little stars" cf. Pope's *Moral Essay III, To Lord Bathurst*, lines 281–82:
Blush, Grandeur, blush! proud courts, withdraw your blaze!
Ye little Stars! hide your diminished rays.
[3] Earlier in the letter JB complains of "bad spirits on account of my Wife's

suffering under a long and alarming illness".

---

[1] Letter CCCI (19 June 1783); Hawkins, pp. 557–58. JB gives the "very full and accurate accounts in letters written by himself" (including the one to Mrs. Thrale), *Life* iv. 228 ff.

that can be of any use, and if not interrupted by the business of your profession, you can have no excuse for not going forward with your great work. You say you abound in Letters, I hope of a very different description from those that have teased us so. I do not think Mason envied Johnson; he only disliked him on account of his insensibility to the excellence of his friends poetry.[2] . . .

To Sir John Hawkins, Wednesday 16 April 1788

MS. Yale (L 634). JB's copy, headed: "To Sir John Hawkins Knight."

Great Queen Street, Lincolns Inn Fields, 16 April 1788

SIR: I have received a letter from Mr. Francis Barber residuary legatee of the late Dr. Samuel Johnson, authorising me to demand from you all books or papers of any sort which belonged to him, that may be in your possession.

You will be pleased to appoint a time when I shall wait upon you to receive them. I am Sir your most humble servant

From Sir John Hawkins, Thursday 17 April 1788

MS. Yale (C 1511). Written, except for the signature, by (presumably) Hawkins's eldest son: see Journ. 19 Apr.

ADDRESS: James Boswell Esq.

[Westminster,] 17th April 1788

SIR,   I have no Books that belonged to Dr. Johnson in my possession; the printed ones are sold, and the value of them accounted for.[1] Those in manuscript, that is to say his Diaries and Notes, have been delivered to Mr. Nichols.[2] Two or three Pamphlets and a few useless Papers are all that remain, and those I wish to be rid of, and shall be ready to deliver to you, on the production of the Order

---

[2] SJ was no more sensible of the excellence of Mason's poetry than Gray's: see *Life* ii. 334–35, iii. 32.

[1] For the sale of SJ's library, see *Life* iv. 405 n., 444–45.

[2] See *ante* From Barber, 9 July 1787, n. 1.

of Mr. Francis Barber, on Saturday next at 6 in the evening.[3]
I am, Sir, Your very humble Servant

JOHN HAWKINS

From Anna Seward, c. 3–4 May 1788

Missing. Sent to London from Lichfield. Received 5 May (Reg. Let.).:
"Miss Seward, a long dissertation against Dr. Johnson etc."

To Edmond Malone, Monday 17 November 1788

MS. Yale (L 940).
ADDRESS: To Edmond Malone Esq., Cobham Park, Surrey.
POSTMARK: NO 17 88.

London, 17 Novr. 1788

. . . During all this time I have laboured at the *Life*, and what I wonder at, have done very well. I am now half done with 1783, so that there remains no more but a year and a half of the first draught to do. But then the Conversation with the King is to be formed into a complete Scene out of the various minutes[1]—my Correspondence with him is to be excerpted—and the whole series of the Composition is to be revised and polished. I intend to make a Skeleton of the Whole, or a Table of Contents in the chronological order, and have it examined by some of the most Johnsonian freinds and by steady Reed[2]—that any omissions may be supplied. Cadel whom I met in the street the other day, raised my hopes by

[3] " . . . Sir John and I settled the business, which we did in perfect good humour. . . . There were but three pamphlets, the three diplomas of degrees from Dublin and Oxford, and a few papers for which I gave a receipt 'as witness my hand at Westminster.' We sat most serenely opposite to each other in armchairs, and I declare, he talked so well, and with such a courteous formality, that every five minutes I unloosed a knot of the critical cat o'nine tails which I had prepared for him. I staid above an hour. How much might human violence and enmity be lessened if men who fight with their pens at a distance, would but commune together calmly face to face. . . . I thought I would spare Hawkins as much as I in justice could" (Journ. 19 Apr.).

[1] *Life* ii. 33–42, 34 n. 1. See *ante* Introduction, p. xlvii, note.
[2] Isaac Reed. See *post* To and From Reed, 21 Apr. 1790.

saying he was convinced mine would be the only Life that would be prefixed to Johnson's Works.[3] I forgot to mention another operation that remains to be performed which is selecting and arranging in proper places the Memorabilia furnished by Langton[,] Maxwell, Steevens[,] Seward. You see my freind Richard is himself again.[4] . . . I shall work assiduously to get my Magnum Opus concluded. It will be something for me to rest upon. . . .

To Sir William Forbes, Friday 12 December 1788

MS. estate of the late Lord Clinton. The *Life* has been interrupted by political, legal and convivial activities. He has reached June 1784 and hopes to publish next May.

[3] The successor to Hawkins's *Life* in the early editions of SJ's *Works* was Arthur Murphy's *Essay* (1792 and following). J. D. Fleeman informs me that JB's *Life* was prefixed to an edition of the *Works* printed at Alnwick in 1816 and re-issued in London in 1818.—Cadell (with W. Davies) succeeded Dilly as the publisher of JB's *Life*, from the fourth through the eighth editions, 1804–16.

[4] Quoting Colley Cibber's *King Richard III* (1700), Act V.

1789

To *William Johnson Temple,*
Saturday 10 January 1789

MS. Pierpont Morgan Library.

London, 10 Janry. 1789

. . . I am now very near the conclusion of my rough draught of
Johnson's *Life.* On Saturday I finished the Introduction and Dedication to Sir Joshua both of which had appeared very difficult to be
accomplished. I am confident they are well done. Whenever I have
completed the rough draught, by which I mean the Work without
nice correction, Malone and I are to prepare one half perfectly, and
then it goes to press, where I hope to have it early in february so
as to be out by the end of May. . . .

To *William Johnson Temple,*
Thursday 5 March 1789

MS. Pierpont Morgan Library.

ADDRESS: To The Reverend Mr. William Johnson Temple, Gluvias
Viccarage.

London, 5 March 1789

. . . Pray (by return of post) help me with a word. In censuring Sir
J. Hawkins's Book I say "there is throughout the whole of it a
dark uncharitable cast which puts the most unfavourable construction on allmost every circumstance of my illustrious freinds conduct." Malone maintains *cast* will not do. He will have malignancy.[1]
Is not that too strong. How would disposition do? Hawky is no
doubt very malignant. Observe how he talks of me as if quite unknown.[2]

I have the pleasure to tell you, that a part of my Magnum Opus
is now ready for the press, and that I shall probably begin to print
next week. . . .

---

[1] JB kept "cast" (*Life* i. 28).
[2] "Mr. James Boswell, a native of Scotland" (p. 472). See *Life* i. 190 n. 4.

From *William Johnson Temple,* Sunday 8 March 1789

MS. Yale (C 2867).

ADDRESS: James Boswell Esqr.

G[luvias] V[icarage,] March 8th 1789

. . . I cannot say I dislike your word *cast* and you have Johnsons authority for it. How do you like, The whole book is tinctured with such a spirit of dark, uncharitable *ungenerous uncandid* INSINUATION as puts— or, such a dark, etc. *insinuation pervades* or *tinctures* the whole book—volume as p⟨uts—⟩ Notwithstanding the Biographers commenda⟨tion⟩ of your friend it is certainly jaundiced ⟨with⟩ a deep tincture of malignity and he richly deserves your censure. . . .

To the Rev. Dr. Hugh Blair, Friday 13 March 1789

Missing. Sent to Edinburgh from London. Reg. Let.: "Rev. Dr. Hugh Blair, for the *date* of a conversation of Dr. Johnson's at the Crown and Anchor . . ."

To Mrs. Mary Cobb, Saturday 14 March 1789

MS. Yale (L 374). JB's copy, headed: "To Mrs. Cobb at Lichfield."

London, 14 March 1789

DEAR MADAM: I am very soon to put my *Life of Dr. Johnson* to the press, and being exceedingly desireous to have as much authenticity as I possibly can obtain, even in the slighter circumstances, I take the liberty of troubling you with this inquiry to ascertain whether it is not related upon good authority that when he solicited his Mother's consent to his marriage with Mrs. Porter and mentioned that "he had told her the worst of him" he said among other things "I have had an uncle hanged"[1] and if he did say so, pray

[1] *Ante* From Seward, 25 Mar. 1785 (end).

286

what uncle was that? or was it said jestingly. You will oblige me much by a speedy answer and I trust you will forgive this freedom for the sake of its motive.

I beg to have my compliments presented to Miss Adye. I am etc.

From the Rev. Dr. Hugh Blair, Wednesday 18 March 1789

MS. Yale (C 164).

ADDRESS: James Boswell of Auchinleck Esqr.

Argyle Square, [Edinburgh,] 18 March 1789

MY DEAR SIR: I am happy to learn that we are at length to have your *Life of Dr. Johnson* from which I expect a great deal of Entertainment. I am not fond of being much brought into publick View, and therefore hope that you will not introduce me without Necessity. Your Anecdote about *the Cow*, in a former Publication,[1] tho' harmless in it self, was very unnecessary and exposed me to some Laughter. My Connection with the Dr. was not such as gives occasion for my making any figure in this work, and therefore I expect either not to find my self in it at all, or at most, for very little.

I Remember very well my having Supp'd at the Crown & Anchor Tavern with the Dr. and You and some other Company, the last time I was in London. It was in 1768, and tho' from any memorandums I have by me I cannot ascertain the day yet I am sure it was about the beginning of June in that Year; and at that date you may certainly fix it.[2] . . .

From Mrs. Mary Cobb, Wednesday 18 March 1789

MS. Yale (C 796). In the hand of Mary Adey. Received 20 Mar. (Reg. Let.).

ADDRESS: James Boswell Esqr.

Lichfield, March th[e] 18th 1789

MY DEAR SIR: I am Sorry I cannot give you any Intelligence of Doctor Johnsons Uncle.

---

[1] The *Tour* (*Life* v. 396 and n. 4).   [2] *Life* ii. 63.

I have made diligent Enquiry of the *oldest* of his Market Street[1] Neighbors. None of them ever remember to have heard of the circumstance that he had an Uncle hang'd, nor can I learn the name, or *who* that Uncle was.[2] I am Inclined to think it might be Said jestingly. Suppose you was to apply to his old Friend Mr. Hector of Birmingham. Perhaps he might procure you better Information.

I hope Soon to have the Pleasure of Perusing your Book. I Shall read it with Satisfaction, as I know you are a Friend to *truth*. Miss Adey unites with me in respectful Compliments and good Wishes. I am Dear Sir, Your Sincere Friend and Humble Servant

MARY COBB

I hope Mrs. Boswell and your Family are Well.

To Mrs. Mary Cobb, Friday 27 March 1789

MS. Yale (L 375). JB's copy.

London, 27 March 1789

DEAR MADAM: I am much obliged to you for your speedy answer. The story of a conversation between Dr. Johnson and his Mother concerning his marriage with Mrs. Porter was communicated to me as having been *told by Mrs. Cobb*.[1] As I find my authority quite erroneous in one remarkable particular, I cannot trust to it for any part. I therefore Madam presume to beg that you yourself will be pleased to inform me whether[2] there really was any such conversation? and if there was, who related it? and what was it?

I offer my best compliments to Miss Adye, and again intreating your pardon for so much trouble, I remain, Madam, Your most obedient humble servant

[1] Or Sadler Street, where SJ was born.
[2] The story remains unsupported. See *Reades*, pp. 154, 234.

[1] This attribution does not appear in Miss Seward's letter, in the state in which we have it (*ante* 25 Mar. 1785, end).
[2] MS. "whethere"

From Mrs. Mary Cobb,
Sunday 29 March 1789

MS. Yale (C 797). In the hand of Mary Adey.

ADDRESS: James Boswell Esqr.

Lichfield, 29 March 1789

MY DEAR SIR: I do not think it a trouble to answer any question you may Ask relating to our good Doctor Johnson. I will answer you with truth and to the best of my rememberance.

I cannot recollect any conversation which past between Doctor Johnson and his Mother concerning his Marriage with Mrs. Porter. *If* I *ever* heard any, it has totally Escaped my Memory.[1] Many things are repeated in Lichfield as being *told* or *Said* by Mrs. Cobb, and not a Syllable of truth in any one of them. I verily believe he never had an Uncle hang'd. I have enquired *Again* and *Again* of the *oldest* Inhabitants of this Place but cannot learn the Smallest circumstance of it—*had* it been So, it wou'd *certainly* have been remember'd, for So faulty is poor human Nature that our misfortunes and our faults are more frequently recorded than the virtues of ourselves or our Ancestors.

[1] In the course of the quarrel between JB and Miss Seward following the publication of the *Principal Corrections and Additions* to the first edition of the *Life* (*Gent. Mag.* Oct.–Dec. 1793), JB observed: "Another story, which she sent me, was a very extraordinary fact, said to have been mentioned in a conversation between his mother and him, on the subject of his marrying Mrs. Porter, which appeared to me so strange as to require confirmation. Miss Seward having quoted, as her authority for it, a respectable Lady of Lichfield, I wrote to that lady, without mentioning the name of the person from whom the report was derived, inquiring only as to the authenticity of it. The lady informed me that she had never heard of the fact alluded to" (*Gent. Mag.*, Nov. 1793, lxiii. 1009). Miss Seward replied: "The conversation which young Johnson is reported to have held with his mother, when he asked her consent to marry the widow Porter, and which formed one of the anecdotes, I sent to Mr. Boswell, and which he suppressed, I have heard frequently and generally mentioned, and credited here. I forget whether or not I quoted to *him* any particular authority for that memoir—yet, to the best of my remembrance, I heard it first from the late Mrs. Cobb, of this place. If I were asked who told me that Johnson said of Chesterfield, 'he is a wit among lords, and a lord among wits,' I should find it difficult to specify an individual from the numbers whom I have heard repeat the sarcasm. Neither can I *now* with *certainty* in this instance—but I never doubted the reality of either story, because there is the Johnsonian spirit in both" (*ibid.* Dec. 1793, lxiii. 1099). Croker (1831, i. 5 n. 1) traced this apocryphal story back to the Rev. Donald M'Nicol's *Remarks on Dr. Johnson's Journey to the Hebrides* (1779, p. 18). JB had included this conversation in the *Life*, as the M.S. proves, but deleted it before sending copy to the printer.

Miss Adey presents her kind Respects. I am Dear Sir, Your obliged Friend

MARY COBB

If you Praise our good Johnson Miss Seward will not love you. I hear She was Critizising the other Evening with two Boys of Eighteen,[2] and finding fault with *Pope* and *Dryden*. I have not a doubt but each thought themselves the better Poet.

Vanity of Vanity
All is Vanity!

From "an Old Officer", Thursday 18 June 1789

MS. Yale (C 2126).

ADDRESS: James Boswell Esq., at Mr. Dillys, Bookseller, in the Poultry.

June 18th 1789

SIR: What You frequently promised Us, in Your entertaining *Tour* with the good and celebrated Dr. Johnson of giving the World what You have preserved of that Great Man, I hope we shall not be dissappointed of, as I am very unwilling to lose the hopes of being agreably entertained as well as improved by Your elegant mode of writing again before I die, and hope and believe You will not deprive the world of what may make it better, from the insolent behaviour of a few worthless individuals,[1] I shall therefore trouble You no farther then to say I hope You will be as good as Your word, and apologize for writing You an anonymous letter (which I have some reasons for doing) and for which I beg Your pardon— and am, Sir Your most obedient Servant—

AN OLD OFFICER

[2] Thomas Lister (1772–1828) and Henry Francis Cary (1772–1844), the translator of Dante, though not yet eighteen, were both protégés of Miss Seward at this time. See *Seward Letters* ii. *passim*; Margaret Ashmun, *The Singing Swan*, 1931, pp. 156 ff.; DNB (for Cary) and Burke's *Landed Gentry*, 1937, p. 1381 and *Alum. Cant.* (for Lister). Lister was employed by Francis Cobb (1724–1807), Mrs. Cobb's stepson, a wealthy Lichfield banker (Ashmun, p. 156; *Johns. Glean.* viii. 169).

[1] The reference is to the abuse of JB in the newspapers. See Lucyle Werkmeister, *Jemmie Boswell and the London Daily Press, 1785–1795* (1963).

To *William Johnson Temple,*
Saturday, Monday 28, 30 November 1789

MS. Pierpont Morgan Library.

London, 28 Novr.[1] 1789

. . . My apology for not coming to you as I fully intended and wished is really a sufficient one; for, the revision of my *Life of Johnson* by so acute and knowing a critick as Mr. Malone is of most essential consequence especially as he is *Johnsonianissimus*, and as he is to hasten to Ireland as soon as his *Shakspeare* is fairly published, I must avail myself of him *now*.[2] His hospitality—and my other invitations—and particularly my attendance at Lord Lonsdale's have lost us many evenings; but I reckon that a third of the Work is *settled*, so that I shall get to press very soon. You cannot imagine what labour, what perplexity what vexation I have endured in arranging a prodigious multiplicity of materials, in supplying omissions, in searching for papers buried in different masses—and all this besides the exertion of composing and polishing. Many a time have I thought of giving it up. However though I shall be uneasily sensible of its many deficiencies it will certainly be to the World a very valuable and peculiar Volume of Biography, full of literary and characteristical Anecdotes (which word by the way Johnson always condemned as used in the sense that the french and we from them use it, as signifying particulars)[3] told with authenticity and in a lively manner. Would that it were in the Booksellers shops. Methinks if I had this *Magnum Opus* launched, the Publick has no farther claim upon me; for I have promised no more, and I may die in peace, or retire into dull obscurity—reddarque tenebris.[4] Such is the gloomy *ground* of my mind, that any agreable perceptions have an uncommon though but a momentary brightness. . . .

---

[1] "30 Novr." appears at the top of the second page.

[2] JB was over-anxious (and Malone over-optimistic): the work was not published until a year (and a day) later.

[3] Tinker noted, *Letters JB* ii. 382: "In 1755 Johnson defined the word as 'something yet unpublished; secret history'.

According to the *New English Dictionary*, the more common meaning entered the language about 1760. This meaning is recognized by Johnson in the fourth edition of his *Dictionary* (1773)."

[4] "and be returned to the darkness" (*Aeneid* vi. 545).

To Francis Barber,
Wednesday 16 December 1789

Missing. Sent to Lichfield from London. Reg. Let.: "Mr. Francis Barber for a little information about his old Master." Enclosed in the following.

To Richard Greene,
Wednesday 16 December 1789

Missing. Sent to Lichfield from London. Reg. Let.: "Mr. Green, Lichfield, enclosing the above."

From the Rev. Dr. William Maxwell,
Thursday 17 December 1789

Missing. Wrapper, Yale (C 1989). Received 29 Dec. (Reg. Let.): "Rev. Dr. Maxwell (from Bath) with some more Johnsoniana." See *ante* From Maxwell, 12 May and 16 June 1787.

ADDRESS: James Boswell Esqr., Great Queen Street, Lincoln's Inn Fields, London.

POSTMARK: DE 17 89.

To the Rev. Dr. William Maxwell,
Friday 18 December 1789

Missing. Sent to Bath(?) from London. Reg. Let.: "Rev. Dr. Maxwell, that I have received his Johnsoniana."

From Francis Barber,
Sunday 20 December 1789

MS. Yale (C 68). In an unidentified hand. Received 24 Dec.; enclosed in the letter from Greene which follows (Reg. Let.).

ADDRESS: James Boswell Esqr.

ENDORSEMENT: Mr. Francis Barber 20 Decr. 1789.

Stowe Street, Lichfield, 20th Decr. 89

HONORED SIR: Agreeable to your request I have Endeavoured to give you as clear an Account of what you desire as I possibly can.[1] I first knew my late Worthy Master early in the year 1752; at my coming to Live with him, I found that Mrs. Johnson was Dead and was Buried about a fortnight, at which period Lord Southwell and my Master were very intimate and Visited each other strictly,[2] as also the Earl of Cork, who then resided in the South side of Lincoln Inn Fields, but cannot recollect the other Gentleman whom you mentioned.

I am extreamly glad that I can oblige you with the Inscription you requested which I have Copied and here inclose, and shall ever be happy to obey any Command wherein I am Capable by any means to give you satisfaction.

Soon after the Death of my Master I made a Journey to Lichfield, in order to take a House, at which time I took the Ring with an intent to Present to Mrs. Porter, being her Mother's Wedding Ring, but she refused accepting the same, and upon my return to Town I had it Enamiled and converted into a Mourning one for my Wife to wear in rememberance of my Master, which she now has in her possession.[3]

Mr. Joddril[4] some time ago, did me the unexpected honor to call upon me, from whom I learned that Sir Joshua, had lost the sight of one Eye, and very likely to lose the other,[5] for which I am extreamly sorry and hope his Case will prove more favorable which with my Earnest Wishes for a continuance of your Health and falicity, I beg leave to Subscribe myself—Your sincere humble Servant

FRANCIS BARBER

[1] Cf. JB's record of Barber's earlier account (*ante* 15 July 1786).

[2] I suppose "regularly" is meant.

[3] *Life* i. 237. The ring, now at the Johnson Birthplace, bears the engraved inscription "Saml Johnson L:L:D: OB: 13 Dec: 1784 AE. 75" (*Johns. Glean.* ii. 56).

[4] Richard Paul Jodrell (1745–1831), classical scholar and dramatist. He was thought to be the last surviving member of the Essex Head Club. See *Life* iv. 437–38; Journ. 22 Feb. 1786, 28 Mar. 1787.

[5] Despite his fears he was spared total blindness (C. R. Leslie and Tom Taylor, *Life and Times of Sir Joshua Reynolds*, 1865, ii. 626). In a letter to Sir William Forbes, 7 Nov. 1789 (estate of the late Lord Clinton), JB gives a detailed report of Sir Joshua's condition and appearance, and identifies the affliction as a *gutta serena* (amaurosis). See Burton Chance, M.D., "Sir Joshua Reynolds and His Blindness and Death," *Annals of Medical History*, 3rd ser., 1939, i. 487–506.

[Enclosure][6]

eheu!
Eliz: Johnson,
nupta. Jul. 9°, 1735.
mortua.   eheu!
Mart. 17°. 1752

From Richard Greene, Tuesday 22 December 1789

MS. Yale (C 1399). Received 24 Dec. (Reg. Let.).

ADDRESS: James Boswell Esqr.

ENDORSEMENT: Mr. Greene Lichfield that he has Dutch weights that belonged to Dr. Johnson.

Lichfield, 22 Dec. 1789

DEAR SIR: I Sent your Letter to F. Barber, and yesterday, received the enclosed[1] *Sealed*: He assures me he has Sent you an exact transcript, I hope you will find it according to your wishes: I should have been better pleased had he permitted my perusal: I Shall my dear Sir, be happy to render you any Service that falls in my Way.

Frank, about a Year Since, presented me with a neat, ancient Box, with a triangular pair of Money-Scales, with 30 Square Brass Weights, Stamped with the Name of each Coin, the date 1656, What use the Dr. made of them I know not or whether he understood the Language: Dutch.[2] They occupy a place in my Museum, but if, as having once been his property they may prove acceptable

---

[6] The inscription, as JB explains (*Life* i. 237), was written on a slip of paper pasted on the inside of a round wooden box in which SJ kept his wife's wedding-ring after her death. Barber's copy is partly written and partly printed on a circular piece of paper about two inches in diameter, and was designed to reproduce the appearance of the original (see next letter), which is now lost. —Barber

transmitted to Strahan one, and perhaps more, of the prayers which SJ composed on his wife's death: see *Diaries*, p. 44 and n.

---

[1] The preceding letter.

[2] SJ took up the study of Dutch twice: in 1773 and again in 1782 (*Life* ii. 263, iv. 21). See also *ibid*. iii. 235.

I shall readily present them to you.[3] I am, with the greatest Sincerity, Dear Sir, your much Obliged Obedient Servant

RICHD. GREENE

Mrs. Greene and my Son[4] join in wishing you the compliments of the Season.

I much wish to see your account of the Doctor.

To Mary, Dowager Countess of Rothes,[1] Wednesday 23 December 1789

MS. F. Hamilton Lacey, Esq. of Sussex (1950); transcribed from a copy.

London, 23 Decr. 1789

DEAR MADAM, I hope Mr. Langton received my letter [in] which I returned thanks for that with which I was honoured by your Ladyship. As I am uncertain where he now is I take the liberty of addressing this to your Ladyship though it refers to particulars which he only can answer. . . . My *Life of Dr. Johnson* is at last very near being put to the press. I am at a loss for a small circumstance or two. When Mr. Langton was asked to look his watch at Oxford and see how much time there was for writing an *Idler* before the post went out, was it half an hour? or how long?[2]

What year was Dr. Johnson at Langton?

Who was the General that was very civil to him at Warley Common and what remark did Johnson make?

What is the *gentlest* account of Sir John Hawkins's putting up a Manuscript Volume of Johnson's and what followed? What were Johnson's various remarks?[3] . . .

---

[3] This is the last extant letter in the correspondence. The eventual disposition of the "Dutch weights" is not known.

[4] That is, the second Mrs. Greene (Theodosia Webb) and their son (his fifth, her only child), Thomas Webb Greene (1763–1842), a Lichfield surgeon (*Johns. Glean.* viii. 156–57).

[1] Mary, Dowager Countess of Rothes (c. 1743–1820), wife of Bennet Langton.

She is said to have been very angry with JB for giving a false, albeit anonymous, account of her domestic economy in the *Life* (iii. 300). See Clifford, *Piozzi*, p. 358.

[2] The first three of JB's queries are answered by Langton in his letter of 16 Apr. 1790 (*post*).

[3] See *Life* iv. 406 n. 1, and *ante* To Brocklesby, 18 Dec. 1784, n. 3.

To Frederick Howard, Earl of Carlisle,[1] Tuesday 29 December 1789

MS. Yale (L 355). JB's copy.

Queen Anne Street West, Tuesday 29 Decr. 1789

Mr. Boswell presents his respectful compliments to Lord Carlisle, and though he has not the honour of being known to his Lordship, presumes to request the favour of a copy of a letter which he is informed by Sir Joshua Reynolds[2] was written by Dr. Johnson concerning his Lordship's Tragedy,[3] and to have permission to insert it in the Life of Johnson which he is preparing for the press.

Mr. Boswell has taken care to record the liberal terms in which Dr. Johnson praised Lord Carlisle's Poems.[4] If there be any impropriety in the present application, trusting to the general courtesy of Literature, it is hoped that Lord Carlisle will be good enough to forgive it.

From Frederick Howard, Earl of Carlisle, Thursday 31 December 1789

MS. Yale (C 759).

ADDRESS: J. Boswell Esqre., Queen Anne St. West.

ENDORSEMENT: Earl of Carlisle.

Gros[veno]r Place, 31 Decr.

SIR: The paper to which your letter refers has been by some accident mislaid, but I trust I shall find it in the course of the day, and

[1] Frederick Howard (1748–1825), fifth Earl of Carlisle, statesman and poet; Lord Lieutenant of Ireland, 1780–82. He was Byron's first cousin once removed and his guardian.

[2] Carlisle composed complimentary verses upon Reynolds's resignation of the presidency of the Royal Academy in 1790, and served as a pallbearer at his funeral in 1792 (Leslie and Taylor, *Reynolds* ii. 557–58, 632).

[3] The letter, dated 28 Nov. 1783, was written to Mrs. Chapone (see *post* 27 Feb. 1791); the tragedy was *The Father's Re-*

venge. The substance and much of the phraseology of the present letter recur in JB's introduction to SJ's letter, *Life* iv. 246–47. SJ wrote two other letters to Mrs. Chapone on the same subject (*Letters SJ* 759.2 and 906.1).

[4] "Johnson praised the Earl of Carlisle's Poems, which his Lordship had published with his name, as not disdaining to be a candidate for literary fame. My friend was of opinion, that when a man of rank appeared in that character, he deserved to have his merit handsomely allowed" (*Life* iv. 113–14).

will, if no objections present themselves to the exposition of its contents, obey your commands, and enclose it to you.

You will much oblige me if you will permit The Revd. Dr. Coombe to be the bearer of the paper to you when found. For which purpose he will call upon you to morrow or the next day at any hour you will appoint.[1] Dr. Coombe lives at No. 93, High St. Marybone. I am Sir your most obedient humble Servant

CARLISLE

From Robert Mylne,[1]
Thursday 31 December 1789

MS. Yale (C 2068).

ENDORSEMENT: Mr. Mylne.

New River head—Islington, 31st Decr. 1789

DEAR SIR: I delayed till now, sending you the paper, I promised,[2] in expectation of getting it copied for you.

But, I am now Obliged, to send it you, in a rough state, such as it is. The left hand Column, was Copied by a Young Girl, out of Hawkins book; and the Notes are blended, along with text. You will see easily, by looking into his book, how it ought to have stood. The Right hand Column, is, what has occurred to me, in as concise a manner, to make you understand. More might have been said, but to you it would be useless. For the Publick, there is too much. If you don't understand, any part of it, I will wait on you. And when you have done with it, I beg you will return it me, as I have no Copy. I am Dear Sir Your much Obliged Servant

ROBERT MYLNE

[1] See *post* To Coombe, 6 Jan. 1790, n. 1.

[1] Robert Mylne (1734–1811), architect and engineer, was the son of Thomas Mylne, city surveyor of Edinburgh and the designer of the Edinburgh Infirmary. See Journ. 23 Nov. 1762 and 6 and 8 Sept. 1774. In the *Life* (i. 351 n. 1) JB notes that SJ "lived with that gentleman upon very agreeable terms of acquaintance, and dined with him at his house".

[2] Neither JB's journal nor Mylne's diary (*Robert Mylne*, ed. A. E. Richardson, 1955) mentions this engagement.

An undated deleted memorandum in the Yale Collection reads: "Write to Milne New River Head about Blackfriars Bridge." Hawkins (pp. 373 ff.) had criticized SJ's participation in the controversy over the design for Blackfriars Bridge in 1759. JB could safely turn to Mylne, the architect who gained the commission, because, while SJ opposed Mylne's design, Hawkins was equally critical of both. In a long note, *Life* i. 351 n. 1, JB defends both SJ and Mylne, in a way which betrays professional assistance—doubtless the missing enclosure to the present letter.

1790

To the Rev. Dr. Thomas Coombe,[1]
Wednesday 6 January 1790

MS. Yale (L 378). JB's copy, headed: "To The Rev. Dr. Coombe."

Queen Anne Street, 6 Janry. 1790

REVEREND SIR: I return the letter, of which I have taken a copy.[2] Upon the expression "a second time" I have made a note thus[:] "Dr. Johnson having been very ill when the Tragedy was first sent to him, he returned it unopened"—Or shall it be *he declined the consideration of it*"[3]—Or is there any better mode of mentioning the fact?

Enclosed is what I intend as my introduction to the letter.[4] You will be pleased to shew it to My Lord Carlisle, that it may be revised and corrected, and if his Lordship will suggest any thing else that he would like better, it shall be adopted. I wish to have the name of the Tragedy, and if it be not presuming too much, I should esteem it a great favour to be indulged with a reading of it.[5]

I beg Sir that you may present my very grateful acknowledgements to Lord Carlisle for his obliging compliance with my request, and I hope you will give me leave to cultivate that acquaintance with you which I have had the good fortune accidentally to obtain.[6] I am Reverend Sir, Your most obedient humble servant

[1] "Saturday 2 January. The Rev. Dr. Coombe, an American who had been Chaplain to Lord Carlisle when Lord Lieutenant of Ireland, waited on me with Dr. Johnson's letter on his Lordship's Tragedy, and drank tea with me. I found him to be a pleasing, well informed man, and very Johnsonian" (Journ.). Thomas Coombe, D.D. (1747–1822), born and educated in Philadelphia, was ordained in the Church of England in 1769. Though he was an advocate of the cause of the Colonies, his ordination oath prevented him from a complete endorsement of the Declaration of Independence, and in 1779 he removed to England, where he passed the rest of his life. After serving the Earl of Carlisle, Coombe became successively chaplain in ordinary to the King, prebendary of Canterbury, and rector to the united London parishes of St. Michael's

Queenhithe and Trinity the Less. He was the author of some poems, including *The Peasant of Auburn, or the Emigrant* (1783), suggested by *The Deserted Village* (DAB).

[2] Paper Apart for MS. *Life*, p. 919 (*Life* iv. 247–48).

[3] The latter: *Life* iv. 247 n. 2. SJ did return it unopened: see *Letters SJ* 759.2.

[4] Not copied. See *ante* To Carlisle, 29 Dec. 1789 and n. 3.

[5] The play was first published in 1783, and was not reprinted until 1800 (*Life* iv. 526). JB notes: "A few copies only of this tragedy have been printed, and given to the authour's friends" (*ibid.* 247 n. 1). This information, together with the name of the tragedy, was probably contained in Coombe's missing reply.

[6] There is no further mention of Coombe in the journal, nor any record of correspondence with him after this date.

From Thomas Steele,[1]
Wednesday 13 January 1790

MS. Yale (C 2542).

ADDRESS: To James Boswell Esq., Queen Ann Street West.

FRANK: Thos. Steele.

ENDORSEMENT: Thomas Steele Esq.

Treasury Chambers, Jan. 13. 1790

Mr. Steele presents his Compliments to Mr. Boswell, he has directed every possible search to be made in the Records of the Treasury and Secretary of State's Office, but he can find no trace whatever of any Warrant having been issued to apprehend the Author of a Pamphlet entitled *Marmor Norfolciense*.[2]

To Sir David Dalrymple, Lord Hailes,[1]
Monday 18 January 1790

Missing. Sent to Edinburgh from London. Reg. Let.: "Lord Hailes, that my life of Johnson is in the press. May I mention some sheets of his Lordship's *Annals* having been corrected by Johnson."

From Sir David Dalrymple, Lord Hailes,
Sunday 24 January 1790

MS. Yale (C 1477). Received 29 Jan. (Reg. Let.).

ADDRESS: James Boswell Esqr.

ENDORSEMENT: Lord Hailes 24 Janry. 1790.

---

[1] Thomas Steele (1753–1823), M.P. for Chichester, 1780–1807 (Judd); joint Secretary of the Treasury, 27 Dec. 1783–91 (Robert Beatson, *A Political Index to the Histories of Great Britain & Ireland*, 1806, i. 418). At this time he was the lessee of Streatham Park (Clifford, *Piozzi*, p. 352).

[2] MS. "Nolfolciense". A deleted memorandum among JB's notes ("Additions and Revisions") for the *Life* reads: "Try Mr. Steel if there be any trace of a Warrant agt Johnson." Steele's reply is quoted in a paraphrase, *Life* i. 141, in rebuttal to Hawkins. See also Clifford, *Johnson*, pp. 213–15.

---

[1] Sir David Dalrymple, Bt. (1726–92), "now one of the Judges of Scotland by the title of Lord Hailes, had contributed much to increase my high opinion of Johnson, on account of his writings, long before I attained to a personal acquaintance with him; I, in return, had informed Johnson of Sir David's eminent character for learning and religion" (*Life* i. 432). For SJ's high opinion of Hailes, see *ibid.* 451–52.

Edinburgh, 24th Janry. 1790

DEAR SIR: You need have no scruple in saying that Dr. Johnson took the trouble of correcting many errors of language in my *Annals*, but it would be wrong to say that he corrected every thing of that nature, for, by such an assertion, the public might be led to suppose that he gave his sanction to whatever he left uncorrected.

Dr. J. never saw the notes to my *Annals* untill they appeared in print.[1]

I have often taken occasion, in conversation, to acknowledge the favour which Dr. J. conferred on me, by his undertaking so very tasteless a labour as that of correcting so long a work, especially to oblige one who [?could claim] so little acquaintance.[2]

Your work will I doubt not, be very entertaining, but I am afraid that your admiration of your friend may lead you to be too minute and to record *dicta* of little moment. I hope that you have observed an advice which I once gave, namely to remember that Dr. J. is the principal figure in the piece. . . .

To Richard Perry,[1]
Thursday 4 February 1790

MS. Yale (L 1069).

ADDRESS: To Mr. Perry, Parish Clerk of St. Andrew's, Holborn.

Queen Anne Street West No. 38, Thursday 4 febry.

SIR: In two different lives of *Richard Savage* it is said he was born 10 January 1697–8 and registered in the parish of St. Andrew's Holborn.[2] When you and I inspected the Register the other day, we could not find the name. But perhaps we did not look at the

[1] SJ's revision of Dalrymple's *Annals of Scotland* is not discussed, but it is mentioned in SJ's correspondence with JB, *Life* ii. 279 and *passim*.

[2] They were introduced at Edinburgh in 1773 (*Life* v. 48). A year and a half afterwards SJ was to refer to "Lord Hailes, whom I love better than any man whom I know so little" (*ibid.* ii. 293). It does not appear that they met a second time.

[1] Richard Perry, "an eminent undertaker, and a man of very exemplary character", was parish clerk of St. Andrew's forty-five years. He died on 30 Dec. 1805, the day after his rector, the Rev. Charles Barton, died (at Bath), and both were buried in St. Andrew's Church (*Gent. Mag.* lxxv. 1242).

[2] The anonymous *Life of Mr. Richard Savage*, 1727, p. 5, and, following it, SJ's (*Lives* ii. 323).

exact place.[3] Please to look again so as to hit the time when according to the date of the birth it is reasonable to conclude the name must appear if really there and let me know how it is, and I will call on you on saturday. I am Sir, your most humble servant

JAMES BOSWELL

From Richard Perry, c. Friday 5 February 1790

MS. Yale (C 2244). Written at the top of the preceding.

[Holborn]

SIR: I have examined the Register Books of Xings for the entry of Richard Savage from the Year 1696 to the Year 1698—do not find any such Entry. I am Sir, Your Humble Servant

RD. PERRY, p. Clk.

To Sir David Dalrymple, Lord Hailes, Thursday 11 February 1790

MS. Sir Mark Dalrymple, Bt., of Newhailes.

London, 11 Febry. 1790

MY DEAR LORD: Many thanks to you for your speedy and obliging answer, and for your kind and judicious hints for the conduct of my *Magnum Opus.*

I am now to trouble your Lordship with a minute inquiry. You no doubt are possessed of a small volume entitled *The Union or Select Scots and English Poems* printed at Edinburgh in 1753. I am pretty sure from memory that the late Mr. William Guthry[1] told

---

[3] "Read in the Parish Record of St. Andrew's and in the Inner Temple Library about Savage" (Journ. 2 Feb. 1790). ". . . it is alleged, that his Lordship gave him his own name, and had it duly recorded in the register of St. Andrew's, Holborn. I have carefully inspected that register, but no such entry is to be found" (*Life* i. 170). JB was thrown off the scent by a wrong date but more irrevocably by a confusion about the name. Savage was baptized 18 Jan. 1696–97 in Fox Court by the minister of St. Andrew's under the name of Richard Smith, son of John and Mary Smith: i.e. the *Christian* name of his reputed father, Lord Rivers, and the assumed surname of his mother. See Clarence Tracy, *The Artificial Bastard: A Biography of Richard Savage*, 1953, pp. 11, 19–20. Malone learned the facts from his friend James Bindley in time for the fifth edition of the *Life* (1807, i. 149): see *Percy-Malone Correspondence*, p. 208.

[1] See *ante* From Hussey, Aug. 1787, n. 10.

me that he was the Authour of a small piece in that collection called *The Eagle and Robin Red-breast a Fable* though it is there said to be written "by Mr. Archibald Scott, before the year 1600."[2] Your Lordship I take it for granted can inform me authentically as to this,[3] and whether the name of Archibald Scott was affixed intentionally (to make it be thought that the Poem was ancient) or by mistake. I observe there are two pieces in the volume "by a late Member of the University of Aberdeen" who it seems directed the Collection. *Who* was this Gentleman?[4] perhaps it may be known. . . . I will be very much obliged to your Lordship for an answer as to Guthry, as soon as may be; for he comes in at an early part of my *Life of Johnson*. . . .

From Sir David Dalrymple, Lord Hailes, Sunday 15 February 1790

MS. Yale (C 1478).

ADDRESS: James Boswell Esqr.

ENDORSEMENT: Lord Hailes 15 feb. 1790.

Edinburgh, 15th Feb. 1790

DEAR SIR: I recollect the Miscellany of Poems which you mention, and I suppose that I have it in the country. I supposed that *Archd. Scot* is a feigned name, and that there is no mistake in it but this that the concealed Author meant to make it pass for the work of a poet in the reign of Q. Mary and called him *Archibald* Scot instead of *Alexander*. Look in Ramsays *Evergreen*. If I recollect right the Poem is there.[1] If Mr. Guthrie was the Author he must have been

[2] Repeated, *Life* i. 117 n. 1.

[3] Hailes was the editor of *Ancient Scottish Poems Published from the MS of George Bannatyne* (1770).

[4] Thomas Warton. The collection was printed at Oxford with the fictitious imprint "Edinburgh: Printed for Archibald Monroe & David Murray". See D. Nichol Smith, "Thomas Warton's Miscellany: *The Union*", RES (1943) xix. 263–75. The pseudonymous poems are : "Ode on the Approach of Summer. By a Gentleman formerly of the University of Aberdeen" (p. 81) and " A Pastoral in the Manner of

Spenser. From Theocritus. Idyll. XX. By the Same" (p. 93). The collection included SJ's "Sprig of Myrtle," attributed to Anthony Hammond: see *Poems*, ed. Smith and McAdam, p. 93.

[1] Allan Ramsay, *The Ever Green, being a Collection of Scots Poems, Wrote by the Ingenious before 1600*, 1724, ii. 232. The name of the author is there given as "AR. SCOT."—which explains Warton's mistake. The poem is not included among the thirty-six by Alexander Scott preserved in the Bannatyne MS. (and edited by

very young at the time of its composition.[2] Mr. Guthrie was an old correspondent of mine, and I thought him very incorrect;[3] he wished to be understood as a man acquainted with every thing. As to the *Aberdeen gentleman* I know nothing about him. . . .

To *Warren Hastings*,[1]
Saturday 27 February 1790

MS. Yale (L 626). JB's draft, headed: "To Warren Hastings Esq."

Queen Anne Street West, 27 Febry. 1790

SIR: Presuming on my having met you at dinner at Sir Joshua Reynolds's[2] I did myself the honour to leave my card at your house in St. James's Place, and afterwards at your house in Wimpole Street wishing to shew my respect for you, when I could not figure any motive of interest except that of enjoying the conversation of a man of distinguished abilities, which has all my life been my chief[3] luxury.

I by no means wish to press my acquaintance upon Mr. Hastings; but knowing that Dr. Johnson wrote to you and finding in one of his letters to Mr. Hoole[4] the following paragraph[:] "Mr. Hastings's packet I received, but do not know that I have a right to

James Cranstoun for the Scottish Text Society, 1896). It has been attributed to Allan Ramsay himself, but, I think, over-ingeniously ("AR. SCOT." = "Allan Ramsay, Scotus"): see W. A. Craigie, "Macpherson on Pinkerton", etc., PMLA (1927) xliii. 437, and D. Nichol Smith, *op. cit.* (n. 4 in preceding letter), p. 270.

[2] Sixteen.

[3] The correspondence may have been over Guthrie's *General History of Scotland* (1767), which, according to DNB, "is painstaking and vigorous, but inaccurate, particularly in the early periods".

porter. See Journ. *passim*; *Letters JB* 329.

[2] "Monday 19 March [1787]. Dined at Sir Joshua Reynolds's with Mr. and Mrs. Hastings, etc. Admired her much; found him a sensible, reserved man, and no more at first. I sat next him. Felt how every thing human tends to diminution. Here was a Man who had been an Oriental Emperour. . . . Tuesday 20 March. . . . Called on . . . Mr. Hastings. In his present situation, to pay him a visit I thought was a liberal compliment: *Valeat quantum valere potest* ['Let it pass for what it's worth': proverbial]" (Journ.). Cf. JB's tribute to Hastings in the *Life*, *post* From Hastings, 14 May 1791, n. 1.

[3] MS. orig. "ambitious"

[4] *Letters SJ* 989. See *post* From Hoole, 17 June 1790, n. 1. JB printed extracts, *Life* iv. 359, omitting the paragraph referring to Hastings.

[1] Warren Hastings (1732–1818), Governor-General of India. From the beginning of his impeachment in 1788 for alleged corruption and cruelty in his Indian administration through his trial and acquittal in 1795, JB was his steady sup-

print it or permit it to be copied"—I should be very glad to have permission to wait upon you in the hope that my *Life of Johnson* may derive some illumination from what you shall be pleased to communicate to me. My Zeal for the object of my present labour will I trust be a sufficient excuse for my giving you this trouble. I have the honour to be with great respect, Sir, Your most obedient humble servant

*From Warren Hastings,
Sunday 28 February 1790*

MS. Yale (C 1503).

ADDRESS: To James Boswell Esqr., Q. Anne Street West.

Park lane, 28th February 1790

SIR: If I have been deficient in the Observance of the form which the custom of civility prescribes, of leaving my Name at your door, in return for that honor done by you to me, I beg, Sir, that you will not impute it to any intentional disrespect, but believe, on my assurance, that I have always held the Name and Character of Mr. Boswell in too high Estimation, not to prize the Offer of[1] his Acquaintance, if my Situation of Life were such as could have permitted me to avail myself of it. Whether mine was such at the Two Periods in which you did me the Favor to call upon me, I cannot say. I can only plead that when I have had it in my Power, I have been most punctual in the return of visits made to me, although at other Times I have been wanting in the Performance of that duty, and, I fear, have given much Offence by it:—unjustly, I think; since if any man living may claim an Exemption from those rules (rules which consume time without yielding or communicating either pleasure or profit), it ought to be allowed to me.

I will not give you the Trouble to call upon me; but will wait upon you to morrow Morning at Eleven o'Clock, and take my Chance of finding you at home. If I should not, be so good as to leave a Note signifying at what other time you may be at Leisure to afford me a meeting. I have the Honor to be with much respect, Sir, Your most obedient and humble Servant

WARREN HASTINGS

[1] MS. "of" omitted; supplied by JB.

To *Warren Hastings,*
Sunday 28 February 1790

MS. Yale (L 627). JB's copy.

Queen Anne Street West, Sunday 28 Febry. 1790

Mr. Boswell presents his most respectful compliments to Mr. Hastings, feels himself highly honoured by Mr. Hastings's letter, and will certainly be at home tomorrow morning at eleven o'clock.[1]

From Bennet Langton,[1]
Monday 1 March 1790

MS. Yale (C 1689).

ADDRESS: To James Boswell Esqr.

ENDORSEMENT: Bennet Langton Esq. 1 March 1790.

Oxford, March 1st 1790

. . . I fancy I had better not keep what I have written, till I have replied to the queries You send relative to Dr. Johnson, as I find

---

[1] On the verso of the present MS. appears the memorandum: "He came accordingly next day. I think I was happy in my mode of addressing him, which was 'Sir I would not deny myself the very great honour of a visit from you, and therefore have availed myself of your most obliging offer. Any temporary difference in your situation I assure you makes no difference in my mind. I was taught by Dr. Johnson that "whatever makes the past, the distant or the future predominate over the present, advances us in the dignity of thinking beings" [see *Life* iii. 173 n. 3, v. 334]. I view you, Sir with the eye of Lord Thurlow as an Alexander; and though I am not surly and proud, I flatter myself I am in some degree a philosopher. Your visit therefore to me may be compared to that of Alexander to Diogenes; for indeed my small hut is not much bigger than a tub. Let me add Sir that you have saved me the trouble of going into the street with a torch at noonday to look for

a Man.' " JB appears to have received a promise of letters at this interview: see *post* To Hastings, 22 Sept. 1790.

---

[1] Bennet Langton (1737–1801), Greek scholar and member of The Club. See *Life* and Journ. *passim.* As I pick up the correspondence at a rather late stage—where JB is just going to press and is putting queries to Langton as they arise in the progress of the printing—it seems advisable to give here a chronology of JB's previous activities in collecting materials from Langton: To Langton, 24 Oct. 1775 (copy by JB's clerk, John Lawrie): "You promised to me or at least resolved to put down in writing all the sayings of Dr. Johnson that you remember. Pray favour me with them, that the crown of his own jewels which I am preparing may be more briliant." Journ. 15 Apr. 1776: "I had engaged to dine with Langton . . . and thought I should get some anecdotes of Johnson from him. . . .

four or five days have stolen on already since I began it—and that might make more addition of delay than I could wish; but I intend resuming the writing and giving my replies almost immediately after dispatching this. I have only one thing further at present to say; which is, that You told me, on my having some apprehension that some of the particulars I had communicated might not be what I should chuse to have published that I should have the reading over of all You had received from me, which I very much wish could have been the case; which to be sure the distance of situation makes something difficult to accomplish—however at present, as I have said, I will send my paper away . . .

I got him to talk of Johnson and he told me some particulars which are to be found in the little book which I keep solely for Dr. Johnson's Life [the *Note Book*]." To Langton, 30 Aug. 1776 (copy by Lawrie): "What says Dr. Johnson? May I beg of you to take the trouble of marking down speedily and collecting for me his sayings of which you have now an opportunity of hearing so many. I am obliged to you already for several. Do not wait for striking opinions, acute detections of fallacy or important remarks. Write any vigourous allusion such as the man 'talking of making gold as—as a Cook Sir of making a pudding' [not included in the *Life*] or any peculiar expression such as 'the gloomy malignity of the dog' (Kenrick) [not used: see a better one at Kenrick's expense, *Life* i. 498]. By sending me sometimes a little packet of *Johnsoniana*, you will delight me in the meantime, and contribute to the future entertainment of the world." Journ. 15 Apr. 1779: "I walked to Langton's house with him, and he obligingly gave me some sayings of Dr. Johnson which I wrote down in his presence." To Langton, 23 Dec. 1779 (copy by Lawrie): "How does our Club go on? Do you see Dr. Johnson often? It will be doing me a kindness for which I shall be very gratefull, if you will write down and send me all the anecdotes concerning him, and all his sayings which you recollect. Pray do I beg it of you." From Langton, 22 May 1780: an account of a meeting with SJ at Mr. Vesey's,

which JB edited and printed, *Life* iii. 424–25. To Langton, 17 Nov. 1780 (copy by Lawrie): acknowledging the favour, but repeating his request "to put down for me in writing at your leisure whatever sayings of his you remember; and I believe you remember many. Some you have already done me the favour to dictate while I wrote; and they are in sure preservat[io]n." Journ. 12 July 1785: "Dined worthy Langton *en famille*, quiet and comfortable. Got Letter to Lord Chesterfield." See *ante* From Brocklesby, 13 Dec. 1784 and n. 8. Journ. 11 Nov. 1786: "Langton, who had come to town last night, his Lady, son, and two daughters drank tea and supt with us comfortably. He gave me Johnsoniana." Journ. 1 Mar. 1787: "Breakfasted with Langton and got from him his letters from Johnson." But not all of the letters, for some were received when the second edition was printing. These first appeared at the end of vol. ii of the second edition, and were put in proper chronological order in the third. To Langton, 17 July 1789 (missing): "To write down Johnsoni[an]a" (Reg. Let.). To Lady Rothes, 23 Dec. 1789 (*ante*). —Langton runs JB a close second in the number of appearances he makes in the *Life* under an anonymous designation. The pattern of his foibles (mainly economic) makes most of the anonyms transparent. See Dr. Powell's Table of Anonymous Persons, *Life* vi (2nd ed., 1964). 431 ff.

From Thomas Percy, Bishop of Dromore, Friday 19¹ March 1790

MS. Yale (C 2235).

ADDRESS (by William Bennet):² James Boswell Esqr., Queen Anne Street West, London.

FRANK: Dublin March the twenty third 1790. Wm. Bennet.

POSTMARK: MR 25 90.

ENDORSEMENT: Bishop of Dromore 19 March 1790.

Dublin, March 19th 1790

. . . I am much indebted to your candid acceptance,³ if you can find any admission for the petty anecdotes I sent you: Which, I am so perfectly sensible are of little value, that I hope you will grant the request, which I now make, viz. that you will not give my *Name* to the public along with them:⁴ but mention if at all necessary that they were communicated by a Person, who had heard them in Conversation from Dr. Johnson himself, or from Mrs. Williams, when he was present and admitted the Particulars to be true. In granting this favour you will much oblige me, and if it should be necessary to cancell a Leaf or two, I will thankfully repay the Loss to the Bookseller. —The indulging me in this Petition, will encourage me to add any supplemental Intelligence, that may hereafter occur when we meet on the other side the Water. . . .

¹ In the dateline of the letter a second (illegible) date is written over "19".

² Chaplain to the Earl of Westmorland, Lord Lieutenant of Ireland; soon (12 June) to become Bishop of Cork and Ross; Bishop of Cloyne, 1794.

³ Letter of 12 Mar. (MS. A. A. Houghton, Jr.; printed, *Letters JB* 272).

⁴ Percy never got over his fear of exposure. In 1805 he wrote to Robert Anderson: ". . . I have at length gone through your Life of Johnson, and submitted such corrections, additions, and notes, as occurred to me, of which you may make what use you please; but I could wish not to have my name unnecessarily obtruded on the reader, and therefore beg you will manage that with your usual prudence and delicacy" (*Lit. Illust.* vii. 158). Percy died in 1811, and Anderson's third edition came out in 1815, with Percy's notes "distinguished by the subscription of his name" (Advertisement, p. vii).

To Joseph Warton, Saturday 27 March 1790

MS. Yale (L 1271). JB's copy.

Queen Anne Street West, 27 March 1790

REVEREND SIR: I take the liberty to beg that you may let me know by return of post which two papers in *The Adventurer* signed T were written by Colman. One of my sheets[1] waits for your answer. I go on steadily, but cannot be out before October. All our common friends are well, and remember you with much regard. I ever am, My Dear Sir, Your faithful humble servant

JAMES BOSWELL

If you can recollect the origin of Johnson's prejudice against G[r]ay's poetry, pray let me have it.

From Joseph Warton, Tuesday 30 March 1790

MS. Yale (C 3064).

ADDRESS: James Boswell Esqr.

ENDORSEMENT: Rev. Dr. Joseph Warton 30 March 1790.

Winton, March 30 1790

DEAR SIR, I do not delay a moment to answer the letter with which you have favoured me, relating to the authors of *The Adventurer*. It was *Thornton*, not *Colman*,[1] who wrote several papers. And it was always imagined, tho I have not positive proof, that Thornton wrote all the papers, marked *A*. viz. Numbers 3, 6, 9, 19, 23, 25, 35, 43. And that *Johnson* wrote ALL marked *T*. except the two from *misargyrus*. That is *all* the papers marked *T*. after n. 45.[2]

---

[1] S (i. 129–36 of the first edition).

[1] Bonnell Thornton (1724–68), miscellaneous writer (see Journ. 24 May 1763); George Colman the elder (1732–94), dramatist and member of The Club (see Journ. *passim*).

[2] Cf. *Life* i. 252 and n. 2, and Malone, 6th ed., 1811, i. 231 n. (where he tentatively acknowledges Warton). SJ's share in *The Adventurer* is thoroughly examined by Dr. Powell in *Samuel Johnson: The Idler and The Adventurer*, ed. W. J. Bate, J. M. Bullitt, and L. F. Powell (Yale Edition of the Works of Samuel Johnson, Vol. II, 1963), pp. 323 ff. See also V. L. Lams, Jr., "The 'A' Papers in the *Adventurer*: Bonnell Thornton, not Dr. Bathurst, Their Author," SP (1967) lxiv. 83 ff.

Just about that time *Thornton* engaged with poor *Colman* in writing the *Connoisseur*.[3] By the two particular freinds[4] Johnson certainly meant—*Hawkesworth* and *Bathurst*. I did not then know *Hawkesworth*.

With respect to our freinds strange aversion to *Gray's* poetry, I never could find any other cause of it, than that he was particularly fond of that sort of poetry, that deals chiefly, in nervous, pointed, sentimental, didactic Lines.[5]

I know not whether you would like to mention that Johnson once owned to me, knowing how enthusiastically fond I was of the Greek Tragedies, that he never had read a Greek Tragedy in his Life.[6]

I long to see your Work, as I am very sure it must be very entertaining and interesting. . . .

To Thomas Warton, beginning of April 1790

Missing. Sent to Oxford from London. Reg. Let.: "Rev. Mr. Tho. Warton, for Johnsonian information."

From Thomas Warton, Wednesday 7 April 1790

MS. Yale (C 3078).

ADDRESS: James Boswell Esq., Queen Anne's Street West.

Woodstock, Apr. 7th, 1790

DEAR SIR: I have just had the favour of yours at this place, eight

[3] See *Life* i. 420. *The Connoisseur* was begun in 1754, *The Adventurer* in 1753. Warton's epithet "poor" refers to Colman's mental breakdown following a paralytic stroke in 1785.

[4] This is a reference to a reference in SJ's letter to Warton of 8 Mar. 1753 (see *ante* From J. Warton, 29 Jan. 1787, n. 2). Warton's information seems gratuitous, unless he is here answering a query of JB's which was omitted from his copy of the preceding letter. Hawkesworth was the founder and editor of the periodical, Bathurst a reputed asociate: see *Life* i. 233–34.

[5] Cf. *Life* i 402–03, ii. 327–28. Warton's analysis is ignored. W. P. Jones's "Johnson and Gray: A Study in Literary Antagonism", MP (1959) lvi. 243 ff. stresses the clash of personalities.

[6] Not used. Cf. *Life* i. 70, 72, iv. 16, 311; *Diaries*, pp. 34, 159.

Miles from Oxford, and therefore do not answer it so soon as you might expect.

At Oxford, *Lodgings* is the word, elleiptically for the *Master's*, or *President's*, etc., *Lodgings*.[1] Thus if I had been visiting our President, I should say, I have been *at the Lodgings*. At Cambridge they say, surely very improperly, the *Lodge*. I am, Dear Sir, very sincerly Yours

T. WARTON

To Bennet Langton, Friday 9 April 1790

MS. British Museum (Add. MS. 36747, f. 50).

ADDRESS: To Major Bennet Langton of the Royal North Lincolnshire Militia, Warley Camp, Essex.

London, 9 April 1790

. . . You may rest assured that you shall see your Johnsoniana before I print them. . . . I have printed twenty sheets of my Magnum Opus. It will be the most entertaining Book that ever appeared. Only think of what an offer I have for it—*A Cool thousand*. But I am advised to retain the property myself.[1]

Now my dear Langton let me request to have your answer to my queries directly; for *one* of the articles will be in the press in a day or two. How *can* you be so indolent? . . .

To Thomas Percy, Bishop of Dromore, Friday 9 April 1790

MS. New York Public Library, Berg Collection. MS. Yale (L 1067): a copy by JB's servant, James Ross.

London, 9 April 1790

. . . As to suppressing your Lordship's name when relating the

---

[1] The term used by Warton in his account of SJ's visit to Oxford in 1754, *Life* i. 272 (see *ante* From T. Warton, 15 Apr. 1786, n. 6). The Master was the Master of Pembroke, Dr. John Ratcliff (1700–75).

[1] The offer was from George Robinson (1737–1801), one of the leading booksellers and publishers of his time. He was very active in the purchase of copyrights and was said to have paid his authors well (Plomer). See *post* To Malone, 25 Feb. 1791.

very few anecdotes of Johnson with which you have favoured me, I will do any thing to oblige your Lordship but that very thing. I owe to the authenticity of my work, to its respectability and to the credit of my illustrious friend,[1] to introduce as many names of eminent persons as I can. It is comparatively a very small portion which is sanctioned by that of your Lordship, and there is nothing even bordering on impropriety. Believe me My Lord you are not the only Bishop in the number of great men with which my pages are graced. I am quite resolute as to this matter.[2] . . .

To Isaac Reed,[1]
Monday 12 April 1790

MS. F. W. Hilles (*L 1094).

ADDRESS: To Mr. Reed, Staple Inn.

[London,] Monday 12 April

DEAR SIR: I shall not apologise for troubling you with this, to beg that you may favour me with the date of Moses Browne's pieces in which Dr. Johnson is mentioned, as also with a sight of the pieces themselves, as also with a chronological note of what you understand to be written by Johnson between 1757 and 1765 inclusive. My servant will call tomorrow before 12 for your answer. Yours sincerely

JA. BOSWELL

[1] MS. "friends"; faithfully copied by Ross, but corrected by JB.

[2] JB compromised only so far as to state, in a foot-note to the second edition (perhaps at Percy's further request), that some of the "conversations in which he is mentioned, [have] been given to the publick without previous communication with his Lordship" (*Life* iii. 278 n. 1). See Tinker's note, *Letters JB* ii. 394.

[1] Isaac Reed (1742–1807), editor of *The European Magazine*, Shakespeare, and of Baker's *Biographia Dramatica*, "whose extensive and accurate knowledge of English literary History I do not express with exaggeration, when I say it is wonderful; indeed his labours have proved it to the world; and all who have the pleasure of his acquaintance can bear testimony to the frankness of his communications in private society" (*Life* iv. 37). Besides contributing to the original *Lives of the Poets* Reed edited and added biographies to the 1790 edition. He was also in all probability the editor of vol. xiv of SJ's *Works* (1788). JB frequently dined in Reed's company, usually at Dilly's or Malone's (Journ. and *Isaac Reed Diaries 1762–1804*, ed. C. E. Jones, 1946, *passim*).

From Isaac Reed,
Tuesday 13 April 1790

MS. Yale (C 2346).

ADDRESS: James Boswell Esq., Queen Anne Street West.

ENDORSEMENTS: Mr. Reed about Dr. Johnson. [*In the hand of JB Jr.:*]
Steady Reid 1790.

Staple Inn, Tuesday

DEAR SIR: You are perfectly right in making no apology. It is
unnecessary. If I can be of any use to you I am at your service. I
do not know that Dr. Johnson is ever mentioned by Moses Browne
more than once and that was in a Book which I am not possessed of.
It was his Edition of Isaac Walton's *Compleat Angler* which was
published either in 1760 or 1761. I am thus particular as to the
time from my recollection compared with Hawkins' Edition of the
same Book.[1] I remember there was a news paper Controversy
between the Knight and the quondam pen maker about the preference which ought to be given to the other's Edition.[2] Johnson had
promised Browne a Life which I believe was never executed.[3]

I am very ready to give you all the information I know about
Johnson's Works in any period of his life. But what you desire cannot be performed within the time you expect. It will require a
reference to a number of books which I cannot readily turn to and
after I have done it You will a thousand to one be already in
possession of all the intelligence I can give you. I do not shrink
from trouble but only from unnecessary trouble and therefore think
you had better send me your own List. I can readily see whether
I can add any thing to it. After all the Search that has been made I
fear you have little new communication to receive. I am, Dear Sir,
Your obedient Servant

ISAAC REED

I waited within untill 1/2 p⟨ast⟩ 12 oClock. Then sent ⟨?this by⟩
the post.

[1] Browne's edition was first published
in 1750, a second edition appearing in
1759. Hawkins's edition was published in
1760. SJ is mentioned in the Preface to
both of Browne's editions as the "ingenious and learned Friend" who suggested the work.

[2] Not traced. The dispute is touched
upon in *Lit. Anec.* ii. 436.

[3] Browne's foot-note (first edition)
identifying his "ingenious and learned
Friend" reads: "Mr. Samuel Johnson, who
may probably, on another Occasion, oblige
the Publick with the Life of Mr. Walton."

From Bennet Langton,
Friday 16 April 1790

MS. Yale (C 1690).

ADDRESS: To James Boswell Esqr.

Oxford, April 16. 1790

. . . I am afraid I cannot speak satisfactorily to the first of Your Queries[1]—*viz.* what was the precise time that Dr. Johnson reduced himself to, in writing a Paper of *The Idler*, at my room—for, unless one could be quite strict in it, it seems not to be of any value to attempt only suppositions or *near* guesses at it. I think it must surely have been more than *half an hour*, the time *You* speak of— but how much more I am afraid it is rather too uncertain to attempt saying.[2]

As to the 2d Query—Dr. Johnson was at Langton in the beginning of the Year 1764.[3]

The General who was so polite to the Dr. was *General Hall*.[4] These answers I apprehend may be sufficient at present—if You will *come*, as You are so kind as to suggest we could then, jointly, pay further regard to such other particulars as I observe in Your Letter. —I am charmed on all accounts to be informed of the magnificent offer You have received; on your own, and on that of our deeply honoured and revered Friend, to observe that his fame by the agency of Your powerful offices of affection and respect is thus striking out deeper and wider Roots, in such sort that one may conceive it as probable for Socrates to cease to be remembered and extolled as for our Friend to experience such a fate. . . .

---

[1] *Ante* To Lady Rothes, 23 Dec. 1789.
[2] JB had left the time blank in the MS. *Life* (p. 180); in the printed *Life* (i. 331) he supplied "about half an hour". The anecdote is told by Hawkins (p. 513 n.), who was content not to specify the time.

[3] *Life* i. 476. JB had originally placed the visit at the end of 1763 (MS. *Life*, Paper Apart for p. 293).
[4] See *post* From Langton, 30 Nov. 1790 and n. 12.

To and From Isaac Reed, Wednesday 21 April 1790

MS. Yale (L 1095).

ADDRESS: To Mr. Reed, Staple Inn.

ENDORSEMENT: with his Notes.

Queen Anne Street West, 21 April 1790

DEAR SIR: I now send you my list[1] from 1760, and shall be obliged to you for any additions.[2] Yours sincerely

J.B.

1760

Dedication to Baretti's Dictionary[3]
Introduction to World Displayed[4]
Address of the Painters to George IIId[5]
Introduction to the Plan for clothing french prisoners[6]

1761

Preface to Rolts Dictionary[7]
Corrections and additions to Thoughts on the Coronation of George III by Gwyn[8]
Review of Tytlers Queen Mary[9]

1762

In this year the preface to the Artists Catalogue is ascribed to him.[10]
Dedication to Kennedys Scripture Chronology[11]

1763

Part of Collins Life in Poetical Calender[12]
Dedication of Hooles Tasso[13]

---

[1] The list is in James Ross's hand. There is also in the Yale Collection a roughly parallel list in JB's hand, with additions by Malone.

[2] Reed's additions are printed in italics.

[3] *Life* i. 21, 353.

[4] *Life* i. 21, 345 (corrected to 1759). Malone entered the work in JB's list, but queried the year.

[5] *Life* i. 21, 352.

[6] *Life* i. 21, 353.

[7] *Life* i. 21, 358. Actually 1756, 1761 being the date of the second issue.

[8] *Life* i. 21, 361.

[9] *Life* i. 21, 354 (corrected to 1760).

[10] *Life* i. 21.

[11] *Life* i. 21, 366.

[12] *Life* i. 22, 382. See *ante* From Percy, 5 and 7 May 1772, and To J. Warton, 3 Aug. 1787 and n. 3.

[13] *Life* i. 22, 383.

1764

Part of a Review of Sugar Cane a Poem. I believe in London Chronicle. Dr. Percy wrote the most of this Review.[14]

1765

His Shakspeare[15]
Dedication of Percys Reliques[16]

1766

Preface to Mrs. Williamss Miscellanies and several pieces in that Volume[17]
Dedication to Gwynns Londo[n] and Westm[inste]r improved[18]
Preface to Adams on the Globes[19]

1767

Aschams Life[20]
Dedication to Adams on the Globes

1768

Prologue to Goodnatured Man[21]

1770

False Alarm[22]

1771

Falklands Islands[23]

1773

Epitaph on Mrs. Salisbury[24]
New edition of Folio Dictionary[25]

[14] *Life* i. 22, 481 ("He told me, that Dr. Percy wrote the greatest part of this review; but, I imagine, he did not recollect it distinctly, for it appears to be mostly, if not altogether, his own."). See *post* From Percy, 12 Mar. 1791, n. 6. The MS. of the review, in SJ's hand with a note added by Percy, is in the Hyde Collection.
[15] *Life* i. 22, 496 and *passim*.
[16] The mention of this Dedication was cancelled in the first edition of the *Life*. See *post* From Percy, 12 Mar. 1791, n. 6.
[17] *Life* ii. 25–26, i. 22.
[18] *Life* ii. 25. This title replaced "Adam's 'Treatise on the Globes'" in the proof (*ibid*. 479).

[19] Deleted by Reed and entered under 1767. JB accepted Reed's correction (*Life* i. 22, ii. 44), but he was right and Reed wrong.
[20] The first issue is dated 1761; the second, undated, came out in 1767. In the *Life* (i. 22, 464) JB assigns the work to 1763. See *ibid*. i. 550.
[21] *Life* ii. 45.
[22] *Life* i. 22, ii. 111.
[23] *Life* i. 22, ii. 134.
[24] *Life* ii. 263.
[25] *Life* ii. 203.

Shakspeare with Steevens *He added only one Note.*[26]
Patriot *Was in 1774.*[27]
Taxation no Tyranny *Was in 1775.*[28]

1777

Dedication and Life prefixed to Pearces Commentary[29]
Writings for Dr. Dodd[30]
Prologue for Kelly's Wido[w] spoken at Cov[ent] Gard[e]n 29 May[31]
In 1773 I believe the preface to Macbean's Dictionary.[32]

From Thomas Percy, Bishop of Dromore, Saturday 24 April 1790

MS. Yale (C 2236).

ADDRESS (by William Bennet): James Boswell Esqr., Queen Anne Street West, London.

FRANK: Dublin April [fourteenth *deleted*] twenty fourth [*initialed* W.B.] 1790. Wm. Bennet.

POSTMARKS: AP 24, AP 28 90.

ENDORSEMENT: From the Bishop of Dromore.

Dublin, April 24th 1790

. . . Be assured, my dear Sir, that I cannot but esteem it an honour to be mentioned in any work of yours: My only scruple was about the peculiar matter with which my Name m[igh]t be connected. As the Anecdotes, I sent you were of the lowest and most trifling kind, I could have wished (and still intreat) that the mention of me expressly by name might be reserved to any Communication which I have sent, or may hereafter send, that may not expose me too much to ridicule from the non-importance of the Particulars. This

---

[26] *Life* ii. 204, ignoring Reed's remark. Reed, who revised the "Johnson-Steevens Shakespeare" for the third variorum edition (1785) would seem to speak with some authority; but Arthur Sherbo (*Samuel Johnson, Editor of Shakespeare*, 1956, pp. 106 ff.) finds that SJ subjected his original commentary to extensive revision and added eighty-four new notes.

[27] *Life* i. 22, ii. 285–86. JB dated this

and the next work correctly in his holograph list.

[28] *Life* i. 23, ii. 312.

[29] *Life* i. 23, iii. 112–13.

[30] *Life* i. 23, iii. 141 ff.

[31] *Life* iii. 113–14. See *ante* From Hussey, Aug. 1787 and n. 15.

[32] *Life* i. 22, ii. 204. See *ante* To and From Barber, 15 July 1786, n. 25.

favour I hope I may obtain from your Friendship that I may be allowed to see before Publication, such Passages as my Name is produced in form to support: as perhaps upon Review I may add something to increase the weight of my Testimony: or the value of my Communication. —If you do not indulge me in this request, I shall really take it ill. —I hope to be in London before Winter, and perhaps that may be soon enough to grant me what I here solicit....

From the Rev. Richard George Robinson, Thursday 6 May 1790

MS. Yale (C 2397).

ADDRESS: James Boswell Esqr., Mr. Dilly's, Bookseller, Poultry, London.

POSTMARK: MA 7 90.

Lichfield, May 6. 1790

DEAR SIR: A few days ago I became acquainted with the Revd. Mr. Weston of Whitney in Oxfordshire, who is a prebendary of Durham,[1] from whence he was returning home, after having kept his residence. He was an intimate friend of Dr. Johnson, by whose recommendation he had been appointed librarian to the king.[2] In the course of our conversation he told me he was possessed of some interesting anecdotes concerning him, having enjoyed much of his society between the years 1766 and 1773. I asked him if he had communicated them to you; he said he had not, and that he could not do it with propriety of his own accord, as he had not the pleasure of being acquainted with you. I replied that I had; and that with his permission, I would write to you and mention these circumstances,

---

[1] Phipps Weston (c. 1738–94) took his B.A., M.A., and B.D. degrees from Magdalen College, where he was a Fellow from 1763 to 1772. He was Rector of Witney, and a prebendary of Durham from 1789 until his death (*Alum. Oxon.*).

[2] "The Bishop of London surprized me today by telling me that Mr. Weston the Librarian at the Queen's House was recommended by Mr. Johnson the celebrated writer to whom you gave a pension, the King having at first thought of appointing Mr. Johnson himself" (Charles Jenkinson to Lord Bute, 18 Jan. 1768;

quoted with the kind permission of the present Lord Bute from the original in his archives). Two letters from SJ to Weston, 22 and 28 Apr. 1768, are printed by Chapman, who guessed wrong in identifying the addressee (*Letters SJ* 203.1, 204.1). Both letters deal with the formation of the King's library (see *post* To F. A. Barnard, 10 June 1790). Dr. Powell, to whom I am indebted for the correct identification, informs me of the existence of a third letter, dated 3 May 1768, in the Hyde Collection.

and also give you his address. He immediately granted it; and told me afterwards he should be in town in a fortnight, or three weeks. It will make me very happy, should you obtain Mr. Weston's communications in time, to be inserted in your life of the doctor,[3] to the publication of which I look forward with a pleasing expectancy; who am, dear Sir, your most obedient humble Servant

RICH. GEO. ROBINSON

To Francis Godolphin Osborne, Duke of Leeds,[1] Saturday 8 May 1790

MS. Yale (L 856). JB's draft.

Queen Anne Street West, 8 May 1790

. . . I presume to mention that Your Grace may contribute towards the illustration of the life of Dr. Johnson in writing which I am now engaged. Should your Grace be so disposed you will oblige me very much if you will be pleased to appoint a time when I may have permission to wait upon your Grace.[2] . . .

From Bennet Langton, Monday 10 May 1790

MS. Yale (C 1691).

ADDRESS: To James Boswell Esqr.

Oxford, May 10th 1790

. . . With regard to the particulars of which You wish me to give some account, and that are now occurring to be treated of in the course of Your Work—I have been dwelling upon them since the

---

[3] Weston is nowhere mentioned in the *Life*.

[1] Francis Godolphin Osborne (1751–99), fifth Duke of Leeds; Foreign Secretary of State, 1783–91; member of The Club, 1792 (*Life* iv. 478). Farington's *Diary* (i. 267) gives an uncomplimentary character of him in his last year. His wife, Amelia Darcy, eloped with John Byron in 1789 and became the mother of Augusta Leigh. (By his second wife Byron became the father of the poet.) Leeds's grandson, Lord William Godolphin (1804–88),

married as his third wife the widow of Hon. Augustus Villiers, Georgina Henrietta, daughter of Viscount Keith and Hester Maria (Queeney) Thrale. It was through Georgina that "the Queeney letters" passed to Lord Lansdowne (Burke's *Peerage*, 1936, p. 1509; *The Queeney Letters*, ed. the Marquis of Lansdowne, 1934, p. xix).

[2] Leeds replied the next day, inviting JB to see him on 10 May. The journal records only the fact of the visit; for the substance of the interview, see *post* To F. A. Barnard, 10 June 1790.

receipt of Your Letter,[1] and have attentively read over what Sir J. Hawkins says,[2] which appears in the main to be correct enough. I am sorry it is out of my power to send You the paper You speak of; that, of Sir Joshua Reynolds's writing, when he put down the Names of those proposed to be applied to for agreeing to meet as a Club—but it unluckily is somewhere among my papers in London, and which I have not any means of giving a direction for finding— but I do not know of any difference that there would be found *in it* from the list given in the 415th page of Sir John's *Life 1st Edition.* On that page it is said that "the first movers in this Association were Johnson and Sir Joshua Reynolds"—whereas it would have been more close to what I remember of the fact if it had been said, that Sir Joshua was the mover of it; as Johnson did not with entire Readiness accede to the Scheme.[3]

You say in yours, that the Commencement of the Club comes in, in the Year 1763. I apprehend that to be a mistake; as exactly as I can trace it in recollection, it was, in the beginning of the year 1764 that it was first talked of, and very soon after it was first named it was actually instituted. I see, in the 425th page of Sir J. Hawkins, he says "the Institution of this Society was in the Winter of 1763" —but it should have been said, "in the Spring of 1764"—it was about eight or ten weeks after the Return of Johnson and me from Lincolnshire—which was, in the beginning of February 1764.[4] I do not know of any other particulars as to the first fixing of the Club that You are not well apprized of at least as I am. . . .

To Frederick Augusta Barnard,[1]
Thursday 10 June 1790

MS. Yale (L 34). A copy by JB's daughter Veronica, endorsed: "copy of a letter to Mr. Bernard."

Queen Anne Street West, 10 June 1790[2]

Sir, I beg leave to renew my request that you would favour me

---

[1] Untraced.

[2] About the founding of The Club (pp. 414 ff.).

[3] "Sir Joshua Reynolds had the merit of being the first proposer of it, to which Johnson acceded" (*Life* i. 477).

[4] JB dates the founding "Soon after his return to London, which was in February"

(*loc. cit.*). See C. N. Fifer, "The Founding of Dr. Johnson's Literary Club", N & Q (1956) cci. 302.

[1] Frederick Augusta Barnard (1743–1830), F.S.A., F.R.S., librarian to George III; knighted, 1828. He was said to be a natural son of Frederick, Prince of Wales

with Dr. Johnsons letter to you,[3] which I really think would be a valuable addition to my Life of that great man, while at the same time it proves his regard for you.

As at our last interview[4] you expressed some difficulty, as if the letter related to the Kings business, I waited on the Duke of Leeds (who had been very obliging as to another article in my work)[5] and stated it to him. His Grace was clear that it was not of that nature as that there could be any objection to its publication, and though he was very ready to do for me all that was proper in his situation, he did not think it fell within his department to mention the matter to his Majesty but suggested it should be done rather by some person in habits of private intercourse with the King and it was agreed that the Bishop of Carlisle[6] should be asked.

It has however occured to me, before giving his Lordship that trouble that you may perhaps be satisfied with the Duke of Leeds's opinion, and may without any application being made to the King, favour me with the letter.

My zeal to render my *Life of Dr. Johnson* as complete as I possibly can, will I trust serve as an apology to you for this importunity, and if you are so good as to comply with my request, I shall be very much obliged to you. I am Sir, Your most obedient humble servant

JAMES BOSWELL[2]

(*Life* ii. 480). The only previous correspondence in the Yale Collection is a copy of a letter to Barnard, 24 May 1785, in which JB "sends another Letter to the People of Scotland, of very interesting concern to that part of the King's dominions; and begs Mr. Barnard may be so good as to convey it to his Majesty the first opportunity".

[2] JB's hand is imitated in the dateline and signature.

[3] Of 28 May 1768, a long letter of advice (patently solicited by Barnard) on

the subject of "ransacking" foreign countries for books for the Royal library (*Letters SJ* 206). The letter is reprinted with a facsimile and a commentary by E. L. McAdam, Jr. in *Dr. Johnson and the King's Library* (privately printed, 1955).

[4] The journal mentions a visit c. 2–3 June to the King's library.

[5] See *ante* To Malone, 22 Mar. 1786 n. 9.

[6] John Douglas, Bishop of Carlisle and Dean of Windsor. See *post* From Douglas 16 May 1791.

From Frederick Augusta Barnard, Friday 11 June 1790

MS. Yale (C 79).

ADDRESS: James Boswell Esqr., Queen Anne Street West.

ENDORSEMENT: From Librarian Barnard.

St. James's, June 11th 1790

SIR: I am sorry to be obliged to repeat my objections to the publication of Dr. Johnsons letter to me, they are of two distinct natures[:] one, because His Majestys business makes the principal sub[j]ect of it, the other, because I do not, on my own account, choose that it should be made public; 'tho you might by the application you mention get the better of the first, yet the latter is insurmo[u]ntable, and you must excuse me for saying, that it is my fixed resolution never to suffer that letter to be published.[1] I am Sir, your most obedient humble Servant

FREDCK. BARNARD

---

[1] "I wished much to have gratified my readers with the perusal of this letter, and have reason to think that his Majesty would have been graciously pleased to permit its publication; but Mr. Barnard, to whom I applied, declined it 'on his own account' " (*Life* ii. 33 n. 4). Mrs. Piozzi had also tried, and failed. In Apr. 1785 she wrote to Lysons from Italy: "Pray enquire for a letter which I *know* Dr. Johnson wrote to Mr. Barnard the King's librarian when he was in Italy looking for curious Books; the Subject was wholly Literary and Controversial, and would be most interesting to the Public; I would give any thing almost to obtain a Copy *now*, and there was a Time when I might have taken twenty Copies" (Clifford, *Piozzi*, pp. 243–44). Lysons replied, 4 July: "Sir Joseph Banks introduced me to Mr. Barnard, who has shewn me the letter which Dr. Johnson wrote to him the day before he left England when going to Italy—but he appears very unwilling to have it brought forward in any way—he says that if he thought it could be interesting to the publick he would give you a copy, but that the observations are quite common place, and by no means in the Doctor's best style, it is very long and consists of remarks on the early printers, of the books most likely to be found in particular countries, what might be most proper for a Royal Collection and concluding with some good Advice—I must own I did not think the language of it so good as he usually wrote" (J. L. Clifford, "Further Letters of the Johnson Circle", *Bull. Rylands Lib.* 1936, xx. 276). Barnard himself printed the letter, with numerous errors and an omission, in the introduction to his *Bibliothecae Regiae Catalogus* (1820), I. iii. For its subsequent printings, see McAdam, *Dr. Johnson and the King's Library*, end-note.

From John Hoole,[1]
Thursday 17 June 1790

MS. Yale (C 1548).

Abinger near Dorking, 17 June

DEAR SIR, When I last had the pleasure of seeing you[2] I mentioned that I would send you a few particulars of our late excellent friend Dr. Johnson and Mrs. Williams, but upon looking them over again, I doubt you will not find much to make use of with respect to the Doctor: however such as they are, I send them to you: they were communicated to me in Letters from Lady Knight,[3] an intimate friend of the Doctor and Mrs. Williams, and I am chiefly induced to put them into your hands on account of what is said of Mrs. Williams, for whose memory and character I have a most sincere regard, and could hope that whenever she is mentioned, it may be to her credit. Lady Knight, you will find, was in long intimacy with her, and knew much of her connexions. I shewed to the Doctor, after Mrs. Williams's death, the passages relative to her and he said that in general the character given of her was just. There was an Account of her in *The London Magazine* in the year 1783, part of which was taken from the same authority.[4] You will be so good, my dear Sir, to recollect that should any use be made of

[1] John Hoole (1727–1803), the translator. See *Lit. Anec.* ii. 404 ff. SJ wrote the Dedications to his Tasso (1763) and Metastasio (1767) and promoted his proposals for Ariosto (1783). JB's journal records several meetings with Hoole. On 8 Apr. 1788 "Mr. Hoole breakfasted with me, and gave me some letters of Dr. Johnson to him, and some notes of his last days". For the letters, see *Life* ii. 289, iv. 359–60; for an acknowledgement of the notes, *ibid.* iv. 406. Hoole's narrative of SJ's last days was first published in *The European Magazine* for Sept. 1799 (xxxvi. 153); it is reprinted, *Johns. Misc.* ii. 145 ff.

[2] 10 May, at breakfast (Journ.).

[3] Phillipina (Deane), Lady Knight (1727–99), widow of Admiral Sir Joseph Knight, R.N. (d. 1775). Hoole printed her account, with notes, in *The European Magazine* for Oct. 1799 (xxxvi. 225–27). The enclosure to the present letter is missing, but the text is very probably that used by Malone in printing extracts in the fourth edition of the *Life* (1804, i. 68 n. †, 429 n. *, and ii. 26 n. ‡). Croker also printed extracts, but apparently from a different copy: see *Johns. Misc.* ii. 171–76. A copy of the *Life* with annotations by Lady Knight is in the Princeton University Library: see C. G. Osgood, "Lady Phillipina Knight and Her Boswell", *Princeton University Library Chronicle* (1943), iv. 37–49.

[4] The account in *The London Magazine* (Dec. 1783, i. 517–21) is signed "B." and concludes with "the expressive words of a lady who had many years known her intimately, and who holds her memory in the highest estimation". This passage is virtually identical with the opening sentences of Lady Knight's account, as printed in *The European Magazine*.

the present materials,[5] Lady Knight desires that *her name may not appear*. I give you the passages from the Letters in her own words. Miss Knight, her daughter, is a woman of extraordinary talents and Author of the little book which I lately published entitled *Dinarbas* as[6] a continuation of *Rasselas*.[7]

I confess I was greatly hurt at the perusal of Mrs. P——s *Anecdotes* which surely impress the general reader, unacquainted with Johnson, with *a very* unfavourable opinion. Among many other passages that offended me, she says page 280 that "Mr. Johnson did not like to read Manuscripts" etc. This might in general be true, but at the same time, the passage seems strongly to imply that *he never* would do an act of kindness of that sort for a friend. Surely the whole passage must give the reader a strong impression of ill nature in the Doctors manner.[8] I could not help inserting in my Copy of the *Anecdotes* this short Note on the passage. "This passage greatly misrepresents his conduct to his friends. I have known him read Manuscripts, and am myself an example of his kindness this way." Being upon this subject I will just mention an instance of his great attention and good nature to me on such an occasion. He had a manuscript Tragedy of mine to read, and knew that I was particularly anxious for his opinion, having had great trouble and much altercation with the Managers and Performers. When he had read part of it, he sent Francis to me to let me know that he was then reading the piece, had gone through three acts and was pleased with it. He finished the reading of the whole that evening and immediately wrote me a Note which you have seen.[9]

[5] None was—by JB.

[6] MS. possibly "or"

[7] Ellis Cornelia Knight (1757–1837), *Dinarbas, a Tale. Being a Continuation of Rasselas, Prince of Abissinia*, 1790. It was published by Dilly; perhaps Hoole meant "which I saw through the press." Miss Knight translated SJ's Latin ode on Skye (*Life* v. 425). See also *ante* From Mickle, 28 Oct. 1786, n. 6.

[8] "Mr. Johnson did not like that his friends should bring their manuscripts for him to read, and he liked still less to read them when they were brought: sometimes however when he could not refuse he would take the play or poem, or whatever it was, and give the people his opinion from some one page that he had peeped into" (*Johns. Misc.* i. 332). In JB's condensed journal for 24 Apr. 1772 appears the following passage, printed with revision, *Life* ii. 195: "Never reads MS. 'Can do no good. If good, very well. If not, cannot help it. No man entitled either to make me be his ennemy or tell a Lie. If they have money, I advise print without name, and try. If for money, go to Bookseller and make best barg you can.' " But cf. *Life* iii. 373 and especially iv. 121, where JB seeks to correct this impression of illiberality.

[9] Printed, *Life* ii. 289. JB identifies the play as *Cleonice*. It was performed, without success, at Covent Garden, and printed in 1775. See *Lit. Anec.* ii. 407.

Surely this was an instance of *attentive*, *kind* and *gentle* manners, that I am apt to think few persons would believe of him from a perusal of the *Anecdotes*. I have repeated obligations to him in these matters.

We have a great loss in this country from the absence of our neighbour my Lord Macartney[10] whom I fear we shall not see again till Winter. I mean to be in town about the end of July when I will do myself the pleasure to call on you.[11]

Mrs. Hoole desires her compliments. Dear Sir, Your obedient humble Servant

JOHN HOOLE

James Boswell Esq.

From the Rev. James Compton,[1] Monday 21 June 1790

MS. Yale (C 816).

ADDRESS: James Boswell Esq.

ENDORSEMENT: Rev. James Compton.

N. 12. Astey Row, Islington, June 21st 1790

SIR: On hearing from Lady Strange[2] that you were on the eve of

[10] George Macartney (1737–1806), Baron (later first Earl) Macartney, colonial administrator; member of The Club. See Journ. *passim*. The Advertisement to the Second Edition of the *Life* concludes with an acknowledgement to Macartney for "his own copy of my book, with a number of notes, of which I have availed myself [e.g. *Life* iii. 243 n. 4, iv. 12 n. 2]. On the first leaf I found in his Lordship's hand-writing, an inscription of such high commendation, that even I, vain as I am, cannot prevail on myself to publish it." Macartney was Hoole's neighbour when in residence at his country-house, Parkhurst, near Dorking. In 1790 he passed some time at his grandfather's estate, Lissanoure, co. Antrim, where he was born (Helen H. Robbins, *Our First Ambassador to China*, 1908, pp. 1, 168, 171). JB was to seek unsuccessfully to join Macartney's mission to China in 1792 (Temple to JB, 30 Mar. 1792; JB to Bishop Barnard, 16 Aug. 1792).

[11] On 19 Aug. JB dined at Reynolds's in company with Hoole (Journ.).

[1] James Compton (living in 1811) was librarian of the Benedictine monastery in Paris which SJ visited with the Thrales in 1775. In 1783, having been shaken by No. 110 of *The Rambler*, he was converted to Protestantism and subsequently became chaplain to the French and Dutch Chapels at St. James's. The story of his relations with SJ, and also of his correspondence—first with JB and later with Malone—about his admission to the *Life*, is told by J. M. Osborn, "Dr. Johnson and The Contrary Converts", in *New Light on Dr. Johnson*, ed. F. W. Hilles, 1959, pp. 297–317.

[2] Isabella Lumisden, Lady Strange (d. 1806), wife of Sir Robert Strange (1721–92), the engraver, and sister of Andrew Lumisden, JB's Jacobite friend.

publishing the life of your respectable friend Dr. Samuel Johnson, I conceived a thought, that perhaps I might have the honour of being mentioned among the living monuments of his universal benevolence. I have been mentioned by Sir John Hawkins in his second edition of the Doctor's life in a manner, respectful indeed to me, but false in the relation.[3] If such anecdotes are to be interwoven in your history, and you choose to hear from myself the nature of my connexions with my excellent patron, I will either send you an account of them in writing or will meet you any *evening* you please to appoint.

I generally spent five or six hours alone with him every evening of the winter of the year 1784, and I believe it is entirely owing to me, that he did not retire to end his days in the Benedictine convent at Paris.[4] How different was that notion from what he inculcates in his 6th N. of *The Rambler*.[5] He little thought that what there he mentions of Cowley would one day be the subject of his own Imitation.

But without entering into farther remarks, for fear of seeming importunate, I will defer them untill I hear whether they come too late, or whether you choose to honour them with your attention. I am, Sir, Your humble Servant

JAMES COMPTON

This letter may reach you several days after the date, as I am to wait on Lady Strange to learn your direction.[6]

To Sir William Forbes, Friday 2 July 1790

MS. estate of the late Lord Clinton. JB reports from Carlisle (where, as Recorder and as Lord Lonsdale's unwilling factotum, he is attending

---

[3] Pages 530–31. In Jan. 1811, at the time Malone was preparing the sixth edition of the *Life*, John Nichols wrote to him introducing Compton, "an old Friend and Acquaintance of Dr Johnson; concerning whom *Boswell* is silent—and Hawkins, (in his *Second* Edition) has greatly blundered". In a subsequent letter he explains: ". . . the Blunder is, that Sir John represents Dr Johnson's having taken Mr Compton under his Protection, and not quitting him till he had obtained

for him *Two Livings*" (Osborn, *op. cit.*, pp. 298, 301).

[4] Cf. *ante* From Adams, 28 Mar. 1785.

[5] On the subject of the futility of seeking happiness by a change of place. Cowley is instanced for his wish to retire to an American plantation "to forsake this world for ever, with all the vanities and vexations of it".

[6] Whenever it was received, it was not answered until 19 Feb. 1791 (*post*).

the election) that 300 pages of the *Life* are now printed; two thirds of the book is still to go to the printer, of which more than 350 pages have not yet been seen by Malone. Both Malone and Nichols have advised against selling the copyright.

From Edmond Malone, Thursday 8 July 1790

MS. Yale (C 1919).

ADDRESS (by Philip Metcalfe):[1] James Boswell Esqr., Carlisle.

FRANK: London, eighth July 1790. P. Metcalfe.

POSTMARK: JY 8 90.

London, July 8, 1790

. . . I happened to be reading his[2] *Essays* last night when the printers boy called; and though I had ordered a sheet of yours for press in the morning, in which you give an account of Johnson's being offended by your urging the subject of death too far, I could not help writing to Mr. Plympsel,[3] if possible to add the following note—to the words—"it will do him no good to whine":[4] because they appear to me admirably to express and *justify* Johnson's notions on the subject; and both from your representation and that of others (Courteney[5] etc.), the reader might him think a *pusillanimous* fellow. Don't however be alarmed, for I am sure you will approve of the insertion.[6] The note was this:

"Bacon in his admirable *Essays*[7] has delivered a congenial

[1] See *post* From Metcalfe, n.d., p. 589.

[2] Bacon's.

[3] J. Plymsell, the compositor.

[4] "To my question, whether we might not fortify our minds for the approach of death, he answered, in a passion, 'No, Sir, let it alone. It matters not how a man dies, but how he lives. The act of dying is not of importance, it lasts so short a time.' He added, (with an earnest look,) 'A man knows it must be so, and submits. It will do him no good to whine' " (*Life* ii. 106–107).

[5] The reference is presumably to the following lines in Courtenay's *Poetical Review of the Literary and Moral Character of the Late Samuel Johnson, L.L.D.*:

A coward wish, long stigmatiz'd by fame,
Devotes Mæcenas to eternal shame;
Religious Johnson, future life to gain,
Would ev'n submit to everlasting pain:
How clear, how strong, such kindred colours paint
The Roman epicure and Christian saint!

[6] The note was not printed, probably because Plymsell could not make room for it.

[7] The second essay, "Of Death."

329

sentiment, which may serve to place Dr. Johnson's notion on this subject in its true light: 'Certainly the contemplation of death, as *the wages of sin*, and passage to another world, is holy and religious; but the fear of it, as a tribute due unto nature, is weak.' " —I happened to light on the words while the boy was waiting. In a former ed[itio]n of the *Essays* printed in 1613, the passage runs somewhat differently, and I had some mind to have taken it from thence as still more apposite.—"Certainly the fear of death, as contemplation of the cause of it and the issue of it, is religious; but the fear of it for itself, is weak."

Your compositor has gone on very smartly; and has not been delayed by me, though I am so busy. I have never seen more than two proofs. The sheet in which was νυξ ερχεται you had ordered for press, and no revise of it came to me: so the errour has gone. It is but a trifle and may be corrected in the Errata.[8] That sheet was Qq. I have had 5 Sheets[:] Rr, Ss, Tt, Uu[,] Xx. The last nearly exhausts Maxwell.[9] It will, I believe, be worked off tomorrow. —I took but one liberty more than I have mentioned, which, I think, upon reflection you will approve. It was to strike out two lines in which you mention an expression which you have heard Johnson used originally in *The False Alarm*, and struck out. Why raise up against him a host of enemies, by telling a thing that need not be told, and in which perhaps your information may have been inaccurate?[10] I do sincerely believe that my friend Lord Charle-

[8] Corrected to Νυξ γαρ ερχεται. This was the inscription on the dial-plate of SJ's watch, "being the first words of our SAVIOUR's solemn admonition to the improvement of that time which is allowed us to prepare for eternity: 'the night cometh, when no man can work' " (*Life* ii. 57). See *ibid.* n. 5. A rough note in the Yale Collection reads: "Ask Steevens as to νυξ γαρ ερχεται." Steevens had come into possession of the dial-plate.

[9] See *ante* From Maxwell, 12 May and 16 June 1787, 17 Dec. 1789; *Life* ii. 116–33. Maxwell's "Collectanea" are missing from the MS. *Life*; the originals evidently served as printer's copy.

[10] The deleted lines are: "Indeed I am well informed that there was struck out from it an expression still more degrading than any that now remain 'Had govern-

ment been overturned by this faction England had died of a *Thyrasis*' " (MS. *Life*, p. 354). The lines concluded the first paragraph of JB's account of the pamphlet, *Life* ii. 111–12. For *Thyrasis*, read *phthiriasis*. "Johnson had a sovereign contempt for Wilkes and his party, whom he looked upon as a mere rabble. 'Sir,' said he, 'had Wilkes's mob prevailed against Government, this nation had died of *phthiriasis*.' Mr. Langton told me this. The expression, *Morbus pediculosus*, as being better known, would strike more. *Lousy disease* may be put in a parenthesis" (*Boswelliana*, p. 274; quoted, *Life* iii. 183 n. 2). I would locate the alleged suppression in the sixth paragraph from the end of *The False Alarm*: "Had *Rome* fallen by the *Catilinarian* conspiracy, she might have consoled her fate by the greatness of her

mont,[11] if he had read that passage in your book, would have
thrown it into the fire. . . . Your very Affectionate

E.M.

I did not know what to do with this. "He repeated Drydens
lines on love (gentle tempestuous, *see further*)" for your compositor
gave me, you see, *asides* and all. I could not find the passage; so
made it—"some lines by Dryden on love, which I have now forgotten."[12]

To Bennet Langton, Friday 27 August 1790

MS. Yale (*L 849.7). Signature cut away.

London, 27 August 1790

MY DEAR SIR: Since I was favoured with your last kind letter[1] I
have been driven about not very pleasingly, having been suddenly
hurried away by Lord Lonsdale[1a] to do duty as Recorder of Carlisle
where I was kept I may say a prisoner in a tedious state of uncertainty,[2] which vexed me the more that the progress of my *Life
of Johnson* was in some degree retarded, though Mr. Malone was
so very kind as to superintend the press in my absence.[3] . . .

I have a very great desire to be with you at Oxford, and your
most kind invitation to accomodate both me and my daughter[4] in
your house warms my heart; for in truth there is very little of such
cordiality to be experienced. My difficulty is in leaving London,

destroyers; but what would have alleviated
the disgrace of *England,* had her government been changed by *Tiler* or by *Ket?*"
Prof. Donald Greene has called my attention to SJ's use of the word in a similar
context in *Thoughts on the Late Transactions respecting Falkland's Islands,* published in 1771, the year after *The False
Alarm* came out.

[11] James Caulfeild (1728-99), first Earl
of Charlemont, Irish politician and member of The Club. See *Life* iii. 342-45, 392;
Journ. 18 Oct. 1762.

[12] Further revised, *Life* ii. 85. The
lines, as Croker conjectured, are from
Tyrannick Love, Act II, Scene 3; they are
quoted by SJ in his *Life of Dryden* (*Lives*
i. 458).

[1] 31 May 1790 (C 1692); to appear in
another volume in this series.

[1a] James Lowther (1736-1802), first
Earl of Lonsdale, became JB's political
patron in 1786.

[2] See Journ. 14 June-15 July 1790.

[3] "Had found that by my kind and
active friend Malone's aid my Book had
gone on in my absence five sheets" (Journ.
19 July 1790). See *ante* Chronology of the
Making of the *Life,* 14 June and following.

[4] Euphemia, who had come to Carlisle
from boarding school in Edinburgh to
join her father and go on with him to
London.

while my *Life of Johnson* is in the press. It will be a much larger work than was calculated. I was very desireous to confine it within one quarto volume, though it should be a very thick one; but I now find that it must be two, and these more than 550 pages each. I have printed as yet only 456; but am next week to put on two compositors, so as to advance in a double ratio.

The Collectanea with which you were pleased to favour me,[5] you may depend upon it shall not be inserted without being revised by you; and ⟨this is one of⟩[6] the reasons which make ⟨me desireous of meetin⟩[6]g with you. Could you without much inconvenience meet me half way, we might pass a comfortable day together, and go through your memorabilia and adjust them, having no interruption, and my visit to you might be deferred till the conclusion of my *Magnum Opus*. Pray try if you can oblige me so much, and if you can, be pleased to fix day and place. I hope this request will induce you to write without delay, before the *mould* of indolence has had time to gather. . . .

From Dr. Charles Blagden,[1]
Saturday 18 September 1790

MS. Yale (C 154).

ADDRESS: James Boswell Esq.

ENDORSEMENT: From Dr. Blagden.

Percy Street, Sep. 18th, 1790

DEAR SIR, Upon further consideration[2] I have no doubt but the term Baretti meant to convey to Dr. Johnson was *"Marc* d'eau

---

[5] See *ante* From Langton, 1 Mar. 1790, n. 1.

[6] The lacunae are the result of the cutting away of the signature.

[1] Charles Blagden (1748–1820), M.D. Edinburgh, 1768; F.R.S., 1772; knighted, 1792; member of the Club, 1793 (though JB noted that he saw him there for the first time on 1 Apr. 1794). See Journ. *passim*. According to Walpole, Blagden said of the *Life* "justly, that it is a new kind of libel, by which you may abuse anybody, by saying, some dead

person said so and so of somebody alive" (*Correspondence with Mary and Agnes Berry*, ed. W. S. Lewis, 1944, i. 275; quoted by Hill, *Life* iv. 30 n. 2).

[2] The first meeting recorded in the journal between JB and Blagden took place on 27 July of this year, when, presumably, the subject of this and the following letter from Blagden (*post* 1 Oct. 1790) was introduced. The business of both letters was to establish points of the text of SJ's diary in France, 10 Oct.–4 Nov. 1775. For the passage explained in the present letter, see *Life* ii. 396.

forte" (which is pronounced *Mar*), signifying the residuum found after the distillation of aqua fortis. Chemically speaking, this, when washed, hardly differs from colcothar prepared expressly by calcining vitriol of iron, though possibly its mechanical properties may not be exactly the same; and as large quantities of aqua fortis are distilled for various manufactures, its residuum may very probably be the principal source of the colcothar used by the glass-grinders. With great esteem I am, dear Sir, Your very faithful humble Servant

C. BLAGDEN

To *Warren Hastings,*
Wednesday 22 September 1790

MS. Yale (L 628). A copy in Veronica Boswell's hand, endorsed: "Copy of a letter to Warren Hastings from J. Boswell Esqr. requesting some letters of Dr. Johnsons."

[London,] 22d Septr. 1790

SIR: I am very sorry to seem importunate. But as you were pleased to say that you would allow me to introduce into my *Life of Dr. Johnson*, some of his letters to you, I request that I may now be favoured with them, as my Work is far advanced. I promise that after I have taken copies of them they shall be speedily and carefully returned. Permit me, Sir, to presume to trouble you with another request, which is that you will be so good as to let me have a few lines, accompanying the letters, expressing your sentiments of Dr. Johnson, with which I am well acquainted. For I should consider it as of important consequence to the memory of my illustrious friend, to shew to posterity that he was regarded by Mr. Hastings. Pray indulge me in this. I have the honour to be with the greatest respect, Sir, your faithful and most obedient humble servant

· JAMES BOSWELL

From *Warren Hastings*,
Friday 24 September 1790

MS. Yale (C 1504).

ADDRESS (by Sir Francis Sykes):[1] Jas. Boswell Esqr., Queen Anne St. West, London.

FRANK: Reading Septr. twenty fourth 1790. Ffree Sykes.

POSTMARK: SE 25 90.

Purley hall,[2] 24th Septr. 1790

SIR: I am ashamed to have given you cause to remind me of my promise. Immediately after the time in which I had last the pleasure of seeing you, I looked over all the Papers which I had of that Class which I thought most likely to comprehend the Letters of Doctor Johnson; but without Success; and I was obliged at that time to desist from the further Search, as in the frequent Changes of my residence I had been obliged to deposit the greatest Part of my Papers, for want of room in the House which I then rented, at my Upholsterers, and in other Places.—On my return to Town, which I hope will not be too late, I will make it my first business to look for the Letters. I will then reply fully to the other Parts of your Letter, being at this time disabled, by a hurt which I lately received, from holding my pen but during a short Interval of time. I have the Honor to be, with very great Respect, Sir, Your most obedient and most humble Servant

WARREN HASTINGS

From *John Moody*,[1]
Monday 27 September 1790

MS. Yale (C 2052).

ADDRESS: James Boswell Esq., London, Queen Anne St. West.

ENDORSEMENT: Mr. Moody the Actor modestly declining to communicate any saying of Dr. Johnson's. Septr. 27 1790.

---

[1] Sir Francis Sykes, Bt. (1732–1804), sometime governor of Cossimbazar, Bengal; M.P. for Shaftesbury, 1771–75, 1780–84, and for Wallingford, 1784 until his death (*Comp. Bar.* v. 214).

[2] Near the village of Purley, Berkshire.

[1] John Moody (?1727–1812), the actor. In the *Life* he makes his sole entrance at the dinner at Davies's, 6 Apr. 1775, where, in attempting to speak, he suffered the humiliation (as construed by Beau-

New Inn, Sepr. 27 1790

MY DEAR SIR: Not being in London for some time past,[2] Your favour[3] lay at Chambers without my seeing it until this day.

In Answer to Yours—The poverty of my Abilities and the place I fill in the world, by no means entitle me to say anything, on paper, of that great man you mention. His doors ever open to me, and a seat at his table, I acknowledge with great gratitude, and, think of them as the foremost honors of my life, not to speak of the great gratification; and, to relate, in my bungling manner, what I heard there, wou'd be baseness in the extreme. I am your very obedient Servant

J. MOODY

From Francis Barber,
Wednesday 29 September 1790

MS. Yale (C 69). In the same unidentified hand as Barber's letter of 20 Dec. 1789 (*ante*).

ADDRESS: James Boswell Esqr. To the Care of Mr. Dilley—Bookseller in the Poultry, London.

POSTMARK: OC 1 90.

Stowe Street, Lichfield, 29th Septr. 1790

HONOURED SIR: It is with much Concern, and Feeling, I pen these Lines, which I hope you will consider and pardon the Liberty I have taken.

I wish I never had come to reside at this Place, but being persuaded by my late poor dear worthy Master, to whom I was, and

clerk) of being "clapped on the back by Tom Davies" (ii. 344), and then is heard no more. The journal shows Moody's part to have been severely, yet perhaps charitably, cut by JB: ". . . Mr. Johnson demolished poor Moody by a word or two, and concluded—'You're an Irishman.' In a little Moody was or affected to be convinced by Mr. J. 'Nay said I, if you go over, *we'll* say you're an Irishman.' Moody was an old acquaintance of mine. Poor Derrick introduced him to me in the year 1760. He sat by today with a kind of timorous humour that durst not play for fear of Mr. J. He was once in danger of a reproof for bringing in scripture too lightly. Talking I think of Reed's Dido a Tragedy, he said it was no more like a Tragedy than the first chapter of Genesis. Tom gave him a significant hush; and Mr. J either did not hear it, or took no notice."

[2] Although associated with Drury Lane for the greater part of his career, Moody frequently acted in country towns (DNB).

[3] Not recovered.

ought, in duty bound, to oblige, was the occasion.[1] Some time ago, I was extreamly ill for a considerable time, which of course incurred a long Doctor's Bill, which when I came to pay astonished me greatly at the Total thereof, however I paid it: viz. 23.5.6, and some few months prior thereto, I observe, I paid him, and another of the Faculty, upon Account of myself, my Wife and Family—14 £. odd.[2]

I have also been at a great Expence in the care an[d] Education of my Children, as it is my wish, upon my Master's Account to see them Scholars.[3]

When I first came here, people never minded, *but rather urged to entrust me* with Articles into the House,[4] but now they see me rather reduced, (but can assure you has not been through my Extravigancy in the least,[5] but trusting in mankind to be honest and just, put too much Confidence in them, who have now rewarded me for my pains,) and through some spiteful Enemy, or busy person, several with whom I dealt, hasteily have sent in their Bills, pressing immediate payment, as if in a manner they would eat me at once, and as my Quarterly payment[6] (as it becomes due) will not be sufficient to discharge the same and to leave me a farthing in Pocket to subsist upon, and having no friend here to assist me, or confide in; beg you will assist me in my distressed situation, and this a Neighbour of mine, a poor honest Man, advises me to do; if you would therefore be pleased to advance me 20 £. I will repay you honestly, by Eight Guineas on every my Quarterly days, with Interest, and for a further Security, will give you a Schedule of part of my household Goods, to such amount, in Case of Non-payment, and this will be the means of Extricating myself from my present difficulties and put me streight into the world once again,

---

[1] JB's remark, *Life* iv. 404 n., that "Mr. Barber, by the recommendation of his master, retired to Lichfield, where he might pass the rest of his days in comfort", is perhaps less a suppression of Barber's complaints than a silent reprimand of them. See *post* To Barber, 11 Oct. 1790.

[2] A similar complaint, leading up to a similar request, is found in Barber's letter to Bishop Percy, 16 Dec. 1788 (*Johns. Glean.* ii. 69–70).

[3] Barber's only surviving son, Samuel, became a preacher in the early Methodist movement, but his formal education ended in about his fourteenth year, when he went into service. Ann, the younger of Barber's two surviving daughters, helped her mother keep a school in Lichfield in 1810 (*Johns. Glean.* ii. 86–87, viii. 80).

[4] SJ's bequest to Barber was apparently widely publicized, thanks in large part to Hawkins's condemnation of it.

[5] For evidence to the contrary, see *Johns. Glean.* ii. 61–64, 72–73, and *post* n. 10.

[6] On his annuity of £70 (*Life* iv. 404 n.; *Johns. Glean.* ii. 58 ff.).

and put my almost broken heart at reast, and for this kind and tender feeling Friend, from whom, 'till I hear, shall be very miserable.[7]

Mr. Burk upon the day of my Master's ffuneral[8] was so obliging to say, that if ever my inclination shou'd lead me to go to Service he wou'd render me his best Assistance—and as things are Circumstanced, I could wish he, you, or some of my Worthy Master's ffriends would get me a Place in the Stamp Office—India-house, etc. I will leave this dead place as I cannot get any Employ therein.[9]

I have my Masters Diploma Box by me and several other Articles, if any of them you should like to have—shall be at your Command.[10]

You will excuse me Writing in my own hand as my Eyes are not so good as they were some time back. I remain Sir, Your distressed and most obedient humble Servant

FRANCIS BARBER[11]

P.S. The Eight G[uine]as Quarterly may be paid to Mr. Dilley, or any person you shall be pleased to name in Town—but my[12] naming Mr. Dilley is on Account being near to the Bank as my Business is negotiated.

From Dr. Charles Blagden, Friday 1 October 1790

MS. Yale (C 155).

ADDRESS: James Boswell Esq., Queen Anne Street West.

ENDORSEMENT: From Dr. Blagden.

Percy Street, Oct. 1, 1790

DEAR SIR, It gives me some satisfaction that I have been able to

---

[7] The incoherence of this passage should probably not be charged to the amanuensis.

[8] Burke was one of SJ's pallbearers (*Life* iv. 419).

[9] Barber subsequently became a schoolmaster at Burntwood, near Lichfield (*Johns. Glean.* ii. 79).

[10] In his financial distress Barber resorted to selling Johnsonian relics (*Johns. Glean.* ii. 76 ff.). On 16 Oct. of this year

Anna Seward wrote to JB: "I am afraid Poor Frank Barber has been very imprudent—that Doctor Johnson's kindness has but little answered its purpose. I have given him three guineas for a carpet so worn, and thread bare, that it is not worth *one*. I was pleased with the idea of treading upon a surface so classical, and did not wish to have a good bargain."

[11] Signed by Barber.

[12] MS. "by"

make out all your difficult words except one.[1] That of Oct. 23d is unquestionably *dregs*, being the usual translation of *Marc*, though in the present case not strictly applicable. In the article of Nov. 2d the first word is *Ant-Bear*, with which animal the description agrees; and the second is *Toucan*, a well-known bird, with a most enormous beak. As to the others, the word after "Two" I cannot decypher; it looks to me like Fansans,[2] but there is no such name that I can find in any language: the words next to "or" are *Brasilian Weesels*; the animal properly so called, however, is not spotted. Can the former word be an adjective of place, like Brasilian? but on that supposition I cannot reconcile the letters to the name of any country.

I shall always receive your commands with great pleasure; and am, very respectfully, dear Sir, Your most obedient humble Servant

C. BLAGDEN

From Bennet Langton, Saturday 2 October 1790

MS. Yale (C 1693). Received 9 Oct. (Reg. Let.).

ADDRESS: To James Boswell Esqr.

Oxford, Octr. 2d 1790

... I observe Your mention of the great kindness of Mr. Malone in having superintended the printing in Your absence,[1] which topick, Mr. Courtenay, who favoured me with a Call not long ago in going through Oxford, explained upon likewise, and mentioned his having deferred an intended Journey to Ireland that he might be of Service in forwarding the work. —I cannot but at times feel a wish, that, instead of merely passing a few hours together, for the reviewing such particulars as have been recovered out of what You have been pleased to style my *Herculaneum*,[2] we might have the means of devoting a quantity of time as much larger as there might

[1] See *ante* From Blagden, 18 Sept. 1790 and n. 2; *Life* ii. 396, 400 and n. 1.

[2] Actually, "fausans" (for "fossanes"): Madagascan civets. See *Life* ii. 400 and n. 2.

[1] See *ante* To Langton, 27 Aug. 1790 and n. 3.

[2] "Very few articles of this collection [of Langton's] were committed to writing by himself, he not having that habit ... I however found, in conversation with him, that a good store of *Johnsoniana* was treasured in his mind; and I compared it to Herculaneum, or some old Roman field, which, when dug, fully rewards the labour employed" (*Life* iv. 1–2). See *post* From Langton, 17 Dec. 1790.

prove to be any topicks to interest relating to our revered Friend, for the endeavouring, by consultation and conference, to throw any additional Light that might be on such parts of his Character and opinions as I happened to have means more peculiarly of knowing from having lived so much with him—but what I speak of I am afraid is not practicable, and to be sure, if at all endeavoured at should have been an earlier proceeding than now, when so much of the work is actually printed. . . .

To Francis Barber,
Monday 11 October 1790

Missing. Sent to Lichfield from London. Reg. Let.: "Mr. Francis Barber that I happen at present to be borrowing money,[1] so cannot lend; but the quarterly offer of 8 guineas for a loan of £20 will satisfy his Creditors. Reminding him that his worthy Master was attacked for the extraordinary liberality of the provision which he left to him. It would be a sad thing if the World should know that even that does not maintain him decently; advising him against leaving Lichfield which his Master recommended as his residence—there he can live much cheaper, and with fewer temptations than in London."

To Sir William Forbes,
Monday 11 October 1790

MS. estate of the late Lord Clinton. The *Life* has swelled to two volumes, one of which is now printed.

From George Steevens,
c. mid-October 1790

MS. Yale (C 2546).

[Hampstead Heath]

I have just been told there is in the King's Library the original MS of Dr. Johnson's *Irene*, containing many unpublished speeches etc. If you have not seen this Curiosity, you may wish to see it. Yours very faithfully

G.S.

[1] At this time JB was negotiating for the purchase of Knockroon, formerly part of the estate of Auchinleck, despite the fact that he was already in financial straits (BP xviii. 287 and n.).

To George Steevens, Saturday 30 October 1790

MS. Hyde.

ADDRESS: To George Steevens Esq., Hampstead Heath.

POSTMARK: Illegible.

[London,] Saturday 30 Octr.

DEAR SIR: My having been in the country[1] has prevented my acknowledging sooner the favour of your polite note.

The Original *materials* of *Irene* Mr. Langton had from Johnson, and presented them with a fair copy made by himself to the King; but with his Majestys permission kept a copy for himself, which he obligingly communicated to me, and I have given some extracts from it.[2] I breakfast every day almost at home at 1/2 past nine. Pray come and *dejeunez* after your walk.[3] I am your most obedient humble servant

JAMES BOSWELL

I go to Kent today and return monday or tuesday.[4]

To Charles Jenkinson, Baron Hawkesbury,[1] Monday 1 November 1790

MS. Hyde. MS Yale (L 632): JB's copy, headed: "To The Right Honourable Lord Hawkesbury Adscombe Place, Croydon."

ENDORSEMENT: London, Novr. the 1st, Mr. Boswell.

Queen Anne Street West, 1 November 1790

MY LORD: I beg that your Lordship may not startle at what you

[1] At Eton, to visit his son Alexander. While there his famous attempt (and failure) to wrest SJ's letters from Fanny Burney took place (*Diary and Letters of Madame D'Arblay*, ed. Austin Dobson, 1904–05, iv. 431–33).

[2] *Life* i. 108 ff. See *ante* From Taylor, 6 May 1785, n. 45.

[3] Steevens habitually walked from his house in Hampstead to London early in the morning, visited his friends, bookshops, and publishing offices, and returned

home early in the afternoon, still on foot (DNB).

[4] See next letter and n. 3.

─────────

[1] Charles Jenkinson (1727–1808), first Baron Hawkesbury and first Earl of Liverpool; Under-Secretary of State to Bute and Secretary to the Treasury under Grenville; "a kind of unofficial minister of propaganda to the government" (Greene, *Politics of Johnson*, p. 191). See *ante* From Robinson, 6 May 1790, n. 2.

will now read from a man who is personally, and perhaps altogether, unknown to your Lordship.

In the *Life of Dr. Johnson* which I have had for some time in the press, after inserting a letter which he wrote in favour of Dr. Dodd to the Right Honourable Charles Jenkinson now Lord Hawkesbury, there is the following paragraph

> Of this letter I am sorry to say no notice whatever was taken, not even the common civility of acknowledging the receipt of it. We may wonder the more at this, that the noble Lord's own great advancement, it might have been thought, would have impressed him with just sentiments of the respect which is due to superiour abilities and attainments. I had prepared something pointed upon this topick, but my high esteem of Lord Hawkesbury's general character restrains me. [2]

In a conversation with Mr. Cator of Beckenham [3] from whence I returned this morning, after passing two days with him, I had the pleasure of being assured that your Lordship did by no means undervalue my illustrious friend; and therefore I presume to give your Lordship this trouble, as you may perhaps enable me to explain a matter which has been much talked of, so as to obviate any unfavourable construction; which I sincerely wish to do; for believe me, My Lord my mind is so happily constituted, that instead of envying, I delight in contemplating a regular, well-founded, wellbuilt prosperity.

I have only to add, that as it so happens that I am just come to

[2] This paragraph is not to be found in the MS. *Life*, having been replaced by a satellite Paper Apart, designated "H.", for p. 619 (*Life* iii. 146–47). The new version, inspired by Hawkesbury's reply (next letter), is much revised, and concludes with the following deleted sentence: "I consider this injurious fiction as a fortunate circumstance because it has been the occasion of producing and transmitting to posterity a *Testimonium* which will be acknowledged to add something to the reputation even of Johnson."

[3] John Cator (1730–1806), a timber merchant much admired by SJ, served with him as trustee and executor of Mr. Thrale's estate. A loose sheet in the Yale Collection (M 57), one of six headed "Boswelliana", explains how this meeting came about: "Seward [William Seward, the anecdotist] having told Boswell that he had asked Mr. Cator to communicate to that biographer some anecdotes of Dr. Johnson and that Mr. Cator had requested that he would bring Boswell to dine with them in order to receive them. So Seward said Boswell you have been *Catering* for me. Yes said Seward and I hope now we shall be *Cater Cousins*." In the *Life* (iv. 313) JB describes Cator's seat at Beckenham, Kent, as "one of the finest places at which I ever was a guest; and where I find more and more a hospitable welcome." See also *ibid.* 537–38, and Journ. *passim.*

that part of my Work in which the Letter from Johnson to your Lordship is introduced, I request that if I am to be favoured with an answer, it may not be delayed. I shall wait for three[4] days. I have the honour to be with great respect, My Lord, Your Lordship's most obedient humble servant

JAMES BOSWELL

From Charles Jenkinson, Baron Hawkesbury,
Tuesday 2 November 1790

MS. Yale (C 1508). MS. Hyde: a copy.

ADDRESS: To James Boswell Esqre., Queen Ann Street West, Cavendish Square.

FRANK: Hawkesbury.

Addiscombe Place, Novr. 2d 1790

SIR: I received this morning the favour of your letter, in which I see to my surprize, that I am supposed to have received a letter from the late Dr. Johnson in favour of Dr. Dodd, to which I never returnd even an Answer of Civility. As far as my Memory will serve me for so distant a period, I can venture to assert, that the letter you mention never came to my hands. I had some letters from Dr. Johnson in the early part of my life, but none as I believe since the year 1766;[1] I recollect these letters and the occasion of them; and if I had received any since that time, I think they would not have escaped my Remembrance. I have sometimes seen Dr. Johnson since the Death of Dr. Dodd, and have had conversations with him; and he never complained to me of any Incivility; and I have consulted the Gentleman, at whose house I sometimes met Dr. Johnson, and he assures me, that he never heard any complaint on this subject from him. Through a long Life of Business, no man has been more punctual than myself in answering all letters, that were proper to be answerd; and it is not probable, that I should have neglected to answer a letter from Dr. Johnson on such a Subject.

---

[4] Written over "two".

[1] The letter in question (*Life* iii. 145) is untraced. Only one letter to Hawkesbury has been recovered; it is dated 26 Oct. 1765 and deals with "papers concerning the late negociations for the Peace" (*Letters SJ* 178.2; *Life* i. 520). See Greene, *Politics of Johnson*, pp. 191–92.

I have always respected the Memory of Dr. Johnson and admire his Writings; and I frequently read many parts of them with pleasure and great Improvement.[2] I am with all due regard, Sir, Your Obedient Humble Servant

HAWKESBURY

From Bennet Langton, Tuesday 30 November 1790

MS. Yale (C 1694). Printed in part, *Life* iii. 361–62. JB edited the MS. for the printer, but in the process of printing further changes were made, as my notes indicate.

Oxford, Novr. 30th 1790

. . . But to come to the point of replying to Your Enquiries.[1] The Book, to which I esteem it as a great honour that You should have remembered my referring, is *The Natural History of Iceland*, translated from the Danish of *Horrebow*. The Chapter is, the 72d and its title,—"Concerning *Snakes*" (not Fishes) and the whole words of the Chapter are,—"There are no Snakes to be met with throughout the whole Island." Though I had forgot having made the Allusion, it occurs easily to see what it pointed to—and I think I feel a little remorse at having been so pert in my remarking, when You say, that the only word or two he *did* utter was, "pretty Dear," to one of the Children—and further, as I owed the means of my having the passage, to make the Allusion, from our Friend himself;—who, as it appeared to me, with an effect of a good deal of Humour, had brought it out in company; when mention was made of Horrebow's Book, he said with an affected gravity "I can repeat an entire Chapter of that Work"; and, when we expected a pretty copious recitation—he *did* repeat it, as above inserted.[2] —There is another such title and Chapter in the Book—"Concerning Owls"[:]"There are no Owls of any kind in the Island."[3] —Next, as to what relates to his visiting the Camp—I believe I had better write down any particulars I remember, loosely as they may occur, and You will then make any use of them or put them in any order that you may

---

[2] This sentence is quoted, *Life* iii. 147.   [2] *Life* iii. 279.
[3] See *ibid*. n. 2.

[1] JB's letter is untraced.

judge proper.—⁴It was in the Summer of the year 1778—that he complied with my Invitation to come down to the Camp at Warley —and he staid with me about a Week. The Scene appeared, notwithstanding a great degree of ill health that he seemed labouring under, to interest and amuse him—as agreeing with the disposition that I believe you know he constantly manifest[ed] towards enquiring into Subjects of the Military kind. He sat, with a patient degree of Attention, to observe the proceedings of a Regimental Court Martial that happen'd to be called in the time of his stay with us— and one Night, as late as at eleven o'Clock, he accompanied the Major of the Regiment, in going, what are styled, the *Rounds*, where he might observe the forms of visiting the Guards, for the seeing that they and the Sentries are ready in their duty on their several posts. He took occasion to converse at times on military topicks, one in particular, that I see the mention of, in Your *Journal*,⁵ which lies open before me—Page 132⁶ as to Gun-powder; —which he spoke of, to the same effect, in part, that you relate⁴— but as You may perhaps, my dear Sir chuse that I should tell you pretty fully what I can recollect, I will venture being tedious rather than being too succinct; and You will make any use, or as little use as You please of any part of what I write. As to the granulating Powder, he observed, that, to a certain degree it is necessary, for if, on the contrary, You reduce it to a state like meal, it will not explode at all; but, what is in that state, consumes in succession; which is what is called wild fire—such, I remember, he said, as the School-boys make for sport. The good, then, of having powder in grains, he said appears to be, the *air* that is by that means admitted; which, being instantaneously⁷ rarified, on firing it, produces the explosion, and the other consequent effects. How *large* the grains ought to be, he said was the matter of next consideration. It would seem that *that* size of them is to be preferred, that, in the same dimensions, would admit of the most air; and, for an experiment to that effect, he said, he would make use of two measures, of a Bushel exactly each; and fill one with Leaden Bullets, the other with small Shot, such as is used in fowling pieces. Then he would weigh them, when so filled—and whichever (as the dimensions of

---

⁴⁻⁴ Quoted, with minor changes, *Life* iii. 361.
⁵ "of a Tour to the Hebrides" interlined by JB.

⁶ Replaced by JB's foot-note: "3 Edit. p. 111."
⁷ MS. "instantanteously"

each Measure were to be exactly equal) proved to be the heavier—would evidently have the least Air admitted. If the bullets weighed heavier, and so appeared, by the larger form in which the Lead was cast, to exclude the air the more—*that* would determine him not to have the Powder in *large* grains. If the small shot weighd heavier—and *so*, excluded air the more—it would induce him not to granulate the powder into smaller grains. He said further, on this article of Gun powder, that, in order to judge whether it was good, his expedient would be, as, in the three Ingredients of it, Salt petre, Sulphur, and Charcoal, the much larger part ought to be Salt-petre (upwards of seventy parts in a hundred—the Charcoal about fifteen, the Sulphur about nine) but that as, from the comparative dearness of Salt petre, the temptation is, to put less of that than its due proportion—he would put a quantity exactly weighed of the powder into *Water*, which would dissolve the Salt petre, and then pour the Water off, which would carry the Salt petre with it—and he would then weigh the mass that remained; which would serve to detect the deficiency (if any) and how great, as to the ingredient most essential and most in danger of being deficient. The above mentioned experiments, I am aware, may, to experienced Men of the military and Chemical professions, possibly appear imperfect and slovenly, in comparison of such as they may be apprized of—but, considering that Dr. Johnson had so little means of being well versed in such discoveries and experiences as belong to professional skill they may perhaps be allowed to be considerable efforts of mind, compared with his means of information—and may lead to the thought, among so many other grounds for the same Idea concerning him—to what his Efforts of Understanding might have attained, if exerted with the same Vigour (in any Profession to which he should have applied) on the stores of knowledge that he would have found therein accumulated. Thus far I had written, when it occurred to me, that, as what has been mentioned as said by Dr. Johnson is of some length, which makes it the more desirable that it should have been founded on correctness of knowledge in the Subject, if there should be thoughts of giving it to the Publick—it might be better to enquire a little, of those qualified to judge, as to the correctness of it—which I have accordingly been doing—and from two respectable Gentlemen of the University whom I conferred with—and to confirm what had been said by them—from our principal Physician here Dr. Wall who was for five years our

Chemical Professor,[8] I learned that what external air there may be among the particles of the Gun powder is by no means to be reputed the cause of the explosion in firing it—but that it is the confined nitre that by its vast expansion occasions it. There being then this alloy, of incorrectness in the Notion—though the expedient proposed by Johnson according to the principle he had supposed is highly ingenious—perhaps you will think it as well not to insert what he said upon it, in any particular manner.[9] And as to the other device, to detect the deficiency of the Salt-petre, Dr. Wall explained upon that head, so as to shew that there would be no certainty in the effect—for that they can adulterate by putting common salt with Salt petre, which has no effect in the explosion, and yet would be equally dissolved by the water that Dr. Johnson proposed to make the trial by—so that if the *remaining* Ingredients, after the water was poured off, weighed no more than they ought in their due proportion still he might be mistaken in thinking that what had been carried off by the water had been only genuine Salt petre. *This* therefore, my dear Sir, in like manner I suppose, you will omit the particular mention of—but I thought I would however send you this paper, both to shew You that I have been at work; and apprehending that You would chuse to have the particulars communicated, for your own amusement and the interest You take in what relates to our Friend—should it not be altogether fit for publication. —I have further to mention—that [10]on one occasion that the Regiment were going through their exercising, He went quite close to the Men at one of the Extremities of it, and watched all their practices attentively, and when he came away his remark was—"the Men indeed do load their musquets and fire with wonderful Celerity[;] the Sportsman is twice as long about it—he first puts in his powder and rams it down and then his Shot which must be rammed down likewise—whereas your Men charge with both powder and ball at once"—which You, I suppose are Soldier enough to know; that what they call the Cartridge, is made up with

[8] Martin Wall (c. 1747–1824), M.D. 1777; Fellow of New College (*Alum. Oxon.*). He was appointed Public Reader in Chemistry in 1781. A professorship in chemistry was not established at Oxford until 1803. See R. T. Gunther, *Early Science in Oxford*, 1923, i. 60–66.

[9] Sewn to the MS. is a paper in JB's hand: "Note on Mr. Langton's Letter at the word *manner*: Although there is it seems a defect in point of experimental science in Dr. Johnson's observations they are so ingenious and shew such a vigorous aptitude of research that I should be sorry to omit them." But he did.

[10-10] Quoted with revision, and omitting "the Sportsman . . . powder and Ball", *Life* iii. 361.

both the powder and Ball. —He was likewise particular in requiring to know what was the weight of the Musquet-Balls in use, and within what distance they might be expected best to take effect when fired off.[10] —[11]In walking among the Tents, and observing the difference between those of the Officers and private Men, he said that the superiority of accommodation, of the better conditions of life, to that of the inferior ones, was never exhibited to him in so distinct a view. —The Civilities paid to him in the Camp were, from the Gentlemen of the Lincolnshire Regiment—one of the Officers of which accommodated him with the Tent in which he slept—and from General Hall,[12] who very courteously invited him to dine with him; where he appeared to be very well pleased with his entertainment—and the civilities he received on the part of the General—the attentions likewise of the General's Aid de Camp, Captain Smith,[13] seemed to be very welcome to him, as appeared by their engaging in a great deal of discourse together. The Gentlemen of the East York Regiment likewise, on being informed of his coming, sollicited his company at dinner—but by that time, he had fixed his departure, so that he could not comply with the Invitation.[11] —The last particular of this tattle that I will offer you is, that he met one day with Dr. Cadogan, who was our Camp Physician, at my tent—who, with a chearfulness and good humour that is constantly prevalent in his manners, asked him as to his state of health. Dr. Johnson, who was clouded with Illness and Uneasiness, replied in a half peevish manner that he was by no means well. Dr. Cadogan then asked him what *plan* he followed with a view to better health. He answered very impatiently "I pursue no plan!" Dr. Cadogan then said I thought very pertinently "if You had said Dr. Johnson that You were in a good health and did not pursue any plan I should have thought you very right, but declaring yourself to be ill, surely it is eligible for you to consider of any Regimen or plan that might give a chance for restor'd health."[14]

[11-11] Quoted, with minor changes, *Life* iii. 361–62.

[12] General Thomas Hall (d. 1809). He was commissioned a major-general in 1777, the year before SJ's visit (*Army List*, 1780, p. 4).

[13] Not identified.

[14] At this point JB has made an X, apparently marking the end of the part of the letter to be printed. But this last anecdote was not used. William Cadogan (1711–97), M.D. Leyden 1737, was the author of *A Dissertation on the Gout* (1771). See *Life* v. 210 and n. 2; and John Rendle-Short, "William Cadogan, Eighteenth-Century Physician", *Medical History* (1960), iv. 288–309. For a discussion of his precepts v. his practice, see *Life* v.

I have not a moment more before the post goes out than to give all our due regards and to say that I am Dear Sir, Yours faithfully

BENNET LANGTON

From Richard Owen Cambridge,[1] November 1790

MS. Yale (C 730).

ADDRESS: To Ja. Boswell Esq.

ENDORSEMENT: R. Owen Cambridge Esq. Novr. 1790.

[?Twickenham]

Mr. Cambridge is in as much haste this morning as the Press, but as no post goes to London tomorrow, he scribbles as quick as he can to give Mr. Boswell something like an answer.[2]

Mr. C. must have known in the year —78 what he is very sure of at this moment: That an Earthquake, which can throw up a hill or mountain, can evidently stop the course of a brook, and even a great river—therefore tho' he remembers nothing of the subject he will try if it be any satisfaction to Mr. B.—if he supposes Mr. C. quoted only to shew a Spanish Quibble.

The Poet observing that most of the Solid Structures of Rome are totally perished, but the Tiber remains the same—adds

> Lo que era Firme *Huió i solamente
> Lo Fugitivo permanece i dura.

Mr. B. will excuse the haste etc.

Ang. *fled. You know H is used by the Spaniards for F.

210 and n. 2. —Towards the end of his life SJ was to show a similar impatience with Dr. Taylor for charging him with "neglecting or opposing" his own health (*Letters SJ* 1028).

[1] Richard Owen Cambridge (1717–1802), poet and essayist. See *Life* ii. 361 ff., iv. 196.

[2] JB's letter is not recovered, but it is clear that he was attempting to complete the record in his journal of Cambridge's

part in the conversation at Sir Joshua's on 9 Apr. 1778 (*Life* iii. 250 ff.). The passage in question reads: "Talking of the brook between Rome & Brundusium in Horace's journey, *Johns.* observed, 'I have often wondered how Small brooks, notwithstanding earthquakes & Agriculture, have kept same place for ages.' *Cambridge*. 'Spanish Writer has the same thought: —— . . .' " At this point in the MS. *Life* (opp. p. 653) appears a blank, and a memorandum: "Send for it." The Spanish writer was Quevedo: see *Life* iii. 518.

From *Warren Hastings,*
Thursday 2 December 1790

MS. Yale (C 1505). Printed, *Life* iv. 66–67.[1]

Park lane, 2d. December 1790

SIR: I have been fortunately spared the troublesome suspense of a long search, to which, in performance of my promise I had devoted this morning, by lighting upon the Objects of it among the first papers that I laid my hands on; my veneration for your great and good friend, Doctor Johnson, and the pride, or I hope something of a better sentiment, which I indulged in possessing such memorials of his good will towards me, having induced me to bind them in a parcel containing other select papers, and labelled with the titles appertaining to them. They consist but of three Letters,[2] which I believe were all that I ever received from Doctor Johnson. Of these one, which was written in Quadruplicate, under the different dates of its respective dispatches, has already been made public,[3] but not from any communication of mine. This however I have joined to the rest, and have now the pleasure of sending them to you for the use to which you informed me it was your desire to destine them.

My promise was pledged with the Condition, that if the Letters were found to contain any thing which should render them improper for the public eye, you would dispense with the performance of it. You will have the goodness, I am sure, to pardon my recalling this Stipulation to your recollection, as I should be loth to appear negligent of that Obligation which is always implied in an epistolary confidence. In the reservation of that right I have read them over with the most scrupulous attention, but have not seen in them the slightest cause on that ground to withhold them from you. But though not on that, yet on another ground, I own, I feel a little, yet but a little reluctance to part with them: I mean on that

[1] The original letter was used as printer's copy, Paper Apart for p. 801.

[2] Printed, *Life* iv. 68–70. A fourth letter, dated 7 July 1780, is in the Hyde Collection.

[3] The last of the three, printed in *Gent. Mag.*, June 1785 (lv. 412). In the British Museum are three holographs of this letter, dated 29 Jan. and 12 June 1781,

and 21 Jan. 1782, the variations in which are slight: see *Letters SJ* ii. 530. The remaining version is doubtless that printed in *Gent. Mag.*; it is dated 9 Jan. 1781, and is the one that JB followed. In one of JB's notebooks recording SJ's publications (M 147) occurs this entry under 1781: "Letter to Mr. Hastings G. M. June 1785."

of my own credit, which I fear will suffer by the Information conveyed by them, that I was early in the possession of such valuable Instructions for the beneficial Employment of the influence of my late Station, and (as it may seem) have so little availed myself of them.[4] Whether I could, if it were necessary, defend myself against such an imputation, it little concerns the world to know. I look only to the effect which these relicks may produce, considered as evidences of the virtues of their author: and believing that they will be found to display an uncommon warmth of private friendship, and a mind ever attentive to the improvement and extension of useful knowledge, and solicitous for the interests of mankind, I can cheerfully submit to the little sacrifice of my own fame to contribute to the illustration of so great and venerable a character. They cannot be better applied, for that end, than by being entrusted to your hands. Allow me, with this offering, to infer from it a proof of the very great esteem with which I have the honor to profess myself, Sir, Your most obedient and most humble Servant

WARREN HASTINGS

turn over

P.S. At some future time, and when you have no further occasion for these papers, I shall be obliged to you if you will return them.

From *A. L. S. R.*,[1]
Thursday 2 December 1790

MS. Yale (C 2340).

ADDRESS: James Boswell Esq., London. To be sent with his other Letters.

POSTMARK: DE 3 90.

ENDORSEMENT: Decr. 1790. Nonsense about Dr. Johnson.

Oxford: Thursday

SIR: Altho the two following anecdotes respecting your late

---

[4] " 'I shall hope, that he who once intended to increase the learning of his country by the introduction of the Persian language, will examine nicely the traditions and histories of the East; that he will survey the wonders of its ancient edifices, and trace the vestiges of its ruined cities; and that, at his return, we shall know the arts and opinions of a race of men, from whom very little has been hitherto derived' " (*Life* iv. 68).

[1] Not identified. No person bearing these initials matriculated at Oxford in this period.

Friend come from one altogether unknowing and unknown to you, you may depend upon their authenticity. As you have generously engaged in an undertaking so valuable to the public as the collecting of the unperishable remains of the great Johnson; and the delineation of his character by a pen like yours, guided by a mind like yours, and amply supplied with materials from the favourable opportunities you enjoyed of marking every, the minutest, trait, I conceive it is the duty of every one to communicate whatever anecdotes concerning him may have fallen within his knowledge. And tho' the information be in itself trifling, who shall say, what consequence it may assume under your direction, when applied by you to illustrate some greater point, to shew the consistency of his opinions or, as in the latter instance it particularly must, to impress upon young minds the inducement to apply themselves with unwearied assiduity to cultivate their understanding and perfect their Sense of moral and Religious duties, by exhibiting the enthusiastic veneration which a mind so fraught draws from others. You Sir, in your habits of intimacy with Dr. Johnson, may probably have heard him speak of some proposals which[2] were submitted to his Judgment, for a Translation of Miltons *Paradise lost* into Greek verse. The projector of this work was a very ingenious young man a Mr. Lawson,[3] who is since dead. Specimens of the Style and manner of executing it were shewn to the Doctor and the Author himself was introduced to him. After some very handsome Compliments and expressions of his approbation of the merit of the performance, he said—"But Sir, it has ever been my opinion, as probably you may have observed, that Milton in his native Language is too ponderous, to engage the attention of most people after their curiosity has been gratified by reading him once. I fear it is too generally the case that we hang over him with admiration in our youth, then throw him by, and in the hurry of our more serious occupations, scarce think of him more or at most but think of him to regret the trouble we find in reading him. Besides Sir, The diffusion of ones particular Language, was of old by Cicero, and is in modern times, by rival States thought an object of national Concern: and if we translate all our best Authors into a more general Lang[uage] for the benefit of Strangers, how can we expect that they will give themselves the trouble of

---

[2] MS. "(which"

[3] Perhaps West Lawson (c. 1761–85),

B.A. Magdalen College, Oxford, 1783 (*Alum. Oxon.*).

acquiring *ours*, to read such trash as escapes even the notice of Translators." This opinion respecting Milton coincides (if I recollect) with a criticism in his Life of that Author.[4] I have not the book by me or I would compare them. That, respecting Translations is I apprehend extremely just. The Passage which he alludes to in Cicero is most probably that *De Archia Poeta*: Quare si hæ res: *etc.*[5] The other Anecdote which I have to communicate may perhaps appear ludicrous, but from that very character it must receive additional force as an effusion of Love and admiration. These Sentiments are probably more strongly expressed by Absurdities than by the most elaborate rational professions. This same Gentleman M. Lawson was so zealous an admirer of the Doctors, that as he could not find such frequent opportunities as he wished of being introduced into his Company, he used to follow him about the town when he was on a visit to Dr. Adams, and endeavour to glean his opinions and Sentiments as much as possible from his Conversation in Public. You will probably call this "pedibus ire in Sententiam."[6] But however: Mr. L. being one day asked what he heard from Johnson: "Heard," said he, "I have heard nothing but the creaking of his Shoes. But even that conveyed more instruction to my mind than the conversation of other People." This was a warm expression to be sure, but if taken properly, not difficult to be understood. And when your Classic Taste suggests to you, as no doubt it will, the example of the great Cicero, when he declared he would rather err with Plato, than be right with the whole world besides,[7] such intemperance in a young devotee must appear very excusable.

If to what I have written my name could give any additional weight, I would with pleasure subscribe it. But as I cannot so flatter myself, I must be content to remain unknown to you till fortune gives me an opportunity of being personally introduced to a Gentleman, whom I so much admire, and whose work I so impatiently expect.

ALSR

---

[4] Cf. *Lives* i. 183–84, 189–91.
[5] *Pro Archia Poeta* x. 23.
[6] "Coming to one's opinions on foot" (a peripatetic approach to knowledge): in allusion to the practice of Roman senators of voting by moving from one side of the senate to the other.
[7] *Tusculan Disputations* I. xvii. 39.

To Edmond Malone,
Saturday 4 December 1790

MS. Hyde.

ADDRESS: To Edmond Malone Esq., Sackville Street, Dublin.[1]
POSTMARK: DE 90.

London, 4 Decr. 1790

. . . The Magnum Opus advances. I have revised p. 216.[2] The additions which I have received are a Spanish Quotation from Mr. Cambridge—an account of Johnson at Warley Camp from Mr. Langton—and Johnson's letters to Mr. Hastings—three in all—one of them long and admirable; but what sets the diamonds in pure gold of Ophir is a letter from Mr. Hastings to me, illustrating them and their Writer. . . .

To Edmond Malone,
Thursday 16 December 1790

MS. Hyde.

London, 16 Decr. 1790

. . . My work has met with a delay for a little while—not a whole day however—by an unaccountable neglect in having paper enough in readiness. I have now before me p. 256.[1] My utmost wish is to come forth on Shrove tuesday (8 March) "Wits are game cocks etc."[2]

I shall probably trouble you with a packet towards the conclusion. I am affraid of having too much Copy.

Langton is in town, and dines with me tomorrow quietly, and revises his *Collectanea*. . . .

---

[1] "Sackville Street, Dublin" deleted; "*Mullingar*" written in. Malone had gone to Ireland in mid-November, when the printing of his edition of Shakespeare was finally completed (Osborn, "Edmond Malone and Dr. Johnson," *Johnson, Boswell and Their Circle*, p. 15).

[2] Of the second volume: *Life* iii. 273–274.

---

[1] *Life* iii. 337–39.

[2] Envy's a sharper spur than pay,
   No author ever spar'd a brother,
   Wits are gamecocks to one another.
   —Gay, *Fables*, "The Elephant and the Bookseller", line 74. Shrove Tuesday was the day for cockfights in the old English public schools.

From Bennet Langton,
Friday 17 December 1790[1]

MS. Yale (M 145). Partly dictated and partly written by Langton. Printed in part, *Life* iv. 2–27.[2] Langton's texts are here given as revised by him; JB's as originally written, including changes evidently made at the first writing. Unless otherwise noted, JB's alterations of Langton's texts may be assumed to have been made in the process of printing; his alterations of his own texts, in the process of revision of the MS. *Life*. As the particulars used by JB occur together and consecutively in the *Life*, it has not seemed worth while to record their locations individually.

[In Langton's hand]

An Edition of Lascaris's Grammar that seems only an imperfect first Draught of the other under his Name.[3]

Theocritus not deserving of very high Respect as a Writer[;] as to the Pastoral part Virgil very evidently superior. He wrote when there had been a larger influx of Knowledge into the World than when Theocritus lived; Theocritus does not abound in description though living in a beautiful Country. The manners painted are coarse and gross. Virgil has much more description, more Sentiment, more of Nature and more of Art. Some of the most excellent parts of Theocritus where Castor and Pollux going with the other Argonauts land on the Bebrycian Coast and there fall into a Dispute with Amycus the King of that Country which is well conducted—a Euripides could have done it—and the Battle well related; afterwards They carry off a Woman whose two

[1] To this MS., or rather series of MSS. (of varying lengths, numbering twenty-seven pages), I have assigned the date on which, according to the preceding letter to Malone, Langton appears to have made his revisions. The collection was compiled on at least two (and probably more) occasions: see *ante* From Langton, 1 Mar. 1790, n. 1.

[2] Further Johnsoniana were added in the second edition, but the MS. is missing. On 11 June 1792 Langton wrote to JB: "perhaps I had better send off what I have writ and defer any thing there may be to

say as to the Johnsoniana till next post, when I propose to dispatch my observations, which however I am afraid will amount to very little; indeed I had thought that you had been aware of all that concerned those few particulars contained in the paper that you have sent me back."

[3] Deleted. On his journey into North Wales SJ visited the library of Blenheim Palace, 22 Sept. 1774, and saw "Lascaris Grammar of the first edition, well printed, but much less than latter Editions" (*Diaries*, p. 221; see also p. 201).

Brothers come to recover Her and expostulate with Castor and Pollux on their injustice but they pay no regard to the Brothers and a Battle ensues where Castor and his Brother are triumphant. Theocritus seems not to have seen that the Brothers have the advantage in their argument over his Argonaut-Heroes. —The Sicilian Gossips a piece of merit. —Callimachus a Writer of little excellence—the chief to be learned from Him accounts of Rites and Mythology which though desirable to be known for the sake of understanding other parts of ancient authors is the least pleasing or valuable part of their writings. —Mattaire's account of the Stephani a Heavy Book. He seems to have been a puzzleheaded Man with a large Share of Scholarship but with little Geometry or Logick in his Head[;] without Method and possessed of little Genius. He wrote Latin Verses from time to time—and published a set in his old age which he called Senilia—in which he shews so little Learning or Taste in writing as to make *Carteret* a Dactyl. —In matters of Genealogy it is necessary to give the bare Names as they are, but in Poetry and in prose of any Elegance in the writing they require to have Inflection given to them. His Book of the Dialects is a sad heap of Confusion. The only way to write on them is to tabulate them with Notes added at the bottom of the page and references.

The Plan for printing Bibles in different Languages that want them a good one.[4] —A Question whether not some mistake as to the methods of employing the Poor seemingly on a supposition that there is a certain portion of work left undone for want of persons to do it—but if that is otherwise and all the materials we have are actually worked up—or if all the manufactures we can use or dispose of are already exe[c]uted—then what is given to the poor who are to be set at work must be taken from some who now have it—as time must be taken for learning—according to Sir Wm Petty's Observation. A certain part of those very materials that as it is, are properly worked up must be spoiled by the unskilfulness of Novices. Sometimes perhaps applicable to well-meaning but misjudging Persons in particulars of this nature what Giannone said to a Monk who wanted what he called to convert Him—Tu sei santo ma Tu non sei Filosofo. An unhappy Circumstance that

---

[4] Deleted. SJ's reasons for advocating the translation of the Bible are given in a letter to William Drummond, the Edin-burgh bookseller, in 1766 (*Life* ii. 27-28).

one might give away £500. a Year to those that importune in the Streets and not do any good.

Castle Howard with the various Buildings seen as You approach to it one of the most magnificent Places any where to be seen. Something in Vanburgh's Designs that has always a striking Effect—the same in Blenheim.[5]

One of the earliest mentions of the isochronous times of the Pendulum in Kircher.[6] —Nothing more likely to betray a Man into Absurdity than Condescention—when he seems to suppose his understanding too powerful for his company.

[In JB's hand]

Having asked Mr. Langton if his Father and Mother had sate for their pictures which he thought it right for each generation of a family to do and being told they had opposed it he said "Sir Among the infractuosities of the human mind I know not if it may not be one that there is a superstitious reluctance to sit for a picture." Cooper related that Soon after the publication of his Dictionary Garrick being asked by Johnson what people said of it Garrick told him among other animadversions they objected that he cited authorities which were beneath the dignity of such a Work and mentioned Richardson. "Nay" said Johnson "I have done worse than that. I have cited thee David."

Talking of expence, he observed with what munificence a great merchant will spend his money both from his having it at command, and from his enlarged views by calculation, of a good effect upon the whole. "Whereas" said he "you will hardly ever find a country gentleman who is not a good deal disconcerted at an unexpected occasion for his being obliged to lay out ten pounds."

When in good humour he would talk of his own writings with a wonderful frankness and candour and would even criticise them with the closest severity. One day having read over one of his *Ramblers* Mr. Langton asked him how he liked that paper? he

[5] At the beginning of the paragraph JB wrote "Sir Joshua Reynolds said", then deleted the whole passage. In discussing SJ's *Life of Blackmore* JB remarks: "In this spirited exertion of justice, he has been imitated by Sir Joshua Reynolds, in his praise of the architecture of Vanburgh" (*Life* iv. 55). In Reynolds's thirteenth *Discourse* Blenheim and Castle Howard are cited as among England's "fairest ornaments".

[6] Athanasius Kircher, *Mundus Subterraneus*, Amsterdam, 1678, i. 50–51. The sentence is deleted.

shook his head and answered "too wordy." And at another time when one was reading his *Tragedy of Irene* to a company at a house in the Country where he was on a visit, he retired to a room, and somebody having said to him "So Sir you would not stay to hear your Play." He replied "I thought it had been better."

Talking of delicate scrupulosity of moral conduct, he said to Mr. Langton "Men of harder minds than ours will do many things at which you and I would shudder; yet Sir they will perhaps do more good in life than we. But let us try to help one another. If there be a wrong twist it may be set right. It is not probable that two people can be wrong the same way."

Of the Preface to Capel's Shakspeare he said "If the man would have come to me I would have endeavoured to 'endow his purposes with words' for he doth 'gabble monstrously.' "

He told that he had once in a dream a contest of wit with some other person, and that he was very much mortified by imagining that his opponent had the better of him. "Now" said he "one may mark here the effect of sleep in weakening the power of reflection, for had not my judgement failed me, I should have seen that the wit of this supposed antagonist by whose superiority I felt myself depressed was as much my own as that which I thought I had been uttering in my own character."

"Ill have a frisk with you." rapping. "Poh—leaving us for a set of wretched unidea'd girls." Garrick said "I heard of your frolick tother night. Youll be in the *Chronicle*." "Sir he durst not do such a thing. His wife would not let him." [7]

One evening in company an ingenious and learned gentleman read a letter of compliment to him from one of the Professours of a foreign university. Johnson in an irritable fit thinking there was too much ostentation said "I never receive any of these tributes of applause from abroad. One instance I recollect of a foreign publication in which mention is made of *l'illustre Lockman*."

Of Sir Joshua Reynolds he said "Sir I know no man who has passed through life with more observation than Reynolds." [8]

An instance of address in Sir Joshua Reynolds occurred one

---

[7] Deleted. The anecdote occurs fully (and intelligibly) written at the end of 1752, *Life* i. 250–51. Malone noted at "frisk" (1811, i. 219): "Johnson, as Mr. Kemble observes to me, might here have had in his thoughts the words of Sir John Brute, (a character which doubtless he had seen represented by Garrick,) who uses nearly the same expression in 'The Provoked Wife,' Act III. Sc. i."

[8] Deleted; then marked "Stet".

evening to which he gave high applause. Johnson Beauclerk and Langton came in upon him unexpectedly when he had a City party with him at cards to whom these friends were entire strangers. "Sir" said he "Reynolds did tonight that which is very hard to accomplish. He so distributed his attention between two parties entirely dissimilar that neither had reason for disatisfaction."[9]

Mem Bacon on the effect of Christs death. Vid Christian Paradoxes.[10]

He repeated to Mr. Langton with great energy in the Greek, our Saviour's gracious expression concerning the forgiveness of Mary Magdalen Ἡ πίστις σου σέσωκέ σε· πορεύου εἰς εἰρήνην Thy faith hath saved thee go in peace. Luke 7. 50. He said "the manner of this dismission is exceedingly affecting."

He thus defined the difference between physical and moral truth[:] "Physical truth is when you tell a thing as it really subsists in itself;[11] moral truth is when you tell a thing sincerely and precisely as it appears to you. I say such a one walked accross the street. If he really did so it was[12] physical truth. If I thought so, though I should have been mistaken, it was[12] Moral Truth.

Huggins the Translator of Ariosto and Mr. Thomas Warton in the early part of his literary life had a dispute concerning that Poet of whom Mr. Warton in his *Observations on Spenser's Fairy Queen* gave some Account which Huggins attempted to answer with violence, and said "I will *militate* no longer with his *nescience*." Huggins was master of the subject, but wanted expression. Mr. Warton's knowledge of it was then superficial,[13] but his manner lively and elegant. Johnson said "It appears to me that Huggins has ball without powder and Warton powder without ball."[14]

Of a friend who boasted[15] that he had never been intoxicated, he said "Sir he is made drunk at dinner by the small beer. But Sir if he gets drunk easily he gets as easily sober again. A draught of wine makes him drunk a draught of water makes him sober. One day

[9] Deleted.

[10] Deleted. *The Characters of a Believing Christian. Set Forth in Paradoxes, and Seeming Contradictions* first appeared in 1645 anonymously and three years later was collected in Bacon's *Remaines*. But the real author was Herbert Palmer (1601–47), Puritan divine. See R. W. Gibson, *Francis Bacon: A Bibliography of His Works, etc.*, 1950, No. 516; DNB s.v. Palmer.

[11] MS. alt. "actually is"

[12] MS. alt. "I told a"

[13] MS. alt. "not so great,"

[14] Cf. *Boswelliana*, p. 274 (where "Tom Wharton" is wrongly identified by Rogers) and Hawkins, p. 257.

[15] MS. alt. "used to boast"

Sir after dinner when he was disputing with me very absurdly, I knew the cause and instead of answering him I called to the servant 'Give the gentleman some coffee.' He was going on. I called again with a louder voice, 'give Mr. —— some coffee.' "[16]

Mr. Colman having told him that Mr. Cumberland brought him a Comedy to offer for the stage and said "You will find it a comedy; for we have had of late things under that name which are *not* Comedies." "Sir" said Johnson "you should have told him you hoped *The Jealous Wife* was a Comedy."[17]

Talking of the Farce of *High Life below Stairs* he said [18]"This shews you the wonderful effect of Stage exhibition.[18] Here is a Farce which is really very diverting when you see it acted; and yet one may read it and not know that one has been reading any thing at all."

He used at one time to go occasionally to the green room of Drury lane Theatre where he was much regarded by the Players and was very easy and facetious with them. He had a very high opinion of Mrs. Clive's comick powers and conversed more with her than with any of them. He said "Clive Sir is a good thing to sit by. She allways understands what you say." And she said of him "I love to sit by Dr. Johnson. He allways entertains me." One night when *The Recruiting Officer* was acted, he said to Mr. Holland who had been expressing an apprehension that Dr. Johnson would disdain the works of Farquhar "No Sir, I think Farquhar a man whose writings have considerable merit." [19]Holland answered "I am glad to hear you say so Sir"; and in his elation of spirit was betrayed into an oath. Johnson calmly checked him "But do not swear." "Sir" said he with respectful concern "I ask your pardon." That evening[20] Mr. Obrien made his first appearance in the part of Captain Brazen. When he came off the stage after having gone through the first scene Johnson called cheerfully to him "Well Sir you have passed the Rubicon now."[19] His[21] friend Garrick was so

[16] Deleted.
[17] Deleted. "We have had many new farces, and the comedy called 'The Jealous Wife,' which though not written with much genius, was yet so well adapted to the stage, and so well exhibited by the actors, that it was crowded for near twenty nights" (SJ to Baretti, 10 June 1761: *Life* i. 364). Colman was the author.

Cumberland's comedy may have been *The Brothers*, produced at Covent Garden in 1769. Colman had become manager of the theatre two years before.
[18]-[18] Omitted in the printing.
[19]-[19] Deleted.
[20] 3 Oct. 1758.
[21] The remainder of the paragraph was deleted, and then marked "Stet".

busy in conducting the Drama that they could not have so much intercourse as Mr. Garrick used to profess an anxious wish that there[22] should be. There might indeed be something in the contemptous severity as to the merit of acting which his old Preceptor nourished in himself that would mortify Garrick after the great applause which he received from the audience. For though Johnson said of him "Sir A man who has a nation to admire him every night may well be expected to be somewhat elated," yet he would treat theatrical matters with a ludicrous slight. He mentioned how one evening he met David coming off the stage drest in a woman's riding hood having acted in *The Wonder*. "I came full upon him and I believe he was not pleased." Once he asked Tom Davies "And what art thou tonight?" Tom answered "The Thane of Ross." "O brave!" said Johnson.

Of Mr. Longley at Rochester a gentleman of very considerable learning whom Dr. Johnson met there he said "My heart warms towards him. I was surprised to find in him such a nice acquaintance with the metre in the learned languages; though I was somewhat mortified that I had it not so much to myself as I should have thought." Then[23] said to Mr. Langton "You Sir possess a good degree of it. Continue to cultivate it." Mr. Langton thanked him for the compliment and said whatever share he had of it was entirely owing to him, as it was by his recommendation that he had prosecuted that kind of study.

A   octavo[24] volume was published attacking his *Journey to the Hebrides*. He lent it to Mr. Seward and jocularly said "The dogs when they mean to abuse me dont know how to go about it. Nobody will read an octavo volume against me. They should keep pelting me with sixpenny pamphlets."

The character of Whirler in the *Idler* is said to have been old Mr. Newberry the Bookseller.

Dr. Johnson could not bear any modern cant phrases. He said

---

[22] MS. "they"

[23] The remainder of the paragraph is deleted.

[24] This item and the next are bracketed by JB, marked "From Mr. Seward", and deleted. The first is printed in a somewhat different version, *Life* ii. 308. The book, "larger than Johnson's own," was the Rev. Donald M'Nicol's *Remarks on Dr. Samuel Johnson's Journey to the Hebrides*

(1779). The second item is omitted entirely. Newbery published *The Idler*. In No. 19 SJ portrays that "great Philosopher *Jack Whirler*, whose business keeps him in perpetual motion, and whose motion always eludes his business". Goldsmith in *The Vicar of Wakefield* (ch. 13) treats Newbery with equal good-natured irony and with a clear recollection of SJ's portrait.

"People pick up cant and then mistake it for elegance." A friend[25] one day used some of these phrases such as the expression "the idling scheme." "Sir" said he "this is about the pitch of golden square." He declared his entire disapprobation of the phrase that *line* to signify any class or description of persons such as the military *line*. A prime minister is said to have most provokingly said to a certain Peer whose profusion made him needy and anxious for a place which he would not give him "I thought you would only chuse to move in the dignified *line*."[26]

Talking of the minuteness with which people will record the sayings of eminent persons a story was told that when Pope was on a visit to Spence at Oxford, as they looked from the window they saw a gentleman commoner who was just come in from riding amusing himself with whipping a post. Pope took occasion to say "That young gentleman seems to have little to do." Mr. Beauclerk observed "Then to be sure Spence turned round and wrote that down," and went on to say to Dr. Johnson "Pope Sir, would have said the same of you if he had seen you distilling." *Johnson* "Sir if Pope had told me of my distilling I would have told him of his grotto."

He would allow no settled indulgence of idleness upon principle and always repelled every attempt to urge excuses for it. A friend one day suggested that it was not wholesome to study soon after dinner. *Johnson* "Ah Sir. Don't give way to such a fancy. At one time of my life I had taken it into my head that it was not wholesome to study between breakfast and dinner."

A friend once attempting at philosophical refinement where some cucumbers were at supper expressed a doubt whether in our cold country we should use them as being the growth of a warmer climate and not of ours they did not seem to be intended for us. *Johnson* "I remember in my younger days I used to argue that a man should not walk with a stick, for if nature had designed he should walk with a stick he would have been born with a stick. Eat cucumbers Sir if you like 'em."[27]

---

[25] MS. "Mr. L" deleted.

[26] Deleted. JB lists "line" (for "department" or "branch") among the "colloquial barbarisms" SJ was "prompt to repress" (*Life* iii. 196). Cf. Hawkins, p. 513 and n. See OED, sb. 28. SJ apparently objected to "golden square" as meaning "golden mean", but if so, it was hardly a *modern* phrase. OED, "square", sb. 1 cites *The Fairie Queene*, II. i. 58. 1 ("golden squire"). I have not found "idling scheme".

[27] Deleted. Cf. *ante* From Astle, Dec. 1786 and n. 8.

Mr. Beauclerk one day repeated to Dr. Johnson Pope's lines

> Let modest Foster if he will excell
> Ten Metropolitans in preaching well

Then asked the Dr. "Why did Pope say this." *Johnson* "Sir he thought it would vex somebody."

Dr. Goldsmith upon occasion of Mrs. Lennox's bringing out a Play said to Dr. Johnson at the Club, that a person had advised him to go and hiss it because she had attacked Shakespeare in her Book called *Shakespeare illustrated. Johnson* "And did not you tell him that he was a Rascal?" *G.* "No Sir I did not. Perhaps he might not mean what he said." *Johnson* "Nay Sir if he lied it is a different thing." *Colman* slyly said (but it is believed Dr. Johnson did not hear him) "Then the proper expression should have been 'Sir if you dont lye you're a rascal.'"

One day when some tarts were brought to the table some of which were baked to a brown colour and others from their paleness seemed a good deal less done Mr. Beauclerk happened to ask what could be the reason of this difference when they were all baked at the same time. "Why Sir" said Dr. Johnson "Perhaps some of them have been nearer the mouth of the oven than others." Upon Mr. Beauclerks seeming to be agreably surprised at the readiness with which he accounted for it, he said "Nay Sir you will find that I have a very minute attention to common things."[28]

He was indeed very fond of possessing and shewing a knowledge[29]

His affection for Topham Beauclerk was so great, that when Beauclerk was labouring under that severe illness which at last occasioned his death, Johnson said (with a voice faultering with emotion) "Sir I would walk to the extent of the diameter of the earth to save Beauclerk."

One night at the Club he produced a translation of an Epitaph which Lord Elibank had written in English for his Lady and requested of Johnson to turn into latin for him.[30] Having read *Domina de North et Gray* he said to Dyer "You see Sir what barbarisms we are compelled to make use of when modern titles are to be specifically mentioned in latin inscriptions." When he had read it once

[28] Deleted.
[29] Deleted.

[30] "vide" is written in the margin, and is deleted. Vide *Life* iv. 477.

aloud and there had been a general approbation expressed by the company, he addressed himself to Mr. Dyer in particular, and said "Sir I beg to have your judgement, for I know your nicety." Dyer then very properly desired to read it over again which having done, he pointed out an incongruity in one of the sentences. Johnson immediately assented to the Observation, and said it had been owing to an alteration of a part of the sentence from the form in which he had first written it; "and I believe Sir you may have remarked that that is a very frequent cause of errour in composition when one has made a partial change without a due regard to the general structure of the sentence."[31]

Johnson being told that a certain Physician[32] had said he was a better greek scholar than Mr. Walmsley, He answered with eagerness "Sir, Walmsley had studied greek sufficiently to be sensible of his own ignorance of the latter language, at which the other never arrived."[33]

He was well acquainted with Mr. Dossie Authour of a treatise on Agriculture, and said of him "Sir of the objects which the Society of Arts have chiefly in view, the chymical effects of bodies operating upon other bodies he knows more than almost any man." Johnson in order to give Mr. Dossie his vote to be a member of this society paid up an arrear which had run on for two years. On this occasion he mentioned as a circumstance which he said was characteristick of the Scotch "One of that nation" said he "who had been one of the candidates against whom I had voted, came up to me with a civil salutation. Now Sir this is their way. An englishman would have stomached it, and been sulky, and never have taken further notice of you. But a scotchman Sir though you vote nineteen times against him will accost you with equal complaisance after each time, and the twentieth time Sir he will get your vote."

Of *Cleone a Tragedy* People will whimper at it.[34]

Talking on the subject of toleration one day when some friends were with him in his study, he made his usual remark that the State has a right to regulate the Religion of the People who are

---

[31] The last part of this last sentence was revised in the printing.

[32] The sentence originally began: "Dr. James"

[33] Deleted. Another version of this anecdote, credited to Langton and naming Beauclerk as SJ's informant, is given in *Boswelliana* (pp. 323–24). It is reprinted, *Life* iv. 33 n. 3.

[34] Deleted. See *post*, n. 49.

the children of the state. A Clergyman having readily acquiesced in this Johnson who loved discussion observed "But Sir you must go round to other states than our own. You do not know what a Bramin has to say for himself. In short Sir I have got no farther than this. Every man has a right to utter what he thinks truth and every other man has a right to knock him down for it. In short Sir Martyrdom is the test."

A man should begin to write soon; for, if he waits till his judgement is matured, his inability through want of practice to express his conceptions will make the disproportion so great between what he sees and what he can at the time attain, that he will probably be discouraged from writing at all. As a proof of the justness of this remark we may instance what is related of the great Lord Granville that after he had written his letter giving an account of the battle of Dettingen he said "Here is a letter expressed in terms not good enough for a tallow chandler to have used."

Talking of a court martial that was sitting upon a very momentous publick occasion he expressed much doubt of an enlightened decision and said that perhaps there was not a member of it who in the whole course of his life had ever spent an hour by himself in ballancing probabilities.

Goldsmith one day brought to the Club a printed Ode which he with others had been hearing read by its Authour in a publick room at the rate of five shillings each for admission. One of the company having read it aloud, Dr. Johnson said "Bolder words and more timorous meaning I think never were brought together." He added "This may be applied to very many literary performances."[35]

It is not perhaps impossible that some unfavourable representation of Dr. Johnson's as if he himself not contented with the Royal Bounty had pressed for a sollicitation to have it enlarged. But in justice to Dr. Johnson's character it has been already shewn that the proposal so far from being suggested by him was made without his knowledge. And so far was he from repining that he said "We must not complain that he who has allready given to a certain degree does not chuse [to] give more"; and upon hearing that the King had inquired after his health, with some earnestness he said in a tone of grateful satisfaction "O tis very pretty Sir 'tis very pretty Sir." And upon its being mentioned again expressed a

---

[35] The last sentence is deleted.

very anxious fear that there would be no more of this favourable notice since his letter to the Lord Chancellor in full contradiction to his intention or expectation had found its way into the Newspapers.[36]

He said "When I was at Oxford I allways felt an impulse to insult the Westminster men who were come there, they appeared to arrogate so much to themselves upon their superficial talent of a readiness in making latin verses; for I have observed Sir that many of them never got farther. And for what I myself have seen of them the well known saying concerning them seemed pretty well to hold[:] Golden freshmen Silver Bachelors and leaden Masters"; but catching himself up with some eagerness said—"Abating that I never saw any golden freshmen."[37]

Talking of Gray's *Odes* he said "They are forced plants raised in a hotbed, and they are but poor plants, they are but cucumbers after all." A Gentleman present who had been running down Ode writing in general as a bad species of poetry, unluckily said "Had they been literally Cucumbers they had been better things than Odes." —"Yes Sir" said Johnson, "for a hog."

His distinction of the different degrees of attainment of learning was thus marked upon two occasions. Of Queen Elizabeth he said "She had learning enough to have given dignity to a Bishop." And of Mr. Thomas Davies he said "Sir, Davies has learning enough to give credit to a Clergyman."

He used to quote with great warmth the saying of Aristotle recorded by Diogenes Laertius that there was the same difference between one learned and unlearned, as between the living and the dead.

It is very remarkable that he retained in his memory very slight and trivial as well as important things. As an instance of this it seems that an inferiour domestick of the Duke of Leeds had attempted to celebrate his Grace's marriage in such homely rhimes as he could make; and this curious composition having been sung to Dr. Johnson he got it by heart, and used to repeat it in a very pleasant manner. Two of the Stanzas were these

[36] Deleted. See *Life* iv. 348–50 and nn., 542–43; *ante* From Seward, 25 Mar. 1785 and n. 6.
[37] Deleted. SJ nevertheless in setting up his school at Edial investigated the discipline of Westminster as one of the "most celebrated Schools" (*Letters SJ* 3.2). See also *Life* iii. 12, and Hill's note on the "remarkable group of Westminster boys", *ibid.* i. 395 n. 2.

When the Duke of Leeds shall married be
To a fine young Lady of high quality
How happy will that gentlewoman be
In his Grace of Leeds's good company

She shall have all thats fine and fair
And the best of silk and sattin shall wear
And ride in a coach for to take the air
And have a house in St. James's square.

To hear a man of the weight and dignity of Johnson repeating such humble attempts at Poetry had a very amusing effect. He however seriously observed of the last Stanza that it nearly comprised all the advantages that wealth can give.

It seems that[38]   when he was shewn the British Museum was very troublesome with many absurd inquiries. "Now, there Sir, is the difference between an Englishman and a frenchman. A Frenchman must be allways talking whether he knows any thing of the matter or not. An Englishman is content to say nothing when he has nothing to say."

His[39] contempt for foreigners was indeed extreme. One evening at Old Slaughter's Coffeehouse when a number of them were talking loud about little matters he said "Does not this confirm Old Meynell's observation 'For any thing I see, foreigners are fools.' "

He said that once when he had a violent toothach, a frenchman accosted him thus "Ah Monsieur Vous etudiez trop."

After passing[40] an evening at Mr. Langton's with the Reverend Dr. Parr, he was much pleased with the conversation of that learned gentleman and after he was gone, said to Mr. Langton "Sir I am obliged to you for having asked me this evening. Parr is a fair man. I do not know when I have had an occasion of such free controversy. It is remarkable how much of a man's life may pass without meeting with any instance of this kind of open discussion."

[In Langton's hand]

Criticism fair between Shakesp. and Corneille as they have alike had the lights which in latter ages have been added, not so just between the Greek and Shakespeare. It may be replied to them on

---

[38] Name illegible.   [40] MS. alt. "Having passed"
[39] "unjust" added in the printing.

Shakesp. that tho' Dariuss Shade had prescience, it does not necessarily follow that he has had all *past* particulars revealed to him.

Spanish play wildly and improbably farcical would please Children here as Children are entertained with Stories full of prodigies their Experience of Life not being sufficient to cause them to be so readily startled at deviations from the natural Course of Life. Machinery therefore of the pagans uninteresting to us. When a Goddess appear[s] in Homer or Virgil we grow weary—still more so when in one of the old Grecian Tragedies—where the nearer approach to Nature is intended. Other Reasons for reading Romances as the fertility of Invention, the beauty of Style and Expression. The Curiosity of seeing with what kind of Performances the age and country in which they were wrote was delighted for it is to be apprehended that at the time when very wild improbable Tales were well received the people were in a barbarous state and so on the footing of Children as above explain'd.

It is evident enough that no one who writes now can use the pagan Deities and Mythology. The only machinery therefore seems that of ministring Spirits[,] the Ghosts of the departed, Witches, and Fairies, tho' these latter as the vulgar Superstition concern[in]g them (which while in its force infected at least the *Imagination* of those that had more advantage in Education and only their Reason set them free from it,) is every day wearing out, seem likely to be of little further assistance in the machinery of Poetry—as I recollect Hammond introduces a Hag or Witch into one of the Love Elegies where the Effect is unmeaning and disgusting.

The man who uses his Talent of Ridicule in creating or grossly exaggerating the Instances he gives—who imputes absurdities that did not happen or when a Man was a little ridiculous described him as having been very much so abuses his Talents greatly. The great Use of hearing those absurdities delineated is to know how far human Absurdity can go—the account therefore absolutely necessary to be faithful. The late Lord Orrery's Character as to the general Cast of it well described by Garrick but a great deal of the Style he expresses it is quite his own particularly in the proverbial Comparisons, "obstinate as a pig" etc.—but Mr. J. apprehends it true enough of Him—that from a too great Lust of Praise and popularity and a politeness carried to absurd Excess he was likely after asserting a thing in general to give it up again in parts, that he was capable enough if he had said Reynolds or any other eminent Artist was the first of painters to have given up as each had been objected to by others his Colouring afterwards his outline, then the grace of the Forms in his pictures, and then to have owned that he was so mere a Mannerist that His dispositions of his Pictures were all alike.

For Hospitality as formerly practised, there is no longer the same Reason—heretofore the poorer people were more numerous, and from want of Commerce their means of getting a Livelihood more difficult, therefore the supporting them was an act of great Benevolence, now that the poor can find maintenance for themselves and their labour is wanted a general undiscerning Hospitality tends to ill by withdrawing them from their work to Idleness and Drunkenness. Then formerly Rents were received in kind, so that there was a great abundance of provisions in possession of the owners of the Lands which, since the plenty of money afforded by Commerce, is no longer the Case.

Hospitality to Strangers and Foreigners in our Country at an end since from the increased Number of them that come to us there have been a sufficient Number of people that have found an Interest in providing Inns and sufficient accommodations which is in general a more expedient method for the entertainment of travellers. Where the Travellers and Strangers are few more of that Hospitality subsists as it has not been worth while to provide places of accommodation[:] in Ireland still in some degree[;] in Hungary and Poland—probably more.

[41]He who constantly has in his View many of the worst of Mankind if he shews a great Humanity of Disposition proves both that he had it to a great degree originally and has since carefully cultivated it. Speaking of the Tenderness and Compassion of Akerman Keeper of Newgate—said to give away not less than 2 £ a week to the Prisoners in Bread and Meat.

When there was a Fire in that Prison He ordered the outward Doors to be locked after him when he went into the Place where the Felons were and not opened on any account wherever the Flames might come, he then told the Felons he had with Him the

---

[41]-[41] Deleted. JB reports the incident at greater length, *Life* iii. 431–32; remarking that "Johnson has been heard to relate the substance of this story with high praise"; and concluding with the opening sentence in Langton's version (revised). For JB's relations with Akerman, see Journ. *passim*.

Keys of the different parts of the Prison and could convey them where they might be preserved, if they would go peaceably with him, but that if they chose to be riotous they might indeed destroy Him but could gain no advantage by it as he had ordered the outward Doors to be locked and on no account whatever to be opened. They paid attention to this and did follow him and were preserved. [41]

[In JB's hand]

Colman in a note on his translation of Terence, talking of Shakspeare's learning asks "What says Farmer to this? What says Johnson?" Upon this he observed "Sir let Farmer answer for himself. *I* never engaged in this Controversy. I allways said Shakespeare had latin enough to grammatacise his english."

A Clergyman whom he characterised as one "who loved to say little oddities" was affecting one day at a Bishops [42] table a sort of slyness and freedom not in character and repeated as if part of "The Old Man's Wish," a Song by Dr. Walter Pope, a verse bordering on licentiousness. Johnson rebuked him in the finest manner, by first shewing him that he did not know the [43] passage he was aiming at, and thus humbling him "Sir that is not in the Song. It is thus." And he gave it right. Then looking stedfastly on him "Sir there is a part of that Song which I should wish to exemplify in my own Life

May I govern my passions with absolute sway. [44]

Being asked if Barnes knew a good deal of Greek? he answered "I doubt Sir he was unoculus inter cæcos."

When I repeated to him Lord Mansfield's saying on the Cause of Hastie the Schoolmaster "Severity is not the way to govern either boys or men" "Yes Sir I believe severity is the way to govern them. I am not so sure if it is the way to mend them." [45]

"As you never seem to love application Sir, by what means did you get so nice a knowledge of latin." "Why Sir my Master whipped me very well, very well indeed. That was the way by

[42] MS. "the Bishop Porteus's" deleted.
[43] MS. alt. "what"
[44] This anecdote was deleted, and then marked "Stet". For SJ's remarks on the Bishop's own breaches of decorum, see *Life* iv. 75 and n. 3, 88–89 and n. 1.

[45] Deleted. The anecdote is printed, *Life* ii. 186. The first "I" is of course JB. Langton was simply reminding JB of the conversation (at the Crown and Anchor, 14 Apr. 1772).

which I got it; for, I am sure I should have done nothing without it. His saying whilst he was whipping his boys used to be 'And this I do to save you from the gallows.' "[46]

He used frequently to observe that men might be very eminent in a profession without our perceiving any particular power of mind in them in conversation. "It seems strange" said he "that a man should see so far to the right who sees so short a way to the left. Burke" (he said) "was the only man whose common conversation corresponded with the general fame which he had in the world. Take up whatever topick you please he is ready to meet you."[47]

A gentleman by no means deficient in literature having discovered less acquaintance with one of the Classicks than Johnson expected, when the gentleman left the room he observed "You see now how little anybody reads." Mr. Langton having mentioned his having read a good deal in Clinardus's greek grammar, "Why Sir" said he "who is there in this town who knows any thing of Clinardus but you and I." And upon Mr. Langton's mentioning that he had taken the pains to learn by heart the Epistle of St. Basil which is given in that grammar as a Praxis, "Sir" (said[48] he) "I never made such an effort to attain greek."

Of Dodsley's *Publick Virtue a Poem* he said "Fine Blanky Sir" (meaning to express his usual contempt for blank verse). "However this miserable poem did not sell—and my poor friend Doddy said Publick Virtue was not a subject to interest the age."

Mr. Langton when a very young man read Dodsley's *Cleone a Tragedy* to him not aware of his extreme impatience to be read to. As it went on he turned his face to the back of his chair and put himself into various attitudes which marked his uneasiness. At the end of an act however he said "Come lets have so[me] more. Lets go into the slaughterhouse. But I am afraid there is more blood than brains."[49] Yet he afterwards said "When I heard you read it I thought higher of its power of language. When I read it by myself I was more sensible of its pathetick effect" and then

---

[46] Deleted. Another version is given, *Life* i. 45–46.

[47] Cf. *ante* From Brocklesby, ?17–18 Apr. 1785.

[48] The completion of this sentence actually belongs to JB's revision. Originally, the sentence ran over to another leaf, which was later discarded.

[49] A rough note in the Yale Collection (M 158) reads: "Of Cleone a Tragedy before it appeared 'People will whimper at it. /I think/ it has more blood than brains.' " (JB's virgules—commonly employed in the MS. *Life*—set off an optional word or phrase.)

paid it a compliment which many will think very extravagant. "Sir" said he "if Otway had written this Play, no other of his pieces would have been remembered." Dodsley himself upon this being repeated to him said it was too much. It must be remembered that Johnson appeared not to be sufficiently sensible of the merit of Otway.

[In Langton's hand]

Snatches of reading—not a Bentley nor a Clarke. To put a child into a Library (where no Books unfit) and let him read at his choice.

Not to discourage a Child from reading any thing that he has an Inclination to—from a notion that it is above his reach or other such reasons. If so, the Child will soon find that out and desist— if not—he of course gains the Instruction—which is so much the more likely to come from the Inclination with which he takes up the study.

[In JB's hand]

Though he used to censure carelessness with great vehemence he owned that he once to avoid the trouble of locking up five guineas hid them, he forgot where, so that he could not find them.

A gentleman* who introduced his brother to Dr. Johnson was earnest to recommend him to the Doctors notice, which he did by saying "When we have sat together some time, Youll find my brother grow very entertaining." "Sir" said Johnson "I can wait."

When the rumour was strong that we should have a war because the French would assist the Americans he rebuked a freind with some asperity for supposing it saying "No Sir National faith is not yet sunk so low."

Towards the end of his life in order to satisfy himself whether his mental faculties were impaired he resolved that he would try to learn a new language and fixed upon the low dutch for that purpose

* One of the Herveys.[50]

[50] Omitted in the printing, perhaps because the Herveys were too numerous for speculation. John, fourth Earl of Bristol, had one son by his first wife and eleven by his second, among whom was SJ's beloved friend, the Hon. and Rev. Henry Hervey (1701–48).

and this he continued till he had read about one half of Thomas a Kempis and finding that there appeared no abatement of his power of acquisition he then desisted as thinking the experiment had been duely tried. Mr. Burke justly observed that this was not the most rigorous[51] trial; low dutch being a language so near to our own; had it been one of the languages entirely different he might have been very ⟨soon⟩[52] satisfied.

Mr. Langton and he having gone out to see a free masons funeral procession and some solemn musick being played on french horns, he said "this is the first time that I have ever been affected by musical sounds" adding that the impression it made upon him was of a melancholy kind. Mr. Langton saying that this effect was a fine one *Johns* "Yes if it softens the mind so as to prepare it for the reception of salutary feelings it may be good, But in as much as it is melancholy *per se* it is bad."

Talking of Dr. Blagden's copiousness and precision of communication He said "Blagden is a delightful fellow Sir."[53]

Goldsmith had long a visionary project that some time or other when his circumstances should be easier, he would go to Aleppo in order to acquire a knowledge as far as might be of any arts peculiar to the east and introduce them into Britain. When this was talked of in Dr. Johnson's company he said "Of all men Goldsmith is the most unfit to go out upon such an inquiry for he is utterly ignorant of such arts as we allready possess and consequently could not know what would be accessions to our present stock of mechanical knowledge. Sir he would bring home a   for grinding knives[54] and think that he had furnished a wonderful improvement."

Greek Sir is like Lace. Every man gets as much of it as he can.

His notion of lace was so high, that he confessed[55]

When Lord Charles Hay after his return from America was preparing his defence to be offered to the Court Martial which he had demanded, having heard Mr. Langton as high in expressions of admiration of Johnson as he usually was he requested that Dr. Johnson might be introduced to him, and Mr. Langton having mentioned it to Johnson he very kindly and readily agreed and

---

[51] Mis-read by the printer as "vigorous".

[52] Obliterated by the tearing of the leaf in half.

[53] In the revision this item was deleted and written in at the end of the MS. When the additional anecdotes were inserted in the second edition, it was again removed to a later position (*Life* iv. 30).

[54] *Life*, "a grinding-barrow, which you see in every street in London,"

[55] Deleted.

being presented to his Lordship while under arrest by Mr. Langton, he saw him several times, upon one of which occasions Lord Charles read to him what he had prepared of which Johnson signified his approbation saying "It is a very good soldierly defence." Johnson said that he had advised his Lordship that as it was in vain to contend with those who were in possession of power, if they would offer him the rank of Lieutenant General and a Government it would be better judged to desist from urging his complaints. It is well known that his Lordship died [56]before the trial came on.[56]

Johnson one day gave high praise to Dr. Bentley's verses in Dodsley's Collection which he recited with his usual energy. Dr. Adam Smith who was present observed in his decisive professorial manner "Very well—Very well." Johnson however added "Yes they *are* well Sir but you may observe in what manner they are well. They are the forcible verses of a man little exercised in writing verse."[57]

Drinking tea one day at Garrick's with Mr. Langton he was questioned if he was not somewhat of a heretick as to Shakspeare. Said Garrick "I doubt he is a little of an infidel." "Sir" said Johnson "I will stand by the lines I have written on Shakspeare in my Prologue at the opening of your Theatre." Mr. Langton suggested that in the line

And panting time toild after him in vain

Johnson might have had in his eye the passage in *The Tempest* where Prospero says of Miranda

—— she will outstrip all praise
And make it halt behind her.

Johnson said nothing. Garrick then ventured to observe "I do not think [that] the happiest line in the praise of Shakspeare." Johnson then exclaimed (smiling) "Prosaical rogues; next time I write I will make both time and space pant."

It is well known that there was formerly a rude custom for those who were sailing as passengers upon the Thames to talk to each other as they passed in the most abusive language they could; generally however with as much satirical humour as they were

---

[56]–[56] Underlined and queried by another hand. See *post* From Langton, c. 30 July 1793 and n. 15.

[57] "for there is some uncouthness in the expression" added in the second edition.

capable of producing. Addison gives a delicate specimen of this in the   Number of the *Spectator* when Sir Roger de Coverley and he are going to Spring Gardens. Johnson was once eminently successful in this species of contest. A fellow having attacked him with some coarse raillery, Johnson answered thus "Sir, your wife— under pretence of keeping a bawdy house—is a receiver of stolen goods." One evening when he and Mr. Burke and Mr. Langton were in company together and the admirable Scolding of *Timon of Athens* was mentioned, this instance of Johnson's was quoted and allowed to have at least equal excellence.

As Johnson always allowed the extraordinary talents of Mr. Burke so Mr. Burke was fully sensible of the intellectual powers of Johnson. Mr. Langton recollects having passed an evening in company with both of them, when Mr. Burke repeatedly started topicks which it was evident he would have discussed with extensive knowledge and richness of expression; but Johnson always seised upon the conversation in which however he acquitted himself in a most masterly manner. As Mr. Burke and Langton were walking home, Mr. Burke observed that Johnson had been very great that night. Mr. Langton joined in this but added he could have wished to hear more from another person. "No no" said Mr. Burke. "It is enough for me to have rung the bell."[58]

From Thomas Barnard, Bishop of Killaloe, Monday 20 December 1790

MS. Yale (C 92).

[St. Wolstans, Leixlip,][1] Decr. 20th

DEAR SIR: In Answer to your very obliging Letter of the 7th,[2] I send you herewith, The True original Round Robin on the Subject

---

[58] Although the expression is common (see e.g. *Life* i. 374), Burke may have been alluding to Swift's comparison of himself to Pope in "Dr. Sw—— to Mr. P——e, While he was writing the Dunciad", last stanza:

Of Prelate thus, for preaching fam'd,
    The Sexton reason'd well,
And justly half the Merit claim'd
    Because he *rang the Bell*.

[1] The place given in Barnard's letter to JB, 2 Jan. 1791 (C 93).

[2] Not recovered. It was enclosed in JB's letter to Malone of 7 Dec. "I shall be indebted to you for half the postage of this; as I enclose a letter to the Bishop of Killaloe to send me the *Round Robin*, and wish to be sure of a *certain* and *speedy* conveyance, and therefore trouble you" (MS. Hyde; *Letters JB* 287).

of Goldsmiths Epitaph according to your Request. (Disclaiming however all Recollection of any *Promise* to that Effect.) I confess that I was a Principal in that Mutinous act, being Employ'd to draw it up at the Table; And though I might be a Little Pot Valiant, when I wrote it, I am still of the Same opinion. I refer you to Sir Joshua Reynolds for the Particulars of the whole Transaction, as it pass'd at his Table. When you have made what use of it you think Proper, I request you to return it to me, that I may preserve it as an archive.[3] . . . Well, I Long for your Shrove Tuesday Cock to make his appearance. But However he will have one Disadvantage; He will be a *Dilly*, (I suppose) and in that Case you Know he must have a great Deal of *Lead* in him. Perhaps you dont call them in Scotland by that Name, and so my Pun is Lost upon you.[4] But whether he be Lead or Feathers Dead or alive I must have him before the Irish Printers get hold of him, and I desire you to order your Printer on the day of Publication to send me one by the mail coach, Directed to the Care of Mr. Jackson Holy head,[5] For the Bishop of Killaloe Dublin. . . .

From Edmond Malone, Thursday 23 December 1790

MS. Yale (C 1921).

Baronston, Decr. 23, 1790

. . . I am very glad to hear the Opus Magnum goes on so well. Pray take care of colloquialisms and vulgarisms of all sorts. Condense as much as possible, always preserving perspicuity and do not imagine the *only* defect of stile, is repetition of words. . . .

---

[3] Malone noted (4th ed., 1804, iii. 84 n. *) that the original remained with Barnard. See *post* Malone to Forbes, 3 Mar. 1804. It is now in the possession of the Earl of Crawford and Balcarres, a collateral descendant of Lady Anne Lindsay, the wife of Barnard's son Andrew. For a facsimile, see *Life* iii, facing p. 83.

[4] A far-fetched joke, dependent upon (1) the puns on "Dilly" and "lead" (JB's

printer or a duck, printer's lead or shot) and, I suppose, (2) the practice of throwing (sticks, etc.) at cocks on Shrove Tuesday, JB's target-date for publication. One can only be grateful that Barnard made nothing of "in the Poultry".

[5] Innkeeper of the Eagle and Child at Holyhead (*Universal British Directory*, 1791, iii. 387).

1791

To Ozias Humphry,[1]
Monday 3 January 1791

MS. F. W. Hilles (*L 645).

ADDRESS: To Mr. Ozias Humphrey.

ENDORSEMENT: Doctor Johnsons Letters from Mr. Boswell—Jany. 3rd 1790 [sic].

Queen Anne Street West, Monday[2]

Mr. Boswell presents his compliments to Mr. Humphrey, and returns Dr. Johnson's letters,[1] with many thanks.

To the Rev. Dr. Samuel Parr,[1]
Monday 10 January 1791

Missing. Printed, *Works of Samuel Parr*, ed. John Johnstone, 1828, viii. 12.

London, 10 Jan. 1791

REVEREND SIR, Having occasion in my *Life of Dr. Johnson* to thank the editor of *Tracts by Warburton and a Warburtonian*,[2] I request to hear by return of post, if I may say or guess that Dr. Parr is he. I should think that I may have the liberty to do my friend the credit of naming the person who has given him just and eloquent praise. I am, Reverend Sir, your most obedient humble servant,

JAMES BOSWELL

---

[1] See *ante* From Malone, 28 Sept. 1787 and n. 1.

[2] Completed by Humphry: "Jany. 3rd 1790 [sic]".

---

[1] Samuel Parr, D.D. (1747–1825). See Warren Derry, *Dr. Parr: A Portrait of the Whig Dr. Johnson*, 1966. "I dined at Langton's with Mr. Wyndham of Norfolk and Dr. Parr, the celebrated greek scholar, whom I had not seen before. His learning, and I may say, eloquence, pleased me . . . though there was something odd in his manner and rather lax in his way of thinking; I do not mean immoral, but not quite orthodox" (Journ. 31 Mar. 1783). Five years later, at Sir Joshua's, "Dr. Parr told us he was to write about Dr. Johnson. He had found out forty points of similarity between him and Plutarch" (*ibid.* 14 Apr. 1788).

[2] *Life* iv. 47 n. 2.

To Edmond Malone,
Tuesday 18 January 1791

MS. Hyde.

ADDRESS: To Edmond Malone Esq., at the Right Honourable Lord
Sunderlin's, Baronston near Mulingar,[1] Ireland.

POSTMARKS: JA 18 91, JA 24, JA 28, JA 28.

London, 18 Janry. 1791

. . . I am really tempted to accept of the £1000 for my *Life of
Johnson*. Yet it would go to my heart to sell it at a price which I
think much too low. —Let me struggle, and hope. I cannot be
out on *Shrove tuesday* as I flattered myself. P. 376 of Vol. II[2] is
ordered for press and I expect another proof tonight. But I have
yet near 200 pages of Copy besides letters[,] and *the death* which
is not yet written. My second volume will I see be 40 or 50 pages
more than my first.[3]

Your absence is a woeful want in all respects. You will I dare
say perceive a difference in the part which is revised only by myself, and in which many *insertions* will appear. . . .

From the Rev. Dr. Samuel Parr,
Saturday 22 January 1791

MS. Yale (C 2183).

ADDRESS: James Boswell Esqr., at Sir Joshua Reynolds's, Leicester Fields.

ENDORSEMENT: Rev. Dr. Parr about inserting his name in a note on my
Life of Johnson.

No. 38 Castle Street, Holborn, Saturday Jan. 22d

SIR: The letter which you lately did me the honour of writing to me,
went from London to Warwickshire, from Warwickshire to Bath
inclosed to a Parliamentary Friend who has left the place, and from
Bath to London, where he was uncertain how to direct it to me. I

---

[1] "Baronston near Mulingar" deleted;
"Gone to Sackville Street Dublin" inserted. Lord Sunderlin was Malone's
elder brother.

[2] *Life* iv. 78–79.

[3] The first volume contained 516
pages; the second, 588.

came to town late on Thursday night, and in the morning I found a large parcel in which your letter was contained.

Permit me to thank you, Sir, not only for the great honour you mean to bestow on what I have written about Dr. Johnson, but for your delicacy in attending to those Circumstances which might induce me to wish for the omission of my Name.

If the passage is not printed, I shall be obliged to you for describing me as a Friend of Dr. Johnson, and the reputed Editor, or as a Warwickshire clergyman. But at all events I beg of you not to use the words, Dr. Parr.[1]

You do not give me the Address of Rd Penn Esq.[2] and I have in vain searched for it in a Court Calendar. I therefore have taken the liberty of directing this letter to the house of Sir Joshua Reynolds, where I once had the pleasure of meeting you.[3] I am Sir your very respectful obedient Servant

S. PARR

From Susanna Davies,[1]
Monday 24 January 1791

MS. Yale (C 909).

ADDRESS: James Boswell Esqr., to the care of Mr. Egerton.[2]

ENDORSEMENTS: Mrs. Davies. *and* N.B. Returned her letters in Decr. 1791.

Monday Jany. 24th 1791, Pimlico

Mrs. Davies best Compliments to Mr. Boswell. The inclosed is all she has been able to find.[3]

---

[1] He is described simply as "the editor".

[2] Richard Penn (1736–1811), grandson of the founder of Pennsylvania and deputy-governor of that colony, 1771–73. He was M.P. for Appleby, 1784–90, Haslemere, 1790–91, 1802–06, Lancaster borough, 1796–1802 (Judd 3559). The transcript of JB's letter given in Parr's *Works* (*ante* 10 Jan. 1791) omits the request—probably in the form of a postscript—that Parr write to him in care of Penn, his neighbour in Queen Anne Street.

[3] See *ante* To Parr, 10 Jan. 1791, n. 1.

[1] Mrs. Susanna (Yarrow) Davies (1723–1801), widow of Thomas Davies, the actor-author-bookseller. For her attentions to SJ after his stroke in June 1783, see *Life* iv. 231, 522.

[2] Perhaps Thomas and John Egerton, booksellers, "Opposite the Admiralty" (*Universal British Directory*, 1791, p. 136).

[3] JB prints two letters and a note from SJ to Davies, *Life* iv. 231 365. In the Yale Collection is an unpublished letter from Davies to SJ, 24 Dec. [1770] (C 905).

To Edmond Malone,
Saturday 29 January 1791

MS. Hyde.

ADDRESS: To Edmond Malone Esq., at the Right Hon. Lord Sunderlin's, Sackville Street, Dublin.

POSTMARKS: JA 29 91, FE 4.

London, 29 Janry. 1791

. . . In this situation[1] then my Dear Sir, would it not be wise in me to accept of 1000 guineas for my *Life of Johnson*, supposing the person who made the offer should now stand to it, which I fear may not be the case; for two volumes may be considered as a disadvantageous circumstance. Could I indeed raise £1000 upon the credit of the work, I should incline to *game* as Sir Joshua says; because it *may* produce double the money, though Steevens *kindly* tells me that I have overprinted, and that the curiosity about Johnson is *now* only in our own circle. Pray decide for me; and if as I suppose you are for my taking the offer, inform me with whom I am to treat. In my present state of spirits, I am all timidity. Your absence has been a severe stroke to me. I am at present quite at a loss what to do. Last week they gave me six sheets. I have now before me in *proof* p. 456.[2] Yet I have above 100 pages of my copy remaining, besides his *Death* which is yet to be written, and many insertions were there room. As also seven and thirty letters exclusive of twenty to Dr. Brocklesby most of which will furnish only extracts.[3] I am advised to extract several of those to others and leave out some; for my first volume makes only 516 pages and to have 600 in the second will seem aukward, besides increasing the expence considerably. The *Counsellor*[4] indeed has devised an ingenious way to thicken the first volume, by *prefixing* the Index. I have now

[1] JB's financial embarrassment, owing to his purchase of Knockroon (see *ante* To Barber, 11 Oct. 1790, n. 1).

[2] *Life* iv. 223–25.

[3] *Life* iv. 353 ff.

[4] Not Mr. Selfe (*Letters JB* ii. 417 n. 1), but Thomas (later Sir Thomas) Edlyne Tomlins (1762–1841), legal writer. At this time, he "having contracted debt was obliged to quit the bar, and was now honestly getting his livelihood by *certain diligence*": viz. working as corrector for Henry Baldwin's press, and, at the moment, making JB's Index (Journ. 14 Feb. 1791). He is called "Counsellor Tomlins" by JB on occasion of a party at Baldwin's celebrating the second edition of the *Life* (*ibid.* 3 Oct. 1793).

desired to have but one compositor.[5] Indeed I go sluggishly and comfortlessly about my work. As I pass your door I cast many a longing look.

I am to cancel a leaf of the first volume, having found that though Sir Joshua certainly assured me he had no objection to my mentioning that Johnson wrote a Dedication for him, he now thinks otherwise.[6] In that leaf occurs the mention of Johnson having written to Dr. Leland thanking the University of Dublin for their Diploma. What shall I say as to it?[7] I have also room to state shortly the anecdote of the College Cook which I beg you may get for me.[8] I shall be very anxious till I hear from you. . . .

To Edmond Malone, Thursday 10 February 1791

MS. Hyde.

ADDRESS: To Edmond Malone Esq., at the Right Honble. Lord Sunderlin's, Sackville Street, Dublin.

POSTMARKS: FE 10 91, FE 14.

London, 10 Febry. 1791

. . . I am anxious to hear your determination as to my *Magnum Opus*. I am very very unwilling to part with the property of it, and

[5] Mr. Plymsell. The other compositor was Mr. Manning, "a decent sensible man, who had composed about one half of his 'Dictionary,' when in Mr. Strahan's printing-house; and a great part of his 'Lives of the Poets,' when in that of Mr. Nichols; and who (in his seventy-seventh year), when in Mr. Baldwin's printing-house, composed a part of the first edition of this work concerning him" (*Life* iv. 321).

[6] Dr. Powell prints the cancelled passage, *Life* iv. 555–56. See also *ibid*. ii. 2 and n. 1.

[7] Unchanged; but separated from the passage on the dedications in the rearrangement of the second edition. See *Life* i. 489, and *ante* From Leland, 29 July 1786 and n. 4.

[8] Malone had written to Lord Charlemont in Nov. 1787, asking his and Dr.

John Kearney's assistance in recovering SJ's letter to "some man who was employed in the College kitchen who had a mind to breed his son a scholar, and wrote to Johnson for advice". (Kearney was Fellow and Professor of Oratory at Trinity, became Provost in 1799, and Bishop of Ossory in 1806.) Charlemont replied on 7 Dec. that the letter was "well remembered, and John Kearney has promised, if possible, to find it, though he seems almost to despair." Two days later he added: "The . . . letter is, I fear, absolutely irrecoverable, as no trace can be found of any papers belonging to the college steward, who has long since been dead." See *ante* From Leland, 29 July 1786, and G. J. Kolb, "Notes on Four Letters by Dr. Johnson", PQ (1959), xxxviii. 379–80.

certainly would not if I could but credit for £1000 for three or four years. Could you not assist me in that way, on the security of the Book and of an Assignment to one half of my rents £700 which upon my honour are always due, and would be forthcoming in case of my decease. I *will* not sell, till I have your answer as to this. . . . I have now before me p. 488[1] in print, the 923 page of the Copy only is exhausted; and there remain 80, besides the Death, as to which I shall be concise though solemn—Also many letters.

Pray how shall I wind up. Shall I give the Character in my *Tour*,[2] somewhat enlarged?

I must have a cancelled leaf in Vol. II of that passage where there is a conversation as to conjugal infidelity on the husband's side, and his wife saying she did not care how many women he went to if he *loved* her alone; with my proposing to mark in a pocket book every time a wife *refuses* etc. etc.[3] I wonder how you and I admitted this to the publick eye; for Windham etc. were struck with its *indelicacy* and it might hurt the Book much. It is however mighty good stuff. No room for compliments. Ever most warmly yours.

J.B.

From John Hurford Stone,[1] Thursday 17 February 1791

MS. Yale (C 2575).

ADDRESS: James Boswell Esqr., No. 47 Great Portland Street.

ENDORSEMENT: John Hurford Stone Esq.

London field, Hackney, ffeb. 17th 1791

I am very happy, Sir, that I had it in my power to furnish you with any thing that you might judge worth recording in your life of Dr. Johnson. The petition which Mr. Seward has been so kind as to transmit to you[2] was given to me by my valued friend the late

---

[1] *Life* iv. 270–72.
[2] *Life* v. 16–20.
[3] Dr. Powell prints the cancelled passage, *Life* iii. 406 n. †.

[2] SJ's original MS. of *The Petition of the City of London to his Majesty in favour of Dr. Dodd*, now in the British Museum. JB printed it, with an acknowledgement to Stone, *Life* iii. 143 n. 1 (first edition, ii. 512 n. 3, having been received too late for proper placing). The intermediary was William Seward, who had previously supplied JB with materials for the *Life* (JB to Mrs. Boswell, 28 Jan. 1789); the occasion may have been on 12 Feb., when,

---

[1] John Hurford Stone (1763–1818), a political refugee from England, became a Girondist and was naturalized as a Frenchman in 1817. I have found no evidence that he was acquainted with SJ.

Dr. Watkinson[3] who received it from the hands of Dr. Dodd the day previous to his death, and it is I think, somewhat of a curiosity considering the person who wrote it, the man for whom it was written and those by whom it was presented.

I am glad to find that your work is so near its conclusion and I thank you much for the pleasure I have received from what you have already written on the subject of Dr. Johnson. Differing from him in almost every thing that regards either politics or religion I have always considered him among the very first in whatever related to morals, classics and criticism. Of his character, tho' enough of evil has been said, no just estimate has hitherto been made. At this distance the light and shade of it may be more accurately distinguished—before the object was too near and new to be distinctly surveyed. From you, Sir, this discrimination is generally expected, and after the sacrifice you have made to friend-ship in the public testimonies you have given of your regard, after having so affectionately honored

>Debitâ lacrymâ favillam
>Vatis amici[4]

We hope to see the stern and faithful historian who will honestly record him as he was. I have the honor to be Sir, Your most obedient and most humble Servant

JOHN HURFORD STONE

To the Rev. James Compton, Saturday 19 February 1791

MS. Yale (L 377). JB's copy or draft, written on side 4 of Compton's letter of 21 June 1790 (*ante*).

London, 19 febry. 1791

REVEREND SIR: I thank you for the offer which you have been pleased to make me; but I have reasons for declining to insert in my

after dining in a large company at John Cator's in the Adelphi, JB and Seward "sat some time after the company was gone" (Journ.). In the revised proofs JB wrote: "I could wish that the form in which p. 512 is were not thrown off, till I have an answer from Mr. Stone the gentleman mentioned in the note to tell me his Christian name, that I may call him Esq."

Stone's letter was evidently not received in time, for his Christian name was not supplied in the printing of the note.

[3] John Watkinson, M.D. (d. 1783). See *Gent. Mag.* (1783) liii. 718; Journ. 31 May 1781.

[4] "the ashes of our friend the poet with a due tear" (Horace, *Odes* II. vi. 23–24).

Life of Dr. Johnson, a narrative of that nature.[1] You will therefore be pleased to excuse me. I am Reverend Sir your most obedient humble servant

To Edmond Malone, Friday 25 February 1791

MS. Hyde.

ADDRESS: To Edmond Malone Esq., Sackville Street, Dublin.

POSTMARK: FE 26 91.

London, 25 Febry. 1791

. . . I am in a distressing perplexity how to decide as to the property of my Book. You must know that I am *certainly* informed that a certain person who delights in mischief has been *depreciating* it,[1] so that I fear the sale of it may be very dubious. *Two Quartos* and *Two Guineas* sound in an alarming manner. I believe in my present frame I should accept even of £500, for I suspect that were I now to talk to Robinson I should find him not disposed to give £1000. Did he absolutely *offer* it, or did he only express himself so as that you *concluded* he would give it? The pressing circumstance is that I *must* lay down £1000 by the first of May, on account of the purchase of land, which my old family enthusiasm urged me to make.[2] You I doubt not have full confidence in my honesty. May I then ask you if you could venture to join with me in a bond for that sum, as then I would take my chance, and as Sir Joshua says *game* with my Book. Upon my honour your telling me that you cannot comply with what I propose will not in the least sur-

---

[1] Though JB declined, Malone was to accept Compton's narrative for inclusion in the sixth edition of the *Life* (1811, iv. 224–27), with the remark that had JB known the circumstances, he would have accepted the account. See J. M. Osborn, "Dr. Johnson and the Contrary Converts", in *New Light on Dr. Johnson*, pp. 308 ff.

---

[1] On 20 Feb. JB walked with Dilly in Lincoln's Inn Fields, "being in great despondency as to *Life of Johnson*. He told me that Stockdale told him it had

been depreciated and on being pressed, owned that Steevens had talked against it. It vexed me to think that this malicious man had I feared access to it at the Printing-House" (Journ.).

[2] "I apprehended Malone had been too sanguine in imagining it had been *offered*. . . . My great tribulation was being *obliged* to lay down £1000 for Knockroon, more than the £1500 which I was to have from Mr. Fairlie upon its security; which if I failed to do, I should be disgraced, and vexatiously lose the purchase" (*loc. cit.*)

prise me or make any manner of difference as to my opinion of your friendship. I mean to ask Sir Joshua if he will join; for, indeed I should be vexed to sell my *Magnum Opus* for a great deal less than its intrinsick value. I meant to publish on Shrove Tuesday. But if I can get out within the month of March, I shall be satisfied. I have now I think *four* or *five* sheets to print which will make my second volume about 575 pages. But I shall have more cancels. That *nervous* mortal W.G.H. is not satisfied with my report of some particulars *which I wrote down from his own mouth*, and is so much agitated, that Courtenay has persuaded me to allow a *new edition* of them by H. himself to be made at H.'s expence.[3] Besides, it has occurred to me that where I mention "a *literary fraud*" by Rolt the Historian in going to Dublin and publishing Akenside's *Pleasures of the Imagination* with his own name, I may not be able to authenticate it, as Johnson is dead, and he may have relations who may take it up as an offence, perhaps a *Libel.* Courtenay suggests that you may perhaps get intelligence whether it was *true.* The Bishop of Dromore can probably tell,[4] as he knows a great deal about Rolt. In case of doubt, should I not cancel the leaf, and either omit the curious anecdote, or give it as a story which Johnson laughingly told as having circulated? There is a glaring mistake into which you and I fell where we agreed, that in No. 39 of *The Adventurer* on Sleep "a translation from Statius marked C.B. is *certainly* the performance of Dr. Charles Bathurst," for unluckily I find that Bathurst's name was *Richard.* I think I may set that right in my Errata.[5] . . .

---

[3] On 3 Mar. JB "Dined at W. G. Hamilton's who had fantastically insisted that some passages in my *Life of Johnson* relative to him should be cancelled, and Courtenay and I were with him some time before dinner to talk of this. Courtenay had been plagued with tedious consultations about it, from the anxiety of Hamilton's vanity. I did not like it; but yielded to a certain degree" (Journ.). See *ante*

From Hamilton, 6 Feb. 1788, n. 9, and *post* To Hamilton, 25 Feb. 1793. Courtenay's own hand appears in the alteration of the MS. of *Life* iv. 48 from "Mr. William Gerrard Hamilton informed me" to "I am well informed".

[4] See *post* From Percy, 6 Apr. 1791.

[5] "Corrections and Additions" (opp. p. 1) for p. 136, line 6; as in *Life* i. 252.

From Mrs. Hester Chapone,[1]
Sunday 27 February 1791[2]

MS. Yale (C 784).

ADDRESS: —— Boswell Esqr., 47 Great Portland Street.

Feby. 27th, Carlisle St.

Mrs. Chapone's compliments to Mr. Boswell, she has no Copy of Dr. Johnson's letter,[3] but has found one from Lord Carlisle to her (occasion'd by her transmitting to him Dr. Johnson's remarks on his Tragedy) which is dated "Piccadilly Novr. 29th 1783." This she *supposes* was nearly if not quite of the same date as the other, but cannot call to mind whether Lord C. sent it *immediately* on the rec[eip]t of the Doctor's letter, or not.

From the Rev. George Strahan,[1]
Friday 4 March 1791[2]

MS. Yale (C 2581).

Extract from *The Political Magazine* for Decr. 1787[3]

Dr. Johnson met a Gentleman of Lichfield who had lately buried his Father,[4] and, after the usual Salutation, he addressed him in Words to the following Effect: "I have not seen you, Sir, since the Death of your worthy Father; he was a Man for whom I had a great

[1] Hester (Mulso) Chapone (1727–1801), the essayist.

[2] The year is deduced from the address: JB moved from Queen Anne Street West to Great Portland Street on 19 Jan. 1791 (BP xviii. 100).

[3] To her on the subject of Lord Carlisle's tragedy: see *ante* To Carlisle, 29 Dec. 1789, and From Carlisle, 31 Dec. 1789. In copying from the original JB omitted the date ("Nov. 1783": *Letters SJ* 911). On the basis of the present information he dated the letter (in the printing) 28 Nov. 1783: *Life* iv. 248.

[1] The Rev. George Strahan (1744–1824), son of William Strahan the printer; Vicar of St. Mary's, Islington; later Pre-

bendary of Rochester and Rector of Kingsdown, Kent. He attended SJ during his last days and edited his *Prayers and Meditations* for publication in 1785: see *ante* From Adams, 12 July 1786 and n. 15. According to Mrs. Thrale (*Thraliana*, p. 204 and n. 8), SJ composed ("I know not how many") sermons for him.

[2] "I walked to Islington where by kind invitation, I dined with the Rev. Mr. Strahan, and talked of Dr. Johnson's last illness" (Journ. 4 Mar. 1791).

[3] xiii. 944–45. The article is headed: "Anecdote of the Late Dr. Johnson." Strahan's transcript alters only the punctuation and a few spellings.

[4] Henry and Thomas White. See *ante* To Pearson, 7 Apr. 1785 and n. 1.

Respect as a Parent and a Clergyman, and I doubt not of your having paid every filial Duty and Respect to his latter Days, alleviating, as far as human Consolation is able, the Struggles of the Mind under the Ruins of the Body. It is a pleasing Sensation to reflect on a due Discharge of Duty to our Parents; you feel the happy Effects of it. From that Source I can derive no Comfort; you very well know, Sir, my Father (and he was a good Father) was a Bookseller, a Bookseller of most inferiour Order. He kept Market, Sir, and he ordered me to get ready to attend him to Uttoxeter; I refused, for I did not like the Office. Pride, Sir, rank Pride was at the Bottom of this Refusal. He intreated, I was obstinate, and so it passed. Some time after my Father's Death, I reflected upon this Act of Disobedience, and upon my visiting Lichfield, I thought some Contrition necessary for such a Breach of Duty. I went to Uttoxeter; it was a Market Day; I went to the Place where my poor Father's Stall stood: it was a rainy Day, Sir; I pulled off my Hat, my Wig, and I stood there for two Hours, drenched in Rain, and I hope the Penance was expiatory."[5]

Johnsoniana[6]

Warburton, he said, was perhaps the last Man that had writ with a Mind full of Reading and Reflection.[7]

Concerning his first Acquaintance with a celebrated Work of Dr. Law he gave this Account to a Friend: "When I was a light young Man, and accustomed to laugh at such Writers as Law, I one Day took up his *Serious Call*, and began to read in it, only to make Sport: But I soon found that I had to do with one much every way above my Match, ceased to laugh at his Seriousness, and read on with Reverance of his Piety.[8]

The man who sate up with him a strange man whom he had never seen before, being asked how he liked his attendant[:] "Not

---

[5] Cf. *Life* iv. 373.

[6] The first two items are in Strahan's hand, the last three in JB's.

[7] Quoted, *Life* iv. 49.

[8] Cf. the similar though rather more momentous version communicated to JB by SJ himself "upon the subject of his religious progress", *Life* i. 67–68. JB first took up the book on 8 Dec. 1793 and

"wondered at [SJ's] approbation of it; for though there is not a little vivacity in it, and many characters very well imagined, the scope of it is to make a Religious Life inconsistent with all the feelings and views which animate this state of being" (Journ.). See Katharine C. Balderston, "Doctor Johnson and William Law", PMLA (1960) lxxv. 382 ff.

at all Sir. The fellow's an idiot; he is as aukward as a turnspit when first put into the wheel and sleeps like a dormouse."[9]

The last time he received the Sacrament he pronounced the following prayer which he afterwards dictated to Mr. Strahan.[10]

He was in much agitation for some time, but became composed for some days before his death.[11]

From Edmond Malone,
Saturday 5 March 1791

MS. Yale (C 1925).

ADDRESS: James Boswell, Esqre., Great Portland Street, Portland Chapel, London.

POSTMARK: MR 9 91.

Dublin, March 5, 1791

. . . The most material part of yours of the 25th of Feb. is that which relates to Robinson. I really forget what words he used, when he talked to me about your book; but the import, I think, was, that he was willing to give 1000 £ for the copy. As it was then to be in one volume, I conceive he could not now offer for two less than 1200 £. —Whenever you fix on your title-page, if you will enclose it to me in Ms, I will examine it very carefully, and perhaps may be able to suggest somewhat.—With respect to the Character in your *Journal*, if you retain it, it certainly should be amplified, and his uniform piety and virtue enlarged upon.[1] Pray omit your

[9] Printed, with revision and without acknowledgement, *Life* iv. 411. Cf. Hawkins, p. 590. The man may have been Cawston, William Windham's servant: see *post* From Byng, 12 Apr. 1791 and n. 4.

[10] Missing, but printed, *Life* iv. 416–17. JB instructed the printer to "take it in" from Strahan's edition of the *Prayers and Meditations*. Strahan had edited the text in copying it from Hawkins (p. 585), and it is not clear whether JB was showing a preference for Strahan's version or had simply overlooked Hawkins. See *Diaries*, pp. 417–18 (where the text is printed from the original, now in the Tinker Collection at Yale) and n. A copy in Strahan's hand is at Pembroke College, Oxford. Another of SJ's prayers, 26 Apr. 1752 (*Life* i. 235–36; *Diaries*, pp. 46–47), was copied for JB by Strahan (who had it from Francis Barber and printed it in his third edition); it first appeared in the second edition of the *Life*, "Additions to the Second Edition" (i. *1).

[11] *Life* iv. 416.

[1] At the very end of the *Life* JB reintroduces the character, remarking in a foot-note: "As I do not see any reason to give a different character of my illustrious friend now. from what I formerly

Canterbury Organ and your *bow wough* entirely.[2] —It will be impossible, I fear, to gain any intelligence of Rolt for you here, unless there was an edition of the *Pleasures of Imagination* published here with *his name*, in which case I might be able to trace it in Faulkner's *Dublin Journal* of which there is a complete set at his successor's, from 1730.[3] Let me know how this is. Dublin is very far from being literary even now, but in 1745 was in complete darkness. . . . *Charles* Bathurst, the *bookseller*, led us into the mistake about the translation from Statius.[4] . . .

To Edmond Malone, Tuesday 8 March 1791

MS. Hyde.

ADDRESS: To Edmond Malone Esq., at Lord Sunderlin's, Sackville Street, Dublin.

POSTMARKS: MR 8 91, MR 10 91, MR 14.

London, 8 March 1791

. . . Dilly proposes that he and Baldwin should each advance £200 on the credit of my Book;[1] and if they do so, I shall manage well enough; for I now find that I can have £600 in Scotland on the credit of my rents; and thus I shall get the £1000 paid in May. . . .

gave, the greatest part of the sketch of him in my 'Journal of a Tour to the Hebrides,' is here adopted" (*Life* iv. 425 n. 1). Somewhat more emphasis is put upon SJ's "piety and virtue", but also upon his intellectual powers, "the art of using his mind". See Introduction, pp. xlv–xlvi.

[2] "Lord Pembroke said once to me at Wilton, with a happy pleasantry, and some truth, that 'Dr. Johnson's sayings would not appear so extraordinary, were it not for his *bow-wow way:*' but I admit the truth of this only on some occasions. The *Messiah*, played upon the *Canterbury organ*, is more sublime than when played upon an inferior instrument: but very slight music will seem grand, when conveyed to the ear through that majestick medium" (*Tour: Life* v. 18). JB had al-

ready included the *bow-wow* in a foot-note, *Life* ii. 326 n. 5.

[3] George Faulkner (?1699–1775), "the prince of Dublin printers" (Swift), began printing *The Dublin Journal* in 1728. At his death, it passed into the hands of his nephew, Thomas Todd Faulkner (d. 1793). See R. R. Madden, *The History of Irish Periodical Literature*, 1867, ii. ch. 1.

[4] Charles Bathurst (c. 1709–86), bookseller and publisher in London. See Plomer. Malone was later to notice another "slight inaccuracy": namely, that the translated lines were from Cowley, who is mentioned in the same paragraph with Statius (6th ed., 1811, i. 229n.; noted also by Hill, *Life* i. 252 n. 3).

---

[1] Which was done. JB settled his accounts with Dilly and Baldwin on 24 Nov. 1792 (Journ.).

Have I told you that Murphy has written *An Essay on the Life and Writings of Dr. Johnson* to be prefixed to the new edition of his Works? He wrote it in a month, and has received £200 for it.[2] I am quite resolved now to keep the property of my *Magnum Opus*; and I flatter myself I shall not repent it.

The charge against Rolt is that he published *The pleasures of Imagination* with *his name* to it. I should think the Bishop of Dromore who once shewed me some[3] letters to Rolt. I would wish to avoid all cause of quarrel or even ill will. The Bishop can probably tell what Rolt was, and what became of him. My Title as we settled it is, The Life of Samuel Johnson, LL.D. comprehending an account of his studies and various works in chronological order his conversations with many eminent persons a series of letters from him[4] to celebrated men and several original pieces of his composition The whole exhibiting a view of Literature and Literary men in Great Britain for near half a century during which he flourished. I think *incidents* should be also introduced. It will be very kind if you will suggest what yet occurs. I hoped to have published today. But it will be about a month yet before I launch. I have now before me in print 560 pages of Vol. 2 and I fear I shall have 20 more. . . .

To Edmond Malone, Saturday 12 March 1791

MS. Hyde.

ADDRESS: To Edmond Malone Esq., Sackville Street, Dublin.

POSTMARK: MAR 15.

London, 12 March 1791

. . . But I am still in great anxiety about the sale of my Book. I find so many people shake their head's at the *two quartos* and *two guineas*. Courtenay is clear that I should sound Robinson and accept of a thousand guineas, if he will give that sum. Mean time the Title Page must be made as good as may be. It appears to me that mentioning his studies works conversations and letters is not sufficient; and I would suggest comprehending an Account in

---

[2] £300, according to *Lit. Anec.* ix. 159. For "*Writings*" read "*Genius*". The *Works*, in twelve volumes, were edited by Murphy and published in 1792.

[3] JB lost the thread of his sentence in starting a new page.

[4] MS. alt. "of his letters"

chronological order of his studies works friendships acquaintance and other[1] particulars[2][;] his conversations with eminent men,[3] a series of his letters to various persons[;] Also several original pieces of his composition never before published[:] The Whole etc. You will probably be able to assist me in expressing my idea, and arranging the parts. In the Advertisement I intend to mention the letter to Lord Chesterfield and perhaps the Interview with the King and the names of the correspondents in alphabetical order.[4] How should *in chronological order* stand in the order of the members of my Title. I had at first *celebrated correspondents* which I don't like. How would it do to say "his conversations and epistolary correspondence with eminent (or celebrated) persons"? Shall it be *different* works, and *various* particulars? In short it is difficult to decide. . . .

. . . Pray could not you be of some service to my Work, by inquiring whether some of the Irish Booksellers would not take some.[5] I trust to be out on the 15 of April. . . .

From Thomas Percy, Bishop of Dromore, Saturday 12 March 1791

MS. Yale (C 2237).

ADDRESS: James Boswell Esqr., Great Portland St., London.

POSTMARK: MR 16 91.

Dublin, March 12th 1791

DEAR SIR, I am happy to find by our Friend Mr. Malone, whom I saw yesterday, that your *Life of Dr. Johnson* may soon be expected: He tells me however, that he thinks 3 or 4 weeks may pass, before you will be able to come forth. This induces me to request a particular Favour, which, if granted, will exceedingly oblige me. It is to beg to be indulged with a sight of that sheet of your book,

---

[1] MS. "various" deleted.

[2] MS. "and anecdotes" deleted.

[3] MS. "persons" deleted.

[4] Not carried out. See *post* From Malone, 14 Apr. 1791 and n. 4.

[5] The Irish booksellers probably lay in wait for the inevitable piracy. As the Dublin edition did not come out until 1792, it "could not have cut into the sale of the first edition to any extent, but it must have injured the market for the second, which it preceded by a year" (*Lit. Car.* p. 167).

wherein you mention a common Friend of Dr. Johnson's and mine,
—Dr. Grainger the Translator of Tibullus:[1] I have a particular
Regard for the memory of poor Dr. Grainger, and as he, thro'
his Wife[2] was connected with some very respectable Families, but
especially as he left an only Daughter[3] a young Lady of great
Beauty and Merit, just now in her bloom, to whom a very considerable Fortune was lately bequeathed by a maternal Uncle, I cannot
but feel a particular solicitude for their and her feelings lest they
should be wounded and her happiness nay even the Chances of her
establishment in Life affected, by any unguarded Account of her
deceased Father, in a book, which She will naturally have on her
Shelf.[4]

Now Dr. Grainger was not only a man of Genius and Learning,
but had many excellent Virtues, being one of the most generous
friendly and benevolent Men I ever knew:[5] yet as there was one
Story, which Johnson used to tell; I mean the Recital of the passage
in his *Sugar-Cane* (where he introduces the Vermin, Rats etc.
which destroy the Canes) by Tom Warton; that I take for granted
you have inserted;[6] I could wish to prevail on you, if not (what I
could most wish) to *omit* that Story, yet to accompany it with a
proper and just representation of what occasioned such a Peculiar-

---

[1] James Grainger (?1721–66), physician and poet. Percy, a staunch friend of
Grainger, was instrumental in the publication of his poetical works and life (ed.
Robert Anderson, 1836). Grainger's Tibullus (which SJ said "was very well done")
appeared in 1758. Percy translated the
first Elegy and Ovid's elegy on Tibullus
(*Life* ii. 454, 534).

[2] Daniel Mathew Burt (named after
her uncle mentioned in the text), daughter
of the governor of St. Christopher in the
West Indies, where Grainger lived from
1759. She was publicly attacked in 1773–
1774 for having allegedly caused her
husband's early death by her infidelity,
but the charge was promptly and vigorously answered by Percy and was withdrawn. See *Life* ii. 534–35.

[3] His only surviving daughter, Eleanor
C. Grainger. Percy was godfather to her,
and later to her eldest son, James Percy
Rousell (*Lit. Illust.* vii. 230).

[4] SJ's character of Grainger as origin-

ally printed by JB was cancelled. See *post*
From Percy, 24 Mar. 1791 and n. 3.

[5] Quoted, *Life* ii. 454 n. 1.

[6] It may be doubted whether Percy's
intuition was not reinforced by Malone's
information; and also whether Percy's
solicitude was for Grainger's reputation
alone. The cancelled passage in the *Life*
includes the following remarks by SJ (the
first part of which was restored in a foot-
note to the second edition, ii. 338): "Percy
was angry with me for laughing at 'The
Sugar Cane;' for he had a mind to make a
great thing of Granger's rats. There was
a review of it in 'The London Chronicle,'
said to be written by me; but I only helped
Percy with it, and was in jest" (*Life* iv.
556). On the question of SJ's authorship
of the review, see *ibid.* i. 481 and n. 4.
JB also cancelled a passage in which he
ascribed to SJ the Dedication to the
Reliques—but this at the urging of Reynolds (see *ante* To Malone, 29 Jan. 1791),
not Percy, Reynolds being mentioned in

ity, in a Poem, which otherwise has great Merit, being the first Collection (I believe) of poetical Flowers, which have ever been gather'd across the Atlantic. —The passage in question was originally not liable to such a Perversion; for the Author having in this Part of his Work occasion to mention the havock made by Mice, Rats, etc.—had introduced the subject with a k⟨ind⟩ of Mock-Heroic, and a Parody of Homer's battle of Frogs and Mice, invoking the Muse of the Old Grecian Bard, in manner that was not ungraceful: and in that State I had seen it: But afterwards unknown to me and his other Friends, he had been overpersuaded to alter the passage, (contrary to his own better Judgment) so as to produce the Unlucky effect above alluded to. —Now this is what I Want to have mentioned in a Note by way of extenuation,[7] accompanied with a just Character of the Doctor[8] who was both a very valuable Man and an ingenious Writer: For his Poem on Solitude, in Dodsley's Misc[ellan]y contains some of the sublimest Images in Nature.[9] He also wrote a very valuable medical Tract on the Treatment of Negroes and their peculiar Maladies.[10] If you will therefore allow me to see your Account of my Friend, I will submit to you such Illustrations or Annotations, as may perhaps induce you to cancell the Leaf (for which I will gladly pay out of my own pocket) and both add to the general Information, Evince your own Candour as well as exceedingly oblige, Dear Sir, Your very faithful Obedient Servant

THO. DROMORE

N.B. Anything bulky will come Post-free under Cover to *The Lord Bishop of Cork*[11] *at the Castle Dublin.*

the same passage as another beneficiary of this talent of SJ's. See *Life* ii. 2 and n. 1, iv. 555–56 and *Percy-Malone Correspondence*, pp. 56–57.

[7] Done, with revision, *Life* ii. 454 n. 1. (In the second edition JB inserted in his text the paragraph beginning "This passage does not appear in the printed work" and in his note the paragraph beginning "The above was written by the Bishop when he had not the Poem itself to recur to".) In 1805 Percy wrote to Anderson: "Boswell's ludicrous account of the 'Sugar Cane' deserves no attention, and need not be mentioned, as the passage was altered in the printed copy" (*Lit. Illust.* vii. 144). But Anderson mentioned it anyway—in

his life of Grainger (*ante* n. 1). See also *Life* ii. 532–34 and G. S. Alleman, "Mice and the Muse," TLS, 13 Aug. 1938, p. 531.

[8] See *ante* n. 5.

[9] "Solitude. An Ode", in *A Collection of Poems in Four Volumes* (1755, iv. 233–43). SJ also praised the poem (*Life* iii. 197).

[10] *An Essay on the More Common West India Diseases; and the Remedies which that Country Itself Produces. To which are added Some Hints on the Management of Negroes,* 1764. It was published anonymously.

[11] See *ante* From Percy, 19 Mar. 1790, head-note and n. 2.

To Charles Jenkinson, Baron Hawkesbury, Wednesday 23 March 1791

MS. British Museum. MS. Yale (L 633): JB's draft or copy, headed: "To The Right Honourable Lord Hawkesbury."

Great Portland Street, 23 March 1791

MY LORD: Circumstances[1] with which I do not presume to trouble your Lordship, have kept my mind in so unpleasing a state, that I have too long delayed to acknowledge your Lordship's very polite and satisfactory letter,[2] for which I return your Lordship my sincere thanks.

Perhaps Mr. Cator, or my old friend your Lordship's neighbour Mr. Claxton,[3] may be so good as to afford me an opportunity of assuring your Lordship in person, of the great respect with which I have the honour to be, My Lord, Your Lordships much obliged obedient humble servant

JAMES BOSWELL

From Charles Jenkinson, Baron Hawkesbury, Thursday 24 March 1791

MS. Yale (C 1509).

ADDRESS: To James Boswell Esqre., Great Portland Street.

FRANK: Hawkesbury.

[London,] Thursday

Lord Hawkesbury presents his Compliments to Mr. Boswell. He received last Night the Favour of his Note. —It is not necessary that Mr. Cator, Mr. Claxton or any one should introduce Mr. Boswell to Lord Hawkesbury. He will be happy to receive him without any Introduction, and begs to have the Pleasure of seeing him Tomorrow Morning at half an Hour after 10 at his House in Hertford Street.[1]

[1] Political frustrations, financial embarrassments, lingering grief over the loss of his wife, and anxiety over the publication of the *Life*: see BP xviii. 96 ff.

[2] *Ante* 2 Nov. 1790.

[3] John Claxton (c. 1740–1811), of Lincoln's Inn, F.S.A., a friend of Gray and Temple. He lived in Shirley, near Croydon (Hawkesbury's residence), Surrey, before retiring to Bath, where he died (*Alum. Cant.*; *Lit. Anec.* i. 169; *Bibliotheca Topographica Britannica* x. 25; *Letters JB* and Journ. *passim*).

[1] There is a gap in the journal between 23 Mar. and 3 Apr.

From Thomas Percy, Bishop of Dromore, Thursday 24 March 1791

MS. Yale (C 2238).

Dublin, March 24th 1791

DEAR SIR, I esteem it quite providential, that by casually[1] mentioning the subject to Mr. Malone I was induced to write you about my poor friend Dr. Grainger, and there by prevented you from suffering the Pain you would have felt at doing injustice to his Memory, and perhaps irreparable Injury to his amiable and innocent Daughter. —I am astonished at the severe Censure which you tell me[2] Dr. J. passed upon that worthy Man: for such I will aver him to have been, from the fullest Conviction and long Acquaintance with him. I knew him much better than Dr. J. and do not recollect a single Instance of Misconduct, or any one Action of his Life (that ever came to *my* knowledge) that could abate my esteem of him. —As to the cruel Censure that he was destitute *of any principle*, or *Obligation of Duty*:[3] I know not how we are to judge of Men's principles, but by their operation on their Conduct: and I do declare, that as to the *relative Duties* Dr. Grainger was quite exemplary: His parents died when he was young, but he was one of the most grateful and affectionate Brothers, of the most indulgent husbands, of the most tender Fathers, and, most disinterested Friends I ever knew: as I could support, if needful, by remarkable Instances. Nor did I ever once hear him throw out any sentiment, even *in sport*, that could justify such a severe Imputation, as that "he was quite destitute of principle I mean any Notion of Obligation to rectitude any principle of Duty," etc. etc. I am persuaded, that Dr. J. would upon reflection have been very sorry to have had, what was perhaps a hasty escape, been made History and certainly to have recorded such a Censure (being, as I believe in my *Conscience* it is, unfounded) would have been as injurious to the Memory of the Relater, as to the Sufferer, and have Entailed Discredit on any Book that should have recorded it. —Excuse me therefore, my dear Friend, if out of regard to the memory of that revered Character, whose Virtues and Talents you wish [to] preserve from

---

[1] See *ante* From Percy, 12 Mar. 1791, n. 6.

[2] JB's letter is untraced.

[3] "He was an agreeable man, and would have done one any service in his power; but was, I think, quite destitute of principle—I mean quite without any notion of obligation to rectitude—any principle of duty" (cancellation, reprinted *Life* iv. 556).

Oblivion: If out of regard to your own future Comfort; and from many other Considerations, which to you I need not urge;—I beg and intreat you before it be too late, to take a retrospect thro' your Book,'and cancel any accidental Escapes of the same kind where Dr. J. has thrown out Severe Censures on the personal Characters of Individuals.—You know how liable he was to Prejudice, and what severe things he would sometimes say of his nearest Friends: Such effusions he never did nor could seriously mean, should be recorded and transmitted to Posterity, as giving their decided Characters. —Allow me also to request the favour of you to let me see the proof Leaf, of your amended Characters of my poor Friend Grainger: If I should propose an amended Sentence or Phrase, you are at last at Liberty to adopt or reject it: What I wrote last was a meer hasty application and I believe incorrect: I think I used the word *ungraceful*, instead of *elegant and well-turned etc.*:[4]—I will repay whatever expence it occasions at press and will return it by first Post. It may come inclosed to me under a Cover To the Lord Bishop of Cork, at the Castle Dublin; and will forever oblige, Dear Sir, Your affectionate and faithful Servant

THO. DROMORE

To Edmund Hector,
Wednesday 6 April 1791

Missing. Transcribed from a facsimile of the original, Francis Edwards Ltd., 1929, N.S., No. 4, p. 9.

London, 6 April 1791

DEAR SIR: This comes to inquire after your health, and to inform you that my *Life of Dr. Johnson* is at last on the eve of publication. I beg to know how I am to send a copy to you[1] as a mark of my regard, and my thankfulness for your communications. I beg to have my compliments presented to Mrs. Careless, and am truly, Dear Sir, your faithful humble servant

JAMES BOSWELL

Please to put your answer under cover of John Courtenay Esq. M.P. London.[2]

---

[4] *Ante* 12 Mar. 1791. Percy's suggested revision, and perhaps others, were incorporated by JB in his note.

[1] A bound book could not be sent by post.

[2] At the foot of the letter is written, in an unidentified hand, "To Mr. Edmund Hector", and, in Hector's hand, "Ans— 8th".

From Thomas Percy, Bishop of Dromore, Wednesday 6 April 1791

MS. Yale (C 2239).

Dublin, April 6. 1791

DEAR SIR, Since I troubled you with my last, Mr. Malone and I have talked over the Anecdote you had heard from Dr. Johnson concerning Mr. Rolt: viz. That coming over to Ireland, he had here printed an Edition of Dr. Akenside's *Pleasures of the Imagination*, as his own Production. —As I wish to prevent every Imputation of Misinformat[io]n from being fasten'd on the Memory of our departed Friend; I have been making it my business to inquire into the truth of this Fact and to day I saw one of the best informed Men of Literature in this Country; One, who I verily believe has seen every Edition of any work of Taste, which has pass'd the Irish Press within this Century: and he had never seen or heard of any Impression of the aforemention[e]d Poem, which had ever been printed by, or attributed to Rolt: Nor did he believe the Fact was true. —I cannot help concluding therefore that Dr. Johnson had been imposed on: And I submit to you, whether in that Case, this Anecdote should not be suppressed.[1] . . .

P.S. Rolt has a Widow living,[2] who may possibly take up the Pen in Vindication of the Character of her deceas'd husband, or get some brother Author of his to do it, if his Memory should be branded with an Imputation false and groundless: Which had better be prevented. . . .

---

[1] See *ante* To Malone, 25 Feb. 1791. In the second edition JB introduced a footnote giving his authorities, and also Malone's opinion "that the truth probably is, not that an edition was published with Rolt's name in the title-page, but, that the poem being then anonymous, Rolt acquiesced in its being attributed to him in conversation" (*Life* i. 359 and n. 2). No edition of Akenside's poem bearing Rolt's name is known (I. A. Williams, *Seven Eighteenth-century Bibliographies*, 1924, p. 89; cited by Dr. Powell, *Life* i. 547).

[2] "His second wife, who survived him many years, was, by her mother, related to the Percys of Worcester. After Rolt's death, Bishop Percy allowed her a pension" (DNB). See also *Lit. Illust.* vi. 572–73, 578–79; *Letters SJ* 247.1.

From Edmund Hector, Friday 8 April 1791

MS. Yale (C 1528).

ADDRESS: James Boswell Esqr.

[Birmingham,] April 8th 91

DEAR SIR: I am favour'd and honoured with your kind intention to me, and your inquiry after mine and my Sisters Health. She, good Woman, is at rest, and my own age and infirmities dayly warn me of my approach to the same Place.[1]

We have made a Subs[c]ription for a Monument of our old Friend, to be plac'd in the Cathedral of Lichd.

The Revd. Dr. Vyse of Lambeth has the conduct of it, in a Letter to me this Week, He says as soon as Mr. Wyatt has given him the design, He will put it into the hands of a Statuary for immediate execution, and hope to have it finish'd this Summer.[2]

If you have any acquaintance with that Gentleman, I think He wou'd be glad of your thoughts about it.[3]

That You may have Health, and long Life to finish (to your own satisfaction) the shining Career You have made, is the sincere and ardent wish of, Dear Sir, Your obliged humble Servant

E. HECTOR

P.S. Mr. Johnson Bookseller in Pauls-Church Yard,[4] if directed to me will con[v]ey them to his Correspondent here.

[1] Mrs. Carless died in 1788, Hector in 1794 (*Reades*, pp. 152–53).

[2] The monument, which was not completed until 1793 (*Life* iv. 472), was the work of "Wyatt, architect, and Westmacott, sculptor" (*Johnsoniana*, p. 464). The designer was probably James Wyatt, although his biographer does not include the project among his works. He was, however, a member of the Essex Head Club with SJ, and was intimately connected with Lichfield Cathedral as superintendent of reparations from 1788 to 1795 (DNB; Antony Dale, *James Wyatt Architect 1746–1813*, 1936, p. 119). The sculptor was Richard (later Sir Richard) Westmacott (1755–1856), later professor of sculpture at the Royal Academy (A. B. Clifton, *The Cathedral of Lichfield*, 1898, p. 73; DNB).

[3] There is no record of any meeting or correspondence between JB and Vyse after Vyse's letter of 9 June 1787 (*ante*).

[4] Joseph Johnson (1738–1809), publisher of Dr. Priestley, Cowper, Erasmus Darwin, and Wordsworth among others. JB had visited his shop on 5 Feb. of this year "and saw two publications to quote from in Johnson's *Life*. Wright the printer [see *post* 7 July 1791] happened to come in, and named me, and afterwards Johnson asked me when my Book was to be ready. I told him in about a month; but that there would be too much of it. 'O no,' said he; 'it will be very entertaining' " (Journ.).

From John Byng,[1]
Tuesday 12 April 1791

MS. Yale (C 721).

ADDRESS: James Boswell Esqr., No. 47 Gt. Portland St.

ENDORSEMENT: Hon. John Byng.

Stamp Office,[2] April 12th 1791

DEAR SIR: You are extremely Welcome to honor my Letter[3] with Publication, if you think it deserving a Place in your Books.

Wou'd you wish for further Particulars, I will send the Person to you who watchd Dr. J. in his last days.[4]

I highly Approve of the Intention of placing his Monument in St. Pauls.[5] I am Dear Sir, Yours Sincerely

J. BYNG

From Edmond Malone,
Thursday 14 April 1791

MS. Yale (C 1926).

ADDRESS: James Boswell, Esqre., Great Portland Street, London.

POSTMARKS: AP 14, AP 19 91.

Dublin, April 14, 1791

MY DEAR BOSWELL, Your letter of the 9th[1] reached me yesterday. I congratulate you on your drawing so near a conclusion. The proof of your last sheet must, I think, have been before you, when you were writing to me. I wish you had enclosed it. The Advertisement in the cover of the *G.M.*[2] makes a very handsome figure:

[1] John Byng (1742–1813), fifth Viscount Torrington, 1812. See *The Torrington Diaries*, ed. C. B. Andrews and John Beresford, 1934–38, i. xxv–lii; Journ. *passim*.

[2] Byng became a commissioner of stamps in 1782.

[3] To Malone, written two days after SJ's death, *Life* iv. 418. The original is in the Hyde Collection.

[4] Cawston, William Windham's servant. It is his account of SJ's last hours that makes up the substance of Byng's letter to Malone.

[5] The committee on SJ's monument met on 15 Apr.; the next day, at a general meeting including the subscribers, it was decided to place the monument in St. Paul's (*Life* iv. 468). Byng is not among the subscribers listed in *Gent. Mag.* for Jan. 1790 (lx. 3–4).

[1] Untraced.

[2] A copy of *Gent. Mag.* for June 1787 in original wrappers, with an advertisement of the *Life*, is in the Tinker Collection at Yale (R. F. Metzdorf, *The Tinker Library*, 1959, p. 76).

but I hope you will not admit into your title-page that heavy word *also*; —("also various" etc.). I suppose it was introduced to avoid ambiguity in consequence of the notice of his Majesty and Lord Chesterfield; but in the title will not be requisite: there it should surely run—"with many eminent persons; *and* various" etc. Your motto will look better if OMNIS stands over *tabella*, with a black line at the beginning:

――――――――― Quo fit ut OMNIS
Votiva etc. . . . . tabella—[3]

Many thanks for your rectification, which comes out rather late, but better late than never. —I have not seen the Letter to Lord Chesterfield advertised. I suppose you will publish it a day or two only before the *opus magnum*.[4] It is singular enough that I should not be in London either at the publication of your or my own,[5] after all the time that we have passed together while both were going on. If by any chance you should be delayed till the 11th or 12th of next month, I may yet be present at the launch, for I hope to see you by that time. . . . I had a good deal of talk the other day with the Bishop of Dromore about Grainger; I am glad you have satisfied him,[6] for he was very earnest about it. . . .

To Sir Joshua Reynolds, Wednesday 20 April 1791

MS. Yale (M 144). See the Dedication to the *Life*.

[3] See the first and second proofs of the title-page, reproduced in *Adam Cat.* ii (leaf preceding p. 37). The quotation is from Horace, *Satires* II. i. 32–34. See *Life* i. 522–23.

[4] Both the letter to Chesterfield and SJ's conversation with George III were separately printed early in 1790 (from the same type as the corresponding texts in the *Life*), but were not circulated. They were entered at Stationers' Hall on 29 Apr. and published on 12 May 1791. Malone's remark makes it clear that JB

had in mind not a separate sale but the protection of his copyright in these valuable passages. See *Lit. Illust.* vii. 344; *Lit. Car.* pp. 137–41; CBEL ii. 650–51; E. K. Willing-Denton, "Boswell and the Copyright of the *Life*", TLS, 1 Dec. 1932, p. 923; and C. J. Horne, "Boswell and Literary Property", N & Q (1950) cxcv. 296–98.

[5] See *ante* To Malone, 4 Dec. 1790, n. 1.

[6] See *ante* From Percy, 12 and 24 Mar. 1791 and notes.

From Joseph Warton,
Sunday 8 May 1791

MS. Yale (C 3065).

ADDRESS: James Boswell Esqr.

ENDORSEMENT: Rev. Dr. Warton.

Winton, May 8 1791

MY DEAR SIR: You make me very happy by saying I shall so soon receive your Great Work, for which I am greatly obliged to you, and return you my warmest thanks. I will beg you to direct them—
    To me—at the College
    Winchester,
    by *Collyer's Coach*, which goes from the White Horse, Piccadilly.[1] I am, Dear Sir, very faithfully your obliged friend and servant

Jos. WARTON

My best Compliments to Mr. Courtenay.

To Sir William Forbes,
Friday 13 May 1791

MS. estate of the late Lord Clinton. JB announces the formal publication of the *Life* on the 16th, reports on the sale to the booksellers, and sends Forbes a complimentary copy.

To Warren Hastings,
Friday 13 May 1791

MS. Yale (L 629). JB's copy, with a memorandum: "On the 13th of May 1791 I sent my *Life of Dr. Johnson* to Mr. Hastings with this inscription upon it [:] To Warren Hastings Esq. / in testimony of very high respect / and sincere attachment / James Boswell. I at the same time sent him the following Note"

Great Portland Street, 13 May 1791

Mr. Boswell presents his most respectful compliments to Mr. Hastings, and begs to know when he may have the honour to wait

---

[1] "Collyer's coach sets off from the White Hart Inn, in this city every morning at seven o'clock, and arrives at the Bell-Savage, Ludgate-Hill, about seven in the evening. Leaves London about four in the morning, and arrives here about three in the afternoon" (*Universal British Directory*, 1791, iv. 918 s.v. Winchester).

on him and deliver Dr. Johnson's letters with which Mr. Hastings was pleased to entrust him.

From Warren Hastings, Saturday 14 May 1791

MS. Yale (C 1506).

ADDRESS: To James Boswell Esqr., Great Portland Street.

Parklane, 14th May 1791

SIR: I had the Honor last night to receive a Note from you, with your valuable Gift of the *Life of Doctor Johnson*, and I immediately sent an Answer containing my Acknowledgm[en]ts by a Servant, who going without a Direction, missed you, and brought it back again. —I am glad of it, because my thanks, though dictated by the fullest Sense of the worth of the prize of which you had put me in Possession, would have expressed but very imperfectly the Obligation which I owed to you, but of which I was not then apprized; having since seen and read the Passage in your book which speaks of me in terms of such high Encomium,[1] of which however unworthy I may deem myself, I yet receive them with pleasure as the pledges of your benevolence towards me, and with pride when I know that the Elegance of Language in which they are clothed, and the reputation of their Authour, will afford to the World so good a Ground to credit them.

I can only offer my Thanks in the common form: but I beg you to believe that I shall be most solicitous to improve your Acquaintance, and to shew myself deserving of the good Opinion to which I am indebted for it. In one respect I am sure I have a Claim to it; I mean, in the Sentiments of Respect which I entertain for your Character, and Esteem for your Abilities. I have the Honor to be, Sir, Your most obedient and faithful Servant

WARREN HASTINGS

---

[1] ". . . a man whose regard reflects dignity even upon JOHNSON; a man, the extent of whose abilities was equal to that of his power; and who, by those who are fortunate enough to know him in private life, is admired for his literature and taste, and beloved for the candour, moderation, and mildness of his character. Were I capable of paying a suitable tribute of admiration to him, I should certainly not withhold it at a moment [January, 1791: *JB's note*] when it is not possible that I should be suspected of being an interested flatterer. But how weak would be my voice after that of the millions whom he governed" (*Life* iv. 66).

From Joseph Warton,
Sunday 15 May 1791

MS. Yale (C 3066).

ADDRESS: James Boswelle Esqr.

ENDORSEMENT: Rev. Dr. Warton.

Wint[on,] May 15 1791

MY DEAR SIR: I seize the very first post to acquaint you that I last night received safe your valuable Volumes, for which I return you my sincerest thanks: and from which, even from what I have already eagerly devoured, I promise to myself the highest entertainment. I am, my Dear Sir, very faithfully and sincerely Yours

Jos. WARTON

From John Douglas, Bishop of Carlisle,[1]
Monday 16 May 1791

MS. Yale (C 1102).

ADDRESS: To James Boswell Esqr., Queen Ann Street, East,[2] London.

FRANK: Windsor, May sixteenth 1791. free J. Carliol.

POSTMARK: MA 17 91.

ENDORSEMENT: Lord Bishop of Carlisle (Dr. Douglas).

Windsor Castle, May 16th 1791

DEAR SIR: I take the earliest Opportunity of expressing my thankful Acknowlegements, for the very unexpected honour conferred upon me, by so valuable a Present. —I had ordered a Copy to be sent me; but your partiality having already supplied me with One, our Library will receive the other, when it arrives.[3] —I hope soon

---

[1] John Douglas, D.D. (1721–1807), Bishop of Carlisle, 1787; Dean of Windsor, 1788; Bishop of Salisbury, 1791 (*Gent. Mag.*, 1807, lxxvii. 476); member of The Club. See *Life* and Journ. *passim*. Douglas is acknowledged in the *Life* for a number of contributions (i. 127, 140, 260 n. 3, 407, 430: the third and last added to the second edition), but no MS. sources have been recovered.

[2] JB had moved from Queen Anne Street, *West* to Great Portland Street on 19 Jan. of this year.

[3] The Chapter Library of the Dean and Canons of Windsor, attached to St. George's Chapel, is apparently meant, though the copy is not to be found there. It is possible, however, that it was removed as the Library became more and more strictly theological. The Royal Library at Windsor Castle did not then exist. I owe this information to the kindness of Miss Olwen Hedley, Assistant at the Royal Library.

to have an Opportunity of thanking you personally at the Deanery;[4] and am, Dear Sir, Your much obliged and obedient humble Servant

J. CARLIOL.

From Edmund Hector, Monday 16 May 1791

MS. Yale (C 1529).

ADDRESS: James Boswell Esqr.

ENDORSEMENT: Mr. Hector. 16 May 1791.

[Birmingham,] May 16/91

DEAR SIR: I take the earliest opportunity of acknowledging the honour and kindness you have shewn me, and congratulate you on the close of your usefull and laborious researches into the life of our honor'd and much lamented Friend. I promise myself, from the perusal of these volumes, much pleasure and entertainment.

If it will not be trespassing upon your time, I may hereafter, if I meet with any inacuracies from your correspondents, observe them to You. If Birm[ingha]m shoud ever happen to be in your Road, You will be sure to meet with a friendly reception by Sir, Your obliged humble Servant

E. HECTOR

From Sir Francis Lumm,[1] Monday 16 May 1791

MS. Yale (C 1807).

ADDRESS: James Boswell Esqr.

ENDORSEMENT: Sir Francis Lumm Bart.

Argyll Street, May 16th 91

Sir Francis Lumm presents his Compliments to Mr. Boswell and

---

[4] JB visited Douglas at Windsor in June (*Letters JB* 302). On 19 Aug. of the following year, on their jaunt to Cornwall, JB and his daughters were entertained at Salisbury. JB found the Bishop "not in the humour for much conversation", but nevertheless extracted from him a number of particulars of his life, which only whetted his appetite for more (Journ.).

[1] Sir Francis Lumm, Bt. (c. 1732–97), of Lummville, King's County, Ireland; Sheriff of King's County, 1755; Governor of Ross Castle, 1762 (*Comp. Bar.* v. 384). See *ante* To Malone, 22 Mar. 1786, n. 9.

requests he will accept his warmest Acknowledgements for the valuable Present, with which Sir Francis has been honor'd, of Mr. Boswell's Work on the Life, Studies, and Writings of Doctor Johnson.

From Capel Lofft,[1] Tuesday 17 May 1791

MS. Yale (C 1763). Enclosed in a letter of the same date to Dilly, in which Lofft says of the *Life*: "It abounds in solid information and continually well supported spirit. It has Ease it has Variety Acuteness Strength."

ADDRESS: To James Boswell Esq. [*completed by Dilly:*] No. 47, Great Portland Street.

ENDORSEMENT: Capel Lofft Esq.

17 May 1791. Trostonhall

. . . Your Letter[2] came farther enriched with a very valuable Present—your *Life of Dr. Johnson*. If I knew nothing previously either of your writings or conversation, I think I should be well authorized, after reading with avidity the first 100 pages (or had it been a tenth of that number) in predicting that it will by no means

---

[1] Capel, or Capell, Lofft (1751–1824), miscellaneous writer; nephew of Edward Capell, the editor of Shakespeare. He was called to the bar in 1775, and succeeded to the family estates at Troston and Stanton, near Bury St. Edmunds, in 1781. An ardent Whig, he opposed the slave trade and the American war, and was a staunch supporter of Napoleon. In 1818 he left Troston, travelled on the Continent, and settled at Turin. Byron introduced Lofft into the second edition of *English Bards and Scotch Reviewers* (1809, line 754) and characterized him in a note as "the Maecenas of shoemakers, and Preface-writer-General to distressed versemen; a kind of gratis Accoucheur to those who wish to be delivered of rhyme, but do not know how to bring it forth." JB first met Lofft at the Dillys' on 19 Mar.

1778: "There came to Coffee with us Mr. Capel Loft, who has celebrated Corsica and me in a Poem called *The Praises of Poetry*, but is now a Counsellor and a Publisher of *Reports*. He was a little, diminutive being, with black clothes and tied hair and a slow formality of speech. He was also shortsighted, and upon the whole struck me more with the idea of a mysterious London Authour, such as I used formerly to have, than any body I have seen of a long time. He was very complimentative to me" (Journ.). JB's correspondence with Lofft deals mainly with legal matters—especially Lofft's writings on the law. Only those letters relating to the *Life of Johnson* are included here.

[2] Untraced.

verify the trite Aphorism μεγα βιβλιον.[3] The eye may be startled (especially the eye of little men) at the first glance of what appears to be two heavy volumes: but beyond this nothing heavy will be found, in any sense in which the Fancy or the Understanding complain of heaviness. I should have seen a third, fourth, fifth or as many more as the language of conveyancing exhibits in prospect of the expected heirs of a great family estate with impressions very distant from those of discouragement or the prospect of fatigue.

But I must not pass even the exterior of the volumes without doing them some justice in this respect. It is very handsomely and agreeably printed—and I think the prefixed Engraving of your Friend seems to have much of characteristic resemblance: and that too of the best kind. It suggests the Idea of a Man whom you would esteem; and not merely admire. You know that I only saw him once on that 17th which you have recorded[4] and of which the Anniversary is now returned after a lapse of seven Years. You allow the possibility of short sighted Persons[5] forming some distinct Idea of those whom they contemplate with attention.

Perhaps when I saw this Morning (for last Night as it came near eleven I confined my reading then to the first volume) what you have said of me,[6] I ought to have been nearly as much surprized as most Readers are when they meet with the intimation from Mallet to Garrick that he would find a Niche for his Friend in the Life of the D. of Marlborough.[7] The little David has been an Appellation preoccupied already by a character of too much celebrity for it to be transferred: otherwise perhaps you would have fixed it on me, by your pleasant and friendly mode of applying it.

I must have been illiberal indeed if I had suffered my difference in metaphysics, religion, or politics to have made me insensible to moral and intellectual excellence of the stamp of Johnson's. Last summer and Autumn I had much cause for renewing and strengthening my opinion of his great and various Merit—his biographical Criticism, his moral Essays his admirable Allegories—by hearing

---

[3] Μέγα βιβλίον, μέγα κακὸν ("Great book, great evil"): proverb derived from Callimachus, *Fragments*, 359.

[4] *Life* iv. 278.

[5] See *ante* n. 1.

[6] ". . . Mr. Capel Lofft, who, though a most zealous Whig, has a mind so full of learning and knowledge, and so much exercised in various departments, and withal so much liberality, that the stupendous powers of the literary Goliath, though they did not frighten this little David of popular spirit, could not but excite his admiration."

[7] SJ's *Life of Mallett*: *Lives* iii. 404–05; quoted, *Life* v. 175 n. 2.

many of them read by the Daughter of a much esteemed Friend of mine and of Mr. Braithwaites[8] . . .

From Capel Lofft, Friday 20 May 1791

MS. Yale (C 1765).

ADDRESS: To James Boswell Esq., at Mr. Dilly's, Bookseller, Mansion House Str[and,][1] London.

ENDORSEMENT: 20 May 1791. Capel Lofft Esq.

[Trostonhall,] 20 May 1791

DEAR SIR, I have now read through your first Vol. Five Days and amidst various interruptions is too short a space to give such a work the discriminated justice it deserves. But it conveys so much so various so important information and in a manner so agreeable that it will be read much and long and repeatedly.

There is the more reason to be solicitous that nothing without necessity should have a place in it which may hurt some Minds and those such as you would not wish to hurt, more than it can please any.

You will allow though such an interposition is a very delicate affair and one to which I little accustom myself this appeal to you as a Friend and will give it what weight you may find it to deserve. You will perhaps at all Events think it has a motive that may endure the trial of Reason better than mere Knight Errantry though it relates to two Ladies in whose cause one might be suspected of such Enthusiasm and if you do consider it as Knight Errantry your attachment to feudal manners will render you as indulgent to it I hope, as your Friend Mr. Burke.[1a]

The first Article is in p. 472:[2] and I suppose all your readers will understand alike who is the political Lady whom your Friend

---

[8] Daniel Braithwaite (c. 1731–1817), "of the Post-office, that amiable and friendly man, who, with modest and unassuming manners, has associated with many of the wits of the age" (*Life* iv. 278–79). See *ibid.* 529–30. The friend and his daughter are not identified.

[1] Dilly's street, the Poultry, extended

from the Mansion House of the Lord Mayor to Cheapside.

[1a] With reference to Burke's lament over the eclipse of Marie Antoinette and the passing of chivalry (*Reflections on the Revolution in France*, 1790, pp. 111 ff.). See Lofft's *Remarks on the Letter of the Rt. Hon. Edmund Burke concerning the Revolution in France*, 1790, pp. 49 ff.

[2] *Life* ii. 336.

represents as impossible to be made ridiculous for a reason expressed by an allusion very vehemently sarcastic.[3] There was a better reason and more worthy of both. Great Minds (whatever may be the effect of a moment of irritability) never can appear, seriously, ridiculous to Minds of similar strength. The splendour of the general character of such minds hides all the little incorrectnesses of outline, which are almost solely observed in characters of less energy and expression. Such Persons whatever they may casually say of each other would not deliberately commit such sentiments to writing.

The other Lady[4] has been always so far as I understand not less distinguished for the amiable simplicity and delicacy of her manners than her Genius. Her Husband[5] is of great respectability and one who in no respect merits to be exposed to a ridicule which among those who are strangers to his worth might have a mixture of contempt. I can not think that their Marriage if Dr. Johnson had been accquainted with them could have appeared to him in such a view as the conversation suggests. The *Lessons for Children*[6] ought not to have degraded her in his estimation, who has spoken with just and emphatic praise of a similar condescension in Watts.[7] And indeed if great Talents seem to stoop on such occasions it is for the noblest purpose and only Genius with much experience of the human Mind is, as you well know equal to such services. And Mrs. L. refers me to a passage, where if Mrs. Piozzi* is not incorrect Dr. Johnson has expressed himself with this liberal justice of the Lady concerning whom I am writing this.

The passage[8] is in p. 515.

* *Anecdotes* p. 16, 7. [9]

[3] "To endeavour to make *her* ridiculous, is like blacking the chimney." The political lady is of course Mrs. Macaulay.

[4] Mrs. Anna Letitia (Aikin) Barbauld (1743–1825). " 'Too much is expected from precocity, and too little performed. Miss —— was an instance of early cultivation, but in what did it terminate? In marrying a little Presbyterian parson, who keeps an infant boarding-school, so that all her employment now is,/"To suckle fools, and chronicle small-beer."/ She tells the children, "This is a cat, and that is a dog, with four legs and a tail; see there! you are much better than a cat or a dog, for you can speak." If I had bestowed such an education on a daughter, and had discovered that she thought of marrying such a fellow, I would have sent her to the *Congress'* " (*Life* ii. 408–09).

[5] The Rev. Rochemont Barbauld (d. 1808), a dissenting minister of French Protestant descent.

[6] *Lessons for Children from Two to Three Years Old*, 1778.

[7] *Lives* iii. 307–08.

[8] That is, the passage in the *Life* (*ante* n. 4).

[9] *Johns. Misc.* i. 157.

410

The delineation of your Friends character is so full and complete, the readiness of his wit, the strength and poignancy of his humour so fully exemplified, that the portrait will lose no particle of resemblance by the omission of these strokes. And as I think you must very soon come to a second Edition I shall feel particular satisfaction if I prevail with you to omit them. I remain, Dear Sir, with true Esteem, Your affectionate and obliged Friend

CAPEL LOFFT

From Capel Lofft,
Thursday–Friday 26–27 May 1791

MS. Yale (C 1766).

ADDRESS: To James Boswell Esq.

ENDORSEMENT: 27 May 1791. Capel Lofft Esq.

[Trostonhall,] 26 May[1] 1791

DEAR SIR, I have at worst the start of all prohibitions if they could be made effectual: for I have read your *Life of Johnson* through yesterday.[2] In having that capacious and richly stored Mind for your Theme, I consider you as Governor General for so many years of an extensive Province. And if I were to lay aside the particular considerations of Friendship and speak as a Stranger I think I should not have many Articles of Impeachment against you: much as I hold of the Republic and you of the Monarchy. But you will accept some few Remarks: as when a Work is before the Public it is open to the sentiments of all; and those which are directly communicated to the Author cannot be generally considered the least candid in the mode of conveyance.

On the negative side hardly any thing occurs. Yet I had rather hoped to have seen mention of Ignatius Sancho, on occasion of de Groote.[3]

---

[1] The date 27 May appears at the end of the letter.

[2] An obscure sentence, which may possibly mean: At however great a disadvantage I may be, I have a head start against all attempts (could they succeed) to prevent me from proceeding with the criticism of your *Life of Johnson*, because I at least have read it through.

[3] For Isaac de Groot, whom SJ befriended, see *Life* iii. 124–25 and *ante* From Vyse, 9 June 1787 and n. 2. Ignatius Sancho (1729–80), Negro writer, was a friend and imitator of Sterne. I do not see the point of Lofft's remark, unless he knew SJ to be one of the literary men who befriended Sancho. But I find no mention of Sancho by SJ, or of SJ by Sancho.

As to my Uncle, I wonder Dr. Johnson should please himself with an allusion that puts Mr. Capel in the place of Caliban. In the place of Timon he might with some plausibility have been put: but he was in person, taste, manner, as unlike to Caliban as I to Hercules.[4]

Let me ask how Dr. Priestley comes into a Note[5] where you briefly glance at the supposed tendency of his Doctrines, and wonder he should be permitted to publish them. If you think it right to attack Priestley's opinions the field is open: the intervention of Government could only narrow it; and if it were possible, as I beleive it is not, that the State and Temper of those times could endure such interference, it could have no other effect than to prevent fair play between the parties to the Controversy. And let me entreat you to weigh the subject with yourself as to the particular opinions which you have noticed. The power of willing and acting upon that will one way or the contrary, when all the circumstances are the same, would make all future Events evidently contingent in their Nature: and that what is so cannot be the subject of Prescience I think you have yourself stated in a manner which could not well be supposed to have left a doubt on your mind. If every thing were contingent in the physical Universe, Chance and not Providence (the thought is as shocking as it is groundless) would govern there: but the physical is of importance only as it relates to the moral Universe: and if there Prescience is excluded, if the strongest and most proper motives may everlastingly fail of their effect, the vice and infirmity of the Creature may prevail against the Wisdom Goodness and omnipotence of the Creator. These I think are true and necessary Results from the Doctrine of freedom as opposed to philosophical Necessity: and as I think such Results contrary to all the Principles of Nature and incompatible with our most clear and certain Ideas of the Deity, and of ourselves, I think Freedom, as so opposed, neither does nor can exist. But you object to the practical consequences. The practical consequences of Truth must always in reality be the best which the Constitution of things admits. And in fact what are they? It destroys moral Government. To my appre-

---

[4] "Of the Preface to Capel's Shakspeare, he said, 'If the man would have come to me, I would have endeavoured to "endow his purposes with words;" for, as it is, "he doth gabble monstrously"'" (*Life* iv. 5). Lofft clearly extends SJ's allusion too far.

[5] *Life* iv. 238 n. 1 (first paragraph; expanded in the second edition: see *post* From Parr, c. 22 Dec. 1791 and n. 17). See also *Life* iii. 291 n. 2.

hension the complete Idea of moral Government is the power of giving to moral causes an efficacy as certain in the given circumstances as we see accompanies those which we call physical Causes. Nothing out of these limits is capable of moral Government. And the Necessity is not an insulated thing, independent of its Natural Causes, like the calvinistic Predestination: on the contrary it is a regular dependence of effects on their proper causes. Hence a rational Assurance of certain Benefit with regard to future Conduct from the cultivation of good Principles and Habits: whereas in the other view complete habitual Villainy to day may convert itself into perfect Virtue to morrow: or the contrary. As to Materialism, be it true or false, it is not substances of which directly we know nothing, but Powers and moral Qualities that are our concern: if Matter *be* capable of thought, consciousness, and voluntary agency, in the philosophical sense, Matter so qualified *is* Mind: the Value and Dignity is in the Powers; not in the Name of the substance to which they belong. I beleive indeed that these Powers, according to my present view, can not exist in Matter: and as I think we have no direct proof, and can have none, of the existence of Matter, and have a direct necessary certainty of the existence of these powers, I think the supposition that Matter does exist (which is merely an unknown supposed something defined by the negation of active powers) is a gratuitous, perplexed, and highly improbable Hypothesis. I, therefore, in my Theory admit nothing but Intellect and it's Modifications: Perception, Idea, Ratiocination, moral Agency. But I am not uneasy concerning the Doctrine of Materialism: which to me amounts to no more than ascribing Powers which undoubtedly exist to an unknown and positively undefinable substance; which can only be distinguished from Intellect, or perception with active power, by the negation of all power. Extension and solidity being merely Ideas: and the Vis inertiæ, which is the Basis of solidity, being only the want of the Power of originating Motion, or consequently of varying its direction, or stopping it. Now if we have no more proof of these supposed primary Qualities than we have of those which are called secondary, as any thing really distinct from Idea and perception, I do not see upon what just Principle of Philosophy we should encumber ourselves with them. But then if we do not we lose the Beauty of the material Universe. Not by any means: Matter is supposed to have no Beauty but what it derives from moral Attributes and Relations: the Perceptions of

Pain, Pleasure, congruity, unfitness and others of that kind. And it is idle in my Idea to object the Deity deceives us if Matter does not exist. The Deity in this, as in all other instances, gives us the simple perceptions: the Cause of those Perceptions, Reason and Experience must indicate to us. And to me these indicate the much greater probability that Matter does not exist than that it does. But if Matter does exist and is capable of thought and consciousness we are deprived of no elevated Principle. Matter as I have said is then Mind: and all it's supposed inertness and other Qualities that impress us with the Idea of the privation of power, and of nothingness, vanish. Lastly as to the future State. Scripture is in a manner silent with regard to the Mode of existence, the employment and the powers which we shall possess in that State. Is it not then right and necessary to guide ourselves, so far as we reason on a Subject so peculiarly interesting to our thoughts, by Analogy. I am persuaded,—and both you and Dr. Johnson incline strongly to the same sentiment,—that our Friendships will continue hereafter. We know that we shall be conscious of our former Conduct; Sentiments, Principles, and Habits derived from them. We know we are in a State of Probation here. Is it not then a very natural Conclusion, that our future State will be analogous to our present? that the knowledge, the activity, accquired here will have its progressive improvement hereafter with reference to Objects to which the present cultivation of those faculties will be really subservient. This is our School: to fit us by a proper Education for our great inheritance. But if every object there, every employment, were totally devoid of Analogy to every thing here we are then educated it would seem as Creatures of one Mind to carry on our existence through Eternity as Creatures of another. This hardly seems compatible with the Notion of moral Identity: with the conception (with your leave and Dr. Johnson's I would still say Idea) of this being a preparatory State. Dr. Priestley supposes it will have great, and at present inconceivable, advantages above this. He supposes that such advantages will ultimately be extended to every intellectual Being: and will render Happiness and Goodness absolutely universal; and unite the whole moral Creation in eternal Gratitude to the Deity, Error, Guilt and Misery becoming finally absorbed by the necessary influence of the ultimately perfective Discipline of the divine Government. And are these debasing or corruptive Ideas of futurity? Is it possible that the human heart can conceive or wish any thing beyond? I am satisfied you will no where find that he has asserted the future world will not be materially different from this. Our restoration from the power of the grave, our being endowed with immortality, our being made conscious of the infinite power and goodness of our Creator, and of such a Result of our short trial upon Earth, these, independent of other circumstances, would make it materially different indeed. And these Dr. Priestley enforces with the truest Energy and feeling. I can refer you to particular passages, if you give me any encouragement to pursue this subject. For myself, the Idea of one human Being eternally miserable—be that Being what it might, and if I were sure of eternal felicity myself and all who were in any degree endeared to me,—would be inconceivably horrid. I do not think it the Doctrine of Scripture. My Heart rejects it. My Reason can not be reconciled to it. And my Veneration towards the Supreme Being does not suffer me to entertain the thought. On the last line relative to Dr. Priestley in your Note[6] I will be wholly silent: from regard to you; and because I think it unnecessary to remark. But if, after all, there must be an Attack, train, collect, and draw up your Forces; bring up the great Guns; and give Battle in Form. But to fire a loose shot over the head of such an Antagonist does not seem to be doing justice to him, to yourself or to the serious importance and extent of the Cause. But perhaps there will be no Contest or permanent Disgust against Dr. Priestley in your Mind.

I think it appears clearly from your *Life of Johnson* that you see much at least of the strength of the Objections against the Doctrine of Contingency. Carry that Doctrine to its utmost, and it plainly annihilates moral Motives and consequently moral Government. It fails of this only in so far as it is defective and inconsistent with itself. The Doctrine of Providence particular or general (though general as rightly observed includes particular,) implies Prescience: and such Prescience can not consist with contingency. For infinite Knowledge must know an uncertainty according to its Nature or in other Terms must be uncertain whether it will happen or not. Human Foresight admits indeed and supposes relative contingency or ignorance as to future particulars: but the Creation and eternal Government of the Universe excludes the Idea of Uncertainty, or Conjecture; or Possibilities contrary to the divine

[6] "I say nothing of the petulant intemperance with which he dares to insult   the venerable establishments of his country."

415

Intention. It excludes I think, most clearly, the Idea of a Creature in eternal Contrariety to the divine Will and suffering ever-lastingly without its perversity being subdued. These Points then seem uniformly connected. The divine Prescience-philosophical Necessity-ultimate universal Reformation: and consequently the Absorption of all Vice and Misery; instead of their everlasting dominion over any part of the Creation. I observe the possibility of Punishment not being eternal favourably entertained by the strong though melancholy Mind of your Friend: and I apprehend the tendency of your own Mind will be understood to be similar on this Point. The Doctrine of philosophical Necessity is the con-necting Medium between these two Ideas;—of the divine Omni-science and the final Happiness of all moral Agents. I do therefore hope you will, if you pursue your Researches, be convinced of the connection and of the Truth of all three: and if this be a System connected by a close and perpetual series of Cause and Effect; if what we are does not arbitrarily but naturally, determine what we shall be, in the next State of Being; there can be no cause to imagine that State will be totally dissimilar to the present. Indeed if Death and the infirmities which lead to it, if the Crimes and Miseries resulting from a want of a full conviction of the divine Government were removed from this present State,—in such a manner as the very existence of a future State, when it shall be experienced, actually will remove the one and consequentially the other—the order, Tranquillity, Benevolence, advancement in moral perfecti-bility and Happiness would be such, even on this Earth, that the Mind in contemplating such a Prospect, is filled with the purest and most elevating Ideas which it is possible for it to form. The Reality I acknowledge will exceed all distinct Idea[s] we can form at pres-ent: but I do not imagine the Transition will be such as to efface all Analogy to human faculties, habits, and Action. I shall conclude this Article in the Language of our great Poet—(the obvious limitations being supposed)

—— What if Earth
Be but the shadow of Heaven; and things therein
To each other like, more than on Earth is thought.[7]

Now then to Earth. . . .

[7] *Paradise Lost* v. 574–76 (Each to other like . . .).

From John Colman Rashleigh,[1]
c. Monday 30 May 1791

MS. Yale (C 2343). Enclosed in a letter to JB from his son Alexander at Eton, dated 30 May 1791 and endorsed by JB: "Master Rashleigh an Eton Boy's Remarks on my *Life of Johnson*." Alexander writes: "As I heard Rashleigh reasoning very sensibly about your book I desired he would write down his observations upon it, which he complyed with as I had lent him the book to read. I think he gives a fair statement of the case for there are many things, which I do not think can strike many readers as very witty."

[Eton]

With deference to a superior Judgement, the following Observation has struck me throughout, in reading Mr. Boswell's book, and at his Son's *earnest* request, I have ventured thus feebly to express it.

The intimate connection Mr. Boswell enjoyed with Dr. Johnson, gave him numberless opportunities of a clearer insight into the mind of that great man, than the public who share the benefit of his labours, could possibly experience. The ebullitions of his mighty mind, were here discovered, and the minutiæ of the Philosopher made Mr. B. master of his opinion on particular less momentous subjects. These are brought forward as the memorabilia of our English Socrates; and the world knows not perhaps, how much it owes to the man, whose assiduous and arduous labours have collected the various smaller scyphons of the great literary Tree. Yet the sanguine feelings of Mr. B. have induced him to insert *some* particular occurrences, whose poignancy and humour are I fear lost upon the generality of those, who have not been as happy as he, in a knowledge of Dr. J. Circumstances in the common course of life occur, which to those who are present afford an infinite Pleasure, from the humorous light a casual trifle may throw on them; The very agents, who must add poignancy to the wit, if unknown, take away a great share of the exquisite Humour that its *Representation* must give the circumstance. Could it be

---

[1] John Colman Rashleigh (1772–1847), eldest son of John Rashleigh, of St. Samson's, Cornwall, first Commissioner and Receiver for Greenwich Hospital. He was admitted to Trinity College, Cambridge in June of this year; became a member of Lincoln's Inn in 1793; and was created a baronet in 1831 (*Alum. Cant.*).

possible for us to divest ourselves of the idea, which the Character of Falstaff naturally brings to our imagination; could we suppose a common speaker to deliver the Knights sentiments, the generality would appear impertinent, and insipid; the mere efforts of low buffoonery: but who will not bear testimony with me (from the sensible pleasure the fat Knight must afford them) to his being replete with *characteristical* genuine humour. Thus what Dr. Johnson sometimes *said*, Dr. Johnson should likewise *accompany*, and his absence flattens those passages greatly to persons *unacquainted* with him[2] personally; One circumstance I can speak more feelingly on, than any of the rest; because having heard almost the same words applied by a very eccentrick character, to almost the same purpose, it instantly recalled a very lively remembrance of the circumstance to my mind and enabled me to enjoy most thoroughly, the humour of the Passage. Johnson asks[3] Tom Davies when drest out and bedizened "And what art *thou?*" Davies. "The Thane of Ross." Johnson. *"Oh brave!"*[4] *All* such passages I have not had a like clue to, nor can I so well figure them in my "mind's Eye." From this one however *I* can readily *conceive* an equal humour attending the others; though I question whether the world can or if it *can* whether it *will*.

From the Rev. Dr. Vicesimus Knox,[1] Wednesday 1 June 1791

MS. Yale (C 1677).

Tunbridge, June 1. 1791

DEAR SIR, I am sorry Mr. Dilly has troubled you with an Application to you on your Censure of me.[2] I wrote to him in perfect Confidence to remonstrate on the Imprudence of his publishing any Thing which tended to degrade his own Authors. He has done this unintentionally more than once.

It appears to me that Writers who publish at the same House and

---

[2] MS. "his". Rashleigh failed to complete his alteration of "his character" to "him personally".

[3] MS. "upon asks"; orig. "upon asking".

[4] *Life* iv. 8: From Langton, *ante* 17 Dec. 1790 (p. 360).

[1] Vicesimus Knox, D.D. (1752–1821), author, and Master of Tunbridge School.

[2] For (1) a "truly ludicrous" imitation of SJ's style, and (2) "ungraciously attacking his venerable *Alma Mater*, Oxford" (*Life* iv. 391 and n. 1).

who meet often at the same Table[3] should consider themselves in some Degree united by their common Connection with their Publisher, and not injure him, or each other, by *public* Attacks. There are enough ready to rejoice at seeing him and his Authors exposed. We should form a Phalanx for mutual Defence, though not for Offence.

You cannot but agree with me that it is *imprudent* in Mr. Dilly to publish Censures of his own Authors. There is a coarse Proverb that says it is an "ill Bird that befouls its own Nest." I meant only to guard him in future against what might alienate some of his best Friends and injure the Sale of his Books. You would probably think him imprudent if he were to publish an Attack of your Publications.

Mr. Dilly is a very good Man and I am sure would not purposely injure any of his Friends. What he has done was done inadvertently. He once published a Pamphlet written by the late Dr. Withers, in which I was virulently abused.[4] He suppressed it, or at least sent all his Copies away, on finding it out. He published not long ago *Essays literary and philosophical*, in which I was attacked[5] and they are still on Sale in his Shop. People may disguise their Feelings or overcome their Resentment, but it is not in human Nature not to be displeased with public Censure.

In the present Case, it appears that you think I was the Aggressor. I do assure you that I was among the most ardent Admirers of Dr. Johnsons Virtues and Abilities. I read every Thing that came out concerning him after his Death and was with many others disgusted with Things that derogated from his Character. You know

[3] Three such meetings at Dilly's table are recorded in the journal: 22 Dec. 1785, 25 June 1786, and 9 Jan. 1790.

[4] Philip Withers, D.D., *A Letter to the Rev. Samuel Dennis, D.D. Vice-Chancellor of Oxford, and President of St. John's College: in Reply to a Letter Signed Vindex, In the St. James's Chronicle of the 16th of October 1788*. It was printed by J. Moore and sold by Dilly among others. Withers, in defending himself against the charges of ignorance and Methodism, first takes up and carries on "Vindex"'s criticism of Knox's exposé of the universities. In a postscript he observes: ". . . if a Shade of Severity be any where visible, it is when

I am speaking of Mr. Knox. It is not my Design to offend that Gentleman, and I entreat him to admit this Apology." Withers died in Newgate, 24 July 1790, while serving a term for a libel on Mrs. Fitzherbert, wife to the Prince of Wales, in his *History of the Royal Malady* (1789). See *Gent. Mag.* (1789) lix. 144, 759, 1140; (1790) lx. 674.

[5] *Essays Philosophical and Moral, Historical and Literary* (1789–91), by William Belsham. Essay XV, "On the Study of Metaphysics", takes as its point of departure Knox's essay "On Logic and Metaphysics" in *Essays Moral and Literary* (1778–79).

there were several such and I dare say disapproved them. I expressed my Feelings in one of my *Winter Evenings*; but I do not remember that any Thing was pointed at you, or could justly be applied to you. Your Name is not mentioned there, and you had not published *The Life of Dr. Johnson*.[6]

Indeed I flattered myself that I possessed some Degree of your Friendship and Confidence; for when I was last in Town, you did me the Favour to shew me one of the Proof Sheets of *The Life* and to take my Opinion on a note.[7] If you had then observed any Mistake in my Books or was displeased with what I had written concerning Dr. Johnson, I did imagine you would have mentioned it. But you did not and I concluded that you were among the Number of my Wellwishers.

You represent me as a mere Imitator of Dr. Johnson. If I were, I might be pardoned, when it is considered that I wrote my *Essays* at the Age of twenty; and between that Age and twenty five.[8] Dr. Johnson wrote his *Ramblers* at the Age of forty and upwards and naturally impressed a young Mind with great Admiration of him and perhaps with a Desire of imitating him. But I have studiously avoided a servile Imitation.[9]

As to my Ignorance of the Laws of my Country, I was not ignorant of the Particular which you mention,[10] though I have certainly expressed myself carelessly and so as to be misunderstood. I would have thanked you for a private Hint or Correction; but true Kindness does not expose the Error it wishes to amend.

[6] In No. xi of *Winter Evenings* (1788; *Works* ii. 348) Knox attacks SJ's biographers for publishing his private conversation. Although the *Life* was not yet published, the *Tour* was.

[7] Perhaps *Life* i. 222 n. 1, citing Knox's authority for SJ's imitation of Sir Thomas Browne, though the reference may well be to a note in which Knox is not mentioned.

[8] On 7 Jan. 1778 JB recorded in his journal: "Read in *London Chronicle* part of *Essays Moral and Literary*. Felt them much superior to my *Hypochondriack*." On 23 Feb. he wrote to Lord Hailes: "I also send You *Essays Moral and Literary* of which I wish to have your opinion. Dilly informs me he does not know who the Authour is. He appears to me to be a young writer but one of more learning and abilities than common. He has however some trite and some superficial reflections. He appears to me to be of the *Johnsonian School*, and to be pretty well tinctured with the Dr.'s *Thinking style* and even *Prejudices*. They have had a good sale." Knox's name appeared on the title-page of the second edition (1779). Dilly published the work on SJ's recommendation (Knox's *Works*, 1824, i. 3).

[9] In the second edition JB qualified his statement of Knox's imitation of SJ's style with the phrase "though not servile" (*Life* iv. 390–91).

[10] That Members of Parliament are not subject to arrest by a bailiff (*Life* iv. 391 and n. 2).

You censure me severely for attacking the Universities.[11] If I am wrong; I have the common Excuse of a good Intention. But I could not foresee that it would draw upon me the public Stricture of the Biographer of Dr. Johnson, who not having been of either english University could not think himself particularly bound to go out of his Way to repell my Attack.

My Displeasure is of no Consequence to you. But I wish to have no Enmities and therefore I declare that I feel no Resentment on the present Occasion. I thank you for the very great Entertainment your *Life of Dr. Johnson* gives me. I am now reading it with great Attention. It is a most valuable Work. It makes me exclaim in the Words of Phædrus

> O suavis Anima! quale in te dicam bonum
> Antehac fuisse, tales cum sint Reliquiæ![12]

Yours is a new Species of Biography. Happy for Johnson that he had so able a Recorder of his Wit and Wisdom.[13]

> Vixêre fortes ante *Agamemnona*
> Multi; sed omnes illachrymabiles
> Urgentur, ignotique longâ
> Nocte, *carent* quia *Vate* sacro.[14]

You are mistaken in saying that I adopted something in my *Winter Evenings* from a Conversation of Dr. J. at Mr. Dillys.[15] Indeed I do not rightly understand what you mean. But I certainly adopted Nothing from it.

I hope to have the Pleasure of meeting you at Mr. Dillys soon with perfect Cordiality. I am, dear Sir, your most humble Servant

V. Knox

[11] *Life* iv. 391 n. 1. Cf. *ibid*. iii. 13 n. 3. In the second edition JB sought to ease the censure by showing that Adam Smith was more at fault in this regard than Knox. He then proceeds to praise Knox for "others of his productions; particularly his sermons".

[12] "Oh sweet soul! What good must have been in you once, when such are your remains!" (*Fabulae* III. i. 5–6).

[13] JB quotes the third, fifth, seventh, and last sentences of this paragraph, *Life* iv. 391 n. 1.

[14] "Many brave men lived before Aga-memnon; but all are crushed unwept, un-known the long night, since they lack a divine poet" (Horace, *Odes* IV. ix. 25).

[15] *Life* iv. 330. JB does not say that Knox adopted something from a conversa-tion of SJ's, but rather that he may have formed the notion of it on this occasion. Hussey noted in his copy of the *Life* (see *ante* Aug. 1787, n. 2) that Knox "posi-tively denied" the charge (as he con-strued it) to him (quoted, *Life* iv. 330 n. 2).

From Mrs. Frances Abington,[1]
Tuesday 14 June 1791

MS. Yale (C 7).

ADDRESS: James Boswell Esqr.

ENDORSEMENT: Mrs. Abington.

[London,] June 14th

Mrs. Abington presents her Compliments to Mr. Boswell; and is much mortified that she was from home when he did her the honor of calling in Pall Mall.

She told Sir Joshua Reynolds[2] how very sensible she was of Mr. Boswells Extreme Kindness in the handsome manner with which it has pleased him to mention her in his *Life of Doctor Johnson*[3] and she had flatterd herself with the hope of meeting Mr. Boswell at a Little Dinner Party, a day or two past, at Doctor Brocklesbys, or she would have made her acknowledgm[en]ts sooner for his goodness in calling upon her.

To Mrs. Frances Abington,
Wednesday 15 June 1791

MS. Hyde. MS. Yale (L 4): JB's copy, written on side 3 of the preceding letter from Mrs. Abington, headed: "Answer."

ADDRESS: To Mrs. Abington.

ENDORSEMENT: Mr. Boswell.

Great Portland Street, 15 June 1791 (Midnight.)

Mr. Boswell present his compliments to Mrs. Abington. It gave

---

[1] Frances (Barton) Abington (1737–1815), the actress. JB was introduced to her on 4 July 1785 and dined in her company several times thereafter (*Journ. passim*). "Mrs. Abington's fame and elegance and vivacity pleased me much, notwithstanding that she was now past fifty and grown very fat" (*Journ.* 15 Feb. 1794). See F. M. Smith, *Some Friends of Doctor Johnson*, [1934,] ch. 2.

[2] "Capricious and wilful as she was, she seems to have been a special favourite with Reynolds. He painted her *con amore*,

and always brought a strong muster of the Club to her benefits" (Leslie and Taylor, *Reynolds* i. 226).

[3] " ' 'Why, Sir, did you go to Mrs. Abington's benefit? Did you see?' JOHNSON. 'No, Sir.' 'Did you hear?' JOHNSON. 'No Sir.' 'Why then, Sir, did you go?' JOHNSON. 'Because, Sir, she is a favourite of the publick; and when the publick cares the thousandth part for you that it does for her, I will go to your benefit too' " (*Life* ii. 330).

him very great pleasure to mention in his *Life of Dr. Johnson,* what that great man said of a Lady whom Mr. Boswell agreed with him in admiring; and he is not a little flattered that Mrs. Abington has been pleased to allow any merit to the Biographer, in that respect.

Sir Joshua Reynolds's communication of Mrs. Abington's goodness in supposing herself at all obliged to Mr. Boswell, emboldened him to call upon her; and happy shall he be, if *a simple act of justice* shall prove the means of his obtaining the friendship of one whose favourable opinion it shall be his study to cultivate.

To John Wilkes,[1]
Saturday 25 June 1791

MS. British Museum.
ADDRESS: To John Wilkes Esq.

Great Portland Street, Portland Place No. 47, Saturday 25 June
MY DEAR SIR: You said to me yesterday[2] of my *Magnum Opus* "it is a wonderful Book." Do confirm this to me so as I may have your *testimonium* in my Archives at Auchinleck.[3] I trust we shall meet while you are in town. Ever most truly yours

JAMES BOSWELL

From William Johnson Temple,
Monday 4 July 1791

MS. Yale (C 2912).

[Gluvias Vicarage,] July 4th 1791
. . . Perhaps no man was ever so perfectly painted as you have painted your hero. You have given us him in every point of view and exhibited him under every shade and under every colour. We think we see him and hear him and are equally entertained whether he contend for Truth or for Victory. You used to say that I did not know him and your Dialogue proves that I did not. Your book must greatly raise and diffuse your Reputation, as it also abounds with many ingenious observations of your own, shews your familiarity and acceptance with persons of the finest discernment, and how eminently you were regarded and loved by such a judge

---

[1] John Wilkes (1727–97), politician. [2] There is no journal for this period. See *Life* and Journ. *passim.* [3] Not found.

as Johnson. Indeed, I can hardly express the pleasure I feel in considering the fame and the profit it must procure you. . . . I need not ask what you are doing. Enjoying, no doubt, the reception you so well deserve. You ought to have come out a little sooner, before the town began to grow empty. . . .

To Thomas Wright,[1]
Thursday 7 July 1791

MS. Yale (L 1306). In the hand of an amanuensis, signed by JB.

London, 7th July 1791

I am verry well satisfied that my friend Mr. Wright Printer shall make a fair Abridgment of the Maxims and Anecdotes in my *Life of Dr. Johnson* to be printed on Account of Himself and Mr. Dilly as may hereafter be Settled, and I trust entirely to their good Pleasure for what Acknowledgment they shall make to me for this Permission.[2]

Signed JAMES BOSWELL

From "Matilda",
Tuesday 12 July 1791

MS. Yale (C 1981).

ADDRESS: To James Boswell Esqr., Great Portland Street, London.

POSTMARK: Shaw.[1]

ENDORSEMENT: Matilda Unknown. Did not answer it.

July 12th 1791

Write on Good Sir, if You *write* you must *delight*; how much ought

[1] Thomas Wright (d. 1797), one of Archibald Hamilton's assistants in the printing of *The Critical Review*, became an independent printer c. 1766, establishing himself first in Chancery Lane, then in Peterborough Court, and finally in Essex Street, Strand (*Lit. Anec.* iii. 398–99; Plomer). See *ante* From Hector, 8 Apr. 1791, n. 4.

[2] In 1798, the year after Wright's death, Dilly brought out *Dr. Johnson's Table-Talk . . . selected and arranged from Mr. Boswell's Life of Johnson*. The Advertisement, dated Mar. 1798, concludes: "It may be proper to add, that this selection was undertaken in the life-time of Mr. Boswell, and with his cordial approbation: had that gentleman lived, it might probably have been rendered more acceptable to the Reader." It seems reasonable to suppose that, despite the date of the Advertisement, the anonymous editor was Wright.

[1] The name of two villages having post-offices, one in Lancashire, the other in Wiltshire.

the thinking part of the *World*, (and here the Expression surely is not exaggerated) be obliged to you for, giving them an opportunity, of becoming So intimately acquainted, with such a genius, who possessed So warm, and feeling a Heart as Dr. Johnson's. His Love of Truth and strong recommendation thereof, is Noble, and Beautiful; and, if properly attended to, few other precepts Either Moral or Divine would be Necessary to Make Mankind good and happy; but there are *those* who say, (and I am sorry to feel they cannot be contradicted) that Dr. Johnsons acknowledged practise, of taking up any Side of an Argument for the Sake of Conversation, is perfectly incons[is]tant with the Love of *strict* truth. If You Sir will take the trouble of answering this by putting a Letter into the *World*, or *Morning Post*, you will Oblige Many, and none more than your Constant Admirer

MATILDA

To Edmund Burke,[1]
Saturday 16 July 1791

MS. Yale (L 335). A copy in an unidentified hand, endorsed by JB: "To The Right Honble Edmund Burke 16 July 1791."

London, Great Portland Street, 16th July 1791

... You were good enough to repeat to me his Majestys Conversation with you concerning that excellent Work Boswells *Life of Johnson*; and the effect was as it should be; for, I have it from undoubted Authority that on his return to Windsor, The King speaking of my Work said "Mr. Burke told me it was the Most entertaining Book he had ever read."

You can do me My Dear Sir a great favour; and I do not recollect your having ever refused me any request that it was proper to grant. I[2] have but an Imperfect recollection of that conversation.

---

[1] In a letter to Sir William Forbes, 11 Oct. 1790 (MS. estate of the late Lord Clinton) JB dates his alienation from Burke from the time of his *Letter to the People of Scotland* (1783), since aggravated by his support of Hastings; however, they have recently dined harmoniously at Sir Joshua's. Cf. Malone's explanation of the

"true cause" of Burke's "coldness" towards JB, *ante* 14 Sept. 1787. The present letter appears to be a calculated, if tacit, rejoinder to that charge. See also *post* From Burke, 20 July 1791, end of first paragraph.

[2] MS. "grant, I"

425

SS*

It is long since I relieved Myself from the Anxious and Laborious task of making minutes of conversations of Value, which however I wish to resume in some degree and am pressed to it by[3] Malone because there is much Wisdom and Wit fresh from the Source in casual talk which should not be lost. You gave me a delicious repast[4] when you Communicated to me what the Sovereign and Yourself said of my Labours, and particularly when you repeated your very friendly defence of my writing down the Conversations of Johnson. If you will in the leisure of Margate take the trouble to let me have for my Archives at Auchinleck a written State of An interveiw so preceious to me I shall be exceedingly Oblidged to you. . . .

From Dr. Charles Burney,[1] Saturday 16 July 1791

MS. Yale (C 705).
ADDRESS: To James Boswell Esqr., Great Portland Street.
ENDORSEMENT: Dr. Burney.

Chelsea College, July 16th 1791

DEAR SIR: So much time has elapsed between the publication of our friend's life and my being possessed of leisure sufficient to finish the perusal of it, that I shall seem to have waited till I could join the general Chorus of your praise. The approbation of an individual can now afford you but small gratification:[2] the effects of praise and abuse are always proportioned to our wants and expectations.

Johnson had enemies, who of course will try to depreciate your

---

[3] MS. "by" inserted by JB.
[4] MS. "repose"

[1] Charles Burney, Mus. Doc. (1726–1814), organist, composer, teacher and historian of music; member of The Club. See Roger Lonsdale, "Johnson and Dr. Burney," *Johnson, Boswell and Their Circle*, pp. 21 ff. Burney furnished JB with anecdotes and sayings of SJ (*Life* i. 397, ii. 406–10, iv. 134: this last surviving in the MS. *Life* in Burney's own hand, Paper Apart "HB" for opp. p. 855), and furnished Malone with notes for the third and succeeding editions. On 3 Nov. 1787

JB "Walked to Chelsea College and breakfasted with Dr. Burney, who gave me some letters from Johnson to him" (Journ.)—not the actual letters, but Burney's own MS. list of the letters, including extracts (two separated parts of which are now in the Hyde and Osborn Collections). The MS. proves that it was Burney and not JB who edited the texts printed in the *Life*. See Roger Lonsdale, "Dr. Burney and the Integrity of Boswell's Quotations", *Papers of the Bibliographical Society of America* (1959) liii. 327–31.
[2] MS. "gratificatification"

work. The number of these will perhaps be somewhat augmented by your success, as well as by the severity of his private opinions;[3] but to all else, the book is so uncommonly alluring, that I have hitherto met with no unprejudiced readers who have not been sorry when they were arrived at the last page.

Some indeed have thought that too many of the weaknesses, prejudices, and infirmities, of this truly great and virtuous Man have been recorded;[4] but, besides the reputation which you will acquire for the fidelity of your narrative in telling all you knew, it will elevate the Character of our Hero: for what other man could have had his private life so deeply and minutely probed, without discovering vices, or at least foibles, more hurtful to Society than those which you have disclosed? The most gratifying information which I can give you concerning the effect of your narrative, is, that it has impressed your most hostile readers with a much more favourable opinion of the goodness of our friends heart than they had before conceived, though some of them were never insensible to his merit as a writer.

I beleive it may be said with truth, that it is impossible to open either of your two Volumes without finding some sentiment of our venerable Sage worth remembering. His wit and his wisdom are equally original and impressive; and I have no doubt but that both will become proverbial to Englishmen, and long continue to direct their taste as well as morals. For my own part, I think myself infinitely obliged to you for embalming so many of his genuine sentiments which are not to be found in his works. Indeed if all his writings which had been previously printed were lost, or had never appeared, your book would have conveyed to posterity as advantageous an Idea of his Character, genius, and worth as Xenophon has done of those of Socrates. I have often found your own

[3] Burney wrote to Malone in Oct. 1798: "It is too late now to soften or expunge the harsh and offensive opinion of living characters and those productions uttered in private conversation by Johnson, without the least idea of their being made public. Among all the good qualities of our friend Boswell, w'ch were very numerous, delicacy had no admission. He was equally careless what was said of himself, or what he said of others. But the memorabilia w'ch his diligence and enthusiastic admiration of the British Socrates have preserved are inestimable and will merit the gratitude of posterity as long as the language of our country shall be intelligible" (Burney's *A General History of Music*, ed. Frank Mercer, 1935, ii. 1032).

[4] Burney among them. In a review of Mrs. Piozzi's *Anecdotes* in *The Monthly Review* for May 1786 (lxxiv. 373ff.), he complained of the exposing of SJ's private opinions and "his failings and his weaknesses". Burney is identified as the reviewer in B. C. Nangle, *The Monthly Review, First Series* (1934), p. 209.

reflexions not only ingenious and lively, but strong; and the latter part of your narrative, though I already knew its chief circumstances, has in it so much pathos, that it renovated all my sorrows, and frequently made me weep like a tender-hearted female at a Tragedy.

I am now more and more inclined to recommend to your diligence, zeal, and biographical abilities, the collecting and writing *Memoirs of the deceased Members of* our *Club*, in your more lively manner than that of Crescimbeni's *"Notizie istoriche degli Arcadi morti."*[5] *Vous aurez beau jeu* in speaking of such men as Garrick, Goldsmith, Lord Ashburton,[6] Bishop Shipley,[7] Beauclerk, Dyer, Chamier, T. Warton, etc.[8] Indeed you may make even Hawkins entertaining, for the first time. If your own manner of pourtraying Johnson had not been so much approved, you might have borrowed the Pencil of Fontenelle or D'Alembert; but the *Eloges* of the former,[9] though admirably written, are rather too much confined to mere panegyric; while *l'Histoire des Membres de l'Academie Françoise*, of the latter,[10] though more miscellaneous and enlivened with anecdotes, has less strength, Originality, and elegance.

It was Johnson's wish that our Club should be composed of the heads of every liberal and literary profession, that we might not talk nonsense on any subject that might be started, but have somebody to refer to in our doubts and discussions, by whose Science we might be enlightened. The Stalls of Divinity, Classics, Civil Law, History, Medecine, Politics, Botany, Chemistry, Criticism, and Painting, were already well filled.[11] *Biography* now claims you as

[5] Published at Rome, 1720–21.

[6] John Dunning (1731–83), first Baron Ashburton, "a great lawyer" (SJ), statesman, and orator. He was elected to The Club in 1777 (*Annals of The Club*, p. 22). See *Life* iii. 240.

[7] Jonathan Shipley, D.D. (1714–88), Bishop of St. Asaph, partisan of American independence and religious toleration at home. He was elected to The Club in 1780 (*Annals of The Club*, p. 26). See *Life passim*.

[8] Other deceased members at this time were: Dr. Nugent; the Rt. Hon. Agmondesham Vesey (d. 1784), Accountant-General for Ireland and husband of Elizabeth Vesey the bluestocking; Adam

Smith; and John Spencer (1734–83), first Earl Spencer.

[9] *Éloges historiques des académiciens morts depuis le renouvellement de l'Académie royale des sciences en 1699*, Paris, 1742.

[10] *Histoire des membres de l'Académie françoise, morts depuis 1700 jusqu'en 1771*, Paris, 1787.

[11] Cf. SJ's and JB's assignment of professorial chairs in the imaginary college at St. Andrews, *Life* v. 108–09. On 14 Aug. 1785 Bishop Barnard wrote to JB: "I am very glad however that you have discretely avoided [in the *Tour*] appreciating the respective Talents of the Present Club in the Same Manner. You

her chairman. Take into consideration how best to fulfill her views in executing the office assigned to you, and beleive me to be with true regard, dear Sir, Your faithful and Affectionate Servant

CHAS. BURNEY

From John Maclaurin, Lord Dreghorn,[1] Tuesday 19 July 1791

MS. Yale (C 1112).

ADDRESS: James Boswell of Auchinleck Esqr. To the Care of Mr. Charles Dilly, Bookseller in the Poultry, London.

POSTMARKS: IY 21, IY 22, JY 25 91.

ENDORSEMENT: Lord Dreghorn.

Edr., North St. Andrews Street, 19 July 1791

DEAR SIR: Not having time sooner to read it I got your book only to day and being informd that you made mention of my information for the Negroe[2] I turnd to the passage and found there a small mistake which I thought it proper to acquaint you of as you might perhaps chuse to correct it in a subsequent edition and that I myself woud incline.

In a Note on p. 180 of Vol. II you say the motto was well-chosn and that it is—nimium ne crede colori. I once thought of that hemistich for the motto but gave the preference to an entire line from the same poet

Quamvis ille niger, quamvis tu candidus esses

and accordingly that is the actual motto to the printed paper[3] and I am clear it is the better as it contrasts the colours and there is something in the quamvis much more delicate but equally forcible with the direct admonition in the former.

Johnston's approbation of that paper gave me at the time great

have wisely taken the sure method to content us all, by Estimating our Merit in the Aggregate."

---

[1] John Maclaurin (1734–96), JB's friend, fellow-advocate, and collaborator in verse. He was raised to the Scottish bench in 1788, when he took the title of

Lord Dreghorn. See *Lit. Car.* pp. 99, 252, 271, 272; Journ. *passim*; *Life* v. 471–72.

[2] Maclaurin's argument before the Court of Session in favour of Joseph Knight, a Negro slave, *Life* iii. 212–13.

[3] Corrected, *ibid.* 212 n. 2. The two quotations occur in sequence in Virgil's *Eclogues* ii. 16–17.

satisfaction[4] and your commemoration of it now no less, the rather that in the negroe-cause I exerted myself as much as I coud, and the paper did not meet with the notice in this country, which I expected. In[5] the preamble it foretold in 1775 the abolition of the slave trade which now in 1791 is I think, thank God, nearly accomplished.

I see you likewise mention a burlesque imitation of Johnstons stile by me and that he said it was the best[6]—according to my recollection the one he saw was in prose and printed in the *C. Mercury*[7] but there is a better one in blank verse[8] which I think I gave you long ago[;] if not I can give it you still. I cannot at present make you any compliments on your book having got it but to day and read the passages only relating to myself but from what I have heard expect great entertainment from it. Tho' I have not seen or heard from you for many years I remain as much as ever, Dear Sir, Your faithful Humble Servant

Jo. MacLaurin

From Edmund Burke, Wednesday 20 July 1791

MS. Yale (C 696).

ADDRESS: James Boswell Esqr., Great Portland Street, London.

FRANK: Margate July twenty first 1791. Free Edm. Burke.

POSTMARK: JY 22 91.

ENDORSEMENT: Right Hon. Edmund Burke.

Margate, July 20. 1791

. . . I wish you all happiness, whenever you retire to Auchinleck from the entertainment of your freinds and the applauses of the publick. We shall I trust find ourselves hereafter as much obliged

---

[4] SJ's approbation was expressed in a letter to JB, 6 July 1776. Maclaurin's satisfaction was reported back in JB's letter of 14 Feb. 1777 (*Life* iii. 88, 101).

[5] MS. "expected in"

[6] *Life* ii. 363.

[7] I have not found this in *The Cale-donian Mercury*, nor does it appear in Maclaurin's *Works* (1798).

[8] The second part of "On Johnson's Dictionary", printed in *The Weekly Magazine, or Edinburgh Amusement* for 14 Jan. 1773 (xix. 81–82); reprinted in Maclaurin's *Works* (i. 29–31). See *post* To Dreghorn, 22 Aug. 1791 and n. 2.

to your invention as hitherto we have been to your recollection. I am sure that something original from you will be well received. Whether, in the present possession of the favourable opinion of the world as you are, it will be prudent for you to risque the further publication of anecdotes, you are infinitely more competent to judge than I am.

As to the conversation I had the honour of having with the King at his Levee with regard to your Work and to Johnson, I gave you the account of it with as much exactness at the time, as I am able ever to relate any thing; not being much in the habit of precision with regard to particular expressions. Since then other things, not of much moment I admit, have made my recollection of the conversation far worse than then it was. I am quite certain, that I am now far less able to furnish you with any detail of that matter; and that you have reason on occasions of this Nature, indeed of any nature, rather to trust to your own Memory than mine. Be assured that this is the fact; and that I do not decline an obedience to your Commands, either from Laziness or inattention to you. In the Substance of the conversation you are certainly right. The King by his manner of questioning me, seemd to be affected properly with the merit of your performance; and I said, what I thought, that I had not read any thing more entertaining; though I did not say to his Majesty, what nothing but the freedom of freindship could justify[1] in my saying to yourself, that many particulars there related might as well have been omitted; However in the multitude of readers perhaps some would have found a loss in their omission. . . .

From Mary Adey,
Thursday 21 July 1791

MS. Yale (C 20).

ADDRESS: James Boswell Esqr. To The care of —— Courtenay Esqr., M.P., London.

ENDORSEMENT: Miss Mary Adye Lichfield.

Lichfield, July th[e] 21st 1791

MY DEAR SIR: Give me leave to Introduce to your Acquaintance a

---

[1] MS. "justifying"

Friend of Mine, and an Admirer of your late valuable Production The Life of our Great and Good Johnson.

Mr. Molesworth[1] who conveys this to you tells me he every Day puts by Some Maxim, or observation worth the Price of The Two Volumes. Indeed the World is much Indebted to you for bringing our deceased Friend So Strongly to our View.

You will be concern'd to hear that my Dear Good Aunt has been Sick and lame ever Since th[e] 13 of April. She is attended by Doctor Jones[2] and our Worthy Friend Mr. Hector of Birmingham has lately paid her a Visit, has examin'd her poor Wounded Limb and has given his advice. He is a very experienced and Skillful Surgeon. He gives me hopes as My Aunt regains her Strength She May in time hobble a little better. She is at present a Miserable Cripple, Supported by a Crutch and her Servant, and Carried to Bed on a Sort of Hammock. She was Seized April th[e] 13th with a giddiness in her head and fell in the Parlor on her left Side, has Straind the Muscles and tendons. Mr. Hector has order'd her a Bandage that reaches to her Hip. She has Suffer'd exquisite Pain. I was fearful her Seizure might be Paralytic. The Faculty tell me it is not, It is a relaxation of The Lymphatic Vessels, and Excruciating Rheumatism has taken Place. She desires her kind Regards to you. We have gone thro' your Voluminous work with Admiration and delight.

You will oblige me by Shewing every civility in your Power to Mr. Molesworth. He is a well Inform'd, Polite, Sensible Man. You will find him worthy your Acquaintance.

I hope your health is good, and that time has in Some degree alleviated the Rememberance of your Great loss.[3] Adieu! My Dear Sir let me have your Prayers for My Dear Aunts recovery and My happiness. I am with Respect and Regard Sincerely yours

MARY ADEY

I walk'd with Mr. Hector to The Cathedral to See where Johnsons monument is to be Placed. Mr. Hector has given ten Guineas. There is already a large Subscription.[4] My Dear Aunt hopes to meet him in Heaven. He will if he *can* make Intercession for her.

---

[1] Probably Richard Molesworth (1737–99), of Dorset Court, London, husband of Katherine Cobb, Mrs. Cobb's step-grand-daughter (*Johns. Glean.* viii. 173–75).

[2] Probably Trevor Jones (*post* 29 Aug. 1791).

[3] The death of his wife, 4 June 1789.

[4] See *ante* From Hector, 8 Apr. 1791.

But I am So Selfish I hope to keep her longer upon Earth, So do all who know her. I am very anxious and uneasy for her. Our Ingenious Good Mr. Greene is declining fast.[5]

> Condemn'd to Hopes delusive mine
> As on we toil from Day to Day,
> By Sudden Blasts or Slow decline
> Our Social Comforts drop away.[6]

Grant me a Place in your Friendship.

From James Elphinston,[1]
Saturday 30 July 1791

Missing. Printed, Elphinston's *Fifty Years' Correspondence*, 1794, vii. 16 (No. 426).

ADDRESS: James Bozwel, Esq., Poartland-street, London.

Izlington, July 30, 1791

SIR, In yoor Life of our late frend *Jonson*, I found too much real enjoyment, not to' hint a few petty instances, in hwich dhe next ediscion may be rendered stil more wordhy dhe candor, conspiccuous in yoor labors.

Ov dhe two' letters to' me, dhe transpozal waz innocent, az won chanced to' hav no date.[2] Dhis dherfore proovs dhe twelth, and dhe oddher but dhe eight'th, ov my *Forty Years' Correspondence.* In yoor

---

[5] Richard Greene (*ante* 29 June 1787) died 4 June 1793, aged 77. His will is dated 17 June 1791 (*Johns. Glean.* viii. 155). Mrs. Cobb died in Aug. of 1793 (*ibid.* 173).

[6] "On the Death of Dr. Robert Levet," 1–4.

[1] James Elphinston (1721–1809), schoolmaster and translator. He brought out the Edinburgh edition of *The Rambler* and "enriched it with translations of the mottos" (*Life* i. 210 and n. 3). SJ took JB to dine with Elphinston at his academy at Kensington on 19 Apr. 1773 (*ibid.* ii. 226). For SJ's character of him, see *ibid.* ii. 171, and cf. *ibid.* iii. 379. In his later

years Elphinston devised a system of phonetic spelling, and in 1791 published *Forty Years' Correspondence between Geniusses ov boath Sexes and James Elphinston,* etc. This was expanded in 1794 and the title changed to *Fifty Years' Correspondence,* etc. Elphinston's system speaks for itself in the two specimens printed here.

[2] *Life* i. 210–11, uncorrected. JB used Elphinston's own transcripts, which are in the same, wrong, order (MS. *Life,* Paper Apart "E" for opp. p. 130); but the restoration of an omitted phrase in the printing shows that JB consulted another source, probably Shaw. See Chapman's discussion, *Letters SJ* i. 428 and iii. 312.

exhibiscion howevver, Sir, boath ar doutles litterally more gennuine pictures, ov dhe oridginals in my pozession: for Inglish Orthoggraphy waz no more known to' dheir Author, dhan to' moast ov my oddher Correspondents.

He might indeed wel retain 'a *scholar's reverence* for *antiquity*,' hoo pronounced (in won ov dhe Ramblers)[3] *'the most polished of modern* European Languages, but barbarous *degenerations*;' and (in an *Idler*)[4] *'the English Tongue* so *little analogical, as to give* few opportunities for *grammatical researches.'* Nor iz it les certain, dhat a scollar, so immersed in dhe diccions ov anticquity, might compoze a Diccionary, valluabel at least for its authorrities, in a *vernacular idiom supposed insusceptible, as unworthy of Orthography.*

But, in yoor seccond vollume, Sir, page (I think) 207,[5] les garded reccolleccion seems to' hav expozed our cellebrated frend, az if rattelling in a manner at wonce unwordhy ov himself, and inconsistent widh dhat kindnes, hwich so onnored me, hwen I first intimated my translacion ov Marsial, az warmly to' say, "I am sorry I waz not yoor first subscriber."[6] Az for Garrics vaporing on dhe subject, no won hoo knows me wil believ, dhat I evver consulted him on anny subject: or dhat I could prostitute to' hiz critticism, hwat I nevver wood submit to' hiz masters.

It iz needles to' tutch here on oddher toppics I cood mension, did yoo wish a conference: for nedher yoor subject, nor its author can evver be indifferent to' a person, hoo so justly vennerates dhe won, and values dhe oddher, az doz, Sir, yoor moast obedient servant,

JAMES ELPHINSTON

[3] No. 169.

[4] No. 91.

[5] *Life* iii. 258: "GARRICK. 'Of all the translations that ever were attempted, I think Elphinston's Martial the most extraordinary. He consulted me upon it, who am a little of an epigrammatist myself, you know. I told him freely, "You don't seem to have that turn." I asked him if he was serious; and finding he was, I advised him against publishing. Why, his translation is more difficult to understand than the original. I thought him a man of some talents; but he seems crazy in this.' JOHNSON. 'Sir, you have done what I had not courage to do. But he did not ask my advice, and I did not force it upon him, to make him angry with me. . . . He would not take my advice. His brother-in-law, Strahan, sent him a subscription of fifty pounds, and said he would send him fifty more, if he would not publish.' "

[6] SJ's subscription to Elphinston's *Epigrams of Martial* (1782) was reported by Roger Lonsdale in *Johnsonian News Letter* (June 1966) xxvi. 8.

From Sir William Scott,[1]
Tuesday 2 August 1791

MS. Yale (C 2441).

ADDRESS: James Boswell Esq., on the Home Circuit.[2]
FRANK: London August second 1791. Wm. Scott.
POSTMARKS: AU 2 91, AU 2 91.

DEAR BOSWELL: You *will* force a Passage[3] and I have only to say that *I* am always glad to see you, let me have what Company I may. But excuse me if I state the true Reason that makes ⌈me⌉ sometimes ask other Friends of our Connexion, when I do not take the Liberty of asking you. I have *other* Acquaintance, Men whom I very much value on many Accounts, but Men who are perhaps more shy and delicate than I am, and who, in my Hearing, have often expressed a proper Respect for your Talents but mixed with a good deal of Censure upon the Practice of publishing without Consent what has been thrown out in the freedom of private Conversation.[4] I don't discuss the rectitude of their Opinion upon that Matter, but I know they are sincere in it; and I really have felt a repugnance to asking Gentlemen to meet, whose Company might excite Sentiments of Uneasiness or Apprehension for a Moment, to each Other. For believe me, it is not the Gaiety of the present Hour nor the most joyous Display of convivial Talents for the Moment, that are an equivalent with many Men for the Pain of being brought out, against their Consent or without their Knowledge, into the Glare of public Light, when they supposed themselves to be merely discussing in a private Society. You will understand me, I am not censuring *You*, but am defending *myself*, for doing what you might otherwise deem to be an Act of Unkindness. *I* shall be glad to see you, I repeat it, as *I* always am; but no *Letter Press* upon the

---

[1] Sir William Scott, Kt. (1745–1836), maritime, international, and ecclesiastical lawyer; D.C.L. 1779; first Baron Stowell, 1821. He was a member of The Club and the Essex Head Club, and was one of the three executors of SJ's will. See *Life* and Journ. *passim*. JB received from Scott, through Malone, the MS. of SJ's French journal from 10 Oct. to 5 Nov. 1775 (*Life* ii. 389–401, 522).

[2] ". . . having resigned the Recorder-ship of Carlisle I am to resume my station on the Home Circuit, which is much more pleasant and promises to be more profitable to me than the Northern" (JB to F. Smythies of Colchester, 23 July 1791). He "did not get a single brief" (JB to Temple, 22 Aug.: *Letters JB* 305).

[3] JB's letter is untraced.

[4] Cf. *ante* From Malone, 14 Sept. 1787.

Occasion! I wish I could remove from my Friends the Apprehension of a Consequence which renders your Company less acceptable than, I am sure, it would be on *Every other* Account. Yours faithfully

W. SCOTT

I dine on Saturday at *5 precise.*

From Sir William Scott, c. Thursday 4 August 1791

MS. Yale (C 2442).

ADDRESS: James Boswell Esq., Queen Ann Street East, Cavendish Square.

[London]

DEAR BOSWELL: I do not know whether you have received from me a Letter upon the Circuit. If you have not, I send this note to say that I shall be very glad to see you at Dinner on Saturday 5 o clock. My Letter contained my Reasons for not asking you before. Yours

W.S.

To Sir William Scott, Friday 5 August 1791

MS. Yale (L 1140). JB's copy or draft, written on side 3 of Scott's letter of 2 Aug.

Great Portland Street, Friday 6 [*sic*] August 1791

DEAR SIR: After receiving your letter communicating a circumstance of which I had not the least apprehension, I certainly could not *force a passage.* I should be curious to know *who* they are that are conceited and absurd enough to imagine that I could take the trouble to publish *their* conversation, because I have recorded the wisdom and wit of Johnson.[1] But I own I wonder my dear Friend at *your* saying *No Letter press upon the occasion.* It is too ridiculous. Yours ever very faithfully

---

[1] At the end of the *Tour* (*Life* v. 414) JB had given the same answer to the same objection by one of his (unnamed) friends. If the friend was Scott, the present exchange is older business than appears.

On 7 Feb. 1794, still smarting, JB was to write to his son Alexander: "... you must be very cautious of letting other people know that you are such an *Observer*, and such a *censor morum*, as they

436

From Sir William Scott,
c. Friday 5 August 1791

MS. Yale (C 2443).

ADDRESS: James Boswell Esq., Queen Ann Street East.

[London]

DEAR BOSWELL: Be so good as to remember that you have published not only the Wit and Wisdom of Johnson, but a little of the Folly of other People mixt with it; amongst the rest, some of your humble Servant's,[1] though I make no grumbling about it. Dont impute to Absurdity and Conceit what is owing to timidity and natural Reserve; you must know that there are Persons who do not choose to face the Light. When I talked of *no Letter Press*, I certainly did it more jocularly than otherwise; and when I talked of *forcing a Passage*, you must suppose that I did it with reference to your own Letter which held out the same Idea; you cannot think me brutal enough to use such an Expression seriously, without supposing that I meant a quarrel, which I should certainly consider as a real Misfortune.

If you dont persist in thinking me *too ridiculous*, pray come. I shall be extremely sorry if you do not, as I go out of Town in a very few Days for the Summer. Yours faithfully

WM. SCOTT

To Sir William Scott,
Tuesday 9 August 1791

MS. Hyde. MS. Yale (L 1141): JB's draft, written on sides 2, 3, and 4 of the preceding letter from Scott.

Maidstone, 9 August 1791

. . . Yesterday I received here your obliging letter, the *principle* of may be apt to misunderstand, and form a wrong notion of you. I speak from experience; because I am certain that there is not in reality a more benevolent man than myself in the World; and yet from my having indulged myself without reserve in discriminative delineations of a variety of people, I know I am thought by many to be ill natured; nay from the specimens which I have given the World of my uncommon recollection of conversations, many foolish persons have been afraid to meet me; vainly apprehending that *their* conversation would be *recorded*."

---

[1] *Life* iii. 261 ff., iv. 91–92. For Scott's embarrassment over a passage in iv. 91, see *post* Scott to Malone, ? early 1799.

which I readily admit, and thank you ⟨?heartily⟩[1] for setting me quite at ease. ⟨But as⟩[2] to the *application*, be so good as to recollect that I have not published any of *your* folly, for a very obvious reason; and what I have published as your share in the Johnsonian Conversations was revised by yourself, upon which occasion I enjoyed one of the pleasantest days I ever passed in my life.[3] *You* therefore, my good Sir William, have no reason even to *grumble*. If others, as well as myself, sometimes appear as shades to the Great Intellectual Light, I beg to be fairly understood, and that you and my other friends will inculcate upon persons of timidity and reserve, that my recording the conversations of so extraordinary a man as Johnson with its concomitant circumstances, was a *peculiar* undertaking, attended with much anxiety and labour, and that the conversations of people in general are by no means of that nature as to bear being registered and that the task of doing it would be exceedingly irksome to me. . . .

From Edmund Hector, Tuesday 9 August 1791

MS. Yale (C 1530).

ADDRESS: James Boswell Esqr.

ENDORSEMENT: 5 [*sic*] August 1791. Mr. Hector, thanking me for my *Life of Dr. Johnson*.

[Birmingham,] Aug. 9th

DEAR SIR: I thank You, most sincerely thank You for the great and long continu'd entertainment your *Life of Dr. Johnson* has afforded me and others of my particular friends.[1]

My intention is not to compliment You upon the execution of your work, but to set you right in regard of a Fabulous anecdote

---

[1] Not in the draft.
[2] So in the draft.
[3] " I dined with Sir William Scott, by appointment, to *sit* upon my Record of the conversation between Johnson and him. . . . We revised my Johnsonian leaves, and I staid supper and sat till the venerable St. Paul's had struck one" (Journ. 10 June 1790). The record in the MS. *Life* is lightly edited, with a few altera-

tions in Scott's hand. There is only one suppression: following "for a considerable time little was said" (*Life* iii. 262, line 4) is the deleted clause, "as Mr. Scott was remarkably cautious of hazarding [*alternatively* risking] himself in his company" (MS. *Life*, pp. 664–65).

---

[1] JB quotes this tribute in the second edition (*Life* iv. 375 n. 2).

communicated to You by the fascinating Eyes and Tongue of the Lichd. Poetess. The *Sprig of Myrtle,* as I think I inform'd You, was wrote as Mrs. Piosie has related it: Lucy Porter was then only a Girl; Mun was the Name he us'd to call me. In a second Edition this may be rectify'd,[2] for which purpose, I will transcribe for you,

[2] *Life* i. 92 n. 2. There is no record of Hector's having previously informed JB of the genesis of the poem. Had he done so, JB would have been spared no little trouble and embarrassment. The trouble began when Miss Seward, in her letter of 25 Mar. 1785 (*ante*), if not before, told JB that the verses were inspired by SJ's romantic affection for Lucy Porter. In the version in Mrs. Piozzi's *Anecdotes,* which appeared the following year, SJ addresses the recipient of both the myrtle and the verses as "dear Mund" (*Johns. Misc.* i. 166–67). Faced with conflicting accounts, JB turned to Miss Seward, and was assured of the authenticity of her version in a (missing) letter, to which he refers in the first edition by way of refuting Mrs. Piozzi (and from which he quotes in the second edition by way of refuting Miss Seward). When the *Life* came out, John Nichols wrote in *Gent. Mag.* (May 1791, lxi. 396) that SJ told him the verses were written "when I was at Birmingham, at the request of a friend" (cf. *post* From Reed, c. Nov. 1792, p. 496). This was not, however, the first disclosure of these two facts: as early as Feb. 1785, in Kearsley's edition of SJ's poetical works, the poem is said to have been "written at Birmingham soon after he left the college, at the request of a friend who aspired to the character of a poet with his mistress". Shaw (p. 22), quoting "one of our monthly publications", gives the same version. (See *Poems,* ed. Smith and McAdam, p. 93, for still earlier statements as to authorship.) It is clear that JB missed these references, for the mention of Birmingham (not in Mrs. Piozzi's anecdote) would surely have led him to question Hector. Upon receipt of the present letter from Hector corroborating Mrs. Piozzi's account, JB was faced with an unpleasant duty. His retraction appeared both in the

Principal Corrections and Additions to the First Edition and, in expanded form, in the second edition (both 1793). But Anna Seward was not one to give up without a fight. In a letter to *Gent. Mag.* for Oct. 1793 (lxiii. 875) she grimly stuck to her guns, though conceding the possibility that the verses may have served SJ in helping out a friend at a later date. (According to Nichols, SJ composed the verses at Birmingham impromptu.) JB replied in the following number (p. 1009), attacking Miss Seward's credibility as a witness. This in turn provoked another blast from Miss Seward in Dec. (p. 1098), in which she answered JB's animadversions, but refrained from any further attempt to defend her story. There the battle might have ended had not Hector, by his letter of 9 Jan. 1794 disclosing the "true history" of the poem, provided JB with more ammunition. For the sequel see *post* From Hector, 9 Jan. 1794 and n. 6.

It remains to tie some loose ends. Hector's belated but positive identification of the suitor in the affair as Morgan Graves must have unsettled JB; for if Hector was not the suitor, then Mrs. Piozzi's anecdote was not accurate after all, nor was Hector accurate in saying that the poem "was wrote as Mrs. Piosie related it". Apparently Hector did not read Mrs. Piozzi's account with care, for he certainly missed the equation of the suitor and "Mund". (That he did read it, and not merely JB's abstract of it in the first edition, is evident: JB does not mention "Mund".) Apparently, also, JB accepted the identification of the suitor as Hector (once he knew that Hector was "Mund"); otherwise he surely would have challenged Mrs. Piozzi on that point. Yet, in the present letter, Hector, in speaking of SJ's ode "to a Young Lady—Sister to the Gentleman

if you think proper Two of the Dr.s Odes, which I have found, one very early wrote of seven Stanza's the other of four to a Young Lady—Sister to the Gentleman the *Myrtle* was wrote for.[3]

This is the first time I have been able to write, having been long confin'd by illness; That You and your Family may enjoy long health and Happiness is the sincere and ardent Wish of Your most humble Servant

E. HECTOR

To John Maclaurin, Lord Dreghorn, Monday 22 August 1791

MSS. Yale (*L 443.1, L 443). The first copy is in an unidentified hand, headed "James Boswell of Auchinleck Esqr. Advocate to John Maclaurin Lord Dreghorn" and endorsed "Johnsoniana Boswell To Lord Dreghorn August 22. 1791," and is signed by JB. The second copy is by James Ross.

the *Myrtle* was wrote for", would seem plainly to dissociate himself from that role. It may be that JB read the letter not wisely but too well. Having been informed that Mrs. Piozzi was right and Miss Seward wrong, JB would, recalling Mrs. Piozzi's version, think of Hector as the suitor, and reading on to the passage concerning the odes, would, not expecting a contradiction, interpret "the Gentleman the *Myrtle* was wrote for" as a circumlocution for Hector himself, and the "Young Lady—Sister to the Gentleman" as meaning Ann Hector (later Mrs. Carless), who was after all SJ's avowed "first love" (see *ante* To Hector, 21 Jan. 1785, n. 1), and a most likely subject for a romantic ode. As for Hector's own unawareness of his misunderstood role in the proceedings, JB's retraction in 1793 would have done nothing to disturb it; for JB wrote only that the verses were "written for Mr. Hector" (*Corrections and Additions*) and that "he was the person for whom Johnson wrote those verses" (second edition)—both statements not inaccurate from the point of view of the suitor's intercessor. But Miss Seward's unambiguous statement, in her first letter to *Gent. Mag.* in Oct. of this year, must have jarred Hector into a recognition of the error: "It is very

likely, however, that Mr. Hector might receive myrtle from a lady in Dr. Johnson's company." (Hector's last letter to JB makes it clear that he followed the debate in *Gent. Mag.*.) In any case, Hector remained silent on this point, and JB discreetly followed suit. A final irony may be noted in conclusion. Had JB been willing to question Mrs. Piozzi before going to press, he would very probably have learned the identity of "Mund", for Mrs. Piozzi (Thrale) had glossed the nickname in the version of the anecdote entered in her diary: "Edmund Hector of Birmingham" (*Thraliana*, p. 163 and n. 2; Prof. Balderston detects no sign of the gloss being added later). With this information JB surely would have approached Hector for the whole story, and while the controversy with Miss Seward could not have been forestalled, the pain of a public apology to Mrs. Piozzi could. Indeed, had JB cared not to scruple, he might have turned her own information to account against her accuracy.

[3] Morgan Graves (c. 1711–70), brother of Richard Graves, the novelist. He had two sisters (T. R. Nash, *History of Worcestershire*, 1781–99, i. 198). See *post* From Hector, 9 Jan. 1794.

440

London, 22 August 1791

MY DEAR LORD, My mistake as to the motto to your case for the Negro has been owing to my trusting to my memory in that instance which I hardly ever did in the course of my late work. I shall take care to correct it both in the next edition and in the Appendix of additions and Errata which is to be printed in Quarto for the purchasers of the present Edition.[1]

I reccollect well your collection of hard words

"Little of Anthropo" etc.[2]

But though laughable enough I cannot consider it as any likeness of Dr. Johnsons Style.[3]

It gives me much pleasure to find that your Lordship remembers me with regard, and great[4] pleasure that I can call you *my Lord*. Be pleased to consider, that had it not been for me neither your Lordship nor Lord Dunsinnane[5] would yet have been upon the bench; and indeed *with submission* the five first Lords who [6]have received and[6] shall receive Commissions since my Pamphlet appeared[7] are in equity bound to acknowledge me, if not by an[8] Years Salary like a Bishop's *first fruits* yet by some offering of Silver plate[9] large enough to admit of[10] a short inscription. In respect whereof etc. Believe me to be allways, my dear Baron McLaren, Your faithful old friend and most humble Servant

JAMES BOSWELL[11]

---

[1] The *Principal Corrections and Additions*, 1793, p. 21.

[2] "Little of *anthropopathy* has he" —the first line of the second part of Maclaurin's burlesque (see *ante* From Dreghorn, 19 July 1791, n. 8). When JB showed SJ these verses in Skye, he "read a few of them, and said, 'I am not answerable for all the words in my Dictionary' " (*Life* v. 273).

[3] "The ludicrous imitators of Johnson's style are innumerable. Their general method is to accumulate hard words, without considering, that, although he was fond of introducing them occasionally, there is not a single sentence in all his writings where they are crowded together ... There is not similarity enough for burlesque, or even for caricature" (*Life* iv. 386–87).

[4] Ross's copy, "much"

[5] Sir William Nairne, Bt., Lord Dunsinane, or Dunsinnan (?1731–1811), Scottish judge. See Journ. and *Tour passim*.

[6-6] Omitted in the first copy; restored from Ross's copy.

[7] "appeared" omitted in Ross's copy. *A Letter to the People of Scotland, on the Alarming Attempt to Infringe the Articles of the Union, and Introduce a Most Pernicious Innovation, by Diminishing the Number of the Lords of Session* appeared in 1785. "As a matter of fact the Bill was killed, and largely through Boswell's efforts" (*Lit. Car.* p. 112).

[8] Ross's copy, "a"

[9] "plate" omitted in Ross's copy.

[10] Ross's copy, "to hold"

[11] Ross's copy preserves at the end the direction "The Honourable Lord Dreghorn Edinburgh".

To James Elphinston,
Tuesday 23 August 1791

Missing. Printed, Elphinston's *Fifty Years' Correspondence* vii. 28 (No. 432). MS. Yale (L 503): a copy by James Ross.

Grait Poartland-street, August 23, 1791

DEAR SIR, Havving been upon dhe Circuit, and at Poartsmouth;[1] yoor obleging Letter haz remained unansered, longuer dhan it shood hav don. I am hurried away to' Scotland, upon particcular biznes. I shal (I hope) be in town aguen erly in October;[2] and shal dhen be glad to' hav a conference widh yoo.[3] Yoo may depend on[4] my acquainting yoo ov dhe time, hwen it wil be in my power to' hav dhat plezzure.

I am, widh sincere regard, Dear Sir, yoor faithfool umbel servant,

JAMES BOZWEL[5]

From Dr. Trevor Jones,[1]
Monday 29 August 1791

MS. Yale (C 1644).

ADDRESS: James Boswell Esqr., Edinburgh [*deleted and re-addressed in another hand:*] Auchinleck, Kilmarnock.

POSTMARK: SE 10.

ENDORSEMENT: Mr. Trevor Jones, Lichfield. 29 August 1791.

Lichfield, 29 Aug. 1791

SIR, In the 2nd volume of your life of Doctor Johnson, page 40,[2] you have the following passage. "I was not informed till afterwards (i.e. after having dined with Mrs. Gastrell) that Mrs. Gastrell's husband was the clergyman who, while he lived at

---

[1] Copy, "etc." The excursion to Portsmouth was to view the Grand Fleet (To Temple, 22 Aug. 1791: *Letters JB* 305).

[2] He arrived at Auchinleck on 28 Aug., his first visit since his wife's death, and left towards the end of Oct. On 22 Nov. he wrote to Temple from London that he "had a very unhappy time in Ayrshire" (BP xviii. 123–24).

[3] The journal fails for this period, and there is no other record that the conference took place.

[4] Copy, "upon"

[5] Following the signature in the copy is the direction: "To Mr. Elphinstone, No. 4 Colebrook Row, Islington."

---

[1] Trevor Jones, M.D., of Lichfield. See *Johns. Glean.* ix. 140, 183.

[2] *Life* ii. 470.

Stratford upon Avon, where he was proprietor of Shakespear's garden, with Gothic barbarity cut down his mulberry tree, and as Dr. Johnson told me did it to vex his neighbours. His lady I have reason to believe participated in the guilt of what the enthusiasts for our immortal bard deem almost a Species of Sacrilege."

Struck with so direct a charge against a gentleman who was remarkable for his charity and generosity and whose mind was far above the influence of the imputed motive of his conduct, and trusting that he might be cleared of the reflection it casts upon his character I enquired into the circumstances thro' a gentleman of the first respectability who resided at Stratford in very intimate friendship with Mr. Gastrell. He favored me with Mr. Gastrell's real motive for cutting down the tree which he had from himself at or very soon after the time it was cut down. "That it was in a decaying state* and that he was apprehensive it would damage an adjoining wall."

It is scarcely necessary that I should remark how completely this simple account overturns the illhumoured sally of Dr. Johnson and the unwarranted inference so hastily suggested against Mrs. Gastrell whose hospitality and politeness you acknowlege and which merited a very different return.

It is possible that Dr. Johnson might hear that Mr. Gastrell cut down the mulberry tree to vex the Stratford people and perhaps from a Stratford man who might suppose that to be his motive and he might repeat it; or he might say it without meaning any thing as he often did give short answers to get rid of a subject; but Dr. Johnson could have no knowlege of the kind himself and I am confident he never would have used an expression (especially could he have conceived it was to come before the public,) injurious to the character of any of the Aston family from whom he had received so many and great obligations. In my visits to him and particularly during my attendance upon him when last in Staffordshire he always spoke in the highest terms of them which I feel myself obliged to declare in justice to Dr. Johnson.

But there is no proof that Shakespear did plant the tree however tradition may have handed down such an opinion. I have often heard that Dr. Johnson planted the Lichfield Willow. Many in

---

* The tree was hollow and some of it's largest branches had been blown down.

Lichfield believe it and it is called his. Dr. Johnson himself told me in the year 1782 that he did not plant it but remembered it's adolescence very well.[3] If your Stratford faith is no better founded there was no gothic barbarity in taking away an object of fond enthusiasm.

The Mulberry tree was cut down in the year 1758[4] and the inhabitants of Stratford did not feel the loss of it till the jubilee ⟨?in⟩ the year 1769. From that period they la⟨ment⟩ed[5] the "hallowed tree." In all probability it would have died of natural decay before now. Those conversant with Mulberry trees know that as they decay the weight of the branches and high winds soon split and destroy them. Of late years this has in some instances been prevented by hooping them with iron where the branches spring.

In thus addressing you I trust you will believe I have no view but to establish truth and do justice to the memory of a very worthy and benevolent character whose act no one has or had a right to complain of.[6] I am Sir your most obedient and humble Servant

TREVOR JONES

[3] In July 1785 Richard Greene had contributed to *Gent. Mag.* (lv. 495–97) an account of SJ's interest in the giant willow and a copy of Jones's letter to SJ, 26 Nov. 1781, written at the latter's request and in considerable horticultural detail. But as neither Greene's account nor Jones's letter contains any implication that SJ was, or was said to be, the planter of the tree, Jones's present recollection of SJ's disclaimer to him "in the year 1782" appears suspect. —Dr. Powell informs me that the fourth descendant of "Johnson's Willow" is now growing in the original spot.

[4] 1756, according to another account (*Life* ii. 541).

[5] JB himself supplied these letters, and the "rd" in "Stratford", obliterated by the breaking of the seal—perhaps a sign that he intended to print Jones's defence. But see the next note.

[6] In the second edition JB inserted a foot-note to the passage in question: "See an accurate and animated statement of Mr. Gastrel's barbarity, by Mr. Malone, in a note on 'Some account of the Life of William Shakspeare,' prefixed to his admirable edition of that Poet's works, Vol. i. p. 118." Cf. Prior's *Malone*, p. 142. Previously, in a letter to *Gent. Mag.* dated 16 Jan. 1792 (lxii. 18), JB had replied to a similar criticism, made in the obituary notice of Mrs. Gastrell in the Dec. number: "I think it necessary, for the sake of truth, and the authenticity of my book, to observe, in answer to your remark (and, at the same time, to a letter signed Trevor Jones, with which I have been favoured on the subject), that I have quoted Dr. Johnson as my informer concerning Mr. Gastrell; and that whoever wishes to see a full account of his Gothic barbarity will find it in the first volume of Mr. Malone's admirable edition of Shakespeare, p. 118, related from the very best authority. Mrs. Gastrell's accession was also told me by Dr. Johnson, though I did not mention his name while she was alive, as it might have given uneasiness to the old lady, to know that one whom she so highly respected had in any degree censured her."

From John Holt,[1]
Friday 23 September 1791

MS. Yale (C 1542).

ADDRESS: James Boswell Esqr., London. Paid.

POSTMARK: SE 26 91.

ENDORSEMENT: Septr. 1791. Mr. Holt, Walton near Liverpool.

Walton near Liverpool, 23d Septr.

SIR: If you have afforded as much pleasure to every reader of your last publication, the *Life of Dr. Johnson,* and of those readers how great the number! as you have given to the writer of this Letter, your time has been more happily employed, than many other that has taken up the pen. Your manner too is original and entirely your own. The many excellent sayings of your friend, and so worthy of preservation, if not owing to your industry, and retentive memory, must have been lost and it would have been a loss, as we see by the treasures thus preserved. Besides the intrinsic value of the work, every serious person must think it seasonable in this Paroxism of the times, when certain notions are but too much propagated. But to praise the whole as it sufficiently deserves, would take up more space, than could be conveyed in this Sheet of Paper. Praise from such an individual as myself is of little value, but I feel a satisfaction in expressing my obligations, from the pleasure received from the fruit of your Labours.

If not trespassing too much on your time, it would afford me additional pleasure, to know how Mr. Francis Barber enjoys his good fortune, and whether engaged in any business—whether the Connexion betwixt this great Man and his Servant had any peculiarities of difference, betwixt Master and Servant[—]what were the principal duties of the latter, whether being so long together, he caught any thing of the manner of his Superior etc.— whether he attended upon him in his excursions at Tables—these are trifling enquiries, I acknowledge but as your friend soared

---

[1] John Holt (1743–1801), schoolmaster and author, settled at Walton-on-the-Hill, near Liverpool, about 1757, where he was parish clerk, highway surveyor, and master of the free grammar-school, as well as conductor, with his wife, of a boarding-school for girls. He was a diligent student of agriculture and contributed the "Meteorological Diary" to *Gent. Mag.* for a long period.

[2] The date appears on the address side.

above the multitude, I wish to know him both in[3] public and in solitude and in every situation. It was never my good fortune to see Dr. Johnson, but I would have travelled many miles to have purchased that pleasure.

It does not appear that your friend, changed or seemed to change his opinion, what he once asserted, that he strenuously maintained, either on conviction in his own mind, or that he could demean himself to yield. I have often compared him with a friend of my own, alas now no more. See an Account of James Park[4] in the obituary of the *Gen. Mag.* May 1789. Bulk and manner, his remaining associates agree,[5] correspond as far as they go with your departed friend; but differed in many particulars. I shall grow tedious. I hope you will not soon lay down your pen, but favour the public with more of your labours. If you can spare a few minutes to an individual, it would add another obligation to Sir, Your obliged and obedient Servant

JOHN HOLT

To Sir William Forbes, Tuesday 27 September 1791

MS. estate of the late Lord Clinton. JB reports on the gratifying reception of the *Life* in England; he expects that the profits will exceed the amount that had been offered to him for the copyright.

From Sir William Forbes, Thursday 13 October 1791

MS. Yale (C 1295).

Edinbg., 13th Octr. 1791

. . . I rejoice exceedingly, My Dear Sir, at the profitable issue of your publication of Dr. Johnson's life, from the perusal of which I derived a very high degree of entertainment. I found in it, indeed, several things that *might*, and some I must honestly confess, that I do humbly think *ought* to have been omitted. Yet I must at the

---

[3] MS. "in both in"
[4] James Parke, of Prospect Hill, in
Everton, retired brewer in Liverpool.
[5] MS. "associates, agree"

same time add, that I met with many an[on]ymous anecdotes, to which I could easily supply a Key, from having formerly heard you relate them to me, and which you have prudently and discreetly foreborn to apply to their Authors by name. I feel regret that You did not oftner use the same precaution. You will pardon me, I hope, for this remark, and allow me the same indulgence in that respect, that You have kindly shown me on former Occasions.[1] . . .

From Capel Lofft,
Wednesday 19 October 1791

MS. Yale (C 1767).

ADDRESS: To James Boswell Esq.

ENDORSEMENT: 19 Octr. 1791. Capel Lofft Esq. mentioning a mistake in my *Life of Johnson* as to the title of a Work by Jonas Hanway.

Trostonhall, 19 Oct. 91

DEAR SIR, By desire of my Friend Mr. Young[1] I write to convey his wishes that you would give your attention to what he and I apprehend to be a slight Mistake in your *Life of Johnson*. Slight in itself and easy to be incurred: but material in the effects which it may produce; as you will easily perceive when I state it.

In p. 341. Vol. I it is said that Mr. Hanway published a *Six Weeks Tour* through the S. of England by which he lost his reputation—or to that general purport.[2] Now as appears to Mr. Young, and to me, from a very strict enquiry into the List of Mr. Hanways numerous works in the Index to the *Monthly Review* Mr. Hanway

---

[1] Forbes had been critical of the *Tour* on just these grounds, and had cautioned JB early (e.g. in his letters of 6 Dec. 1785 and 25 July 1787)against giving offence in the *Life*. The subject of JB's candour (judged to be imprudent though innocent) makes up an interesting exchange between Forbes and Beattie, 9 Jan. and 12 Feb. 1786 (Forbes, *An Account of the Life and Writings of James Beattie, LL.D.*, 1806, ii. 181 ff.).

---

[1] Arthur Young (1741–1820), agriculturist and author of travel books, notably *Travels in France* (1792). His political sympathies and friendships were akin to Lofft's, and like Lofft he was an avowed admirer of JB's *Account of Corsica*. On 14 Mar. 1768 he wrote to JB requesting information about the agriculture of some Scottish parishes for use in a book; for JB's reply, see *Letters JB* 83.

[2] "Speaking of Mr. Hanway, who published 'A Six Weeks Tour through the South of England,' 'Jonas, (said he,) acquired some reputation by travelling abroad, but lost it all by travelling at home' " (quoting Dr. Maxwell).

published no *Six Weeks Tour*, but a *Ten days Tour*;[3] which probably is the work alluded to by Dr. Johnson.

As the Title by which the Tour is mentioned is so distant from that of the work of Hanway, to which it appears meant to refer, and coincides with a well known Publication of Mr. Youngs,[4] it might lead many to imagine that the Name of the Author and not that of the work had been mistaken, and that Mr. Youngs Tour was meant; an essential misapprehension in prejudice of him and the work: which I believe it would hurt you should [he] be supposed to have been thus mentioned by your Friend.

I lose not a days time after having been apprized of this, as Mr. Young is struck with the probability, which also occurs to me, that a second Edition may now be printing. I remain, Dear Sir, Yours sincerely

CAPEL LOFFT

James Boswell Esq.

From Sir William Forbes, Saturday 29 October, Friday 4 November 1791

MS. Yale (C 1296).

Edinbg., 29th Octr.[1] 1791

. . . I hope, on your meeting with your Bookseller, you have found all your first impression of your *Life of Dr. Johnson* disposed of; and the public ready for a second edition. It was with a view to this second edition, that I took the liberty of hinting in my last letter, that I had found some things in the Book, which I cannot help thinking might be better omitted. And if Mr. Malone is returned to London, I would really use the freedom of suggesting the idea to you of your looking over the whole again with him. I am persuaded you will, on such a review, see the propriety of making

[3] JB altered the title to "An Eight Days' Journey from London to Portsmouth", *Life* ii. 122. The actual title was *A Journal of Eight Days Journey from Portsmouth to Kingston upon Thames*, etc. (1756). Hanway published no *Ten Days' Tour*, etc., nor does the *Index* to the *Monthly Review* say he did. In the list of SJ's reviews for *The Literary Magazine*, *Life* i. 309, JB had given the (short) title correctly.

[4] *A Six Weeks' Tour through the Southern Counties of England and Wales*, 1768. JB read a little of it during his tour of the Hebrides with SJ (*Life* v. 294–95).

[1] At the end of the letter appears the date 4 Nov.

some few alterations on some passages, just as you did in the second edition of your *Hebridian Tour*.[2] It is really a most entertaining and interesting work, for which I am sure the public are under very great obligations to you; and therefore it is, that I would fain have any thing removed from it, at which any person may be supposed to take Offence or exception. As I said in my former letter, I am sure, My Dear Sir, you will do justice to my Motive in troubling you with this hint; for which the intimate freindship that has now subsisted between us for so long a term of years, will, I hope, plead my excuse. . . . I lately met with a periodical paper published at Oxford by the title of the *Olla Podrida*, in one of the Numbers of which (I think the 42d)[3] are strictures on the Character of Dr. Johnson, extremely well written. Has it come in your way? . . .

From Edmund Hector, Monday 31 October 1791

MS. Yale (C 1531).

ADDRESS: James Boswell Esqr.

ENDORSEMENT: 31 Octr. 1791. Mr. Hector with two odes by Johnson in his early years[1] and praising my Book.

[Birmingham,] 8ber 31 91

DEAR SIR: For the pleasure You have given me and many of my friends who knew Dr. Johnson, I most gratefully and sincerely thank you.

If hereafter, it shou'd ever lie in my power to do you any service, You may command Your oblig'd humble Servant

EDMD. HECTOR

The daffodill was the first production of his Pen I ever saw, and as He thought it not characteristick[2] of the flower gave no copy.[3]

---

[2] See *Lit. Car.* pp. 117–18.
[3] Rather, the 13th: see *ante* From S. Adams, 13 June 1787 and n. 3. SJ is mentioned in the 42nd, which deals with the theme of the contrarieties of human character, but as the biographer of Savage, not as a specimen himself.

---

[1] The two odes and the fragment that

follows them occupy the first two pages of the letter, preceding the letter proper. The first of the odes, "The Daffodil", duplicates Hector's earlier offering (*ante* 1 Feb. 1785). For the texts, see *Poems*, ed. McAdam and Milne, pp. 3, 38, and 69.
[2] MS. "chararist"
[3] Cf. *ante* From Hector, 1 Feb. 1785.

From the Rev. Dr. Samuel Parr, Sunday 11 December 1791

MS. F. W. Hilles (*C 2184).

ADDRESS: James Boswell Esqr., at Sir Joshua Reynolds's, Leicester Square, London.

ENDORSEMENT: No. 1. Rev. Dr. Parr. Decr. 11, 1791.

Hatton, December 11th

DEAR SIR: By few works has my attention been seized so forcibly, detained so agreeably and rewarded so fully, as by your late publication. It is copious without prolixity, and splendid without glare, it forms a noble piece of Biography, which, in my judgement, will never disgrace the memory of that man who stands on the highest pinacle of fame for biographical writing.

Amidst such a multiplicity of facts, and such a variety of subjects, different readers will contend for different rules of selection. The man of vanity will affect to wish for the omission of a tale which he already knows, and the man of curiosity will wish for amplification, because he desires to know more. The Whig will blame you for inserting political opinions which he does not like, and the Tory will blame you for not suppressing those qualifications, by which the vigour of Johnsons understanding and the honesty of his heart controuled the wantonness of dogmatism. But, in my opinion, the best rule is the most comprehensive. Of such a man as Johnson, it is more pleasant to Scholars, and more advantageous to the world, for the Biographer to say too much, than too little. Nothing, indeed, has been said by you, which some body or other will not approve, and nothing could have been omitted, the absence of which I for one should not have regretted. I will therefore commend and thank you, for not "sparing your paper," for such were the words of Johnson, when he was conversing in my presence with Dr. Horsley about the life of Newton;[1] and depend upon it, Sir, that Mr. Boswels memoirs of Dr. Johnson are not among the *Chartae periturae*.[2] —Of objections there is no end, and with such an ample stock of character you ought to have no fear of objectors—

---

[1] Samuel Horsley, D.D. (1733–1806), Bishop of St. David's, Rochester, and St. Asaph; member of the Essex Head Club. The work referred to is probably Hors-ley's edition of *Isaaci Newtoni Opera*, etc. (1779–85), although there is no life contained in it.

[2] "writings that will perish."

happy is he who recording so many interesting facts, and so many brilliant conversations, can produce two quarto volumes with excellences so numerous, and imperfections so few.

Upon the general merit of your work I have told you my opinion very sincerely, and perhaps I am not very foolish in supposing that you would be glad to know it.

My particular acknowledgments are due to you, not only for the honourable mention you have made of my attainments, but for your spirited defence of my motives in a work,[3] which for obvious reasons, has been abused by those, who at this moment think what I say, and who, after the death of a certain prelate,[4] will venture to say for themselves what I have justified them in thinking of him.

But the chief cause for which I trouble you with this letter is, that I may tell all I have to say, and ask what you have to say farther, upon a striking passage in the 582d page of the second Volume. Your words are "to compose his epitaph has incited[5] the warmest competition of genius," and as those words express, not an opinion, but a fact, I must beg your permission to explore the whole extent of your meaning.

Since the death of Johnson, I have, in random conversation, been now and then asked to write his epitaph,[6] and I refused to write it, from a consciousness of the difficulty which must accompany such an attempt. In the course of this year some applications were made to me in a more formal manner, and in a long correspondence with our most respected friend Sir Joshua Reynolds, I stated fully the reasons which deterred me from promising to do, what, for the sake of Johnson, I wished to be done consummately well. My arguments were impartially considered, my conditions were un-equivocally admitted, and at last, my objections were completely vanquished.[7] But the passage above mentioned has given me serious alarm—I never meant to triumph over a competitor, and, before the perusal of your book, I never understood that any

---

[3] *Tracts by Warburton and a Warburtonian*. See *Life* iv. 47 n. 2, and *ante* To Parr, 10 Jan. 1791.

[4] Bishop Hurd, the "Warburtonian" of the *Tracts*.

[5] Actually, "excited"; see next letter.

[6] See Parr's *Works* iv. 678–714; H. B. Wheatley, *Johnson Club Papers by Various Hands*, 1920, pp. 221–38; *Life* iv. 469–72.

[7] In the *Life*, after quoting from a letter of Parr's to William Seward, in which he expresses his fear of being unable to rise to the occasion, JB remarks: "But I understand that this great scholar, and warm admirer of Johnson, has yielded to repeated solicitations, and executed the very difficult undertaking" (*Life* iv. 423 n. 3).

competition at all existed. I entered upon the station which I now occupy, without a spirit of invasion, I hope to fill it without dishonour, and I am prepared to retreat from it without reluctance. You will not wonder then, that, upon a business of such delicacy, I am sollicitous for a little explanation, and if you know any learned man, who either has written Dr. Johnsons epitaph, or intends writing it, or has been asked to write it, I beg of you to inform me unreservedly. My time has not been misspent, either in composing the inscription, or in reading those works of antiquity which alone could enable me to compose it properly. But my sensibility will be very much hurt indeed, if, without my consent, I am to be staked as a rival, where I intended only to perform the part of a friend.

I beg of you to present my best respects to Sir Joshua Reynolds, and have the honour to be, Dear Sir, your very faithful and Obedient Servant.

SAMUEL PARR

To the Rev. Dr. Samuel Parr, Wednesday 14 December 1791

MS. Yale (L 1028). JB's copy, headed: "To The Rev. Dr. Parr."

London, 14 Decr. 1791

DEAR SIR: You could not have done me a greater kindness than by communicating to me your very favourable opinion of my *Life of Dr. Johnson*. As I have full confidence in Dr. Parr's sincerity, such praise from him is a high gratification indeed. I trust it is unnecessary for me to do myself the honour of repeating how sensible I am of his other qualities. I return you my very sincere thanks for this spontaneous, full, and allow me to add hearty applause.

Let me hasten to make you perfectly easy with respect to the passage in my Book which I am not a little sorry has disturbed your sensibility, and I own with apparent good reason. In short I have expressed myself inaccurately. I should not have said that to write Johnson's Epitaph *has excited the warmest competition of genius*; but that *it will no doubt excite*—or *must certainly excite*;[1] for though various sepulchral inscriptions for him appeared in the fugitive publications, no man of genius has been asked to write his epitaph,

---

[1] Changed in the second edition to: "To compose his epitaph, could not but excite" etc. (*Life* iv. 423).

yourself excepted, who it was universally agreed would do it the best; nor is there to be any comparative examination, or any kind of rivalship. I ask pardon for assuming or rather carelessly expressing as *in Esse* what my imagination was filled with as *in posse*.

Keep your station, then Sir, as the *Lapidicirist* of Johnson, with I hope also a glowing sentiment of *Paulo Majora canamus*.[2] A critical display of the various excellencies of his Works by your forcible pen will accumulate glories on my illustrious friend.

Sir Joshua Reynolds begs I will make his excuse to you for not writing. He has for a considerable time had such a depression of spirits, as to be almost unfit for any exertion. This most distressing of all states (as I have often sadly experienced it to be) has in his case been owing to an apprehension of losing his other eye by inflammation, and in consequence of that, reducing himself very low, which at sixty eight must not be done. I am happy to inform you that Dr. Warren is clear that his eye is in no danger, and has prevailed on him to live more generously, so that he is returning to us.[3] I am very much with him to be of any service I can.

Mr. Courtenay sends you his best compliments. He says you are *liberally orthodox*. You will oblige me much if you will let me know that I have satisfied you. I am, Dear Sir, Your very faithful humble servant

From Anne Gardner, Thursday 22 December 1791

MS. Yale (C 1332).

ADDRESS: James Boswell Esqr., Great Portland Street, Oxford Street. No. 47.

ENDORSEMENT: Mrs. Anne Gardner.

Park Street, Dec. 22. —91

SIR: I flatter myself you will excuse this address when you know the motive.

I have lately been very highly entertained in reading your *Life of*

---

[2] "Let us sing a somewhat higher strain" (Virgil, *Eclogues* iv. 1). "Lapidicirist" appears to be a coinage of JB's.

[3] Against his inclination Reynolds on 10 Dec. was re-elected President of the Royal Academy; on 23 Feb. he died. See *Letters of Sir Joshua Reynolds*, ed. F. W. Hilles, 1929, p. 228 n. 1.

Dr. Johnson—the life and conversations of such a man, related by such a friend, must edify and entertain all who read it. But there is one short paragraph in it (with all due deference I speak it) that I believe the Dr. did not perfectly understand, relative to the late Mr. Gardner, Printer, opposite St. Clements Church in the Strand, and his connexion with Mr. Smart when *The Universal Visitor* was published.[1]

I, Sir, have the honour of being Mr. Gardner's eldest daughter— his true character as a *Christian*, and a *Gentleman in the real sense of the word*, makes it no impropriety for me to esteem it an *honour* to be so nearly related to him. His memory is deservedly dear to all who really knew him, as well as to me. Your benevolent disposition will therefore lead you to make every allowance for the feelings of an affectionate child—hurt at the least appearance of shade cast over the character of a much revered parent.[2]

I will suppose the book must be reprinted—which prompts me to solicit the favour of you to permit that whole paragraph to be left out—it begins, *"Old* Tom Gardner," etc. My dear Father Sir was but fifty-two when he died. This was of no consequence, nor should I have marked it, only with submission to observe that as the worthy Dr. was misinformed in one particular, he might also in another. I hope, for the credit of human-nature, it was not from Mr. Edmund Allen[3]—because *he* had received numberless kindnesses from my father and mother.

I ought Sir to make many appologies for giving you this trouble. May the subject plead for me, and then I will assure myself of your

[1] "We spoke of Rolt, to whose Dictionary of Commerce, Dr. Johnson wrote the Preface. JOHNSON. 'Old Gardner the bookseller employed Rolt and Smart to write a monthly miscellany, called "The Universal Visitor." There was a formal written contract, which Allen the printer saw. . . . They were bound to write nothing else; they were to have, I think, a third of the profits of this sixpenny pamphlet; and the contract was for ninety-nine years. I wish I had thought of giving this to Thurlow, in the cause about Literary Property. What an excellent instance would it have been of the oppression of booksellers towards poor authors!' (smiling)" (*Life* ii. 344–45). Thomas Gardner was a printer and publisher, Cowley's Head, without Temple Bar, Strand, 1735–56 (Plomer). The original contract, abstracted by Dr. Powell, *Life* ii. 345 n. 2, would appear to substantiate SJ's complaint. For SJ's contribution to the periodical, identified by Miss Gardner, see R. B. Botting, "Johnson, Smart, and the *Universal Visiter*," MP (1939), xxxvi. 293–300.

[2] See JB's benevolent foot-note, added in the second edition; and Miss Gardner's acknowledgement, *post* 6 Aug. 1793.

[3] Edmund Allen (1726–84), printer, Bolt Court; SJ's landlord, "a worthy obliging man, and his very old acquaintance" (*Life* iii. 269). See *Life* and *Letters SJ passim*.

pardon. Whatever censure it may incur, the blame is wholly mine —having acted entirely from the dictates of my own mind, without consulting any one. I tresspass no longer on your time than to assure you that I am Sir! with great respect, Your very humble servant

No. 40 Park Street, Grosvenor Square   ANNE GARDNER

From the Rev. Dr. Samuel Parr, c. Thursday 22 December 1791

MS. Yale (C 2185).

ADDRESS: James Boswel Esqr., at Sir Joshua Reynolds, Leicester Square, London.

POSTMARK: DE 23 91.

ENDORSEMENT: No. 2 Rev. Dr. Parr Decr. 1791.

Decr. —91, Hatton

DEAR SIR: The applause I gave to your *Life of Johnson* was I am sure "hearty," and glad I am that you think it "full." Months often roll over my head in which I have no access to three of those publications which for a time have too much influence upon general opinion. I do indeed read *The English review* and there I have seen a querulous and impotent letter from Dr. Ogilvie, in which he censures you for saying, what he has himself substantially said even in his explanation.[1] —Before I sat down to your book, I certainly had in conversation heard many objections, and after reading it, I found very few of them were just. In respect to Johnson you have displayed him in a new, and luminous, and a most advantageous point of view by producing the arguments which he drew up upon legal cases.[2] He brings into the field such numerous forces, He draws them up in such formidable array, he furnishes them with such gorgeous armour, that I consider him, as "more than conqueror in the day of *trial.*"[3] There is no levity in appliing scriptural

[1] John Ogilvie, D.D. (1733–1813). His letter (*English Review* for Nov. 1791, xviii. 397–400; *Edinburgh Magazine* for same date, xiv. 355–57) attempts to correct or tone down details of JB's account of his part in the conversation at the Mitre, 6 July 1763, during which he is alleged to have claimed for his native Scotland "a great many noble wild prospects", thus drawing upon himself SJ's famous retort (*Life* i. 425). The day before (*ibid.* 421) SJ had criticized Ogilvie's poems as having "no thinking in them".

[2] *Life* ii. 183–85, 196–200, 242–46, 372–73, 373–74, iii. 59–62, 202–03, iv. 74, 129–31.

[3] Cf. *Romans* viii. 37.

language to the moral opinions of a man, by whom scripture was reverenced. —As to the composition of the book I upon the whole think it very good, and so good as to justify you in making it better for a future edition. —Two passages struck me very forcibly —the one was, where you quote the magnificent criticism of some modern scholar upon the *Life of Young* by Herbert Croft and you must excuse me for asking even with importunity who the critic was.[4] The other was the grand comparison between the Gladiator driving back the wild beasts into their dens without destroying them, and Johnson struggling with his passions without vanquishing them.[5] I read it with admiration, and with envy, such as Johnson is said to have felt when he desired our friend Sir Joshua to read him again some splendid passage in his lectures and exclaimed, "why did not I write that."[6] The former instance of triple effort reminded me of what Homer says about the descent of Neptune from Samothrace to Ægæ—τρὶς δ'ωρέξατ ἰών[7]—and of the latter I would say in the strong and vivid language of Quintilian, ad summum pervenit non nisu, sed impetu.[8] In this comparison you have the advantage. I am now satisfied about the Epitaph.[9] It has been written long ago, and I shall bring it with me to London in the close of January. My books were all removed, and my papers thrown into confusion during the riots,[10] and from that dismal time to the present, I have not once looked at the inscription. It is written according to the plan which I mentioned to Sir Joshua. He

[4] *Life* iv. 59. The critic was Burke (Journ. 8 May 1781), and so identified by Malone in the third edition (*Life* iv. 59 n. 2).

[5] *Life* ii. 106. See Introduction, p. xlix.

[6] Cf. *Life* iv. 320: "Though he had no taste for painting, he admired much the manner in which Sir Joshua Reynolds treated of his art, in his 'Discourses to the Royal Academy.' He observed one day of a passage in them, 'I think I might as well have said this myself'".

[7] Τρὶς μὲν ὀρέξατ' ἰών ("Three times he stretched himself as he went"): *Iliad* xii. 12.

[8] Read "non pervenit": "He reaches the top not by work but by a shove" (*Institutio Oratoria* VIII. iv. 9).

[9] The business of the epitaph was not settled until 1795, after JB's death. One of the last letters JB wrote was to Malone on 13 Apr. 1795 (*Letters JB* 327), protesting Parr's high-handed forcing of his epitaph on the committee for SJ's monument sight unseen. The letter was "written at Malone's request for Parr's perusal" (BP xviii. 275–76).

[10] The Birmingham Riots of July 1791, over the celebration of the anniversary of the French Revolution by local dissenters. Because of his friendship with Dr. Priestley, whose library was destroyed by the rioters, Parr had expected similar treatment at nearby Hatton parsonage, but order was restored in time. The next year he published *A Letter from Irenopolis to the Inhabitants of Eleutheropolis, or a Serious Address to the Dissenters of Birmingham*, in which he sought (successfully) to dissuade them from holding a second celebration (DNB; Parr's *Works* iii. 278, 299 ff.).

was pleased to approve of the plan, and I am answerable for the execution. It is very short, and very plain, because Antiquity has left no good inscription but what is short and plain. You will look in vain for one splendid phrase, one nice discrimination, or one structure of Sentence apparently artificial. If I should ever be induced to write a critical life of Johnson, depend upon it that I shall not forget the hint which you have given me with so much pleasantry. All my classical reading, all my literary knowledge, all my powers in criticism and in philosophy will be brought to the task.[11] —I am not weak enough and arrogant enough to say that mine will be the magnæ mentis opus, but I may apply the remainder of the passage when I say that the life of Johnson must be mentis opus non de lodice paranda Sollicite, satur est cum dicit Horatius Ævoe.[12] When a prebend furnishes me with a cushion and a rectory with a footstool, I probably shall sit down to the work with ardour. But in my present Curatical condition I have neither leisure to read nor inclination to write, and your friend Mr. Pitt will not resign his place to give me an opportunity of scribbling about Johnson, and while he keeps his place I must toil for my daily bread.[13]

I have met with few men whom I think more agreable, or better informed, than Mr. Courtenay. I have seen him in many companies, and heard him upon many subjects. His wit is gay but not acrimonious, and his knowledge is various but not ostentatious. I[14] am

---

[11] In 1825 Parr wrote to Joseph Cradock: "For many years I spent a month's holidays in London, and never failed to call upon Johnson. I was not only admitted, but welcomed. I conversed with him upon numberless subjects of learning, politics, and common life. I traversed the whole compass of his understanding; and, by the acknowledgment of Burke and Reynolds, I distinctly understood the peculiar and transcendental properties of his mighty and virtuous mind. I intended to write his life; I laid by sixty or seventy books for the purpose of writing it in such a manner as would do no discredit to myself. I intended to spread my thoughts over two volumes quarto, and if I had filled three pages the rest would have followed. Often have I lamented my ill fortune in not building this monument to the fame of Johnson, and let me not be accused of arrogance when I add, my own" (Parr's *Works* viii. 23). See also Wheatley, *Johnson Club Papers*, p. 223, and *Bibliotheca Parriana*, 1827, pp. 706–08.

[12] Juvenal, *Satires* vii. 66–67, 62; for "non" read "nec" and for "Sollicite" read "attonitae". Parr is saying that his projected work may not be that of a great mind, but must at least be that of a mind not distracted by the problem of securing a livelihood (Horace has a full stomach when he cries "Evoe!").

[13] As an outspoken member of the Whig Opposition Parr of course stood little chance of preferment. In 1787 he had specifically attacked Pitt in print. See DNB.

[14] MS. "ostentatious, I"

not sorry that he calls me "literally[15] orthodox," though I suspect that if he knew me more he would see my orthodoxy rather in the spirit than in the letter. Believe me Dear Sir, wise and good men, as Johnson says of Whigs and Tories, do not much disagree in their principles,[16] and as to their prejudices, I have seen so many of them upon all sides, that no small portion of my time has been laid out in correcting my own—for this reason I totally [differ] from yourself, and from Dr. Johnson in the treatment which ought to be given to infidel writers[17] and as to the heretical I equally differ from ⟨the⟩ method which Bishop Horsley has pursued,[18] Whether or no you think this orthodox, I know it to be right, and if I should hereafter, take up my pen, neither you nor Johnson will escape with total impunity upon this subject. And yet in the serious belief of religious truths, and in a serious concern for them I will not yeild the superiority to either of you. I am glad to have Dr. Warrens opinion of Sir Joshua, you love your friends, and your friends know how to value you, cherish Sir Joshua with your company, and enliven him by your conversation. In taste, in judgement, in felicity of stile, and urbanity of manners, he is among the first of men, and there are qualities of a yet higher order which give him a place among the best of men. Pray remember me to him, and to Mr. Courtenay in the most respectful terms. I hope to have the pleasure of seeing you when I come to town. In the mean time I have the honour to remain Dear Sir, your most obedient faithful Servant

SAMUEL PARR

Was our friend Mr. Windham the eloquent critic on poor Crofts? it is his manner.

[15] A misreading of "liberally" (*ante* To Parr, 14 Dec. 1791)—unless JB miswrote it in the original.
[16] *Life* iv. 117–18.
[17] *Life* ii. 442–43, where JB in a long speech objects to "treating an infidel writer with smooth civility," and where SJ "coincided" with him.
[18] The tear in the MS. may have obliterated a word at this point.

1792

From Charlotte Lennox,[1]
Tuesday 3 January 1792

MS. Yale (C 1725).

ADDRESS: James Boswell Esqr., Great Portland Street.

ENDORSEMENT: Mrs. Charlotte Lennox.

[London,] Janry. 3d 1792

SIR: At the same time that I hear from every mouth the highest praises of your *Life of Doctor Johnson*, I hear likewise of the honourable mention you make of me in that elegant performance.

What I could not hope for from my own writings you have bestowd upon me, and by recording your illustrious friend's favourable judgment of me,[2] have given me a share in that immortality which your own pen confers on your self. I am with great respect, Sir, Your Obligd, and very humble Servant

CHARLOTTE LENNOX

My compliments to the Ladies of your family whom I had the pleasure to see at Mrs. Reynolds's.[3]

---

[1] Charlotte (Ramsay) Lennox (b. ?1729–32, d. 1804), author. See *ante* From Percy, 5 and 7 May 1772 and n. 26. An account of the recently discovered Lennox papers, among which are thirteen letters from SJ and one from JB to Mrs. Lennox, is given by Duncan E. Isles in TLS, 29 July and 5 Aug. 1965, pp. 666 and 685. In Feb. 1793 JB wrote at Mrs. Lennox's request *Proposals for publishing a new and improved edition of Shakespeare Illustrated*; copies are in the Yale (P 151) and Hyde Collections and Lennox papers, now at Harvard. The MS. *Life* (Paper Apart for p. 430) contains a copy—the only one as yet brought to light—of SJ's printed Proposals for her projected *Works*, dated 14 Feb. 1775. JB crossed out all but SJ's text: see *Life* ii. 289–90.

[2] " 'I dined yesterday [14 May 1784] at Mrs. Garrick's, with Mrs. Carter, Miss Hannah More, and Miss Fanny Burney. Three such women are not to be found: I know not where I could find a fourth, except Mrs. Lennox, who is superiour to them all' " (*Life* iv. 275). This preference is confirmed by Bowles in one of his "memorandums" (quoted by Dr. Powell, *ibid.* 524). SJ wrote, 10 July 1781, "She has many fopperies, but she is a Great genius" (*Letters SJ* 736.1).

[3] Frances Reynolds, Sir Joshua's sister. Mrs. Lennox seems to have kept up the acquaintance. There is a letter in the Yale Collection (C 1727) from her to JB's daughter Veronica, 26 (misdated 28) Apr. 1794, commenting on JB's paper war with Anna Seward.

From James Abercrombie,[1]
Wednesday 25 January 1792

MS. Yale (C 1).

ADDRESS: James Boswell Esqr. of Auchinleck. To the Care of Mr. Charles Dilly, Bookseller, London.[2]

Philad[elphi]a, Jany. 25th 1792

SIR: Your Benevolence and Urbanity will I flatter myself induce you to pardon the liberty I take in thus addressing you, without the introduction of a mutual friend; being irresistibly impell'd thus to trespass on your time and attention, by the following motives.

In the first place, Sir, I beg leave to offer you my most grateful thanks, for the very superior degree of entertainment and instruction I have received from your lately published *Life of Dr. Johnson*; which I have been most anxiously expecting, ever since your promise of it at the end of your *Tour to the Hebrides,*[3] printed in 1785, and to which I have attached an additional value, from its being the only literary production I have ever yet met with, which amply gratified (nay in this instance far exceeded) that luxurious

[1] James Abercrombie (1758–1841), a graduate of the College of Philadelphia in 1776, was at this time in business. He was ordained deacon in St. Peter's Church, Philadelphia in 1793, and priest the following year. In 1804 he received a D.D. from the College of New Jersey. Besides serving as assistant minister of Christ Church and St. Peter's, he was Principal of the Philadelphia Academy, which he helped to found in 1810 (W. B. Sprague, *Annals of the American Pulpit*, 1859–69, v. 392; *Appletons' Cyclopædia of American Biography*, ed. J. G. Wilson and John Fiske, 1888–89, i. 8). A Tory in his politics, he frequently attacked Jefferson in his sermons after 1800 (J. T. Scharf and Thompson Westcott, *History of Philadelphia, 1609–1884*, 1884, i. 506). Abercrombie's interest in SJ's writings, shown throughout his correspondence with JB, culminated c. 1809–10 in Proposals (by J. and A. Y. Humphreys, Philadelphia) for a complete edition of his works, but the project was abortive. The Prospectus reads in part: "The Rev'd James Aber-crombie, D.D. the editor of the proposed edition, from his early and profound respect for the character, and his admiration of the writings of Dr. Johnson, has, for many years past, spared neither pains nor expense to obtain whatever has been published, either by or in relation to that distinguished author. Through the activity of several kind friends, and the indulgent attention of James Boswell, Esq. with whom Dr. A. corresponded for some years before his death, he is now enabled to give to the world that *complete* collection of Dr. Johnson's writings, so long and so justly desired." SJ's sermon on his wife's death (*ante* To Barber, 20 Mar. 1788 and n. 2) was included by Abercrombie in a collection of consolatory writings, *The Mourner Comforted* (1812).

[2] The covering letter to Dilly is dated 26 Jan. and postmarked 16 Apr. It is endorsed by JB: "From Mr. Abercrombie Philadelphia. 25 Janry. 1792. Answer Within."

[3] That is, in the Advertisement.

indulgence of hope, to which my too sanguine imagination often subjects me.

My second inducement for this address, is to transmit you copies of two letters of your venerable friend. Justly have you observed, that "every thing however small which fell from his pen, like the filings of diamonds, is of inestimable value."[4] I trust therefore the enclosed will be acceptable. Gladly Sir would I have sent you the originals, but being the only relics of the kind in America, they are considered by the possessors, of such inestimable value, that no possible consideration would induce them to part with them.[5] They are now before me; and being honored by an intimate acquaintance with both the gentlemen to whom they are addressed, I readily obtained their permission to transmit you copies of them. One of the gentlemen complied with my solicitation, on condition that I would promise not to transcribe his name at full length, as he had several times refused your personal application to him for it when in England. He is himself an American, practised the Law with success at the English Bar during the late war, and now resides here in a public character of considerable dignity.[6] The other, address'd to Mr. White (now Doctr. and Bishop of the Episcopal church in Pennsylvania) is in some degree connected with it, being enclosed in the packet entrusted by Dr. Johnson to Mr. B——d. During Dr. White's first visit to England in 1771 as a candidate for Holy Orders, he was several times in company with Dr. Johnson, and in one of their conversations told him that an edition of

[4] A free paraphrase of an observation, not by JB, but by Dr. Maxwell, *Life* ii. 117.

[5] This sentence, combined with a part of the last sentence of this paragraph, was inserted in the second edition, followed by the letters, *Life* ii. 206–07.

[6] Paraphrased, *Life* ii. 207 n. 1. SJ's correspondent was first named, and briefly identified, in the Edinburgh edition of his letters (1822). Phineas Bond (1749–1815), like Abercrombie a native Philadelphian and graduate of the College of Philadelphia, was appointed British consul for the Middle States in 1786, having been a loyalist during the Revolution. At the outbreak of hostilities in 1812 he retired to England, where he passed his remaining years (Scharf and Westcott,

History of Philadelphia ii. 923; *Letters of Benjamin Rush*, ed. L. H. Butterfield, 1951, i. 447 n. 4). He is doubtless the same Mr. Bond with whom JB dined at Dilly's on 8 Jan. 1793 (Journ.): see *post* From Abercrombie, 17 May 1793 and n. 22. Chapman's conjecture (*Letters SJ* 297 n.) that the partial suppression of Bond's name indicated his unwillingness "to be known as corresponding with the author of *Taxation No Tyranny*" is overturned by the present passage and also the fact of Bond's loyalist background. For an account of Bond and other prominent Americans mentioned in Abercrombie's correspondence with JB, see M. J. Quinlan, "Johnson's American Acquaintances," *Johnson, Boswell and Their Circle*, pp. 190–207.

his *Rasselas* had been printed in America. The Dr.'s expressing a wish to see it, induced Dr. White to send him a copy immediately on his return, which occasioned the enclosed reply.[7] Their internal evidence of style will readily convince you of their authenticity, and [8]in some future publication of yours relative to that great and good man, may perhaps be thought worthy of insertion;[8] at any rate I doubt not they will be well received by you.

From my enthusiastic veneration for Doctr. Johnson, I have diligently endeavoured to collect every work of his, and every publication relative to him which has hitherto come within my information. Those in my possession are,

1. His *Works* by Sir John Hawkins, with the additional vols. amounting to 16 Octavos[9]
2. Your lately published *Life of Dr. Johnson*, 2 Vols. 4to
3. Your *Tour to the Hebrides*, 8vo
4. The last 4to edition of his *Dictionary*, 2 Vols.[10]
5. Dr. Johnsons letters to Mrs. Thrale, 8vo
6. His *Prayers and Meditations*
7. Mrs. Piozzi's *Anecdotes*
8. His edition of Shakespeare, 10 Vols.[11]

[7] Paraphrased, *Life* ii. 207 n. 2. William White, D.D. (1748–1836), also a native Philadelphian and graduate of the College, was the first Protestant Episcopal bishop of the diocese of Pennsylvania. He was ordained deacon in London in 1770 (not 1771) and remained there until 1772, when he was of age to be ordained priest (DAB; J. H. Ward, *Life and Times of Bishop White*, 1892, p. 21). A brief account by White of his acquaintance with SJ, and also with Goldsmith, is given in Ward, pp. 23–24, and reprinted in part, *Life* ii. 499. The *Rasselas* which White sent SJ was a copy of the first American edition (Philadelphia, 1768): see *Life* ii. 499; C. B. Tinker, *Rasselas in the New World* (1925); and R. F. Metzdorf, "The First American 'Rasselas' and Its Imprint", *The Papers of the Bibliographical Society of America* (1953) xlvii. 374–76.

[8–8] Quoted, *Life* ii. 207, followed by the letters. The original of the letter to White is in the Hyde Collection (see

Adam Cat. i. 186); the original of the letter to Bond is untraced.

[9] Hawkins's edition of the *Works*, including the *Life*, ran to eleven volumes (1787). Two additional volumes consisting of the *Debates in Parliament* were brought out in the same year by John Stockdale, who added a third of miscellaneous writings the following year. In 1789 appeared an edition of SJ's translation of Lobo's *Abyssinia* by George Gleig together with some tracts (Courtney, p. 162; Chapman-Hazen, pp. 164–65). The sixteenth volume, as Abercrombie goes on to say, consisted of the two volumes of the *Sermons Left for Publication by John Taylor* (1788–89), bound together.

[10] Either the sixth edition (1785) or Jarvis and Fielding's edition (1785).

[11] That is, the edition by SJ and Steevens: either the first (1773), the second (1778), or the third, revised by Isaac Reed (1785). The original edition by SJ alone (1765) was in eight volumes.

9. *The Beauties of Johnson,* 2 vols. 12mo[12]
10. *Lexiphanes*[13]
11. *Dinarbas*—a continuation of *Rasselas.*[14]

Are there any other publications by or of that illustrious character, the possession of which could add to the enjoyment of one of his most ardent admirers? If there are I will thank you Sir for their titles.

Two thin Octavo Vols. of his *Sermons* (*left for publication by Dr. Taylor*) bound together, form my 16th Vol. of his works. Can you inform me Sir, whether any more of the Forty he is said to have written have yet been discovered, or whether any other of his writings yet remain to be published.

In the fullest confidence that your goodnature will excuse the length of this epistle, I now subscribe myself with great respect, Sir, Your most humble Servant

JAS. ABERCROMBIE

From James Hutton,[1]
Sunday 29 January 1792

MS. Yale (C 1576).

ADDRESS: James Boswell Esqr., No. 47 Great Portland Street.

POSTMARKS: JA 31 92, FE 1 92.

ENDORSEMENT: Rev. Mr. Hutton of the Unitas Fratrum.

Oxtead near Godstone, Surrey, Jan. 29. 1792

DEAR SIR: I saw you[2] and thankd you for what you have so well wrote of my dear Respected Friend in his *Life,* I was not pleasd

---

[12] Published by George Kearsley in 1781 in one volume octavo. Abercrombie probably owned one of the several 1782 editions, or reprints: see *Life* iv. 500. The editor of the collection appears to have been SJ's early biographer, William Cooke; see A. T. Hazen, *MP* (1938) xxxv. 289–95.

[13] *Lexiphanes, a Dialogue. Imitated from Lucian and Suited to the Present Times . . . Being an Attempt to Restore the English Tongue to Its Ancient Purity and to Correct as well as Expose the Affected Style, Hard Words, and Absurd Phraseology of Many Late Writers, and Particularly of our English Lexiphanes, the Rambler.* The work was published anonymously in 1767 by Archibald Campbell. See *Life* ii. 44.

[14] See *ante* From Hoole, 17 June 1790 and n. 7.

[1] James Hutton (1715–95), founder of the Moravian Church in England. See *Thraliana,* pp. 926–27. JB dined in his company at Aubrey's tavern in London, 19 Apr. 1785 (Journ.). Parts of the conversation are recorded in *Boswelliana* (p. 300, where Hutton is wrongly identified).

[2] On 24 Jan., as Hutton later says. There is no journal for this period.

with that part of what you wrote in the *Tour to the Hebrides*, relating to a conversation of His with some Clergymen at Edinburgh, as if the Relation of the Success of the Missions was not worthy of the Credit it assumed.[3] I happen to know that Relation of the Success of the Moravian Missions, far from exceeding the Bounds of Veracity, falls far short. This was not necessary for me to attack as I know not that He intended it against our Missions, but I met lately again with that charming work and was sorry to read it. When one of our very expensive Missions to the Coast of Labradore, [4]for which as much expence was incurrd by our Society of plain middling men not one of which was I suppose owner of 1000 £ to fit out a Vessel and to furnish yearly Provisions, Cloaths and Refreshments for our poor Volunteers serving and working as a speculation Commercial requires, and this continued year by year,[4] required the Contributions of richer People, Dr. Johnson on my applying to him, then at Mr. Thrale's Grosvenor Square,[5] introduced me to Mr. Thrale then at Breakfast, who on whispering to Dr. Johnson gave me 5 Gs towards the Expences of that year. The Success of which Mission in civilising at least the Eskimaux on that Coast, formerly the most traitorous murtherers known on any Coast, procured me from Dr. Franklyn a Letter to be taken with the Ship in case it should be attacked by the American Ships of War,[6] that the Endeavour had been of so much use to the General use and Peace universal of every Trading Nation, that He was sure the Congress would approve of their letting our Vessel so charit-

[3] "Dr. Erskine and Mr. Robert Walker, two very respectable ministers of Edinburgh, supped with us, as did the Reverend Dr. Webster. —The conversation turned on the Moravian missions, and on the Methodists. Dr. Johnson observed in general, that missionaries were too sanguine in their accounts of their success among savages, and that much of what they tell is not to be believed" (*Life* v. 391).

[4-4] Read as a parenthesis.

[5] The ailing Thrale rented a furnished house in Grosvenor Square the end of Jan. 1781 and died there on 4 Apr. (*Thraliana*, pp. 478, 487). See *Life* iv. 72 and n. 1.

[6] Hutton's letter to Franklin, requesting immunity from American armed ships, is dated 21 Jan. 1778 (Franklin Papers, American Philosophical Society). The passport is printed in *Works of Franklin*, ed. Jared Sparks, 1836–40, v. 122–23; and Franklin's covering letter, dated 23 June 1778, in *Writings of Franklin*, ed. A. H. Smyth, 1905–07, vii. 162. Both documents were first printed in *Memoirs of Franklin*, ed. W. T. Franklin, quarto edition, 1818, i. 326–27. I owe this note to Prof. L. W. Labaree.

ably employd Pass without Molestation, The same sort of Protection Pass was given me every year during the Remainder of the
War, by the Court of France, on my sending back the Pass, on the
same Grounds. They renewd the Pass every year. Dr. Johnson
had contributed his Share kindly and we got him Greenland Testament and Hymns, so curious was He as to every Language He
could hear of. I was glad to have met you at kind Mr. Metcalfe's
the 24th to have opportunity of thanking you for the true Pleasure
you gave me in your charming *Life* of dear great good Dr. Johnson
to whose Imperfections I was no Stranger, much less so his brave
Virtues, to day I find my Name, where I can be proud of it, among
those whom He liberally honourd with his friendship and returnd
His.[7]

The same Day Jan. 24 I had a Stroke of the Apop. sort in the
Park at returning home after a Day of too much Fatigue for my
years born Sept. 3, O.S. 1715 and was led home by a Soldier,
coverd with Blood from the Fall on my Nose, and was carried on
the 28th to this kind most hospitable Cottage by an adopted
Daughter[8] to be kept Quiet, and nursd as dear Dr. Johnson frequently was, with ten thousand fewer Merits than His.

I found lately an Error in Mrs. Piozzi's Italian Tour where she
approximated a kind Idea on her being informd some where in
Hungary of a Moravian Chapel reminding her of me.[9] The
Moravian Brethren have not to the best of my knowledge any
Chapel in those Parts. What is pleasing is her kind Recollection of
me. What Baretti wrote of her was wrote as with a Stilletto dipt
in Mud.[10] The Provocation she gave non erat tanti.[11] It seems I am
some what recovered from the Effects of that Stroke of Jan. 24, but
my Head resents the assault of that Day. I do not find my Name or

---

[7] "It is to the mutual credit of Johnson
and Divines of different communions,
that although he was a steady Church-of-
England man, there was, nevertheless,
much agreeable intercourse between him
and them. Let me particularly name the
late Mr. La Trobe, and Mr. Hutton, of
the Moravian profession" (*Life* iv. 410).
[8] Hutton passed his last years at Oxted
Cottage with the Misses Biscoe and
Shelley. He was married, but had no
children of his own (DNB).

[9] *Observations and Reflections Made in
the Course of a Journey through France,
Italy, and Germany*, 1789, ii. 291.
[10] Baretti's "Strictures" on the publication of Mrs. Piozzi's *Letters To and
From Johnson* appeared in *The European
Magazine* for May, June, and Aug. 1788
(xiii. 313–17, 393–99, xiv. 89–99). See
Clifford, *Piozzi*, pp. 322 ff.
[11] "was not worth the trouble"
(of retaliating): proverbial. Cf. *Life* iv.
112.

that of Mr. La Trobe[12] who frequented him 10 times more than I and had great Merit indeed towards poor Dodd at my Request, and being Neighbour to Will. Strahan who shewd me from his Accounts that I had been one of his very first Employers, by the Recommendation of the younger Wesley, used to visit Strahan daily, by him introduced to Dr. Johnson, saw much of Him and Loved Him. We both ardently wishd our dear Doctor J. more of the Luminous Comforts of the Gospel than He ventured to embrace and apply to his own Case. This was unfortunate. I recollect having heard in Derbyshire that Dr. Taylor had boasted at a Table there that Dr. Johnson had consulted Him about the admissibility of Suicide, and that He had set him right by the most paltry common place Stuff that could be. I grew so angry and so disgusted that I despised Taylor as unworthy of Society, if what He utterd was in any Degree True, as a Confessors Breach of Confession Fidelity, and if not True, it certainly was not, how disgraceful. I desire my Love and my poor Thanks to every one who really Loved and esteemd Dr. Johnson. Take yourself as large a share as you like. I thank kind Mr. Metcalfe for the Brighton Kindness and for his Taste. So Langton and Sir Joshua, Dr. Brocklesby, Heberden, Cruikshanks and every Soul of Man that is kind. I am generally at this Place, as little as possible in Town at my House next to the Turnpike Pimlico. The Quiet of the Cottage hinders me from over Exertions, and the kindness of Conversation makes my great Infirmities lighter to me. May you find Friends always and every where, you deserve them. I am, Dear Sir, your most obedient Servant

JAMES HUTTON

[12] The Rev. Benjamin La Trobe (1728–86). See *Life* iv. 552; Croker, 1860, pp. 805 n. 3 and 846; and M. J. Quinlan, "An Intermediary between Cowper and Johnson," RES (1948) xxiv. 141–47. As Hutton has already referred to the place in the *Life* where both he and La Trobe are mentioned (*ante* n. 7), the present reference would seem to be to SJ's letter to JB, 28 June 1777, on the death of Dr. Dodd: ". . . he had a Moravian with him much of the time" (*Life* iii. 121–22).

From the Rev. Ralph Churton,[1]
Friday 9 March 1792

MS. Yale (C 787). Inside the address side appears the postscript: "Coming unexpectedly to London to morrow, I shall bring the packet in my portmanteau. Mar. 12."

ADDRESS: James Boswell Esq.

ENDORSEMENT: Rev. Mr. Ralph Churton and Rev. Dr. Townson. 9 March 1792.

Brasen Nose College, Oxford, March 9. 1792

SIR, Your candour will pardon a letter from an unknown hand, as it may be proper to explain the occasion of the inclosed extract, which I give on a separate paper that it may not appear in company unworthy of it, and may also, if You please, be preserved when this is committed to the flames. The first volume of the *Life of Johnson* I read last summer at my friend Dr. Townson's,[2] and most of it to Him, with great delight to both parties. The second volume, which He read shortly afterwards, I had no opportunity to go on with till the Christmas holidays, when I read it with equal avidity and satisfaction. This pleasure I expressed to my friend, and suggested to Him a wish, that, if He thought proper, he would make a present of his Book[3] to the Author of a Work which in common we so much admired. The extract now sent is his answer to that part of my letter. As for the attendant volume,[4] which solicits Your acceptance, I ought certainly to apologize for such intrusion; but this paper will itself, I fear, in what follows still more require an apology. For I am going, without further preface, but with all deference, to submit to Your consideration one or two strictures on the work which I have hitherto extolled and cordially approve. The chief part[5] of what I have to observe is contained in the following

---

[1] The Rev. Ralph Churton (1754–1831), M.A. Brasenose College, Oxford, 1778; Bampton Lecturer, 1785; Archdeacon of St. David's, 1805. He was the author of a number of sermons and biographies. See *Lit. Anec.* ix. 736.

[2] Thomas Townson, D.D. (1715–92), Rector of Malpas, Cheshire, where Churton attended school. After the death of Churton's parents Townson befriended him and helped sponsor his education at Oxford.

[3] *Discourses on the Four Gospels*, etc., 1778. See *Life* iv. 300 n. 2 (p. 302).

[4] Churton's Bampton Lectures: *Eight Sermons on the Prophecies respecting the Destruction of Jerusalem*, 1785. See *Life* iv. 300 n. 2 (p. 302), 534.

[5] Churton's letter from this point to the end is quoted, with very little editing, in the second edition (*Life* iv. 300 n. 2, 212 n. 4).

transcript from a letter to a friend, which with his concurrence I copied for this purpose; and, whatever may be the merit or justness of the remarks, You may be sure that being written to a most intimate friend without any intention that they ever should go further, they are the genuine and undisguised sentiments of the writer.

Jan. 6. 1792

Last week I was reading the second volume of Boswell's *Johnson* with increasing esteem for the worthy Author, and increasing veneration of the wonderful and excellent Man who is the subject of it. The writer throws in now and then very properly some serious religious reflexions; but there is one remark, in my mind an obvious and just one, which I think he has not made, that Johnson's "morbid melancholy" and constitutional infirmities were intended by Providence, like St. Paul's thorn in the flesh, to check intellectual conceit and arrogance; which the consciousness of his extraordinary talents, awake as he was to the voice of praise, might otherwise have generated in a very culpable degree. Another observation strikes me, that in consequence of the same natural indisposition and habitual sickliness (for he says he scarcely passed one day without pain after his twentieth year) he considered and represented human life as a scene of much greater misery than is generally experienced. There may be persons bowed down with affliction all their days; and there are those no doubt whose iniquities rob them of rest; but neither calamities nor crimes, I hope and believe, do so much and so generally abound as to justify the dark picture of life which Johnson's imagination designed and his strong pencil delineated. This I am sure, the colouring is far too gloomy for what I have experienced, though as far as I can remember I have had more sickness (I do not say more severe, but only more in quantity) than falls to the lot of most people.* . . . But then daily debility and occasional sickness were far over-balanced by intervenient days and perhaps weeks void of pain and overflowing with comfort.* . . . So that in short, to return to the subject, human life, as far as I can perceive from experi-

* What is omitted respected the writer solely, not the argument nor the work criticised.

ence or observation, is not that state of constant wretchedness which Johnson always insisted it was; which misrepresentation (for such it surely is) his Biographer has not corrected, I suppose because, unhappily, he has himself a large portion of melancholy in his constitution, and fancied the portrait a faithful copy of life.

I have conversed with some sensible men on this subject, who all seem to entertain the same sentiments respecting life with those which are expressed or implied in the foregoing paragraph. It might be added that as the representation here spoken of appears not consistent with fact and experience, so neither does it seem to be countenanced by scripture. There is perhaps no part of the sacred volume which at first sight promises so much to lend its sanction to these dark and desponding notions as the book of Ecclesiastes, which so often and so emphatically proclaims the vanity of things sublunary. But "the design of this whole book," as it has justly been observed, "is not to put us out of conceit with life, but to cure our vain expectations of a compleat and perfect happiness in this world; to convince us, that there is no such thing to be found in mere external enjoyments"; and "to teach us to seek for happiness in the practice of vertue, in the knowledge and love of God, and in the hopes of a better life. For this is the application of all: *Let us hear* etc." xii. 13. "Not only his duty, but his happiness too; *For God* etc." ver. 14. *

The New Testament tells us indeed and most truly that "sufficient unto the day is the evil thereof"; and therefore wisely forbids us to increase our burden by forebodings of sorrow; but I think it no where says that even our ordinary afflictions are not consistent with a very considerable degree of positive comfort and satisfaction. And accordingly one whose sufferings as well as merits were conspicuous assures us, that in proportion "as the sufferings of Christ abounded in them, so their consolation also abounded by Christ." 2 Cor. i. 5. It is needless to cite, as indeed it would be endless even to refer to, the multitude of passages in both Testaments holding out in the strongest language promises of blessings even in this

* Sherlock on Providence, p. 299.[6]

[6] William Sherlock, *A Discourse concerning the Divine Providence*, 1694, p. 245 (elliptically quoted).

world to the faithful servants of God. I will only refer to St. Luke xviii. 29, 30 and 1 Tim. iv. 8.

Upon the whole, setting aside instances of great and lasting bodily pain, of minds peculiarly oppressed by melancholy, and of severe temporal calamities, from which extraordinary cases we surely should not form our estimate of the general tenor and complexion of life; excluding these from the account, I am convinced that as well the gracious constitution of things which Providence has ordained, as the declarations of scripture and the actual experience of individuals authorise the sincere Christian to hope that his humble and constant endeavours to perform his duty, chequered as the best life is with many failings, will be crowned with a greater degree of present peace serenity and comfort, than he could reasonably permit himself to expect if he measured his views and judged of life from the opinion of Dr. Johnson often and energetically expressed in the memoirs of him, without any animadversion or censure by his ingenious Biographer. If He himself upon reviewing the subject shall see the matter in this light, He will in an octavo edition, which is eagerly expected, make such additional remarks or corrections as He shall judge fit; lest the impressions which these discouraging passages may leave on the reader's mind should in any degree hinder, what otherwise the whole spirit and energy of the work tends and I hope successfully to promote, pure morality and true religion.

I will only beg Your patience, if You have read thus far, to one slight correction. [7]The passage in the Burial Service, quoted vol. ii. 450, does not mean the resurrection of the person interred, but the general resurrection; it is "in sure and certain hope of *the* resurrection," not "*his* resurrection." Where the deceased is really spoken of, the expression is very different: "as our *hope* is this our brother doth" (rest in Christ,) a mode of speech consistent with every thing but absolute certainty that the person departed doth *not* rest in Christ, which no one can be assured of without immediate revelation from heaven. In the first of these places also "eternal life" does not necessarily mean eternity of bliss, but merely the eternity of the state, whether in happiness or in misery, to ensue upon the resurrection; which is probably the sense of "life everlasting" in the Apostles' creed. See Wheatly and Bennet on the Common Prayer.[7]

[7-7] Quoted, *Life* iv. 212 n. 4, with the omission of the reference to the first edition. Wheatly is Charles Wheatly, *The Church of England Man's Companion, or a*

Not having Your address I shall send the packet to Your Bookseller, who I presume will deliver it to You. Once and only once I had the satisfaction of seeing Your illustrious Friend; and as I feel a particular regard for All whom he distinguished with his esteem and friendship, so I derive much pleasure from reflecting that I once beheld though but transiently near our college gate One whose works will for ever delight and improve the world, who was a sincere and zealous son of the Church of England, an honour to his country, and an ornament to human nature. I am with much respect, Sir, Your very humble servant

RALPH CHURTON

[Enclosure]⁸

Extract of a letter from the Rev. Dr. Townson to
Mr. Churton, dated "Malpas, Feb. 16. 1792

Mr. Boswell is not only very entertaining in his works, but they are so replete with moral and religious sentiments, without an instance, as far as I know, of a contrary tendency, that I cannot help having a great esteem for him; and if you think such a trifle as a copy of the *Discourses*, *ex dono authoris*, would be acceptable to Him, I should be happy to give him this small testimony of my regard."

From the Rev. *William Beville*,¹ *Tuesday 13 March 1792*

MS. Yale (C 149).

ADDRESS: James Boswell Esq., Great Portland St.

ENDORSEMENT: Reverend Mr. Beville.

March 13th 1792, Edgware Road No. 17 [London]

DEAR SIR: I presume upon the very polite attention which you

Rational Illustration of the Harmony . . . and Usefulness of the Book of Common Prayer, 1710; Bennet is Thomas Bennet, *A Paraphrase with Annotations of the Book of Common Prayer*, 1708.

⁸ Endorsed by JB: "Extract of a letter from the Rev. Dr. Townson to the Rev. Mr. Ralph Churton."

¹ William Beville (d. 1822), B.A. 1778, M.A. 1781, and Fellow of Peterhouse, Cambridge. He preached in London, first at Great Queen St. Chapel and later at the chapel in Spring Gardens; at the time of his death he was Rector of Exford, Somersetshire (*Gent. Mag.* xcii. 188; Courtney, p. 136). JB heard him preach and received him at his house on several occasions during 1787–88 (Journ. *passim*). He is described in the journal as "quite a genteel clergyman and *in character*", and as having a "mild, elegant manner of preaching" (29 Apr. 1787, 27 Apr. 1788).

most obligingly paid me, during your attendance at Queen St. Chapel, to present to your notice, a little pamphlet of mine, entitled *Observations on Dr. Johnson's Life of Hammond*. It was written ten years ago; and I am persuaded, that, with *you*, the ardour of youth will be some apology for the rashness and ignorance of such a publication.[2] As an atom in that field of Literary History, on which you have raised an immortal column to the memory of your illustrious friend, I hope I shall be pardoned for pointing it out to your inspection. With my respectful Compliments to the Miss Boswells, I have the honour to be, Dear Sir, Your most obedient and much obliged humble Servant

WILLM. BEVILLE

From *William Elford*,[1] *Friday 16 March 1792*

MS. Yale (C 1186).

ADDRESS: James Boswell Esqr., London.

ENDORSEMENT: William Elford Esq.

Bickham near Plymouth, 16 March 1792

SIR: I am willing to believe that men of Eminence in the literary world, are sometimes troubled with letters from perfect strangers, and that this of mine is not among the first intrusions of that kind. If, however, I am guilty of taking an undue liberty, I am prompted to it, by, what I trust will in some measure plead my excuse, an invincible desire to tell You how very great a pleasure I have received from the perusal of Your *Life of Dr. Johnson*, which to my great regret I have just finish'd. When Your *Journal of a Tour to the Hebrides* was publish'd, I read it with an avidity, I had never experienc'd before, and I need not say, with what anxiety I ex-

---

[2] In the second edition JB added a note to his discussion of the narrow attacks upon SJ's *Lives of the Poets*, excepting Beville's "ingenious though not satisfactory defence of Hammond. ... It is a juvenile performance, but elegantly written, with classical enthusiasm of sentiment, and yet with a becoming modesty, and great respect for Dr. Johnson" (*Life* iv. 63 n. 4).

[1] William Elford (1749–1837), banker, politician, scientist, and artist. He was Mayor of Plymouth in 1797, M.P. for Plymouth, 1796–1806, Fellow of the Royal Society and of the Linnean Society, 1790, and was created a baronet in 1800.

pected the appearance of this last work, which does so much honor to Your Friend and Yourself. This kind of Biography appears to me perfectly new, and of all others the most excellent—it constitutes a fund of the highest intellectual entertainment, by giving the portrait of the mind of perhaps the greatest man the world has produc'd—enliven'd with anecdotes, and conversations of most of the great literary characters of his time—and as these works of Yours are, I believe the first of their kind, so it will be long before Your example will be follow'd, for Your plan requir'd not only great Ability, and Capacity of selection, but a degree of labour and attention which very few persons will be found willing to submit to. In short instead of describing Your characters, You exhibit them to the Reader. He finds himself in their Company, and becomes an Auditor of Conversations, which have all the dignity of the best moral writings, soften'd by the ease, the wit and the familiarity of Colloquial manners.

Will You permit me, Sir, to add, that I have also another reason for troubling You with this letter, which is, that I am very sollicitous of the honor of being known to You, and that If I am not discouraged, I shall request some mutual friend to do me the favor of introducing me to You, on my Arrival in London in April. Had the late Sir Joshua Reynolds been alive[2] I might quickly have obtain'd that favor from him.

I shall send this letter to my Friend Mr. Cranstoun of the Navy Office,[3] who will be so good as to transmit it to You, by means of Your Brother,[4] with whom I believe he has the pleasure of being acquainted. I have the honor to be, Sir, Your Very Oblig'd and Obedient Servant

WILLM. ELFORD

[2] He died 23 Feb. Elford and Reynolds were neighbours in Devonshire, and Elford was himself an artist, contributing to the Royal Academy exhibitions from 1774 until his death.

[3] Henry Kerr Cranstoun (c. 1756–1843) was assistant to the Inspector of Seamen's Wills and Powers of Attorney, Inspectors Branch of the Pay Office (*London Calendar*, 1792, p. 132). He was the grandson of William, fifth Lord Cranstoun (*Scots Peer*. ii. 598).

[4] T. D. Boswell was a clerk in the same branch.

To the Rev. Ralph Churton,
Thursday 5 April 1792

Missing. Transcribed from a photostat of the original, which, in 1950, was in the estate of Gabriel Wells. MS. Yale (L 369): a copy by James Ross, headed by JB: "To The Reverend Mr. Ralp[h] Churton."

ENDORSEMENT: Recd. Apr. 9. Ans. Apr. 10.

London, 5 April 1792

REVEREND SIR: My worthy friend Mr. Langton had given me the satisfaction of knowing your favourable opinion of my *Life of Dr. Johnson*, before I had the honour to receive your very obliging letter, for which I sincerely thank you, and I beg you may present my best respects to Dr. Townson with my acknowledgements for his kind expressions concerning my Works. Such spontaneous praise I feel as the best reward of my labours. You and he, Sir, will also be pleased to accept of my thanks for the Books you have been so good as to present to me, of which I have read enough already to perceive that I shall derive more than pleasure from them.

Be assured Sir, that I take in very good part the remarks which you have made upon my Book; and you will be convinced of my sincerity when you have read what I am now to say.

As to Johnson's notion of the unhappiness of human life, I have when mentioning *The Rambler* (Vol. 1 p. 186)[1] in some degree obviated any reflections against him on that head; and when mentioning *Rasselas* (Vol. 1, p. 186)[2] I suggest that his "morbid melancholy" may have made life appear to him more miserable than it generally is. But the truth, Sir, is as you have judiciously observed, that I myself have a large portion of melancholy in my constitution, for which I am satisfied that allowance should be made. Your remark upon this important subject is so good, that if you will give me permission, I will insert it as a note on "the unhappiness of human life" in my second Volume p. 242.[3]

I am much pleased with your remark on the passage concerning the Burial service, and shall be very happy also to insert it.

In both instances, I request that the sanction of your name may not be refused.

[1] *Life* i. 213.
[2] *Life* i. 343.
[3] *Life* iv. 300 n. 2. JB's own remarks, as given in this paragraph, are inserted in the note (p. 302).

My Octavo edition is now in the press; and therefore you will be so good as to let me hear from you with your first convenience. I shall esteem it a happiness to obtain your personal acquaintance, whenever an opportunity offers, and I am, Reverend Sir, your much obliged humble servant

JAMES BOSWELL

Please to write to me under cover of John Courtenay Esq. M.P. London.

To *William Elford,*
Thursday 5 April 1792

MS. Yale (L 500). A copy by James Ross, headed by JB: "To William Elford Esq."

London, 5 April 1792

SIR: I should much sooner have gratefully acknowledged the honour of having received your most obliging letter; but upon my word it is not affectation nor words of course when I say that I have felt no small difficulty to express my feelings on an occasion so unexpected and so flattering. Your praise, Sir, carries with it undoubted evidence of intrinsick value by exhibiting in its conveyance the mind of him who gives it. I shall not attempt to make any other return to your liberal and elegant testimony than to request your acceptance of my very sincere thanks and to assure you that I feel such spontaneous praise as the best reward of my labours.

You have no need Sir, of any mutual friend to introduce you to one who will esteem a personal accquaintance with [you] a great favour. My house is No. 47 Great Portland Street, and if you will be pleased when you come to town, to let me know where you are, I shall hasten to pay my respects to you. I am Sir, Your much obliged humble Servant

(Sign'd) JAMES BOSWELL

To William Ellford Esq.

From Dr. John Mudge,
Saturday 7 April 1792

MS. Yale (C 2062).

ADDRESS: To James Boswell Esq., London.

ENDORSEMENT: Dr. Mudge, introducing Mr. Elford.

Plym[ou]th, April 7th 1792

DEAR SIR: Had I enjoy'd the happiness of being more intimately known to you[1] I should have felt a confidence on this Address which I do not possess, and must, therefore, rest my Apology for it on the kindness, and goodness of your Heart. Mr. Elford, the Bearer of this, is a Gentleman of Fortune in this Neighbourhood; a Man of most amiable Manners; excellent Understanding, and a Good Naturalist; an admirer of Dr. Johnson even to Idolatry, and is, consequently, so strongly impress'd with a respect for his Biographer, that he much wishes to have the honor of being introduced to him. If I may be permitted, without the imputation of Arrogance, to present him to you, I am sure the acquisition of this Gentleman, for whom I have the highest regard, to the number of your Friends will not be displeasing to you, and you will much Oblige, Dear Sir, your most Humble Servant

JOHN MUDGE

From the Rev. Ralph Churton,
Tuesday 10 April 1792

MS. Yale (C 788).

ADDRESS: James Boswell Esquire.

ENDORSEMENT: 10 April 1792. Rev. Mr. Ralph Churton.

Malpas, April 10. 1792

SIR, I had the favour of Your letter forwarded to me from college yesterday; and am certainly much obliged and flattered by the attention You have shewn to the remarks I ventured to submit to You in regard to Your work. I am very glad the octavo edition is in the press; and if You think the observations may be at all useful,

---

[1] See their correspondence, *ante* 30 Oct. and 13 Nov. 1787.

they are, with all their imperfections on their head,[1] at Your service and Your mercy. I took a hasty copy of the letter I sent You to shew it to a very excellent and intimate friend, who sees most of my trifles "warm from the brain." If on my return to college next wednesday I see any thing material in this copy to alter I will write to You on the subject; but I would not delay acknowledging Your favour.

The remark on the Burial service occurred at once on reading Your work, and is so far my own. But when I looked in Wheatley and Bennet I think I found the same thing in both of them; and as I read Bennet about fourteen Years ago I believe, it might be reminiscence in me, not invention. If you think proper to use the passage, You may refer to one or both of those books. Pearson on the Creed I think understands "the life everlasting" in the same general sense;[2] which I think I did not mention, nor is it perhaps necessary.

Possibly in adapting Your Index to the octavo edition You may make it a little fuller; and if You do I shall not be sorry to see my friend Dr. Loveday's name in it, who furnished, as You mention, one or two letters written to Mr. Bagshaw.[3]

I came hither to see my most dear and esteemed friend Dr. Townson; who, now entering his 78th Year I believe, is I fear sinking fast[4] under a dropsy and asthma, which came upon him about Christmas. His strength decays, though I hope without much pain, but that it is almost impossible to know from his unexampled patience and cheerfulness. I take up with me a work of his on our blessed Saviour's resurrection,[5] which has long been finished, but which he even now is revising. His memory of present as well as past occurrences is equal to the best. I made Your respects to him.

And now since I have said so much about Dr. Townson and as Mr. Langton has done me the honour to mention my name to You, perhaps You will be pleased to hear, as well as I can give it from

---

[1] *Hamlet*, I. v. 74.

[2] John Pearson, *An Exposition of the Creed*, 1659, Article 12.

[3] *Life* ii. 258 n. 3. The latter part of the note was added in the second edition: "This worthy gentleman [Loveday], having retired from business, now lives in Warwickshire. The world has been lately obliged to him as the Editor of the late Rev. Dr. Townson's excellent work, modestly entitled 'A Discourse on the Evangelical History, from the Interment to the Ascension of our Lord and Saviour Jesus Christ'; to which is prefixed, a truly interesting and pleasing account of the author, by the Reverend Mr. Ralph Churton."

[4] He died on the 15th of this month.

[5] The *Discourse* (*ante* n. 3).

memory, what Dr. Townson said to me in one of his letters concerning him; and the more as it in part regards Your work, which
he had then just perused: "Your friend Mr. Langton," he observed,
"seems the most perfect character of all Dr. Johnson's acquaintance; and what he communicated[6] is by no means one of the least
sensible and shining parts of the work."

You are very kind in expressing a wish to be personally acquainted with your present correspondent; and I should be very
happy to wait upon You if I have opportunity in London or if You
come to Oxford before I leave residence there, in July 1793. But
of this I can very honestly assure You, that if from my letter or
from the too indulgent representation of a friend You have entertained some favourable opinion or hopes of me, an interview will
greatly disappoint You. In this however I trust I shall never
disappoint You, as a friend, according to my poor abilities, to
religion and truth; and as being with sincere esteem, Sir, Your
much obliged and most obedient humble servant

RALPH CHURTON

From John Perkins,[1]
Monday 23 April 1792

MS. Yale (C 2240).

ADDRESS: James Boswell Esqr.

Southwark, 23 April 1792

Mr. Perkins Compliments to Mr. Boswell. In[2] Answer to his
Note[3] acquaints him that the Property purchased by Mr. Barclay
and himself from the Ex[ecut]ors of Mr. Thrale was £135000.[4]

---

[6] See ante From Langton, 1 Mar. 1790,
n. 1 for a survey of his contributions.

---

[1] John Perkins (?1730–1812) "was for
a number of years the worthy superinten-
dant of Mr. Thrale's great brewery, and
after his death became one of the pro-
prietors of it; and now resides in Mr.
Thrale's house in Southwark ... in
which he continues the liberal hospitality
for which it was eminent. Dr. Johnson
esteemed him much" (*Life* ii. 286 n. 1).
JB dined with him at the Thrales, 1 Apr.

1781 (*ibid.* iv. 80 ff.). In the journal for
this date he is referred to as "the confidential Clerk of the Brewhouse". See
Peter Mathias, *The Brewing Industry in
England 1700–1830* (1959), pp. 265–76.

[2] MS. "Boswell in"

[3] Untraced.

[4] In the first edition (i. 268) JB had
given the figure as £130,000, but he had
also printed SJ's letter to Langton, 16
June 1781 (*Life* iv. 132), in which it is
given as £135,000. In the second edition
JB corrected his statement. See also *Life*
iv. 86 n. 2.

From William Elford,
Tuesday 24 April 1792

MS. Yale (C 1187).

ADDRESS: James Boswell Esqr., London.

ENDORSEMENT: William Elford Esq.

Bickham, 24th April 1792

SIR: I had arrived at Bath in my way to Town about ten days ago, when Your letter was sent to me thither, and I hope You will do me the Justice to believe, that the politeness and consideration with which You treated my application to You, affords me the most sensible pleasure; But I am unable to express my mortification, when I say, that the very letter in which Your's came inclos'd, convey'd the intelligence that my Wife's mother was at the point of Death, and that my return hither was indispensibly necessary. On my Arrival I found She had died soon after the date of my Summons, and the necessity of my presence in settling her affairs, precludes me from all hopes of seeing London this Spring. I am thus depriv'd of the enjoyment of many happy hours. Some of my friends are now in Town, whom I am not likely soon again to find there—particularly Mr. Pennant of Wales,[1] with whom, being fond of Zoology, I have long corresponded, but never had an interview, and from whom, I had just received a letter to say he hop'd we shou'd now meet. In the first Rank of the pleasing expectations I had form'd, are to be plac'd those which Your letter had afforded me, and I hope You will permit me to look forward to some future opportunity of cultivating an Acquaintance from which I must derive so much honor and pleasure.[2] I observe in some part of Your late Work You Speak of having been to visit a friend in Devonshire; but we are left in the dark as to what part of the County he resides in.[3] Shou'd You, Sir, find Yourself about to make him another Visit this Summer, and will extend Your journey to the western part of the County, You will make me very happy. I can scarcely hope for a favor, to which I can offer so few inducements.

[1] Thomas Pennant (1726–98), traveller and naturalist. See *Life passim*.

[2] Elford was JB's guest in London sometime this spring. In a letter dated 10 June 1792 (C 1188) he acknowledges the kindness of JB's daughters and pays his respects to JB Jr.

[3] *Life* iii. 122 n. 2 (p. 123). The visit was to Temple, at Mamhead. Both person and place are mentioned, *ibid*. ii. 371.

You will see a part of the Kingdom, which has certainly some beauties peculiar to itself, particularly the Port and Harbour of Plymouth, from which my house is but Seven Miles distant; where I will treat You with[4] excellent Mutton, fed on the Downs near me, some very good Port, and the Conversation of a few sensible men, who are, of course, Your admirers.[5]

I am asham'd of having trespass'd so long on You, and hasten to add that I am, Sir, with true respect and esteem, Your most oblig'd and humble Servant

WILL. ELFORD

From James Beattie,
Thursday 3 May 1792

MS. Yale (C 109). Printed in part, *Life* ii. 148 n. 2.

ADDRESS: James Boswell Esqr., London.

Edinburgh, 3 May 1792

. . . As I suppose Your great work will soon be reprinted, I beg leave to trouble You with a remark or two on a passage of it, in which I am a little misrepresented. Be not alarmed; the misrepresentation is not imputable to You; [1]it is in one of Dr. Johnson's letters.[1] Not having the book at hand, I cannot specify the page, but I suppose You will easily find it. Dr. Johnson says, speaking of Mr. Thrale's family, "Dr. Beattie *sunk upon us* that he was married" or words to that purpose.[2] I am not sure that I understand *sunk upon us*, which is a very uncommon phrase; but it seems to me to imply, (and others, I find, have understood it in the same sense) *studiously concealed from us his being married.* Now, Sir, this was by no means the case. I could have no motive to conceal a circumstance, of which I never was nor can be ashamed;[3] and of which Dr. Johnson seemed to think, when he afterwards became acquainted with

[4] MS. "will"

[5] JB and his daughters stopped at Bickham c. 21 Sept. (*Letters JB* 311) towards the end of their jaunt to Cornwall (Aug.–Sept. 1792). The journal breaks off short of this date.

[1-1] Beattie misremembered the context, and JB, in editing his letter for the *Life*, deleted this clause.

[2] *Life* ii. 148. JB introduced the relevant part of the present letter in a footnote to this passage, "from my respect for my friend Dr. Beattie, and regard to his extreme sensibility . . . though I cannot but wonder at his considering as any imputation a phrase commonly used among the best friends".

[3] See the notes by Hill and Dr. Powell, *Life* ii. 148–49.

Mrs. Beattie, that I had, as was true, reason to be proud.[4] So far was I from concealing her, that my wife had at that time almost as numerous an acquaintance in London as I had myself; and was, not very long after, kindly invited and elegantly entertained at Streatham by Mr. and Mrs. Thrale.[5]

My request therefore is, that You would rectify this matter in Your new edition. You are at liberty to make what use You please of this letter. . . .

From Sir William Chambers,[1] Tuesday 29 May 1792

MS. Yale (C 782).

ADDRESS: To James Boswell Esq.

ENDORSEMENT: Sir William Chambers concerning his Chinese Architecture 29 May 1792.

[London,] 29 May 1792

DEAR SIR: I could not get a Copy of my Chinese book[2] in town, was therfore obliged to defer giving an answer to your Note of the 22[3] til I had been at Whitton, where I found a Copy which is herewith Sent, and when you have done with it, please to return it, as it is the only Copy I have, and the book is out of print.

I have looked over my part of the preface, and think it *mediocre* enough, not withstanding Johnsons approbation. You will see at once where he left off, and where I begun.

If You mean to put it among his Works in Your publication, You

---

[4] *Life* ii. 145, 149.

[5] On 13 Aug. 1773, along with Sir Joshua and Miss Reynolds, Baretti, Goldsmith, and others (*James Beattie's London Diary 1773*, ed. R. S. Walker, 1946, p. 81).

[1] Sir William Chambers, Kt. (1726–96), "that great Architect, whose works shew a sublimity of genius, and who is esteemed by all who know him, for his social, hospitable, and generous qualities" (*Life* iv. 187–88). On 21 Dec. of this year, at the Royal Academy Club,

Chambers proposed that JB write a history of the Academy, for which he would turn over "great Collections" (Journ.). The following summer JB visited Chambers at his country house at Whitton, Middlesex. "In this Journal I am not to *expatiate* on the comfort and elegance of Sir William Chambers's living. But it dwells on my mind" (4 Aug. 1793).

[2] *Designs of Chinese Buildings, Furniture, Dresses, Machines, and Utensils. . . . From the Originals drawn in China by Mr. Chambers, Architect*, 1757.

[3] Untraced.

must do me the Justice to say that I my Self pointed it out to you, and mentioned it as his.[4] The book was published in the Spring of 1757.

I wish a Country man of Yours, Lord Kaimes, had been honest enough to confess what he Stole from his neighbours, the Six last pages of the book I now send you, would in such Case, have been published in my Name, not under that of his Lordship.[5]

I think Miss Windham[6] dined with us once since her arrival, and that is the only time I have Set Eyes on her Charms since last Year. I ought Certainly to have informed you of her being in town, but hope you will pardon the Omission, when I assure you it was neither prepense nor malicious, but entirely oweing to forgetfulness. I am very truely, Dear Sir, Your faithful and obedient humble Servant

W. CHAMBERS

To James Abercrombie, Monday 11 June 1792

Missing. Printed, *The Port Folio*, 1801, i. 10. MS. Yale (L 1): a copy by James Boswell Junior, headed by JB: "Copy To James Aberc[r]ombie Esq. Philadelphia"; and bearing a note by him on the back: "Sent by Mr. Allen."[1] Although neither text is perfectly reliable, the print seems on the whole superior.

London, June 11,[2] 1792

SIR:[3] The packet, with which your spontaneous kindness has been pleased to honour me, after being a little while delayed by the ship's[4] having put into Ireland, came safely to my hands. The two letters from Dr. Johnson to American gentlemen, are a valuable

[4] In the second edition JB inserted a brief mention of SJ's interest in the volume, and in a foot-note quoted SJ's contribution: viz. the first two paragraphs of the Preface, *Life* iv. 188 and n. 1. JB does not say that Chambers pointed it out to him, but the phrasing implies it.

[5] Lord Kames's account of Chinese gardening in his *Elements of Criticism* (1762, ch. XXIV) follows Chambers's *Designs* (pp. 14–19), at times in a very close paraphrase.

[6] Perhaps a sister of George Wyndham of Cromer (Windham's *Diary*, p. 91; Burke's *Commoners*, 1835, ii. 244). I find no further mention of her among JB's papers.

[1] Not identified.

[2] Copy, "11 June": JB's characteristic style.

[3] Copy, "My Dear" deleted. The salutation is in JB's hand.

[4] *Port Folio*, "ships". *Lit. Illust.* vii. 314, in reprinting this letter from *The Port Folio*, makes the correction silently.

acquisition. I received them in time to be inserted in the second edition of my life of that great man, which is now in the press. It is to be in three volumes octavo, and will contain a good[5] many additions. A copy *from the author* shall be sent to you, hoping that you will allow it a place in your library.[6] Meantime, sir, my grateful acknowledgements to you shall be wafted across the Atlantic.[7]

In the letter to bishop White, I observe Dr. Johnson says, "I take the liberty which you give me,[8] of troubling you with a letter, of which you will please to fill up the direction." There must therefore have been a third letter of my illustrious friend's sent to your continent. If the respectable gentleman, under whose care it was transmitted, can procure a copy of it for me, I shall be much obliged to him, and to you, of whom I beg pardon for giving you more trouble after what you have done for me.

You are, I find, sir, a true Johnsonian; and you may believe that I have great pleasure in being of any service to one of that description. I have not yet been able to discover any more of his sermons, besides those *left for publication by Dr. Taylor.* I am informed by the lord bishop of Salisbury, that he gave an excellent one to a clergyman, who preached and published it in his own name, on some public occasion.[9] But the bishop has not as yet told me the name, and seems unwilling to do it. Yet I flatter myself I shall get at it.

Your list of Johnson's works, and of what has been written concerning him, has what is most valuable. There have, however, been various other publications concerning him, several of which I have mentioned in my book. If you think it worth your while to collect all that can be had, I will do all that[10] I can to assist you, though some of them attack me with a good deal of ill nature, the *effect*[11] of which, however, I assure you, is by no means painful.

I now send you a poetical review of Dr. Johnson's literary and moral character,[12] by my friend Mr. Courtenay, in which, though I

---

[5] Copy, "a good" omitted.

[6] It is now in the Hyde Collection.

[7] JB uses this phrasing in his printed acknowledgement to Abercrombie, *Life* ii. 206.

[8] Copy, "me" omitted. SJ's original letter confirms "give me".

[9] An anniversary of the Gunpowder Plot (5 Nov.), as JB later discovered (*post* To Abercrombie, 28 July 1793). This is clearly not the sermon written for,

and published by, the Hon. and Rev. Henry Hervey Aston ("Harry Hervey"): see *Life* v. 483–84. JB's informant, John Douglas (see *ante* 16 May 1791), was famous for exposing frauds, notably the forgeries of William Lauder and the affair of the Cock Lane Ghost. See *Life* i. 228–29, 407.

[10] Copy, "that" omitted.

[11] Not underlined in the copy.

[12] Copy, "a Poetical Review etc."

except to several passages,[13] you will find some very good writing.

It will be kind, if you will be so good as to let me know if any thing be published in the New World, relative to Johnson. My worthy bookseller, Mr. Dilly, will take care of whatever packets you may have to send me.[14]

I am, sir, your much obliged humble servant,

JAMES BOSWELL

To the Rev. Dr. Andrew Kippis,[1] c. Saturday 11 August 1792

MS. Yale (L 833). JB's copy.

[London]

DEAR SIR: In my second edition of the *Life of Dr. Johnson* I am to insert the following note on the passage concerning the *Biographia*.[2]

> * In this censure which has been carelessly uttered I carelessly joined. But in justice to Dr. Kippis, who with that manly candid good temper which marks his character set me right[3] I now with pleasure retract it; and I desire it may be parti-

[13] In the *Life* (i. 222) JB takes exception only to Courtenay's "too great partiality for one of his friends"—namely, himself; cf. *ibid.* 316. But he had criticized the poem in detail in his correspondence with Malone.

[14] Copy, "send to me". So printed in *Lit. Illust.*

[1] Andrew Kippis, D.D. (1725–95), Nonconformist divine, was pastor of the Presbyterian congregation in Princes Street, Westminster, from 1753 until his death. He is best known as editor of the second edition of the *Biographia Britannica*, only five volumes of which were completed. See Journ. *passim*.

[2] *Life* iii. 174, where JB, after first mentioning that SJ had declined the undertaking and then praising Kippis's work, goes on to express a regret that

the task had not been assigned to " 'a friend to the constitution in Church and State'. We should not then have had it too much crowded with obscure dissenting teachers, doubtless men of merit and worth, but not quite to be numbered amongst 'the most eminent persons who have flourished in Great-Britain and Ireland' ". In a postscript to a letter to Temple, 28 Nov. 1789 (*Letters JB* 269), JB had observed: "Dr. Kippis makes a strange kettle of fish of the *Biographia*." In a letter to JB, 12 July 1791, Kippis professes his loyalty to the King and "though I conscientiously dissent from the Church of England, I have always done it with Moderation and Candour, and with the greatest Respect for the distinguished Ornaments of that Church".

[3] No letter from Kippis setting JB right has been recovered, and there is no journal for this time.

cularly observed that in the new edition of the *Biographia Britannica* there have been introduced of the dissenting Clergy only

(*Here please to fill up*

and (*here mention the* CHURCHMEN

The expression "a friend to the Constitution in Church and State" was not meant as any reflection upon this Reverend Gentleman as if he were an ennemy to the Constitution of his country as established at the Revolution; but from my steady and avowed predilection for a *Tory*, were [*sic*] quoted from Johnson's *Dictionary* where that distinction is so defined.

Be pleased Dear Sir to return this paper filled up, and that without delay, as I am about to take a jaunt into Devonshire and Cornwall.[4] I am always yours with regard

JAMES BOSWELL

From the Rev. Dr. Andrew Kippis, Sunday 12 August 1792

MS. Yale (C 1666).

ADDRESS: To James Boswell Esq., No. 47, Great Portland Street.

ENDORSEMENT: Rev. Dr. Kippis as to *Biographia Britannica* for my second edition of Johnson's *Life*.

Westm[inste]r, Aug. 12. 1792

DEAR SIR: I am much obliged by your kind Note, with which I am perfectly satisfied. Herewith I enclose a Paper, of which You will make what Use You think proper.[1] I am, with sincere Regard, dear Sir, your very obliged and obedient Servant,

AND. KIPPIS

---

[4] To visit Temple. See Journ. 17 Aug. and following.

[1] The paper is missing. See *Life* iii. 174 n. 3.

From the Rev. Charles Edward De Coetlogon,[1] Saturday 15 September 1792

MS. Yale (C 917).

ADDRESS: James Boswell Esqr.

ENDORSEMENTS: Rev. C. E. De Coetlogon *and* Answer Within.

[London,] Septr. 15th 92

SIR: If it be possible, there should be a Copy of your Life of the immortal Johnson remaining unsold, I could find it in my heart to solicit the Benefaction. The apparent Indelicacy of such a Hint, is as painful to my Feelings, as it may be surprizing to your's. I know therefore, how much it becomes me, to state any Reason, I can offer, for such an application, from a Person, whose comparative obscurity has thrown him out of the Sphere of your Knowledge.

I have read your Work, with a sort of Admiration, I shall not attempt to describe. It contains, in my humble Opinion, the first Specimen of biographical Composition, and of unaffected Liberality of Mind and Sentiment, I have ever met with. I must naturally wish to have it in my possession; and should certainly have purchased it, were not the Expence an inconvenient Trespass upon a very limited Income. The Fact is, I am an unbeneficed Clergyman, with an unprovided Family.

Considering you, as brought up at the Feet of One, who, had he lived in the apostolic Age, would, at least, have been another Gamaliel, I repose myself upon the Idea, your Book has taught me to entertain, of your Generosity, Confidence, and Secrecy—as, to any third Person, such an Application would wear an Aspect, with which my own Sensibilities might perhaps be shocked. I am not however unwilling to add, that the Present from Yourself would stamp a Value upon it, much superior to what it could derive from any Quarter besides.

It is needless for me to say, that, you are at perfect Liberty to leave the Writer entirely unnoticed. He will suffer the less, in that Case, as he has long been habituated to wait, in vain, in the great Hall of Expectation. But, should you be disposed to indulge him,

---

[1] The Rev. Charles Edward De Coetlogon (?1746–1820), Calvinist preacher and writer; editor of *The Theological Miscellany*, 1784–89; Vicar of Godstone, Surrey, 1794. In 1793 he published an edition of Young's *Night Thoughts*, with notes and a life (BM *Cat.*).

your Favour will reach him at Mr. Edwards's, Bookseller, in New Bond Street. Whatever be the Event of this rather awkward Proceedure, he has the Honour to subscribe himself, Sir, Very respectfully Your unknown Admirer

C. E. DE COETLOGON

From the Rev. John Fawcett,[1] Saturday 22 September 1792

MS. Yale (C 1240).

ADDRESS: James Boswell Esq., with Mr. C. Dilly, Bookseller, Poultry, London.

POSTMARK: SE 24 92.

ENDORSEMENTS: Mr. J. Fawcett and Answer Within.

Brearley Hall, Halifax, Yorkshire, Sep. 22. 1792

DEAR SIR, I have had more entertainment from your writings than from any one man's I can name, excepting those of Dr. Saml. Johnson. Your *Journal of a Tour to the Hebrides* has, ever since its first publication, been a favourite book with me. But how shall I express my gratitude for your *Life of Dr. Johnson?* I could not rest till I had purchased the copy, though we have it in a public Library of which I am a proprietor.[2] It contains a rich fund of instruction and entertainment, for which the public is greatly indebted to you. No man, I think, is a greater, or more enthusiastic admirer of Johnson than myself. Mr. Bewley begged the cover of a letter to preserve as a relic;[3] if I thought it would not be deemed impertinent in a stranger to request some small, very small favour of the same kind, from the Writer of his life, I should urge my solicitation with all the pathos I could muster. If this request cannot be granted, I shall still love and admire you; but if you could indulge me with the smallest token, you would contribute, in a very high degree, to the gratification of, Dear Sir, Your most grateful and obedient Humble Servant

JOHN FAWCETT

[1] The Rev. John Fawcett (1740–1817), Baptist minister and author. See J. Horsfall Turner, *Halifax Books and Authors*, Idel, Bradford, 1906, pp. 65–71.
[2] The Halifax Free Library.

[3] *Life* iv. 134. For William Bewley and his fanatical devotion to SJ, see Roger Lonsdale, "Johnson and Dr. Burney," *Johnson, Boswell and Their Circle, passim.*

489

UU*

From James Abercrombie,
Wednesday 10 October 1792

MS. Yale (C 3).

ADDRESS: James Boswell Esqr., London.

ENDORSEMENT: James Abercrombie Esq. Philadelphia 10 Octr. 1792.

Philadelphia, Octr. 10th 1792

DEAR SIR: The very high degree of pleasure with which I perused your polite favor of 11th June can only be conceived by those who have been gratified with the receipt of letters from characters of the first eminence in the circles of science and polite literature; and much indeed does it flatter me, to find, that the offering I have already made has proved an acceptable one. Be assured, Sir, no exertion on my part shall be wanting to effect the repetition of what you are pleased to honor with the appellation of "kindness." I feel much satisfaction in assuring you, that if the letter you are desirous of obtaining is now in existence, there can be little doubt of my procuring it for you. Dr. White has at length recollected (which he long despaired of doing) the name of the gentleman to whom it was addressed; I find it to be The Revd. Jonathan Odell, an Episcopal Clergyman, but now Secretary of the province of New Brunswick—Nova Scotia.[1] From that gentleman's former intimacy

[1] White was mistaken: the addressee was not Odell (*post* From Abercrombie, 17 May 1793 and n. 4), but William Samuel Johnson (1727–1819), of Stratford, Connecticut (see *Letters SJ* 299), one of the framers of the Constitution and the first president of Columbia College, 1787–1800, where the original is preserved. From 1767 to 1771 he resided in England as a special agent of the General Assembly to defend the Colony of Connecticut in a property case involving the Mohegan Indians (DAB). In a letter to his father, the Rev. Samuel Johnson (1696–1772), first president of King's College, dated Westminster, 2 Nov. 1769, he wrote: "For the sake of the Name, & because I think him one of the best of the Modern Writers, I made an Acquaintance some time ago, with Dr. Sam[u]el Johnson Author of the Dictionary &c— ... He has shining Abilities, great Erudition, exact & exten-

sive Knowledge, is ranked in the first Class of the Literati, & highly Esteemed for his strong sense & Virtue; but is as odd a Mortal, in point of Behaviour & Appearance, as you ever saw. You would not, at first sight, suspect he had ever read, or thought, in his life, or was much above the degree of an Idiot. But Nulla Fronti Fides [*Fronti nulla fides* ("Trust not to outward show"): Juvenal, *Satires* ii. 8], when he opens himself, after a little Acquaintance, you are abundantly repaid for these first unfavourable Appearances—" (MS. Connecticut Historical Society: courteously transcribed for me by Frances A. Hoxie; printed in E. E.Beardsley, *Life and Times of William Samuel Johnson, LL.D.*, 1876, p. 71). Hill mistakenly called Johnson "Reverend", having confused him, I suppose, with his father. Chapman's Index preserves the error.

in my family, I am confident of his disposition to oblige me in any instance; and I indulge the most sanguine hope of obtaining *more than one* letter of your illustrious friend to him, as Dr. White informs me Mr. Odell was the gentleman who introduced him to Dr. Johnson, and he doubts not that a correspondence was supported between them.[2] I have accordingly written to Mr. Odell on the subject, and enforced my solicitation by your request; all my fear is, that from the variety of changes he has experienced since the year 1773, those letters may have been mislaid or lost. He is a gentleman who would justly estimate the value of such epistles, but in the convulsions of a civil war, and the consequent change of places and property, 'tis much to be feared they may not have been preserved; you shall however hear from me as soon as I am informed. I have inquired of Mr. Odell whether he knows of any other letters addressed by Dr. Johnson to America.

Accept my most grateful thanks Sir, for your kind promise of a copy of your 2d edition. I shall consider its own singularly intrinsic value much increased, by being honor'd with it *immediately from the author*; and most deservedly shall it occupy the most conspicuous shelf in my library.

I feel much indebted to you Sir, for Mr. Courtenay's Poem, and read it with that singular degree of pleasure, which the effusions of every pen recording the virtue and superior excellence of the immortal Johnson, never fails to excite.

Sorry I am that I cannot communicate to you as favorable an account of the progress of literature in this country as I could wish. Small is the list of American authors; and of that small list very few indeed are possessed of real merit. Of those who are now in the highest estimation, our late Judge of the Admiralty, Francis Hopkinson,[3] is generally allowed to be one of the first. I have taken the liberty of transmitting to the care of Mr. Dilly, a copy of his miscellanious works just published,[4] in 3 Vol. 8vo of which I beg Sir you will honor me with the acceptance. Some account of the

---

[2] None has been recovered.

[3] Francis Hopkinson (1737–91) was a member of the Continental Congress from New Jersey, 1776–77, a judge of the admiralty, 1777–89, and U.S. district judge in Pennylvania, 1789. Besides being a poet and essayist, he was an artist, an inventor, and an accomplished musician (DAB).

[4] *The Miscellaneous Essays and Occasional Writings of Francis Hopkinson.* He had himself prepared the collection for publication before his death.

author was published in a Magazine[5] soon after his death which I have also sent. You will find by the exaggerated praise there bestow'd upon his genius and abilities, that an author who is possessed of either, is a rara avis amongst us. The best productions of his pen do not in my opinion rise above mediocrity; the general suffrage however is highly in his favor, and had we a Temple dedicated to Minerva[6] and The Muses, his name would most certainly appear there in very conspicuous characters. Many of the pieces contained in his works, will be altogether unentertaining to you, as their subjects are of a local or personal nature, and many of them alluding to incidents which can only be interesting to those who were spectators of, or in some degree concerned in them. Such however as they are, I have forwarded them for your inspection, and most sincerely regret, that I have nothing of greater literary merit to present to you. Judge Wilson's Lecture has received much praise, and perhaps deserved some. None but the Introductory has yet been published.[7]

In a new Country like this, the universal object of eager pursuit which engrosses the attention of all orders of men, is the acquisition and accumulation of property. The various objects of Speculation, which, in consequence of our recent existence as an Independent Nation, presented themselves, were too fascinating not to attract general attention; in proportion however as the different States become organized, their governments settled, and the different ranks of society clearly designated, we shall have leisure to attend to the advancement of Literature, and in that proportion will the

---

[5] "Account of the late Francis Hopkinson, Esq.", *The Universal Asylum and Columbian Magazine* (1791) vi. 291. The article, unsigned, was written by Benjamin Rush, who expanded it from an entry in his commonplace-book made on the day of Hopkinson's death (*Autobiography of Benjamin Rush*, ed. G. W. Corner, 1948, p. 192). Hopkinson had been one of the editors of *The Columbian Magazine* and a frequent contributor (G. E. Hastings, *Life and Works of Francis Hopkinson*, 1926, pp. 433–34).

[6] Probably with a secondary reference to Hopkinson's poem, *The Temple of Minerva* (1781), written to celebrate the alliance between France and America

(DAB). An extract was printed in *The Columbian Magazine* for Apr. 1787 (i. 391–92), but it was not otherwise published (Hastings, *op. cit.*, pp. 314–18).

[7] James Wilson (1742–98), a Scottish emigrant, was a dominant force in the Constitutional Convention, and in 1789 was appointed Associate Justice of the Supreme Court. In Dec. of the same year, as newly appointed professor of law at the College of Philadelphia, he delivered the first in a series of lectures ("the Introductory"), which was published at Philadelphia in 1791. The remaining lectures, given in 1790–92, were first published in his collected works, 1804, ed. Bird Wilson, Philadelphia.

superior merit and abilities of your illustrious friend be acknowledged and revered[;] at present his writings and real character are known but by a few, owing, partly to the causes I have already suggested, but more to Political prejudices against him. His *Taxation No Tyranny* will long rankle in the minds of Americans.[8]

You ask me whether any thing relative to Johnson has been published in the New World. To this I answer in the negative, but should any thing appear, either respecting him, or on any literary subject worthy your perusal, I shall not fail to transmit it to you.

I thank you for your polite offer to collect for me *all* that has been written concerning Johnson, but from your assurance that I am already in possession of every thing that is most valuable, I shall confine my request to two small Pamphlets which I should be glad to have. First, a Criticism on Gray's *Elegy*, said to be written by a Mr. Young. This, in your *Life of Johnson*, you mention as the best imitation of his style which has appeared.[9] The other is the Funeral Sermon preached before the University of Oxford, by Mr. Agutter.[10]

I have now to entreat your pardon for this trespass upon your time and attention, and to assure you that I am with much esteem and respect, Dear Sir, Your most humble Servant

JAS. ABERCROMBIE

To the Rev. John Fawcett, Friday 12 October 1792

MS. The John Rylands Library (Rylands English MS. 343/43). MS. Yale (L 535): JB's copy, written on side 2 of Fawcett's letter of 22 Sept. 1792 (*ante*); headed: "Answer."

London, 12 October 1792

SIR: I am very much flattered by your letter which though in a high strain of compliment, appears to me to be sincere, and therefore gratifys both my vanity and my benevolence; for, believe me, Sir, the hope of giving instruction and entertainment is a great motive to my literary labours.

I should have thanked you for your letter, and complied with your request sooner; but to make amends for the delay, I enclose

---

[8] See *Life* ii. 312–13; and cf. Journ. 18 Mar. 1775.

[9] *Life* iv. 392.

[10] See, coincidentally enough, *post* From Agutter, 17 Oct. 1792.

you a small piece of the handwriting of my illustrious friend.[1] I am, Sir, your much obliged humble servant

JAMES BOSWELL

To John Fawcett Esq., Brearley Hall, Yorkshire

From the Rev. William Agutter,[1] Wednesday 17 October 1792

MS. Yale (C 26).

ADDRESS: James Boswell Esqr., Portland Street.

ENDORSEMENTS: Rev. Mr. Agutter. 17 Octr. 1792. *and* Answer Within.

Octr. 17. 1792, No. 7 Furnivals Inn Court, Holborn

DEAR SIR: As a small mark of my respect and as a Testimony of the pleasure and profit I have derived from a perusal of your interesting *Life of Dr. S. Johnson*, particularly of his Conversations I beg leave to present you with the enclosed discourse[2] which I hope is calculated to be useful in these critical and eventful Times.

If a second Ed⌈itio⌉n of the *Life* is called for I have some few Corrections and Remarks which I will help you to. I am obliged to you for mentioning my Sermon which I have not yet printed.[3] I am, Sir, Your obedient humble Servant

W. AGUTTER

To the Rev. William Agutter, Wednesday 24 October 1792

MS. Yale (L 14). JB's copy, written on side 3 of the preceding.

Great Portland Street, 24 Octr. 1792

Mr. Boswell presents his compliments to Mr. Agutter, with thanks

[1] Very likely SJ's invitation to JB, in behalf of Mr. Thrale, printed by Mary Hyde in "Not in Chapman," *Johnson, Boswell and Their Circle*, p. 314. The note is docketed: "This is a piece of the handwriting of Dr. Samuel Johnson. James Boswell."

[1] The Rev. William Agutter (1758–1835), a scholar of Magdalen College, Oxford, from 1780 to 1793, was renowned as a preacher. In 1797 he became chaplain and secretary to the Asylum for Female Orphans in London. It does not appear that he was personally known to either SJ or JB.

[2] Missing. But see next letter.

[3] "A sermon upon that event [SJ's death] was preached in St. Mary's church, Oxford, before the University, by the Reverend Mr. Agutter, of Magdalen College" (*Life* iv. 422). It was published in 1800 under the title *On the Difference between the Deaths of the Righteous and the Wicked. Illustrated in the Instance of Dr. Samuel Johnson and David Hume, Esq.*

for his *Christian Politicks.*[1] A strong infusion of such salutary doctrine seems to be very necessary at present.

Two volumes and a part of a third of an Octavo Edition of Mr. Boswell's *Life of Dr. Johnson* are already printed. If Mr. Agutter has any remarks which will be in time for what remains to be printed, he will be pleased to communicate them.[2]

From the Rev. Dr. William Maxwell, Thursday 15 November 1792

MS. Yale (C 1990).

ADDRESS: James Boswell Esqr., Great Queen Street, Lincoln's Inn Fields,[1] London.

POSTMARKS: NO 16, NO 22 92.

ENDORSEMENT: 15 Novr. 1792. Rev. Dr. Maxwell.

Falkland, Nov. 15th 1792

DEAR SIR: There has lately been published An Irish Edition of your Valuable *Life of Johnson*, not very accurately printed,[2] for we want here good Correctors of the Press. The Work has been very generally demanded, and Universally Esteemed, as it well deserves, for A Work more replete with Instruction and Amusement has seldom appeared. I beg leave to offer you my best thanks for the pleasure I have received from this latter, as well as your former Publications. You appear so well qualifyed for Biographical Writing, that I hear A general Wish expressed, that you may continue to Amuse and Instruct Mankind by Compositions of that Nature. You have described our Illustrious Friend with so much Spirit, Truth and Justice, that I make no doubt, but your Name will descend to Posterity, as A Commentator worthy of the Great

---

Hill noted: "Neither Johnson nor Hume is mentioned in the sermon itself by name. Its chief, perhaps its sole, merit is its brevity."

[1] *Christian Politics; or the Origin of Power and the Grounds of Subordination,* 1792.

[2] Agutter replied (in a missing letter), giving JB an abstract of his sermon on SJ (*Life* iv. 422 n. 1) and (probably in the same letter) a brief dialogue between SJ

and Agutter's friend, the eccentric scholar, John Henderson (1757–88), on the reasoning powers of non-jurors (*ibid.* 286 n. 3). Both items were included in the second edition, a copy of which JB sent to Agutter (MS. list, Yale).

---

[1] JB was now living in Great Portland St.

[2] For a description of this edition, see *Lit. Car.* pp. 156–57.

Original. Wishing You most *gratefully* all Imaginable Happiness I remain, with great Esteem, Dear Sir, Your most Faithfull and Obedient Humble Servant

WM. MAXWELL

From Isaac Reed, c. November 1792[1]

MS. Yale (C 2347).

ENDORSEMENT: Mr. Reed's Corrections and Additions for the Second Edition of my *Life of Dr. Johnson*.[2]

P. 13: There is an Account of Bishop Green by Mr. Duncombe in the *Gent. Magazine*. Vol. 49. p. 234.[3]

P. 33: Spenser was not of Oxford but Cambridge. From the reference to Nash's *History* it appears that Spence the Author of *Polymetis* was the person mistaken for *Spenser*.[4]

P. 35: In Garricks *Poems* is a Song by Mr. Walmsley.[5]

P. 42: Floyer's worth preserving] This was Floyer's Treatise on Cold Baths. *Gent. Mag.* 1734. p. 197.[6]

The Verses in this page were not to Miss Porter. Mr. John Nichols had an account of the manner of their production from Dr. Johnson himself.[7]

P. 70: The prize Poem on the Attributes was given to Moses Brown. See his poems.[8]

[1] The date is inferred from the apparent connexion between the postscript in JB's letter to Reed of 26 Nov. 1792 (*post*) and Reed's promise in the present MS. to give JB his copy of Edward Young's "Proposals".

[2] The MS. contains several of JB's own notes on the first edition. Except for two which relate to Reed's notes, they are omitted here.

[3] John Duncombe (1729–86), preacher and author. His account of Green remains unnoticed in the *Life* (i. 45).

[4] Spenser's name was omitted in the second edition (*Life* i. 75).

[5] JB expanded his note on Walmesley for the third edition (*Life* i. 81 n. 2), but this detail was not included. The Song, "sung by Mr. Lowe, at Drury-lane Theatre, 20th November, 1740", is

printed in Kearsley's edition of Garrick's *Poetical Works* (1785, ii. 362–64), where it is said that the third stanza was added by Garrick himself.

[6] Reed's reference is misleading, and so is JB's note in the second edition, which simply copies it (*Life* i. 91 n. 1). In writing to Cave SJ speaks of the printing of "loose pieces, like Floyer's", by which he means not Floyer's "Treatise" but his letter on the same subject written after the book was out (*Gent. Mag.*, 1734, iv. 197).

[7] See *ante* From Hector, 9 Aug. 1791 and n. 2.

[8] This information was not used. See *Life* i. 136 and n. 3. Browne's poem, the fourth and last in the series, was printed in *Gent. Mag.* for June 1738 (viii. 313–15) and collected in his *Poems on Various*

P. 80: would your Society etc.] This does not allude to the Royal Society but a Society then existing of which Dr. Birch was a leading Member and called the Society for the Encouragement of Learning. It continued from about 1736 to 1746 when having incurred a considerable debt it was dissolved. Their object was to assist Auth[o]rs in the printing of expensive works.[9]

P. 91: This character of the *Life of Savage* was not by Fielding who had then quitted all connection with *The Champion*. I have the minutes of the partners of that paper in my possession by which it appears that James Ralph succeeded Fielding in his share of the paper and was I doubt not the Author of this Eulogium.[10]

P. 94: In a late *European Magazine* are some strictures upon this Note relative to Savage.[11]

P. 96: The reasoning about Sir Thos. Hanmer does not seem conclusive. A rival Editor of Shakspeare might not be very partial to the Oxford Edition yet a Brother Tory might have a great respect for the Tory Politician. He might censure in one capacity and praise in the other. Surely the verses have Johnson's stamp on them.[12]

P. 107: There is in Aaron Hill's Letters his Account of *Irene* after having seen it. I think it would be worth preserving. If you think so I will copy it.[13]

Subjects (1739, pp. 428–40). It won the largest share of the £40 in prize money. Hawkins wrote (p. 46 n.) that Browne was the chief support of the poetry section of *Gent. Mag.* at this time and was the winner of most of the competitions. See C. L. Carlson, *The First Magazine*, etc., 1938, pp. 221 ff.

[9] JB's foot-note in the first edition read: "It is strange, that a printer who knew so much as Cave, should conceive so ludicrous a fancy as that the Royal Society would purchase a Play." In the second edition the note was changed, following Reed almost verbatim (*Life* i. 153).

[10] In the first edition, commenting on the "liberal praise" given to SJ's *Life of Savage* in *The Champion*, JB noted: "This paper is well known to have been written by the celebrated Henry Fielding. But, I suppose, Johnson was not informed of his being indebted to him for this civility; for if he had been apprised of that circumstance, as he was very sensible of praise, he probably would not have spoken with so little respect of Fielding, as we shall find he afterwards did." This passage was omitted in the second edition, and replaced by a foot-note following, and acknowledging, Reed (*Life* i. 169 and n. 2).

[11] Unchanged, *Life* i. 173 n. 3. The strictures, signed "G. H.", appeared in the Jan. number of *The European Magazine* (1792, xxi. 38–40).

[12] Unchanged, *Life* i. 177 ff.

[13] Opposite this item in the MS. is a note in JB's hand: "A letter to Mr. Mallet: I was in town at the *anomolous* Mr. *Johnson's* benefit and found the Play his proper representative strong sense ungrac'd by sweetness or decorum. Vol. 2. p. 355." This became the foot-note added in the second edition (*Life* i. 198 n. 4).

P. 116: It is a mistake to say *The Rambler* was first published in four Vols. octavo. It was first collected in 6 Vols. 12mo. Afterwards in four.[14]

[P.] 173: Soame Jenyns's name is always spelt wrong. It was not *Jennings*.[15]

[P.] 180: Dr. Burney is not accurate in saying that the controversy *now* raged (i.e. in 1758) between the friends of Pope and Warburton. It had been over many years.[16]

[P.] 181 l. 6: For Newberry read *Newbery*.[17]

[P.] 190: If Francis was liberated in consequence of Smollet's application the precise time could hardly be three days before the King's death[:] a full year and a half intervened.[18]

[P.] 194: Rolts *History of the War* was not the same on which Johnson had thoughts of employing his pen. Rolts war was that of 1739.[19]

[P.] 195: Mr. Boswell is totally wrong about Innes's Book. It was not on the Authen[ti]city of the Gospel History but on Moral Virtue. Mr. Reed will get the title as it ought to be before it is wanted.[20]

Q. If he is not also wrong about Douglas's poem. Mr. Reed remembers to have seen a poem called *The Resurrection* by Dr. Douglas in folio about 1747 but not *The Redemption* which he believes does not exist.[21]

P. 196: It is not fair to take the Letters to Baretti with[ou]t acknowledg[in]g that they come from *The European Magazine*.[22]

[14] Corrected in the second edition (*Life* i. 212). Cf. *ante* From Percy, 5 and 7 May 1772 and n. 4.

[15] Corrected in the second edition (*Life* i. 315).

[16] For "Warburton" read "Bolingbroke". JB did not correct the statement, *Life* i. 329, but Reed was right: the pamphlet-war ended in 1749 (DNB s.v. Warburton and Mallet).

[17] Corrected in the second edition (*Life* i. 330). But for "Newbery" read "Payne" (*ibid*. n. 3).

[18] The first edition read: "He [Francis Barber] recollects the precise time to be three days before King George II. died." The sentence was omitted in the second edition (*Life* i. 348–50).

[19] First edition: "Rolt, who wrote a great deal for the booksellers, particularly a History of the War, on which, as

we have seen, Johnson himself once had thoughts of employing his pen, was, as Johnson told me, a singular character." In the second edition the middle of the sentence ("particularly . . . pen") was omitted (*Life* i. 359).

[20] First edition: "The Reverend Dr. Campbell, of St. Andrew's, wrote a book on the authenticity of the Gospel History, the manuscript of which he sent to Mr. Innys, a clergyman in England, who was his countryman and acquaintance." In the second edition JB corrected the title to "An Enquiry into the original of Moral Virtue", altered "Innys" to "Innes", and added a foot-note, as in *Life* i. 359.

[21] The first edition mistakenly gave the title as "Redemption", although JB knew better. See *ante* From Blair, 25 Aug. 1787.

[22] Rectified in the second edition (*Life* i. 361 n. 2).

P. 200: As *The Gentleman's Magazine* has mentioned that the letter here printed was in favour of Mr. Sewards Nephew Mr. Hunter of Sydney why should it be omitted here.[23]

P. 237:[24] Q. Could Garrets in the Temple ever be employed as a printing house?[25]

P. 243: Mrs. Macauley has given a different Account of this Conversation. Q. Should it not be noticed?[26]

P. 270: with a concise account of *each* play] Not of each. Some he omitted.[27]

P. 319: Q. If not Loveling who wrote Latin Bawdy verses here ment[ione]d.[28]

P. 330: There are no such lines in Blackmore as are here quoted. They are from Howard's *British Princes*.[29]

P. 370: Patterson was charged by the Reviewers with having imitated Sterne. On which he printed a pamphlet which I have got in which he produced the evidence of his printers and Bookseller to prove that his work was written before Sterne's was known.[30]

P. 374: It is not very lucky for the credit of this story that there is no such name as Pendengrast either for or against Sir John Friend. At Charnocks tryal about the same time a Capt. Pendergrass was an Evidence. Perhaps he is the person meant.[31]

[23] Unchanged, *Life* i. 368. Christopher Hunter (c. 1746–1841) was admitted sizar at Sidney Sussex College, Cambridge 2 June 1762 (*Alum. Cant.*), or six days before the date of SJ's letter, in which his admission is viewed as problematic. For Chapman's suspicions about the text, see *Letters SJ* 141 nn. I have not found the reference in *Gent. Mag.* "Mr. Hunter of Sydney" called on Reed on 6 Oct. 1790 (*Reed Diaries*, ed. Jones, pp. 185–86).

[24] Actually p. 236.

[25] In the second edition "printing-house" was altered to "warehouse" (*Life* i. 435).

[26] Unchanged, *Life* i. 447. See *post* Johnsoniana Transmitted by Astle, n.d., p. 587.

[27] Unchanged, *Life* i. 497. SJ did not write "General Observations" (as they came to be called) for either *A Comedy of Errors* or *Much Ado About Nothing*. Those for *The Tempest* first appeared in the 1773

edition. See Arthur Sherbo, *Samuel Johnson, Editor of Shakespeare*, 1956, p. 87.

[28] Unchanged, *Life* ii. 91. Reed's guess is supported by the same identification proposed independently by Edward Bensly (*ibid.* 488).

[29] In the second edition JB altered "I defended Blackmore's lines" to "I defended Blackmore's supposed lines", and added a long foot-note on the question of their authorship, with an acknowledgement not to Reed but to "An acute correspondent of the European Magazine, April 1792 [xxi. 267–68; signed 'G.G.']" (*Life* ii. 108 and n. 2).

[30] In the second edition a foot-note to this effect was inserted (*Life* ii. 175 n. 4); in the third edition a further note on Paterson was added (*ibid.* n. 3).

[31] Unchanged in the second edition; in the third the name was changed (perhaps by Malone) to "Prendergast" (*Life* ii. 182–83). See *ibid.* 183 n. 1.

P. 476: For *The Visitor* read *The Universal Visitor*.[32]

Q. Should not Mrs. Lenox's mention of Johnson in *The Female Quixote* be noticed. It is one of the first times he is introduced into any literary work with his name.[33]

p. 408:[34] On the Extract from *Eugenio* two lines are omitted. The Author was a Wine Merch[an]t at Wrexham and just after the publication of the Poem cut his throat. If you think it worth while to have it right I believe I can find the Poem.[35]

p. 119: Sandys History of all Religions] Q. If there is such a Book. I believe not and that it is a mistake for Sandy's's *Europa Speculum* or view or survey of the State of Religion in the Western parts of the World.[36]

Vol. II

p. 29: The quotation from Shenstone is not accurate.[37]

[P.] 55: Mr. Ballow mentioned in this page was a deformed man and wrote a book called *The Principles of Equity*. There is an Account of him in Hawkins's *Life of Johnson*.[38]

[P.] 58: *The Patriot* was only indirectly insinuated to be Johnson's. There is no mention of him in the printed copy. It was only in the Advertisem[en]ts.[39]

[32] Corrected in the second edition (*Life* ii. 345). But for "*Visitor*" read "*Visiter*" (cf. *ibid.* i. 306).

[33] *The Female Quixote*, 1752, Book VI, Chapter XI, where *The Rambler* receives high praise ("the finest System of Ethics yet extant"). On the verso of the first leaf of the present MS. JB noted: "At wrote Proposals for Charlotte insert her early compliment to Johnson in a Note." "Wrote Charlotte's Proposals" is an entry in SJ's diary for 2 Jan. 1775; JB quotes it, *Life* ii. 289, but does not mention there or elsewhere the reference in *The Female Quixote*. The Dedication to the novel was ascribed to SJ by JB on internal evidence (*Life* i. 19); and the authorship of the eleventh chapter of Book IX has also been claimed for SJ (see Hazen, p. 95).

[34] Actually p. 409.

[35] See next letter.

[36] Corrected in the second edition (*Life* i. 219). Reed gives the title of the 1625 edition of the work. It first appeared in 1605 as *A Relation of the State of Religion*, etc.

[37] An explanatory note was added in the second edition (*Life* ii. 452).

[38] The reference to Hawkins was inserted in the second edition (*Life* iii. 22 n. 4). The work was entitled *A Treatise on Equity*; Henry Ballow (1707–82) was the probable author. See *Life* iii. 472–73.

[39] The reference is to the tragedy by Joseph Simpson, not the political piece by SJ. The first edition read: "['The Patriot'] . . . was positively averred to have been written by Johnson himself." JB drafted his revision in the present MS.: "was advertised as having been written by Johnson himself." In the second edition (*Life* iii. 28) the passage came to read: ". . . was fallaciously advertised, so as to make it be believed to have been written by Johnson himself."

[P.] 114: its design being supposed favourable to the Ministry it fell etc.] This is by no means the fact. There was nothing of the least political tendency in the play. The offence given to the popular party by Kelly was writing in *The Ledger* against them.[40]

[P.] 174: Mr. Boswells Eulogium on Beckford's Speech to the King is unfounded. Not a word of it was spoken. It was written by Mr. Horne Tooke and authenticated (if we may so say) by a trick.[41]

[P.] 208: the Siege of Something] It was called *The Siege of Aleppo*. The Author was Mr. Hawkins formerly professor of Poetry at Oxford and of Pembroke College there. This play was printed in his *Miscellanies* 3 Vols. 8vo. 1758.[42]

[P.] 212: Danl. de Foe never was a Silversmith. He had been at one time a Hosier.[43]

[P.] 213: Q. Are these verses in Dodsley's *Collect[io]n*. I do not immediately recollect them.[44]

[P.] 235: Videt et erubuit etc.] This line is Crashaw's. See his life *Biog. Britt.*[45]

[P.] 243: for *translator* of Demosthenes read *Editor* of Demosthenes.[46]

[P.] 334: I think Mr. Langton is inaccurate in saying that Dossie was the Author of a treatise on Agriculture. He wrote a treatise on Brandy and 2 Vols. called *The Handmaid of Arts* in which there is I believe nothing about Agriculture.[47]

[40] The reference is to Hugh Kelly's *A Word to the Wise*. In the second edition (*Life* iii. 113–14) the passage quoted by Reed was altered to: "he being a writer for ministry, in one of the news-papers, it fell" etc.

[41] Unchanged, *Life* iii. 201. See *ibid.* n. 3 and pp. 511–12.

[42] This information was given in a foot-note in the second edition (*Life* iii. 259 n. 1).

[43] First edition: "a man, who, bred a silversmith"; second edition: "a man, who, bred a tradesman" (*Life* iii. 267–68).

[44] Unchanged, *Life* iii. 269. Malone (who either had access to Reed's list or was following JB's MS. notes in the margin of his partially revised copy of the second edition: see *ibid.* i. 14–15) searched in vain for the verses, as did Hill (*ibid.* iii. 269 n. 2).

[45] The identification was made by

Malone in a foot-note to the third edition (*Life* iii. 304 n. 3). Reed's reference is to the second edition of *Biographia Britannica* (iv. 432).

[46] Corrected in the second edition (*Life* iii. 318). For another notice of the error, see *ibid.* 524.

[47] Unchanged, *Life* iv. 11. Langton was right: Robert Dossie was the author of *Memoirs of Agriculture, and Other Oeconomical Arts* (3 vols., 1768–82). The BM *Cat.* lists among other works *An Essay on Spirituous Liquors; with regard to their effects on health; in which the comparative wholesomeness of Rum and Brandy are particularly considered* [1770] and *The Handmaid to the Arts* (1758). JB met Dossie at Gen. Paoli's on 23 Mar. 1775: "We had at dinner ... a Mr. Dossie, who writes on agriculture, etc., a fat, pale faced englishman who affected to treat religion lightly, saying, 'I forget

[P.] 342: for Seldon in the verses read Selden.[48]

[P.] 345: There was another person from whom Dr. Johnson received more assistance than from all that are here mentioned put together. That person however does not desire to be mentioned.[49]

[P.] 402: Mr. Young's Account that his father lost in the South Sea money got by *The Universal Passion* cannot be true. The South Sea year was 1720 and the poem was not published untill 1726 and 1727.[50] Young however had issued Proposals for an expensive Edition of his Works of which I have a Copy. He might also have raised money by it and lost it. I will find the Proposals before Mr. Boswell wants the information.[51]

[P.] 453: Mallocks name so spelt is to the second Edition of Thomson's *Winter*.[52]

[P.] 513: The line here quoted I think was in Brooke's *Earl of Essex* and I believe suppressed in the last Edition.[53] This fact I will ascertain.

how many sacraments we have'. He however knew Mr. Johnson a good deal, and respected him highly" (Journ.; quoted in part by Dr. Powell, *Life* iv. 11 n. 2).

[48] Corrected in the second edition (*Life* iv. 23 n. 3).

[49] In the second edition JB expanded the passage naming those who assisted with the *Lives of the Poets*, concluding: "But he was principally indebted to my steady friend Mr. Isaac Reed, of Staple-inn, whose extensive and accurate knowledge of English literary History I do not express with exaggeration, when I say it is wonderful; indeed his labours have proved it to the world; and all who have the pleasure of his acquaintance can bear testimony to the frankness of his communications in private society" (*Life* iv. 37).

[50] Unchanged in the second edition; a note on the chronology by Malone appeared in the third edition (*Life* iv. 121 n. 3). See also *ibid.* 493–94.

[51] Reed edited the last volume of Young's *Works* (6 vols., 1778–79). I have not found any other mention of these Proposals.

[52] Noted by Malone in the third edition (*Life* iv. 217 n. 1).

[53] Not noted, *Life* iv. 312. Hill identified the play and quoted the passage—the speech of the Queen at the end of the first act—from the first edition (1761). In the 1778 edition (*A Collection of Pieces formerly published by Henry Brooke, Esq.*, 4 vols., ii. 239 ff.), the whole speech is altered. Nor is this the only one. The Advertisement states: "There are some few Passages in the following Tragedy different from those which are spoken on the stage; the reason of which has been, that in dramatic writings, many things may appear well in the closet, which would not have a good effect in the representation." SJ, it will be remembered, attacked (ironically) the suppression of Brooke's first play, *Gustavus Vasa*, in *A Compleat Vindication of the Licensers of the Stage* (1739).

From Isaac Reed,
c. November 1792

MS. Yale (C 2348).

ADDRESS: James Boswell Esq., No. 47 Great Portland Street.

Conclusion of Eugenio or Virtuous and Happy Life. A poem.
4to 1737

Say now, ye fluttering, poor assuming Elves,
Stark full of Pride, of Folly, of—yourselves,
Say where's the Wretch of all your impious crew,
Who dares confront his character to view?
Behold EUGENIO—view him oer and o'er;
Then sink into your selves and be no more;
Or be, what Nature and Religion meant,
Men to some purpose—Christians with Intent:
In vain with Balaam else, you'll wish to die
EUGENIO's Death—like him ascend the sky.
    Gracious and Good! Oh late remove him hence
To thy own Heaven! To Joy refin'd from Sense!
Transplant his virtues to their native C⟨lime,⟩
To baffle Death and triumph over Time.

The Writer of this Poem was Mr. Thos. Beach Wine Mer-
ch⌈an⌉t at Wrexham in Denbighshire. Just after this publication
viz. 17 May 1737 he cut his throat with such desperate resolution
as almost to sever his head from his Body. It appears by Swifts
works that this Poem was communicated to him and received
some of his corrections.[1]

To Isaac Reed,
Monday 26 November 1792

MS. Yale (*L 1096). JB's copy.

⌈London,⌉ Monday 26 Novr.

DEAR SIR: Will you do me the favour to dine with me at my house
No. 47 Great Portland Street near Portland Chapel *on thursday*

---

[1] This information (with the author's
name suppressed) and the text of the
verses were included, with acknowledgement to Reed, in the second edition
(*Life* ii. 240 n. 4).

next at half past four, to meet Malone and some more friends? My servant will call for an answer tomorrow morning.[1] Yours sincerely

JAMES BOSWELL

Have you found Young's Proposals for his *Love of Fame?*

From an Anonymous Correspondent, Monday 10 December 1792

MS. Yale (C 3186).

ADDRESS: James Boswell, Esqre.

ENDORSEMENT: Anonymous Decr. 10. 1792.

London, Dec. 10th 1792

SIR: My chief Object in addressing these ill-written Lines to you, after having been both amus'd and instructed by your entertaining Account of Johnson is to rouse your sleeping Ambition for "liberal Praise and well earn'd Pelf."[1]

Publish, as soon as you can, the Collection respecting the feudal Antiquities of Scotland, mentiond p. 308 of your second Volume.[2] And upon this Subject you may find some collateral Information in Dornfords Translations of Putters History of the Germanick Empire,[3] and still more in your own Countryman's, Gilbert Stuarts, *View of Society in Europe.*[4] A Work too little known for its Merits.

Publish some Travels of your own, mention'd in some part of

---

[1] "This day I gave a dinner, a kind of feast, two courses and a desert upon the success of my first edition of Dr. Johnson's *Life*—present Mr. Malone, Mr. Deputy Nichols, his son in law the Rev. Mr. Pridden, Mr. Reed, Mr. Dilly, Mr. Baldwin, and his son Charles printer with him, Squire Dilly, my brother T.D., my daughters Veronica and Euphemia and son James. . . . We drank 'Church and King'—'Health and long life to the *Life of Dr. Johnson*'—'the pious memory of Dr. Johnson' etc. etc." (Journ. 29 Nov. 1792).

[1] Not located.

[2] "I have a valuable collection made by my Father, which, with some additions and illustrations of my own, I intend to publish" (*Life* iii. 414 n. 3).

[3] Johann Stephan Pütter, *An Historical Development of the Present Political Constitution of the Germanic Empire*, etc., translated by Josiah Dornford, 1790.

[4] Gilbert Stuart, *A View of Society in Europe, in Its Progress from Rudeness to Refinement*, 1778. Stuart's "bluntness did not please" JB, "though his strong mind did" (Journ. 1 June 1785).

the same Volume, which I cannot find. Whatever Dr. Johnson might have said to disencourage you, be assur'd that he was mistaken.[5]

Publish the Anacreon alluded to in p. 467.[6] If a Dislike to the dull Business of editing deter you, or, if you suspect, that from disuse you may have lost a critical, and accurate Knowledge of the Greek Language, your friend Dr. Langton may himself assist you, and what is more procure you the requisite Assistance from that saucy fellow, Porson,[7] who must be allowed the merit, in spite of his Sauciness of being the most acute and well informed of all our Greek Philologists. Should his Character deter you from making an Application to him, you might by Dr. Langton's means obtain an introduction to another of our present Literati, scarcely inferior to Porson in an accurate Knowledge of the Greek Language, and infinitely his superior in every other literary attainment, and in those qualities of the heart and temper, which unite and endear us to each other. I mean, the Revd. Thos. Burges.[8]

Of Ellis' Translation of Ovid mentiond p. 54[9] a large Class of

---

[5] "I expressed some inclination to publish an account of my *Travels* upon the continent of Europe, for which I had a variety of materials collected. JOHNSON. 'I do not say, Sir, you may not publish your travels; but I give you my opinion, that you would lessen yourself by it. What can you tell of countries so well known as those upon the continent of Europe, which you have visited? . . . Why, Sir, most modern travellers in Europe who have published their travels, have been laughed at: I would not have you added to the number. The world is now not contented to be merely entertained by a traveller's narrative; they want to learn something' " (*Life* iii. 300–01). "I believe, however, I shall follow my own opinion; for the world has shewn a very flattering partiality to my writings, on many occasions" (*ibid.* n. 1). Previously SJ had encouraged JB to publish his travels (*ibid.* i. 409–10). JB wrote to Sir William Forbes on 11 May 1793 (MS. estate of the late Lord Clinton) about his plans for publication, but the work never materialized.

[6] "I wrote to him . . . and mentioned

that 'Baxter's Anacreon, which is in the library at Auchinleck, was, I find, collated by my father in 1727, with the MS. belonging to the University of Leyden, and he has made a number of Notes upon it. Would you advise me to publish a new edition of it?' " (*Life* iv. 241). SJ suggested in his reply that JB consult Lord Hailes. See *ibid.* 525.

[7] Richard Porson (1759–1808). One of his saucier *divertissements* was an ironical panegyric on Hawkins's *Life of Johnson* (*Gent. Mag.*, 1787, lvii. 652–53, 751–53, 847–49).

[8] MS. apparently "Thosʰ". Thomas Burgess, D.D. (1756–1837) was successively Bishop of St. David's and Bishop of Salisbury.

[9] "This Mr. Ellis [John Ellis, 1698–1790] was, I believe, the last of that profession called *Scriveners* . . . He was a man of literature and talents. . . . He shewed me a translation which he had made of Ovid's Epistles, very prettily done" (*Life* iii. 21 n. 1). According to an account of Ellis in *The European Magazine* (1792, xxi. 5), "Dr. Johnson frequently recommended the publication

readers would be glad to see the publication, and would think themselves much indebted to Mr. Boswell, if he could accelerate the Publication.

In p. 149—in the Note—You mention a projected History of the *Affair* of 1745,6—by Mr. John Home, who was himself gallantly in the field for the reigning family.[10] I wish it were published, and wish that it may be as well written as the account given of the *Affair* of 1715, in Tindal's Continuation to Rapin's *History*.[11] But why should a History written by James Boswell, be composd in such a Spirit, as to make it necessary to go to a foreign Press?[12] Should you seriously think of writing it, or should you wish to add to Mr. Homes' Source of Information, I will venture to say that if you will take a Journey into the Parts of Wales, contiguous to Shropshire and Cheshire you will meet with Anecdotes very much to *your Taste* from many of the Gentlemen, resident in those parts, who are very little removed from Jacobitism. The present Curate of Wrexham,[13] had given to him, a Collection of all the Newspaper Squibbs, Manifestos, etc. stuck up, or dispersd over that part of the Kingdom by the Adherents to the "good old Cause." He *may* have them *still*.

Of Mrs. Caroline Rudd, mention'd in p. 90—A Narrative written by you, or some person as capable,[14] would be extremely acceptable to the generality of Readers, and let me add to minds of a higher Order than the Generality. A very well-written Narrative was given of that extraordinary Forger, Charles Price, better known by the Name of old Patch, who is the very identical small-beer

---

of his translation of Ovid's Epistles, and Dr. King . . . commended it in very warm terms, declaring 'that he differed from other translators so much as to warrant him to say, what he read was not Ellis, but Ovid himself' " (quoted, *Life* iii. 472).

[10] *Life* iii. 162 n. 5. John Home (1722–1808), who was taken prisoner at the battle of Falkirk, published his *History of the Rebellion in the Year 1745* in 1802.

[11] Tindal's continuation of Rapin (5 vols., 1732–51) brought the *History* from the Revolution of 1688 down to the accession of George II in 1727.

[12] SJ had suggested that JB print his projected *History of the Civil War*, etc. in

Holland, but JB thought he might write it so as to be acceptable at home: *Life* iii. 162.

[13] The Rev. Edward Edwards, M.A., Curate of Wrexham, Denbighshire, from 1763 to 1804 (A. N. Palmer, *History of the Parish Church of Wrexham*, Wrexham and Oswestry, [1886,] p. 82).

[14] *Life* iii. 79. For a narrative by JB of his interview with the celebrated criminal (in the form of a letter, unsent, to his wife), see BP xi. 303–11; for an account of her by Prof. Pottle, *ibid.* 297–300 (somewhat expanded in *Boswell: The Ominous Years*, 1963, pp. 352–55). See also Journ. *passim*.

Brewer of p. 84.[15] Perhaps your varied and extensive acquaintance in this Metropolis may enable you to gather some Anecdotes of the Aunt of Prices' Wife, by Name Hickeringhall,[16] a Woman, as artful an⟨d as⟩ able, tho' not so elegant as Mrs. Rudd.

Will you not satisfy the Public Curiosity with the Life of Sir R. Sibbard [*sic*], mention'd p. 189[17]—Nor with the Anecdotes of Pope and Bolingbroke, which you had from Lord Marchmont—p. 259?[18]—which, by the bye, you might bring forward in the Notes to a new Edition of John Dennis's Critical Works.[19]

And now permit me, with all due Respect to your Feelings and to your Character, to suggest to you that the Public have a very strong Claim to an 8vo Edition of your Work—Which it should be your Business to expedite as soon as possible from motives of Liberality to that Publick, whose Approbation has so amply rewarded your Labours, and likewise from the Wish to extend still farther, your own and the Reputation of your illustrious friend.

Whenever it shall be published I hope the Index will be very much enlarged.[20] I would likewise suggest a Division like that of Mason's in his *Memoirs of Gray*.[21] Perhaps after all, a mere Table of Contents prefixed to each Volume, besides an enlargement of the Index to the whole might answer the purpose. In this Table of

[15] *Life* iii. 70. Mentioned by SJ in telling an anecdote of Foote. See *Memoirs of a Social Monster, or the History of Charles Price . . . Commonly Called Old Patch*, etc., 1786.

[16] Actually, Hickeringill; alias Mrs. Poultney, Price's accomplice in counterfeiting. See *Memoirs*, p. 326 and *passim*.

[17] "I mentioned that I had in my possession the Life of Sir Robert Sibbald, the celebrated Scottish antiquary, and founder of the Royal College of Physicians at Edinburgh, in the original manuscript in his own handwriting; and that it was I believed the most natural and candid account of himself that ever was given by any man. . . . I talked of some time or other publishing this curious life" (*Life* iii. 227–28). Cf. Journ. 18 Aug. 1776 ("I thought of printing it with additions by myself."). JB never carried out his design. It was first published by James Maidment, anonymously, in 1833 from the Auchinleck MS. See *Life* iii. 515–16.

[18] ". . . I waited on the Earl of Marchmont, to know if his Lordship would favour Dr. Johnson with information concerning Pope, whose Life he was about to write. . . . I availed myself of this opportunity to hear from his Lordship many particulars both of Pope and Lord Bolingbroke, which I have in writing" (*Life* iii. 342, 344). These materials form a part of JB's journal for 12 May (and following) 1778.

[19] "He said, he wished to see 'John Dennis's Critical Works' collected. Davies said they would not sell. Dr. Johnson seemed to think otherwise" (*Life* iii. 40).

[20] The prefixed index ("Alphabetical Table of Contents, to Both Volumes") runs to fifteen pages, double column, in the first edition. In the second edition it was somewhat enlarged.

[21] Where the table of contents (following the Memoirs) gives brief abstracts of both the narrative and the letters.

Contents You might give in a brief manner the topics of any remarkable Letter, Argument, or Discourse. Remember, if you should be inclined to smile with Contempt at my merely *Book making* suggestions that there are many works, which will always be read by *snatches* and resorted to for illustration of particular Subjects however splendid and entertaining the Abilities of their Authors may prove. With powers of Entertainment and Instruction, equal, at least, to many other admired writers, You must like them, yield to the Necessity of, the overpowering Influence, I mean, of your Subject.

And now, Sir, I take my leave of You, with many thanks for the Entertainment which you have afforded me, and with many wishes for your *domestic* Happiness. This you may have a better Chance to secure by not carrying your feudal Prejudices into the Bosom of your family. [22] By respecting the weakness of our common Nature in your Daughter. By not making a Merit of disinheriting a poor Girl (vd the 2d Vol.) for consulting her own Happiness upon a point, in which She only can be the real judge, and where no Parent has a right to force the Actions of his Child. [23] I am, Sir, Your sincere Well-wisher and frequent reader, tho' one of ⟨"?the⟩ Hounds of Whiggism"—vd 2d Vol. [24]

[22] The reference is to the discussion of the Auchinleck entail, *Life* ii. 412 ff. JB had anticipated the objection, *ibid.* 420 n. 1: "Yet let me not be thought harsh or unkind to daughters; for my notion is, that they should be treated with great affection and tenderness, and always participate of the prosperity of the family." He had also avowed, if not "feudal Prejudices", at least his "old feudal principle of preferring male to female succession" (*ibid.* 387 n. 1).

[23] I have found no such passage in the second volume of the first edition. But cf. *Life* ii. 328–29, where SJ and JB, in opposition to Mrs. Thrale, condemn "A young lady who had married a man much her inferiour in rank."

[24] "Against his Life of MILTON, the hounds of Whiggism have opened in full cry" (*Life* iv. 40).

1793

From *Andrew Erskine*,[1]
Monday 14 January 1793

MS. Yale (C 1213).

ADDRESS: James Boswell Esq. [*completed in another hand:*] No. 47 Great
Portland Street, London.

POSTMARKS: JA 17 93, JA 18 93.

ENDORSEMENT: Honourable Andrew Erskine.

Edinburgh, Janry. 14th 1793

. . . I am happy in this opportunity of thanking you for the very
honourable niche you have given me in your modern Pantheon.[2]
I read your book, (the copy you presented Lord Kellie,)[3] with
infinite avidity, and whenever it begins to fade a little from my
memory shall read it again, it is an inexhaustible mine of wit and
good sense, you have raised the character of your Hero, and have
shown clearly that his fits of fretfulness and bursts of rudeness
proceeded from no innate acrimony of disposition, but from that
nervous irritability, to which from his constitution he was so unhappily subject. You and I my dear Boswell who from melancholy
experience have been taught, that in the long list of human calamities, it is the most oppressive and severe, and how tyrannically
it rules the mind,[4] can find an excuse in that deplorable malady, for
all the failings of your venerable friend. He seems to have loved
you with sincere affection, and to have gain'd the heart of such a
man as Dr. Johnson does you infinite honour. I am fond of your
Style, it is not the solemn march of your friend, but the careless and
easy walk of a Gentleman. . . .

---

[1] The Hon. Andrew Erskine (1740–
93), JB's early friend and collaborator.
See *Letters between The Honourable
Andrew Erskine, and James Boswell, Esq.*
(1763) and Journ. *passim.*

[2] ". . . my friend the Honourable

Andrew Erskine, himself both a good
poet and a good critick" (*Life* iii. 150).

[3] Erskine's brother Archibald, seventh
Earl of Kellie (1736–97).

[4] Erskine was a suicide in Oct. of this
year. See BP xii. 240.

From John Stuart, Earl of Bute,[1] Thursday 21 February 1793

MS. Yale (C 719).

ADDRESS: James Boswell Esqr., Royal Academy, Somerset-place, London.

FRANK: Luton, twenty-one February 1793. Cardiff.[2]

POSTMARK: FE 22 93.

Luton Park,[3] 21 February 1793

Mr. Boswell's attention to collect every thing, which in any shape concerns the late Doctor Johnson, induces Lord Bute to send him, with his compliments, copies of two letters addressed to his late Father.

[Enclosure][4]

Cambridge, Nov. 15. 1761

MY LORD, I take the liberty of troubling your Lordship with a petition the completion of which will redound not only to your own honour but to that of the whole kingdom. We are at this time my Lord perhaps the happiest nation in the world; enjoy in the amplest manner every species of civil and religious liberty in their fullest extent and are blest with a prince on the throne, who seems likely to rival, in the virtuous part of their characters the Tituss and Antonines of old. Yet notwithstanding these fortunate circumstances there yet is wanting something to fill up the proper measure of national and kingly glory. I mean in the patronage and protection of those, who have eminently distinguished themselves

[1] John Stuart (1744–1814), fourth Earl and first Marquess of Bute. As Lord Mountstuart he figures prominently in JB's journal of his grand tour, 1765. In the *Life* (iv. 209) he is characterized at length, though anonymously.

[2] Mountstuart was created Baron Cardiff of Cardiff Castle in the peerage of Great Britain, 20 May 1776 (*Scots Peer.* ii. 305). See Journ. 11 May 1776.

[3] On 4 June 1781 SJ and JB together visited "Lord Bute's magnificent seat" in Bedfordshire (*Life* iv. 127–28). For an account of the estate, see *ibid.* 496–97.

[4] I give here the (anonymous) letter to Lord Bute which JB did not print (MS. Yale C 3182). The other, SJ's acknowledgement of the intended pension, 20 July 1762, was included by JB at the end of the second volume of the second edition, and was put in its proper chronological place in the third (*Life* i. 376–77). A second letter from SJ to Bute was printed in the second edition from a copy by Lord Macartney, "from the original, which was found, by the present Earl of Bute, among his father's papers" (*Life* i. 380).

in the literary way. And as your Lordship is said to have the honour of being consulted by His Majesty oftener than most of those, who are about his person;[5] this has emboldened me to put you in mind of a truly great Author, who deserves every reward that this nation can bestow on him, but who hitherto has remained exposed to the conflicts of indigence and want. The writer I mean is *Mr. Samuel Johnson*, who has not only immortalized as it were our language; but in every work that he has produced has done his utmost to the promotion of every moral and religious duty. I will not anticipate your Lordships reflections by desiring you to consider the great disgrace it reflects on this nation that this learned and virtuous man still remains unpensioned and left to procure himself a precarious subsistence by the bounty of Booksellers. If it be objected that his political principles render him an unfit object of His Majesty's favor, I would only say that he is to be the more pitied on this account, and that it may sometimes happen that our opinions, however erroneous, are not always in our power. Add to this that a disregard to this would be a further prosecution of his Majesty's noble plan, the total abolition of all party distinctions. The particular reason of my troubling your Lordship with this is, that popular fame represents your Lordship as a man of letters and a patron of all useful arts,[6] this therefore has prompted me to put you in mind of a man, whom, in the multiplicity of affairs, you may perhaps have omitted to take notice. 'Tis not private friendship but admiration of this truly great man that has made me to give myself and your Lordship this trouble. I never, that I know of, ever saw Mr. Johnson, but have made many enquiries into his character, which tho' tarnished with some human failings is on the whole extremely aim[i]able and benevolent. What pleasure therefore would it afford to you to rescue such a man as this from the approach of poverty and all it's sad attendant circumstances and how would both His Majesty's and your character be encreased in the estimation of all who are the friends to learning and virtue. It is said that the King has conferred a pension of £200 pr. ann. on Mr. Kennicott; I do not call in question the propriety of His Majesty's bounty, he most certainly did it with the purest and best

---

[5] Bute was virtual Prime Minister from the accession of George III, having been the Prince of Wales's chief companion and confidant. He became Prime Minister in name as well on 28 May 1762.

[6] Especially (it was alleged) as practised by Scotsmen.

intentions. Yet what are the merits of this man compared to those of Johnson? will the world be in possession of any one undiscovered moral or religious truth when *he* (viz. Kennicott) has completed his scheme?[7] but, with respect to the other, I may venture to say that he hath done more by his writings to the advancement of real piety and valuable learning than almost any other man now living. Your Lordship must be sensible that when the opportunity is gone, we regret that such men as this man I am now writing about should die unrewarded. We have then nothing left but to pay the empty tribute of a sepulchral monument to their memories. For once my Lord let this sad maxim be contradicted and enjoy the exalted satisfaction of making a worthy man happy. I hope your Lordship is not above making use of such information as I now send you. True wisdom as well as true greatness disdains no method of growing wiser and refuses to reject any council if it be good in whatever manner it be offered. Consider my Lord 2 or 300 £ pr. ann. pension would deliver this great author from every fear of penury and indigence, would fill his heart with gratitude and at the same time instigate him to shew himself worthy of the royal favor by every means in his power. I am told that his political principles make him incapable of being in any place of trust, by incapacitating him from qualifying himself for any such office. But a pension my Lord requires no such performances—and my Lord it would seem but a just condescension to human infirmity that the man who has endeavored in such a forcible manner to correct all our failings and errors should be excused one himself. I think it high time to ask your Lordships pardon for this long interruption from public business. But perhaps you may have disregarded this long before you have read thus far and may perhaps have looked upon it as the production of one whose intellects have been, by some accident overturned. But I can assure your Lordship of the contrary; tho' indeed this is nothing to the purpose, if the matter is reasonable in itself. My only design in this is to do good to the man, and tho' I am altogether unknown to your Lordship, I cannot help flattering myself that it may not be wholly without

---

[7] Kennicott's lifelong devotion to Biblical scholarship was crowned by his *Vetus Testamentum Hebraicum cum Variis Lectionibus* (1776, 1780). "Ot Dr. Kennicott's Collations, he observed, that though the text should not be much mended thereby, yet it was no small advantage to know, that we had as good a text as the most consummate industry and diligence could procure" (*Life* ii. 128, quoting Dr. Maxwell).

effect. I have long meditated such a design, but the oddness and unusualness of the attempt for a long time discouraged me, I have now put it in execution and your Lordship's general character made me address myself to you. I am, my Lord your Lordships most obedient Servant

Your Lordship at the opening of this[8] and seeing no name subscribed to it, will perhaps be tempted to reject it immediately; but let me request the favor of you to give it a patient perusal some time when you are entirely at leisure.

You will perceive that I aim not in this at elegance in the composition, I wrote it immediately from the feelings of the heart. I thought that if the subject would not persuade it was in vain to have recourse (supposing I had been able) to the arts of eloquence and I have purposely wrote it in a handwriting quite different from what I commonly use; no probability of a discovery of the real Author may be conjectured; but of this there is no danger as I am not known to any one to whom your Lordship can shew this, *though I hope from your Lordships known prudence*, you will only consider the contents without making them known to anyone.

To be delivered into my Lord Bute's own hands.

It is requested that if this comes to the Secretary of State's office that they do not open it, for it contains no public business but only something to be considered of in private by his Lordship himself.

To John Stuart, Earl of Bute, Monday 25 February 1793

MS. Yale (L 349). JB's copy.

Great Portland Street, 25 Febry. 1793

Mr. Boswell presents his compliments to Lord Bute, and returns many thanks for the obliging communication concerning Dr. Johnson, with which his Lordship has been pleased to favour him.

---

[8] Apparently this paragraph and the next were originally written on a covering leaf, and the instructions which follow them, on the outside.

To *William Gerard Hamilton,*
Monday 25 February 1793

MS. Yale (L 622). JB's draft.

Great Portland Street No. 47, Feb. 25. 1793

Sir: I am sorry to intrude upon you, [1]but forgive me for mentioning that you owe me[1] two pounds sixteen shillings for Cancels made at your desire.[2] I am, Sir, Your most humble servant

JAMES BOSWELL

To The Right Honourable William Gerard Hamilton.

From *William Gerard Hamilton,*
Tuesday 26 February 1793

MS. Yale (C 1491).
ADDRESS: Js. Boswell Esq., Great Portland St., No. 47.
ENDORSEMENT: Right Hon. W. G. Hamilton 1793.

[London,] Tuesday

Sir, I send you by the Bearer the Sum I am indebted to you, and I consider myself as much obliged to you. Yours truly,

W. G. HAMILTON

To the Rev. Dr. *William Maxwell,*
Tuesday 26 February 1793

MS. Yale (L 962). A copy in Veronica Boswell's hand, headed: "To the Reverend Dr. Maxwell, Falkland, Tynan, Ireland."

Gt. Portland St., London, 26 Feb. 1793

DEAR SIR: It gives me much pleasure to hear from you that you think so well of my *Life of Dr. Johnson.* It has indeed been re-

---

[1-1] JB made several attempts at phrasing this passage. The original version was: "but rather than trouble a third person give me leave to mention to you myself that you are indebted to me . . ."

[2] See *ante* From Hamilton, 6 Feb. 1788, n. 9, and To Malone, 25 Feb. 1791 and n. 3. The cancels are described by Dr. Powell, *Life* iv. 556–57.

ceived by the World in the most flattering manner to its Authour. I am sorry that the Irish Edition is not accurate. I shall soon have a second edition published here with corrections and considerable additions. Pray let me know how I shall convey a set to you. Why do you not come amongst us. We should be heartily glad to see you. Come then in summer and let us *Johnsonise.* I am, Dear Sir, Your obliged and most obedient Servant

Signed JAMES BOSWELL

To Andrew Erskine, Wednesday 6 March 1793

MS. Yale (L 531). A copy by JB's son Alexander, endorsed: "Copy of a Letter From James Boswell To The Honour[a]ble Andrew Erskine after a cessation of correspondence."

Auchinleck, 6 March 1793

MY DEAR ERSKINE: I have received a great many letters in commendation of my *Life of Dr. Johnson,* none of which gave me greater pleasure than yours,[1] for, I say it most sincerely I respect your judgement much, and am sure of your sincerity. The praise you so kindly bestow is the more valuable that I well recollect you were rather a heretick with regard to my illustrious Friend: But I have persevered with confidence to make his real character known; and *St. Andrew* is now added to the Johnsonian Calendar. To be canonised (in your own lifetime at least) is probably more than you expected. Since you truly like my *Magnum Opus,* you shall no longer read Lord Kellys Copy. I will send you my second Edition in three volumes, octavo which will come forth early in April,[2] with corrections and several sheets of additions with which I have been favour'd by the Bishop of Salisbury,[3] Lord Bute[,][4] Mr. Windham,[5] Mr. Langton[6] and many others. I am to publish them separately in Quarto to accommodate the purchasers of the first Edition of which 1689 sets have been sold (the rest of the impression of 1750 having gone to the ent[r]y in Stationershall[,]

[1] *Ante* 14 Jan. 1793.
[2] It was published 17 July.
[3] See *ante* From Douglas, 16 May 1791, n. 1.
[4] See *ante* From Bute, 21 Feb. 1793, n. 4.
[5] *Life* iv. 415.
[6] Langton's "additions" at this time were letters from SJ (see *ante* 1 Mar. 1790, n. 1); "corrections" were still to come (*post* c. 30 July 1793).

presents etc.) and many more would have gone off could they have been had. . . . Dr. Ogilvie I find has written a letter to *The English Review* questioning petulantly enough the authenticity of Johnsons humourous retort to him on the *noble wild prospects.*[7] I reccollect your telling me at Ayr that you had a letter from me at *the time* mentioning it. I will be much obliged to you for that letter.[8] . . .

To Edmond Malone, Wednesday 20 March 1793

MS. Yale (L 944). JB's copy, written on the inside of a wrapper.

ADDRESS: To Edmond Malone Esq.

Auchinleck, 20 March 1793

MY DEAR MALONE: I return the last part of Vol. Second. I am sorry that seeing it reminded you of *both* books and swains *alone*, as I differ so sturdily from you. Remember you defied me, and said I might add what I pleased in answer.[1] Nevertheless I submit great Commentator! to your revision of my retort, which please to correct if[2] it require correction though I think it is very well. If the Sheet and half can be delayed till I get to *Town* which *must* be at farthest on the 4th of April we may discuss the matter or rather the *manner* over good Oporto. . . .

---

[7] See *ante* From Parr, c. 22 Dec. 1791, n. 1.

[8] A letter in the form of journal, 5–22 July 1763, entitled "A Minced Pye of Savoury Ingredients For The Honourable Andrew Erskine". The account of the exchange between SJ and Ogilvie is virtually the same as that in JB's journal proper, 6 July, and *Life* i. 425. In his reply, 11 Mar., Erskine offered JB the letter if he would stop over at Edinburgh on his way to London. JB did so, but the letter remained among Erskine's papers. In 1955 Yale acquired JB's letters to Erskine from Sir Ralph Anstruther of Balcaskie, a descendant of Erskine's sister Janet.

---

[1] The reference is to JB's stricture on Malone's stricture on SJ's stricture on a passage in Parnell's *Hermit*, *Life* iii. 392–93, 393 n. 1. Hill mistakenly observed that "This note is first given in the third edition"; it appears in the second edition, ii. 611. Malone had the last word in the third edition, iii. 419 n. See, coincidentally, next letter, at n. 32.

[2] MS. "if if"

From the Rev. John Campbell,[1]
Friday 19 April 1793

MS. Yale (C 749). See JB's point-by-point reply *post* 26 July 1793.

ADDRESS: James Boswell Esqr. of Auchinleck, London.

ENDORSEMENT: Rev. Mr. Campbell Minister of Kippen.

Kippen, April 19. 1793

SIR: The general Benevolence of your mind, so strongly marked in your writings, encourages me to hope, that you will not be very much offended, though an entire stranger presume to request for a little, your attention and indulgence. To intrusions of this kind indeed, a Gentleman of your eminence in the literary world, must, I suspect, be not unfrequently exposed. If my presumption excite disgust, I hope you will lose nothing more than the short time that is spent in reading my Paper. If you are disposed to hear me with indulgence, your condescending notice will not only impress me with gratitude, but in some measure gratify the curiosity (I trust not unallowable) of one, who has read some of your Productions with pleasure, and learnt from them to respect both the Character and the Talents of the Writer.

I have lately perused with very peculiar pleasure your *Life of Dr. Johnson*. That Work must be gratifying in a high degree to all who were particularly acquainted with its illustrious Subject. They will find their great Friend and Master as it were embalmed in your Narrative; and may daily live over those scenes which are long since past. To the Lovers of Literary Biography it will furnish a rich and ample feast. Philosophers and Theologians are here provided with abundance of materials, by means of which they will be enabled to enlarge our knowledge of human nature. As I proceeded in the History, I felt myself more and more interested in the great man to whom it relates. I thought for the time that I lived and conversed with him, and made one of those happy Societies and Companies, which he instructed by his Wisdom, or entertained with his Wit. And when at length I came to the closing scene, I felt a sensation of regret, as if I had just parted from a venerable Friend, in whose Society I had long been happy.

[1] The Rev. John Campbell (1758–1828), Minister of Kippen, Stirling. He was the author of the account of Kippen in Sir John Sinclair's *Statistical Account of Scotland*, 1796, xviii, 317–57, and of *Sermons* (posthumously published, Edinburgh, 1829).

It is none of the least satisfactions I received from your Work, to find that the name of Johnson may now be recorded amongst the sincere and stedfast friends of Religion. In a day when the Evidences of Divine Revelation are overlooked or opposed, and when its peculiar Doctrines are scoffed at by many Pretenders to Reason and Wit, it is pleasing to observe that the sagacious mind of Johnson acquiesced in the solidity of those Proofs by which its Truth is established, and could perceive no absurdity even in those Doctrines which are most currently received and surely believed amongst Christians. Above all, when we observe the support which he derived from Religion in his last moments, and the happy state of his mind when he died "full of Resignation, strengthened in Faith, and joyful in Hope";[2] must not such a Scene give strength and consolation to every pious heart, and for ever confound the Irreligious and Profane? "Let me die the death of the Righteous, and let my last end be like his"![3]

I cannot help regretting that Dr. Johnson should have expressed himself so strongly with respect to the impossibility of a good man in this present life attaining to an assured hope of Eternal happiness. This sentiment occurs frequently: E.G. Vol. II. p. 229, 230, 506, etc.[4] His own opinion may easily be accounted for, by that "morbid Melancholy," which was so deeply interwoven with his constitution. But to say, as he does, Vol. II. p. 230,[5] that "he would not think better of a man who should tell him on his Deathbed he was sure of Salvation," is certainly going a great deal too far. I am well aware that many extravagant assertions have been advanced on the article of Assurance, and an unguarded representation of this doctrine may open a wide door to Enthusiasm. At the same time I cannot see any Absurdity in supposing that a Man of uniform Piety and Virtue, may, on the principles of Christianity experience that "Peace and Joy in Believing," that "good Hope through Grace," which elevates the mind above Despondency and Doubt, and fills it with the well-grounded assurance of Life and Immortality. Not to insist on those examples that occur in the sacred writings, how easy would it be to mention Thousands in the present as well as in former times, who, living and dying, have declared on the most rational grounds their triumphant hope of Eternal Life! From the multitude that might here be mentioned,

[2] *Life* iv. 419.
[3] *Numbers* xxiii. 10.
[4] *Life* iii. 294 ff., iv. 299–300.
[5] *Life* iii. 295.

let me select the names of Dr. William Leechman, late Principal of the University of Glasgow;[6] Mr. James Hervey, the Author of many popular writings;[7] and the eminently worthy Dr. Philip Doddridge of Northampton.[8] If you have never seen the Memoirs of Dr. Doddridge's life, written by Mr. Job Orton[9] permit me to recommend it to your attention. It is indeed but a Medallion, when compared with your full length Picture. It is however a piece of well-written and instructive Biography; and the last Chapter, in a particular manner, will excite the tender sensibility of every heart which is warmed with the love of exalted Virtue. Nay when we think of the influence of natural temperament in disposing different men to admit or refuse Comfort from Religion as well as from other sources, may we not justly consider the calm tranquillity at which Johnson himself arrived previous to his dissolution, as an equal or perhaps greater example of the power of Christian Faith and Divine Grace, than even that more assured confidence and Joy which holy men of more chearful and sanguine tempers have frequently displayed? Excuse my dwelling on this subject. Nothing is farther from my intention than to draw you into any Theological discussion. Whilst you have discharged the duty of a faithful Biographer in recording the opinions as well as actions of your great Friend, as they really were, you are certainly on no account responsible for either.

After having provided so ample a fund for the entertainment of your Readers, you will perhaps be surprised that any of them should wish for more information concerning the great Subject of your work. I must own however there is one particular with respect to which my Curiosity is not quite allayed. I should like to have a clear idea of Johnson's means of Subsistence from the time of his coming to London, till the period when he rose to easy circumstances and established Reputation. His only occupation seems to have been writing for the Booksellers. When we consider the paultry sums he received for his two Poems,[10] we are led to conclude

---

[6] SJ and JB visited him on 29 Oct. 1773 (*Life* v. 370).

[7] The Rev. James Hervey (1714–58). SJ ridiculed his *Meditations* (1746, 1748) and JB confessed himself "not an impartial judge; for *Hervey's Meditations* engaged my affections in my early years" (*Life* v. 351–52).

[8] Philip Doddridge, D.D. (1702–51), Nonconformist divine. See *Life* v. 271.

[9] See *Life* v. 271.

[10] "The profits of a single poem, however excellent, appear to have been very small in the last reign, compared with what a publication of the same size has since been known to yield. I have men-

that his annual emoluments must have been very small. The penurious System referred to in Vol. I. p. 49,[11] might have enabled a single man to protract a wretched existence; but we must remember that Johnson had a Wife who resided in London, and sometimes had lodgings in the Country, which was "an unsuitable expence," (p. 129);[12] so that his circumstances were far from being easy, so far down as 1751. Nay it does not appear that they ever became quite easy till he got his Pension. Though the sum he received for his *Dictionary* was greater than he had ever received before, yet it appears to have been mostly anticipated.[13] I propose these difficulties with no other view, than to procure some satisfaction to my own curiosity as to the mode in which this great man procured his living for so long a course of years. If he contrived to live on the fruits of his own industry, such as they were, his Œconomy is certainly entitled to the highest praise. If you do not think my inquiries impertinent, and will be so obliging as to satisfy them, I shall esteem your communications a real favour.

In going over your Work, I frequently marked down with my

tioned, upon Johnson's own authority, that for his LONDON he had only ten guineas; and now, after his fame was established, he got for his 'Vanity of Human Wishes' but five guineas more, as is proved by an authentick document in my possession" (*Life* i. 193). The receipt for the copyright of *The Vanity of Human Wishes* is in the Hyde Collection.

[11] The system of SJ's Irish painter friend who assured him "that thirty pounds a year was enough to enable a man to live [in London] without being contemptible. He allowed ten pounds for clothes and linen. He said a man might live in a garret at eighteen-pence a week; few people would inquire where he lodged; and if they did, it was easy to say, 'Sir, I am to be found at such a place.' By spending three-pence in a coffee-house, he might be for some hours every day in very good company; he might dine for six-pence, breakfast on bread and milk for a penny, and do without supper. On *clean-shirt-day* he went abroad, and paid visits" (*Life* i. 104–05).

[12] "I have, indeed, been told by Mrs. Desmoulins, who, before her marriage, lived for some time with Mrs. Johnson at Hampstead, that she indulged herself in country air and nice living, at an unsuitable expence, while her husband was drudging in the smoke of London" (*Life* i. 237–38).

[13] "He had spent, during the progress of the work, the money for which he had contracted to write his Dictionary" (*Life* i. 304). Cf. Hawkins (pp. 345–46): "... Johnson, who was no very accurate accountant, thought a great part [of the £1,575 stipulated] would be coming to him on the conclusion of the work; but upon producing, at a tavern-meeting for the purpose of settling, receipts for sums advanced to him, which were indeed the chief means of his subsistence, it was found, not only that he had eaten his cake, but that the balance of the account was greatly against him. His debtors were now become his creditors: but they, in a perfect consistency with that liberal spirit which, in sundry instances, the great booksellers are known to have exercised towards authors, remitted the difference, and consoled him for his disappointment by making his entertainment at the tavern a treat."

Pen such observations as occurred at the time, relating either to apparent mistakes, or to matters concerning which some farther elucidation seemed desireable. The most considerable of these have probably occurred already to your own observation, or have been pointed out by some of your friends. Yet I will take the liberty of submitting my remarks to your Judgement. Nothing would be more ungenerous, and I can assure you nothing is farther from my intention, than to dwell "with invidious severity," on such inaccuracies as may be expected in so extensive and complicated a work.[14] It is rather surprising that those which are to be found in it, are so few and trivial. I trust I need make no other apology for the freedom I have taken, to a Gentleman who is so attentive to the minutiae of exactness; and if my labours shall in any degree contribute to the improvement of a new Edition of the *Life of Dr. Johnson*, this circumstance I shall certainly consider as a distinguished felicity and honour.

IN VOLUME I. The dates of the Marriage and Death of Dr. Johnson's Wife, seem involved in some degree of obscurity. In Vol. I. p. 44,[15] the Marriage day appears to have been, July 9. 1735. In p. 128,[16] from Johnson's inscription on the Box, it seems to have been 1736. Again from that inscription, as well as the dates in pp. 127, 129, She appears to have died March 17. 1752. But in Vol. II. p. 536,[17] the Dr. says in his letter to Mr. Bagshaw that it was "in 1753, he committed to the ground his dear Wife." The mistakes probably, are merely typographical; if not they may be ascribed to a slip of memory in Johnson.

P. 55. Note.[18] The enumeration which you give of Johnson's Works, and the pains which you have employed for ascertaining their authenticity, by distinguishing those which he himself acknowledged from those which are ascribed to him only on the probable ground of internal Evidence, is certainly a valuable part of your undertaking. Permit me to observe that if Editions should be multiplied, typographical Omissions or alterations of the

[14] Echoing JB's "Advertisement to the First Edition", *Life* i. 6–7.

[15] *Life* i. 96.

[16] *Life* i. 237.

[17] *Life* iv. 351.

[18] "While in the course of my narrative I enumerate his writings, I shall take care that my readers shall not be left to waver in doubt, between certainty and conjecture, with regard to their authenticity; and, for that purpose, shall mark with an *asterisk* (*) those which he acknowledged to his friends, and with a *dagger* (†) those which are ascertained to be his by internal evidence. When any other pieces are ascribed to him, I shall give my reasons" (*Life* i. 112 n. 4).

discriminating marks might easily take place, which might tend in a great measure to frustrate your good intentions. Besides it would no doubt be gratifying to many of your Readers, to see at one view a complete catalogue of Dr. Johnson's Productions thus distinguished, and arranged in a Chronological series. Would it not be a real improvement to collect these together in a separate paper, and subjoin it as an Appendix to your Work. Where a number of these pieces is mentioned at once without particular observation, (as is sometimes the case,) they might easily be classed together with such references, as to render the insertion of them in the text unnecessary. This remark appears to myself one of the most important I have presumed to offer.

P. 97. It is objected by the great Critick there referred to, against the probability of Johnson's being the Author of the Verses on Lord Lovat's execution, that the word "Indifferently" is used in the sense of "without con[c]ern";[19] I leave it to your own determination whether the word "Indifferent" is not used by Johnson in this sense, in his Letter to Lord Chesterfield, p. 142;[20] and in his letter to Dr. Wetherell, Vol. II. p. 13. l. 20?[21]

P. 269. When I first read the account of his introduction to Mr. Thrale's family, I supposed that he then gave up his own lodgings,[22] and wished to know what became of Miss Williams. But in p. 274,[23] I find him again in his own house in Johnson Court, with Miss Williams and Mr. Levett as members of his family. I presume then that he resided at his own house or Mr. Thrale's occasionally, as inclination for the time directed. There is nothing extraordinary in his visiting Mr. and Mrs. Thrale in their Country Villa at Streatham; but it seems rather peculiar that he should leave his own house in the City, and sojourn with them for any length of time in the Borough of Southwark.[24]

P. 286.[25] "Mrs. Thrale the *Author* of that Poem." I am glad to have the sanction of your authority for applying the term *Author*

---

[19] *Life* i. 180. The critic was no doubt Malone.

[20] *Life* i. 262. Noted by Hill, *ibid.* 180 n. 1.

[21] *Life* ii. 425.

[22] ". . . he accepted of an invitation to dinner at Thrale's, and was so much pleased with his reception, both by Mr. and Mrs. Thrale, and they so much pleased with him, that his invitations to

their house were more and more frequent, till at last he became one of the family, and an apartment was appropriated to him, both in their house in Southwark, and in their villa at Streatham" (*Life* i. 493).

[23] *Life* ii. 4–5.

[24] The next item is deleted: "P. 279 [*Life* ii. 14]. last line but one, 'Sat *by* us,' should it not be, *beside* us."

[25] *Life* ii. 26.

to a female Writer. I look upon *Authoress*, *Poetess*, etc., as unnecessary affectations in language.[26]

P. 190.[27] What is the reason that so long an interval elapsed between Dr. Smollett's letter to Mr. Wilkes, March 16. 1759, and Barber's Release, which did not take place till Octr. 1760?

P. 288. Dr. Johnson has alluded to the worthy man employed in the Gaelic Translation of the New Testament.[28] Might not this have afforded you an opportunity of paying a proper tribute of respect to the memory of the Rev. Mr. James Stuart, late Minister of Killin, distinguished by his eminent Piety, Learning and Taste. The amiable simplicity of his life, his warm Benevolence, his indefatigable and successful exertions for civilizing and improving the Parish of which he was Minister for upwards of 50 Years, entitle him to the gratitude of his Country, and the veneration of all good men. It would certainly be a pity if such a Character should be permitted to sink into oblivion.

P. 331. "Tenth of October." Read November; see line 6th of this Page, and date of Johnson's letter.[29] This should have been put into the Errata; as also in P. 478, "*May* 8th," which is another Typographical Mistake; from the preceding and subsequent dates it should be April.[30]

P. 362. It may seem rather a deviation from the design of these remarks to enter into the merits of any of those Questions which were agitated between Johnson and his friends. Yet excuse me if I venture to suggest a reason for the concern expressed by Dives for his Brethren in the Parable, which appears to me at least more probable than that approved of by the great man and his Biographer.[31] May we not suppose that he had been active in leading

---

[26] SJ, according to Beattie, called Hannah More "the most powerful versificatrix" in the English language (quoted by Hill, *Life* iii. 293 n. 5).

[27] *Life* i. 348–50, 350 n. 1.

[28] *Life* ii. 28–29, the end of SJ's letter to William Drummond, the Edinburgh bookseller. JB quotes Campbell's remarks, with minor revision, n. 2.

[29] Corrected, *Life* ii. 110. For the sixth line of p. 331, see the last line of ii. 109.

[30] *Life* ii. 349. Noted by Hill, n. 2.

[31] On the subject of friendship in a future state: "JOHNSON. . . . 'We shall either have the satisfaction of meeting our friends, or be satisfied without meeting them.' BOSWELL. 'Yet, Sir, we see in scripture, that Dives still retained an anxious concern about his brethren.' JOHNSON. 'Why, Sir, we must either suppose that passage to be metaphorical, or hold with many divines, and all the Purgatorians, that departed souls do not all at once arrive at the utmost perfection of which they are capable.' BOSWELL. 'I think, Sir, that it is a very rational supposition.' JOHNSON. 'Why yes, Sir; but we do not know it is a true one'" (*Life* ii. 162).

his Brethren into wickedness, or in preventing their reformation; he therefore did not wish to meet with them in the place of Torment, from a conviction that their presence there would only serve to aggravate his own misery?

VOLUME II. pp. 184, 293.[32] May I be permitted again to dissent from the opinion of the ingenious COUNSEL, and the decision of the venerable Judge, and to give in a *Reclaiming Petition*,[32a] requesting another Hearing for Dr. Parnell? I would then beg leave to offer in behalf of my Client, that the apparent inconsistency arises from the ambiguity of the word "knew," and the different acceptations in which the words "know," and "knowledge" are used in common language. If it is maintained that these terms are always used in so unlimited a sense as to extend to every species and degree of acquaintance with things, by whatever means attained, then the Cause must be given up, and the sentence irreversibly established. But do we not find that in ordinary Speech, some kinds or degrees at least of knowledge are considered as so small and mingled with so much uncertainty and error, as hardly to deserve that name? Particularly that knowledge of human Nature and human Life which is derived from Books and Speculation is generally reckoned so defective and erroneous, as to render the mere *Scientific* in some measure the object of commiseration or Ridicule. On the contrary that acquaintance with Mankind which is acquired by actual observation and commerce with Society, is held so far superior to the other as to be dignified exclusively with the apellation of "the knowledge of the World." Now our Hermit, it is supposed was deeply conversant with Books, but his *knowledge of real Life**
was derived only from those few Swains who nightly resorted to his Cell. He therefore wished to extend his sphere of observation, to view Society in its different aspects, that thus, when he should "know the world by sight," those doubts which he had entertained

* "A man of a great deal of knowledge of the world, fresh from life, not strained through books." Dr. Johnson. See his *Life*, Vol. I. p. 49.[33]

[32] *Life* iii. 220, 392–93, on a controversial passage in Parnell's *Hermit*. See *ante* To Malone, 20 Mar. 1793.

[32a] "A reclaiming bill or petition is a written pleading stating the grounds on which a judgement of the Lord Ordinary or of the whole Court is expected to be altered" (Robert Bell, *Dictionary of the Law of Scotland*, 1807).

[33] *Life* i. 105. Said by SJ of the Irish painter, *ante* n. 11.

might be cleared, and he might attain to just apprehensions of the ways of God and the Characters of men.

P. 188.[34] I cannot find "Lord Trimblestown" in my Almanack amongst the Irish Peers. Very probably it is an Omission in that compilation.

P. 269.[35] In this page, Mr. Welch's Daughter is called Anne; in the next, Dr. Johnson calls her "Nancy," which in this country is the contraction for Agnes.

P. 280.[36] Might not a single page, or part of one, have been spent without any impropriety in giving some of the circumstances of Garrick's Death, who was so eminent a man, and so intimate a friend of Johnson. Many of your Readers will never have access to see any account of him.

P. 515.[37] Upon the principle of truth-telling which Johnson himself avowed, and on which you yourself have acted in reporting freely so many of his Sentiments and sayings, is there any great reason for wishing that Mrs. Thrale had concealed that expression, "vile agents etc.," supposing him to have really used it?

Since these Remarks were written, it has occurred to me to inquire if you know who the Clergyman in the Bishopric of Durham was, to whom David Hume declared, that "he had never read the New Testament with attention." Vol. I. p. 276.[38] This anecdote is repeated by Johnson; and I own it gave me great satisfaction to learn, that so acute and keen an enemy of Christianity had never been at pains to make himself acquainted with that Religion which he so zealously attacked. In this light, the fact appears to me of great importance, and it must be very desirable that its authenticity should rest on the firmest foundation. Might not the name of the Clergyman be inserted with propriety in the next edition?

---

[34] "When we were at tea and coffee, there came in Lord Trimlestown, in whose family was an ancient Irish peerage, but it suffered by taking the generous side in the troubles of the last century" (*Life* iii. 227). The spelling of the name was corrected in the third edition. By "suffered" JB refers to the fact that the title was forfeited in 1641.

[35] *Life* iii. 217, 218.

[36] *Life* iii. 371, JB's letter to SJ, 2 Feb. 1779, commenting on the death of Garrick.

[37] "Mrs. Thrale has published, as Johnson's, a kind of parody or counterpart of a fine poetical passage in one of Mr. Burke's speeches on American Taxation. It is vigorously but somewhat coarsely executed; and I am inclined to suppose, is not quite correctly exhibited. I hope he did not use the words '*vile agents*' for the Americans in the House of Parliament; and if he did so, in an extempore effusion, I wish the lady had not committed it to writing" (*Life* iv. 317-18).

[38] *Life* ii. 9.

I suspect I have already trespassed too much upon your patience. I shall therefore only add, that I am with esteem, Sir, Your most Obedient humble Servant

JOHN CAMPBELL

P.S. My address is, Minister of Kippen by Stirling.

From Richard Owen Cambridge, Spring 1793[1]

MS. Yale (M 146:6). In the hand of an amanuensis. Printed, *Life* iv. 195–96.

ENDORSEMENT: Communication from Richard Owen Cambridge Esq. Pray return this.

Johnson ask'd Mr. Cambridge if he had read the Spanish translation of Sallust, said to be written by a Prince of Spain, with the assistance of his Tutor, who is professedly the author of a Treatise annexed on the Phoenician language.

Mr. Cambridge commended the work particularly as he thought the Translator understood his Author better than is commonly the case with Translators. But said, He was disappointed in the purpose for which he borrow'd the book[:] To see whether a Spaniard could be better furnishd with Inscriptions from monuments coins or other antiquities which he might more probably find on a coast so immediately opposite to Carthage than the Antiquarians of any other countries. Johnson. "I am very sorry you was not gratified in your expectations." Cambridge. "The Language would have been of little use as there is no History existing in that tongue to ballance the partial accounts which the Roman writers have left us." Johnson. "No Sir. They have not been *partial*. They have told their own story without shame or regard to equitable treatment of their injured enemy. They had no compun[c]tion no feeling for a

---

[1] This contribution was received too late for inclusion in the text of the second edition, published 17 July 1793. It appears, along with the last of Dr. Maxwell's "Collectanea", sent to JB 4 May 1793 (next letter), among the "Additions to Dr. Johnson's Life Recollected, and Received after the Second Edition was Printed" prefixed to the first volume, p. *xix. In the third edition it was placed among SJ's miscellaneous sayings, iv. 203–04. The manuscript was edited by another hand (which does not appear to be Malone's); on side 3 is written, in the same hand, JB's eulogistic acknowledgement to Cambridge, *Life* iv. 196.

Carthaginian. Why Sir, They would never have borne *Æneas's treatment of Dido if she had been any thing but a Carthaginian."

[In Cambridge's hand]

[*] If you should think, (for I dont exactly remember or see the difference) that He said *Virgil's* treatment, You'll put which of two you or Mr. Malone think best.[2]

Im sorry I could not make the whole shorter but, you'll print it or not as you chuse.

From the Rev. Dr. William Maxwell, Saturday 4 May 1793

MS. Yale (C 1991).

ADDRESS: James Boswell Esqr., Great Portland Street, London.

POSTMARK: MA 10 93.

ENDORSEMENT: Rev. Dr. Maxwell. 4 May 1793.

Falkland, May 4th 1793

DEAR SIR: Most sincerely do I thank you for the Hon[ou]r of your obliging letter, and the kind present you intend me, which I request you will please to keep for me, till we meet next Autumn. The Irish Edition, I hear, sold very well, tho' indeed not accurate; with Pleasure I read in our Parl[iamentar]y Debates, that you were Styled the *Illustrious Biographer*, and that too by Men of the 1st reputation.[1] Indeed I think, they are most entertaining Volumes, and highly Instructive too that have been exhibited to the Publick. I send you with this 4 Folio sides of *Johnsoniana*,[2] as nearly as I can possibly recollect *in his own Words*. I recollect these Anecdotes

---

[2] " 'Why, Sir, they would never have borne Virgil's description of Æneas's treatment of Dido, if she had not been a Carthaginian.' "

[1] JB is called the "illustrious biographer" (of Paoli, not SJ) by Patrick Duigenan (1735–1816) during a debate on the Catholic Bill, 4 Feb. 1793 (*The Parliamentary Register: or, History of the Proceedings and Debates of the House of Commons of Ireland*, 1793, xiii. 130).

[2] This last instalment of Maxwell's "Collectanea" (see *ante* 12 May and 16 June 1787, 17 Dec. 1789) was included in the second edition among the "Additions to Dr. Johnson's Life Recollected, and Received after the Second Edition was Printed" (i. *v–*x). In the third edition it was placed in proper sequence (*Life* ii. 129, line 15 following), but in the process the last two items of the group printed in the first edition became transposed.

since I sent you the former Papers. The Authenticity is Indubitable, and you may do with them what you please. They may afford yourself some little Amusement, whether you insert them or not in Another Edition. I am, Dear Sir, Your Oblig'd, Affectionate and Obedient Servant

WM. MAXWELL

From Edmond Malone, Monday 13 May 1793

MS. Yale (C 1927).

ADDRESS: James Boswell, Esqre.

ENDORSEMENTS: Edmond Malone Esq. May 13, 1793. A strange letter. *and* Answer Within.

[London,] Monday May 13. 1793

DEAR BOSWELL: You have an undoubted right over your own reputation, and to expose yourself in any way you think proper; but you certainly have no right whatsoever over the reputation of others. If therefore you should persevere in printing the wild Rhodomontade which by accident I yesterday saw at the press, as an addition to your new Advertisement,[1] I entreat, not as a favour, but a *right*, that you would cancel whatever relates to me in the former Advertisement:[2] for *noscitur a socio* is a very true[3] adage, and you cannot degrade yourself without injuring at the same time the characters of those whom you mention as your friends. Poor Sir Joshua is in his grave, and *nothing can touch him further*;[4] otherwise he could not but blush, that his name should appear at

---

[1] In his letter to Forbes, *post* 5 July 1798, Malone states that he had persuaded and helped JB to rewrite the original version of the Advertisement but was unable to restrain him from adding the (four) puffing paragraphs with which the Advertisement now concludes (*Life* i. 12–13). An offprint of what must have been a part of the original Advertisement is in the Yale Collection. It reads: "It is impossible for me an enthusiastic *Tory*, not to tell the world what I feel, and shall express with that reverential fondness which characterises

a true royalist. Soon after the death of my illustrious friend, HIS MAJESTY one day at the levee, after observing that he believed Dr. Johnson was as good a man as ever lived; was graciously pleased to say to me, 'There will be many lives of Dr. Johnson: do you give the best' [Journ. 20 May 1785]. —I flatter myself that I have obeyed my SOVEREIGN'S commands."

[2] *Life* i. 7–8.

[3] MS. "wise" deleted.

[4] Cf. *Macbeth* III. ii.

the head of a dedication, followed by such an Advertisement as the compositor has now in his hands. Yours always very sincerely in *private*, but by no means wishing to be *pilloried* with you in *publick*,

E.M.

To Edmond Malone,
Friday 17 May 1793

MS. Yale (L 945). JB's copy.

[London,] 17 May 1793

DEAR MALONE: I knew that Steevy's stabs had hurt you;[1] but I did not apprehend to that degree of irritation which your *hyper*critical letter indicated. I could make no answer to it; but just let it cool.

Jack Courtenay however came yesterday, and talked with calm and kind earnestness on the subject. I assured him as I do yourself, that I was fully satisfied you acted with real friendship towards me; but I could not help thinking very erroneously; for surely every man is at liberty to put himself forward in the style he likes best[2] and his praise of his friends in a very different style must not be confounded with his own personal Rhodomontade. But since mine for my second edition has struck you so strongly I am to submit the proof to John of Sarum[3] and let him decide. . . . I ever am "blow high blow low" with true regard very faithfully yours

[1] The reference is almost certainly to Steevens's strictures on Malone in the fourth edition of his Shakespeare, published this year. See especially the Advertisement. Steevens had fallen out with Malone over some of Malone's notes controverting him in the edition of Shakespeare superintended by Reed (1785), but he nevertheless urged Malone in the undertaking of his own edition. Shortly after it came out, JB warned Malone of Steevens's intended treatment of him (*Letters JB* 288). For Malone's reaction to Steevens's new edition, see *Johns. Misc.* ii. 24 n. 2, and Prior's *Malone*, pp. 121, 206.

[2] "There are some men, I believe, who have, or think they have, a very small share of vanity. Such may speak of their literary fame in a decorous style of diffidence. But I confess, that I am so formed by nature and by habit, that to restrain the effusion of delight, on having obtained such fame, to me would be truly painful. Why then should I suppress it? Why 'out of the abundance of the heart' should I not speak?" (*Life* i. 12).

[3] John Douglas, Bishop of Salisbury (see *ante* From Douglas, 16 May 1791). There is no journal, and no correspondence with Douglas, for this period.

From James Abercrombie, Friday 17 May 1793

MS. Yale (C 4).

ADDRESS: James Boswell Esqr., London.[1]

ENDORSEMENTS: James Abercrombie Esq. Philadelphia 17 May 1793. *and* Answer Within to this, and to his letter of 10 Octr. 1792.

Philad[elphi]a, May 17th 1793

DEAR SIR: Naturally of a sanguine disposition, I have been all my life time "condemn'd to toil in Hope's delusive mine,"[2] and, notwithstanding my frequent conviction of her treachery, am too often induced by her to promise myself the enjoyment of those gratifications which I most ardently wish for. Our London vessels are now all arrived, and none of them the bearer of a single line from you. This is indeed a source of the most poignant regret, and dis-appointment to me, having solaced the gloom of the last winter, with the pleasing expectation, that the earliest breezes of the spring, would waft an epistle to me from you across the Atlantic, in reply to a long one I addressed to you, under cover to Mr. Dilly, last autumn.[3] Yet, notwithstanding my chagrin on this occasion, I am induced to rely so far upon the benevolence of your heart, as, in direct opposition to the restraint which your unexpected silence should impose upon me, to venture, once more, to obtrude upon your attention some gleanings of information with respect to that great and good man, that *Unique* of writers and of moralists, your truly estimable friend Dr. Saml. Johnson. Before I enter upon it, however, I must tell you the result of my application to Mr. Odell, for the letter mentioned by Dr. Johnson in his to Dr. White.[4] Here also I experienced another instance of the futility of the promises of Hope. Mr. Odell thus replies to my application

---

[1] "entrusted to the care of one of the passengers on board the Pigou" (*post* From Abercrombie, 22 Aug. 1793).

[2] See *ante* From Adey, 21 July 1791 and n. 6.

[3] *Ante* 10 Oct. 1792.

[4] See *ante* 10 Oct. 1792 and n. 1. The Rev. Jonathan Odell (1737–1818) studied for holy orders in England, where he was ordained priest in 1767. He became an ardent loyalist, composing essays and verse satires against the American position, and served as liaison in the negotiations between British headquarters and Benedict Arnold. After the war he settled in New Brunswick, where he held the posts of registrar and clerk of the province, with a seat in the executive council (DAB).

It was not, my dear Sir, till within these few days past, that I had the pleasure of receiving your letter of the 10th Octr. a pleasure for which I lament that it is not in my power to repay you, by the communication of the letter you mention from the late Dr. Johnson. It is, alas! irrecoverably lost—a misfortune, which you will do me the justice to attribute to unavoidable circumstances, and not to inattention or neglect. For it would argue something more than a want of taste in any one who had shared in the happiness of Dr. Johnson's acquaintance, not to cherish the effusions of his pen, as relics, sacred both to Genius and to Virtue.

When you write to Mr. Boswell, to whom I have not the honor of being known, do me the favor to assure him of my regret on this occasion; and permit me, Sir, to avail myself of the same opportunity, to convey my part of the tribute of thanks and applause, due from the Republic of Letters, to Doctor Johnson's Biographer.

The information with respect to Dr. Johnson which I have alluded to, I obtained from a very worthy and intimate friend of mine, Dr. Benjn. Rush, Professor of Chymistry in the University of Pennsylvania;[5] who, knowing my[6] attachment to the writings and character of that great moralist, told me, that while he was in England, he once had the pleasure of dining in company with Dr. Johnson, he repeated some of the conversation which pass'd, and, at my request, committed it to paper, with permission to transmit a copy of it to you. It is as follows,[7]

[5] Benjamin Rush (1746–1813), the celebrated Philadelphia physician, received his M.D. from the University of Edinburgh in 1768. He became the first professor of chemistry at the College of Philadelphia in 1769, and professor of medicine at the newly organized University of Pennsylvania in 1791 (DAB).

[6] MS. "great" deleted.

[7] Abercrombie printed Rush's letter, or another copy of it, in *The Port Folio* (1804, iv. 393), with the prefatory remark that "Mr. Boswell received it with many thanks, and intended to insert it in his third edition of the life of his illustrious friend, Dr. Samuel Johnson. He lived not, however, to execute that

intention." That intention is nowhere indicated in the correspondence. Rush's letter is reprinted in L. H. Butterfield, *Reminiscences of Boswell and Johnson* (1946) and in *Letters of Rush* (ii. 632–33). Rush's *Autobiography*, composed several years after the letter to Abercrombie, contains another, less full account of the dinner (pp. 58–59). The copy sent to JB differs from the printed version in a number of particulars, some of which are given in the notes that follow. One omission from JB's copy is understandable enough:

A book [*Account of Corsica*], which had been recently published, led to some remarks upon its author. Dr.

DEAR SIR: During my residence in London in the winter of 1768,[8] I was introduced by our worthy countryman Mr. West,[9] to Sir Joshua Reynolds, who favor'd me a few days afterwards, with a card to dinner. At his table I met a group of Authors, among whom was the celebrated Doctr. Johnson. The day was to me one of the most memorable I passed while abroad, on account of the singular display which I witnessed both of Talents and of Knowledge. Dr. Johnson came late into company. Upon his entering the room, he found Sir Joshua consoling one of his guests under the pain he felt from having been handled very severely by the reviewers.[10] "Dont mind them" (said Johnson to the unfortunate author) "Where is the advantage of having a great deal of money, but that the loss of a little will not hurt you? And where is the advantage of having a great deal of reputation, but that the loss of a little will not hurt you?"

At dinner I sat between Dr. Johnson and Dr. Goldsmith. The former took the lead in conversation. He instructed upon *all* subjects. One of them was Drunkenness, upon which he discovered much of that original energy of thought and expression, which were so peculiar to him.

After the cloth was removed, Dr. Goldsmith addressed several questions to me, respecting the manners and customs of the North American Savages, which Dr. Johnson at last interrupted, by saying[,] "I'm surprized, Goldsmith that you

Goldsmith, addressing himself to Dr. Johnson, said, "He appears, Doctor, from some passages in his book, to be one of your acquaintances." "Yes," said Johnson, "I know him." "And pray, what do you think of him?" said Goldsmith. "He is well enough—well enough," said Johnson. "I have heard," said Goldsmith, "he is much given to asking questions in company." "Yes, he is," said Johnson, "and his questions are not of the most interesting nature. They are such as this— 'Pray, Doctor, why is an apple round, and why is a pear not so?' "
Rush's later and condensed version of the anecdote (*Autobiography*, p. 59) names JB. A flaw in the story is evident: Goldsmith, who had met JB in 1762 (Journ. 25 Dec.),

knew perfectly well of SJ's friendship with him (see, e.g., Journ., 23 Feb. 1766, when Goldsmith and JB go to call on SJ together). Mrs. Piozzi noted another version in her copy of the 1816 edition of the *Life* (quoted by Dr. Powell, *Life* iii. 519).

[8] In the print, 1769. Rush arrived in London from Edinburgh late in Sept. 1768 (*Autobiography*, p. 52).

[9] Benjamin West (1728–1820), the painter. He was born near Springfield, Pennsylvania, went to Italy in 1760 to study art, visited England in 1763, and remained there the rest of his life (DAB). In 1792 he succeeded Reynolds as President of the Royal Academy. See Journ. *passim*.

[10] Unidentified.

can ask the young man so many frivolous questions. I am sure none but a *Savage* could think of plaguing him so." "I'm sure Doctor," said Goldsmith, "that none but a *Savage* could interrupt a man so abruptly in his conversation."

The *Anemone Maritima* was named by one of the company, about which Naturalists have disagreed, whether it belonged to the vegetable, or animal kingdom. "It is an animal," said Dr. Johnson, "for its ashes have been analized and they yield a *Volatile* Alkali, and this we know is the criterion of animal matter, as distinguished from vegetable, which yields a *fixt* alkali." I was much struck with this remark, for I did not expect to hear a man, whose studies appeared from his writings, to have been confined to moral and philological subjects, decide so confidently upon a controversy in Natural History and Chymistry. The Doctr. delivered the prevailing opinion of the day upon that controversy, but some late experiments have proved, that it was erroneous; for, several plants have been found to yield a *volatile* instead of a *fixed* alkali.[11]

Doctr. Johnson was then drawn into a dispute with Mr. E. W. about the riot in St. George's fields; and the well known steps which were taken by Government to quell it.[12] Mr. W. condemned the conduct of government in very harsh terms, and said that Col[one]l —— of the Guards, had declared, that he could have suppressed the riot without firing a gun or killing a man.[13] "That may be," said Johnson, "Some men have a *Nack* in quelling riots which others have not, just as you Sir have a *Nack* in defending them which I have not."

I regret that I cannot gratify you by detailing the whole of the Doctors conversation during the course of the day. I should not have ventured after the lapse of near five and

[11] This last sentence is omitted in the print. For a present-day perspective on this controversy, see *Letters of Rush* ii. 634 n. 5.

[12] The riot took place on 10 May 1768 in protest against the imprisonment of Wilkes. See *Life* iii. 46 and n. 5. "Mr. E. W." is identified as "Mr. Eaton [i.e. Heaton] Wilkes, brother of Jno. Wilkes" in Rush's *Autobiography* (p. 59).

[13] In an abstract of a trial issuing from the riot, the following bit of testimony is

recorded (*Annual Register*, 1768, 3rd ed., p. 232): "that Col. West was there . . . he said he could have drove them all away without breaking their shins, there was no reason to hurt any of them." The Hon. George West (1733–76), second son of John, first Earl De La Warr, was colonel in the Army and captain and lieutenant-colonel in the 1st Regiment of Foot Guards in 1768 (Collins's *Peerage* v. 396; *Army List*, 1768, p. 47).

twenty years, to have given you the above from my memory,[14] had they not been impressed upon it by my having occasionally related them among my friends.

I concur with you in your partiality to the genius and writings of Dr. Johnson; and, after making some deductions from his character on account of his ecclesiastical and political bigotry, I am disposed to consider the single weight of his massy Understanding in the Scale of Christianity, as an overbalance to all the Infidelity of the Age in which he lived. With great regard I am, Dear Sir, Your Sincere Friend

BENJN. RUSH

22d April 1793

Dr. Rush tells me he once had the pleasure of dining in company with you at Sir Alexander Dicks.[15] He some time ago received from a particular friend of his, The Revd Mr. Hall,[16] who is Chaplain to the British Factory at Leghorn in Italy, some *original* Letters from eminent characters to Doctr. Smollet, who died there, and in whose trunk the said letters were found. Dr. Rush has deposited them as Curiosities, in the Museum of our City Library. The Letters are from Lord Shelburne, Mr. Pitt, Mr. Richardson, Mr. D. Hume, Dr. Armstrong, Dr. Hunter, Mr. Colman, Mr. Derrick, and one from yourself, Sir; together with an *original* letter from Dr. Smollet to Mr. Renner at Leghorn;[17] *all* which I

[14] Rush kept a journal of his stay in Great Britain and France in 1768–69, but the London record is missing (*Autobiography*, p. 58, n. 52).

[15] Sir Alexander Dick, Bt. (1703–85), physician, whose life JB "cherished a design of writing" (Journ. 13 Dec. 1775; see *Lit. Car.* p. 304). Rush was introduced to him by a letter from Benjamin Franklin c. 1766–67 (*Letters of Rush* i. 27 and n. 1). JB's journal records many dinners at Sir Alexander's, but Rush is nowhere mentioned.

[16] The Rev. Thomas Hall (*Letters of Rush* ii. 897 n. 4).

[17] Ten of these letters were printed in the first volume of *The Port Folio* (1801). Between Jan. 1800 and Jan. 1801 Hall donated "Original Letters of Hume, Robertson, Armstrong, Garrick, and John Gray, to Dr. Smollet" to the Massa-

chusetts Historical Society (*Proceedings, 1791–1835*, p. 136). In the appendix to vol. i of his third edition of Smollett's *Works* (1803), Robert Anderson printed the letters owned by the Society and reprinted those in *The Port Folio*. No letter from Derrick to Smollett has been recovered, and I suspect a mistake: Derrick for Garrick. A letter from George Colman, 28 Sept. 1770, one of five to Smollett now in The Free Library of Philadelphia, is printed in Lewis Melville, *Life and Letters of Tobias Smollett* (1926, p. 241). The letter from Smollett to Renner, his agent at Leghorn, is printed in *Letters of Tobias Smollett, M.D.*, ed. E. S. Noyes (1926, p. 109). The letter from JB to Smollett, 14 Mar. 1768, printed in Melville (p. 229), is now owned by F. W. Hilles.

have carefully copied. The substance of your letter to Dr. Smollet, is, the informing of him that you had just published your *History of Corsica*, and that you had been told by Mr. Douglas of Douglas, that Dr. Smollet had taken amiss what you had said of him in your book. 1st With respect to an *error* in Paoli's age, which you say had found its way into Dr. Smollet's *History*. 2dly Respecting an oath against the Republic of Genoa, which it was said the Corsicans took, but which Paoli assured you was altogether a fiction.

I take the liberty to enclose you a copy of the letter from Dr. Armstrong to Dr. Smollet; because, by a paragraph in it, you will I think be led to believe, that your censure of Dr. Smollet in your note upon his letter to Mr. Wilkes, in favor of Francis Barber, is perhaps not well founded. Is it not probable from Dr. Armstrong's letter, that Mr. Wilkes in the original publication of the letter, is in error; and not Dr. Smollet; Mr. Wilkes having mistaken in Dr. Smollet's hand writing, which is not very plain, *Cham* for *Chum*; as Dr. Armstrong distinctly writes it "the *Cham of Literature.*"[18]

In your *Life of Dr. Johnson*, Vol. 1st pp. 409, you say, that "Dr. Johnson had a great contempt for that species of wit call'd punning, but deigned to allow that there was one good pun in 'Menagiana,' I think on the word *Corps.*" Now, Sir, I have diligently searched the *Menagiana*, and conceive the following to be the pun alluded to. I request your opinion.

> Mad[a]me de Bourdonne, Chanoinesse de Remiremont, venoit d'entendre un Discours plein de feu et d'esprit, mais fort peu solide et tres irregulier. Une de ses amies, qui y prenoit interêt pour l'Orateur, lui dit, en sortant: Eh bien Mad[a]me que vous semble-t-il de ce que vous venez d'entendre? Qu il y a d'esprit! Il y en a tant, repondit Mad[a]me de Bourdonne, que je n'y ai pas vû de *Corps*. —*Menagiana*, Tom. 2d pp. 64, 3me Edi[tio]n a Amsterdam, 1713.[19]

I have just been perusing the Supplement to *The Gentleman's Magazine* for 1792, and most sincerely unite in Sentiment with Mr. Nicholls's Dublin correspondent Z. who annexes the following Postscript to his letter relative to the collection of[20] materials for

---

[18] See *post* To Abercrombie, 28 July 1793 and n. 18.

[19] See *post* To Abercrombie, 28 July 1793 and n. 19.

[20] MS. "of of"

publishing the Life of Sir Joshua Reynolds. "Mr. Boswell's *Histy of Corsica* has afforded me so much pleasure, that I should be happy to learn, that he proposed to favor the public with a History of his, (Sir Jos[hu]a Reynolds's) Tour to the Netherlands."[21]—Permit me to ask, Sir, whether you really have such intentions, and how soon you mean to indulge the world with the execution of them.

I am very anxious, Sir, to be informed by you, whether you have yet prevailed on The Lord Bishop of Salisbury to tell you, for what Clergyman Dr. Johnson wrote the Sermon you mentioned in your letter to me, and whether it, or any other of Dr. Johnson's works have been discovered, since you did me the honor to write to me.

My good friend Mr. Bond,[22] agreeably to my request, sent me out this Spring from England, two exceedingly fine engraved Portraits, one of you Sir, by Sir Joshua Reynolds, engraved by Jones;[23] the other of Doctr. Johnson, painted by Opie, and engraved by Townley.[24] They are of equal size, in similar frames, and I consider them the *best* ornaments of my *best* room. Dr. Johnson's portrait is one of the finest Mezzotinto's I ever saw, and has been admired with rapture by several of our first Connoisseurs. Mr. Bond joins me in opinion that it is one of the few which were struck off, before the plate was unfortunately destroyed, as mentioned by you in your list of the different likenesses of Dr. Johnson.[25]

I have the pleasure to present you, Sir, with three late publications, which may perhaps afford you half an hours entertainment. I have delayed the closing of my letter to the last day, in hopes of being able to transmit you a curious Dissertation on the Elements of written language, which lately obtained the prize medal of our Philosophical Society, and in which the author has some severe strictures on Dr. Johnson.[26] I perused it in manuscript and think it

---

[21] *Gent. Mag.* lxii. 1200; freely rendered.

[22] The fact that Abercrombie no longer attempts to conceal the name indicates that Bond had revealed himself to JB as the addressee of SJ's letter: see *ante* From Abercrombie, 25 Jan. 1792 and n. 6.

[23] See *ante* From Greene, 9 Sept. 1787 and n. 1.

[24] Reproduced, *Life* iii. opp. 245. For an account of the three states of this engraving, see *ibid.* iv. 462–63.

[25] *Life* iv. 421 n. 2 (p. 422).

[26] William Thornton, *Cadmus, or a Treatise on the Elements of Written Language*. The title-page announces the work as the "Prize Dissertation, which was honored with the Magellanic gold medal, by the American Philosophical Society, January, 1793". The book is a plea and a prospectus for a distinct American language constructed on a phonetic orthography, and takes to task the English grammarians, particularly SJ, for their "ignorance" and their "learned absurdities".

an ingenious tho an impracticable system; as, if adopted, it would render useless all the books which have already been written. Had the sailing of the Pigou been postponed a few days, I should have been gratified by sending you a copy by her, but as there are yet three sheets to be printed I must defer that pleasure till the next opportunity.[27]

An invincible desire of receiving frequent and long letters from intelligent correspondents, often leads me into error, by inducing me to scribble such prolix addresses. For the unwarrantable length of this epistle, I am sensible, Sir, that my powers of invention are inadequate to the task of forming a sufficient apology; I shall not therefore attempt it, but trusting to your benevolence for forgiveness, assure you that with the most perfect respect and esteem, I am, Dear Sir, Your most humble Servant

JAS. ABERCROMBIE

From James Sedgwick, Jr.,[1] Monday 3 June 1793

MS. Yale (C 2452).

ADDRESS: To James Boswell Esqr., 47 Great Portland Street.

ENDORSEMENT: Mr. James Sedgwick Junior.

19 Bedford Street, Covent Garden, 3d June 1793

SIR: I should apologize for the Liberty I take in addressing You, were I not convinced that the detail of any Circumstance relative to the Subject of it, however unimportant it may appear to many will not, by You be considered as triffling. If Mrs. Piozzi has represented Dr. Johnson as disinclined to do small acts of kindness, you have well defended him from the charge.[2] As a further vindication of this great and worthy Man, permit me to enclose You what I

---

[27] *Post* 22 Aug. 1793.

[1] Perhaps James Sedgwick (d. 1851), legal writer. He was the son of James Sedgwick of Westminster, matriculated from Pembroke College on 30 Oct. 1797 (but failed to graduate), and was called to the bar at the Middle Temple in 1801. According to his obituary in *Gent. Mag.* (xxxv, n.s., 436), he was born in 1775; according to *Alum. Oxon.*, in 1772. In

either case he was very young at the time of SJ's death; but it may be noted that he makes no claim to first-hand information in this letter. Two subsequent letters from Sedgwick, 14 Mar. and 1 Apr. 1795 (C 2453, 2454), concerned primarily with JB's proposing him for membership in, it seems, the Essex Head Club, will appear in another volume of this series.

[2] *Anecdotes: Johns. Misc.* i. 279-80; *Life* iv. 201, 344.

esteem a literary curiosity, it is probable you may never have seen it, as, that it was written by the Author of *The Rambler* is a Circumstance little if at all known. Dr. Johnson frequently visited at Mr. H——'s.[3] A[4] little time after his death (*Mr. H.'s*) Mrs. H—— mentioned one Evening before Dr. Johnson the necessity that the Shop-Card should be alter'd and her fears of not acquitting herself in the alteration to her own Satisfaction, he immediately offered to write one, she of course accepted the offer, and he wrote the Card I have enclosed.[5] It was written I beleive in the year 1783 as Mr. H—— died in that year.

Dr. Johnson inserted an Account of his Death in the Newspapers of that time, to the following purport. That he was a Man of unimpeached Integrity and unrivalled Skill, and brought the Manufacture of Glass to its present Perfection. And that his Chandeliers were sent abroad and exhibited in the palaces of paris as the Manufacture of France. He died 13th Feby. 1783. I have searched the Magazines of that and the following Month, expecting to find the Account copied into them but have not succeeded. However if you wish it I will endeavour to obtain a correct Copy of it.[6] —Your venerable friend was always highly delighted with the different vitreous Manufacture which were shewn him. "I love Glass" (said he) "it is a Child of our own."[7]

The following is another instance of the goodness of his Heart. Mrs. H—— served the Gloucester Family. The Duke[8] called one Day and ordered some Lustres desiring Mr. H—— to send such as he thought proper of a certain size. A Stranger called a day or two afterwards enquiring for some Lustres of a certain number of Branches of which they had not any. This person related at the Duke's that none could be had at Charing Cross of that description.

---

[3] Coleborn Hancock's (see n. 6).

[4] MS. "H——'s, a"

[5] Missing.

[6] Sedgwick's copy of the obituary notice is preserved in the Yale Collection. It is endorsed by JB: "Character of Mr. Hancock by Dr. Johnson inserted in 1783"; and reads: "April 1783. —On the sixteenth Inst. died Coleborn Hancock Master of the great Glass Shop in Cockspur Street Charing Cross after a very afflictive and tedious disorder. He was in his Manners a Man of unimpeached Integrity and in his Art of eminent and unrival'd Skill who did honour to his Country as a Manufacturer of Ornamental Glass. His Chandeliers were carried into France, and shewn to Englishmen in the palaces of paris as incontestible proofs of french Superiority." I have not discovered a printed source, which, one expects, would settle the conflict in dates.

[7] See SJ's detailed account of looking-glass-making in France, *Life* ii. 396.

[8] William Henry, fifth Duke of Gloucester (1743–1805), brother of George III.

The consequence was, he, being in the Trade obtained the Order and sent it in himself. Mr. H—— was then alive but unfortunately deranged in his intellects. Fearful[9] to lose the custom of the family, Mrs. H—— applied to Mr. Lowe[10] (who also was intimate there) to relate the Circumstance to Dr. Johnson and to beg the favor of him to write a Letter for her which she might send to the Duke. When Mr. Lowe mentioned it "Certainly my dear" (was the reply) "I will do it with all my heart." He immediately wrote one which was copied by Mrs. H—— and sent by the post to the Duke. Such was the prevailing power of his Language that[11] the Duke sent one of his pages in less than two hours after he receiv'd it to say "He was sorry it had so happened, that it was entirely without his knowledge And that he had given strict Orders that whatever Articles in their Trade he in future might want, they should supply."

He wrote also to Lord Southwell in behalf of Mr. Lowe, and in Answer obtain'd a promise from his Lordship to allow him £30 a year. This Answer was the Letter left at the Corner of Hedge Lane when You call'd with him in a Coach and which he said "was good News for a Man in distress."[12]

This Sybyl Leaf contains the few fragments I have been able to collect concerning a Man whose Memory above all others I revere. I wish they had been more—but your retentive Memory and accurate Research has left little unrecorded. I am willing to impute to a more amiable principle than Vanity the pleasure I feel in sending them to You. Should this letter inform You of what You had before known—Receive it, my dear Sir, as an uninterested Tribute of Gratitude from one, who thanks you from his heart, for the Amusement and Instruction he has received from Your writings. The engagements of intellectual Life give you I doubt, but little Leisure. I should be highly gratified however to hear that these

9 MS. "intellects, fearful"

10 Mauritius Lowe (1746–93), the painter. See *Life* and *Letters SJ passim*, and *ante* From Hector, 1 Feb. 1785, n. 3.

11 MS. "Language. That"

12 *Life* iii. 324. Peter Cunningham identified the "man in distress" as Lowe (*ibid.* n. 2). The point of SJ's writing to Lord Southwell in his behalf was that Lowe was the natural son of his father, SJ's "qualitied" friend, now dead (see *ante* To and From Barber, 15 July 1786, n. 42). That letter is untraced; but see SJ's letter to the Viscountess Southwell, written 9 Sept. 1780, less than two weeks after her husband's death, petitioning for a continuance of the allowance to Lowe (first printed by Malone in the fourth edn. of the *Life*, 1804, iii. 476–77; *Letters SJ* 705; the original MS. has been located by G. J. Kolb: see PQ, 1959, xxxviii. 382).

little Communications have not been unwelcome.[13] I regret that I am not within the Circle of your Acquaintance. But shall always remember with pleasure that I once subscribed myself, Dear Sir, Your most obedient and most humble Servant

JAS. SEDGWICK

J. Sedgwick Junr.

From *"Poll" Carmichael*,[1]
Friday 28 June 1793

MS. Yale (C 761).

ADDRESS: Mr. Boswell, No. 47 Great Portland Street, Oxford road.

ENDORSEMENT: Mrs. Carmichael.

St. Martins Street No. 25, Leicester Square, June 28. 1793

Mrs. Carmichael with most respectfull Compliments to Mr. Boswell hopes he is perfectly recovered.[2] Should Esteem it a particular favor he would Lend her his *Life of Dr. Johnson* as her Circumstances will not permitt her to be a purchaser at present. She having Dined Last Sunday with some Ladies who have had Great pleasure in reading it, which renewd in her mind a desire She has Long had of doing the Same hopes Mr. Boswell will pardon so Bold a request if he Should not Comply with it.

From *"Poll" Carmichael*,
Tuesday 16 July 1793

MS. Yale (C 762).

ADDRESS: Mr. Boswell.

ENDORSEMENT: Mrs. Carmichael.

St. Martins, July 16. 1793

Mrs. Carmichael with most respectfull Compliments to Mr. Boswel thanks him Sincerely for his Condesention, and so would

---

[13] They were not used.

[1] One of SJ's tribe of dependants; a "Scotch Wench" (*Thraliana*, p. 184). See *Life* ii. 215, 503, iii. 222, 368, 462–63,

and *Letters SJ passim*. She called on JB on 21 Apr. 1790, but the journal records nothing further of this meeting.

[2] See *post* To Churton, 26 July 1793 and n. 3.

Dr. Jhonson if there was a posibility of his knowing it. Her[1] friends had pleasure but She has been Delighted and thought she almost heard his very Voice. The Bearer will Bring Vol. 2 if Mr. Boswell should approve.

To the Rev. John Campbell, Friday 26 July 1793

Missing. Printed, *Letters JB* 316. MS. Yale (L 354): copy by James Ross.

ADDRESS: To the Reverend Mr. John Campbell, Minister of Kippen, by Stirling.[1]

London, 26 July 1793

REVEREND SIR, Your long, intelligent, and very obliging letter upon my *Life of Dr. Johnson*[2] gave me very great pleasure; and perhaps I should upbraid myself for not having thankfully acknowledged it sooner. The truth is that I was in hopes that a second edition of my work would soon be finished, and I wished to accompany my thanks with a copy of the book to which you have done so much honour. Unforeseen delays have happened; but at length a new impression corrected and augmented is come forth,[3] and I request your acceptance of a copy which will come in a parcel to Mr. Adam Neill, printer in Edinburgh,[4] who will deliver it to your order. I shall, however, send this letter in the meantime, hoping that you will be so good as to excuse my seeming inattention to so valuable a correspondent.

I agree with you, Sir, in regretting that my illustrious Friend's morbid melancholy darkened so much his views of religion, both with respect to himself and others. Your suggestions of a contrary tendency, and the instances which you mention are very consoling. But still it must be allowed that much depends on temperament;[5] and also that, however severely Johnson suffered from his anxiety concerning his future state, he erred on the safe side.

---

[1] MS. "it, her"

[1] Supplied from the copy.

[2] *Ante* 19 Apr. 1793. JB quotes himself in quoting Campbell, *Life* ii. 28 n. 2.

[3] The second edition was published on 17 July, having been in the press about a year. For an account of the publication and the disorganized state of this edition, see *Lit. Car.* pp. 167–69.

[4] Adam Neill (d. 1812), printer of JB's *Letter to Lord Braxfield* (1780). See Plomer; and Journ. 4 Jan. 1776, 28 Apr. and 1 May 1780.

[5] As Campbell himself allowed (*ante* 19 Apr. 1793, p. 521).

Your extraordinary and minute attention to the subject of my work entitles you to all the information or explanation that I can possibly give you, and it will afford me real satisfaction, if by answering the different particulars in your letter as well as I can, I shall in any degree contribute to your amusement.

It is true that Johnson received very inconsiderable sums for his two admirable imitations of Juvenal. But we must not argue from that circumstance that the profits arrising from his labours during the many years in which he "lived by literature"[6] were not sufficient to afford him a subsistence. Poetry is generally of less value in the *market* than almost any other species of writing; and we may be certain that the *work*, as it may be called, which he performed for Cave and others, much of which will remain undiscovered, was paid for, much dearer, when quality is considered. At the same time there is no doubt, that this great man was always in straitened circumstances, till the pension was granted to him.

Volume I.

p. 44 compared with p. 128. It is clear that I have inadvertently erred as to the date of his marriage by making it the year 1735, when it is fixed by his own inscription to have been in 1736. I have corrected this.[7]

The variation which appears as to the date of his wife's death, Vol. I mentioning 1752, and Vol. II, 1753, is owing to the difference of the old and new style. You know the year formerly began in March.[8]

p. 55, note. I am indebted to you for a very good hint. You will

[6] " 'No man (said he) who ever lived by literature, has lived more independently than I have done' " (*Life* i. 443). Cf. *ibid*. iv. 326.

[7] In the list of Corrections prefixed to the second edition: but the discrepancy went unresolved in the third edition. The correct date is 1735, not 1736, the true cause of the error being the printer's misreading of JB's ambiguous "5" in the MS. *Life* (Paper Apart "E" for p. 148). It is doubtful that JB consulted his manuscript before making the "correction", though the ambiguity is such that he could have misread his own writing; it is

certain that he did not consult his source —Barber's copy of SJ's inscription (*ante* 20 Dec. 1789)—for there the date is clear.

[8] JB had stated, *Life* i. 234, that the date 17 Mar. 1752 was Old Style. On the first day of 1753 SJ adopted New Style "which I shall use for the future", and on 28 Mar. he "kept this day as the anniversary of my Tetty's death" (*Diaries*, pp. 49, 50). When, in 1784, he arranged for a gravestone and inscription, he first recalled the year New Style (*Life* iv. 351–52), but later "rectified" it to Old (*Letters SJ* 1032).

find a chronological table of his Works with distinct marks, prefixed to my second edition.

p. 97. There is no question as to the adjective *indifferent*; the doubt is whether the adverb *indifferently* can be properly used in the sense of *without concern*.[9]

p. 269. Mr. Thrale's house in the Borough of Southwark was at a considerable distance from Johnson's own; and was so much more agreable on many accounts that there is no wonder he spent much of his time there.

p. 190. Probably Francis Barber is mistaken as to the time of his release. I have struck out what he told me.[10]

p. 288. I have introduced your character of the worthy translator of the New Testament into Erse.

p. 331. October is corrected to November in my Errata.[11] I am sorry I have omitted to mention April for May in p. 478.

p. 362. Your supposition may also be allowed. It is, however, selfish.

Volume II.

pp. 184, 293. Your argument is ingenious; but still the *inaccuracy* of *expression* must remain. You will find Mr. Malone on the same side with you in my second edition.[12] I have tried several acute friends, by propounding my objection to the passage. They have all defended it in a different manner.

p. 188. Lord Trimblestown's peerage was forfeited. I have mentioned[13] his family having suffered.

p. 269. In Scotland "Nancy" is used for Agnes; but in England for Anne.

p. 280. Garrick was not so intimate a friend of Johnson as he should have been. His death was not attended with any remarkable circumstances.

p. 515. I object to reporting the phrase "vile agents," even if used by Johnson in the heat of party spirit, because Mr. Burke was a zealous friend to him.

[9] See *Life* i. 180 n. 1, and OED, "Indifferently", 3.

[10] See *ante* To and From Barber, 15 July 1786, n. 13, and From Reed, c. Nov. 1792 and n. 18.

[11] Corrections, i. 567, line 17.

[12] ii. 611 n. 6, on *swains alone*. See *ante* To Malone, 20 Mar. 1793 and n. 1.

[13] In the first edition. Malone noted in the third edition (*Life* iii. 227 n. 3) that the attainder had since been reversed and the peerage restored.

I am sorry I did not endeavour to be informed *who* was the clergyman in the bishoprick of Durham to whom Mr. David Hume owned that he had never read the New Testament with attention, as Johnson informed me.

I have thus, Sir, done my best to comply with the desire of your letter, for which I again thank you; and I shall be most ready, upon every occasion, to prove to you with what grateful regard I am, Reverend Sir, Your much obliged humble servant,

JAMES BOSWELL

P.S. My *Journal of a Tour to the Hebrides with Dr. Johnson* will also come to you, as it is indeed a part of his Life written by me.

To the Rev. Ralph Churton, Friday 26 July 1793

Missing. Transcribed from a photostat of the original, which, in 1950, was in the estate of Gabriel Wells. MS. Yale (L 370): a copy by James Ross, headed by JB: "To The Reverend Mr. Ralph Churton."

ADDRESS: To The Reverend Mr. Ralph Churton with a parcel.

ENDORSEMENT: (waited with the books for my return to College. Recd. Sept. 18. Ans. 20.).

London, 26 July 1793

REVEREND SIR: You will now be pleased to accept of a copy of the second edition of my *Life of Dr. Johnson* corrected and augmented, and I flatter myself that as you thought so favourably of the Work before, you will now be still more pleased with it.

You have laid me under additional obligations by the presents of your sermon on the General Fast,[1] and of the late venerable Dr. Townson's *Evangelical History from the interment to the ascension of our Saviour*, with your excellent Account of the Authour.[2] I have read all of them with more than ordinary satisfaction. They indeed served as cordials to me, while I was under confinement, in consequence of having been knocked down, cut and bruised by one of those street robbers with which London has been grievously in-

[1] *A Sermon, preached before the University of Oxford . . . on Friday, April 19, 1793, being the day appointed for a General* Fast.
[2] See *ante* From Churton, 10 Apr. 1792, n. 3.

fested this year.[3] I am now I thank GOD greatly recovered, though I have not yet regained my usual strength.

You have made me so well acquainted with Dr. Townson's character, that I regret much my never having seen him; and though you tell me, that an interview with yourself will disappoint me, I am very desireous to try; for you appear from your writings to be so much a man according to my own heart, that I cannot doubt of being happy in your society. Believe me to be most sincerely, Reverend Sir, your much obliged humble servant

JAMES BOSWELL

To the Rev. Charles Edward De Coetlogon, Friday 26 July 1793

MS. Yale (L 408). JB's copy, headed: "To The Reverend Mr. C. E. De Coetlogon."

Great Portland Street, 26 July 1793

REVEREND SIR: Before I was favoured with your letter, the first impression of my *Life of Dr. Johnson* was disposed of; and I hoped long e'er now to have had a second edition finished. I waited for that, to acknowledge the very obliging terms in which you are pleased to speak of my Work, that I might at the same time request your acceptance of a copy of it corrected and augmented, which I now send, trusting that you will be assured I have not been neglectful of the attention shewn me by a Gentleman who must not suppose that he is unknown to his most obedient humble servant

---

[3] "Last Wednesday night as James Boswell, Esq. was returning home from the city, he was attacked in Titchfield street, knocked down, robbed, and left lying in the street quite stunned, so that the villain got clear off. A gentleman happening to pass that way, with the assistance of the watchman and patrole, conducted him safe to his house in Great Portland-street, when it was found he had received a severe cut on the back part of his head, and a contusion on both his arms; he has ever since been almost constantly confined to his bed with a considerable degree of pain and fever" (*London Chronicle*, 8–11 June).

To James Abercrombie,
Sunday 28 July 1793

MS. Yale (L 2). A copy by James Ross.[1] Printed (from the original, now untraced), *The Port Folio*, 1801, i. 10.

London, July 28. 1793

DEAR SIR: I have this very day received your packet containing[2] your letter of 17[3] May and as a Vessel sails for Philadelphia tomorrow I shall not delay till that morrow,[4] to express my sincere thanks for your accumulated favours.

I am very sorry that you have experienced any uneasiness at not hearing from me in answer to your obliging letter of 10[5] Octr. 1792, which came safe to my hands together with Mr. Hopkinsons *Miscelleaneous Works* and the Magazine giving an account of that gentleman. The truth is, I delayed writing to you again, till I could send you the second edition of my *Life of Dr. Johnson* which I supposed would be ready long before this time; but it has been retarded by various causes; one of which you will not regret, I mean my having had some valuable additions lately communicated to me. The Work is at length finished, and you will be pleased to receive your copy of it *from the Authour*. It will be accompanied with Mr. Youngs Criticism on Grays celebrated *Elegy*, in imitation of Dr. Johnsons manner[6] which I persuade myself will entertain you a good deal.

I think a kind of national modesty in a *Young race* if I may so express myself has led you to rate your Countryman Hopkinson[7] lower than he deserves.[8] I do not mean to estimate him as a first rate Genius, but surely he had good abilities, and a wide and various range of application. I have not time to consider the Writings which you have kindly sent me with your last letter so as to give any opinion upon them by this opportunity. But I shall certainly presume to tell you in a future letter what I think of them. I shall be glad to have the curious Dissertation on the Elements of writ-

---

[1] The copy is on the whole superior to the print.

[2] *Port Folio*, "concerning"

[3] *Port Folio*, "17th"

[4] *Port Folio*, "till that morrow" omitted.

[5] *Port Folio*, "10th"

[6] See *ante* From Abercrombie, 10 Oct. 1792, p. 493.

[7] *Port Folio*, "Hopkinson" omitted. But to no avail, the editor having neglected to suppress the name in the second paragraph.

[8] *Ante* 10 Oct. 1792, pp. 491–92.

ten language though you mention that it contains some severe strictures on Dr. Johnson.[9] I am not afraid. I know what he can bear.

Mr. Agutters Sermon on his death has not yet been published.[10] Should it appear you may depend on my taking care to transmit you a copy of it.

I cannot warmly enough acknowledge the zeal with which you have exerted yourself in order to gratify me. I am verry sorry that Dr. Johnsons letter to your friend Mr. Odell is lost,[11] But that is one of the many evils occasioned by that unjust Civil War which I reprobated at the time when a bad Ministry carried it on[12] and now look back upon with a mixture of wonder and regret. Let us not however get upon that subject. I beg you may present my compliments to Mr. Odell with thanks for his polite[13] mention of me. I also beg to be respectfully remembered to Dr. Rush[14] who I am pleased to find recollects having met me[15] at the hospitable table of my old friend Sir Alexander Dick who was truly a *Corycius Senex*.[16] The Johnsoniana which Dr. Rush[14] has obligingly allowed you to send me have the characteristical stamp; and I like much the Doctors expression[17] "the single weight of Johnsons massy understanding in the scale of Christianity is an over ballance to all the infidelity of the age in which he lived."

You will find in my second edition a correction of *Chum* to *Cham* suggested to me by Lord Palmerston. I am glad to have it confirmed by the letter from Dr. Armstrong and should my Book come to another edition that confirmation shall be added[18] as shall your discovery of the pun upon *Corps* in *Menagiana* in which you are I think clearly right. You will find an ingenious conjecture concerning it in my second edition by an unknown correspondent.[19]

I have not yet obtained from the Bishop of Salisbury the name of

---

[9] *Ante* 17 May 1793, p. 538.
[10] *Ante* From Abercrombie, 10 Oct. 1792 (p. 493), and From Agutter, 17 Oct. 1792.
[11] *Ante* 17 May 1793, pp. 532–33.
[12] See Journ. and *Life passim*.
[13] *Port Folio*, "very polite"
[14] *Port Folio*, "Dr. Rush" left blank.
[15] Copy, "recollects me"
[16] Virgil, *Georgics* iv. 127, alluding to

Dick's horticultural accomplishments. See *Life* iii. 103, iv. 263 n. 1.
[17] *Port Folio*, "his expression that"
[18] It was added by Malone in the third edition (*Life* i. 348 n. 5).
[19] See *post*, p. 592 and n. 6. JB revised the note for the third edition to include Abercrombie's discovery, "which renders the preceding conjecture unnecessary, and confirms my original statement".

the Clergyman to whom Johnson gave a Sermon which was preached on the fifth of November; for that I find was the public occasion.[20] I will endeavour if possible to find it out.

Sir Joshua Reynolds Tour to the Netherlands is much better written by himself than I could do it, for it is I understand almost entirely an Account of the Pictures. It is to be subjoined to an edition of his *Discourses to The Royal Academy* which is now in the press under the care of that accurate Critick my friend Mr. Malone.[21]

By your name Sir, you must be of Scottish extraction. May I presume to ask how long your Family has been settled in America.[22] I have a great wish to see that Country and I once flattered myself that I should be sent thither in a station of some importance.[23]

I am with a very grateful sense of my obligations to you, Dear Sir, Your most obedient humble servant

(Signed) JAMES BOSWELL

To James Abercrombie Esq., Philadelphia

[20] See *ante* To Abercrombie, 11 June 1792.

[21] *A Journey to Flanders and Holland* was published as part of the first collected edition of Reynolds's works, brought out in 1797 by Malone, Sir Joshua's literary executor. See F. W. Hilles, *Literary Career of Sir Joshua Reynolds*, 1936, pp. 73–81.

[22] Abercrombie's father, James, was a native of Dundee and a relation of General Sir Ralph Abercromby (1734–1801). He was engaged in the East India trade, was an officer in the British navy, and settled in America in 1753. In 1760, two years after the birth of his son, he "was lost in the German ocean" (W. B. Sprague, *Annals of the American Pulpit*, v. 392).

[23] In 1789 Richard Penn had promised to make JB his secretary in the event that he was appointed ambassador to the United States (Journ. 3 Dec.). JB nursed the same ambition as early as 1783, when, in a letter to General Oglethorpe, 14 Feb., he exclaimed: "Let us not look back, but forward—and behold the grand prospect of Peace with our Bretheren of America and all its consequences! I have a warm wish to visit that Continent. Could I but have the honour to accompany Genl. Oglethorpe thither! Why are you not to be Ambassador to the United States? With what alacrity and satisfaction should I act as your Secretary." See also JB to Burke, 8 Mar. 1778 (*Letters JB* 182).

From the Rev. Dr. William Vincent,[1]
Tuesday 30 July 1793

MS. Yale (C 3042).

ADDRESS: James Boswell Esqr., Upper Portland Street.
ENDORSEMENT: 30 July 1793. Rev. Dr. Vincent.

Deans yard, July 30 1793

DEAR SIR: I thank you for Johnson.[2] —I have long been acquainted
with him, but never in so agreeable a Character as you introduce
him. I never thought him, in the very few hours I have seen him,
the man you describe, but I sincerely wish a good man, and a good
Christian to descend to posterity in an amiable light. —With many
thanks believe me, Your faithful Servant

W. VINCENT

From Bennet Langton,
c. Tuesday 30 July 1793

MS. Yale (C 1697). Headed by JB: "Bennet Langton Esq. from Warley
Camp 1793."

Accept, my dear Sir, of my best thanks for your welcome present;[1] it
is unnecessary to attempt explaining to you *how* welcome it must be
to me, to dwell on the Scenes of the Life of a Man, whom I so much
honoured[,] by whom I was so kindly regarded, Scenes in which
I had so frequent a share, and in the accounts of which the mention
of course is introduced of a Set of men eminent for their abilities,
with most of whom I was in a state of intimacy, and with some of
particular friendship. I have been of course rivetted to the perusal
and re-perusal of the Volumes by night and by day since their
arrival—a few mornings ago, it happened that the thundering
Morning Gun, which you were in such a state of fearful preparation for, surprized me not yet gone to bed, and if I was not at the
moment reading your book, it had at least been accessary to my

[1] William Vincent, D.D. (1739–1815),
classical scholar; Headmaster of Westminster, 1788–1802; Dean of Westminster, 1802. JB met with Vincent
several times, beginning early in 1790,
when he was preparing to enrol his son
James at Westminster (Journ. *passim*).

[2] The second edition. See *post* From
Wingfield, 31 July 1793, n. 1.

[1] Two copies of the second edition
(JB to Langton, 24 July 1793).

sitting up so late. —One thing, my dear Sir, occurs to me as I am writing, as a subject of regret, which is that I have never found an opportunity of requesting you to allow me the perusal of the Letters of thanks and praise of your Work that you have had the satisfaction of receiving, particularly the Letter you received from such a Man as Dr. Parr[2]—it must have been a high delight to me to see feelings and opinions so corresponding with my own so much better expressed, as they would of course be by him, and perhaps by many others of those who have writ to you, than I could presume to suppose my having the power of doing.

Now that I have given some vent to expressions, of admiration on this reperusal of your Work, and of the delight it has given me —let me take up an opposite task—that of pointing out some mistakes—wherein I am naturally led to one, that is in front of those communications of mine that you have judged proper to make use of, and which communications unluckily stand forward and prominent, as being premised to the mass of the work[3] and therefore should, you will allow me, be more than commonly correct, as well as good in their kind. I do not know whether it may not be the best way of managing what I have to say to tell you, that, on my being desired to lend the book, which I think need not be objected to in instances where it does not particularly appear that a copy of it would otherwise be purchased, (I speak of the unfairness it would be in me to lend a book that you had presented me with, unless the circumstances were as I have said that there seemed not to be an intention of purchasing it—and *then* I think it may contribute in no small degree, by diffusing its reputation to increase the chance of its being purchased, if occasions are taken of *so* lending it)—on lending the book, I drew up a corrected form of two passages, which I laid between the leaves,[4] as not chusing that my poor contributions should go out with their imperfections on their heads[5]—and this paper which I put into the book I will transcribe, and shall be glad to receive word of what occurs to you on the matter. The following is the Copy of it—

The Communication from Mr. Langton in Page Xth of the

[2] *Ante* 11 Dec. 1791.

[3] i. *x–xiii.

[4] One of these sheets of corrections is now owned by F. W. Hilles. JB had them hastily printed on a separate leaf (p. *xxxviii) entitled "Additional Correc-

tions", which was belatedly bound with the other preliminary matter of the second edition. See *Lit. Car.* pp. 158–59.

[5] Cf. *ante* From Churton, 10 Apr. 1792 and n. 1.

Additions to *Dr. Johnson's Life* premised to the first Volume, by some accident is very much mis-stated[6]—it should have been to the following effect.

> "On occasion of Dr. Johnson's publishing his Pamphlet of *The False Alarm* there came out a very angry answer (by many supposed to be by Mr. Wilkes). Dr. Johnson determined on not answering it, but, in conversation with Mr. Langton mentioned a particular or two, that, if he *had* replied to it, he might perhaps have inserted. In the Answerer's Pamphlet, it had been said with solemnity 'Do you consider, Sir, that a House of Commons is to the People as a Creature is to its Creator?' 'To this Question,' said Dr. Johnson, 'I could have replied, that, in the first place, the idea of a Creator,' "

—and so on, as it is in the printed book, down to the figure, "*3*", that refers to the Note in all which latter part the statement given by Mr. Boswell is correct.[7]

The Remark then, was not a general one, which it surely would have been unnecessary for Johnson to make, as containing only such very evident truth; but its excellence was in its particular application to what his Opponent had said.

In Page XIII of the Additions, there is a confusion in the statement of the Remark on the Shield of Achilles[8] which will be disentangled if we read it as follows, and as it should have been given—

> " '*He may hold up that Shield against all his enemies,*' was an observation on Homer, in reference to his description of the Shield of Achilles, made by Mrs. Fitzherbert Wife to Mr. Fitzherbert of Derbyshire and respected by Dr. Johnson as a very fine one. He had in general"

etc. as in the book.[9]

---

[6] " 'TALKING reverently of the SUPREME BEING, he uttered these sentences:

'Do you consider, Sir?

'In the first place—the idea of a CREATOR must be such as that he has power to unmake or annihilate his creature.

'Then it cannot be conceived that a creature can make laws for its CREATOR[3]' " (second edition, i. *x).

[7] Corrected in "Additional Corrections"; see *Life* iv. 30–31 and n. 1.

[8] " '*He may hold up that* SHIELD *against all his enemies;*'—was an observation by him on Homer, when referring to the description of the shield of Achilles, made by Mrs. Fitzherbert, wife to his friend Mr. Fitzherbert of Derbyshire, and respected by Dr. Johnson as a very fine one. He had in general a very high opinion of that lady's understanding" (second edition, i. *xiii).

[9] Corrected in "Additional Corrections"; see *Life* iv. 33.

WW*

I trust then, my dear Sir, that you will see the necessity there is
for explaining and correcting the Passages I have been noticing.
A few more mistakes I have marked—which I will enumerate—
"Bender," Vol. 2d. P. 37, should I have no doubt be, "Belgrade."[10]
Oglethorpe served against the Turks under Prince Eugene—and I
am almost certain that *He* never besieged Bender. Apothegm,
surely should be spelt Apophthegm.[11] —The Greek word Vol. 3d.
P. 360—is wrong printed—ευσροποι—which should be ευστροφοι.[12]
In Vol. 3d. P. 582. It is said that Mr. Burke stood forth in defence
of his Friend, which perhaps might be the case, but the Person
that I heard Johnson speak of as his defender on that occasion
was Mr. Fox, as I particularly well remember;—perhaps Mr.
Burke might also have come forwards.[13] Vol. 1st. 525—You
say Mr. Gibbon was chosen Professor of ancient Literature in the
Academy—having previously said that *that* was *my* Professorship,
—Mr. Gibbon's is—of ancient *History*.[14] Vol. 3d. P. 269—The
errour continues—of saying "it is well known that the Trial of
Lord Charles Hay never came on." The Trial did come on, and was
carried through—and, at the Time of Lord Charles's death, the
Sentence was probably according to the usual forms before the
King for his consideration.[15] In Vol. 2d. P. 274[16] The expression as
you give it from Johnson's Journal "little more than half as much
for" (In this erased part I had not at first taken the import right,
but, on a re-attention, my difficulty disappears.) —Vol. 2d. P. 284
—"Frenon," the Journalist, I am pretty sure should be *Freron*.[17]
—These I think are all the Errata I have observed—and have only

[10] Corrected in "Additional Corrections"; see *Life* ii. 181.

[11] The spelling of the second (and the
first) edition was changed in the third;
see *Life* ii. 348. "The spelling *apothegm*
was the more usual till preference was
expressed in Johnson's Dict. for *apophthegm*, which is now more frequent in
England. Webster adopts *apothegm*,
which Worcester also thinks 'perhaps best
supported by common usage' " (OED).
In the entry for "Apothegm" SJ remarks:
"[properly *apophthegm*; which see.]."

[12] This word was listed in the "Additional Corrections" and corrected in the
third edition (*Life* iv. 106 n.).

[13] Unchanged, *Life* iv. 318; but Langton was right: see *ibid.* n. 3.

[14] Corrected in the third edition; see
Life ii. 67 n. 1.

[15] Revised to read: "It is well known
that his Lordship died before the sentence was made known" (*Life* iv. 23). See
ante From Langton, 17 Dec. 1790 and n.
56–56.

[16] Page 273, last line; see *Life* ii. 396.

[17] Corrected in the "Additional Corrections"; see *Life* ii. 406. The name
appears correctly spelled in SJ's French
journal, *Life* ii. 392. The error in the
present case should doubtless be charged
to the printer: "n" for "r" is an easy
misreading of JB's hand. But as the
sentence in question was added to the
second edition, and no MS. has survived,
the theory cannot be tested.

remaining time to insert my Compliments and my Sons to the Young Ladies and Gentlemen—and those of all the Gentlemen of our Corps to yourself and am Dear Sir, Your faithful humble servant

B. LANGTON

From the Rev. John Wingfield,[1]
Wednesday 31 July 1793

MS. Yale (C 3143).

ADDRESS: James Boswell Esqr.

ENDORSEMENT: 31 July 1793. Rev. Mr. Wingfield.

Deans Yard, July 31st 93

SIR: I return you my best thanks for your last Edition of Dr. Johnson's *Life* and promise myself much entertainment from the perusal of it during our recess.

It would be superfluous in me to add anything in commendation of the work itself. The general approbation, which it has experienced in the world, is the best testimony of its merits. I have the honour to be, Sir, Your much Obliged and faithful Servant

J. WINGFIELD

From the Rev. James William Dodd,[1]
Wednesday 31 July 1793

MS. Yale (C 1090).

ADDRESS: James Boswell Esqr.

ENDORSEMENT: 31 July 1793. Rev. Mr. Dodd.

[1] John Wingfield (1760–1825), Under Master at Westminster, 1788–1802, succeeding Vincent as Headmaster. He became D.D. in 1799, Prebendary of Worcester in 1803 and of York in 1812 (John Sargeaunt, *Annals of Westminster School*, 1898, p. 211). JB visited Wingfield on 29 May 1790 to prepare the way for his son James's entrance and "found him to be an intelligent, civil man" (Journ.). According to L. E. Tanner (*Westminster School, A History*, 1934, p. 35), "The boys called him 'Grubby Wingfield', and he seems to have been singularly ineffective." On the same day as the present letter was written JB wrote to his sons: "I have presented the Provost, the Head-Master, and Under Master of Eton, and the Head Master, Under Master, and Mr. Dodd, Usher of Westminster, with the second edition of my *Life of Dr. Johnson*. It goes off wonderfully well." Of the six donees mentioned, acknowledgements have been preserved from all but two: George Heath, D.D., Headmaster of Eton, 1792–1802, and William Langford, D.D., Under Master of Eton, Canon of Windsor, and Chaplain to George III. See Sir Henry C. M. Lyte, *A History of Eton College 1440–1898*, 1899, pp. 361–63.

[1] James William Dodd (d. 1820), son of the actor of the same name (see DNB),

Dean's Yard, West⸢minste⸣r, July 31st 1793

DEAR SIR: I beg you will allow me to return my best thanks for your polite favour of the Books—which I had the pleasure of receiving yesterday—and from which I promise myself, with the greatest certainty, the most ample amusement. I remain, Dear Sir, Your Very Obliged Humble Servant

J. W. DODD

From Richard Owen Cambridge, after July 1793[1]

MS. Yale (C 731).

ENDORSEMENT: Mr. Cambridge.

Vol. 1 Page 362

The Translator of Drelincourt, finding his book had no sale, employd Defoe to write the Story of this pretended Apparition, and the book, from thence grew as popular as *Robinson Cruso*.

Vol. 1 489 *Beggars opera*

—— saved by the innocent looks of Polly in the Song *Oh Ponder well* when she came to those two lines which exhibit at once a painful and ridiculous *image*

> For on the Rope that hangs my Dear
> Depends poor Polly's life.

Vol. 2 Page 203

We may[2] believe Horace more when, confessing his Infirmity, he says,

> Romae Tibur amem ventosus Tibure Romam

than when he boasts of his consistency

> Me constare mihi scis et decedere tristem
> Quandocunque trahunt invisa negotia Romam.

---

was Usher at Westminster from 1784 until his death. He received his B.A., 1783, and M.A., 1786, from Peterhouse, Cambridge; became Vicar of Swineshead, Lincolnshire, in 1800, and Rector of North Runcton, Norfolk, in 1812 (Joseph Welch, *Alumni Westmonasterienses*, 2nd ed., 1852, p. 411). Dodd was JB Jr.'s private tutor at Westminster: see Journ. *passim*.

[1] This material first appeared in the third edition, in the form of (1) a note by Malone, (2) a revision of the text, and (3) an expansion of the text. Cambridge's references are to the first edition. See *Life* ii. 163 n. 4, ii. 368, and iii. 252.

[2] MS. "may" inserted by JB.

From Anne Gardner,
Tuesday 6 August 1793

MS. Yale (C 1333).

ADDRESS: James Boswell Esqr.

ENDORSEMENT: 6 August 1793. Mrs. Anne Gardner.

Park Street, August 6. —93

Mrs. Gardner's acknowledgements to Mr. Boswell for his attention to her, in adding *his note* to the paragraph in the *Life of Dr. Johnson* on her late dear Father,[1] whose memory is so justly revered by her. Had Dr. Johnson *really* known him he could not even *in joke* have spoke so very lightly of so good a man—and his humanity would have suffered if he had known that by that lightness he was giving a lasting wound to the feelings of an affectionate daughter.

Mrs. Gardner adds her best wishes for Mr. Boswell's health and happiness, which must ever be interesting to those who have the pleasure of his acquaintance, or the perusal of his works.

From John Hoole,
Tuesday 6 August 1793

MS. Yale (C 1550).

ADDRESS: To James Boswell Esq., No. 47, Great Portland Street, Oxford Street, London.

ENDORSEMENT: 6 August 1793. John Hoole Esq.

Hazel Hall by Guildford, 6th August 1793

DEAR SIR, I am much obliged by your very kind attention in the letter forwarded to me by Mr. Dilly, which did not come to my hands till yesterday, being sent by him in a parcel to my Sister in Kent, where I resided last year, but which I have left some time and have since been in Surrey,[1] which circumstance I imagine slipt Mr.

---

[1] See *ante* From Gardner, 22 Dec. 1791.

[1] After resigning from the India House late in 1785, Hoole retired in Apr. 1786 with his wife and son, the Rev. Samuel Hoole, to the parsonage at Abinger, Surrey. "He afterwards lived at Tenterden, Kent, with his aged mother and two sisters" (DNB).

Dilly's memory. I was some time in Guildford and have, for about two months past, settled my habitation at this place, in a most pleasant but retired country.

Accept my best thanks, my good Sir, for your kind and most valuable present and you may be sure I will take care and insert in the blank page the name of Mr. Boswell to whom I am indebted for this testimony of his regard and for so valuable a memorial of my ever respected Friend.

I congratulate you on your happy recovery from your alarming attack in the streets. I hope you know I made inquiry after your health, when I was last in town, and am very sorry that my very short stay prevented my seeing you. I am, Dear Sir, With Mrs. Hooles compliments, Your obliged and obedient Servant

JOHN HOOLE

Compliments to the Ladies.

From James Abercrombie, Thursday 22 August 1793

MS. Yale (C 5).

ADDRESS: James Boswell Esqr., London.

ENDORSEMENT: James Abercromby Esq. Philadelphia August 22. 1793.

Philad[elphi]a, Augt. 22d 1793

DEAR SIR: I have now the pleasure to present you, agreeably to promise, with The Essay on the elements of written language;[1] a performance in which you may possibly discover something worthy of commendation, but certainly will find much to censure, particularly the criticism on the style and principles of your illustrious friend. Dr. Thornton's system is doubtless an ingenious one, but I imagine altogether impracticable.

You are, before this time I trust, Sir, in possession of the packet which I entrusted to the care of one of the passengers on board the Pigou.[2]

With the exhilarating expectation of being soon honor'd by an epistle from you, I remain with sincere respect and esteem, Dear Sir, Your most humble Servant

JAS. ABERCROMBIE

[1] See *ante* 17 May 1793 and n. 26.   [2] *Ante* 17 May 1793.

From the Rev. Charles Edward De Coetlogon, ?August 1793

MS. Yale (C 918).

ADDRESS: James Boswell Esqr., Great Portland street.

ENDORSEMENT: Rev. Mr. C. E. De Coetlogon 1793.

Thursday, Lg[1] Place

SIR: On my Return from a little Excursion into the Country, I find myself favoured with your polite Civility;[2] for which you will have the goodness to accept my respectful Acknowledgments, and believe me, Sir, Your much obliged humble Servant

C. E. De COETLOGON

From the Rev. Thomas Stedman,[1] Monday 2 September 1793

MS. Yale (C 2537).

ADDRESS: To James Boswell Esqr., to be left at Mr. Dilly's in the Poultry, London.

POSTMARK: SE 5 93.

ENDORSEMENT: 2 Septr. 1793. Rev. Mr. Thomas Stedman Vicar of St. Chad's Shrewsbury.

Shrewsbury, Sept. 2d 1793

SIR: You have pleased and edified me so much by the second Edition of your admirably well written *Life of Dr. Johnson*, that I am willing you should know it, and at the same time am desirous of testifying my respect and gratitude. I have therefore desired Mr. Longman[2] to deliver to you a Copy of Dr. Doddridge's *Letters*,[3] which I hope you will do me the honour to accept. Whilst I was engaged in reading the *Life* an Episcopal Friend of your's called

---

[1] MS. doubtful: perhaps "LG" (Lower Grosvenor Place?). De Coetlogon was chaplain to Lock Hospital in Grosvenor Place in 1793 (*Royal Kalendar*, 1793).

[2] See *ante* 26 July 1793.

---

[1] The Rev. Thomas Stedman (c. 1747–

1825), B.A. and M.A. Pembroke College, Oxford, 1787; Vicar of St. Chad, Shrewsbury, 1783–1825 (*Alum. Oxon.*).

[2] See *ante* From W. Strahan, 1 June 1785 and n. 4.

[3] *Letters To and From ... Philip Doddridge ... Published with Notes ... by T. Stedman*, Shrewsbury, 1790.

upon me—to whom I mentioned it.[3a] He desired to see it—then to have it—and while I was deliberating, drew out his purse and put down the price of it. I could not deny his request, tho' I had written some remarks in it, and had considerably enlarged the Index. I wish I had thought of it in time to have communicated to you some Anecdotes of different persons mentioned in the Account. I hope you will now favour us with your *own Life*, after the manner of several Biographers, which would be peculiarly interesting and instructive.

You will find in Doddridge's *Letters* one written by the poet Blair,[4] whom you notice in your 2d Volume.[5]

I shall long to see Walton's *Lives* republished by Mr. Boswell.[6] Mention is made of them in an Account of Dr. Townson, lately published by Mr. Churton of Oxford.[7]

If I knew how to direct to Mr. Home (ii. 547)[8] I should be disposed to send him for his Account some Letters written by several Scotch Noblemen to Dr. Doddridge concerning the Civil War in 1745. Indeed I have many Letters to him from divers of the Scotch Nobility, of whom I should be glad to receive some information. Wishing your health, and much enjoyment from your useful labours, I am, Sir, with much respect, Your obliged and very humble servant

THOMAS STEDMAN

I much wish to procure the print of Dr. Johnson prefixed to the 4to Edition of the *Life*,[9] if it may be had separately, to add to my Illustrious Heads, especially to a Collection of portraits of eminent

[3a] Probably Bishop Percy, who was very interested in changes made for the second edition. He and Stedman both came from Bridgnorth, Shropshire (*Alum. Oxon.*).

[4] Letter LXXIX, p. 253. Dated Athelstaneford, 25 Feb. 1741/42, it requests a reading of his MS. poem, "The Grave" (published in 1743).

[5] *Life* iii. 47–48.

[6] "Pray get for me all the editions of 'Walton's Lives.' I have a notion that the republication of them with Notes will fall upon me, between Dr. Horne and Lord Hailes" (JB to SJ, 4 Apr. 1777: *Life* iii. 107). Cf. JB to SJ, 30 Aug. 1774: *Life* ii. 283–84. Malone noted in the third edition: "None of the persons here

mentioned executed the work which they had in contemplation. Walton's valuable book, however, has been correctly republished in quarto, with notes and illustrations, by the Rev. Mr. Zouch" (quoted, *Life* iii. 488).

[7] See *ante* From Churton, 10 Apr. 1792 and n. 3. "He read Isaac Walton's Lives during his illness; with a view, no doubt, to trim his lamp and prepare for his Lord, by comparing his conduct with the examples of those meek and holy men, described by the pleasing and faithful biographer" (p. xci).

[8] *Life* iii. 162 n. 5. See *ante* From Anon., 10 Dec. 1792 and n. 10.

[9] *Life* i, frontispiece.

Men who were educated at Pembroke College Oxford; of which College I myself was formerly a member, and have since married a Niece of the late worthy Master.[10] Have you seen, Sir, the elegant and appropriate Epitaph for Dr. Adams? which I wish to see inserted in a future Edition of Dr. Johnson's *Life*.

From the Rev. Dr. Jonathan Davies,[1] Wednesday 11 September 1793

MS. Yale (C 895).

ADDRESS: James Boswell Esqr., to be left at Mr. Cadel's, Bookseller, strand, London.

POSTMARK: SE 12 93.

ENDORSEMENT: 11 Septr. 1793. Rev. Dr. Davies Provost of Eton.

Eton College, Sepr. 11th 1793

DEAR SIR, I am quite ashamed of having so long neglected to return you thanks for your obliging present of your new Edition of the *Life of Johnson* in three vols. Octo.; but I will tell you the real case, and then appeal to your goodness to excuse, or submit to your justice in condemning me.

When the books came, it was our Election week,[2] full of business; and on that account, had I discover'd that I owed them to your kindness I might not have been able to write; but I thought that my Bookseller, Faulder,[3] from whom I had the 4to. Editn.[4] had sent them for me to look at, and to return them, as He often does. Just as I found out my mistake, My Brother Provost[5] was going away, and desired that He might take them with Him to Denham

---

[10] Catherine Adams (c. 1754–96). The marriage was licensed 14 Dec. 1785, and among the witnesses was a William Adams, doubtless the Master of Pembroke. In 1804, as his second wife, Stedman married Jane Woodward, widow (*Shropshire Parish Registers* xvii. 1588, 1825, 1881).

---

[1] Jonathan Davies (1736–1809), Headmaster of Eton, 1773–91; Provost, 1791. On 17 Sept. JB visited Eton with Temple (who was preparing to place his son John James) and introduced him the next day to Davies, "whose vivacity pleased him much" (Journ.). See Lyte, *History of Eton College*, pp. 357 ff.

[2] "Year after year for some four centuries, the Provost of King's rode to Eton about the end of July, in order to take part in the election of scholars suitable for his college at Cambridge and of others to fill their places in the school" (Lyte, *op. cit.*, p. 57).

[3] See *ante* From S. Adams, 13 June 1787 and n. 4.

[4] That is, the first edition.

[5] Dr. Cooke (next paragraph).

(his Living near Uxbridge) for his amusement and family; He did not bring them back, till three or four days ago, with many thanks for the great entertainment they had afforded Him, and the strongest approbation of your labours, being of opinion that there was hardly any sentence spoken or written by that great man, but what ought to have been recorded.

I have receiv'd no less entertainment from what I have read, and think you have made very valuable additions; Dr. Cooke[6] form'd his opinion, not only from Dr. Johnson's works, but from having been in company with Him two or three times, when He was brought to Eton by Mr. Beauclerk.[7] He was happy in that respect; I am amongst those, who never had the pleasure of hearing or even seeing Him, which I have often regretted; but your works have introduced me to his acquaintance, and tho you wou'd say "Quid si Ipsum audîsses, quid si Ipsum vidîsses,"[8] yet by this second-sight, this second hearing, which you have given me so animated and lively, that regret is much diminish'd, to the great entertainment and satisfaction of, Dear Sir, Your very faithful humble Servant

JONATH[A]N DAVIES

From the Rev. Ralph Churton, Friday 20 September 1793

MS. Yale (C 789).

ADDRESS: James Boswell Esq.

ENDORSEMENT: 20 Septr. 1793. Rev. Mr. Ralph Churton.

Brasen Nose, Sept. 20. 1793

SIR, My absence from Oxford ever since July prevented an earlier acknowledgement of Your very valuable present of the Second Edition of the *Life of Dr. Johnson*, rendered still more agreeable by Your very kind and obliging Letter which accompanies it.[1] For both these You will now be pleased to accept my sincere thanks. I was not entirely ignorant of the many and interesting additions

---

[6] William Cooke, D.D. (1711–97), Provost of King's College, Cambridge, from 1772. He had been both a Fellow and Bursar of Eton.

[7] Beauclerk had a summer residence at Windsor, where SJ visited him (see *Life* i. 250). The visits to Eton, which I have

not seen recorded elsewhere, no doubt took place on these occasions.

[8] "What if you had heard the man himself, what if you had seen him": evidently a quotation, but I have not been able to locate it.

---

[1] *Ante* 26 July 1793.

made in Your Work, having seen the volumes at the house of a friend; who, having been highly gratified with a perusal of the first edition, was looking with avidity at the improvements in the second, and preparing to read the whole again with fresh pleasure. I am much concerned to hear of the dangerous assault and hurt You met with, and sincerely wish a perfect and speedy reestablishment of Your health and strength. The high regard You express for the excellent Dr. Townson and his works is extremely gratifying to me; nor is it certainly unwelcome intelligence that the account which I have given of that ever dear person affords some satisfaction to One who is in every respect so good a judge of biography. You are very kind in wishing for an interview, which I also much long for, and do not despair but it may sometime happen; though probably now that I am leaving Oxford (this day indeed) and going to reside at my living of Middleton,[2] I may be in London less frequently than heretofore. If I should come to town when You are there, I shall be happy to wait upon You, and it was not without regret that in one or two instances when I was in London lately, I heard of Your absence. Though I am quitting college, a line directed hither or to Middleton near Banbury will always find me,[3] and if in any way I can forward Your literary labours or otherwise serve You, it will give me great pleasure to do it; being very sincerely, Sir, Your much obliged and faithful humble servant

R. CHURTON

From the Rev. John Campbell, Saturday 21 September 1793

MS. Yale (C 750).

ADDRESS: James Boswell Esqr., [*deleted line of address illegible*] London.

ENDORSEMENT: Rev. Mr. Campbell at Kippen 21 Septr. 1793.

Kippen, Sept. 21. 1793

SIR: When I first committed to writing my remarks on your *Life of Dr. Johnson*, I must own I had no higher object in view, than a little temporary amusement to myself. I afterwards thought it incumbent upon me to transmit them, as a small tribute of respect

---

[2] The college rectory at Middleton Cheney, Northamptonshire, to which he was appointed in 1792 (DNB).

[3] No further correspondence has been recovered, nor is there any record of a meeting between JB and Churton.

and Gratitude, to the ingenious Authour, from whose labours I had derived so much entertainment. Your favourable acceptance of them would have much more than overpaid my labour, if the small trouble of transcribing these remarks, deserves to be dignified with such a name. But the very high remuneration with which your approbation of them is accompanied, so far transcends their intrinsic merits, that it only convinces me, that your Candour and Generosity as a Gentleman, are not inferior to those accomplishments as an ingenious and elegant Writer, which have procured you the admiration and applause of all the Friends of Polite Literature. The Volumes which you promised to send me, came to hand a few days ago in good order; and I cannot delay acknowledging with lively Gratitude, the signal honour you have conferred upon me, by so handsome a Present. Their value, intrinsically great, I must ever consider as enhanced in a high degree, when I view them as a testimony of regard from Mr. Boswell, the Friend of Johnson, and the Friend of Paoli.

The full and satisfying manner in which you have replied to my several inquiries and remarks, leaves me room only to express my grateful sense of the condescending attention with which you have honoured them. I shall certainly employ my earliest leisure in again going over a Work, every perusal of which, I am sure, will give new delight. If any farther observations should occur to me, or if I could be useful only in the humble task of detecting typographical Errata, I should willingly send them to you, if I were sure that the repetition of such minute communications would not excite disgust.

I am happy to observe that you have promised to favour the World with a complete Edition of Dr. Johnson's Poetical Pieces.[1] My retired situation precludes me from knowing what the Voluminous Edition of his Works consists of, beside those larger Productions with which the World has long been familiar. If those Biographical and Critical Pieces, which your Catalogue[2] mentions as inserted in the several Periodical Misscellanies with which he was concerned, are not included in that large Collection, I doubt not that the separate publication of them in two or three moderate Volumes, would furnish a most elegant and delicious Repast to the numerous admirers of Johnson, and indeed to all the Friends of

---

[1] *Life* i. 16 n. 1.
[2] "A Chronological Catalogue of the Prose Works of Samuel Johnson, LL.D."

(*Life* i. 16 ff.). The catalogue was Campbell's suggestion (*ante* pp. 523–24).

Literature. If such a Collection should be carried on under your inspection, the Public would be assured of its authenticity; and the Editor, I doubt not, would find his account in the undertaking.

The Justice, Sir, which the World has done to your Talents as a Biographer, must powerfully encourage you to continue your exertions in that pleasing species of Composition. Such another Subject indeed, and such ample materials as contribute to form the *Life of Johnson*, you can hardly expect to find. At the same time however, I am firmly persuaded that no Production will ever come from your Pen, which shall not promote your own Reputation, as well as "the instruction and entertainment of Mankind." Would not the Life of Lord Hailes be a desireable acquisition?[3]

Your kind proffer of personal regard I accept with real pleasure; and can only in return assure you, that I am with sincere Esteem and Gratitude, Sir, Your most Obedient humble Servant

J. CAMPBELL

From Claud Irvine Boswell,[1] Saturday 21 September 1793

MS. Yale (C 312).

ADDRESS: James Boswell Esqr., London.

ENDORSEMENT: 21 Septr. 1793. Claud Boswell Esq.

Balmuto by Kinghorn, Septr. 21. 1793

DEAR SIR: I was much pleased with receiving your handsome present of the *Life of Johnson* not so much on account of the Value of the Book as that I esteemed it a mark of your regard and friendship which believe me will give me singular pleasure to cultivate.

The Book I shall transmit to my Son[2] as a proof of our friendship and which I shall inculcate in him to keep up with your Sons.

I was very happy in seeing James. He is really a fine Lad[—] Boy I cannot call him; Sandie is no less so. You really have great cause to be pleased with your young Men.

[3] There is to this day no full-scale biography of Hailes.

[1] Claud Irvine Boswell (1742–1824), later (1799) Lord Balmuto; Lord Auchin- leck's cousin. JB found him an uncongenial spirit. See Journ. *passim*.

[2] John (d. 1863), who succeeded his father as laird of Balmuto. See Burke's *Landed Gentry*, 1952, p. 229.

All here join in best Compliments to you and the Young Ladys and I ever am Dear Sir, Very sincerely Yours

Claud Boswell

From John Perkins,
Thursday 26 September 1793

MS. Yale (C 2241). In the hand of an amanuensis, except for the street address on the address side.

ADDRESS: Jas. Boswell Esqr., Great Portland Street, Portland Place.

ENDORSEMENT: Mr. Perkins 26 Septr. 1793.

Park St., Southwark, Septr. 26. 1793

DEAR SIR, As I presume by this time you have properly used those letters of Dr. Johnson's, I had the honor of lending you last Christmass,[1] the return of those Memorials of my deceased Friend will much oblige—Dear Sir, Your most faithful and obedient humble Servant

John Perkins

To the Rev. Thomas Stedman,
Thursday 3 October 1793

MS. Yale (L 1185). JB's draft, headed: "To The Reverend Dr. Stedman."

London, 3 October 1793

REVEREND SIR: Owing to a variety of causes I have been prevented from sooner owning[1] the receipt of your very obliging letter,[2] and the present of the Collection of Dr. Dodridge's letters with which you have been pleased to honour me. I now gratefully acknowledge your kind attention to me.[3] Your approbation of my *Life of Dr. Johnson* in such strong terms gratifies me not a little; and I take the liberty to request that you will be good enough to let me have the remarks you have made upon it, and your anecdotes of

---

[1] There is no earlier mention of this contribution. JB inserted five letters from SJ to Perkins chronologically in the second edition: *Life* ii. 286, iv. 118, 153, 257, 363. Chapman prints twenty. See his article, "Johnson's Letters to Perkins," RES (1926) ii. 97–98. See also Mary Hyde, "Not in Chapman," *Johnson, Boswell and Their Circle*, pp. 316–17.

[1] MS. "acknowledging" deleted.
[2] *Ante* 2 Sept. 1793. MS. "and also of the present of" deleted.
[3] MS. "and hope that you will excuse the delay which I am truly sorry has happened" deleted.

different persons mentioned in it. I shall be particularly glad to see the Epitaph on Dr. Adams whom I loved and respected, and whose memory I should be happy in any degree to illustrate.

Whether I shall ever write my own Life I cannot tell; but I hope to give a new edition of Walton's *Lives* with notes. I observed the notice of them in Mr. Churton's excellent account of Dr. Townson to which you refer.

My regard for the character of Dr. Dodridge would have made me value any correspondence of his: But what you have published is interesting on many accounts. I was surprised to find in the letter from the Authour of *The Grave* that a Poem of such merit and which has attained to such extensive popularity, was at first subjected to a mortifying discouragement.[4] I should be curious to trace it's progress, and to see Mr. Blair's letters to Dr. Watts.

If you will let me know the names of the Scotch Noblemen from whom Dr. Dodridge had letters I may probably be able to give you some information concerning them.

I shall take care to have a good impression of the[5] engraved portrait of Dr. Johnson prefixed to my first edition of his *Life* conveyed to your Bookseller Mr. Longman, and I beg your acceptance of it. Give me leave to offer my compliments to Mrs. Stedman; and be assured that I am, Reverend Sir, your much obliged humble servant

Any letters to me may be put under cover to John Courtenay Esq. M.P. London.

[4] "Yesterday I had a letter from the Dr. [Watts] signifying his approbation of the piece in a manner most obliging. . . . But at the same time he mentions to me, that he had offered it to two booksellers of his acquaintance, who, he tells me, did not care to run the risk of publishing it. They can scarce think (considering how critical an age we live in with respect to such kind of writings) that a person living three hundred miles from London could write so, as to be acceptable to the fashionable and polite. Perhaps it may be so: though at the same time I must say, in order to make it more generally liked, I was obliged sometimes to go cross to my own inclination, well knowing that whatever Poem is written upon a serious argument, must upon that very account lie under peculiar disadvantages: and therefore proper arts must be used to make such a piece go down with a licentious age which cares for none of these things" (Blair to Doddridge, pp. 254–55).

[5] MS. "plate" deleted.

From the Rev. Thomas Stedman, Monday 7 October 1793

Missing. Wrapper, Yale (C 2538).

ADDRESS: James Boswell Esqr. By favour of Mr. Courtenay.

ENDORSEMENTS: 7 Octr. 1793. Rev. Mr. Thomas Stedman Vicar of St. Chad's Shrewsbury. *and* N.B. Epitaph on Dr. Adams enclosed.

To John Perkins, Thursday 10 October 1793

MS. O. T. Perkins, Esq., Chagfield, Devonshire; from a transcript made by R. W. Chapman. MS. Yale (L 1068): JB's copy, dated 11 Oct.

ADDRESS: To Mr. Perkins, Southwark.

Great Portland Street, 10 October 1793

Mr. Boswell presents his compliments to Mr. Perkins, and hopes he will excuse him for not answering his note before this day. He now returns him with many thanks all the letters and cards from Dr. Johnson obligingly communicated to him by Mr. Perkins, who he trusts will not take amiss that a note is written upon one of the letters.[1] Mr. Perkins is requested to accept of a copy of the second edition of Mr. Boswell's *Life of Dr. Johnson*.[2]

To Sir William Forbes, Thursday 24 October 1793

MS. estate of the late Lord Clinton. JB continues their friendly argument over the question of literary freedom (now apropos of the projected publication of his "travels"), and adopts the traditional defence of the satirist as one who writes under an obligation to expose unworthy and ridiculous individuals. He reports that the second edition is selling as well as could be expected.

[1] *Life* iv. 118 n. 1, identifying Perkins's partner, Barclay.

[2] On 20 Nov. JB "Wandered over London Bridge all the way to Thrale's Brewhouse, and paid a visit to Mr. Perkins, one of his successors, thinking I might dine with him, but I found that he was as yet at his Country house" (Journ.).

From Sir William Scott, Saturday 2 November 1793

MS. Yale (C 2445).

ADDRESS: James Boswell Esq., Portland Street, Queen Ann Street.

ENDORSEMENT: Sir William Scott (without date but) 2 Novr. 1793.

[London]

DEAR SIR: I am much obliged to you for the Present of your Additions[1]—but it was unnecessary, because I had bought your 8vo Edition; as I cannot do without having the Book in a portable convenient form, fit for a Post-Chaise—jucundus comes in vehiculo.[2] —I hope Malone did not take amiss my deserting Him; there are few Men whom I should be less willing to disoblige. Yours etc. etc.

WM. SCOTT

From the Rev. Thomas Stedman, Sunday 3 November 1793

MS. Yale (C 2539).

ADDRESS: James Boswell Esqr.

ENDORSEMENT: Novr. 3. 1793, Rev. Mr. Stedman Vicar of St. Chad's Shrewsbury.

Shrewsbury, Sunday Novr. 3. 1793

DEAR SIR: I return you very many thanks for your picture of Dr. Johnson; which I shall preserve with the greatest care, and transmit to my Children as your present. You have won my heart by your Writings, and this instance of your good nature. Were I possessed of any thing that I knew would be acceptable, it should be conveyed to you as a testimony of my respect and gratitude.[1] I am, Your obliged and most humble servant

THOMAS STEDMAN

---

[1] That is, the *Principal Corrections and Additions to the First Edition* (1793).

[2] "Comes jucundus in viâ pro vehiculo est" (An agreeable companion on the road is as good as a coach.—Publilius Syrus).

[1] In addition to the *Letters of Doddridge* (*ante* 2 Sept. 1793), Stedman had presented JB with his edition of Job Orton's *Letters to a Young Clergyman* (Shrewsbury, 1791). See Journ. 25 Oct. 1793.

From John Davidson,[1]
Saturday 16 November 1793

MS. Yale (C 894).

ADDRESS: To James Boswel Esqr., London.

ENDORSEMENT: 16 Novr. 1793. John Davidson Esq.

Edin., 16 Nov. 1793

DEAR SIR: I found here on my return from the Country, a very elegant 8vo Copy of your estimable work on the life of Doctor Johnson, as a present from you, for which I am much obliged to you and return you my most gratefull thanks and am, Dear Sir, Your most humble Servant

JOHN DAVIDSON

P.S. Mr. Claud Boswel directed me to send this under cover to Mr. Courtenay.

James Boswel Esqr.

From James Abercrombie,
Sunday 15 December 1793

Missing. Sent to London from Philadelphia. ". . . my long address to you of Decr. 15th . . . contained my grateful acknowledgment of the receipt of your 2d Edition of the *Life of Dr. Johnson*, and the information of my resolution to enter into Holy Orders" (*post* From Abercrombie, 28 June 1794).

---

[1] John Davidson (d. 1797), of Stewartfield and Haltree, Crown Agent (*A History of the Society of Writers to Her Majesty's Signet*, 1890, p. 53). He makes three brief appearances in the journal: 5 Feb. 1768, 2 Sept. 1774, and 22 Dec. 1775.

To the Rev. Thomas Stedman, Thursday 19 December 1793

MS. Yale (L 1186). A copy, including signature, in three different hands: Veronica Boswell's, JB Jr.'s, and John James Temple's;[1] headed: "Copy of a letter to the Revd. Mr. Stedman [*in JB's hand:*] Shrewsbury."

London, 19th Decr. 1793

REVEREND SIR: I am very uneasy to think that I am in your debt for no less than three letters.[2] Pray do not suppose me to be insensible of your goodness. But indeed I have been in that state of indisposition which makes it painful to me to write. Perhaps I yield too much to it. The year shall not close without my acknowledging your favours.

I am glad that the engraved Portrait of Dr. Johnson has been received in good condition and I have read with much satisfaction Mr. Ortons letters to you for which please to accept my thanks. They are not only piously instructive but truely liberal, and may be of general use.

The Epitaph on Dr. Adams pleases me much and should my *Life of Dr. Johnson* come to a third edition, it will be a suitable and agreable addition.[3] I should be sorry to give you extraordinary trouble but if at your leisure you will let me have any of your remarks on my Book which you think should be communicated, and also Copies of the other two letters from the Authour of *The Grave* I shall take it kindly. If I can obtain sufficient materials I wish to publish some account of that Poet.[4]

The success which I have had in writing the life of one most eminent with whom I was long and intimately acquainted and for doing which I had many other peculiar advantages must not make it be thought that I could write the lives of other persons in the same manner. There is a very good account of Dr. Townson by Mr. Churton.[5] Dr. Horne (whose letter I return) has left many

---

[1] John James Temple, fourth son of JB's friend, was with the Boswells 11 to 24 Dec. for a part of his holidays from Eton.

[2] *Ante* 2 Sept. and 3 Nov. 1793. For the third letter, see *post* n. 6.

[3] Malone saw to it that the epitaph,

which was inscribed upon Adams's monument in Gloucester Cathedral, was included in the third edition (iv. 399). Dr. Powell reprints it, corrected, *Life* iv. 548.

[4] See *Life* iii. 47 n. 3.

[5] JB forgot that Stedman knew of this account (*ante* 2 Sept. 1793).

friends able to do justice to his memory[6] and why should not you Sir be the biographer of Dr. Adams. Though Sir John Hawkins has preceded me writing the life of Isaac Walton[7] I shall nevertheless write a new life of him and prefix it to my edition of his lives and I now know of some additional circumstances which will be interesting. I am happy to understand from you that there is a picture of him at Salisbury. Mr. Malone I find knew of it some time ago and has recommended to an engraver to have a print made from it. . . .

[6] For instance, the Rev. William Jones, of Nayland (1726–1800), who published in 1795 *Memoirs of the Life . . . of . . . George Horne*. For Horne, see *ante* From S. Adams, 13 June 1787, n. 3. On 11 Nov. 1793 Stedman wrote JB (C 2540) about a portrait of Walton: "I mention this to encourage you in your laudable design of publishing a new Edition of Walton's *Lives*. For the same reason I enclose you the Bishop of Norwich' Letter (tho' there is not much in it) but which I shall be glad to have returned at your leisure."

[7] Prefixed to his edition of *The Complete Angler* (1760).

1794

1794

From Edmund Hector,
Thursday 9 January 1794

Missing. Facsimile montage, *Johnsoniana*, opp. p. 316. Printed, *Life* i. 92 n. 2.[1]

ADDRESS: James Boswel Esqr.

ENDORSEMENT: Mr. Hector Birmingham sending the Original Copy of Dr. Johnson's Verses on a sprig of Myrtle.

Birm[ingha]m, Jany. 9th 94

DEAR SIR: I am sorry to see you engag'd in altercation with a Lady, who seems unwilling to be convinc'd of her errors;[2] surely it woud be more ingenuous to acknowledge, than to persevere.

Lately, in looking over some papers I meant to burn, I found the original manuscript of the *Myrtle*, with the date on it, 1731, which I have inclosed.[3]

The true history (which I could swear to) is as follows: Mr. Morgan Graves, the elder brother of a worthy Clergyman near Bath,[4] with whom I was acquainted, waited upon a lady in this neighbourhood, who at parting presented him the branch. He shewed it me, and wished much to return the compliment in verse. I applied to Johnson, who was with me, and in about half an hour dictated the verses which I sent to my friend.

I most solemnly declare, at that time Johnson was an entire stranger to the Porter family; and it was almost two years after, that I introducd him to the acquaintance of Porter,[5] whom I bought

---

[1] I give here a hybrid text, transcribing the whole of the facsimile and incorporating the missing paragraphs (second, third, and last) from the normalized version in the *Life*.

[2] See *ante* From Hector, 9 Aug. 1791, n. 2.

[3] Missing. W. H. Craig rightly pointed out (N & Q, 8th ser., 1896, ix. 201–02) that Hector's MS. was hardly decisive evidence against Miss Seward's contention, but his general defence of her position is no more convincing. —JB printed the poem from Mrs. Piozzi's text (see *Poems*, ed. Smith and McAdam, p. 95). In the MS. *Life* (p. 46) the verses appear in a shortened and garbled form.

A space left blank in one of the lines indicates a MS. rather than a printed source—very likely Miss Seward's reconstruction. As the MS. version is not cancelled, and bears no direction to a printed text, we may suppose that the substitution was made at the printer's.

[4] See *ante* From Hector, 9 Aug. 1791 and n. 3.

[5] Miss Seward had stated that SJ wrote the verses to Lucy Porter two or three years before his acquaintance with her mother. It is possible, though not probable, that SJ met Lucy at her grandfather Hunter's in Lichfield before he knew her parents in Birmingham.

my Cloaths of. If you intend to convince this obstinate woman and to exhibit to the publick the truth of your Narrative you are at liberty to make what use you please of this statement.[6]

I hope you will pardon me for taking up so much of your time. Wishing you *multos et felices annos,* I shall subscribe myself Your obligd humble Servant

E. HECTOR

From Mary Palmer, Countess of Inchiquin,[1] Friday 24 January 1794

MS. Yale (C 1580).

ADDRESS: James Boswell Esqr.

ENDORSEMENT: 24 Janry. 1794. Countess of Inchiquin.

Leicester Square, Jany. 24

Lady Inchiquin presents her Compliments to Mr. Boswell and returns him many thanks for his valuable present, she hopes soon to have the pleasure of thanking him in person. Best Compliments to the Miss Boswells.

[6] With this authoritative document in hand, JB felt obliged to reopen the debate, and wrote again to *Gent. Mag.* on 20 Jan. (lxiv. 32), giving Hector's letter in evidence. In the third edition of the *Life* (1799) JB's report of the later history of the controversy, including Hector's letter, is tacked on to the note printed in the second edition, with no notice being taken of the unanswered questions which still remained. See *ante* From Hector, 9 Aug. 1791, n. 2. —Mrs. Piozzi wrote in her diary, Apr. 1794: "Mr Boswell & Miss Seward are good Antagonists for each other—made on purpose one would think: I wonder which will have the last word about poor dear old Johnson's Sprig of Myrtle.—Boswell's Cause is best certainly, but his Opponent out-writes him—Miss Seward has ten times his Powers. The Epigram that went about this Winter is very pretty.

Fye Bozzy! Hector and talk big!
  Away th' unworthy Quarrel;
Here, take your Master's Myrtle-Sprig,
  But spare a Lady's Laurel" (*Thraliana*, p. 878).

[1] Mary Palmer (1750–1820), Countess of Inchiquin, later Marchioness of Thomond; Sir Joshua Reynolds's niece, amanuensis, and residuary legatee. See *Journ. passim.*

To the Rev. James Abercrombie, c. Tuesday 24 June 1794[1]

MS. Yale (L 3). JB's draft, headed: "Rev. Mr. Abercrombie."

[London]

I received your very obliging communications by the Pigou, and since that yours of 22 Augt. 1793 with Dr. Thornton's *Elements of written language* which are ingenious and fanciful and have in some measure been preceeded by Mr. Elphinston[2] who furnished Mottoes to *The Rambler*. It was a remarkable circumstance that just before receiving the Essay I had read over from beginning to end Dr. Johnson's English Grammar prefixed to his *Dictionary*. The other publications have merit[3] in their different ways.

I now write to you as a Revd.[4]

From the Rev. James Abercrombie, Saturday 28 June 1794

MS. Yale (C 6).

ADDRESS: James Boswell Esqr., London.

ENDORSEMENT (by Alexander Boswell): Jas. Abercrombie, Philadelphia.

Philad[elphi]a, June 28th 1794, Pine Street No. 101

DEAR SIR: I have indulged till the moment of the Pigou's departure, the hope of being honor'd with a reply to my long address to you of Decr. 15th, which contained my grateful acknowledgment of the

---

[1] The date is supplied from a leaf of rough notes (J 118.1) containing the memorandum: "Write to Abercromb Philadelph." The notes were made in preparation for JB's journey to Auchinleck on 26 June.

[2] See *ante* From Elphinston, 30 July 1791 and n. 1.

[3] MS. "though not a great deal of novelty" deleted.

[4] See *ante* From Abercrombie, 15 Dec. 1793, head-note. The MS. continues: "Mem. Dr. Cooper in his best moments./ Bradford's Enquiry into the punishment of death in Pensylvania *read*. The other

two *with* you." For Dr. Cooper, see *ante* From W. Strahan, 4 Jan. 1779, n. 1. The second reference is to the works sent by Abercrombie, presumably with his missing letter of 15 Dec. 1793, and the sense is: "You have read Bradford's *Enquiry* and can leave it behind. Take the other two with you to be read." William Bradford's *An Enquiry How Far the Punishment of Death is Necessary in Pennsylvania* (Philadelphia, 1793) led to the abolition in that state of the death penalty for all capital crimes except murder in the first degree (DAB).

receipt of your 2d Edition of the *Life of Dr. Johnson*, and the information of my resolution to enter into Holy Orders, which event took place on the 1st Sunday after Christmas. I am now established here, as an Assistant Minister in the Episcopal Churches.

I beg your acceptance of my friend Dr. Rush's account of the Fever which prevailed here last summer.[1] His opinion is opposed to that of many other gentlemen of the Faculty in this city, which is, that it was imported. In a late *Gentlemans Magazine*, I observed a letter from Dr. Lettsome on the subject,[2] who thinks that it was carried from the coast of Africa to Granada, from thence to the other West India Islands, and so to Phila[delphi]a. In this judgment a large majority of the Physicians coincide.

Dr. Coxe, the bearer of this, is an amiable young man, and intelligent, tho' his studies have been hitherto much confined to the profession he is just entering upon. He was a pupil of Dr. Rush. His connexions are in the first line of respectability in this place. His grandfather [is] President of the College of Physicians.[3] With sincere respect and esteem, I am, Dear Sir, Your most humble Servant

JAS. ABERCROMBIE

[1] *An Account of the Bilious Remitting Yellow Fever, As It Appeared in the City of Philadelphia in the Year 1793*, Philadelphia, 1794. See Winthrop and Frances Neilson, *Verdict for the Doctor: The Case of Benjamin Rush*, 1959.

[2] John Coakley Lettsom (1744–1815), Quaker physician, philanthropist, and author. His letter, signed "Medicus Londinensis", appears in the Jan. number (lxiv. 3). A decade later, Rush and Lettsom were still arguing it out in correspondence: see *Letters of Rush* ii. 880, 917. Lettsom makes one appearance in the *Life*, at Dilly's dinner for SJ and Wilkes, 15 May 1776 (iii. 68). For JB's subsequent meetings with him, see Journ. *passim*.

[3] John Redman Coxe (1773–1864) had just received his M.D. degree from the University of Pennsylvania and had come abroad to continue his studies in the hospitals of London, Edinburgh, and Paris. He returned to Philadelphia in 1796 to practise, but went on to lecture and write and edit a number of medical works. From 1809 to 1819 he was professor of chemistry at the University of Pennsylvania (DAB). His grandfather, John Redman (1722–1808), M. D. Leyden, 1748, was Rush's teacher, as Rush was Coxe's. Redman was the first president of the College of Physicians of Philadelphia, 1786–1804 (DAB).

1795

From Sir Michael Le Fleming,[1]
Tuesday 27 January 1795

MS. Yale (C 1718).

ADDRESS: James Boswell Esqr., 47 Great Portland Street, London.

FRANK: Kendal, Twenty eighth January 1795. M[ichae]l le Fleming.

POSTMARK: JA 31 95.

> Rydall, 27 Jan. 1795, near Kendal

DEAR BOSWELL: I have this moment left off "for the present" reading your *Life of Johnson* which has realy been of more use to me during my confinement than all the assistance I have had from my Physician Medicines Friends or visitors. The Gout has kept me in the House for above a month. Thank God I have not had much pain and have always been in good spirits. It appears a long time to me since I had the pleasure of hearing from you or seeing you.[2] Hearing of you I certainly have which is always very pleasing to me. I see you are favoring the World with a new Edition of Your Friends Life.[3] I never heard of a Book that was so much commended as yours is in Ireland and indeed "now" every wheres[,] but there by the first people[4] as containing more information and real anecdote than any other publication. I drink my Bottle *exactly* every day and I often wish for your Company at that Sociable moment. I have laid in a tolerable stock of wine and I hope you will contrive some time or other to Honor me with your Company to taste it with the Heir apparent and any friends that may be with you.

What think you of the loss of Holland.[5] Our Minister[6] may have the *gift of the Gab* but he has not the foresight and wisdom necessary at this moment for the director of our affairs. —Favor me with a line. I hope to be in Town ere long. Have you seen the great

---

[1] Sir Michael Le Fleming, Bt. (1748–1806), M.P. for Westmorland from 1774 until his death (*Comp. Bar.* iv. 193). See Journ. *passim.*

[2] The last meeting recorded in the journal was on Christmas day, 1792, at JB's house in London; the last known letter is JB's of 31 July 1793 (*Letters JB* 318).

[3] The third. Though in preparation, it was not published until 1799, four years after JB's death.

[4] Cf. *ante* From Maxwell, 4 May 1793.

[5] To the French, Dec.–Jan. 1794–95. See *Annual Register*, 1795, pp. 43 ff.

[6] Pitt.

Earl[7] lately. Pray my best Compliments to the young Ladies and Beleive me to be with real regard Your very devoted Friend

MICHAEL LE FLEMING

Are you to be the *Law Chief* of Corsica.[8]

To Sir Michael Le Fleming, Tuesday 3 March 1795

MS. Hyde.

ENDORSEMENT: Mr. Boswell.

London, 3 March 1795

MY DEAR SIR MICHAEL: Many thanks to you for your very agreable letter of 29[1] Janry.; and I take shame to myself for not acknowledging it sooner. Such praise of my *Life of Dr. Johnson* from such a man as you my elegant friend is the most pleasing reward of my labours. I have indeed great reason to be satisfied with the share both of gold and fame which that work has procured me.

Be assured that your long absence from Town has been felt with real sensibility by me; and no man will rejoice more to see you here again. For we have congenial souls in many respects, as ancient Gentlemen as lovers of good books and good conversation good— in short good every thing. I went to Ayrshire in June, staid full seven months and returned to London in January; since which time I have been relishing the Metropolis with avidity.[2]

I rejoice to hear of your stock of wine; and shall joyously taste it I hope before this year is gone round. My son and heir your Eton acquaintance who loves and admires you is at Edinburgh College this winter.[3] He comes up to me early in May.[4] I would give him welcome orders to take Rydell in his way; but hope that his Father shall see you long before then.

---

[7] Lonsdale. Le Fleming was an associate of his, and had in 1790 unsuccessfully urged JB's candidacy as representative for Carlisle (Journ. 15 June).

[8] United with Great Britain, June 1794.

---

[1] 27.

[2] See the digest of JB's activities for this journal-less period, BP xviii. 274–75.

[3] Alexander entered the University of Edinburgh in Oct. 1793, remaining three years but not taking a degree. Le Fleming, a fellow-Etonian, had visited him when he was still at school (JB to Alexander Boswell, 17 Nov. 1789, 24 Feb. 1791).

[4] To his father's deathbed. JB died on 19 May at two o'clock in the morning.

The great Earl after a long *vacuum* asked me to dinner last summer. *I was engaged.* He asked me *again* and I went. There was a good party and excellent doings. I have left my Card since I came to town; but have not seen him nor heard of him. You know him perfectly.

I am not going in any publick capacity to Corsica, which is not well in those who rule us *à lheure qui'l est. N'importe.*[5] *Vive la gayete de Coeur!* I have published a second edition of my *Life of Johnson.* You shall have the additions separate when you come. One of them is a just, and I think a happy compliment to you by name.[6]

My daughters are flattered by your polite remembrance of them; and return you compliments. Pray gratify me with intelligence *when* we shall see you. I have the honour to remain, with sincere regard, My Dear Sir Michael, Faithfully and affectionately and cordially yours

JAMES BOSWELL

I passed two hours this morning with Lord Macartney and was deliciously entertained with his Chinese Embassy.[7]

---

[5] JB had applied to Dundas to be Minister or Commissioner to Corsica but was rejected (Journ. 17 and 26 Mar. 1794).

[6] In a note to the designation "a very fashionable Baronet": "My friend Sir Michael Le Fleming. This gentleman, with all his experience of sprightly and elegant life, inherits, with the beautiful family Domain, no inconsiderable share of that love of literature, which distinguished his venerable grandfather [*read* great uncle], the Bishop of Carlisle" (*Life* i. 461 and n. 4). JB had advertised this compliment in an earlier letter to Le Fleming, 31 July 1793 (*Letters JB* 318).

[7] See *ante* From Hoole, 17 June 1790, n. 10.

UNDATABLE MANUSCRIPTS

Johnsoniana transmitted by the Rev. Daniel Astle

MS. Yale (C 60). In an unidentified hand, presumably that of "————— Baldwin Esqre." which Astle has supplied at the foot of the text.

ENDORSEMENT (in Astle's hand): Revd. Mr. Astle.

One day Dr. Johnson and several of his friends were walking in Richmond, and upon their turning in at the Garden gate, the Dr. called out to know, where they were going—they said "into the[1] Gardens to be sure"—upon which he instantly turned about and said—"I'l not walk in the gardens of an Usurper!"

Some time after this, Lord Bute having introduced him to his Majesty,[2] he became so much better informed, by the gracious and amiable manner in which he was received, that he told his friends that the KING, was the most accomplished Prince in Europe.[3]

Being in company with several friends and the late well known Dr. Rose of Chiswick,[4] the conversation turned upon eminent Scotch writers, when Johnson said—there had not been *One*, since the days of Buchanan.[5] Rose insisted there had been several— Johnson defied him to name *One*—Rose paused,—Johnson urged him stil more, when Rose named Lord Bute! The Dr. started at the name, and in an alterd tone of voice, said, he had the highest respect for Lord Bute, but that he had never heard that he was a Writer, and desired Dr. Rose to name the work. Rose, again kept him some time in suspence. Johnson became more and more urgent when Rose with an archness peculiar to him, dryly said,—"the three lines that conveyed to you your Pension." Johnson was so much hurt by this pointed sarcasm, that he instantly took up his hat, and quited the company.[6]

Dr. Johnson being in an afternoon at Mrs. Macaulays with much

---

[1] MS. "to"

[2] There is no evidence that Bute introduced SJ to George III.

[3] Cf. *Life* ii. 40–41.

[4] William Rose, LL.D. (1719–86), schoolmaster, translator, and one of the principal contributors to *The Monthly Review*. JB was associated with him in 1769 in a London club to which Benjamin Franklin also belonged ("the club of honest whigs": *Writings of Benjamin Franklin*, ed. A. H. Smyth, 1906, vi. 430), and described him then as "a bold

honest fellow and a man of coarse Abilities" (Journ. 21 Sept.).

[5] Cf. *Life* iv. 185–86, v. 57 n. 3.

[6] JB gives a different version of the anecdote as an illustration of the many stories told of "imaginary victories" over SJ, *Life* iv. 168 n. 1. According to this version, SJ, far from being offended, acknowledged the truth of Rose's jest. But JB hastens to add that SJ denied the whole story. For still another version, Arthur Murphy's, see *ibid.* iv. 509.

company, the lady in a long harangue endeavourd to prove the necessity and propriety of an equality among mankind. The[7] Dr. made no reply, but when the Servant came in with the Tea things, he asked Mrs. Macaulay his Christian name. She[8] said "John," upon which, quiting the chair, on which, next to the lady, he had some time sat silent, he said in a loud voice—"here John come and sit down between Catherine Macaulay and me"—when she, not a little surprised, said, "Dr. what do you mean by this?" —The[9] Dr. said, "why have you not been labouring to prove that all mankind are equal."[10]

Here allow me to add, that I have been much surprised to see a blunder so long continued in Dr. Johnsons celebrated *Dictionary*, for under the word—Rackoon, the explanation is—a New England animal etc. etc. And the word *Rattoon* is made to signify a west India fox. Now the fact is, that the suckers or offsets from the Sugar Cane, after the first years growth, are called by the West India Planters *Rattoons*, and they describe their Crops to each other, by saying, they have so many Acres of Plants and so many Acres of Rattoons to cut, meaning thereby, Canes of one and two years standing; for after the Rattoons are cut, they are generally dug up and the ground replanted; So that a Rattoon is a vegetable and not an animal.[11]

[7] MS. "mankind, the"

[8] MS. "name, she"

[9] MS. "this?—the"

[10] The anecdote is told by SJ himself in July 1763 and again on 15 May 1776 at the famous dinner at Dilly's attended by Wilkes, *Life* i. 447, iii. 77–78. For still another version, see *Johns. Misc.* ii. 4. Charles Fortescue-Brickdale, a lineal descendant of Mrs. Macaulay, maintains (N & Q, 1930, clix. 111) that SJ took liberties in reporting the incident and that JB showed little judgement in accepting his account. He cites Mrs. Macaulay's own version in her *Letters on Education*, published the year before the *Life* came out, according to which the servant was not in the room, she was not offended by SJ's proposal, and she met it intelligently with the explanation that her argument was not against inequality of property, which is unavoidable, but against political distinctions.

[11] "Rattoon" is a variant both of "racoon" and of "rattan". In the first sense it is the name given to the West Indian fox; in the second, that given to second-growth sugar cane, as described in the present passage. Had SJ's critic looked in the *Dictionary* under "ratan", he would have found the definition, "An Indian cane".

Johnsoniana from Philip Metcalfe[1]

MS. Yale (M 145). In JB's hand. Printed in part, *Life* iv. 159–60 (Paper Apart for MS. *Life*, p. 861).

Mr. Metcalf

He met Mr. Metcalf often at Sir Joshua Reynolds's and other places and was a good deal with him at Brighthelmstone in 1782. Mr. Metcalf shewed him great respect and sent him a note that he might have the use of his carriage whenever he pleased. Johnson (3 Octr. 1782) returned this polite Answer "Mr. Johnson is very much obliged by the kind offer of the carriage but he has no desire of using Mr. Metcalf's carriage except when he can have the pleasure of Mr. Metcalf's company." Mr. Metcalf could not but be highly pleased that his company was thus valued by Johnson, and he frequently attended him in airings. One day Johnson expressed a wish to see Cirencester.[2]   said he was born there.[3] "I'll carry you" said Mr. Metcalf. "Sir" said he "I shall be obliged to you." They accordingly went, and he was much satisfied with what he saw. They visited Petworth and Cowdery the venerable seat of the Lords Montacute. "Sir" said Johnson "I should like to stay here four and twenty hours. We see here how our ancestors lived."[4]

He made Mr. Metcalf a present of his *Lives of the English Poets* with this inscription "To Mr. Metcalf from the Authour March 29, 1783." Upon the blank leaf of the first volume Mr. Metcalf has written "This Work Mr. Edmund Burke pronounced to be the best Body of Criticism in the English Language. —Of stile—that Addison's was the truest English (He attended to Anglicisms).

[1] Philip Metcalfe (1733–1818), M.P., F.R.S., was an intimate friend of Sir Joshua Reynolds and one of his executors. SJ appointed him trustee of the annuity to Francis Barber. See *Life* iv. 505. According to Farington's *Diary* (i. 95–96), JB and Metcalfe "did not always go on pleasantly together." Metcalfe would call him 'Bozzy' which the other would only willingly permit from Dr. Johnson, but Boswell in return called Metcalfe 'Mettie', which was equally disagreeable for him. Sir Joshua Reynolds proposed Metcalfe to be a member of the Literary Club, at which Boswell expressed much dislike. One black ball excludes and Metcalfe was blackballed, which Her Ladyship [Mary Palmer: *ante* 24 Jan. 1794] is convinced was done by Boswell, but Metcalfe does not know it." See also *Journ. passim*.

[2] MS. "Chiches" deleted. Nevertheless the place was Chichester, not Cirencester.

[3] It was no doubt the poet William Collins who SJ said was born at Chichester.

[4] This paragraph was revised and printed, *Life* iv. 159–60. See *ibid.* 506–07 and *Diaries*, p. 348. The passage "One day . . . he saw." is deleted. The rest of the paper, though revised also, was also deleted.

That Johnson's would translate best. —*A conversation at Sir Joshua Reynolds's table the day of the Dr.'s interment in Westminster Abbey which we attended."*

In an extempore prayer of great energy, he mentioned a strong tendency to insanity from the age of 22.[5] This accounts for an expression to me[6] when we went together to Chichester in Octr. "that he had suffered more pain of body and *distraction of mind* than most men." See likewise his Preface to his great Work the *English Dictionary*, written he says "not in the soft obscurities of retirement, or under the shelter of academick bowers, but amidst inconvenience and distraction, in sickness and in sorrow."

Johnsoniana from Thomas Warton

MS. Yale (C 3079).

Among the *Idlers*, Numbers 33, 93, and 96, are written by Mr. Warton.[1]

A small copy of Verses *On presenting a Sprig of Myrtle to a Lady*, common in our Miscellanies, is often attributed to Dr. Johnson.[2] I have heard old Mr. Dodsley the Bookseller say, that it was written by Hammond, author of the *Love-Elegies*.[3] It first appeared in Dodsley's *Museum*.[4]

Old Mr. Dodsley gave Johnson a guinea, in 1756, for writing the introductory Discourse to a Newspaper, called *The London Chronicle*, still publishing.[5] Davies reprinted it in his *Fugitive Pieces*,[6] vol. ii. p. 153. It first appeared in the *first* Number of that Paper.

---

[5] Cf. *ante* From Hector, 1 Feb. 1785 and n. 23, 28 Mar. 1785 and n. 37.

[6] Metcalfe. In his revision of the MS. JB inserted the year "1782" after "Octr." in this sentence, which makes it clear that this is the same visit as recounted in the first paragraph. SJ was with Metcalfe several days in Oct., but the excursion which took them to Chichester did not take place until 8–10 Nov.

---

[1] *Life* i. 330.

[2] See *ante* From Hector, 9 Aug. 1791, n. 2.

[3] Warton had included the poem with this ascription in his collection, *The Union* (see *ante* To Hailes, 11 Feb. 1790 and n. 4). See SJ's *Life of Hammond* (*Lives* ii. 314–15) and *Life* v. 268 for his strictures on the *Love Elegies*.

[4] 1747, ii. 429; anonymously.

[5] *Life* i. 317. See Hazen, pp. 131–32.

[6] *Miscellaneous and Fugitive Pieces* (1773).

The Preface to Lauder's pamphlet about Milton, is *undoubtedly* written by Johnson.[7]

I believe Johnson's *Life of Barretier* was a sixpenny pamph[l]et, for Cave, 1745.[8]

Johnson's friend Gilb. Walmesley, son of William a gentleman of Lichfield, was admitted a Commoner of Trinity College Oxford, aged 17, in 1698. He has many Latin verse translations in *The Gentleman's Magazine*. One is of *My time O ye Muses*, etc.[9]

From an Anonymous Correspondent

MS. Yale (M 159).

Queries? arising from the *Life of Dr. Johnson* by Jas. Boswell Esqr.

Vol. I

P. 106. "Sir William *Young.*" Q. If the Writer of the *Epilogue* to the *Tragedy of Irene* 1749 might not have been William Young Esqr. who was created a Baronet 1769; and not the late Right Honble. Sir William *Yonge* Bart. K.B.?[1] Mr. Young, then living in Kent, had theatrical Propensities; and about that time play'd the Part of *Othello*, for a publick charity, at Canterbury. Mr. Urban's old Correspondent Mr. Gemsege (if he be living)[2] was one of his audience.

[7] *Life* i. 228–29, 231. See Hazen, pp. 77 ff.

[8] 1744. See *Life* i. 161.

[9] Revised and quoted in a foot-note to the second edition (expanded in the third): *Life* i. 81 n. 2. But Warton was mistaken in identifying the author of the Latin version of "My time, O ye Muses" (who signs himself "G. Walmsley") as SJ's friend; he was Geoffrey Walmsley (1725–73), of Sidney Sussex College (*Life* iv. 2nd ed., 1964, p. 488, Errata). The original English poem, "Colin and Phoebe," was by John Byrom.

[1] In the second edition JB altered the spelling of the name from "Young" to "Yonge" and inserted the phrase "as Johnson informed me". Dr. Powell suggests (*Life* i. 197 n. 4) that the insertion was aimed at Murphy, who had cast doubt upon the attribution; another prompting is now apparent. Sir William Yonge, Bt. (d. 1755), was Secretary at War in the Walpole Administration. See *Life* ii. 161; and Pope's *Epistle to Arbuthnot*, line 115; *Epilogue to the Satires* I. 13, 68; and *Essay on Man* iv. 278. Sir William Young (1725–88) was Lieutenant-Governor of the Island of Dominica. He was twice married, both times to women of Kent. His son William (c. 1750–1815) married as his second wife Barbara, daughter of Richard Talbot, of Malahide Castle, co. Dublin (*Comp. Bar.* v. 153).

[2] Samuel Pegge (1704–96), antiquary, contributed to *Gent. Mag.* from 1746 to 1795 under this and other pseudonyms.

P. 363. "Mrs. Veal." Q. if it has not been confess'd that the Story of the Ghost was added to force the Sale of the Book?[3]

P. 408. "The Whole Duty of Man." Q. If this Work were not written by Lady Packington, the Wife of Sir John Packington Bart. and a Daughter of the Lord Keeper Coventry? The Question is investigated in Mr. Ballard's *Memoirs of British Ladies*; tho' it is suggested in the Baronetage 1741 (Article Packington).[4] Mr. Ballard's Book was perhaps not publish'd when this Conversation took place.[5]

P. 409. "Corps." Q. If not on the word *Fort?* A vociferous French Preacher said of Bourdaloue,—"Il preche *fort bien*, et moi *bien fort.*" (*Menagiana.* See also *Anecdotes Litteraires*, Article Bourdaloue.)[6]

P. (Page and Volume forgotten.) Q. If the Reason why Dr. Johnson collected the *Peels* of *squeez'd Oranges* be not given in the 358th Letter in Mrs. Piozzi's Collection?[7]

Vol. II

P. 151. For Lambe read Lombe. Q. from Hutton's *History of Derby* whether the Silk-Mill were not brought hither by *John* Lombe, who was succeeded by his Brother *William:*—and if Sir Thomas, who was their Cousin-German, were not the

---

[3] Malone noted in the third edition: "This fiction is known to have been invented by Daniel Defoe, and was added to Drelincourt's book, to make it sell. The first edition had it not" (*Life* ii. 163 n. 4). See also *ibid.* 493–94.

[4] Not used, *Life* ii. 239. *The Whole Duty of Man* is now ascribed to Richard Allestree, D.D. (1619–81). In the *Baronetage of England* ("Pakington, of Ailsbury, Buckinghamshire": 1771 ed., i. 188–89) Lady Pakington is described as "the most accomplished person of her age for wisdom and piety", and "equal to such an undertaking, though her modesty would not suffer her to claim the honour of it". The attribution rests finally, for the writer of the article, on the fact that "the manuscript under her own hand now remains with the family". In George Ballard's *Memoirs of Several Ladies of Great Britain* (1752) the argument for her authorship, which takes note of the *Baronetage*, is made more elaborately.

[5] It was. The conversation in the *Life* took place on 30 Apr. 1773.

[6] Quoted by JB in a foot-note to the second edition, *Life* ii. 241 n. 3. But see *ante* To Abercrombie, 28 July 1793 and n. 19.

[7] JB introduced the suggestion in the second edition, *Life* iv. 204 n. 5. For "358th" he read "558th", despite the fact that he actually consulted Mrs. Piozzi's edition, from which he quotes a phrase. The letter is to Hill Boothby (*Letters SJ* 79). There are two references in the *Life* to SJ's practice of collecting orange peels, and it is to the first, longer, and more portentous one (ii. 330–31) that JB's correspondent doubtless refers. And it is to this passage, rather than the other, that one should have expected JB to attach his foot-note (as indeed Hill attached his). That JB was not constrained in his choice is clear from the location of the other additions derived from this MS.

FROM ANONYMOUS, n.d.

Third Proprietor?[8] Sir Thomas was a Knight, and it appears
that a Sheriff of London, of both his Names, was knighted
July 8. 1727.

[8] The first edition states: "After
dinner, Mrs. Butter went with me to see
the silk-mill which Sir Thomas Lambe
had a patent for, having brought away
the contrivance from Italy." Second
edition: "After dinner, Mrs. Butter
went with me to see the silk-mill which
Mr. John Lombe had had a patent for,"
etc. JB also added a note citing and
praising Hutton's *History*. JB's correspondent is correct in his report on
Hutton's facts, but he gives no indication
of the liveliness of the account (pp. 191–
209). The DNB, in defiance of Hutton,
gives Sir Thomas greater prominence
than John, and entirely ignores William.

MALONE'S CORRESPONDENCE ABOUT
THE *LIFE* AFTER THE DEATH OF BOSWELL

From Sir William Forbes to Malone, Tuesday 22 May 1798

MS. Yale (C 1309).

Edinbg., 22d May 1798

DEAR SIR: I troubled Mr. T. D. Boswell to state to you a doubt that had occurred to me, in regard to the proposed new edition of Mr. Boswells *Life of Dr. Johnson*. I will now take the liberty of explaining a little more particularly what I had then in view.

As I mentioned in my letter to Mr. T. D. B., and, indeed, as I had often said to our late friend himself, I had always thought, there are a good many things in the Book that *might*, and some that certainly *ought* to have been omitted in the publication.[1] It was to those last only that I alluded in my letter.

In every work of that Kind the author, in my humble opinion, ought scrupulously to take care not to say any thing that could prove injurious to the reputation of any person *dead*, or that could hurt the feelings of any one *living*. This rule, however, he had certainly not attended to, in some instances. I appeal, for example, to the Conversation and Correspondence between Dr. Johnson and the Bishop of Dromore, the publication of which, Mr. Boswell himself owned to me, had hurt the Bishop so much, that it was with difficulty he could be prevailed on ever to speak to him again; or even to come to the Literary Club when Mr. Boswell was present.[2] I am well persuaded, that in that, or any similar passage, Mr. Boswell never intended to hurt any body, and that he erred in judgement merely: but certainly when he found the case to be otherwise, he ought to have omitted that part in any new edition: and if we publish it of new, are we not aiding in the propagating of a story, which though very well told, gave the Bishop so much offence and uneasiness. I do not beleive there are many such passages, which one would chuse to omit; for as to such parts of the Book as may be thought by some to be scarcely deserving of insertion, since Mr. Boswell thought otherwise, I do not see that we have any thing to do with them. And I am far from thinking that a few judicious omissions would do any harm to the Sale. On

[1] See *ante* From Forbes, 13 Oct. 1791 and n. 1.

[2] They were present together at least six times between the publication of the *Life* and JB's death. For an account of their estrangement, see C. N. Fifer, "Boswell and the Decorous Bishop", *JEGP* (1962), lxi. 48–56.

the other hand, if you either think that we are not warranted to make any alteration, or if Mr. Dilly will not publish it in any other form than as it was at first printed; how far shall I discharge my duty rightly to the Younger Children, if I deprive them of the Share of the profits of this new edition by refusing to accept of Mr. Dilly's Offer, which you think in other respects a reasonable one?

You will Oblige me extremely by favouring me with your opinion on this head, in which I justly place great Confidence. I remain with much respect, regard, and esteem, Dear Sir, Your most Obedient and faithful humble servant

WILLIAM FORBES

Edmund Malone Esq.

From Malone to Sir William Forbes, Thursday 5 July 1798

MS. estate of the late Lord Clinton. Replying to the preceding, Malone gives his opinion that JB's text may be altered only where errors of fact can be corrected from documents left for the third edition. The objectionable matter in the *Life*, which does not amount to much, was reduced by Malone's own prudential exertions; but further changes of this nature are clearly unwarranted now that the author is dead. As for Percy, JB altered the offensive passage in the second edition according to his own directions,[1] and their friendship was subsequently renewed. Malone's own clash with JB—over the Advertisement to the second edition—is recounted (see *ante* 13 and 17 May 1793).

[1]

First Edition	Second Edition
ii. 215 Dr. Percy still holding himself as the heir male of the ancient Percies,	iii. 53 (*Life* iii. 271) Dr. Percy knowing himself to be the heir male of the ancient Percies,
ii. 217 for there was a gentleman there who had recently been admitted into the confidence of the Northumberland family, to whom he hoped to appear more respectable, by shewing him how intimate he was with the great Dr. Johnson; and now the gentleman would go away with an impression much to his disadvantage, as if Johnson treated him with disregard, which might do him an essential injury.	iii. 58 (*Life* iii. 275) for there was a gentleman there who was acquainted with the Northumberland family, to whom he hoped to have appeared more respectable, by shewing how intimate he was with Dr. Johnson, and who might now, on the contrary, go away with an opinion to his disadvantage.

From Sir William Scott to Malone, ?early 1799

MS. Yale (C 2449).

[?London]

DEAR SIR: The insertion of that Passage[1] gave me great Pain, as I knew it would give great offence to Blackstone's family, and I have Reason to think that It had that effect. I remonstrated sharply with Boswell about It, and He did in a later Edition or in some Corrections by Way of Addenda, modify it in some Degree.[2] —The Expression as it stands rather appears to give Blackstone a *sottish* Character, and the Amendment inserted was to take off that Character (which He by no means deserved) and to represent Him

First Edition	Second Edition
ii. 217 you will be kind enough to put in writing as an answer to that letter, what you have now said, and in short all that you can say to Dr. Percy's advantage; and as	iii. 58 (*Life* iii. 276) you will be kind enough to put in writing as an answer to that letter, what you have now said, and as
ii. 217 Johnson's letter was studiously framed to place Dr. Percy's unquestionable merit in the fairest point of view;	iii. 58 (*Life* iii. 276) Johnson's letter placed Dr. Percy's unquestionable merit in the fairest point of view;
ii. 217 Thus our friend Percy was raised higher in the estimation of those by whom he wished most to be regarded.	iii. 59 (*Life* iii. 276) Thus every unfavourable impression was obviated that could possibly have been made on those by whom he wished most to be regarded.

In the present light, JB's statement in the foot-note added in the second edition (*Life* iii. 278 n. 1) that this information "has been given to the publick without previous communication with his Lordship" seems unaccountable, unless JB first wrote the note to apply to the version in the first edition (in order to keep Percy from looking doubly foolish—both as a principal in the conversation and as

sanctioning its publication), and then, being persuaded by Percy to tone down details of the account itself, inadvertently left the foot-note standing. As the foot-note calls attention to the affront, it seems unlikely that JB was attempting to cover the tracks of his revision. For the cancel made in the first edition at Percy's request, see *ante* 12 Mar. 1791 and nn. 4 and 6.

---

[1] *Life* iv. 91. Cf. *ante* From Scott, c. 5 Aug. 1791 and n. 1.

[2] First edition, ii. 383: "Dr. Scott . . . related, that Blackstone composed his 'Commentaries' with a bottle of port before him." Second edition, iii. 344–45

(*Principal Corrections and Additions*, p. 27): "Dr. Scott . . . related, that Blackstone, a sober man, composed his 'Commentaries' with a bottle of port before him; and found his mind invigorated and supported in the fatigue of his great Work, by a temperate use of it."

only as a Person who felt his faculties invigorated by a temperate Use of Wine—and I could wish that a note to that Purpose was inserted.[3] Yours faithfully

W. Scott

From Malone to Sir William Forbes, Saturday 3 March 1804

MS. estate of the late Lord Clinton.

Queen Anne Street, East, March 3. 1804

Dear Sir, In looking once more over our late friend's *Life of Dr. Johnson*, of which a new edition is now passing through the press,[1] two or three little matters have occurred, which induce me to trouble you with a few lines. —In vol. 3. p. 84 (last edition)[2] Mr. Boswell says "Sir Wm Forbes writes to me thus: 'I enclose the *Round Robin*'" etc. From these words, I conceived that you had sent Mr. B. the original, and stated the matter so, some time ago at Mr. Metcalfe's, in the presence of the present Bishop of Limerick (Barnard). But he said it was in his possession; and was so piqued at the contrary supposition, that he immediately got into his carriage which was then at the door, went to his lodgings, and brought it to us in his hand. —I suppose therefore that which you sent to Mr. B. was a copy. But as the fac similes could not be[3] engraved without the original, it seems strange that he should desire a copy from you, if he were possessed of the original. Perhaps the solution is, that at the time of his corresponding with you on this subject, he had not obtained the original, and procured it from Bishop Barnard at a subsequent period.[4]

In Johnson's Letter to Mr. B. of July 3, 1778 (vol. 3. p. 388) third paragraph,[5] we have in the printed editions,—"without *asserting* Stoicism"—. I am strongly inclined to think that Johnson

---

[3] JB's revision plainly served the purpose, and Malone wisely refrained from inserting a note. According to Prior, Malone had privately, in a letter to Blackstone's family, apologized for the publication of the anecdote (*Life* iv. 91 n. 2).

[1] The fourth, published this year.
[2] *Life* iii. 83.

[3] MS. "be be"
[4] Malone's conjecture was perfect. See *ante* From T. Barnard, 15 Oct. 1785 and n. 3; From Forbes, 19 Oct. 1787; and From T. Barnard, 20 Dec. 1790.
[5] *Life* iii. 362–63. The phrase occurs in the fourth paragraph, not the third. The third begins with a dash, creating an optical illusion that it is part of the second.

wrote—*"affecting"*—and request the favour of you to examine that letter, if in your possession, to see whether I am right in my conjecture.[6]

In the last line of Johnson's Letter of Nov. 21. 1778, (vol. 3. p. 394,) we find in the printed copy—"I hope soon to send you a few lines to read." —Surely Johnson must have written *lives*[7] (namely his *Lives of the Poets*, of which the proof sheets were collected after they were done with, and sent to Mr. B.).[8]

In Vol. 3. p. 143. Johnson in a letter dated *Nov. 1. 1777*,[9] quotes a line from a Sonnet of Sir Ph. Sidney's which is thus exhibited— "leave it, as Sidney says,

To virtue, fortune, *wine*, and woman's breast."

The word which I have underscored seemed to stand so oddly, and it seemed so strange that *wine* should have any influence in determining whether they should undertake another expedition together, that I was induced to consult the original from which Johnson quoted, where I found the word was—*time*, and so I have no doubt he wrote: but his hand being very small and often difficult to read, these words might easily be confounded, especially by our friend, who unfortunately set more value upon *wine*, than *time*. In the former part of the line there is an errour; for Sydney wrote—"To *nature*, fortune" etc. but this was doubtless Johnson's own mistake, for he always quoted from memory, which sometimes deceived him.[10]

[6] Malone's note in the fifth edition (1807, iii. 391) reads: "I suspect that this is a misprint, and that Johnson wrote 'without affecting stoicism'; —but the original letter being burned in a mass of papers in Scotland, I have not been able to ascertain whether my conjecture is well founded or not. The expression in the text, however, may be justified" (quoted, *Life* iii. 529). Chapman thought Malone's conjecture "more than probable" (*Letters SJ* 578 n. 5). Ironically, the printing of Malone's conjecture created a more vexed question: Did he in fact write "burned", or did the printer misread "buried"? See Prof. Pottle's arguments for "buried" in his forthcoming history of the Boswell Papers.

[7] He did, and it was so printed in the first edition. The error crept into the second. Malone corrected it silently in the fourth. See *Life* iii. 369.

[8] See *ante* To Barber, 22 Jan. and From Barber c. 20 Feb. 1779 and notes.

[9] *Life* iii. 131–32. The letter is dated *Sept.* 1, 1777.

[10] In the fourth edition Malone pointed out the error of "wine" for "time" and what he thought was SJ's error of "virtue" for "nature", quoting Sidney's sonnet as printed in Harington's *Orlando Furioso* (1591, p. 87). But SJ was remembering the second edition of the *Arcadia* (p. 196): "To vertue, fortune, time & womans brest" (*Life* iii. 493). The original of SJ's letter is untraced. For a more

Perhaps after all, the letters may not be in your possession, but in the hands of Mr. Boswell at Auchinleck; if so, I beg the favour of you to forward these inquiries to him, and remain, dear Sir, with sincere regard and esteem, Your most faithful and obedient humble Servant,

EDMOND MALONE

In vol. 3. p. 285 (last edit.),[11] the author says,—"And yet I have in my large and various collection of his writings a Letter to an eminent friend, in which he expresses himself thus: 'My godson called on me lately' " etc.

As I suppose among Mr. B.'s papers he could not have had many *original* letters from Johnson, not addressed to himself, perhaps this letter may not be difficult to be found. If you should stumble upon it, I request to know, to whom it was addressed; for it seems odd that it was not inserted *entire*, according to the general plan observed in the work. Perhaps the contents may explain this matter, and furnish the reason of its omission.[12]

In various parts of Mr. B.'s work, he has mentioned certain papers, in manuscript, as if they had been deposited by him in the Museum etc.; intending doubtless to deposit them very speedily in the places mentioned. In conformity to his intention I deposited in the Museum after his death one of the *copies* of Johnson's Letter to Lord Chesterfield, corrected by Johnson[13]—which I mended and covered, that it might remain to posterity. The other yet remains to be deposited.[14] —Johnson's famous letter to Macpherson, in Mr. B.'s handwriting, but corrected by Johnson, was intended for the same repository: but I know not where it is.[15] Would it not be right to send it there? So also in vol. 3. p. 381; he says, he meant to deposit a slip of paper in the Bodleian Library, in which Johnson authorised him to make a correction in one of the Verses of his poem, entitled *London*.[16] This certainly has not been done.

technical analysis of how "wine" and "time" might be confused in reading SJ's hand, see *Letters SJ* 541 n. 1.

[11] *Life* iii. 266.

[12] The letter was to Dr. Mudge, 9 Sept. 1783. For the reason of its omission, see *ante* From Mudge, 13 Nov. 1787 and n. 4.

[13] The copy dictated to Baretti and presented to Langton: see *ante* From Brocklesby, 13 Dec. 1784 and n. 8.

[14] The copy dictated to JB in 1781: see *ante* From Adams, 17 Feb. 1785, n. 27.

[15] See *ante* From Hussey, Aug. 1787, n. 14.

[16] Rather, *The Vanity of Human Wishes*. See *Life* iii. 357–58 and 358 n. 1. The slip of paper was preserved among the Boswell Papers and was presented by Col. Isham to the Bodleian Library in 1947 (*Bodleian Library Record*, 1947, ii. 179).

From Malone to Sir William Forbes, Monday 23 April 1804

MS. estate of the late Lord Clinton. JB's account of the Round Robin having been printed off, it is too late to alter it; but any misconception will be prevented by Malone's note stating that the original is in the possession of Bishop Barnard (4th ed., 1804, iii. 84 n.*).

From Malone to Sir William Forbes, Wednesday 2 May 1804

MS. estate of the late Lord Clinton.

Queen Anne Street, East, May 2. 1804

DEAR SIR, I had the favour of yours of the 25th of April[1] a few days ago, and am sorry to find that my inquiries occasioned you so much trouble. —The Materials from which Mr. Boswell formed his book is an immense mass; but I conceive the paper we are in quest of (I mean Dr. Johnson's original letter to Mr. Boswell, dated Ashbourne Sep. 1. 1777,) will not be found among them.[2] I apprehend he kept all Dr. Johnson's letters to himself in one bundle, and arranged in the order of time; and this bundle must be either in your possession or at Auchinleck.[3] —I have ventured to print *time* instead of *wine*, agreably to Sidney's sonnet; and am confident that whenever Johnson's letter is found, we shall see that the errour arose from the transcript made from it and sent to the press.[4] . . .

Whenever the Letter I have mentioned shall turn up, or the other papers that Mr. Boswell promised to deposite in the Museum and Bodleian Library, I shall hope to hear from you, and in the mean time beg you will believe me to be with sincere respect and esteem, Dear Sir, Your most humble and obedient Servant,

EDMOND MALONE . . .

---

[1] Not recovered.
[2] See *ante* 3 Mar. 1804 and n. 9.
[3] Only one of SJ's letters to JB was found at Fettercairn; three others have been recovered; the rest are missing. See *Letters SJ* iii. 276, and Mary Hyde,

"Not in Chapman," *Johnson, Boswell and Their Circle*, p. 314. For JB's letters to SJ, see *ante* From Brocklesby, 27 Dec. 1784 and n. 23.
[4] See *ante* 3 Mar. 1804 and n. 10.

From Malone to Sir William Forbes, Friday 4 May 1804

MS. estate of the late Lord Clinton.

Queen Anne Street, East, May 4. 1804

DEAR SIR, Though I wrote to you so lately, a circumstance has since occurred,[1] which induces me to trouble you again. Doubts having been entertained concerning the external appearance of Mrs. Johnson, I have taken some pains with a view to obtain information on that point. —In the last letter which Doctor Johnson wrote to his step-daughter Lucy Porter, dated *Dec. 2. 1784*, only eleven days before his death, he sent her a translation of the Latin Epitaph which he had then recently written for his wife, in which he describes her as *formosa*. Mr. Boswell has printed this letter, but has, I know not why, omitted Johnson's translation of this epitaph;[2] which is the more singular, as he was so very anxious to obtain from Johnson a translation of the very short inscription on his Picture of Mary Queen of Scots.[3] —Wishing to print this letter at full and without any mutilation, I requested Dr. Vyse of Lambeth, (a Lichfield man,) to write to Mrs. Porter's executor, to obtain from him Johnson's original letter of the date above given; but I learned from his answer yesterday, that Mr. Boswell had not returned it, and of consequence, that it must be among his papers,[4] and probably in the very place to which it properly belongs, near the end of his work being, I think, the last *letter* in the book, and coming in immediately before Johnson['s] death and Will. —I shall be much obliged to you therefore, if you can hunt out this Letter, and transmit it to me. —I had conceived, as I believe I mentioned in my last, that Mr. Boswell had kept Dr. Johnson's Letters addressed to himself in a distinct parcel; but if this is not the case, and they are blended with the other materials of his work, would it not be adviseable to take them *all out*, and arrange them in chronological order, to be preserved as an honourable testimony to the Author, in the Library at Auchinlecke? As Johnson's handwriting is so remarkable, I should hope it would not be attended

---

[1] MS. "occcurred"

[2] *Life* iv. 394. Malone let it stand without comment. See *Letters SJ* 1041.

[3] *Life* ii. 270, 283, 293 n. 2.

[4] See *ante* From Pearson, 2 Apr. 1785 and notes.

with much trouble. —With respect however to the letter in question, being addressed to Mrs. Lucy Porter, it doubtless will be found in its proper place, under December 1784, with the other matter respecting his last illness and death.[5]

They are proceeding at the printing-house with great rapidity, yet if I hear from you in the course of a week, I think I shall be able to make the insertion I propose, the letter in question coming in at p. 421 of the 4th volume, according to the last edition. —Believe me, Dear Sir, with great sincerity and esteem, Your most faithful and obedient Servant,

EDMOND MALONE

From the Rev. Dr. William Maxwell to Malone,
Thursday 10 May 1804

MS. Yale (C 1992).

ADDRESS: Edmond Malone Esqr., Queen Anne Strt. East, London.

Bath, May 10th 1804

DEAR SIR: I had the honor of your letter[1] A few days since, and was much flattered by your Obliging recollection of me. I made all possible Search to find the lines alluded to, but to no purpose. I perfectly recollect Johnson's repeating them, more than once, owing I presume to the Congeniality of the Sentiment with his own Ideas upon that Subject. I should think it most probable those lines might be found in Spencer, or Cowley, or perhaps Blackmore or Crashaw.[2] I left my books in Ireland, and I could not get Sight of Crashaw or Blackmore here. I am very happy to hear that A new Edition of Boswell's *Life of Johnson,* is soon to appear under your Auspices; It could not be in better hands, and am persuaded the Publick will be much oblig'd to you. If by chance I should discover, where those lines may be found, I shall do Myself the honor to

---

[5] The MS. *Life* shows that the original letter was sent to the printer as one of the Papers Apart for Dec. 1784. At a later date it was restored to the packet of Lucy Porter's letters which Pearson had sent to JB and was found among them at Fettercairn.

[1] Not recovered.

[2] The verses, transcribed by Maxwell in his "Collectanea", were later discovered by JB Jr. as being taken from William Walsh's *The Retirement,* and so noted by Malone in the sixth edition. See *Life* ii. 133 and n. 1, 491.

inform you, and remain, Dear Sir, with very Sincere respect, Your most faithfull and Obedient Servant

WM. MAXWELL

From Malone to James Boswell Junior,[1] Wednesday 28 September 1808

MS. Yale (C 1930).

ADDRESS: To James Boswell Esqre., Auchinleck, Machline, N.B.

POSTMARK: SE 28 808.

London, Sept. 28. 1808. Wednesday

. . . If you will turn to the following Letters,[2] I think we shall be able to make some valuable corrections.

1. In Johnson's letter (to your father) of May 27, 1775, towards the end—"I *would* be glad to have them"

2. In the same nearer the end,—"because I *would* be loath to leave any out." —Q. in both these places—"I *should*"—[3]

3. In Letter of Aug. 27, 1775—about 18 lines from the beginning, in the printed copy—"and by reading sometimes easy and sometimes curious." Q. curious *books*.[4]

4. In Letter Sept. 1, 1777. Quotation from Sidney. Q. whether the line runs thus:

"To *virtue*, fortune, *time*, and woman's breast."[5]

5. In Letter to Dr. Brocklesby (if you have it)—beginning July

[1] JB Jr. had furnished notes to the third and succeeding editions, and is credited in Malone's Advertisement to the sixth edition with having "read over" the whole. The year following Malone's death he contributed a biographical memoir to *Gent. Mag.* (1813, lxxxiii. 513–20); it was separately issued for private circulation (with additions) in 1814. In 1821 he brought out a new edition of Malone's Shakespeare (the "third variorum").

[2] From the issue of these inquiries it is apparent that James failed to find *some* of the letters to which Malone refers, and I am inclined to think that he found *none*.

[3] *Life* ii. 380. Virtually all of SJ's letters to JB, including those mentioned

here, are missing. Malone let the readings stand without comment. So did Chapman.

[4] Malone misquotes: "curious" for "serious". In the third edition a comma had been inserted after "reading"— probably by Malone, and probably for clarification: " 'For the black fumes which rise in your mind, I can prescribe nothing but that you disperse them by honest business or innocent pleasure, and by reading, sometimes easy and sometimes serious' " (*Life* iii. 382). Malone did not express his suspicion of the passage in subsequent editions.

[5] See *ante* Malone to Forbes, 3 Mar. 1804 and n. 10. No change was made in the sixth edition.

20 1784, (5th line of print)—"when accident *recovers* me." I think, it should be, *"removes* me." I fear you have not this letter; but if there be even a copy of it, it may be worth while to see how it stands in the copy.[6]

6. In Letter to Langton, Aug. 25, 1784,—"I had the consolation to find." I think some word before *consolation* has been omitted. So Q.—I applied to Langton about this; but he had not the letter; so I suppose it is with you.[7]

7. In Letter to Perkins, October 4, 1784. *"Please make."* I know not how Johnson came by this Scotticism. But I fear you have not the original letter. If the copy should be in your fathers hand-writing, he perhaps, from old habit, may have written thus:—or Johnson himself inadvertently omitted *"to."*[8]

Your father in various notes, in his book, has said that he *had* deposited certain papers in the Museum, etc. meaning to do so at some subsequent time. One of these I found; Johnson's Letter to Lord Chesterfield,—the Copy that Langton had, corrected by Johnson himself. This I mended and pasted on strong paper, and deposited in the Museum, as he intended.[9]

Johnson's Answer to Macpherson, in your father's handwriting —corrected I think by Johnson, if you can find it, should likewise go to the Museum, being promised.

A Slip of paper on which Johnson made the correction of the word *spreads*, substituting *burns* in its place, in the poem of *"London."* This was promised to the Bodl[eian] Lib[rar]y.

I cannot recollect other promised pieces:[10] but I have a faint recollection of something being promised to be given to Pembroke College.[11] . . .

---

[6] The original, found at Fettercairn, confirms Malone's conjecture (which he had noted in the third edition, iv. 369 n. *). The letter is dated 21 July, not, as JB states, the 20th (*Life* iv. 353).

[7] The original, found at Fettercairn, confirms the reading of the *Life* (iv. 361). Malone had noted his doubt and conjectures in the third edition, iv. 381 n. *. See *Letters SJ* 999 n. 3. Again, JB dated the letter one day too early.

[8] The word was dropped out in the printing of the fifth edition (iv. 391). It is surprising that Malone should have overlooked so elementary an explanation, or indeed that he should have trusted to so late an edition for questions regarding the text. In the sixth edition the error is preserved without comment. JB returned the original to Perkins: see *ante* 10 Oct. 1793.

[9] For this and the two items following, see *ante* Malone to Forbes, 3 Mar. 1804 and nn. 13, 15, and 16.

[10] See *Life* ii. 297 n. 2, 307 and 514, 399 n. 2 and 522.

[11] Not in the *Life*.

APPENDIX

Johnson's Sermons

Introductory Note

These "Fragments" from the notebook of the Rev. Daniel Astle (*ante* Dec. 1786) constitute portions of two sermons included in the collection published by the Rev. Samuel Hayes as *Sermons on Different Subjects Left for Publication by John Taylor, LL.D.* (1788, 1789): No. V in the first volume and No. XI in the second. It was an open secret in SJ's lifetime that he composed sermons for Taylor and other clergymen, and when Hayes's first volume appeared, SJ's authorship of a part if not the whole was suspected at once. See *Monthly Review* (1788) lxxix. 528; Hawkins, pp. 391–92; Davis, *Johnson Before Boswell*, pp. 93–94, 196–97. Hussey (*ante* Aug. 1787 and n. 2) noted in his copy of the *Life* that the sermons "were generally copied in his own study by those that employed him, and when finished he always destroyed the original in their presence" (quoted, *Life* iii. 507). Astle's fragmentary texts may have been transcribed directly from Taylor's own copies of the originals (in which case a number of the variants must be charged to Hayes's editing). In answer to JB's inquiry as to their authenticity, he writes: "The papers which I have already communicated to you, were long ago intrusted to me under a strict injunction of secrecy; so that you may safely rely upon their being authentic. The Originals [i.e. the original copies?] from whence these were taken, are now in London, where it is not in my power to obtain access to them" (*ante* 23 Jan. 1787). The injunction of secrecy would be a natural precaution for Taylor to take, and the presence of the "Originals" in London fits the fact that Taylor was Rector of St. Margaret's, Westminster. There can be little doubt that JB recognized the fragments for what they were. He remarks to Astle, "I *guess* at the way in which the *Fragments* are known to be authentick; but shall not express it, in my Compilation" (*ante* 14 Feb. 1787). And writing to Abercrombie after the *Life* was published, he says, "I have not yet been able to discover any more of his sermons, besides those *left for publication by Dr. Taylor*" (*ante* 11 June 1792). In his account in the *Life* of his visit with SJ at Ashbourne in Sept. 1777, JB takes up the matter of the sermons: "I have no doubt that a good many sermons were composed for

Taylor by Johnson. At this time I found, upon his table, a part of one which he had newly begun to write: and *Concio pro Tayloro* appears in one of his diaries [*Diaries*, p. 277]. When to these circumstances we add the internal evidence from the power of thinking and style, in the collection which the Reverend Mr. Hayes has published, with the *significant* title of 'Sermons *left for publication* by the Reverend John Taylor, LL.D' our conviction will be complete" (iii. 181). JB might have adduced the present fragments and reported Astle's claim for their authenticity, but as this evidence afforded no absolute proof of authorship, there was no reason not to stand by his promise not to publish his speculations in the *Life*.

For the canon of SJ's sermons, see J. H. Hagstrum, *Modern Philology* (1943) xl. 255, and the forthcoming edition of the sermons in the Yale Edition of the Works of Samuel Johnson. In the collations which follow, variants in spelling, punctuation, and paragraphing have been ignored. For Astle's scribal idiosyncrasies, see *ante* From Astle, Dec. 1786, n. 2.

A fine Sentiment.[1]

To be able to soften the calamities of Mankind, and to inspire gladness into a heart oppressed with want is indeed the noblest privilege of an enlarged fortune: but to exercise that privilege in all its generous refinements, is an instance of the most uncommon elegance both of temper and understanding.

In the ordinary dispensations of bounty, little address is required: but when it is to be applied to those of a superiour rank and more elevated mind, there is as much charity discovered in the manner as in the measure of one's benevolence. It is something extremely mortifying to a well-formed spirit, to see it-self considered as an object of compassion: as it is the part of improved humanity to humour this honest pride in our nature and to relieve the necessities without offending the delicacy of the distressed.

I have seen charity if charity it might be called insult with an air of pity, and wound at the same time that it healed. But I have seen too the highest munificence dispensed with the most refined tenderness and a bounty conferred with as much address as the most artful employ in soliciting one.

JOHNSON.

[1] These reflections, not mentioned by Astle in his letter, are closely paralleled in Sermon VI of the second volume.

A Fragment.
On the Miseries of Life.

Nehemiah IX. v. 33[2]

It is indeed hardly possible to write without falling upon this copious and extensive topic, for all science is little more than the art either of bearing Misery or avoiding it.[3]

*　　*　　*　　*

Some have endeavoured to engage us in the contemplation of the evils of life for a very wise and good end. They have proposed by laying before us the uncertainty of prosperity, the vanity of pleasure and the inquietudes of power, the difficult attainment of most earthly blessings, and the short duration of them all, to divert our thoughts from the glittering follies and tempting delusions that surround us, to an enquiry after more certain and permanent felicity; felicity not subject to be interrupted by sudden vicissitudes, or impaired by the malice of the revengeful, the caprice of the inconstant or the envy of the ambitious.[4]

*　　*　　*　　*

Others have taken occasion from the dangers that surround, and the troubles that perplex us, to dispute the wisdom or justice of the Governour of the world or to murmur at the Laws of divine Providence, as the present state of the world, the disorder and

[2] The verse is quoted in the *Sermons*: "Howbeit thou art just in all that is brought upon us, for thou hast done right, but we have done wickedly."

[3] In place of this sentence the printed sermon begins: "There is nothing upon which more Writers, in all ages, have laid out their abilities, than the miseries of life; and it affords no pleasing reflections to discover that a subject so little agreeable is not yet exhausted."

[4] The printed sermon continues: "They have endeavoured to demonstrate, and have in reality demonstrated to all those who will steal a few moments from noise and show, and luxury, to attend to reason and to truth, that nothing is worthy of our ardent wishes, or intense solicitude, that terminates in this state of existence, and that those only make the true use of life, that employ it in obtaining favour of God, and securing everlasting happiness."

confusion of every thing about us, the casual and certain evils to which we are exposed, and the disquiet and disgust which either accompany or follow those few pleasures that are within our reach, seem in their opinion to carry no marks of infinite benignity. This has been the reasoning by which the wicked and profligate in all ages have attempted to harden their hearts against the REPROACHES OF CONSCIENCE, and to[5] delude others into a participation of their CRIMES.

By this Argument weak minds have been betrayed into doubts and distrust, and decoyed by degrees into a dangerous state of suspen[ce][6] though perhaps never depraved[7] to absolute infidelity. For few men have been made infidels by argument and reflection, their actions are not generally the result of their reasonings, but their reasonings the result[8] of their actions, yet those[9] reasonings though they are not strong enough to pervert a good mind, may yet when they coincide with interest, and are assisted by prejudice contribute to confirm a man already corrupted, in his impieties, and at least retard his reformation if not entirely obstruct it.

Besides, notions derogatory[10] from the Providence of God tend even in the best men if not timely eradicated, to weaken those impressions of reverence and gratitude which are necessary to add warmth to his devotions and vigour to his virtue: for as the force of corporeal motion is weakened by every obstruction, though it may not be entirely overcome by it, so the operations of the mind are by every false notion impeded and embarrassed and though they are not wholly diverted or suppress'd, proceed at least with less regularity and with less celerity.

But these doubts may easily be removed and these arguments confuted by a calm and impartial attention to religion and to reason; it will appear upon examination, that though the world be full of Misery and disorder, yet God is not to be charged with disregard of his Creation, that if we suffer, we suffer by our own Fault, and that "He has done right, but we have done wickedly."

[5] *Sermons,* "to" omitted.
[6] Here and elsewhere in the MS. Astle has left some letters blank. In every case the reason appears to be some doubt about the proper spelling. In every case I have supplied the spelling of the printed version.

[7] *Sermons,* "betrayed"
[8] *Sermons,* "the result" omitted.
[9] *Sermons,* "these"
[10] *Sermons,* "thus derogatory"

APPENDIX

We are informed by the Scriptures, that God is not the Author of our present state, that when he created man, he created him for happiness, happiness indeed depend[e]nt upon his own choice, and to be preserved by his own conduct, for such must necessarily be the happiness, of every reasonable being; that this happiness was forfeited by a breach of the conditions to which it was annexed, and that the posterity of him that broke the Covenant, were involved in the Consequences of the[11] Fault.

Thus Religion shews us, that Physical and Moral Evil entered the World together, and reason and experience assure us, that they continue for the most part so closely united, that to avoid Misery, we must avoid Sin, and that while it is in our power to be virtuous, it is in our power to be happy, at least to be happy to such a degree, as may have little room for murmur and complaints.

Complaints are doubtless irrational in themselves, and unjust with respect to God, if the remedies of the evils we lament, are in our own[12] hands, for what more can be expected from the Beneficence of our Creator, than that he should place Good and Evil before us, and then direct us in our Choice.

That God has not been sparing in[13] his Bounties to Mankind, or left them even since the original Transgression of his Command, in a state so calamitous as discontent and melancholy have represented it will evidently appear if we reflect

First how few of the Evils of Life can justly be ascribed to God.

Secondly how far a general piety might exempt any community from those evils.

Thirdly how much in the present corrupt state of the world, particular men, may by the practice of the duties of Religion, promote their own happiness.

First how few of the Evils of Life can justly be ascribed to God.

In examining what part of our present Misery is to be imputed to God, we must carefully distinguish that which is actually appointed by him, from that which is only permitted, or that which is the consequence of something done by ourselves and could not be prevented, but by the interruption of those general and settled Laws which we term the *Course* of *Nature*, or the established order of the Universe. Thus it is decreed etc.[14]

---

[11] *Sermons*, "his"
[12] *Sermons*, "own" omitted.
[13] *Sermons*, "of"

[14] The MS. breaks off at this point, having covered approximately one-third of the printed sermon.

A Fragment.

Proverbs XXIX. v. 2.

When the righteous are in authority,
the people rejoice: but when the wicked
beareth rule, the people mourn.[15]

This is a Truth which it would be very superfluous to prove by authorities or illustrate by examples.[16] Every Page of History whether sacred or profane will furnish us abundantly with instances of rulers that have deviated from justice, and of[17] subjects that have forgotten their allegiance, of nations ruined by the tyranny of governours, and of governours overbourn by the madness of the populace.

Instead of a concurrence between governour and subject[18] for their mutual advantage, they seem to have considered each other not as allies or friends to be aided and supported but as enemies whose prosperity was inconsistent with their own, and who were therefore to be subdued by open force or subjected by secret stratagems. Thus have slavery and licentiousness succeeded one another and anarchy and despotick power alternately prevailed, virtue has at one time stood exposed to the punishments of vice, and vice at another time enjoyed the security and privileges of virtue.[19]

Man is for the most part equally unhappy when subjected without redress to the passions of another or left without controul to the dominion of his own. This every man however unwilling he may

---

[15] Only the first half of the verse appears in the printed sermon.

[16] This is the second sentence of the printed sermon. The first reads: "That the institutions of government owe their original, like other human actions, to the desire of happiness, is not to be denied; nor is it less generally allowed, that they have been perverted to very different ends from those which they were intended to promote."

[17] *Sermons,* "of" omitted.

[18] *Sermons,* "subjects"

[19] The printed sermon continues: "Nor have communities suffered more, when they were exposed to the passions and caprices of one man, however cruel, ambitious, or insolent, than when all restraint has been taken off the actions of men by publick confusions, and every one left at full liberty to indulge his own desires, and comply, without fear of punishment, with his wildest imaginations."

617

be to own it of himself will very readily acknowledge of his neighbour.

No man knows any one except himself whom he judges fit to be set free from the Coercion of Laws, and to be abandoned entirely to his own Choice. By this consideration have all civilized nations been induced to the enaction[20] of penal Laws, of[21] Laws by which every man's danger becomes every man's safety, and which[22] tho' all are restrained yet all are benefitted.[23]

Corrupt[24] governments operate with equal force and efficacy to the destruction of a people, as good governments to their preservation. But that authority may never swell into tyranny, or languish into supineness, and that subjection may never degenerate into slavery nor freedom kindle into rebellion it may be proper both for those from whom obedience is required[25]

If it be true in general that no man is born merely for his own sake, to consult his own advantage or pleasure unconnected with the good of others who are exalted into high rank dignified with honours and invested with authority,[26] their superiority is not to be considered as a sanction for laziness, or privilege for[27] vice. They are not to conceive that their passions are to be allowed a wider range, or their appetites set more free from subjection to Reason than those of others. They are not to consult their own glory at the expence of the lives of others or to gratify their avarice by

---

[20] *Sermons*, "enactions"

[21] *Sermons*, "of" omitted.

[22] *Sermons*, "by which"

[23] The printed sermon continues: "Government is therefore necessary, in the opinion of every one, to the safety of particular men, and the happiness of society; and it may be considered as a maxim universally admitted, that *the people* cannot *rejoice*, except *the righteous are in authority*; that no publick prosperity, or private quiet, can be hoped for, but from the justice and wisdom of those to whom the administration of affairs, and the execution of the laws, is committed."

[24] *Sermons*, "For corrupt"

[25] The sentence breaks off, and a space of several lines is left blank before the text is resumed. The incomplete sentence contains a scribal omission, due no doubt to the repetition of "those". The printed sermon reads: "both for those who are intrusted with power, and those from whom obedience is required, to consider," and proceeds: "/First, How much it is the duty of those in authority to promote the happiness of the people. /Secondly, By what means the happiness of the people may be most effectually promoted. /Thirdly, How the people are to assist and further the endeavours of their governors. /First, How much it is the duty of those in authority to promote the happiness of the people."

[26] The omission of a phrase in the MS. obscures the meaning of the entire passage. The printed sermon reads, after "good of others": "it is yet more evidently true of those" etc.

[27] MS. "ofor"

plundering those whom diligence and labour have entitled to affluence. They are not to conceive that power gives a right to oppress and to punish those who murmur at oppression. They are to look upon their power and their greatness as instruments placed in their hands to be employed for the public advantage, they are to remember that[28] they are placed upon an eminence, that their examples may be more conspicuous and that therefore they must take care lest they teach those vices which they ought to suppress. They must reflect that it is their duty to secure property from the attempts of rapine and robery, and that those whom they protect will be very little benefitted by their care if what they rescue from others, they take away themselves.[29]

Nothing then can equal the obligations of governours to the people, and nothing but the most flagrant ingratitude can make them careless of the interests or unconcerned at the misfortunes of those to whom they owe that for which no danger has been thought too dreadful to be encountered no labour too tedious to be undergone and no crime too horrible to be committed.

Gratitude is a species of justice; *he* that requites a benefit may be said in some sense to pay a debt, and consequently[30] *he* that forgets favours received may be accused of neglecting to pay what he cannot be denied to owe.[31]

It is with the greatest[32] reason that large revenues pompous titles, and all that contribute[33] to the happiness of life are annexed to those[34] high offices; for what reward can be too great for him to whom multitudes are indebted for the secure enjoyments[35] of their possessions, for him whose authority checks the progress of

[28] *Sermons*, "that" omitted.

[29] The printed sermon continues: "/It appears from those struggles for dominion, which have filled the world with war, bloodshed and desolation, and have torn in pieces almost all the states and kingdoms of the earth, and from those daily contests for subordinate authority, which disturb the quiet of smaller societies, that there is somewhat in power more pleasing than in any other enjoyment; and, consequently, to bestow upon man the happiness of ruling others, is to bestow upon him the greatest benefit he is capable of receiving."

[30] *Sermons*, "and, of course,"

[31] The printed sermon continues: "But this is not the only sense in which justice may be said to require from a Governour an attention to the wants and petitions of the people. He that engages in the management of publick business, takes a trust upon him, which it was in his power to decline, and which he is therefore bound to discharge with diligence and fidelity; a trust which is of the highest honour, because it is of the greatest difficulty and importance, a trust which includes, not only the care of the property, but of the morals of the people."

[32] *Sermons*, "justest"

[33] *Sermons*, "contributes"

[34] *Sermons*, "these"

[35] *Sermons*, "enjoyment"

vice, and assists the advancements[36] of virtue, restrains the violence of oppression,[37] and asserts the cause of the injured and the innocent.[38] These are doubtless merits above the common rate, merits which can hardly be too loudly celebrated or too liberally rewarded.

But it is to[39] be observed that he only deserves the recompence who performs the work for which it is proposed, and that he that[40] wears the honours and receives the revenues of an exalted station[41] without attending to the duties[42] is in a very high degree criminal both in the eyes of God and Man.[43]

In political as well as natural disorders the great erro[ur] of those who commonly undertake either cure or preservation is that they rest in second Causes without extending their search to the remote and original sources of evil, they therefore obviate the immediate evil, but leave the destructive principle to operate again, and have their work forever to begin like the Husbandman who mows down the HEADS of noisome weeds instead of pulling up the *roots*.

The only uniform and perpetual Cause of publick happiness is public virtue. The Effects of all other things which are considered AS ADVANTAGES, will be found casual and transitory; without virtue nothing can be securely possessed or properly enjoyed.

In a Country like ours the great Demand which is for-ever repeated to our Governours is for the security of property, the confirmation of liberty, and the exten[s]ion of commerce. All this we have obtained and all this we possess in a degree which perhaps was never granted to any other people, yet we still find something wanting to our happiness, and turn ourselves round on all sides with perpetual restlessness to find that remedy for our Evils which neither power nor policy can afford.

That established prosperity[44] and inviolable Freedom are the greatest of political felicities no man can be supposed likely to deny. To depend upon[45] the Will of another to labour for that of which

[36] *Sermons*, "advancement"
[37] *Sermons*, "the oppressour"
[38] *Sermons*, "and the innocent" omitted.
[39] *Sermons*, "always to"
[40] *Sermons*, "who"
[41] *Sermons*, "nation". The MS. is doubtless correct.
[42] *Sermons*, "duties of his post,"
[43] The printed sermon continues: "/It

is, therefore, the certain and apparent duty of those that are in authority, to take care that the people may rejoice, and diligently to enquire, what is to be considered. /Secondly, By what means the happiness of the people may be most effectually promoted."
[44] *Sermons*, "property"
[45] *Sermons*, "on"

arbitrary power can prohibit the enjoyment is the state to which want of reason has subjected the Brute.[46]

Human Laws however honestly instituted or however vigorously inforced must be limited in their effect, partly by our ignorance and partly by our weakness.

Daily experience convinces[47] us that all the avenues by which Injury and Oppression may break in upon LIFE cannot be guarded against[48] by positive prohibitions; every man sees and may feel evils which no laws[49] can punish. And not only will there always remain possibilities of guilt which legislative foresight cannot discover, but the laws will be often violated by wicked men whose subtelty eludes detection and whom therefore vindictive Justice cannot bring within the reach of Punishment.

These deficiencies in civil life can be supplied only by Religion. The mere observer of human laws, avoids only such offences as the laws forbid and those only when the Laws can detect his Delinquency.

But he who acts with the perpetual consciousness of the DIVINE PRESENCE and considers himself as accountable for all his Actions to the irreversible and unerring Judgment of Omniscience has other motives of action and other reasons of forbearance; he is equally restrained from evil in publick[50] and in secret solitude, and has only one rule of action, by which he does to others what he would that others should do to him and wants no other enforcement of his Duty than the fear of future Punishments[51] and the hope of future Rewards.[52]

* * * *

The wisdom of Mankind has been exercised in enquiries how riches may be gained and kept; how the different claims of men may be adjusted without violence, and how one part of the community may be restrained from encroachments on the other.

[46] At this point the printed sermon departs from the MS. for a little more than a page, after which it proceeds, first with the conclusion of the fragment ("The Wisdom of Mankind" etc.) and then with the section following the point of departure ("Human Laws" etc.).

[47] *Sermons,* "may convince"

[48] *Sermons,* "against" omitted.

[49] *Sermons,* "law"

[50] *Sermons,* "publick life,"

[51] *Sermons,* "punishment,"

[52] The remaining seven pages of the printed sermon complete the discussion of the second theme ("By what means the happiness of the people may be most effectually promoted") and briefly treat the third theme ("How the people are to assist and further the endeavours of their Governours").

For this end governments have been instituted in all their various forms, with much study and too often with much blood-shead; but what is the use of all this if when these ends are obtained there is[53] so much wanting to felicity. I am far from intending to insinuate that the studies of political wisdom or the labours of legislative patriotism have been vain and idle. They are useful but not effectual, they are conducive to that end which yet they cannot fully gain. The legislator who does what human power can attain towards the felicity of his fellow creatures is not to be censured, because by the imbecility of all human endeavours he fails of his purpose, unless he has become culpable by ascribing too much to his own powers, and arrogated to his Industry or his Wit that Efficacy which Wit and Industry must always want unless some higher power lends them Assistance.[54]

The husbandman may plow his fields with industry and sow them with skill, he may manure them copiously and fence them carefully, but the harvest must depend at last on celestial influ-ences[55] and all his diligence is frustrated unless the Sun sheds its warmth and the Clouds pour down their moisture.

Thus in all human affairs when prudence and industry have done their utmost the work is left to be compleated by a[56] superior agency, and in the security of peace, and stability of possession our policy must at last call for helps[57] upon RELIGION.

*　　*　　*　　*

[53] *Sermons*, "is yet"
[54] *Sermons*, "and co-operates with them."

[55] *Sermons*, "influence"
[56] *Sermons*, "a" omitted.
[57] *Sermons*, "help"

Index

The following abbreviations are used: D. (Duke), M. (Marquess), E. (Earl), V. (Viscount), B. (Baron), JB (James Boswell), SJ (Samuel Johnson), *Life* (Boswell's *Life of Johnson*). For convenience in alphabetical arrangement, "Boswell" and "Johnson" are not abbreviated at the beginning of sub-entries. The sub-entry "letters" under personal names refers not to the letters that make up this volume (these are listed in the Alphabetical Table of Correspondents, pages xiii–xix) but to others that are cited, quoted, or mentioned.

Abercrombie, James, father of following, d. 1760, 550 *n.* 22.

Abercrombie, James, D.D., 1758–1841, account of, 462 *n.* 1, 550 *n.* 22; Johnson's letters to American correspondents, mentioned by, 463–64, 490–91 *and n.* 1, 532–33; Johnson's works, edition planned by, 462 *n.* 1; letter from Rush to, on SJ, text, 533–36 *and n.* 7; *Life* presented to, 548; portraits of JB and SJ received by, 538; on Rush's collection of Smollett's letters, 536–37.

Abercromby, General Sir Ralph, 1734–1801, 550 *n.* 22.

Abington, Frances (Barton), actress, 1737–1815, account of, 422 *n.* 1, *n.* 2; benefit for, 422 *n.* 3.

Adams, George, d. 1773, *Treatise on the Globes*, preface by SJ, 318.

Adams, Sarah (Mrs. Benjamin Hyett), dau. of William Adams, 1746–1804, account of, 11 *n.* 4, 155 *n.* 1; Boswell calls on, 216 *n.* 2, 217 *n.* 5; memorandum on SJ reported lost by, 216–17; mentioned, 11, 20, 42, 112, 128, 161, 162 *and n.*

Adams, Sarah (Hunt), wife of William Adams, d. 1785, account of, 11 *n.* 4; death, 112 *n.* 2; mentioned, 11, 20, 42.

Adams, William, D.D., 1706–89, account of, 10 *n.* 1, 11 *n.* 4, 12 *n.* 2, *n.* 3; Boswell visits, 10 *n.* 1, 20 *n.* 1, *n.* 6, 21 *n.* 1, 152 *n.* 1; epitaph for, 561, 567, 568, 571 *and n.* 3;

Johnson, contributions on, xxxvii,

21–25, 56–63, 159–62, Chesterfield, quarrel with, 21–22 *and n.* 1, *n.* 7, 24–25, 60–62, *Irene*, first performance, xxviii–xxix, 22 *and n.* 9, *n.* 10; last visit, 62 *and n.* 33, 161, melancholy, 24 *and n.* 20, 161, at Oxford, 23 *and n.* 13, 57–58 *and n.* 10, *n.* 11, prayers, 62, 161, 161–62 *and n.* 15;

Johnson influenced by, 207; Johnson visits, 20 *n.* 1, *n.* 6; letter to SJ from, 11 *n.* 1; letter to Scott from, 62 *n.* 33; letters from SJ to, 82 *and n.* 4, 128, 155–56, 159 *and n.* 4; portrait by Opie, 217 *and n.* 6; mentioned xxxviii, 352, 561 *n.* 10, 572.

Addison, Joseph, 1672–1719, 72, 589; *see also Spectator.*

Adey, Mary (Mrs. John Sneyd), 1742–1830, account of, 54 *n.* 1; Johnson, contributions on, 63–71; Johnson's letter to Simpson copied, 67–70; letters to Mrs. Piozzi from, 67 *n.* 15, 68 *n.* 18, 69 *n.* 34, 70 *n.* 41; mentioned, 52 *n.* 1, 56, 66 *n.* 13, 287, 288, 290

Adventurer, The, 164 *n.* 4, 168 *n.* 32, 169 *n.* 40, 201 *n.* 2, 311 *and n.* 1, *n.* 2, 312 *and n.* 3, *n.* 4, 387; Johnson's contributions to, 5, 311.

Adye (? Adee), Swithin, M.D., 152 *n.* 1.

Agutter, Rev. William, 1758–1835, account of, 494 *n.* 1; *Christian Politics*, 495 *and n.* 1; sermon on death of SJ, 493, 494 *and n.* 3, 495 *n.* 2, 459.

Akenside, Mark, poet, 1721–70, *Pleasures of the Imagination*, Rolt's publication of, 387, 391, 392, 399 *and n.* 1.

INDEX

Beville, Rev. William, 1755–1822, 473 *n.* 1; *Observations on Dr. Johnson's Life of Hammond*, 474 *and n.* 2.

Bewley, William, surgeon, 1726–83, 489 *and n.* 3; specimen of SJ's handwriting sent to, 494 *and n.* 1.

Bible, *Luke*, 358; *Romans*, 455 *n.* 3; translations of, 355 *and n.* 4.

Binning, Charles Hamilton, Lord, *later* 8th E. of Haddington, 1753–1828, 143.

Birch, Thomas, D.D., 1705–66, 497.

Birmingham, Johnson and JB visit, 11 *n.* 3; Johnson lives in, 86–87 *and n.* 7, *n.* 10, 172 *and n.* 16; Music Festival, 236 *n.* 4.

Birmingham Journal, The, 87, *and n.* 12.

Birmingham riots, 1791, 456 *and n.* 10.

Blackmore, Sir Richard, author and physician, ?1650–1729, 356 *n.* 5, 499 *and n.* 29, 605.

Blackstone, Sir William, 1723–80, anecdote of, in *Life*, 599–600 *and n.* 2, *n.* 3.

Blackwall, Rev. Anthony, 1674–1730, *Introduction to the Classics*, 200 *and n.* 20.

Blagden, Charles, M.D., 1748–1820, account of, 332 *n.* 1, *n.* 2; Johnson on, 372; Johnson's words in diary interpreted, 332–33, 337–38.

Blair, Hugh, D.D., 1718–1800, account of, 71 *n.* 1, *n.* 4; at Crown and Anchor with SJ and JB, 287; Johnson's writings criticized by, 71–73; journal, requests for, 230, 237; letter to JB from, 140; *The Resurrection*, poem by Blair and Bannatyne, 230–31, 232 *and n.* 2.

Blair, Rev. Robert, poet, 1699–1746, 560 *and n.* 1, 567, 571; letter to Doddridge from, 567 *n.* 4.

Blenheim Palace, Oxfordshire, 356; library, 354 *n.* 3.

Bolingbroke, Henry St. John, 1st V., 1678–1751, 158 *n.* 4; Pope and, 498 *n.* 16, 507 *and n.* 18.

Bond, Phineas, 1749–1815, 463 *and n.* 6; letter from SJ to, 463, 464, 484–85, 538 *n.* 22; portraits of JB and SJ sent to Abercrombie, 538.

Boothby, Sir Brooke, 1710–89, 198 *n.* 2, 237 *n.* 4.

Boothby, Brooke, son of preceding, 1744–1824, 237 *n.* 4.

Boothby, Hill, 1708–56, letters from SJ to, 198 *n.* 2, 237 *and n.* 4, 592 *n.* 7.

Boswell, Alexander, son of JB, 1775–1822, at Edinburgh University, 582 *and n.* 3; at Eton, 340 *n.* 1, 417; letters from JB to, lxxi, lxxiv, lxxviii, 436 *n.* 1, 582 *n.* 3; letter to JB from, 417; letters copied by, 258, 517; mentioned, 565, 577, 581.

Boswell, Claud Irvine, *later* Lord Balmuto, 1742–1824, 565 *n.* 1; *Life* presented to, 565; mentioned, 570.

Boswell, David. *See* Boswell, Thomas David.

Boswell, Elizabeth, dau. of JB, 1780–1814, 474, 481 *n.* 2, 566, 576, 582, 583.

Boswell, Euphemia, dau. of JB, 1774–1837, 331 *and n.* 4, 406 *n.* 4, 474, 481 *n.* 2, 482 *n.* 5, 504 *n.* 1, 566, 576, 582, 583.

Boswell, James, 1740–1795.
> *Letters from:* to Barnard, 41 *n.* 4; to Boswell, Alexander, lxxi, lxxiv, lxxviii, 436 *n.* 1, 555 *n.* 1, 582 *n.* 3; to Mrs. Boswell, lvi, lxv; to Dempster, lxxv; to Erskine, 518 *n.* 8; to Forbes, 213 *n.* 2, 293 *n.* 5, 425 *n.* 1; to Garrick, 9 *n.* 1, *n.* 3; to Hailes, 420 *n.* 8; to Johnson, lii, returned, xxiv *and n.* 1, 34 *and n.* 23; to Langton, 270 *n.* 13, 308 *n.* 1; to Malone, lxiv, lxix, 119 *n.* 2, 456 *n.* 9; to Oglethorpe, 550 *n.* 23; to Percy, lxviii; to Mrs. (Thrale) Piozzi, lii, liii; to Anna Seward, 163 *n.* 1, in *Gentleman's Magazine*, 289 *n.* 1, 576 *n.* 6; to Smollett, 536 *and n.* 17; to Temple, lii, lxviii, lxxv, lxxvii, lxiv–lxvi, 442 *n.* 1, *n.* 2; 489 *n.* 2; to Thurlow, 28 *and n.* 11; to Walker, 117 *n.* 4.

> *Letters to:* from Barnard, 428 *n.* 11; from Blair, 140; from Boswell, Alexander, 417; from Johnson, xxiv, 15 *n.* 1, 52 *n.* 1, 140 *n.* 7, 468 *n.* 12, 490 *and n.* 1, in *Life*, 600–1, 606, original manuscripts, 603 *and n.* 3, 604, 606 *n.* 3; from Langton, 354 *n.* 2; from Malone, 119 *n.* 2; from Anna Seward, 163 *n.* 1, 337 *n.* 10, in *Gentleman's Magazine*, 289 *n.* 1; from Stedman, 571 *n.* 2, 572 *n.* 6.

626

INDEX

INDEX

Johnson, Joseph, bookseller, 1738–1809, and n. 4.

Johnson, Michael, father of SJ, 1656–1731, bookshop in Birmingham, 86–87; death, 57 n. 11, 58, 80 and n. 17; epitaph, 225 n. 1; Johnson disobeys, does penance at Uttoxeter, 389; and Johnson's epitaph on a duck, 64 n. 2; Pope's *Messiah*, SJ's translation, printed for, xxxvii, 104 and n. 40; mentioned, 56, 81 n. 19.

Johnson, Rev. "*Samuel*". *See* Johnson, Rev. John.

Johnson, Rev. Samuel, father of William Samuel Johnson, 1692–1772, 490 n. 1.

JOHNSON, SAMUEL, LL.D., 1709–1784.
Biographical: advocate, thinks of becoming, 58 n. 16, 59 and n. 17, 161; Baretti, trial of, 151 and n. 21; in Birmingham, 86–87; Chesterfield, quarrel with, 21–22 and n. 1–n. 7, 24–25, 60–62, 218 and n. 1, 234–35 and n. 11; childhood: Dame Oliver, teacher at Lichfield, 205, epitaph on a duck, 64 and n. 2, 79–80, in Lichfield Cathedral, 64, touched by Queen Anne for scrofula, 85 and n. 3; death, xl–xli, 48 and n. 4, 135, 390, Boswell's reaction to, 29 n. 1, Brocklesby describes, xl–xli, 25–28, 31–35; degrees: diplomas, JB asks Hawkins for, 271–72 and n. 1, 275, 276, LL.D. (Dublin), 174–75 and n. 1, n. 2, D.C.L. (Oxford), 62, 153, M.A. (Oxford), 62, 145 and n. 5, 160, 212 n. 2; epitaph by Parr, 451 and n. 6, n. 7, 452, 456 and n. 9, 457; Essex Head Club, formation of, 136; Garrick, relationship with, 148–50; George III, interview with. *See* George III; illness: asthma, 19 n. 1, 85 n. 3, dropsy, 19 n. 1, 91, last, 91, 100–01, 277 n. 3, sarcocele, 256 and n. 4, scrofula, 85 n. 3; at Lichfield with JB, 11 and n. 1, 21 n. 1, 53 n. 1; Literary Club, formation of, 268–69; lives of, before JB's work, 35 and n. 26, 40 n. 2; London, arrival in, 207 and n. 18, advised to be a porter, 233 and n. 5; London residences: Bolt Court, 133 n. 3, 524, Fetter Lane, 107, Gough Square, 90 and n. 35, 164, 166 and n. 15, Inner Temple Lane, 165 n. 14; love affairs, 90 n. 31, Ann Carless, 42 n. 1, Olivia Lloyd, 88 and n. 22,

Mrs. Paul (false story), 89–90, "a seducing man," 89 and n. 27; marriage, 172 and n. 15, 235 and n. 13, 523, 544 and n. 7, asks his mother's consent, 81, 286, 288, 289 and n. 1; monument to, in Lichfield Cathedral, 400 and n. 2, 432; monument to, in St. Paul's, 401 and n. 5; at Oxford as student, 23 and n. 13, 51 and n. 29, 57–58 and n. 10, n. 11, 102–4, 207, 365; penance at Uttoxeter, 389; pension, 218 n. 1, 219 and n. 2, 264, 364–65, JB's petition for addition to, 28 and n. 11, Brocklesby's offer rejected, 28 and n. 12, 30 and n. 2, letter to Bute (anonymous), text, 512–15, Rose's sarcasm on, 587; Mrs. Piozzi (Thrale), relationship with, 141, 143, 251 n. 42, 265 n. 2, correspondence on her second marriage, 273 and n. 3; at school: Latin exercises, 188, Lichfield, xxxii–xxxiii, 49–50, 85, 97, 99–100, 101–02, Stourbridge, 51, 88, 91, 206, 245, translations, exercises, 229, 238, 244 and n. 3; as schoolmaster: applications for employment, 58 and n. 14, 121 n. 5, 170 and n. 8, 173 and n. 19, Edial, 171 n. 10, 172, 172 n. 18, Market Bosworth, 86 and n. 6, 170–71; sermon on his death, by Agutter, 493, 494 and n. 3, 495 n. 2; "uncle hanged," 286–87, 287–89; will, 35 and n. 27, 39 and n. 2, 134 n. 5, legacy to Barber, 39, 220 n. 2, 336, Lichfield house, 62–63 and n. 35, 83 and n. 8, value of estate, 77 and n. 6.

Contributions on: by Adams, xxviii–xxix, 21–25, 56–63, 159–62; by Mary Adey, 63–71; by Astle, 180–92, 587–88, *see also* Writings, sermons, *post*; by Barber, 163–69; by Bowles, 245–55; by Brocklesby, xl–xlii, 25–28, 31–35, 93–95; by Burney, 426 n. 1; by J. Dodsley, 158–59; by Hamilton, 263–65; by Hector, 47–51, 85–91, 169–73; by Langton, 316, 338 n. 2, 343–47, 354–74, chronology of, 308 n. 1; by Maxwell, 214, 215 n. 2, 219, 224; by Metcalfe, 589–90; by Mickle, xxviii, xxx–xxxi, 177–80; by Percy, 5–8, 204–8; by A. L. S. R., 350–52; by Reynolds, 119–22; by Rush, 533–36; by Sastres, 133–36; by Sedgwick, 539–42; by Anna Seward, 54 and n. 2, 55 n.

INDEX

JOHNSON, SAMUEL (*cont.*)

5, 76–81; by Steevens, 146–52; by W. Strahan, 107–8; by Taylor, xlii, 98–107; by T. Warton, 590–91. *Letters from:* to Adams, 82 *n.* 4, 128, 155–56, 159 *and n.* 4; to Astle, 180 *n.* 1, 202 *n.* 2; to Elizabeth Aston, 225 *n.* 6; to Bagshaw, 479, 523; to Barber, 119, 266; Barber gives to JB, 133 *and n.* 1; to Baretti, 207 *n.* 21, 359 *n.*; to F. A. Barnard, 323 *and n.* 3; to Beattie, 241, 243 *and n.* 4, 273; to Bond, 463, 484–85, 538 *n.* 22; to Hill Boothby, 198 *n.* 2, 434, 592 *n.* 7; to Boswell, xxiv, 15 *n.* 1, 53 *n.*, 140 *n.* 7, 468 *n.* 12, 490 *and n.* 1, in *Life*, 600–1, 606, original manuscripts, 603 *and n.* 3, 604, 606 *n.* 3; to Bowles, 111, 137, 138, 156, 256–57, 258–59 *and n.* 2; to Brocklesby, 93 *n.* 1, 382, 606–7; Fanny Burney refuses to give JB, 340 *n.* 1; to Bute, 512 *n.* 4; to Cave, 180 *n.* 1, 202 *n.* 2; to Chambers, 144 *n.* 1; to Mrs. Chapone, 296 *n.* 3; to Chesterfield, 21, 24–25, 27 *and n.* 8, 61 *and n.* 27, 246, 308 *n.* 1, 524, deposited in British Museum, 602, 607, printed separately, 402 *and n.* 4; to Clark, 276 *and n.* 3; to College cook (lost), 175 *n.* 5, 383 *and n.* 8; to Davies, 381 *n.* 3; to Dodsley, text, 158; to Drummond, 355 *n.* 4, 525 *n.* 28; to Forbes, 213; to Fothergill, 153 *and n.* 1, 212 *and n.* 2; to Jane Gastrell, 225 *n.* 6; to Greene, 223, 225 *and n.* 3; to Hastings, 306, 308 *n.* 1, 333, 334, 349–50 *and n.* 4, 353; to Hawkesbury, 340–42; to Hector, 49 *and n.* 10, 62 *n.* 33; to Heely 107 *n.* 1; to T. Hervey, 157 *n.* 2; to Hoole, 306–7, 325 *n.* 1; to Humphry, 238 *and n.* 1; to Hussey, 239; to W. S. Johnson, offered by Abercrombie, 464, 484–85, 490 *and n.* 1, 532–33, 549; to Langton, 205 *n.* 4, 607; to Lawrence, 236 *and n.* 2; to Miss Lawrence, 236 *and n.* 2; to Leland, 175 *and n.* 2, *n.* 4, *n.* 5, 383; to T. Levett, 79 *and n.* 10; to Macpherson, 235 *and n.* 14, 602, 607; to Maxwell, 211, 213; to Mudge, 256, 602 *n.* 12; to Nicol, 180 *n.* 1; to O'Conor, 109–10, 113–14 *and n.* 4, *n.* 5, 121 *and n.* 1; to Percy, 96 *n.* 3; to Perkins, 566 *and n.* 1, 568, 607; to

Mrs. Piozzi, 33 *n.* 13, 167 *n.* 26, 175 *n.* 5, 273 *and n.* 3; to Lucy Porter, 77 *n.* 4, 92–93 *and n.* 3, *n.* 4, 604–5; to Reynolds, 212 *n.* 2, 266 *n.* 5; to Sastres, 133; to Simpson, text, 67–70, 181, 193; to Steevens, 147–48 *and n.* 3, *n.* 5; to W. Strahan, 107 *n.* 1, text, 13–14; to Mrs. Strahan, 107 *n.* 1; to Taylor, 56 *n.* 7, 98 *n.* 1, 106 *n.* 45; to Thurlow, 28 *n.* 12, 77 *and n.* 6; to Vyse, 214–15 *and n.* 3, *n.* 4; to J. Warton, 201 *and n.* 2; to T. Warton, 59 *n.* 18, 123–24 *and n.* 2, 127, 129, 144 *n.* 1, *n.* 3, 145 *n.* 4, *n.* 5, 146; to Weston, 320 *n.* 2; to Wetherell, 211–12 *and n.* 1, 524; to Windham, 236–37 *and n.* 3.

Letters to: from Boswell, lii, returned, xxiv *and n.* 1, 34 *and n.* 23; from W. Cowley, 82 *and n.* 4; from T. Davies, 381 *n.* 3; from Forbes, 213; from T. Jones, 444 *n.* 3.

Opinions and Sayings: abusive language in boat on Thames, 374; American Revolution, 252, 371; Aston, Elizabeth, 78–79; Mrs. Barbauld, 410 *n.* 4; barometer, 250; Bible, translations of, 355 *and n.* 4; Blagden, 372; books recommended to Astle, 188, 193, 197–200; Boswell, 533 *n.* 7; brooks, 348 *n.* 2; Burke, 93–94 *and n.* 2, 370; Bute, 264; cancer, lady with, 101; cane (stick), 181–82, 361; cant phrases, dislike of, 360–61; capital punishment, 179–80; Carlisle, E. of, 296 *n.* 4; chemistry, interest in, 253, 345, 361, 535; Chesterfield, 234 *n.* 11, 289 *n.* 1; Mrs. Cibber, 181 *and n.* 7; compliments in foreign publications, 357; conversation, 253–54, 370; Creator and creature, 553 *and n.* 6; cucumbers, 361, 365; death, attitude toward, xlii, xlix, 254, 329 *and n.* 4, of friends, 248, meeting friends after, 525 *n.* 31; debts, 69 *and n.* 33; discovery, voyages of, 178; dream of contest of wit, 357; drinking, 140 *n.* 3, 143, 247 *and n.* 16, *n.* 17, 248, 358–59; duels, 257 *and n.* 3; Duke of Leeds, verses on his marriage by a servant, 365–66; education, 248; employment of the poor, 355–56; equality, conversation with Mrs. Macaulay, 587–88 *and n.* 10; Fielding, Henry, 177; fireworks, 151–52; for-

INDEX

INDEX

INDEX

INDEX

647

INDEX

Port Folio, The, 484 and n. 4, 533 n. 7, 536 n. 17.

Porter, Harry, first husband of Mrs. Johnson, 1691–1734, 80 and n. 17, 88 and n. 20, 575.

Porter, Lucy, stepdau. of SJ, 1715–86, account of, 45 n. 1; death, 65 and n. 11; Johnson leaves her nothing in his will, 65 and n. 9; on Johnson's epitaph on a duck, 64 n. 2; Johnson's relationship with, 56 n. 7, 65, 69 n. 34; letters from SJ to, 77 n. 4, 92–93 and n. 3, n. 4, 604–5; ring belonging to her mother, 293; "Sprig of Myrtle" verses said to have been written for her, 80 and n. 16, 439 and n. 2, 575 n. 5; mentioned, 44, 52 n. 1, 56 and n. 7, 66 n. 13, 69, 77, 79, 80, 96 n. 1, 172 n. 15, n. 18, 191, 496.

Porteus, Beilby, Bishop of London, 1731–1808, 369 n. 42, n. 44.

Pott, Percival, surgeon, 1714–88, 257 and n. 2.

Pottle, Frederick A., xxxvi, 601 n. 6.

Powell, L. F., 87 n. 15, 140 n. 2, 147 n. 2, 246 n. 8, 320 n. 2, 444 n. 3.

Prendergast, Sir Thomas, ?1660–1709, 499 and n. 31.

Preston, Sir Charles, Bt., of Valleyfield, c. 1735–1800, 42 and n. 4, 45.

Price, Charles, counterfeiter, 1723–86, 506–7 and n. 15.

Prideaux, Dr. Humphrey, Orientalist, 1648–1724, The Old and New Testament Connected, 199 and n. 12.

Pridden, Rev. John, 1758–1825, 504 n. 1.

Priestley, Joseph, LL.D., theologian and scientist, 1733–1804, Johnson's comment on, 253; library destroyed in Birmingham Riots, 456 n. 10; in Life, 412, 414, 415; published by Joseph Johnson, 400 n. 4.

Pringle, Sir John, Bt., 1707–82, 13 n. 1; letter from JB to, 13 and n. 1.

Pritchard, Hannah (Vaughan), 1711–68, account of, 22 n. 9; acts in Irene, xxviii–xxix, 22 and n. 9.

Proceedings of the Committee . . . for Cloathing French Prisoners of War, introduction by SJ, 317.

Public Advertiser, The, 269 n. 1; "Observations on the Character of Dr. Johnson," 176 and n. 1.

Publilius Syrius, 1st century B.C., 111 n. 6, 569.

Pufendorf, Baron Samuel von, 1632–94, Introduction to the History of the Principal Kingdoms and States of Europe, 199 and n. 7.

Pulteney. See Johnstone-Pulteney, William.

Pütter, Johann Stephan, 1725–1807, An Historical Development of the Present Political Constitution of the Germanic Empire, 504 and n. 3.

Queensberry, Catherine Hyde, Duchess of, 1701–77, memoirs, 116 and n. 2.

Quevedo y Villegas, Francisco Gómez de, author, 1580–1645, 348 n. 2.

Quintilian, 1st century A.D., Institutio Oratoria, 456 and n. 7.

Ralph, James, ?1695–1762, review of Life of Savage, 497.

Ramsay, Allan, poet, 1686–1758, The Ever Green, 305 and n. 1.

Rashleigh, John Colman, 1772–1847, 417 n. 1; Life, criticism of, 417–18.

Ratcliff, John, D.D., Master of Pembroke, 1700–75, 313 n. 1.

Reed, Isaac, editor, 1742–1807, account of, 314 n. 1; at Boswell's dinner, 503–504, 504 n. 1; Dido, a tragedy, 334 n. 1; Life, corrections and additions, list, 496–502; list of SJ's works by JB annotated, 317–19; praised in Life, 502 n. 49; Shakespeare, SJ's edition, revised by, 319 n. 26, 464 n. 11, Steevens's edition superintended by, 531 n. 1; Young's works edited by, 502 n. 51; mentioned, 281.

Renner, Mr., agent for Smollett at Leghorn, 536 and n. 17.

Reynolds, Frances, sister of Sir Joshua, 1729–1807, 119 n. 2, 461 and n. 3; letter to Veronica Boswell from, 461 n. 3; mentioned, xxxix n. 1, 483 n. 5.

Reynolds, Sir Joshua, 1723–92, Frances Abington's friendship with, 422 and n. 2, 423; at Baretti's trial, 151 n. 21; blindness, danger of, 293 and n. 5, 453; death, 453 n. 3, 475 n. 2; Discourses, 356 n. 5, 550; SJ's praise of, 456 and n. 6; Earl of Carlisle's verses on, 296 n. 2; Garrick on, 368; Johnson,

652

INDEX

655

INDEX

INDEX

Townley, Charles, ?1746–1800, engraving of Opie's portrait of SJ, 538.

Townley, James, dramatist, 1714–78, *High Life below Stairs*, 359.

Townshend, Charles, 1725–67, 100 *and n.* 7.

Townshend, George, 4th V. and 1st M. Townshend, 1724–1807, 100 *and n.* 6.

Townson, Thomas, D.D., 1715–92, account of, 469 *n.* 2; *A Discourse on the Evangelical History*, 479 *n.* 3, 546; *Discourses on the Four Gospels*, 469 *and n.* 3, 473; letters to Churton from, 473, 480; memoir of, by Churton, 479 *n.* 3, 560, 567, 571; mentioned, 469, 476, 547, 563.

Trimlestown, Robert Barnewall, 12th B., d. 1779, 527 *and n.* 34, 545 *and n.* 13.

Trysull Grammar School, Staffordshire, 173 *n.* 19, 204 *n.* 1, 206.

Tyers, Thomas, 1726–87, *Biographical Sketch of Dr. Samuel Johnson*, 35 *n.* 26, 146 *n.* 1, 151 *n.* 23; characterized in *Idler*, 147 *n.* 2; epigram on SJ, 147 *n.* 2; Steevens's epigram on, 147 *and n.* 2; mentioned, 246 *n.* 10.

Tytler, William, historian, 1711–92, *History of Mary Queen of Scots* reviewed by SJ, 317.

Union, The, or Select Scots and English Poems, 304–5 *and n.* 4.

Universal Asylum and Columbian Magazine. See Columbian Magazine.

Universal Chronical (*Payne's Universal Chronicle*), 169 *n.* 40.

Universal Visiter, The, 454 *and n.* 1, 500.

Uttoxeter, SJ's penance at, 389.

Vallancey, Charles, 1721–1812, 114 *n.* 2; *Collectanea de Rebus Hibernicis*, SJ's contributions to (not found), 115.

Vanbrugh (Vanburgh), Sir John, dramatist and architect, 1664–1726, 356.

Vertot, Abbé René Aubert de, French historian, 1655–1735, *History of the Knights of Malta*, et al., 199 *and n.* 8.

Vesey, Rt. Hon. Agmondesham, d. 1784, 308 *n.* 1, 428 *n.* 8.

Vesey, Elizabeth (Vesey), wife of preceding, ?1715–91, 428 *n.* 8.

Victor, Benjamin, d. 1778, 89 *n.* 24;

false story of SJ's affair with Mrs. Paul, 89–90.

Villiers, Thomas. *See* Clarendon.

Vincent, William, D.D., 1739–1815, 551 *n.* 1; *Life* presented to, 551 *and n.* 2; mentioned, 555 *n.* 1.

Virgil, 70–19 B.C., *Aeneid*, 228 *n.* 2, 291 *n.* 4; *Eclogues*, 186 *n.* 31, 429 *n.* 3, 453 *n.* 2; *Georgics*, 549 *n.* 16; Johnson's opinion of, 354, 529.

Vyse, Richard, son of following, 1746–1825, 103 *and n.* 37.

Vyse, William, 1709–70, account of, 103 *and n.* 37; gives shoes to SJ, 103–04; letters from SJ to, 214–15 *and n.* 3, *n.* 4.

Vyse, William, D.C.L., son of preceding, 1742–1816, 103, 103 *and n.* 7, 604; monument to SJ in Lichfield Cathedral, 400.

Walker, Joseph Cooper, 1761–1810, account of, 109 *n.* 1; *Historical Memoirs of the Irish Bards*, 110 *and n.* 3, 112; and Johnson's letter to O'Conor, 109–10, 113–14, 124 *and n.* 1; letter from JB to, 117 *n.* 4; letter from Percy to, 117; suggests JB write book on Ireland, 125; and Walpole's *The Mysterious Mother*, 117 *n.* 4.

Walker, Rev. Robert, 1716–83, 466 *n.* 3.

Wall, Martin, M.D., c. 1747–1824, 152 *n.* 1, 345–46 *and n.* 8.

Walmesley, Gilbert, ?1680–1751, account of, 78 *n.* 8; Johnson on, 78–79, 363; song by, in Garrick's poems, 496 *and n.* 5; mentioned, 207 *n.* 18, 591 *and n.* 9.

Walmesley, Magdalen (Aston), wife of preceding, 78 *n.* 8, 225.

Walmsley, Geoffrey, 1725–73, verses, 591 *n.* 9.

Walpole, Horace, 1st B. Walpole of Wolverton, 1678–1758, Pitt's speech against, written by SJ, 246 *and n.* 9, *n.* 10.

Walpole, Horace, 4th E. of Orford, 1717–97, 332 *n.* 1; *The Mysterious Mother*, 117 *n.* 4.

Walsh, William, 1663–1708, *The Retirement*, 605 *n.* 2.

Walton, Izaak, 1593–1683, *The Compleat Angler*, Browne's edition, 314, 315 *and*

657

INDEX

Whitehorn, William, of Jamaica, at Oxford, 104 *and n.* 39.

Whole Duty of Man, The. See Allestree, Richard.

Wickins (? James, fl. 1772–81), draper in Lichfield, anecdote by, 187 *n.* 33.

Wilcox, bookseller (?John, fl. 1721–62), advises SJ to be a porter, 233 *and n.* 5.

Wilkes, Heaton (Eaton), brother of following, 535 *and n.* 12.

Wilkes, John, 1727–97, and Barber's discharge from Navy, 165 *n.* 13, 525, 537; at Dilly's dinner with SJ, 578 *n.* 2, 588 *n.* 10; Johnson's *False Alarm*, reply to, 553; Johnson's opinion of, 330 *n.* 10; *Life* praised by, 423; *Lives of the Poets* presented to, 252 *and n.* 47; riot against his imprisonment, 535 *n.* 12.

Wilks, Joseph (Dom Cuthbert), 82–83 *and n.* 6.

Williams, Anna, poetess, 1706–83, death, 39 *n.* 3, 248; Lady Knight's letters on, 325; lives with SJ, 166, 524; *London Magazine*, account of, 325 *and n.* 4; *Miscellanies in Prose and Verse*, 6 *and n.* 10, preface by SJ, 318; mentioned, 5, 7, 9 *n.* 3, 24, 169, 205, 248 *n.* 24, 310.

Wilson, James, 1742–98, 492 *and n.* 7.

Wilson, Mr., druggist in Lichfield, 226.

Wilson, Thomas, D.D., 1703–84, 97, 98 *n.* 6.

Windham, Miss, 484 *and n.* 6.

Windham, William, 1750–1810, account of, 237 *n.* 3; diary quoted, 28 *n.* 12; letters from SJ to, 236–37 *and n.* 3; protest against Hawkins's *Life of Johnson*, 221 *n.* 1; mentioned, 34 *n.* 20, 266, 379 *n.* 1, 384, 458, 517.

Wingfield, John, D.D., 1760–1825, 555 *n.* 1; *Life* presented to, 555 *and n.* 1.

Withers, Philip, D.D., d. 1790, Knox criticized by, 419 *and n.* 4.

Wolcot, John (Peter Pindar, pseud.), 1738–1819, *Poetical and Congratulatory*

Epistle to James Boswell, Esq., 139–40.

Woodfall, William, journalist, 1746–1803, 117 *and n.* 5.

Wordsworth, William, 1770–1850, 400 *n.* 4.

World, The, Chesterfield's papers in, 60 *and n.* 23.

World Displayed, The, introduction by SJ, 317.

Wright, Thomas, printer, d. 1797, account of, 424 *n.* 1; maxims and anecdotes in *Life*, publication suggested, 424 *and n.* 2; mentioned, 400 *n.* 4.

Wyatt, James, architect, 1746–1813, monument to SJ in Lichfield Cathedral, 400 *and n.* 2.

Wyatt, John, inventor, 1700–66, 89 *n.* 25.

Wyndham. *See* Windham.

Xenophon, ?434–?355 B.C., *Cyropaedia*, 251; *Memorabilia Socratis*, edited by Edwards, 82 *and n.* 4, 160; mentioned, 427.

Yonge, Sir William, Bt., d. 1755, 591 *and n.* 1.

Young, Arthur, agriculturist and author, 1741–1820, account of, 447 *n.* 1; *A Six Weeks' Tour through the Southern Counties of England and Wales*, 448 *and n.* 4.

Young, Barbara (Talbot), 2nd wife of William Young, d. 1830, 591 *n.* 1.

Young, Edward, poet, 1683–1765, life of, by Croft, 456, 458; *Love of Fame*, 188, 504; *Night Thoughts*, 488 *n.* 1; proposals for works, 496 *n.* 1, 502; works edited by Reed, 502 *n.* 51.

Young, Prof. John, c. 1746–1820, criticism of Gray's *Elegy* in style of SJ, 493, 548.

Young, Sir William, 1725–88, 591 *and n.* 1.

Young, William, son of preceding, c. 1750–1815, 591 *n.* 1.